Mediation has burst its banks and spilled over into many fields. It is no longer a meandering stream or a quiet backwater. It has left behind romantic beginnings and entered many new waterways. Read this book and be carried along in the surge.

John Winslade, California State University—San Bernardino, USA

In *The Mediation Handbook*, we have a wonderful new resource that provides insight from some of the most innovative thinkers and practitioners in the mediation world. Drawing on the best lessons of the past and a broad vision of the demands of the future, the handbook offers a wide range of practical approaches for deepening and extending the reach of mediation in the twenty-first century.

Bernie Mayer, Creighton University, Canada

THE MEDIATION HANDBOOK

The Mediation Handbook gathers leading experts across fields related to peace, justice, human rights, and conflict resolution to explore ways that mediation can be applied to a range of spectrums, including new age settings, relationships, organizations, institutions, communities, environmental conflicts, and intercultural and international conflicts. The text is informed by cogent theory, state-of-the-art research, and best practices to provide the reader with a well-rounded understanding of mediation practice in contemporary times.

Based on four signature themes—contexts; skills and competencies; applications; and recommendations—the handbook provides theoretical, applicable, and practical insight into a variety of key approaches to mediation. Authors consider modern conflict on a local and global scale, emphasizing the importance of identifying effective strategies, foundations, and methods to shape the nature of a mediation mindfully and effectively. With a variety of interdisciplinary perspectives, the text complements the development of the reader's competencies and understanding of mediation in order to contribute to the advancement of the mediation field.

With a conversational tone that will welcome readers, this comprehensive book is essential reading for students and professionals wanting to learn a wide range of potential interventions for conflict.

Alexia Georgakopoulos is a Professor in the Department of Conflict Studies at Nova Southeastern University, USA. She is the Director of the Institute of Conflict Resolution and Communication, a mediation and conflict resolution training, and consulting firm specializing in delivering educational training and mediation certification to professionals. A world-class scholar and practitioner in mediation with numerous articles, book chapters, and speaking engagements, she was featured on NBC's *Today Show* to discuss peace in the diverse world.

THE MEDIATION HANDBOOK

Research, Theory, and Practice

Edited by Alexia Georgakopoulos

Routledge
Taylor & Francis Group
NEW YORK AND LONDON

First published 2017
by Routledge
711 Third Avenue, New York, NY 10017

and by Routledge
2 Park Square, Milton Park, Abingdon, Oxon OX14 4RN

Routledge is an imprint of the Taylor & Francis Group, an informa business

© 2017 Taylor & Francis

The right of Alexia Georgakopoulos to be identified as the author of the editorial material, and of the authors for their individual chapters, has been asserted in accordance with sections 77 and 78 of the Copyright, Designs and Patents Act 1988.

All rights reserved. No part of this book may be reprinted or reproduced or utilised in any form or by any electronic, mechanical, or other means, now known or hereafter invented, including photocopying and recording, or in any information storage or retrieval system, without permission in writing from the publishers.

Trademark notice: Product or corporate names may be trademarks or registered trademarks, and are used only for identification and explanation without intent to infringe.

Library of Congress Cataloging in Publication Data
A catalog record for this book has been requested

ISBN: 978-1-138-12420-2 (hbk)
ISBN: 978-1-138-12421-9 (pbk)
ISBN: 978-1-31564-833-0 (ebk)

Typeset in Bembo
by Taylor & Francis Books

This handbook is dedicated to all the Mediators around the world for their remarkable work and inspiring commitment to peace and conflict transformation!

CONTENTS

LIST OF ILLUSTRATIONS

Figures

Tables

CONTRIBUTORS

Mohammed Abu-Nimer, Ph.D., is Professor of International Peace and Conflict Resolution and Director of the Peacebuilding and Development Institute at the School of International Service, American University. He has conducted interreligious conflict resolution training and interfaith dialogue workshops in many conflict areas around the world. In addition to his articles and publications, Dr Abu-Nimer is co-founder and co-editor of the *Journal of Peacebuilding and Development.* He holds a Ph.D. in Conflict Analysis and Resolution from George Mason University.

Oliver Leighton Barrett is a Senior Research Fellow at the Center for Climate and Security, where he focuses on the impacts of environmental degradation and climate change on the stability and security of states and populations with an emphasis on Latin America. He is also the founder of Janus Advisory Inc., a company that provides climate change resilience advisory services to national governments and communities. In 2014, he led a multi-author effort to draft the Pentagon's Environmental and Energy Issues for Militaries report—a collaborative multi-national assessment of the impacts of climate change on Latin America and Caribbean militaries' operations and installations. A retired naval officer, Oliver began his military career as an enlisted US Marine deploying to Somalia in support of humanitarian assistance operations, and later commanded sensitive reconnaissance missions in support of Operation Enduring Freedom. He worked as an advisor to US Southern Command for eight years (2006–14) managing partner nation public-private cooperation outreach efforts as well as environmental and energy security initiatives. Oliver is also a Contributing Writer for *Foreign Policy Association,* with published articles on fragile states, environmental security, and emerging diplomacy and defense issues.

RaJade M. Berry-James (Ph.D., Rutgers University—Newark) is an Associate Professor of Public Administration and Resident Research Fellow of the Genetic Engineering and Society Center at North Carolina (NC) State University where she teaches courses in Social Equity, Program Evaluation, and Cultural Competence. Her scholarly research focuses on cultural dimensions and has appeared in several publishing outlets, including the *Review of Public Personnel Administration, Journal of Black Political Research, Public Performance and Management Review, International Journal of Public Administration, International Journal of Humanities, Journal of*

Public Budgeting, Accounting and Financial Management, and *Journal of Public Management and Social Policy*. Dr Berry-James is past Chair of the NASPAA Commission on Peer Review and Accreditation (COPRA) and the NC State University Diversity Advisory Committee (UDAC).

Tommie V. Boyd, Ph.D., is the Professor and Chair of the Department of Family Therapy at Nova Southeastern University. She has over 30 years of clinical and supervision experience and is the recipient of an American Association for Marriage and Family Therapy (AAMFT) Leadership Award. She is trained as a mediator. She has developed programs helping to employ marriage and family therapists in mediation and medical settings, and was a key player in developing guidelines for marriage and family therapist employments in military settings.

Benjamin J. Broome, Ph.D., is Professor in the Hugh Downs School of Human Communication at Arizona State University. He was the recipient of the IACM Jeffrey Z. Rubin Theory-to-Practice Award for 2016 in New York, NY. This award recognizes his important contributions to the nexus between the theory and practice of conflict management. His work focuses on developing ways to help groups, organizations, and communities respond to conflict through dialogue rather than violence. Over the past 30 years, he has facilitated design workshops in North America, Europe, and the eastern Mediterranean, working with educational institutions, nongovernmental organizations, professional associations, government entities, and indigenous nations and communities. During the past two decades, his work has concentrated on peacebuilding efforts in Cyprus, bringing together Greek-Cypriot and Turkish-Cypriot communities for facilitated dialogue. He has published books, journal articles, and book chapters on a variety of topics, including the application of interactive design processes to promote peace in ethnic conflicts; building a culture of peace through intergroup dialogue; understanding relational empathy and its role in transforming intercultural conflict; developing a collective vision of the future in divided societies; and challenges and promises of the third-party role in intractable conflicts.

Sean Byrne, Ph.D., and Jessica Senehi founded in 2003 the Arthur V. Mauro Centre for Peace and Justice at St Paul's College, University of Manitoba, and in 2006 a Ph.D. program in Peace and Conflict Studies (PACS). Together with Brian Rice, Anna Snyder and Dean Peachey in 2010 they co-founded a Joint Master's in PACS between the University of Manitoba and the University of Winnipeg. His research on ethnopolitical and international conflicts has been funded by grants from the United States Institute of Peace, and the Social Sciences and Humanities Research Council of Canada. He is interested in peacebuilding efforts in societies transitioning out of protracted conflict and violence, children and war, women and peacebuilding, and the critique of the liberal peacebuilding model.

Colleen Chiochetti was trained in the Conflict Resolution Program at Georgetown University. Previously she studied at Juniata College, where she graduated with a degree in Conflict and Russian Studies. She has previously worked for Nonviolence International and GlobalSolutions.org researching and writing about nonviolent movements, peace initiatives, and the Responsibility to Protect as it applies to the United Nations Security Council.

Patrick James Christian, Ph.D., is a retired US Army Green Beret officer with 24 years of experience in the practice and research of intra-state violence, civil war, and tribal conflict. He has led field teams conducting combat advisory missions, tribal engagement and counterinsurgency operations in Caquetá, Putumayo and Los Amazonas, Colombia; Puerto Francisco de Orellana in Ecuador; Darfur, Sudan; Bilate and Ogadin regions of Ethiopia; and Baghdad and Taji, Iraq. For the past year and a half, he has served as a Special Forces inter-agency field team leader with US Africa Command's Special Operations Command—Africa, conducting counter-terrorism, intelligence analysis, international security, and military operations (advise/assist/accompany) in the northern reaches of the Republic of Niger in the Central Sahel. His doctorate is in the psychopathology of ethnic and cultural conflict and he is an Adjunct Research Professor at the Joint Special Operations University, Tampa, Florida.

Kenneth Cloke, Ph.D., is Director of the Center for Dispute Resolution and a mediator, arbitrator, facilitator, coach, consultant and trainer, specializing in communication, negotiation, and resolving complex multi-party disputes, including marital, divorce, family, community, grievance and workplace disputes, collective bargaining negotiations, organizational and school conflicts, sexual harassment, discrimination, and public policy disputes; and designing preventative conflict resolution systems. He is an internationally recognized speaker and author of *Mediation: Revenge and the Magic of Forgiveness*; *Mediating Dangerously: The Frontiers of Conflict Resolution*; *The Crossroads of Conflict: A Journey into the Heart of Dispute Resolution*; *Conflict Revolution* (1st and 2nd editions); and *The Dance of Opposites: Explorations in Mediation, Dialogue and Conflict Resolution Systems Design*; and co-author with Joan Goldsmith of *Thank God It's Monday! 14 Values We Need to Humanize the Way We Work*; *Resolving Personal and Organizational Conflict*; *The End of Management and the Rise of Organizational Democracy*; *The Art of Waking People Up: Cultivating Awareness and Authenticity at Work*; and *Resolving Conflicts at Work: Ten Strategies for Everyone On the Job* (1st–3rd editions). He has done conflict resolution work in over 20 countries, and is founder and first President of Mediators Beyond Borders. He received his BA from the University of California (UC), Berkeley; JD from UC Berkeley's Boalt Law School; Ph.D. from UCLA; LLM from UCLA Law School; and did postdoctoral work at Yale University School of Law. He is a graduate of the National Judicial College.

Jerrell D. Coggburn (Ph.D., University of South Carolina) is Professor and Chair of Public Administration in North Carolina State University's School of Public and International Affairs (SPIA). His main research interests are in public human resource management and public management. His research has appeared in *Public Administration Review*, *Review of Public Personnel Administration*, *Journal of Public Administration Research and Theory*, *American Review of Public Administration*, *Public Performance & Management Review*, *International Journal of Public Administration*, *Public Administration Quarterly*, and other scholarly outlets. He is a life member of the American Society for Public Administration (ASPA) and serves as President of the ASPA Research Triangle Chapter.

Lynn Cole, currently President and CEO of BRDGES Academy at www.BRDGESAcadem y.com, is the recent past President and Chair of the Board of Mediators Beyond Borders, International. She has served for over 13 years as a full-time mediator in the US, is Harvard trained and circuit-civil certified in Florida. She also is internationally certified by the International Mediation Institute (IMI) in The Hague. From 2005 to present, she has served as a United States Agency for International Development (USAID) Mediation Specialist designing national court-related mediation programs in Bulgaria, Jordan, Kosovo and, currently, Sri Lanka. She is a recognized author on the explosive global growth of international mediation and a trainer in mediation for students in domestic and international universities and law schools, judges, attorneys, and mediators from Jordan, Oman, Lebanon, Saudi Arabia, Iraq, Slovenia, Bulgaria, Serbia, Croatia, Greece, Kosovo, Cypress, and Turkey.

Harold Coleman Jr. is Senior Vice President for mediation at the American Arbitration Association (AAA), a global leader in dispute resolution services, and executive director/ mediator for mediation.org, a division of the AAA. He also trains new AAA arbitrators and aspiring mediators in basic/advanced arbitration case management techniques and basic/ advanced mediation skills. Coleman is a licensed attorney, licensed real estate broker, and credentialed mediator, arbitrator, and educator who since 1987 has served the international business and legal communities in resolving complex litigated and non-litigated disputes through innovative alternative dispute resolution (ADR) applications of interest-based negotiation, facilitation, mediation, independent fact finding, early neutral evaluation, and binding arbitration. He is a professional trainer, who routinely trains corporate management teams in ADR, communication, conflict management, claims prevention, strategic planning, and critical thinking/problem solving, among other enterprise risk-management themes. As a trainer, Coleman's corporate clientele has included The Boeing Company, the global aerospace leader. A former multi-disciplinary project manager and complex litigation attorney, Coleman has mediated and arbitrated hundreds of litigated and non-litigated disputes during a 28-year law and ADR career. He is a Fellow and Director of the College of Commercial Arbitrators (CCA), a director of the International Mediation Institute (IMI), and former member of the AAA's international board of directors. Coleman serves the ADR community from the Association's Los Angeles and New York offices.

Robin Cooper, Ph.D., is a Professor of Conflict Resolution and Ethnic Studies and Chair of the Department of Conflict Resolution Studies (DCRS) at Nova Southeastern University (NSU). Prior to joining the faculty at DCRS, Dr Cooper served as a faculty member of public health and Director of the Interprofessional Primary Care Education Project at NSU's College of Osteopathic Medicine. In this capacity, she developed training and education in collaborative practices in health care, with funding from the Department of Health and Human Services. Dr Cooper has published and taught in such areas as identity-based conflict, diversity, collaborative practices in organizational contexts, and qualitative research. She co-edited *Peace and Conflict Studies Research: A Qualitative Perspective* with L. Finley in 2014 (Information Age Publishing).

Dorit Cypis, artist, addresses aesthetics and ethics critically from studio art to education, conflict mediation and community building. Cypis explores psychosocial aspects of history, knowledge, and experience that inform identity and social relations. Current projects: *The Sighted See the Surface*—performative exhibition on sight and blindness, *North East Youth Council*—interaction between police, youth and community, and *The Future of Policing*—dialogue between police and community. Cypis has exhibited internationally and has been a recent recipient of a Guggenheim Fellowship as well as many other awards and fellowships. She has taught on identity and social relations internationally and is the founder of Kulture Klub Collaborative—artists working with homeless youth to bridge survival and inspiration. She earned a Master's in Fine Art at California Institute for the Arts and a Master's in Dispute Resolution, Pepperdine University.

Dennis M. Daley (Ph.D., Washington State University) is a Professor of Public Administration at North Carolina State University. He previously taught at the University of

Mississippi, Iowa State University, and Minnesota State University (Mankato). He is the author of *Performance Appraisal in the Public Sector: Techniques and Applications* (1992) and *Strategic Human Resource Management* (2002), along with numerous refereed articles and book chapters. His research focuses on the relationship that human resource and organizational behavior managerial practices and techniques have on organizational effectiveness. He teaches classes in Human Resource/Personnel Management, Organizational Behavior, and Negotiations & Mediation. He served as the elected Chair of the Faculty (2003–05), PSPA Interim Department Head (2006), and Public Administration Director (1988–90) at North Carolina State University. He also served as Public Administration Director (1987–88) at the University of Mississippi.

Thomas DiGrazia received a JD from Notre Dame Law School and an MA in Political Science from Rutgers University. He has practiced law in South Dakota, Indiana, Alaska, and Hawaii. He was an RKF Fellow working with the Lakota in South Dakota (1970–72); and he practiced Public Interest Law with Native Americans all over the USA. He is a Peacemaker, Lawyer and Director of the Mediation Center—Windward Oahu. He has been an Adjunct Professor at Hawaii Pacific University, teaching graduate classes in Mediation and Conflict. Currently, he is a senior teacher, co-founder and co-director of the Yoga School of Kailua and Hawaii Yoga Prison Project. He is author of *Peacemaker: A Sicilian American Memoir* (2013) and *Light on Peacemaking: A Guide to Appropriate Dispute Resolution and Mediating Family Conflict* (2016).

Daniel Druckman, Ph.D., is Professor of Public and International Affairs at George Mason University, an eminent scholar at Macquarie University, an Honorary Professor at the University of Queensland, and a Visiting Professor at several universities. He has published widely on such topics as international negotiation, nationalism, nonverbal communication, peacekeeping and research methodologies. He is the recipient of a Lifetime Achievement award from the International Association for Conflict Management. He has also received outstanding book awards for *Doing Research: Methods of Inquiry for Conflict Analysis* and *Evaluating Peace Operations*, with Paul F. Diehl.

Cheryl Duckworth, Ph.D., is an Associate Professor of Conflict Resolution and Peace Education at Nova Southeastern University. Her teaching, community collaborations, and research focus on peace education and intercultural dialogues, especially where contested historical narratives of conflict are involved. She is the author of numerous chapters and articles on historical memory and peace education. Her latest book, *Teaching Terror: 9/11 and Collective Memory in America's Classrooms*, was published by Routledge in 2014.

Marcelle E. DuPraw, Ph.D., is a consensus-building practitioner with 35 years of experience in environmental and cross-cultural collaborative problem solving and conflict resolution. She serves as the Director of Practice Development as well as Managing Senior Mediator and Facilitator at the Center for Collaborative Policy, California State University, Sacramento; she is also President of Collaborative Choices, LLC. She holds a doctorate in Conflict Analysis and Resolution with a concentration in culture and ethnicity; a Graduate Certificate in Qualitative Research Methods; and a Master's degree in Natural Resource Policy, Economics, and Management. Dr DuPraw is a recipient of the Sharon M. Pickett Award for Achievements in Environmental Protection through Alternative Dispute Resolution. She serves on the steering committee of the University Network for Collaborative

Governance, and is on the mediator rosters of the US Institute for Environmental Conflict Resolution, the Institute's Native Network, and the US Environmental Protection Agency (EPA).

Farshad Farahat is an award-winning Hollywood actor and a peace activist. He is working on his doctorate degree in conflict resolution. He graduated from the University of Massachusetts Amherst with a degree in political journalism. He is a spokesperson for Global Zero, an international movement for the elimination of nuclear weapons, and a board member of Ploughshares Fund, a US-based security foundation. Farshad is an organizer with the National Iranian American Council in promoting diplomatic initiatives between Iran and the USA. Farshad's acting credits include *300*, *CSI*, *The Tonight Show*, and *Conan*, the NBC series *State of Affairs*, and *House of Cards*. In 2011, he was cast as Azizi in Warner Bros.' true story, *Argo*. The Screen Actors Guild Awards honored Farshad Farahat for outstanding performance by a "Cast in a Motion Picture." In 2013, he produced an educational short called *Eviolent*, exploring the potential of non-violent civil resistance against unchecked authority. He is currently cast as Cyrus the Great in the upcoming adaptation of Alex Jovy's novel, *I Am Cyrus*.

Thomas Fiutak is currently Senior Fellow in the Technological Leadership Institute, University of Minnesota—Twin Cities, as well as adjunct faculty in Conservation Biology. Dr Fiutak has taught Conflict Management and Mediation Systems in the Humphrey Institute for Public Affairs at the University of Minnesota, and initiated and directed the Conflict and Change Center, which coordinated research in the areas of negotiation, mediation models, and conflict management systems. An active community mediator in the Dispute Resolution Center of St Paul, Minnesota, he also has been requested to mediate refugee disputes in Germany, fishing rights treaties between Native American Tribes and the Department of Natural Resources in Minnesota, water rights issues among Minnesota, North Dakota, and Manitoba, Canada, intra-organizational disputes in the Environmental Policy Institute of the Czech Republic, territorial disputes in the Gagauz region of Moldova, and provide mediation support to the political conflict among a range of political organizations, as well as combatants and ceasefire teams involved in the Philippines/Moro Islamic Liberation Movement. A founding member of Mediators Beyond Borders, International, he co-leads the Climate Change Project and has observer status with the United Nations Convention on Climate Change, having attended conferences in Copenhagen, Panama City, Bonn, Bangkok, and Warsaw.

Joseph P. Folger, Ph.D., is a Professor of Adult and Organizational Development at Temple University in Philadelphia, Pennsylvania. He is a co-founder and fellow of the Institute for the Study of Conflict Transformation (www.transformativemediation.org). His work at the Institute included assisting with the design and delivery of the US Postal Service REDRESS mediation program, as well as conducting assessment and benchmarking research for numerous organizations and mediation agencies. He has worked extensively as a third-party intervener in organizational, community, court, and small group disputes. Folger has delivered keynote addresses at conferences held by the Academy of Family Mediators, Mediation UK, Mediator's Institute of Ireland, National Mediation Conference of Australia, Universal Forum of Cultures—Barcelona, Spain, Congreso Mundial de Mediación and the Congreso International de Mediación, the Rakmo Institute of Slovenia, and IMAB in São Paulo, Brazil. He won the Peacebuilder of the Year award from the New York State Dispute Resolution Association in 2006. Folger has published extensively in the areas of communication and conflict, mediation, and third-party intervention processes. His books include the award-winning volumes, *Working through Conflict: Strategies for Relationships, Groups and Organizations* (7th edition, with M.S. Poole and R.K. Stutman), and *The Promise of Mediation* (with R. Bush, 1st and 2nd editions). He edited (with R. Bush) *Designing Mediation: Approaches to Training and Practice within the Transformative Framework*, and most recently he edited (with R. Bush and D. DellaNoce) *Transformative Mediation: A Sourcebook—Resources for Conflict Intervention Practitioners and Programs*.

Alexia Georgakopoulos, Ph.D., is currently a Professor in the Department of Conflict Studies at Nova Southeastern University. She is the Director of the Institute of Conflict Resolution and Communication (ICRCtraining.com), a premier mediation and conflict resolution training, consulting firm specializing in educational training and mediation certification. She also delivers Florida Supreme Court Mediation Certification and continuing mediation education (CMEs) to the public. She is a practicing mediator in diverse forms of mediation (family, corporate, environmental, and multinational mediation) as well as a facilitator, arbitrator, dispute systems designer, conflict coach, and peacebuilder in both domestic and international contexts. She served as part of the Middle East Initiative Group of Mediators Beyond Borders, works as a lead facilitator with a House Representative who has been charged by the White House to address policy issues concerning Climate Change and National Security, and she continues to train thousands of mediators throughout the world in classroom and training contexts. She designed a grant awarded Youth Peace Leadership Mentorship Program titled READING PEACE PALS where she has trained youth to be Peace Ambassadors and plans to roll out this program on national and international levels. She works with the Crime Commission to promote safer communities with her work on workplace bullying, community policing, illicit narcotics, and at-risk youth programs. She is an authority on Conflict Management Systems and Adult Workplace Bullying and regularly delivers training workshops on these topics for organizations. As a professor, trainer, practitioner, and world-class expert in mediation and conflict resolution with two decades of work in the field, she is a nationally and internationally sought speaker and trainer. She was interviewed and appeared on NBC's *Today Show* to discuss global peace. She also provided conflict resolution consulting to Olympic athletes.

Charles Goesel, Ph.D. in Conflict Analysis and Resolution. He evaluates peace education programs and conducts research on refugees and most recently examined the lived experience of Syrian refugees. Charles has published on the use of mediation in a domestic violence context and on war and domestic abuse. Charles was formerly the Content Coordinator for the National Partnership for Community Training (NPCT), a program of Gulf Coast Jewish Family and Community Services. At NPCT, Charles researched and developed innovative content to aid social service providers in identifying, referring, assisting, and serving survivors of torture. Charles has published on the effectiveness of group treatment with survivors of torture. He also has extensive experience teaching English as a Second Language both domestically and internationally.

William Hall, Ph.D., coaches federal clients, convenes environmental collaboration and conflict resolution (ECCR) cases, supervises contracted neutral facilitators and mediators, and manages the evaluation research program for the US EPA's Conflict Prevention and Resolution Center—the EPA's primary resource for services and expertise in the areas of consensus building, collaborative problem solving, alternative dispute resolution, and environmental conflict resolution. During his 15 years at the Center, he has been responsible for ECCR cases involving enforcement and compliance, hazardous waste cleanup, water pollution control, and environmental civil rights. He is also an Adjunct Professor in Georgetown University's MA in Conflict Resolution program.

Toran Hansen, Ph.D., is a Professor in the Department of Conflict Analysis and Dispute Resolution in the Fulton School of Liberal Arts at Salisbury University in Maryland. He earned his Ph.D. in Social Work from the University of Minnesota and has a Master's degree in Conflict Analysis and Resolution. He has worked as a Research Associate for the Center for Restorative Justice and Peacemaking, the Center for Urban and Regional Affairs, and the Institute for Child Health Policy. He has also worked as a mediator and facilitator for the Minnesota Department of Corrections, the Palm Beach County Courthouse, and elsewhere. In addition, he worked with medium- to high-risk juveniles for the Focus Foundation of Canada. Toran has written a variety of scholarly articles and taught courses relating to both restorative and transitional justice. He is also the author of *The Generalist Approach to Conflict Resolution* (Lexington Books).

Brian L. Heisterkamp (Ph.D., Arizona State University) is Professor in the Department of Communication Studies at California State University, San Bernardino. His research interests involve the relationship between social action and social structures, and the manner in which conversation can be examined to understand mediator behavior, conflict, and interpersonal relationships, particularly gay and lesbian relationships. Currently, he is examining disputant storytelling during community mediation. He is also researching the memorable messages individuals convey regarding work-family balancing. He teaches courses in conflict and mediation, relational communication, nonverbal communication, research methods, and various graduate seminars.

Randy Heller, Ph.D. in Family Therapy. She is a Licensed Marriage and Family Therapist, Licensed Mental Health Counselor, Certified Supreme Court Family Mediator, Qualified Parenting Coordinator, Certified Hypnotherapist, and founder of The Family Network, Collaborative Counseling Center for Positive Growth and Change, established in 1994. Additionally, Dr Heller serves as a board member for numerous national and international organizations focused on an interdisciplinary approach to working with families transitioning through divorce. Dr Heller has published research on *Competency and the Role of the Mental Health Counselor in Collaborative Family Law*. She has also published research results in the *Collaborative Review: Research Edition*, two book chapters on the mental health professional working in divorce, and taught the first course in Florida on Collaborative Divorce for graduate students at Nova Southeastern University's Department of Family Therapy.

Evan Hoffman, Ph.D., is a Senior Associate at the Canadian International Institute of Applied Negotiation (CIIAN). He has worked closely with the Ottawa Police Service to revise their mediation program and he oversaw its operation for several years. Stemming from this, he was then invited to develop and deliver conflict resolution training for new recruits joining the force. Dr Hoffman has published numerous articles on the themes of conflict prevention and resolution, peacebuilding, and mediation. He has provided consulting services to Global Affairs Canada (GAC), the Carter Center, the United Nations, the European Union, the Vietnamese Ministry of Justice, and others on these topics. Over the last ten years, he has conducted workshops and training sessions with hundreds of community leaders, students, police officers, and government officials from around the world.

Jessica Katz Jameson (Ph.D., Temple University, Philadelphia, Pennsylvania) is Associate Professor of Communication at North Carolina (NC) State University. She studies conflict management within organizations with an emphasis on interpersonal and group conflict. Her research has focused on mediation and dispute system design with attention to the roles of identity and emotion in conflict transformation. Jessica has published in journals such as *International Journal of Conflict Management*, *Negotiation Journal*, and *Western Journal of Communication*, and co-authored a chapter on conflict in health care in the *Handbook of Conflict Communication* (2013). Dr Jameson is a mediator for the NC State University employee mediation program and serves as President of the International Association for Conflict Management (2016).

S. Ayse Kadayifci-Orellana, Ph.D., is Associate Director of Georgetown University's MA Program in Conflict Resolution. Her research focuses on the role of religio-cultural traditions in resolving conflicts and building peace; peacebuilding in Muslim communities; gender and peacebuilding; and evaluation of peacebuilding and development programs, among others. Dr Kadayifci-Orellana has authored *Standing on an Isthmus: Islamic Narratives of War and Peace in the Palestinian Territories*, and co-authored the edited volume, *Anthology on Islam and Peace and Conflict Resolution in Islam: Precept and Practice*. She also served as the Associate Director at Salam Institute for Peace and Justice, a non-profit organization for research, education, and practice on issues related to conflict resolution, nonviolence, and development, and was a consultant for the Religion and Peacebuilding Program at United States Institute of Peace.

Neil H. Katz, Ph.D. After more than three decades as a Professor and director or co-director of five conflict resolution programs in the Maxwell School of Citizenship of Syracuse University, Neil has taken on a new challenge as Professor and recent Chair of the Graduate Department of Conflict Studies at Nova Southeastern University in Fort Lauderdale, Florida. Neil also continues consulting and training while serving as head of his own consulting firm, Dr. Neil Katz and Associates. In these capacities, he has worked with many prestigious public and private sector organizations throughout the USA in the areas of conflict resolution, negotiation, mediation, facilitation, and emotional intelligence. Dr Katz has authored numerous books, book chapters, and articles. Among his awards and honors, he received the Martin Luther King Jr. Human Rights Award from the Syracuse community for his career-long commitment to nonviolent conflict resolution and the principles embodied in Dr King's life and work.

Michael Kern, MPA, is the Director of the William D. Ruckelshaus Center. He has a Master of Public Administration degree from the University of Washington's Evans School of Public Policy and Governance, and almost 25 years of experience helping diverse groups reach common ground on public policy issues in the State of Washington and the Pacific Northwest. Prior to joining the Ruckelshaus Center, he was a Senior Associate at Triangle Associates Inc. in Seattle, providing facilitation, mediation, public involvement, strategic planning, project management, and other services. He has also provided these services at non-profit organizations, academic institutions and as a sole practitioner for the North Cascades Initiative, Hatchery Reform Project, Hanford Openness Workshops, and other projects.

Mark Kleiman, Esq., began his career as an attorney with Legal Aid Society Juvenile Rights Division. Recognizing the inadequacy of the courts, he left and founded Community Mediation Services, Inc. (CMS, 1983). CMS grew to become the community mediation center for Queens with up to 20 court diversion programs for families, youth, and the community. The programs utilize a range of intervention strategies from mediation, dialogue, restorative practices, conflict coaching, and cognitive social work approaches. Each offers the skills of collaborative problem solving inducing better communication, and understanding within and between tens of thousands of individuals. He is a founding member of the New York state and city divorce mediation councils and Mediators Beyond Borders. A state court-certified trainer, he is the 2011 winner of the NYSDRA Lawrence Cooke Award for Innovation in Mediation and the Association for Conflict Resolution's 2013 John M. Haynes Distinguished Mediator Award.

Sabine T. Koeszegi, Ph.D., is a Professor, Head of the Institute of Management Science, and Academic Director of the MBA Program Entrepreneurship & Innovation at Vienna University of Technology. She has been visiting scholar—amongst others—at the University of Ottawa and at Victoria University, Melbourne. Her work is published in such international peer-reviewed journals as *Group Decision and Negotiation, Decision Support Systems*, and *Journal of Managerial Psychology*. Her current research interests are management of conflict and diversity in organizations, workplace bullying, negotiation support and e-mediation, and flexible work arrangements.

Ran Kuttner, Ph.D., teaches at the University of Haifa and serves as an academic advisor to Givat Haviva, an organization that aims at building a shared society and dialogue among Jews and Arabs in Israel. Ran recently returned to Israel after seven years in the USA, during which he was an Associate Professor of Negotiation and Dispute Resolution at the Werner Institute, Creighton University. Preceding his arrival at Creighton, Ran was a Visiting Scholar at the Program on Negotiation at Harvard Law School for three years, where he served as an Associate Director of the Dispute Resolution Project and where among other research projects he helped redesign and teach the Harvard mediation course, a joint course for law and MBA students. Ran completed his Ph.D. at the Program on Conflict Management and Negotiation at Bar-Ilan University, Israel. His focus is on relational approaches to conflict resolution and he has published articles on mindfulness in mediation, dialogue, leadership, and negotiation in leading academic journals. He is a certified mediator and mediation teacher in Israel and consults to organizations and community mediation centers that work toward a more dialogic Israeli society in implementing collaborative, relationally oriented conflict engagement approaches.

George A. Lopez, Ph.D., is the Hesburgh Chair in Peace Studies, Emeritus at the Kroc Institute, University of Notre Dame. Lopez's research focuses on economic sanctions, human rights, and various topics in peace studies. He has written or co-edited a dozen books and numerous articles. Lopez's research with David Cortright detailing the success of sanctions on Iraq and the unlikely presence of weapons of mass destruction there appeared before the war in "Disarming Iraq" in *Arms Control Today* (September 2002) and then further articulated after the war in *Containing Iraq: the Sanctions Worked* in *Foreign Affairs* (July/August, 2004). From October 2010 until mid-July 2011, he served on the United Nations (UN) Panel of Experts for monitoring and implementing UN Sanctions on North Korea. From September 2013 to July 2015, he served as Vice President of the Academy for International Conflict

Management and Peacebuilding at the United States Institute of Peace in Washington, DC. For 2015–16, he is co-leader of a Kroc Institute-United Nations University research project assessing 25 years of UN economic sanctions.

Perry Mars, Ph.D., was Professor Emeritus at Wayne State University in Detroit and recognized for his work on Caribbean and African studies. He also taught several other courses in the Africana Studies department, including Black Social and Political Thought, Race and Racism in America, and Black Social Movements. He was considered by many to be among one of the most significant civil rights leaders of the 21st century and his violent murder in 2016 was a terrible loss for everyone he has impacted along with everyone who knew him or his remarkable work. Mars was educated at the University of Guyana where he received his Bachelors degree in History, and Carleton University in Ottawa where he obtained both a Masters degree in International Affairs and a PhD in Political Science. He served in various university positions before going to Africana Studies at Wayne State, including a professorship of Political Science and Development Studies at the University of Guyana and various visiting positions at the University of California (Berkeley), California State University (Los Angeles), The New School for Social Research (New York) and the University of West Indies (Mona, Jamaica). Professor Mars was also the recipient of several academic awards including two Fullbright professorships, and a MacArthur fellowship award. His books include *Ideology and Change: The Transformation of the Caribbean Left*, jointly published by Wayne State University Press and University of the West Indies Press in 1998, and an edited book (with Professor Alma Young) entitled *Caribbean Labor and Politics: Legacies of Cheddi Jagan and Michael Manley*, also published by Wayne State University Press in 2004.

Raffi Mnatzakanian currently serves in the US Army Civil Affairs Regiment. He currently serves as a Civil Affairs Liaison Officer for US Army Europe to 1/10 Special Forces Group in Stuttgart, Germany. His experience includes time as a Civil Affairs Team Leader in Eastern Europe working with various echelons of the Department of Defense, Department of State, and various foreign ministries. He has extensive experience in accessing, developing, and coordinating civil-military operations relevant to the human domain. He recently published in *The Small Wars Journal* on "SOF Mediators: The Application of Understanding-based Model of Mediation as a Non-Lethal Effect." He is a veteran of Operation Iraqi Freedom where he served as a Military Police Platoon Leader in 2009. He is a graduate of the US Military Academy at West Point with a degree in Russian Studies.

Christopher W. Moore, Ph.D., is a Partner in CDR Associates, an international stakeholder engagement, collaborative decision-making and conflict management firm. He has worked in the field of complex multiparty decision making and conflict management for close to four decades as a mediator, facilitator, dispute resolution systems designer, trainer, and author. Internationally, he has consulted in more than 50 countries or political entities and provided assistance to governments, the private sector and civil society organizations to negotiate peace accords, make decisions on national political issues, settle ethnic and religious differences, resolve environmental controversies, and promote sustainable development. Chris worked in the Middle East and Africa to help address a range of transboundary and public policy issues. He has also provided dispute resolution system design and capacity-building assistance for new or existing systems in Liberia, Mongolia, the Philippines, and Sri Lanka to improve access to justice; and in Afghanistan, Jordan, Lebanon, Liberia, South Sudan, Sri Lanka, and Timor Leste to resolve post-environmental crises and post-conflict housing, land

and property disputes. Some of his clients include the United Nations, UN Development Programme, the World Bank, USAID, GTZ (the German Technical Cooperation Agency), the Asia Foundation, and the Norwegian Refugee Council. Domestically, Chris specializes in collaborative decision making, mediation, and facilitation and dispute resolution systems. Some of his domestic clients include Levi Strauss, Pitney Bowes, United Airlines, and the US Army Corps of Engineers, multiple Department of the Interior agencies, the EPA and multiple state governments. He is the author of *The Mediation Process: Practical Strategies for Resolving Conflict* (4th edn, 2014); *Housing, Land and Property: Handbook for Collaborative Decision-Making and Dispute Resolution* (2012); and co-author of *The Handbook on Global and Multicultural Negotiation* (2010); and *A Guide for Developing and Implementing Grievance Mechanisms for Development Projects* (Washington, DC: Office of the Compliance Advisor/Ombudsman of the International Finance Corporation, 2008). Chris holds a Ph.D. in Political Sociology from Rutgers University.

Douglas E. Noll, JD, MA, is a peacemaker, mediator, author, and teacher, specializing in difficult, complex, and intractable conflicts, and was named Lawyer of the Year in 2014 by Best Lawyers in America (www.bestlawyers.com). Along with his colleague Laurel Kaufer, Mr Noll was honored by *California Lawyer Magazine* as California Attorneys of the Year in 2012 for their pro bono Prison of Peace project. He is the creator of Negotiation Mastery for the Legal Pro, an online legal negotiation training course, Negotiate a Centered Life, an online life skills and relationship course, and is author of *Elusive Peace: How Modern Diplomatic Strategies Could Better Resolve World Conflicts* (Prometheus Books, April 2011), *Sex, Politics & Religion at the Office: The New Competitive Advantage* (Auberry Press, 2006, with John Boogaert), and *Peacemaking: Practicing at the Intersection of Law and Human Conflict* (Cascadia, 2002).

Marie Olson Lounsbery (Ph.D., Wayne State University) is an Associate Professor of Political Science at East Carolina University in Greenville, North Carolina, where she teaches courses on international relations, research methods, and war. Her research examines the causes, processes and resolution of intra-state conflict, as well as the impact of foreign military intervention. Recent work examines the organizational dynamics of rebel and terrorist groups. She has published articles in *The Journal of Peace Research, International Interactions*, and *Political Violence and Terrorism*, among others. Dr Olson Lounsbery's book, co-authored with Frederic Pearson, examines various aspects of civil war (2009, published by the University of Toronto Press).

Vitus Ozoke, Ph.D., is originally from Nigeria where he practiced law before moving to the USA. He obtained a Master of Laws (LLM) and a doctorate in Conflict Analysis and Resolution. Due to his primary background in law, he continues to explore areas of synergy between the conventional adversarial approach to conflict and the alternative dispute resolution mechanisms. His research interests include civil wars and other ethno-political conflicts—their dynamics and resolution, multiculturalism, indigenous systems of conflict resolution, civil societies and mass movements, and their roles in conflict, governance, governmental institutions and legal reforms, social identity and its conflict dynamics, social media, gender, race, human rights, and social justice. As a faculty member in the Department of Conflict Analysis and Dispute Resolution, Salisbury University, he teaches courses in diverse areas, including: Race and Race Relations in America; Research Methods; Cross-cultural Conflict Analysis and Resolution; Gender, Sexuality, Human Rights, and Conflict; Negotiation and Conflict Management in Business; and Workshops, Training, and Conflict Coaching. He is a mediator, negotiator, workshop facilitator, ADR trainer, and conflict coach.

Frederic Pearson, Ph.D., is Director of the Center for Peace and Conflict Studies, Professor of Political Science, and Gershenson Distinguished Faculty Fellow at Wayne State University (WSU). He was previously Professor and Research Fellow at the University of Missouri—St Louis and twice a Fulbright Scholar in the Netherlands and UK. His dissertation (University of Michigan) was on Middle East conflict systems, and his numerous books include topics such as civil war solutions, Arab styles of conflict resolution, military intervention, and arms control. Recent research projects have dealt with intergovernmental organization collaboration in peacemaking missions and with insurgent group structures, networks, and violence levels. He was a governmental consultant in 2000 on US National Security, 21st Century, in Washington, DC. As part of his work at WSU, Dr Pearson has brought visiting study delegations from the Middle East and groups of immigration experts to the Detroit community. He is involved in the local and international peace efforts of Rotary International, where he has served as a board member and club president, and has initiated anti-violence projects at several Detroit high schools.

Brian Polkinghorn, Ph.D., is a Distinguished Professor in the Department of Conflict Analysis and Dispute Resolution, Executive Director of the Bosserman Center for Conflict Resolution at Salisbury University and Fulbright Alumni Ambassador with the Council for the International Exchange of Scholars. He has worked in the conflict intervention field since 1985 as a mediator, arbitrator, facilitator, trainer, researcher, academic program developer, conflict coach, dispute systems designer and ombudsman. His primary research and publications are in the areas of environmental and natural resource disputes, graduate program developments in the English- and Spanish-speaking world, international post-conflict development projects, ADR court program assessment, and the evaluation of major government ADR programs. He was a Fellow with the Program on Negotiation (PON), Harvard University Law School, a National Fellow with the US EPA, a United States Presidential Fellow, University System of Maryland Wilson Elkins Professor, and more recently a Senior American Fulbright Scholar with the Evens Program in International Conflict and Mediation at Tel Aviv University.

Daniel Rainey is recognized internationally as an expert practitioner in the fields of ADR and online dispute resolution (ODR). He is a Fellow of the National Center for Technology and Dispute Resolution, a member of the editorial board of *Conflict Resolution Quarterly*, and a co-Editor-in-Chief of the *International Journal of Online Dispute Resolution*. Rainey has authored many publications addressing the ethics and practice of ODR, and he is a co-author and editor of the first comprehensive sourcebook on ODR, *Online Dispute Resolution: Theory and Practice*. He has been active in the integration of technology into dispute resolution practice for two decades, and he has designed technology elements for domestic and international dispute resolution systems. Rainey teaches graduate classes in ODR, negotiation, mediation, and international dispute resolution for Creighton University, Dominican University, and Southern Methodist University. He was one of the instructors for the first ODR course offered by a university (University of Massachusetts, Amherst), and he was the co-designer of the first ODR course to be required as part of a graduate dispute resolution degree (Werner Institute, Creighton University). He is a principal in the consulting firms Holistic Solutions, Inc., and Fourth Party Solutions, a board member of the InternetBar.org, a board member of the Northern Virginia Mediation Service, a member of the advisory board for Modria.com (a leading ODR service provider), and he is the Chief of Staff for the National Mediation Board.

Christian Ramthun is a retired career US Army Foreign Area Officer for sub-Saharan Africa with experience as a Defense Attaché in the Republics of Namibia and Guinea, and command of United Nations troops in Skopje, former Yugoslav Republic of Macedonia. He served on the Theater Special Operations Command-Africa and the United States Special Operations Command as a joint regional strategist, strategic planner, and special operations integrator. Currently, he serves as a course director at the Joint Special Operations University (JSOU) within the United States Special Operations Command, where he oversees the quality and educational effectiveness of Counter Terrorism Fellowship Program (CTFP) courses. In this role, he develops and manages the curriculum of courses involving the combat of violent extremism and an inter-ministerial collaboration course.

Timothy Seidel, Ph.D. from the School of International Service at American University in Washington, DC. Drawing from discourse and postcolonial theory, his research interests include the theoretical and theological foundations of peacebuilding, conflict resolution, and nonviolent resistance.

Jessica Senehi, Ph.D., is Associate Professor of Peace and Conflict Studies at the University of Manitoba, Winnipeg, Canada. Peace and Conflict Studies offers a Ph.D. and Joint MA, and is administered by the University's Faculty of Graduate Studies and housed in the Arthur V. Mauro Centre at St Paul's College at the University. Dr Senehi's scholarship focuses on the role of storytelling for peace, and young people affected by violence. She is Managing Editor of *Storytelling, Self, and Society: An Interdisciplinary Journal of Storytelling Studies.* With Sean Byrne, she is the author of *Violence: Analysis, Intervention, and Prevention* (Ohio University Press, 2012). In 2006, she established the annual Winnipeg International Storytelling Festival: Storytelling on the Path to Peace. She is a board member of Humankind International. She has served as a volunteer mediator in Syracuse, New York, and Fort Lauderdale, Florida. She holds a Ph.D. in Social Science from Syracuse University.

Dan Simon, JD, MA, practices and teaches transformative mediation in St Paul, Minnesota and Los Angeles. He mediates in a wide variety of settings, including divorce and family disputes, and employment conflicts with the US Postal Service. He currently writes a blog on transformative practice for the Institute for the Study of Conflict Transformation (www.transformativemediation.org).

Rebecca Storrow, Ph.D., Vice President in the Commercial Division of the American Arbitration Association (AAA), is in charge of the AAA Miami Regional Office, managing large commercial cases, arbitrators, and mediators in Florida. She is the AAA's Director of a Florida Court Mortgage Mediation Program, holds Florida Supreme Court certification in family, child dependency, circuit, and county mediation, was a Florida Court ADR Program Director, and was appointed to the Florida Supreme Court Foreclosure Taskforce. Rebecca previously founded a community mediation program and is a qualified restorative justice trainer through the University of Minnesota Center for Restorative Justice and Peacemaking. She has conducted indigenous conflict resolution processes including Ho'oponopono and circle processes for courts, businesses, and families.

Matt Swiderski holds a Master of Arts from Salisbury University in Conflict Analysis and Dispute Resolution. Swiderski has served as a Research Fellow at the Bosserman Center for Conflict Resolution at Salisbury University since 2013. During his tenure at Salisbury, he created a database strictly dedicated to mediation articles. Also as a fellow, he served as a research assistant on the Maryland ADR Statewide Research Project. Additionally, while working for the Institute for Public Affairs and Civic Engagement, he served as a research assistant for the Institute's Civic Enhancement across the Curriculum program. Swiderski is a certified mediator and a proud recipient of the Ben Carson Scholarship. He also has instructed undergraduate and graduate courses in International Conflict Resolution and Dispute System Design.

Alan Tidwell, Ph.D., is currently the Director of the Center for Australian, New Zealand and Pacific Studies located in the Edmund A. Walsh School of Foreign Service at Georgetown University. From 2001 through 2004, he was a program officer with the United States Institute of Peace, where he focused on conflict resolution and education. His area of specialization includes work on conflict in the Australasian region. Prior to joining the Institute in 2001, he was a Senior Lecturer in Management at Macquarie Graduate School of Management in Sydney, Australia, where he taught courses in conflict resolution and negotiation. Tidwell holds a Ph.D. in International Relations from the University of Kent in the UK.

Mark Umbreit, Ph.D., is a Professor and founding Director of the Center for Restorative Justice and Peacemaking at the University of Minnesota, School of Social Work. He serves as a Visiting Professor at the Marquette University Law School in Milwaukee and has served as a Fellow of the International Center for Healing and the Law. He is an internationally recognized practitioner and scholar with more than 37 years of experience as a mediator, peacemaker, trainer, researcher, and is author of seven books and more than 180 other publications in the fields of restorative justice, mediation, spirituality, forgiveness, and peacemaking. Dr Umbreit has conducted training seminars and lectures throughout the world. As a practitioner, he facilitates peacebuilding circles in the community between members of diverse cultures and restorative dialogues between family survivors of homicide and the offender in their quest for healing and strength. Mark has initiated a Muslim Outreach project in the Twin Cities and is working with colleagues in Northern Ireland, South Africa, Liberia, and Israel and Palestine on peacebuilding initiatives. Dr Umbreit serves on the faculty of the Center for Spirituality and Healing in the Academic Health Center at the University of Minnesota, teaching courses on Peacemaking and Spirituality, and Forgiveness and Healing.

Siniša Vuković, Ph.D., is a Professor for the Conflict Management Program and Global Policy Program at Johns Hopkins University's School of Advanced International Studies (SAIS). He also holds visiting professorships at the Universities of Amsterdam, Leiden and Nijmegen. He received his Ph.D. and MA from Leiden University and The Netherlands Institute of International Relations Clingendael, and his BA (laurea) in Political Science from University of Rome La Sapienza. He is the recipient of many research grants. His research and teaching focus on various forms of international conflict resolution, negotiation and mediation. He has published in journals such as *Foreign Affairs*, *Washington Quarterly*, *Millennium Journal of International Studies*, *International Journal of Conflict Management*, *International Negotiation*, *Cooperation and Conflict*, and *Acta Politica*, and contributed chapters to several edited volumes. His book *International Multiparty Mediation and Conflict Management* (2015) is published by Routledge.

LaVena Wilkin, Ph.D., is the Director of the Ph.D. program at Sullivan University. Before accepting that position, she served for five years as the Dean of Conflict Management programs at Sullivan and for three years as the Dean of the College of Business Administration. Currently, she is the Editor of the *Journal of Conflict Management*, a scholarly journal that publishes research in many of the multidisciplinary areas of managing conflicts. Before joining Sullivan University, Dr Wilkin spent 26 years in the construction industry, and three of those years she co-owned a commercial masonry sub-contracting company. Dr Wilkin has facilitated workshops, presented at conferences, and written articles on workplace bullying, forgiveness, emotional intelligence, communication, organizational conflict, conflict styles, interpersonal conflict management, and change management. She is the Treasurer for the Leadership Council at Unity Church of East Louisville. Additionally, she serves on the board of directors of the Society for the Prevention of Aggressiveness and Violence among Adolescents (SPAVA).

John Winslade, Ph.D., is an Associate of the Taos Institute and a Professor at California State University San Bernardino (CSUSB). He teaches counseling and until recently was the Associate Dean of the College of Education at CSUSB. For ten years previously he was at the University of Waikato in Hamilton, New Zealand. He has also taught narrative mediation at California State University Dominguez Hills and the Universitat Oberta de Catalunya in an adjunct capacity. He is a regular contributor to the teaching programs of the DISPUK Institute in Denmark and the Conrad Grebel College at the University of Waterloo in Canada. John has co-authored ten books on narrative therapy, narrative mediation and multicultural counseling, as well as many articles and book chapters. He is a founding editor of *Narrative and Conflict*, an online journal on narrative conflict resolution. His books include *Narrative Mediation: A New Approach to Conflict Resolution* (with G. Monk) and *Practicing Narrative Mediation: Loosening the Grip of Conflict* (with G. Monk). His work has been translated into Japanese, Korean, Chinese, Russian, Spanish, German, and Danish.

Anthony Yost, MA, is currently the Mediator Education Coordinator with the New York Peace Institute. Anthony manages a team of over 400 mediators covering thousands of cases every year. He is also part of the training team focused on delivering conflict resolution skills to organizations all over New York. Anthony earned his MA and BA in Conflict Analysis and Dispute Resolution from Salisbury University. He is a Senior Practitioner who mediates, facilitates, trains, and continues to collaborate on research projects with the Bosserman Center for Conflict Resolution. He has conducted research, published, and presented on a number of topics in conflict resolution including international mediation and peace agreements, dispute systems design, and mediation process.

Craig Zelizer, Ph.D., is a faculty member in the Conflict Resolution Program at Georgetown University and the founder/CEO of the Peace and Collaborative Development Network. He has over two decades of experience in conflict resolution practice and research around the world. His areas of expertise include working with youth from violent conflict regions, civil society development and capacity building, the role of the private sector in peacebuilding, and integrated peacebuilding. Dr Zelizer is co-editor of the book *Building Peace: Practical Reflections from the Field* (Kumarian, 2009), and his latest edited book is *Peacebuilding: Innovative Approaches to Transforming Conflict* (Westview Press, 2013).

John Zivojinovic, Ph.D. in conflict resolution studies, is the founder and President of Legacy University. He has served the non-profit sector for almost 30 years. He has written a chapter entitled "The Work of Resolution" in the volume *The Inside Out Youth Worker* (2006). He is a professional speaker, entrepreneur, consultant, mediator, coach, facilitator, trainer, visionary, and strategist. He served for several years as a Lead Pastor of a large congregation in the greater Denver, Colorado area.

Zena D. Zumeta, JD, is a former board member and President of the Academy of Family Mediators (now merged into the Association for Conflict Resolution), past President of the Michigan Council for Family and Divorce Mediation, and past Regional Vice President of the Society of Professionals in Dispute Resolution. She is a member of the Editorial Board of the American Bar Association's *Dispute Resolution Magazine*. She has taught at Hamline University School of Law, and is an Adjunct Professor at Pepperdine University School of Law's Straus Institute for Dispute Resolution, and Cooley Law School. She is the recipient of the Family Mediation Council-Michigan Lifetime Achievement in Mediation Award; the National Education Association/Saturn Corporation Award for Union-Management Collaboration; the John Haynes Distinguished Mediator Award from the Association for Conflict Resolution; and the Kumba Award from the National Conference on Minorities in ADR. As President of the Mediation Training and Consultation Institute, Zena is also a highly respected mediation trainer. She is also a former labor negotiator and continues her work with labor-management cooperation as President of The Collaborative Workplace.

ACKNOWLEDGEMENT

This handbook reflects the contributions of a brilliantly talented team of individuals whom I respect and appreciate tremendously for sharing their wisdom and knowledge. I would like to extend my utmost gratitude and heartfelt thanks for the determination and support of all the remarkable contributing authors who not only provided their precious time and talents to this project, but who also tirelessly dedicate their lives to the pursuit of peace, justice, human rights and conflict resolution through their work in mediation. These leaders in the field face among some of the most difficult conflict conditions in human history given the crossroads of global change and conflict crisis we face in the world today. Words cannot express the gratitude I have for these exceptional human beings whom I treasure not only as colleagues, but most especially as friends. It was a blessing to have worked with such an inspiring and talented group of individuals who were able to balance the complexity of this project with a very sophisticated sense of professionalism and creativity. It was a lifetime honor to work with them all! These nearly 60 contributors are true gifts to this world. I am certain that it is through their innovative work and creative spirits that the world has indeed become a better place!

I would like to express very special thanks to my exemplar team. Charles Goesel led in masterfully assisting me in this project and he was my right hand throughout this project. His meticulous attention to perfection and his leadership was appreciated profoundly; he was a true blessing. It was his ambitious support and assistance that made this project a reality. He is a well-rounded and talented scholar, practitioner, and researcher whom I consider a dear and respected colleague as well as friend, and I look forward to working with him for years to come! Diane Gaston, April Coan, and Sheila Northrop provided exceptional support in the aspects of organization and compilation of this project. I was surrounded by the best support team I could imagine. They provided unwavering support and assistance that was outstanding and they are incredible assets to the field of conflict resolution. I appreciated the entire team's commitment to this project and their professional interface with all the contributors. I can only imagine what wonderful things they will do in their careers given the level of professionalism they displayed during this project.

I extend heartfelt thanks to those who supported me at my university. I appreciated their interest and recognition of this project. Also the loyalty and commitment along with the hard work of all my talented graduate students, who are amazing change agents and peacemakers and continue to inspire me in my work in this beautiful field.

Also, I would like to extend my utmost gratitude to the dedicated and professional staff at Routledge for their assistance and guidance throughout this process, as their professional team helped me turn my vision into a reality from inception to completion. It is with their commitment and hard work that this project came to fruition. It was a pleasure working with such a steadfast and professional team who treated me like a part of the family. I am especially grateful to Sharon Golan, Erin Arata and Ruth Bradley for their interest, support, and production of this handbook.

Finally, I must pay a special tribute to my entire beloved family who supported me over the course of several years to make this handbook a reality. Thank you from the bottom of my heart for your love, support, and sacrifice—to my mother and father, husband Stavros, children Vassilios, Alexandra and Christina, and my brothers Nick and Greg along with their families.

PREFACE

The world of mediation is pervasive in terms of growth and development in the current diverse landscape where conflict is widespread. Today's world requires professionals alongside everyday citizens to emerge as mediators and peacemakers to influence positive change in an ever-changing world. This handbook presents disparate interdisciplinary perspectives and applications of mediation from multiple lenses and serves as a bridge between theory, research, and practice in the conflict resolution field. It is relevant for a diverse audience with topics that span across disciplines that encompass conflict resolution, peace, justice and human rights, and it is relevant for individuals with different levels of expertise from the novice to the seasoned professional across various disciplines.

The story behind this handbook began 20 years ago when I began working in the conflict resolution field with the simple idea that mediation is an amazing form of conflict resolution that has a number of possibilities. Since then I have taught mediation to thousands of master's and doctoral students in one of the earliest conflict resolution departments in the nation to offer a doctoral degree, taught conflict resolution to undergraduates at three prominent universities, and trained and certified thousands of professionals as mediators as the Director of the Institute of Conflict Resolution and Communication (ICRC), as well as had the unique opportunity to personally work with a very brilliant group of practitioners and scholars from across the world in the field of conflict resolution.

While my formal training and work have provided me with the honor to serve in the field of peace and conflict resolution, it is my personal story that encompasses my background and history, largely complemented by my family members and lived experiences, that provided me with a strong inclination for the field and an enduring commitment to it that only grows with time. My grandfather was an immigrant who arrived on the shores of the USA with his father and brother at the age of 16 in 1930 with only one small bag that contained his personal belongings. He would never return to his Greek village to see his mother again who would suffer the sights of genocide and other atrocities by several invasions of their small village located in the historic region known as Epirus in Europe. He served in the US Air Force during World War II. His sacrifice of three years in the war and his near loss of life when US battleships were targeted by bombs and sunk directly in front and behind his own battleship was far more than I could imagine. What inspired me even more is that he drew from his faith as a spiritual leader and led the crew of young soldiers in prayer for what they thought would be their last moments of life. This story is a testament of authentic courage and hope; it strongly resonates with me every day and has placed me on a life trajectory to promote peace in the world, as humbling as this can be for any individual.

As a child, my family members worked abroad for the US Department of Defense, so I was exposed to disparate cultures that faced revolutions and lacked basic liberties like the freedom of speech, human rights, fair justice, and religious freedoms. The people in these countries were profoundly warm, compassionate, and peaceful, but the political climate was volatile and hostile at times. I saw people who were regularly wrongfully accused and persecuted. A close family friend accused of speaking about the corruption of government was placed in jail. He was informed weekly that he would be executed, yet he was released over a decade and a half later after being physically and mentally tortured. Today he is free and inconceivably optimistic about life and the world. He champions peace, compassion, and love toward others in his work despite the hate that invaded his life. He is a vessel of peace, an emergent mediator, and an inspiring role model for me and others.

My story is only one story, but all the contributors to this handbook have traveled on their own personal journeys. I am confident that their stories continue to inform their work. You will have an opportunity to explore their work within this handbook. Indeed, as you read each chapter, I hope you recognize that stories like experiences provide the nexus between theory and praxis and your personal story is significant as well as relevant to the work you conduct or will conduct in the future. What connects all the contributors to this handbook is that they are profoundly committed to promoting peace and they view mediation as one formidable conflict resolution approach to that end.

Along with my personal journey, as a professor, trainer, researcher, and practitioner in mediation, I saw a need to develop a unique handbook of mediation that was valuable, practical, and applicable for individuals who had an earnest desire to learn from thought leaders, notable practitioners, forefront authorities, and distinguished educators in the mediation field. This project was only possible because of the collective commitment and dedication of these world-class professionals, of whom several are well-noted pioneers, to the expansion and development of the field. Presented collectively, these chapters present a kaleidoscope of meanings and applications of mediation for present-day conflict resolution scholars, professionals, practitioners, and students (undergraduate, graduate, and postgraduate).

This handbook was designed to complement the resources available to mediators and conflict resolutionists in order to provide these individuals with a more nuanced understanding about mediation and conflict resolution approaches. It is intended to aid in the development of mediators' competencies and skills as well as promote a more holistic understanding of most contemporary mediation theory, research, and practice. Each chapter is arranged according to the context where it best applies. Applications to disparate settings are presented in a manner to showcase where mediators are working, what services they render, and/or what mediation concepts are beneficial in these settings. It is noteworthy that many of these concepts are applicable across mediation settings. My hope is that there is something for everyone, whether you desire simply to explore and learn about mediation or aspire to advance your mediation career and techniques. My personal perspective is that mediation requires mediators to be lifelong learners and my hope is that these chapters will be valuable to you in your endeavors—both in your personal and professional life. Finally, my greatest desire is to incite remarkable people to be remarkable mediators to render better alternatives of conflict management in order to improve the human condition and support peace for people around the world who face conflict.

As I convey to my students at the conclusion of every mediation class, after you complete this class, or in this case complete reading this handbook, it is not the end, but merely the beginning of this journey. I encourage you to continue this exciting journey of lifelong learning, dialogue, and exploration into mediation as it has so much to offer you, and you have so much to contribute to it as well. I wish you a journey that is both fulfilling and memorable!

Please feel free to contact me about this or future editions.

Alexia Georgakopoulos
icrctraining@comcast.net or georgako@nova.edu

INTRODUCTION

Revealing the world of mediation

Alexia Georgakopoulos

> The more affects we allow to speak about one thing, the more eyes, different eyes we can use to observe one thing, the more complete will our concept of this thing, our objectivity, be.
>
> *(Nietzsche in* The Genealogy of Morals*)*

The practice of mediation traces back to ancient times and across ancient civilizations, and interestingly the field of mediation continues to grow and advance in contemporary times around the globe. The resounding significant applications and impacts of mediation across contexts point to its remarkable influence. This handbook features invaluable theories, research, and practice of world-class professionals who have dedicated their lives to the craft and study of mediation.

Aristotle poignantly stated, "experience seems almost the same as science and art, but in fact science and art come to men [people] through experience ..." (MacMahon, 1943, p. 5). This statement underscores the importance of experience in the advancement of knowledge, especially in the world of mediation where the ebb and flow of mediation is fluid and dynamic. Revealing the world of mediation is also about a story, so it is through the diverse experiences of the contributing authors of this handbook that a story of mediation emerges—of its past, present, and future—which is a collective narrative that professionals in the mediation field should continue to share as it develops education, research, theory, practice, and spirit—which all encompass the hallmark, progress, and development of mediation. As with any form of progress, it does not come without recognition, struggle, and action. Thus, mediators are encouraged to reflect on who they are as mediators, what guides their behaviors, what shapes them, how they shape mediation, and what is necessary to improve their effectiveness.

Who mediators are and what they have experienced influences their personal, ethical, and theoretical standpoints; therefore, it is essential that mediators are reflective and mindful in practice because they are largely responsible for shaping the nature of every mediation. Introspection into the questions "Who am I?" and "What does it mean for me to be a mediator?" are important questions that all mediators should ask themselves. It is important to qualify that mediators are largely a product of their cultural and social blueprints. Many aspects of decoding information, making sense of data, and responding to parties are automatic, heuristic, and unconscious.

There may be a level of implicit bias for mediators on diversity such as culture, ethnicity, faith, gender, age, race, politics, disability, and class, to name a few. Mediators should better understand their conscious and unconscious biases. These aspects are among the most pressing issues facing mediators as they concern their effectiveness, trustworthiness, and credibility across settings. Therefore, it is essential for mediators to engage continuously in the reflexivity process. Mediators should condition themselves to be aware of their bias (self and other) and the power of language (use of words such as adversaries versus partners in peace, custody versus co-parenting, plaintiff and defendant versus collaborators). These elements punctuate and prime the direction of the communication interaction as well as impact parties' responses. Mediators should be held to high standards to ensure trustworthiness in the profession. Their demonstration of credibility emits largely from effectively being guardians of the process. Effectiveness as a mediator is only possible in action when mediators are aware of their values, norms, and biases. Effective mediators may navigate a landscape of contrasting values and norms while performing mediation ethically and professionally with a gold standard when they recognize their own biases, take concerted action to prevent biases from infringing on the mediation process, and become transparent about their goals and perspectives of mediation.

Identity is multi-faceted, so mediators should be cognizant about how they position themselves in terms of addressing who they are in relation to the parties and their subscribed mediation framework. It is important to recognize that mediators are value-bound in the following ways: 1) the viewpoints or mindset mediators have about conflict, how they frame conflict, and focus on it (some see it as an opportunity, others see it as a problem); 2) who mediators are as individuals and how they see their roles as mediators as well as how they view parties; 3) what choices mediators make concerning their frameworks, practices, and/or approaches in mediation; and 4) what questions mediators decide to ask parties given the power of language and how questions or statements punctuate discourse responses (i.e. glass half full questions from a more optimistic perspective or glass half empty questions from a more pessimistic perspective). By recognizing their mindsets, viewpoints, biases, and processes, mediators may become more intentional while building solid toolboxes that will improve their craft.

While mediators shape the mediation context because they are guardians of the process, they are concurrently and commensurably shaped by it as well. Mediators often share that there are transcendental, even spiritual moments in mediation that inherently transform them along with parties. This is best described as a positive energy or source that is experienced. Through the nexus of supporting party empowerment, transformation, and self-determination, mediators often experience the byproduct of being deeply impacted and transformed themselves. This should not be a self-serving goal, yet it is a common outcome as the essence of mediation can be very spiritual in nature. By being authentic, compassionate, intentional, and meaningful, a mediator may open a space for spirituality to emerge naturally for everyone involved in mediation. Perhaps since humans cannot experience compassion without struggle, it is through mediation that compassion emerges with transcendental moments. When mediators harness the power of mediation and embrace spiritual opportunities of connectedness and inclusiveness in mediation, they develop as professionals, but more importantly as human beings. While individuals in other professions may envy mediators, this profession unquestionably is not free of frustration, uncertainty, difficulty, and complexity to the highest degree, yet it is often the inclination of the mediator to face the challenges and tackle the responsibilities associated with mediating complex disputes because mediators are often internally driven by the simple yet powerful desire to help people in a time of need or turmoil when there are high stakes in conflict.

Albeit as mediators shape mediation and are shaped by it, context also plays a significant role in mediation. Thus, importance should also be placed on contextual features in mediation given the dialectical and significant impact these features have on mediation and mediators. Mediation cannot be understood in a vacuum. Mediators and parties are situated to a large extent by communication and interaction that place them juxtaposed within the rich parameters of context, culture, and history. Without recognition of these formidable contextual features, mediators may not be able to navigate the changing landscapes and complex meanings involved in mediation processes.

The famous sociologist E.T. Hall argued that "communication is culture and culture is communication" (Hall, 1959, p. 186). Thus, mediators must come to understand contextual features as they provide mediators with nuanced cultural meanings that are couched within every interaction, both domestically and internationally. For instance, a particular party may have a preference to discuss historically significant narratives that are couched in the past while another party desires to speak of only future-oriented solutions. These preferences have developed over time and cultures; thus effective mediators should open a space and invite all parties to participate so their needs may be met. Without an understanding of rich meanings associated with context, mediators can be compared with pilots who are deprived of navigational equipment in vast open skies.

Diverse perspectives and applications of mediation will continue to grow just as demand is typically met with supply. As mediation continues to grow by its application in relationships, organizations, communities, and cultures across the globe, mediators will be called to better understand and carefully consider creative processes, indigenous approaches, specialized processes, creative frameworks, along with global preferences. The idea of one size fits all will never be reflective of the practice of mediation, but rather mediation will expand with the ebb and flow of conflict that will differ across issues, people, and settings.

The field of mediation requires the establishment of a gold standard in the industry and often this standard will derive best from the various contexts where mediation is utilized or unique tenets that rest within particular mediation theories. Logically, internationally acceptable standards should be established to support the reputation and integrity of the field around the world. Like specialized and professional fields of medicine and law, mediation requires a code of conduct that a highly regarded and respected community of professionals can develop and agree upon that provides openness for the formation of new theories and applications of mediation. An oversight body would promote quality control and maintain integrity of the profession. Mediators should be held to the highest standards of conduct with oversight and accountability woven directly into the fabric of their practice and field. This handbook reveals a solid collection of mediator characteristics and skills that may contribute to the advancement of solid standards for the conduct of mediators.

As you will discover, this handbook is organized around a number of significant contexts where mediators work and the sequence of contexts is as follows: *new age, relational, organizational and institutional, community, environmental, intercultural and international mediation contexts.* Each section is informed by solid theory, state-of-the-art research, and best practices to provide the reader with a well-rounded scope and understanding of mediation praxis in contemporary times.

Part I involves dynamic, creative, and innovative concepts as well as a survey of trends that impact mediation in the new age. This section covers careers, ethics, and values involved with mediation, as well as mediation infused with technology, improv, storytelling, and spirituality. This section features what many individuals might consider to be unconventional techniques in mediation, yet these are techniques, skills, and processes that have the potential to promote the dynamic nature of mediation. The chapters in this section illustrate that mediation may benefit substantially from new ways of operating and thinking that go beyond standard mediation processes of the past.

Part II focuses on mediating conflicts within intimate and/or family relational settings, which can arguably be among the most sensitive settings because of the close bonds and/or emotional ties surrounding these types of relationships. In this section, formidable mediation concepts are underscored to aid mediators who are involved with the challenging task of mediating infractions in disparate relationships that can result in strong emotions such as anger, hurt, fear, pain, despair, and disappointment. The chapters in this section illustrate that by tapping into authentic forgiveness, restorative justice, transformative mediation, narrative mediation, genuine mindfulness, collaborative approaches, and embraced spirituality, a mediator potentially can promote parties to experience renewed hope, heartfelt shifts, transformational moments, real reconciliation, powerful restitution, and/or life-changing new stories.

Part III features mediating disputes within organizational settings such as criminal justice, governmental, health care, court, commercial (private and public sector), and other institutional settings. With the continuing rise of court costs coupled with the length of time it takes to litigate disputes within these settings or the toll conflict takes on both the organization and its employees who avoid addressing conflict within these contexts, mediation can serve as an impressive alternative process of dispute resolution or conflict management system that has the potential of restoring relationships or fixing problems through parties' own decision making and self-determination. Indeed, relationships could otherwise be impaired to perpetuity in alternative adversarial forums. The chapters in this section provide a framework for mediating conflict where parties, whether they be victim vs. offender, doctor vs. patient, employee vs. supervisor, academics vs. leadership, or colleague vs. colleague, may engage in a consensual process to address conflict, collaborate in crafting creative solutions, or experience renewed empowerment, validation, or confirmation by participating in this process.

Part IV centers on constructively mediating conflict matters within community contexts and building peaceful communities by having individuals take personal accountability for the resolution of the conflict and control of the outcomes. Community mediation often serves as a form of conflict management to strengthen relationships and build connections between individuals, groups, and organizations for the preservation and enhancement of the community and subsequently the society as a whole. It is typically designed to avoid destructive confrontation, uninformed ignorance, costly litigation, or violence within communities. The chapters of this section feature mediation involved with community policing, peer programs, family services, intergroup dialogues, cooperative citizenship, and juvenile development.

Part V addresses mediating in the unprecedented and undeniably most complex conflict in human history—environmental conflict. The chapters in this section problematize environmental issues and impacts such as climate change, natural disasters, depleted resources, national security, and land use that have pervasive impacts across the world. Humankind's greatest challenge to solve environmental crisis is not a question of *if* it requires action and attention, but *when* humans can effectively address this conflict and in *what* manner, as it is a matter of human survival. Mediation seems to be a course of action that may be needed more frequently in phases that pertain to preemptively planning for versus reactively responding to large-scale environmental conflict and crisis. This section will underscore how mediators can be instrumental in discussions, dialogues, and policies, debates, and action plans that surround urgent issues in environmental conflict.

Part VI discusses mediating in the age of complex conflicts in dynamic international and intercultural settings where diverse cultural standpoints in norms, values, ethics, and mindsets often result in protracted conflict and escalating tensions. Raging war is often the consequence of unsettled conflict on international fronts; however, war is costly, and it leaves a significant imprint on human memory with often catastrophic results such as human loss. Moreover, it often leaves destruction in its path with no renewal or graver consequences such as aggravating the conflict and worsening relations to more volatile conditions. There are no bombs big enough to build relationships. When there is no relationship, there can be no trust; when there is a relationship, trust can be built. While many people may argue that it takes courage to go to war, the chapters in this section collectively illustrate that it takes courage to promote peace, and an alternative dispute resolution approach that has profound promise in this arena includes mediation, which has proven to support invaluable outcomes such as the following: trust building, committed diplomacy, newfound understanding, cooperative narratives, genuine dialogue, humanistic connection, trust restoration, relationship transformation, and sustainable peacebuilding. The chapters in this section cover mediating conflict in challenging cultural contexts with topics such as politics, religion, and war as well as conditions, processes, and techniques that impede or assist mediators in these diverse global contexts.

This handbook underscores the following four signature themes: 1) *contexts* where mediators have significantly contributed (and can contribute more in the future); 2) *skills and competencies* that inform best practices for mediators; 3) *applications* of mediation that provide examples of success and critiques of mediation; and finally 4) *recommendations drawn from theory, research, and practice* for mediators. The chapters are delivered by thought leaders, forefront authorities, and/or notable practitioners in the field of mediation. In approaching the readings, the reader is advised to be reflective while keeping an open mind to the nuanced differences and similarities across the chapters. This approach would be similar to having an open dialogue at a conference where individuals would be encouraged to pose questions to better understand the perspective of others while gaining better insight into their own perspectives. Mediators have much to gain from exploring the experiences, work, and approaches of other mediators. This approach is best captured by Bernstein's (1983) notion of a dialogic community where different voices from different scholarly camps and disciplines may share their work with others, which can effectively inform science, understanding, and praxis. Bernstein's (1983) notion of truth and meaning goes beyond objectivism and relativism as it is only through dialogue that different interpretations and meanings are shared for a more holistic understanding of the thing that we desire to understand. It is my desire for each reader to expand his/her horizon and experience a more holistic view of mediation from reading the multiple perspectives and applications of mediation presented in this handbook.

If one assumes that conflict is a natural part of any relationship and a relationship is characterized as individuals or groups who are interdependent, then conflict is pervasive across all types of relationships across domestic and global contexts. There may be no greater need for future generations than the ability to effectively mediate conflict issues that pertain to relationships, communities, nations, resources, sustainability, trust, security, and war. This is a time when conflict conditions are volatile and unprecedented in the history of the human race, with financial crises, environmental variability, threatening diseases/viruses, scarcity of resources, population explosions, outbreaks of violence, and new uncharted problems that face humans. One response to the human condition could be to participate as observers in what inextricably could be defined as circumstances outside anyone's control, or mediators along with other alternative dispute resolution professionals may be decisive to participate in the movement to improve the world by tackling conflict. At times, conflict circumstances call for the attention of mediators and at other times, mediators inherently take action to address conflict. Through global citizenship, it seems fitting that mediators with civility, integrity, humility, compassion, intentionality, and commitment should be part of mediating the complex discourse, debates, solutions, public policies, and action plans that impact humans during crossroads of change and sometimes crisis across contexts for a more promising and peaceful future.

Mediators who have a commitment to translating theory and research into best practices for meaningful societal and humanistic impact are adaptable to real world applications. It is substantially changing the way we think and do things by way of our own and others' experiences that teaches us powerful lessons about ourselves and mediation. As mediators face disparate conflict milieux with complex challenges that are unprecedented in history, it is imperative to produce highly skilled and specialized mediators who are master learners equipped with unparalleled competencies, who are trained to tackle local and world problems in order to help change and improve the world. What is more, the world needs large-scale grassroots efforts to grow the most influential mediators as promoting pervasive peace rests with ordinary people who work as change agents like teachers, parents, mentors, neighbors, role models, friends and even strangers. It is my hope that readers of this handbook learn from the extensive breadth and depth of experiences informed by theory, research, and/or practice of the contributing authors, and are inspired to harness their own strengths to face present and future conflict challenges that face humans.

References

Bernstein, R.J. (1983) *Beyond Objectivism and Relativism*. Philadelphia, PA: University of Pennsylvania Press.

Hall, E.T. (1959) *The Silent Language*. New York: Doubleday (1990 re-issue by Anchor Books, a division of Doubleday).

Nietzsche, F. (2006). *On the Genealogy of Mortality*. C. Diethe (trans.), K. Ansell-Pearson (ed.). Cambridge: Cambridge University Press. Retrieved from www.inp.uw.edu.pl/mdsie/Political_Thought/GeneologyofMorals.pdf.

MacMahon, J.H. (1943) Metaphysics. In L.R. Loomis (ed.), *Aristotle: On Man in the Universe* (pp. 3–40). New York: Walter J. Black.

PART I

Promoting dynamic mediation in the new age

1

MEDIATION CAREER TRENDS THROUGH TIME

Exploring opportunities and challenges

Craig Zelizer and Colleen Chiochetti

This chapter explores the opportunities and challenges regarding applied careers in mediation. The first section explores the concept of mediation and the associated skills needed to advance a career. This is followed by a discussion of the various paths to building skills, ranging from gaining practical experience, to undertaking short-term training programs, to pursuing undergraduate or graduate degrees. The diverse range of mediation career opportunities is highlighted with strong emphasis on the need to integrate the process across diverse sectors. Throughout the chapter, particular attention focuses on the ethical and practical challenges for those seeking to advance their career in mediation. A critical focus of the chapter is the need to approach the process and skills of mediation in a holistic manner and the importance of not limiting a career in mediation to positions that fit the traditional definition of the process.

Over the past few decades, mediation has rapidly grown from a small nucleus of individuals and organizations to a burgeoning sector with dedicated job opportunities, emerging career tracks, and many individuals seeking to advance a career in the field. This tremendous growth in the USA, and around the world, has been largely motivated by the desire for more participatory and effective means of addressing diverse inter-person, intergroup, community, and international conflicts. However, the number of individuals seeking to engage in mediation both on a voluntary and professional basis far exceeds the number of paid opportunities available.

What is mediation?

Mediation generally refers to a third-party process conducted by a mediator, with no formal stake in a particular dispute or conflict issue, who helps to facilitate a participatory process in which the stakeholders or parties that are in dispute with one another find a mutually satisfactory and beneficial outcome. As Dr Christopher Moore, one of the pioneers in the field, explains:

> Mediation is a conflict resolution process in which a mutually acceptable third party, who has no authority to make binding decisions for disputants, intervenes in a conflict or dispute to assist involved parties to improve their relationships, enhance communications,

> and use effective problem-solving and negotiation procedures to reach voluntary and mutually acceptable understandings or agreements on contested issues.
>
> *(Moore, 2014, p. 8)*

It is essential to note that mediation, as a process, has existed for centuries (Barrett & Barrett, 2004; Moore, 2014). For as long as there have been one or more individuals or groups in conflict that they are unable to solve directly, third parties have been present to try to help facilitate a resolution. The notion of pursuing paid employment as a full-time mediator is a relatively recent development which came about in the mid-20th century, as the field of Alternative Dispute Resolution began to emerge. Prior to this, individuals in many professional and personal capacities, such as diplomats, religious leaders, business leaders, political figures, or simply trusted individuals, would help facilitate a process through which parties could reach an agreement. As Moore (2014) explains, "[f]or the most part mediators in other ages and cultures learned their crafts informally and fulfilled their role as mediators in the context of other functions and duties" (p. 69).

Much of the modern mediation practice emerged from four main trends. The first was the incredibly turbulent history of US labor/management relations in the 19th and 20th centuries. During this period, there were hundreds of strikes by workers seeking better working conditions, better pay, and a voice in their workplaces, while many employers sought to prevent the ability of workers to organize. It was only in the post-Depression era that a social contract was formed and an emerging field of labor relations or industrial relations developed, in which mediators began to play an increasingly important role in helping to mediate strikes and worker–management issues. The US federal government played a key role in helping to facilitate more positive and peaceful relations through the creation of agencies such as the National Mediation Board (designed to help prevent railway strikes in 1926) and the Federal Mediation and Conciliation Services (FMCS) in 1947, with the mission of "preventing or minimizing the impact of labor-management disputes on the free flow of commerce by providing mediation, conciliation and voluntary arbitration" (FMCS, 2015). The US government had a strong interest in helping to ensure more peaceful relations between workers and management, particularly in critical industries, as disruptions greatly affected the economy (Kovick, 2005).

The second major trend in expanding mediation as a career option was the growth of community mediation programs in the 1970s. During this period, as part of the larger movement for social justice in the late 1960s and 1970s, combined with frustration regarding the increasing number of disputes going to the courts, a movement emerged promoting mediation as a quicker, fairer and more just solution. In court-based approaches, the process and the outcome are far removed from the parties who are in dispute. For example, legal counsel often represents the parties, a jury or judge imposes a decision, and usually one side emerges as the winner and the other as the loser. Conversely, mediation allows the parties to represent their interests directly, and formulate an agreement where both sides can emerge as winners.

In addition to the push by community justice organizations for fairer and more inclusive processes, there was recognition by some in the legal and governmental communities that the legal system was not always the best avenue to resolve disputes. Clogging up courts with cases was overwhelming the capacity of local and state systems. Thus, what began as a largely community social justice-orientated push, also started to become institutionalized (Kovick, 2005). Apart from the potential for more collaborative solutions than court-based options, mediation can also save time and money for the parties involved in the process.

The third major trend in the growth of mediation was the dramatic expansion of the conflict resolution and peacebuilding fields on a global scale after the end of the Cold War. Although, as highlighted earlier, mediation practices and institutions were present in all societies, it was during this period that the practice, scholarship, and funding of domestic, regional, and international conflict resolution institutions increased dramatically. For example, as Zelizer (2013) explains, "[w]hat was initially carried out by a select group of scholars, citizen diplomats, and nongovernmental organizations is now being integrated into official discourse, policies and practices" (p. 4). For many years, the term conflict resolution was used to refer to the larger field of scholarship and practice. However, over recent decades, peacebuilding has become a more dominant term encompassing international conflict resolution practices, while conflict resolution is a more frequently used term in the domestic and sometimes academic arenas (Zelizer, 2013). Many use peacebuilding as a term to refer to larger structural and relational changes, while conflict resolution is often thought of as a "narrower set of specific tools (negotiation, mediation, facilitation, conflict analysis, communication skills and their theoretical underpinnings)" (Zelizer, 2013, p. 7).

The fourth area that has led to a dramatic use of mediation and alternative dispute resolution (ADR) practices is the institutionalization of conflict resolution practices in private and public organizational settings. For many years, mediation practices in institutions were often relegated to the sidelines or seen as an extension of human resources. However, as the conflict resolution field began to expand, there was also a significant push to create more effective, participatory, and transparent conflict-sensitive systems. Although a number of federal agencies had mediation and/or ADR programs, Congress passed the Administrative Dispute Resolution Act of 1996, which made it easier for federal institutions to adopt ADR processes (Pou, 1997). This act builds on earlier legislation that started to encourage the more widespread use of ADR. As Pou (1997) explains, the act shows that "Congress, along with many federal agencies, have moved beyond an initial skepticism and concern over potential abuses to a point where they have begun to view ADR methods as safe and effective" (para. 10). President Clinton issued an executive order requiring federal agencies to use "dispute resolution in all civil cases" involving the government (Reporters' Committee for Freedom of the Press, 1996, para. 1).

Since then, conflict resolution as a process to help organizations run more effectively internally and externally and increase employee morale has grown substantially. This is across an array of institutions as many private companies, schools, universities, and public agencies have set up ADR, Conflict Management, and Ombuds offices to help prevent, manage, and mitigate conflicts.

It is important to understand the four general trends that have helped fuel a growth in the mediation field, as each of these also corresponds to a potential career path in which one may use mediation skills and knowledge to develop a career. The next section of the chapter outlines the skills needed for a mediation career, followed by an overview of career opportunities, and finally challenges and opportunities for practicing mediators.

Skills, knowledge and training needed to be a mediator

Skills

Mediators need many skills in order to be effective in their work. These skills can be broken down into three main areas, including communication, managing the process, and personal awareness. One of the main differences between negotiation (when two or more parties directly communicate) and mediation is that mediation is a form of "third party facilitated communication" (Moore, 2014, p. 8).

Thus, a mediator needs to be highly skilled in numerous communication skills including:

- *Questioning*—The ability to ask appropriate and reflective questions encouraging parties to engage in a conversation and move beyond zero-sum position discussions.
- *Listening*—This is one of the most essential skills that a mediator can possess. It is critical since often in situations of heightened conflict, parties stop listening to each other. They might only listen for weaknesses in the adversary's position, not understanding. A mediator can help parties by modeling good listening practices, and it is through listening mindfully and reflectively (combined with questioning) that a mediator can help the parties uncover the roots of a conflict.
- *Body language*—The use of one's body and positioning is a critical component of the communication process. Although there is strong emphasis on verbal communication, a great deal of research has shown that upwards of 55 percent of communication takes place through body language and nonverbal cues (Jensen, 2012). Mediators can model both open and encouraging behavior to inspire parties to do the same.
- *Paraphrasing/summarizing*—In a mediation session, a crucial step is making sure the parties feel their story or perspective has been heard and acknowledged. Thus, mediators can use their communication skills to summarize and ensure that how a party has framed their experience has been heard correctly.
- *Reframing*—In many escalated conflict settings parties will say hurtful or escalatory statements. Therefore a mediator often needs to be skilled in taking potentially damaging comments and removing the bite, but keeping the essence to help the mediation continue in a positive direction.

Process

Mediators need to possess familiarity and ease with the mediation process. Part of building a successful career in mediation is learning the basic steps of mediation, and then unlearning them to some degree, so as to be able to adapt them to the ebb and flow of each mediation. Knowing the process and the general steps is like having a compass as an aid to know the general direction in which mediation may proceed. For example, many mediations will reach a point where parties may seem stuck or reluctant to move on. Being comfortable with letting the parties proceed on their own while also knowing when to help encourage progress is important.

Managing the mediation process may also be akin to riding a bike, while juggling and talking on a cell phone. It is necessary to keep many contradictory items in balance. A mediator needs to listen deeply to the parties, but at the same time be thinking about what comes next, exploring potential roadblocks, checking in with a co-mediator, if there is one, being comfortable with the emotional highs and lows of mediation, managing the process, but not scripting too closely, etc. This may seem like a daunting series of tasks or challenges, and initially it is, but with time, experience, and practice the process becomes intuitive and mediators are then able to more comfortably adapt to their own preferred mediation style(s). Effectively managing the process is a critical step in increasing the chances of having a successful outcome.

Knowledge

Being an effective mediator requires an in-depth knowledge of the dynamics of conflict, and understanding what might motivate individuals to pursue behaviors that, on the outside at least, may not be rational or in their own self-interest. Knowledge of conflict dynamics includes psychological and emotional elements of what causes conflict escalation and de-escalation. In addition, understanding how to analyze conflicts is a central process in mapping and understanding the key parties' underlying interests, issues, and more (Moore, 2014). One of the most challenging aspects of the mediation process is helping two or more parties with mutually incompatible truths to at least be able to acknowledge the perspective and legitimacy of the other side's perspective. A mediator needs to be skilled in breaking down complex conflicts into common issues through which the parties can begin to find common ground.

Mediators should also have knowledge of the larger conflict resolution and peacebuilding industry. It is necessary to understand how one's work fits within the larger field and what the key trends are in one's particular area, whether it be working on organizational conflicts or helping to mediate land disputes in violent contexts overseas. This also includes an understanding of who is providing funding for mediation practice and why.

Personal awareness

The idea of mediation is that a third "neutral" party helps disputants find common ground and find a self-directed and participatory resolution to the issue. In reality, being a mediator is an inherently personal process and being reflective, critical, and self-aware are crucial components to success in the field. There is also the issue of "mediator burnout," as oftentimes working with parties in highly charged situations can be emotionally draining. As Kolb (2001) explains, "[a] good deal of mediator burnout appears to derive from the parties, whose emotional pain, limited motivation for resolving their difficulties, combativeness and general resistance often conspire to frustrate and demoralize even the most tenacious and resourceful mediator" (p. 484).

Many mediators work in teams, and it is necessary to develop a positive working relationship with one's co-mediator. This can help ensure a more productive session with parties, and also is essential to help them reflect on what worked well and what needs to be changed. Being aware that mediators may have their own emotional reactions, and being able to discuss and engage with a colleague can be helpful in keeping one's sanity in difficult situations.

Training

To build a career in mediation there are several options to get the necessary training. This includes basic training, pursuing advanced academic training, and/or getting applied experience. Many individuals in the USA, and some other countries as well, initially choose to participate in a 40+-hour mediation training course offered by a community mediation center or another entity. These programs generally offer their participants basic education in the mediation process, overview, practice of communication and process skills, and awareness of legal and ethical issues that may arise in mediation. Most states in the USA require certified mediators, meaning they have the ability possibly to run mediations through a court-referred program. Therefore after training, many choose to gain experience as an apprentice mediator. This means that a junior mediator might co-mediate or watch a number of mediations with a more experienced practitioner. After a certain number of sessions, and with mentoring, the junior mediator is then able to apply for certification and/or help lead mediations.

There are both positive aspects and challenges to 40+-hour mediation training programs. Some of the former include enabling individuals from diverse backgrounds to gain exposure and practice with mediation. Furthermore, at least in the community-based programs, the costs are usually not prohibitive. Lastly, these programs are a great way for mediation enthusiasts to jump into the field. Challenges to this model include the complexity of conflict and human relations. The limited training that aspiring mediators might receive may not sufficiently equip them with the experience needed to be effective as much more training and insight is needed (even if mentorship is provided). Second, in some states and locations there are tensions regarding mediation being open to anyone who has completed such training, versus lawyers who may add mediation as one of their process offerings. Third, there is a great deal of mediation training offered in the USA at various outlets, and many individuals might pursue such training with the goal of building a mediation career; however, the reality in many locations is that the number of people being trained in mediation and the supply of mediators is much greater than the demand. This has led to a fundamental mismatch between training programs and the goals of people being trained, who may grow frustrated at not having adequate opportunity to advance their skills, and even more so at the challenging environment in which they have to build a potential career.

Pursuing advanced academic training

Although the conflict resolution academic field began in the 1950s, it is only in the past two decades that there has been a virtual explosion of academic degrees at the undergraduate, graduate, and doctoral levels in conflict resolution and related fields. Currently, there are hundreds of institutions offering degrees in conflict resolution, peacebuilding, and alternative dispute resolution around the world.

For many individuals passionate about obtaining a much deeper understanding in both the theoretical and applied practice of conflict resolution, pursuing a degree can be a useful option to explore. Having the time and ability to delve into the complex sources of conflict in a community, to refine one's skills through applied mentorship and intensive coaching, and to be engaged in shaping the larger field can be invaluable experiences. Moreover, advanced training can greatly aid individuals by expanding their skills and enhancing their professionalism. They can learn about the larger conflict resolution field, and related processes, while increasing their skills, knowledge, and marketability. This can greatly aid mediators in expanding their toolkit of conflict resolution processes and building a career.

Possessing academic credentials can aid in the job search by providing skills and knowledge employers seek in potential hires. However, academic training may not always be the right choice for individuals for several reasons. First, a number of academic programs in the field are not providing students with sufficient integration of skills/theory training (Carstarphen et al., 2010). Second, while quite a few programs may offer a mediation class, it does not always include the possibility of direct "live" experience outside the classroom. The classes might include training in mediation theory, practice, and process largely through simulations, which can be invaluable, but direct experience is critical. Third, the financial cost of pursuing higher education opportunities can be prohibitive. However, for those seeking broader training in the field, academic training can still be a very effective option in many cases.

Applied experience

There are many around the world who use mediation skills and practices who may not have formal academic or professional training. Rather they have gained significant experience through direct groundwork. In fact, the majority of conflicts in the world are still resolved through informal (nonprofessional) mediation. As Beer and Packard (2012) explain, "[t]hough professional mediators offer valuable experience and a large set of facilitation tools, in real life most conflicts are mediated by trusted people who are near at hand" (p. xii).

While professional and academic credentialing is becoming increasingly important, particularly for individuals who seek to work in court-based or organizational settings, many who work in communities, particularly in developing countries, may have obtained work in the field only through direct experience. For example, many mediators working for local community-based organizations or nonprofits may work with identity groups in conflict or small-scale land disputes, only falling into their positions out of the need to do something rather than a conscious decision to pursue a career in mediation. While it is certainly possible to build a career in mediation by informal work, having some type of training and/or academic certification is becoming more important for an individual to advance their career.

Types of careers

The diversity of career options in which mediation can be used in part or in whole is growing. As Picard (2004) explains, about the growth in the process, "[m]ediation is now accessed through community conflict resolution programs, workplace mediation programs, tribunals, government and court mandate programs, and public policy consultations" (p. 313). Picard (2004) refers to the increasing "institutionalization of mediation" in a growing number of organizations as setting up processes to help better manage and prevent disputes (p. 316).

The traditional image of a mediator is someone who might set up a sole mediation practice and have a host of people seeking their services to help address disputes between neighbors, small businesses, family matters, and more. While there are many sole practitioners out there, the growth of mediation positions in a range of institutions is a very positive development for the field. Such positions might include working in the World Bank's Mediation program, helping to address disputes between staff members, working as a peer mediation teacher in a school-based setting, helping students resolve conflicts directly, working for a large tech company doing online dispute resolution or mediation for a company such as eBay, and a host of other opportunities. There are also many jobs in international and local nongovernmental organizations, where mediation might be a central area of work, such as working for Search for Common Ground helping to design mediation and conflict resolution programs in conflict-affected countries, or working to help set up mediation laws and systems in newly democratizing countries. It is important to emphasize that for those seeking to work in the broader field of conflict resolution, mediation is an important but not always sufficient skill set to have. Having knowledge of the larger field of scholarship and practice in conflict resolution and peacebuilding is also critical.

Many jobs in which mediation is a core component may not have "mediator" in the title, but could be a position located within a conflict systems office such as human resources. Often positions might be located in the fields of international development, humanitarian relief, or peacebuilding, where mediation is a process that will be used as part of one's job (Zelizer, 2013). In exploring the future of mediation it is essential for individuals to use creativity to define mediation broadly, and to explore the diverse range of sectors and institutions in which such skills may be needed. Too many individuals seeking work in mediation limit their vision to being a community mediator, the next US Secretary of State, or UN Secretary-General, mediating major national and international disputes. However, very few people can reach a career in mediation at the top level.

One of the most important ideas in considering a career in mediation is the idea of integrating mediation skills and processes into diverse areas that may not normally link (Zelizer,

2013). Individuals with strong mediation skills can often play a very important role in helping to foster more positive relations between diverse groups, as well as organizational cultures. For example, there is an increasing need for individuals working on projects in IT companies to be able to foster more positive relations with clients and staff, and to address potential disputes. Therefore, while a project manager in the technology sector might traditionally be focused on executing a project, helping to improve team relations and communication with clients has become essential.

Recommendations, opportunities and challenges

Recommendations

There are many reasons why mediation can be seen as an attractive process to be used in a wide variety of settings, ranging from improving relationships, to cost effectiveness, to fostering improved workplace morale. In exploring a career in mediation or trying to infuse mediation within a particular environment, mediators need to be advocates for mediation, and provide the data needed to make the case for the process. It is not enough to say that mediation works; evidence-based explanations and advocates for increased use of the process also need to be provided (Kolb, 2001).

Many institutions seeking to implement mediation programs internally or with their external partners may not be swayed by the moral argument that mediation is important to consider because parties should be able to determine the outcome of their disputes. However, the economic arguments are key. As mediator Phil Neiman comments:

> Litigation is inherently inefficient. It consumes an inordinate amount of resources, both public and private. Mediation, on the other hand, offers better results for a smaller investment of time and money. The return on mediation is significantly greater almost every time.
>
> *(Neiman Mediation, 2012, para. 28)*

This is an argument many favoring mediation make, but there is a need to provide more metrics to support such statements. For example, the National Conflict Resolution Center (2013) estimates that the average divorce case costs about US$20,000 per person, while mediation costs between $2,000–$5,000 for the entire process ("10 Reasons," para. 1).

Another case mediators can make to help increase support for the process is going beyond the financial aspects to stress that the process in which parties craft and decide their own solution is often more durable and effective than ones imposed by judges or managers. The rates of success for mediation agreements generally range between 60–80 percent. Even more important, as an example, is that 80 percent of child support agreements through mediation are complied with, compared to around 40 percent for court-based agreements (Neiman Mediation, 2012). Similarly, Mediate.com reports that mediation generally has an 80–85 percent success rate (Edwards, n.d.). This success rate is highly dependent on the ability of the mediator, making advanced training key (ADRR, 2000).

Opportunities

The mediation industry has seen extraordinary growth in recent decades. This process has proven the industry's ability to help diverse constituencies more effectively address disputes, build more effective, healthier organizations, and reduce costs. There are tremendous opportunities for individuals seeking development or wanting to advance in the field to help further expand it, and bring the process and skills to diverse areas.

One example of this is the increasing conflict surrounding health care provision and delivery in the USA, and around the world. There is a tremendous opportunity to increase the role of mediators and conflict professionals in hospitals and health service settings. As highlighted earlier, the explosion of the tech industry and the increasing amount of companies providing services online has led to the growth of a field of online dispute resolution. For example, eBay (2016) has an online dispute resolution process that encourages buyers and sellers to try to come to a solution. Yet if they are unable to do so, eBay (2016) implements a mediation process.

One of the greatest opportunities for those employed in the mediation field is the satisfaction resulting from having a positive impact on parties. Although many mediation positions may not boast the largest salary, for those individuals pursuing careers in institutional settings, such as private sector or government agencies, or those who have legal training and offer mediation as a service, these salaries can be comfortable (Velikonja, 2011).

Another opportunity for those looking to become full-time mediators are the many organizations whose membership provides connections and opportunities to find employment. The Association of Conflict Resolution (2015) offers its members access to training programs, a membership directory, and eligibility for their referral list. The Dispute Resolution section of the American Bar Association (2016) also offers many connections for aspiring mediators with over 18,000 members. These organizations can provide invaluable opportunities for their members, providing an entry point into the field for beginners. The Alliance for Peacebuilding (2016), the main US-based network for the global peacebuilding community, can also be very useful for those seeking work on international conflict issues.

Challenges

There are several key challenges to advancing one's career in mediation, including defining the field, supply versus demand, and ambiguous career paths. A key challenge in mediation is defining the boundaries and scope of the field. Although most would agree that mediation means third-party assistance to disputants in finding a voluntary and mutually satisfactory resolution to their conflict, the term is also used sometimes as a wider catch-all for conflict resolution or ADR approaches in general. There is also the challenge, and sometimes battle, over who can define mediation. Is it something that lawyers and the legal sphere do, or is it more focused on community justice (Adler, 2009)? Adler (2009) also cautions that the field runs the risk of trying too hard to professionalize without realizing that mediation is something that comes naturally to many. Instead, to have the maximum impact, we need to infuse the approaches and tools as widely as possible (Zelizer, 2013).

Another challenge is the significant gap between the supply of mediators and the demand from potential employers or clients. Many people dream about being a mediator, and will undertake training in the hopes of advancing a successful and high-paying career. However, as original research by Urska Velikonja (2011) shows:

> The private mediator market is similar to markets for entertainers or professional athletes, instead of the professional job markets from where many mediators are drawn; a few mediators at the top of the pyramid are wealthy, while the vast majority of mediators make little or no money.
>
> *(Velikonja, 2011, p. 3)*

In statistics drawn from the US Department of Labor (2016), the average wage in the USA for arbitrators and mediators was estimated in 2013 to be $69,060. While this is a healthy number, it is important to note that this category includes mediators and arbitrators, who make a much higher amount, and the total number of people employed is listed as 6,380, which is a very small number (US Department of Labor, 2016). Other groups estimate the average annual salary for mediators to be anywhere from $48,000 (SimplyHired, 2016) to $71,000 (Indeed, 2016). While these statistics only include people working for institutions, they provide valuable insight into the financial difficulties many mediators face.

Picard (2004, p. 334) notes only 20 percent of mediators in Canada do mediation full time, and most mediators have a host of other activities they use to sustain themselves financially. Velikonja (2011, p. 20) remarks that most mediators in the USA are volunteers, do not make any money, or receive a very small stipend, and in fact often have to spend resources to be trained. As Velikonja (2011) explains, "[t]he vast majority of mediators offer their services on a part-time basis, either by choice or, more commonly, because of lack of demand" (p. 11). Adler (2009) explains, "[b]eyond the steps of the courthouse, however, many mediators seem to struggle for work and identity" (para. 18). Similarly, the National Association for Community Mediation (2011) reports that while there are over 400 community mediation programs throughout the USA, the average program only has three full-time staff, supported by 50 volunteers.

Conclusion

Mediation as a field has grown tremendously in recent decades, with people now pursuing careers in part or in whole as mediators. However, it is prudent for individuals seeking to advance their career to think creatively in terms of skill sets and career options, and for institutions training mediators to be transparent about the still limited professional opportunities (Adler, 2009). Unfortunately, the supply side of individuals seeking to do mediation is often much greater than the demand side of institutions willing to pay for such services. This does not mean that being a mediator is not a viable career. Rather, to be successful, a career in mediation often requires individuals to obtain substantial experience through largely volunteer activities. On the other hand, for those who pursue advanced degrees in conflict resolution or related fields, this training can be a strong asset in developing a more diverse skills portfolio. Yet practical experience is still key.

It is also essential to see mediation as a process and skill set that can be used in a wide variety of careers and sectors. For example, many people might use mediation as part of their overall responsibility at work, but may not be employed as full-time mediators. Project managers, human resources, educators, or almost anyone engaged in work with or managing others, can certainly benefit from learning and refining mediation skills.

Institutions training mediators also need to be more transparent and realistic in the information they provide to individuals seeking a career in this sector. Anyone pursuing training should learn how mediation is situated within the larger conflict resolution and peacebuilding fields, to be able to see beyond the training. That is, know that mediation is one process with a set of skills that can be very effective in a wide variety of conflict contexts. However, there is a much larger field with many other processes ranging from facilitation to dialogue, collaborative problem solving, etc. Those that catch the mediation bug and want to do more should be encouraged to engage with the larger field. Moreover, mediation at large needs to do a better job of providing evidence-based arguments detailing the benefits of mediation in a wide variety of areas, as well as explaining when mediation is and is not a viable option for different contexts.

References

Adler, P. (2009) The end of mediation: An unhurried ramble on why the field will fail and mediators will thrive over the next two decades. *Mediate.com*. Retrieved from www.mediate.com/articles/adlerTheEnd.cfm.

ADRR. (2000) The truths behind mediation. *ADRR.com*. Retrieved from adrr.com/adr3/other.htm.

Alliance for Peacebuilding. (2016) *Missions and Programs*. Retrieved from www.allianceforpeacebuilding.org.

American Bar Association. (2016) *American Bar Association Section of Dispute Resolution: Membership*. Retrieved from www.americanbar.org/groups/dispute_resolution/publications.html.

Association of Conflict Resolution. (2015) ACR member benefits. Retrieved from www.imis100us2.com/acr/ACR/Membership/WhyJoin/ACR/Membership/Why_Join_ACR_.aspx?hkey=3b1f6a76-2c85-433d-8faa-fa94641664f1.

Barrett, J.T. & Barrett, J.P. (2004) *A History of Alternative Dispute Resolution: The Story of a Political, Cultural, and Social Movement*. San Francisco, CA: Jossey-Bass.

Beer, J.E. & Packard, C.C. (2012) *The Mediator's Handbook: Revised & Expanded Fourth Edition*. Cabriola Island, BC: New Society Publishers.

Carstarphen, N., Zelizer, C., Harris, R. & Smith, D.J. (2010) Graduate education and professional practice in international peace and conflict. United States Institute of Peace. Retrieved from www.usip.org/publications/graduate-education-and-professional-practice-in-international-peace-and-conflict.

eBay. (2016) Dispute resolution overview. Retrieved from pages.ebay.com/services/buyandsell/disputeres.html.

Edwards, C. (n.d.) Alternate dispute resolution. *Mediate.com*. Retrieved from www.mediate.com/tegci/pg1.cfm.

Federal Mediation and Conciliation Service (FMCS). (2015) A timeline of events in modern American labor relations. Retrieved from www.fmcs.gov/aboutus/our-history/.

Indeed. (2016) Mediator salary. Retrieved from www.indeed.com/salary?q1=Mediator&l1.

Jensen, K. (2012) The naked truth: How body language reveals the real you. *Forbes*. Retrieved from www.forbes.com/sites/keldjensen/2012/06/12/the-naked-truth-how-body-language-reveals-the-real-you/.

Kolb, D.M. (2001) *When Talk Works: Profiles of Mediators*. San Francisco, CA: Jossey-Bass.

Kovick, D. (2005) Twenty years of field-building 1984–2004. The Hewlett Foundation's Conflict Resolution Program. Retrieved from www.hewlett.org/uploads/files/HewlettConflictResolutionProgram.pdf.

Moore, C. (2014) *The Mediation Process: Practical Strategies for Resolving Conflict*. San Francisco, CA: Jossey-Bass.

National Association for Community Mediation. (2011) The state of community mediation. Retrieved from www.nafcm.org/Resources/state.

National Conflict Resolution Center. (2013) Divorce mediation group. Retrieved from www.ncrconline.com/Divorce/MediationVsLitigation.php.

Neiman Mediation. (2012) Marin county community mediation center white paper. Retrieved from www.neimanmediation.com/conflict-resolution/marin-county-community-mediation-2/.

Picard, C. (2004) *The Art and Science of Mediation*. Toronto, ON: Emond Montgomery.

Pou, C. (1997) Federal ADR and negotiated rulemaking acts receive permanent reauthorization. *Administrative & Regulatory Law News*, 22(2). Retrieved from apps.americanbar.org/adminlaw/news/vol22no2/adr&rneg.html.

Reporters' Committee for Freedom of the Press. (1996) Clinton orders agencies to use alternative dispute resolution. Retrieved from www.rcfp.org/browse-media-law-resources/news/clinton-orders-agencies-use-alternative-dispute-resolution.

SimplyHired. (2016) Mediator salaries. Retrieved from www.simplyhired.com/salaries-k-mediator-jobs.html.

US Department of Labor. (2016) Occupational employment and wages, May 2015: Arbitrators, mediators, and conciliators. Retrieved from www.bls.gov/oes/current/oes231022.htm#nat.

Velikonja, U. (2011) Making peace and making money. *Dispute Resolution*, 17(2): 20–23, 29.

Zelizer, C. (2013) *Integrated Peacebuilding: Innovative Approaches to Transforming Conflict*. Boulder, CO: Westview.

2

ONLINE TECHNOLOGY

The new frontier for mediation and conflict engagement

Daniel Rainey and Alan Tidwell

Mediation in the digital age

Information and communication technologies (ICT) now link the globe, yet even with their tremendous growth and innovation, we have barely begun to feel the depth of their impact. The International Telecommunication Union (2015) announced that as of 2015, "there are more than 7 billion mobile cellular subscriptions worldwide, up from less than 1 billion in 2000. Globally 3.2 billion people are using the Internet, of which 2 billion are from developing countries" (p. 1). The fledgling world of online dispute resolution, including mediation, peacemaking, and peacebuilding, has yet to be fully realized. The impact of this ever increasingly networked world has the potential to remake conflict engagement.

Any observer of the conflict engagement movement would acknowledge its diverse and wide-ranging character. Mediators, peace activists, lawyers, aid workers, community organizers, and more coalesce under the broad conflict engagement banner. That same diversity of practice and perspective is replicated in the world of online dispute resolution (ODR). Before delving into the diverse ways in which technology is being used by conflict engagers, we offer a definition and make two caveats. First, online dispute resolution was initially used to describe the ways in which the internet could be used to facilitate mediation, negotiation, or other similar processes in the realm of e-commerce. Over time, however, ODR has broadened to include the use of any ICT through the broad range of dispute resolution and prevention. We suggest that the most useful definition is that ODR is the intelligent application of information and communication technology to any of the varied modes that make up the practice of conflict engagement.

The first caveat concerns our use of the phrase conflict engagement to include a broad church of practitioners, scholars and readers including those interested in alternative dispute resolution, mediation, peacemaking, peacebuilding and many more. We do this because there are many ways that we, as third parties, engage with those who are in the cycle leading up to conflict, are in active conflict, and are dealing with the aftermath of conflict—and not all of our intervention efforts are aimed toward resolution. So, we will use the broader term to suggest that the entire sweep of conflict engagement is, and should be, affected by the use of ICT. The second caveat is that technology has been an integral part of conflict engagement since its inception. It simply was not often noticed. Just as a fish does not notice water, people have a hard time recognizing the ways in which the technology surrounding them affects their work. Our argument is that because of the ubiquitous nature of ICT in our everyday lives, it is absolutely inevitable that ODR technology will play a central role in all forms of conflict engagement—especially for our purposes here the practice of mediation—as we move further into the 21st century.

Mediators, and indeed all conflict engagement professionals, do three things wherever they work: they help parties manage communication; they help parties deal with and understand data; and they help parties manage group dynamics. Three of the basic features of ICT and ODR are that they create and use a vast array of communication channels; they help us deal with and understand information in ways not possible in the past; and they help us redefine and expand the concept of what a group is. Given these parallels, how can ODR technology *not* basically impact mediation and conflict engagement?

The last quarter of the 20th century witnessed a growing acknowledgement that technology would play a role in conflict engagement. SchWeber's (1989) article on telephone mediation signaled a growing awareness that technology had a role to play. MacDuff (1994) described the use of ICT in carrying out a mediation session simultaneously in three different countries. Today, these experiments seem almost naive. Tidwell (1996) voiced issues needing resolution for ODR to move forward, by writing "[r]ecord keeping and privacy are ... important issues. How will records be kept? Who will keep them? ... Does the mediation need protection by encryption software to ensure privacy, and if so, do both parties have such software?" (p. 246).

Most of the issues of access have been addressed by market penetration of computers and mobile phones, and the issues related to privacy and ethics are beginning to be addressed (Rainey, 2014). In our view, and in the views of many of our colleagues, technology now is simply integral to all types of human interaction, including mediation and other forms of conflict engagement.

New frontiers in mediation

Conflict engagement and mediation stand at a frontier brought about by innovations in technology. Three conceptions of the frontier of ODR suggest themselves—two that have dominated work and discussions in the field to date, and one that has been less discussed, but which is a significant frontier left to those of us who work in conflict engagement.

The two frontiers with which we have been most concerned during the past 15 years are first e-commerce, and second traditional conflict engagement modes, examples of which include the alternative practices of mediation and facilitation. The new frontier we want to suggest involves much more of the world of conflict engagement at large, and includes modes of practice that heretofore have been unavailable to mediators and other practitioners.

e-Commerce

In order to understand the ODR options available to mediators today, it is necessary to understand the origins of the concept of online dispute resolution. Application of ICT to online commerce was the first ODR frontier, and it was probably natural and inevitable that e-commerce was the first place that ODR emerged. When the National Science Foundation (NSF) lifted the ban on commerce in 1992, a new type of dispute emerged—one born online and capable of being resolved only online. Ethan Katsh's early work with eBay to set up an ODR system, and Katsh and Janet Rifkin's creation of the term "fourth party" to describe the role of technology in ODR, grow out of the massive numbers of disputes created by online commerce, and the impossibility of handling those disputes using traditional face-to-face methods (Katsh & Rifkin, 2001). Simply put, in the history of humankind we had never seen anything like the e-commerce environment, and we had no idea how huge it would become, but we realized early on the capacity of this mode of exchange to create disputes. The earliest approaches to these online disputes were a straight application of traditional mediation to the new online environment. eBay's groundbreaking ODR system initially featured a corps of mediators operating in a text environment (using email) using traditional mediation techniques to handle consumer disputes. The volume of disputes created online quickly made traditional mediation approaches inadequate.

As ODR has rolled out across the many online commerce sites around today, there has developed what we will call "the funnel theory" of disputes generated by online commerce. An overwhelming number of buyers have what they perceive to be a problem (eBay once reported handling 60 million of these disputes each year—given all the e-commerce sites operating today, it is probably not an exaggeration to say that there are billions of these disputes created each year). These individuals are given entry into the first level of e-commerce ODR systems, using relatively simple algorithms to elicit basic information about the complaint and, with no human intervention, provide basic information that resolves a very large number of the problems. The next layer, with fewer cases because of the filtering effect of the first set of algorithms, uses more complex algorithms to troubleshoot and problem solve, again without human intervention. The final layer, the small end of the funnel, leads the individual to a customer service representative who takes care of those problems not resolvable through the technology, using techniques that would be familiar to any traditionally trained mediator. This model has been repeated over and over again in e-commerce, and has even found its way into speculation about how we can reform the justice system.

Evolution of online mediation—the justice system

e-Commerce is relevant to everybody involved in any kind of conflict engagement, including mediation, because much of the development of the basic technology that can be used for conflict engagement more broadly has come from the e-commerce environment, and will eventually be available to the rest of us. Like e-commerce, the justice system experienced its own growth of technology use. Whereas the problems faced in e-commerce were born largely from novelty and unfamiliarity, the problems facing the use of ODR in the law are born of the very nature of the legal territory itself.

It is not surprising that the first developments in ODR for the law were designed to make the current system work more efficiently. Just as in e-commerce, we kept doing the same things we always did, we just did them using technology. Take as an example the developments in e-discovery. Online tools and smart applications allow firms to store, search, and evaluate massive amounts of information contained in documents produced in discovery in a way that was not possible before the advent of ICT in the law. ODR systems that deal with filing cases, scheduling cases, and other normal aspects of the justice system continue to be developed and come online.

However, there are some efforts to totally rethink the justice system, using ODR as a way to change the basic nature of the justice process. The Online Dispute Resolution Advisory Group's (2015) report, "Online Dispute Resolution for Low Value Civil Claims" is the product of work commissioned by the Lord Chief Justice of England and Wales, and produced by a working group led by Sir Richard Susskind. It takes an essential form from ODR developed for e-commerce and uses that approach to reimagine access to justice as a service instead of a physical location. Interestingly, but not surprisingly, the basic format the report suggests is the funnel that e-commerce has used so successfully, but the report leaves the way open for broad discussions about the nature of the law and the practice of law in the internet age. The report imagines tiers of service and access, with a reallocation of financial resources away from the bricks and mortar legal institutions to online resources aimed at early interventions and alternative approaches to issue resolution.

The report also acknowledges that this suggested use of ODR technology in the justice system may be perceived as disruptive by lawyers and judges—but the technology has proven its utility in e-commerce, and use of the same general technology would move the legal system much closer to being a service that could actually be accessed to obtain justice. Projects are underway in Canada to apply ODR technology to the justice system, and as those projects and others move forward, we predict that the standards set by development of e-commerce systems will cease to be the *de facto* standards for the law (Thompson, 2014).

An interesting feature of the adaptations being considered in the justice arena is the central place that ADR, including mediation, will play as technology becomes more integral to the overall justice system. A recent publication by the leaders of the UK justice system calls for the creation of online courts, with mandatory online mediation (Briggs, 2015, p. 75). Online mediation can reduce costs and increase access, but it will require mediators, especially in traditional legal fields, to acclimate new methods and to use technology in new ways.

Challenges in developing and implementing online mediation

Since ODR in e-commerce served as the proof-of-concept for ODR generally, there have been attempts to develop ODR applications for mediation, facilitation, peacebuilding, etc. One barrier that existed early in the development of ODR was the cost of developing and hosting applications. A format was already there. Early attempts to create ODR platforms for mediation, for example, simply took the standard North American Model of mediation and put it online. These attempts failed for two reasons. First, successful ODR does not simply create online an analog of mediation offline. NSF research from 2004 through 2010 demonstrated that there are inherent differences between offline and online work, and that there are some things unique to the ODR environment (National Science Foundation, 2007). Second, the cost of systems like The Mediation Room and Juripax were high because of the cost of development, and the user base was small because of the novelty of the ODR approach. Simply put, the overhead was too high to make use of ODR platforms feasible. This situation has begun to change rapidly.

Platforms with the capability to be the entry point that makes general ODR use possible exist, but most of the developers are concentrating on high-volume caseloads and are not marketing to small firms or sole practitioners. On the other hand, the market is beginning to see applications that allow for online negotiation, online arbitration, and online mediation in a way that invites small firms and practitioners to use the platform. For another traditional form of conflict engagement, ombudsmanship, Rainey and Fowlie (2015) detail the use of ODR platforms in ombudsman offices over the past decade and a half.

Current options for online mediation

So, what are the options for conflict engagement at large, including mediation? What does conflict engagement at large mean? In part, we mean things that would be recognizable to anyone who has gone through a course in dispute resolution in a university—mediation, facilitation, dialogue, reconciliation, and peacebuilding—all of the traditional forms. However, in addition, we are referring to conflict engagement possibilities that are either created by the existence of ODR technology, or can be reimagined through ODR technology. For mediators, it is possible to think of comprehensive programs that allow mediation work to be done completely online. However, it is probably more productive to think of ODR as a way to fulfill various functions that are a part of the steps in the standard North American Model of mediation.

For intake and for convening, many applications allow the mediator to schedule, execute agreements to mediate, and exchange pre-mediation information. There are audio and video applications that allow for storytelling and information exchange, and there are several mind map applications that allow for brainstorming and option generation. To rate and rank ideas, there are many polling and multi-voting applications. For producing agreements, single text editing programs are available for joint writing. Any of these functions can be addressed as part of a totally online process, or they can be used to enhance face-to-face work. Ultimately, the question should be, does the use of technology add value to the mediation process? If not, traditional face-to-face methods may be best.

The future of online mediation

As we have said, the first wave of technology adaptation usually allows us to do the things we do by tradition, but do them using technology. That is where we are now with mediation. There are other efforts under way, however. Let us highlight some examples of technology changing the nature of traditional conflict engagement.

e-Jurgas in Afghanistan

At a United States Institute for Peace conference a few years ago, some of our colleagues introduced the idea of the "e-Jurga." In Afghanistan, traditional access to justice was through *Jurgas*—councils of elders who heard both sides and helped parties reach a proper resolution. Convening Jurgas in Afghanistan was dangerous for all concerned. It was suggested that through using mobile phones, parties could record their presentations to the Jurga members, the Jurga could listen to the presentations, and then make its recommendations by recording them on a service that all had access to, and through this approach, the essence of the traditional justice system could be maintained. This is very important in an environment where a formal justice system is all but nonexistent.

Reducing election violence in Kenya

In Kenya, election violence is a real threat to general social order. One of the more notable ODR projects there is called Ushahidi Crowdmapping, which uses crowdsourcing to pinpoint sites of violence and links that information to interveners who try to prevent or blunt the impact of the violence. An even more frontier project is Sisi ni Amani (n.d.), which is a project using mobile phones to counteract hate speech.[1] After the last round of election violence, researchers talked to a large number of individuals who had been involved in the violence, asking them two questions. First, what kind of language or messages incited you to engage in violence? Second, is there any kind of message or language that, if you had heard it, would have made you think twice about engaging in violence? The researchers took the data and put together a database of violence prevention messages that could be quickly disseminated by a text messaging system. They then created a messaging network by offering various kinds of free information to anyone who would sign up, and they got over 30,000 participants. The project operates like this: when one of the members hears messages that sound like the ones that incite violence, it is reported to the system and non-violent messages go out to all 30,000 members before the violence occurs. The ultimate success is still being evaluated, but try replicating that kind of conflict engagement without ODR technology.

PeaceTones® and ODR technology

In 2007, Aresty and Rainey (personal communication) developed the basic concept behind a successful ODR conflict engagement project called PeaceTones®. A couple of assumptions were driving their thinking. Their first thought was that in the run-up cycle before conflicts break out, and in the post-conflict cycle after direct conflict has occurred, it is the lack of opportunity to obtain even the basic necessities of life that drives groups toward conflict and nurtures the tendency toward renewed conflict. Second, the assumptions behind much of the existing conflict engagement programs were that there had to be a strong intervener presence on the ground, there had to be a large pool of money (by developed country standards) to make a difference, and that there had to be a responsible agent associated with the interveners on hand to guide decisions about how to use resources. Further, there seemed to be a bias toward tradition: access to justice programs tend to target building up the courts; infrastructure projects tend to build radio stations, build hospitals, and drill water wells. All of that is good, at least on one level, but in a fundamental way, they take attitudes and forms from the developed world and transfer them to the developing or undeveloped world with the expectation that if they worked here, they will work there.

Aresty and Rainey's (personal communication, 2007) concept for PeaceTones® as an ODR project was different. First, they recognized that in a place where the population is living on one or two dollars per day per person, you do not have to raise a million dollars to make a difference. Second, they redefined access to justice as access to rights and opportunity, not as access to local court systems. Third, they looked for items produced by local populations that had value that could not be unlocked using traditional methods. Finally, they were committed to using ODR tools as the means of intervention and the means of sustaining the results of our conflict engagement.

PeaceTones® goes into pre- or post-conflict zones, identifies musicians who are creating socially positive music, and helps them record and sell their music. PeaceTones® teaches them about intellectual property and how to protect themselves and do business in an e-commerce environment, and how to run their business on a day-to-day basis. PeaceTones® helps them record and sell their music in exchange for a promise to put a substantial amount of any money they make back into their communities in projects they and their neighbors choose and manage. PeaceTones® could not exist without ODR technology (PeaceTones®, 2016).

Online mediation in space and international peacebuilding

In the early days of the development of what we came to call the Internet and the World Wide Web, one of the primary researchers, J.C.R. Licklider, suggested calling this creation "The Intergalactic Network" (Pelkey, 2007). In October 2015, at the Association for Conflict Resolution conference, a colleague who has been working on an ODR conflict engagement platform serving the International Space Station presented an ODR platform that is one step closer to intergalactic. With NASA funding, James Cartreine, of Brigham and Women's

Hospital, designed and produced an interactive computer-based program "to assist astronauts in managing real, ongoing conflicts during long-duration missions" (Cartreine, 2013, p. 1).

ODR tools that enhance communication channels and quickly share information have been in use for over a decade. Among the first of the successful examples is that of ICT4-Peace (2016) and GroundViews (2016), projects created to facilitate conflict engagement during the Sri Lankan civil war. Using citizen journalism, conflict mapping, secure online meetings, and other channels, what we think was the first transformational ODR campaign worked throughout the war and is still working in the peacebuilding process after the war (ICT4Peace, 2016; GroundViews, 2016).

Language and artificial intelligence in ODR

As we look to the future, one of the great possibilities we see for ODR technology relates to the development of smart systems and artificial intelligence, machine language studies and natural language studies. Artificial intelligence "may contribute to develop ODR processes that will deal with other sorts of problems, namely complex multi-party, multi-issue, and multi-contract ones" (Carneiro et al., 2014, p. 215). Using such technologies will also facilitate developing processes that mimic the cognitive processes of human experts, leading to more efficient ODR tools (Carneiro et al., 2014, p. 215).

In the late 1990s, the United States Department of Agriculture (USDA) first used an online tool, email, to accept public comments about a standard for labeling food as organic. They had been used to getting hundreds of comments when they went out to the public via mail and local meetings. Using email for the first time, they got thousands of comments. Teasing out the threads of interest and truly understanding all of the comments from that large a community of interest is, for a human, difficult or impossible. For a good smart program, using algorithms and artificial intelligence (AI), such a task goes from complex to simple. The City of Austin, Texas, uses a variety of online platforms and tools to engage citizens in public debate and to manage public participation projects in a way that is not possible using traditional offline methods. In short, the work being done in varied ODR platforms, AI, and natural-language research is going to revolutionize how we do public participation engagement.

Conclusion

In the CERN museum in Geneva there is a case that contains the original concept paper that Tim Berners-Lee wrote, laying out the essential framework of what became the World Wide Web. At the top of the first page, one of his colleagues had written a note: "vague but exciting" (CERN, 2008). There will always be those who are caught in the past, and those who do not immediately grasp the potential of new ideas, but let us leave you with a gentle exhortation. We have the frontier of e-commerce behind us—we are in the middle of rethinking how ODR can improve the justice system and traditional practice—and we have in front of us the final frontier.

No escaping online mediation and conflict engagement

Most of us began working in the area of conflict engagement because there is something compelling and rewarding about being able to work with people under stress and in distress, helping them feel better, live better, be better. Whether it is working to make sure people feel they are being treated fairly when a purchase goes wrong, or feeling that there really is access to justice, or offering ways to reduce or eliminate the cycle of violence, the work we do is important. In doing this work, we cannot ignore the new social reality in which we find ourselves—if your clients and parties can buy anything imaginable online, if they can talk to the grandchildren on the other side of the world online, if they can find someone to marry online, they are going to wonder why they cannot interact with conflict engagement professionals online.

Challenges

There are many things we could do with technology in any given venue. We need to look for those things we should do to make sure we are using ODR technology to offer our customers, clients, and parties the best customer service, counsel, and support possible. Much work still needs to be done with regard to privacy and ethics. The eruption of privacy as a linchpin issue should not be surprising. In 1993, concern was raised about email encryption, again in 1998 when the Clinton Administration attempted to obtain encryption keys for law enforcement, and again with the development of the clipper chip. The challenge for conflict engagement professionals now is not to find ODR platforms that can be used in every imaginable form of practice, but to find ways to use the ODR tools in an ethically sound manner, offering advantages to the parties without creating disadvantages.

Recommendations

- Think of ODR as offering some assistance during each of the major phases of the traditional mediation process rather than as a "cradle to grave" use of ODR technology for every phase of a mediation. Most practitioners who use ODR technology do so for specific functions, integrating with face-to-face practice. Think of using online survey tools for intake and signing agreements to mediate. Use bulletin boards and shared documents for storytelling. Use mind maps for brainstorming. Use instant survey platforms for rating and ranking options, and use online workspaces with single-text editing to create agreements.
- Try small steps before jumping in with both feet. Find applications that do one or two things that are necessary for almost every case, and experiment with them before pushing them out to clients.
- Look at your practice to see where time and geography cause problems—see if ODR can help there.
- Use some ODR platforms for your own purposes so you can develop facility with the applications. For example, if you want to use mind maps for brainstorming, start by using mind maps to keep track of your own to-do list. This forces you to touch the platform every day and ensures that when you use it with parties you are able to focus on the parties, not on the application.
- Be open to ODR innovations. Just because something does not look like traditional conflict engagement does not mean that it is not useful, or even groundbreaking.

Note

1 Sisi ni Amani, Program Summary, at www.youtube.com/watch?v=dxSv34YxoY4.

References

Briggs, M. (2015) *Civil Courts Structure Review: Interim Report.* Judiciary of England and Wales. www.judiciary.gov.uk/wp-content/uploads/2016/01/ccsr-interim-report-dec-15-final1.pdf.

Carneiro, D., Novais, P., Andrade, F., Zeleznikow, J. & Neves, J. (2014) Online dispute resolution: An artificial intelligence perspective. *Artificial Intelligence Review*, 41(2): 211–240.

Cartreine, J.A. (2013) Countermeasure for managing interpersonal conflicts in space. National Space Biomedical Research Institute. Retrieved from nsbri.org/researches/countermeasure-for-managing-interpersonal-conflicts-in-space/.

CERN. (2008) Tim Berners-Lee's proposal. Retrieved from info.cern.ch/Proposal.html.

GroundViews. (2016) About. Retrieved from groundviews.org/about/.

ICT4Peace. (2016) ICT4Peace history and FAQ. Retrieved from ict4peace.org/?page_id=773.

International Telecommunication Union. (2015) ICT facts and figures: The world in 2015. Retrieved from www.itu.int/en/ITU-D/Statistics/Documents/facts/ICTFactsFigures2015.pdf.

Katsh, E. & Rifkin, J. (2001) *Online Dispute Resolution: Resolving Disputes in Cyberspace.* San Francisco, CA: Jossey-Bass.

MacDuff, I. (1994) Flames on the wires: Mediating from the electronic cottage. *Negotiation Journal*, 10(1): 5–15.

National Science Foundation. (2007) Grant No. IIS-0429297: Process technology for achieving government online dispute resolution. National Science Foundation Division of Information and Intelligent Systems. Retrieved from www.nsf.gov/awardsearch/showAward?AWD_ID=0429297.

Online Dispute Resolution Advisory Group. (2015) Online dispute resolution for low value civil claims. Retrieved from www.judiciary.gov.uk/wp-content/uploads/2015/02/Online-Dispute-Resolution-Final-Web-Version1.pdf.

PeaceTones®. (2016) What we do. Retrieved from peacetones.org/about/.

Pelkey, J. (2007) An interview with J.C.R. Licklider. *A history of computer communications: 1968–1988.* Retrieved from www.historyofcomputercommunications.info/Individuals/LickliderJCR/InterviewJCRLicklider.html.

Rainey, D. (2014) Third party ethics in the age of the fourth party. *International Journal of Online Dispute Resolution*, 1(1): 37–56.

Rainey, D. (2015) Glimmers on the horizon: Unique ethical issues created by ODR. *Dispute Resolution Magazine*, 21(2): 20–23.

Rainey, D. & Fowlie, F. (2015) Leveraging technology in the ombudsman field: Current practice and future possibilities. *Journal of the International Ombudsman Association*, 8(1): 61–72.

SchWeber, C. (1989) Your telephone may be a party line: Mediation by telephone. *Mediation Quarterly*, 7(2): 191–196.

Sisini Amani. (n.d.) SMS programming. Retrieved from www.sisiniamani.org/what-we-do/programs/sms-programming/.

Thompson, D. (2014) *The Growth of Online Dispute Resolution and its Use in British Columbia.* Civil Litigation Conference 2014. Retrieved from www.cle.bc.ca/PracticePoints/LIT/14-GrowthODR.pdf.

Tidwell, A. (1996) Handling disputes in cyberspace. *Australian Journal of Dispute Resolution*, 7(3): 245–248.

3

STORY-BASED INTER-GROUP MEDIATION

Jessica Senehi

Story-based mediation draws on the power of storytelling to address social divisions and inter-group conflicts. Storytelling is an important tool for working, in the context of conflict, with the intangibles of conflict, including knowledge, identity, emotion, morality, time, and cultural geography. Story-based mediation follows key principles of mediation, including belief in the capacity of people to solve their own problems, separating the people from the problem, the importance of acknowledgement and creative problem solving for mutual benefit. Three examples are reviewed: To Trust and Reflect, Toward Healing and Understanding, and Jerusalem Stories. The potential of story-based mediation to address some of the limits of mainstream mediation is explored. Guidance in developing a story-based mediation is provided.

Broad social conflicts cannot be mediated in one go. International agreements do not remove hostilities at the grassroots level with the swoosh of a pen (Lederach, 1997). Throughout the world, political, structural, and cultural violence harm whole groups of people. While these issues may be addressed in different ways in interpersonal or international mediation, there is a need for processes at the more middle level to process, negotiate, educate, heal, reconcile broad social conflict issues and to re-envision relationships and society. Story-based inter-group projects are an important way to mediate these social divisions at a juncture between the personal and political, where personal agency and voice may shape interpersonal relationships and the world.

Storytelling

Most simply, storytelling is someone telling someone else that something happened (Smith, 1981, p. 228). Oral (or signed) storytelling involves a teller and at least one listener; such storytelling is a social interaction (Ryan, 1995). Stories can be related in non-verbal forms; written, visual art, theater, film, and digitally. The storyteller is seen to be in a position of power in the social construction of meaning (Bauman & Briggs, 1990). Through stories, people negotiate meaning.

Knowledge

All cultures have a body of stories that encoded their knowledge. The experiences of groups of people with a shared history and experience also encode knowledge, and this knowledge can be accessed through these stories. Such stories form a voice of resistance to whole groups otherwise excluded from the "authoritative" discourse of first-world journalism, academia, and literature (Gugelberger & Kearney, 1991; Randall, 1991).

Identity

Stories create and give expression to personal and collective identities. The process of storytelling and narration fosters empathy as listeners identify with the characters in a story. Cultural and dominant discourses shape people's identities, and at the same time persons and groups draw on the power of their own stories—through human rights movements and truth commissions—to shape social thought and action (Schaffer & Smith, 2004; Truth and Reconciliation Commission of Canada, 2015).

Emotions

Stories engage the mind and heart. Addressing emotions is critical in post-peace accord peacebuilding. Storytelling, in the context of interpersonal conversation, dialogue groups, art forms, or truth commissions can be a means of healing in the aftermath of political and inter-communal violence.

Storytelling is a way to work with many of the intangibles of social life and social conflict. Stories always imply how things should be; they have moral import. Stories have a linear dimension of time, and interpretations of the past and visions of the future are encoded in stories. Geographic locations, for example, Jerusalem, national territories, and neighborhoods, are given significance through stories. In all cultures and religions, storytelling is a primary way of teaching.

Storytelling is not inherently positive. As with any form of language, storytelling can be used for innumerable purposes, and can be constructive or destructive (Senehi, 2002). Destructive storytelling is associated with coercive power ("power over" rather than "power with" or "power for"), exclusionary practices, a lack of mutual recognition, dishonesty, and a lack of awareness. Such storytelling sustains mistrust and denial. Constructive storytelling is inclusive and fosters collaborative power and mutual recognition; creates opportunities for openness, dialogue, and insight; a means to bring issues to consciousness; and a means of resistance. Constructive storytelling builds understanding and awareness, and fosters voice. Story-based mediation draws on the power of constructive storytelling.

Story-based mediation

A variety of story-based projects seek to promote understanding between groups and are forms of mediation. These story-based projects can take many forms, from private encounters to theatrical performances that form a collective narrative of different stakeholders in a conflict. All of these projects encompass key principles of mediation.

People have the capacity to solve their own problems

Participants in story-based projects profoundly influence the shape projects take. Participants generate the knowledge that is mobilized through the project. The Jerusalem Stories theater piece was based on the real stories and words of real people (Jerusalem Stories, 2015). Theatre of Witness productions are not only grounded in the stories of real people, but they are enacted by those same people whose stories are being shared (Sepinuck, 2013). When people draw on the power of their own knowledge and leverage these stories for healing and non-violent social change, this is empowering and reverses processes of internalized oppression that may result from longstanding interpersonal or social conflict.

Separating the people from the problem

Story-based projects do not focus on attributing blame, but rather how people are affected by the situations that have challenged them. When the stories of both parties are brought together, it is a chance to see how the situation has harmed both parties or how both parties face a shared challenge (Rothman, 1997). Storytelling, which is always about people facing a particular situation, is a natural way to externalize a problem and at the same time promote understanding of the point of view of the speaker.

The need for recognition and acknowledgement

Mediation is based on an assumption that each side needs to have their interests and/or needs acknowledged. Story-based projects have the potential to allow for this type of recognition. Where there has been a longstanding inter-communal struggle, recognition of harm done cannot be a one-off event, but rather must be an ongoing process that gradually affects more people, more profoundly.

Creative problem solving for mutually beneficial solutions

Mediation allows for the possibility for processing conflict in innovative ways that meet individuals's particular interests and circumstances. In the case of longstanding inter-communal conflicts, a story-based project does not prescribe a solution, but it holds the potential to open up a space for its participants to begin to imagine different possibilities. Such mediation is a place where new seeds of peacemaking germinate (Bush, 2011).

Mediator support

Mediation is based on the assumption that while people have the power and knowledge to solve their own problems, they may benefit from the facilitation and expertise of a mediator to steer them through the rapids of uncertainty, anxiety, and the strong emotions of conflict. Similarly, such guidance brings value to story-based projects. Key individuals have developed models, brought their vision and expertise to the process, and even worked to develop structures of support so that the projects are economically viable and sustainable.

Examples of story-based inter-group mediation

Increasingly, practitioners have drawn on the power of storytelling to mediate conflicts between identity groups. These innovative approaches are often at a junction between mediation and art or, perhaps, more accurately, are a fusion of mediation and art. Three examples are discussed below: To Trust and Reflect, which addressed the divide between Palestinians and Israelis; Toward Healing and Understanding, which addressed the divide between Catholic nationalists and Protestant unionists in Northern Ireland; and Jerusalem Stories Performance, Exhibit, Dialogue.

To Trust and Reflect

Israeli psychiatrist Dan Bar-On developed encounter meetings, most of which were held during 1990–95, often over an extended period, such as weekend retreats, which brought together the children of survivors of the Holocaust with the children of parents who were convicted of war crimes during that period (Bar-On, 1989). Central to Bar-On's work has been an exploration of reconstructing personal stories (Bar-On, 1995) and how to conduct conversations and reconstruct relationships after trauma (Bar-On, 1999).

In 1995, he developed a similar project, held over a period of three years, called To Trust and Reflect, supported by the Körber Foundation, which included Palestinians and Israelis. An evaluation of To Trust and Reflect emphasized that storytelling was the key aspect of the process that was cited by the participants as promoting understanding and insight among them (Maoz, 2000). While this project is small scale, Wolf Schmidt, State Secretary Plenipotentiary to the Federation, the European Union, and for Foreign Affairs, stated: "Change is never initiated by majorities; it requires individuals who start asking critical questions and thinking in new ways. And then they have to find allies in the media, religious communities, political parties, trade unions, business associations, etc." (Schmidt, 2000, p. 16). In this process, mediated encounters across the divide of historical and current strife require healing from the past and can also be a basis of forging new relationships and long-term social change.

Toward Healing and Understanding

At the community-based peacebuilding organization, The Junction in Derry/Londonderry, Northern Ireland, Maureen Hetherington was inspired by Dan Bar-On's project, in which she participated, and also on a project called *An Crann* in Gaelic, or "The Tree." An Crann was founded by Northern Irish poet and playwright Damian Gorman to facilitate persons' telling and hearing stories of the Northern Ireland conflict. In 2002, Hetherington developed Toward Healing and Understanding, which draws on the power of storytelling to develop a project that brings together people from both sides of the Northern Ireland conflict, who were directly affected by violence, some of whom were former combatants (O'Hagan, 2008a).

Participants are brought together for weekend-long retreats, and storytelling is central to the program. It includes, for example, an exercise where participants create a string of beads to share their life story. In a video on the program, a participant expresses that when presented with the bead process, he was at first skeptical (O'Hagan, 2008b), but almost immediately, he saw a shiny black bead and knew that this bead would represent the day he lost his son to the violence. An evaluation of Toward Healing and Understanding found that the program helped people to heal in the aftermath of trauma, promoted conversation and understanding in the present, and led to the collaborative development of ideas on how to go forward, in particular, around the challenge of honoring the past without rekindling hostilities (Bush, 2011).

Jerusalem Stories Performance, Exhibit, Dialogue

In 2007, American Carol Grosman developed a project called Jerusalem Stories, which drew on the power of storytelling through oral history, theater, and photography to explore and promote within-group dialogue (that is, dialogue among Israelis, and dialogue among Palestinians) about what the ongoing Palestinian–Israeli conflict and the city of Jerusalem meant to both Palestinian and Jewish Jerusalemites (Jerusalem Stories, 2015; Senehi et al., 2008). Grosman interviewed more than 60 people about how they had been impacted by the conflict and asked them for metaphors that got at what Jerusalem meant to them. From among these interviews, six personal narratives were selected, three of Palestinians and three of Israelis, which formed the basis of a play written, originally in English, by Palestinian playwright Mohamed Thaher.

The play was translated into both Hebrew and Arabic. Two parallel theater productions were developed, one with Palestinian actors to deliver the Arabic version of the play in East Jerusalem, and one with Jewish actors to deliver the Hebrew version of the play in West Jerusalem. All the performances were presented at no cost to the public. Accompanying the play was an exhibit of 22 portrait photographs taken by photojournalist Lloyd Wolf. The program began with the play, followed by a reception and viewing of the photo exhibition, and then audience members were invited to join one of several small-group conversations that were facilitated by people experienced in mediation and conflict resolution. This project is distinguished from among other mediated co-existence encounters because it involved a broader public both in the development of the content and in the execution of the program to public audiences in West and East Jerusalem.

Addressing the limits of mediation

Story-based approaches to conflict resolution may help address some of the limitations of mediation: limitations of time, scope, and culture. Typically, mediation is time limited and short term, which may limit the possibilities for personal change and empowerment. Story-based approaches, on the other hand, are often more lengthy and more in-depth. In Theatre of Witness, participants work with and develop their stories in community over a period of time, and then the final production is shared with the audience, and may endure in the form of film or digital media (Sepinuck, 2013).

Interpersonal mediation reaches only those individuals involved, and confidentiality may prevent insights or solutions from setting a precedent for others. International mediation may not address the cultural and emotional concerns of people at the grassroots. Story-based projects at the community level may be an important way to foster social and cultural awareness, dialogue, and change (Senehi & Byrne, 2006).

While forms of mediation are found across cultures, how a particular mediation process takes shape may differ across cultures. Further, it is difficult to address issues of power in mediation if there is historical hurt that has not been acknowledged. Storytelling, which is a way of knowing across cultures and is accessible to people of different ages and educational levels, is often an effective and compelling way to include diverse people in the processes of creating, receiving, and negotiating knowledge.

Considerations in development of a story-based mediation project

Storytelling is an inexpensive, accessible, and highly flexible form of working collectively to negotiate identity, power, and knowledge. A story-based mediation project could be developed in infinite ways, and there could be no prescriptive roadmap for how to do this. Rather, such projects are best developed inductively. Because storytelling is a form that is used in all cultures and a process in which everyone can participate, story-based approaches are a good approach for appropriate and ethical intervention. Below are some guidelines for developing a story-based mediation project.

What is the purpose?

A project starts with a purpose or *raison d'être*. A project is inspired by a larger purpose or quest for healing, understanding, trust, or reconciliation between or among groups. A story-based project may address broad social divisions, conflicts within a particular organization, or build awareness and knowledge to close a gap of understanding.

Identify an advisory group

In order to develop a project that is ethical and appropriate, it is usually advantageous to develop some key partners and stakeholders to participate in the project. An advisory group can take on different parameters in terms of size, formality, and constituency; and it can have different roles in terms of its relationship to the project. The key thing is for the project initiator to consider to whom they may be accountable, and who can bring insight and wisdom to the project.

What are the project goals and objectives?

While a general purpose will inspire a project, goals and objectives are also identified. Goals are abstract and intangible intentions. Different types of goals can be addressed with story-based mediation, such as the development of personal healing and reconciliation among a core group, developing a body of knowledge about how people have been affected by a conflict and sharing that knowledge, or for education.

Who is a storyteller?

It is important to give due consideration to who the storytellers are for a project. For a story-based mediation project, the storytellers will usually include people from both sides of the conflict divide. There are many considerations: the setting in which stories will be told, the type of stories that are most relevant to the project, how the storyteller will be treated, and what will be done with the stories. Storytelling is not necessarily cathartic. Consider how storytellers will be treated to honor, acknowledge, and validate them, and how to prevent re-traumatization; this is a process of witnessing (Weingarten, 2003; Denborough, 2008).

Who is the audience?

Consider who will be the audience for a particular project. The audience may be participants in a workshop, school students, or the public. A digital storytelling project may have an online audience. Consider what might be expected of an audience, how the audience will be selected or invited, and how an audience might be impacted by a story-based mediation project. Consider how to tell stories in ways that make us stronger, and be aware that a story-based project may also trigger past trauma or distress the person who listens to the story.

What is the story?

Consider the type of story that is being sought. Stories are elicited through the process, and story-based mediation does not aim to deliver a prescribed narrative. If questions are being used to solicit stories, develop those questions thoughtfully. Many types of stories might be used in a single project, even folktales. It is always more useful to elicit stories about things that have happened or about concrete things rather than abstract ideas. Carol Grosman asked Palestinian and Israeli Jerusalemites what Jerusalem was to them, generating powerful metaphors (Jerusalem Stories, 2015): "Jerusalem is like the sea and I am like the fish," said Samir al Jundi (para. 2); "Jerusalem is filled with faces that I know," said Emmanuel Stein (para. 3).

What is the format of story-based mediation?

While certain principles of mediation, for example, "separating the people from the problem," as discussed above, will always be present, the format of story-based mediation can take innumerable forms. The best place to start is where you are. Consider the resources, skills, and access available in developing a project. An educator might involve students. Someone who works for a nongovernmental organization might develop the project under the aegis of that organization. Develop projects gradually: start small, evaluate, adapt, and build from there.

Evaluate your project through thick description

Take time to evaluate your project. It is best if someone not directly involved in the project can provide a qualitative analysis drawing on interviews with a variety of project participants as well as survey data. It is advisable to allocate funds for an evaluation in grant applications.

Share your model

Talented and visionary peacemakers are developing innovative story-based mediation projects all over the world. Often, few people, other than the participants or the audience for those projects, are aware of them. Find a way to share your model with others through training manuals or research scholarship.

References

Bar-On, D. (1989) *Legacy of Silence*. Cambridge, MA: University of Massachusetts Press.

Bar-On, D. (1995) *Fear and Hopes*. Cambridge, MA: Harvard University Press.

Bar-On, D. (1999) *The Indescribable and the Undiscussable*. Budapest: Central European University Press.

Bauman, R. & Briggs, C.I. (1990) Poetica and performance as critical perspectives on language and social life. *Annual Review of Sociology*, 19: 59–88.

Bush, K. (2011) *The Evaluation of Storytelling as a Peace-building Methodology*. International Conflict Research Institute. Coleraine, Northern Ireland: University of Ulster.

Chornenki, G.A. & Hart, C.E. (2015) *Bypass Court: A Dispute Resolution Handbook* (5th edn). Toronto: LexisNexis Canada.

Crowshoe, R. & Manneschmidt, S. (2002) *Akak'stiman: A Blackfoot Framework for Decision-making and Mediation Processes*. Calgary: University of Calgary Press.

Denborough, D. (2008) *Collective Narrative Practice*. Adelaide: Dulwich Centre.

Denborough, D. (2010) *Kite of Life: From Intergenerational Conflict to Intergenerational Alliance*. Adelaide: Dulwich Centre.

Gugelberger, G. & Kearney, M. (1991) Voices for the voiceless: Testimonial literature in Latin America. *Latin American Perspectives*, 18(3): 3–14.

Jerusalem Stories. (2015) *The Jerusalem Stories Project*. Retrieved from www.jerusalemstories.com.

Lederach, J.P. (1997) *Building Peace*. Washington, DC: United States Institute of Peace.
Maoz, I. (2000) Expectations, results, and perspectives: The evaluation report. In D. Bar-On (ed.), *Bridging the Gap* (pp. 135–164). Hamburg: Körber-Stiftung.
O'Hagan, L. (ed.). (2008a). *Stories in Conflict*. Derry/Londonderry: Yes!
O'Hagan, L. (ed.). (2008b). *Training Manual with DVD*. Derry/Londonderry: Yes!
Randall, M. (1991) Reclaiming voices: Notes on new female practices in journalism. *Latin American Perspectives*, 18(3): 103–113.
Rothman, J. (1997) *Resolving Identity-based Conflict*. San Francisco, CA: Jossey-Bass.
Ryan, P. (1995) *Storytelling in Ireland*. Derry/Londonderry: The Verbal Arts Centre.
Schaffer, K. & Smith, S. (2004) *Human Rights and Narrative Lives*. New York: Palgrave.
Schmidt, W. (2000) Peace through storytelling. In D. Bar-On (ed.) *Bridging the Gap* (pp. 13–17). Hamburg: Körber-Stiftung.
Senehi, J. (2002) Constructive storytelling: A peace process. *Journal of Peace and Conflict Studies*, 9(2): 41–62.
Senehi, J. & Byrne, S. (2006) From violence toward peace: The role of storytelling for youth healing and political empowerment after social conflict. In S. McEvoy-Levy (ed.) *Troublemakers or Peacemakers?* (pp. 235–258). South Bend, IN: University of Notre Dame Press.
Senehi, J., Kahanoff, M. & Shibli, N. (2008) *Evaluation of Jerusalem Stories, Exhibit, Dialogue*. Unpublished report.
Sepinuck, T. (2013) *Theatre of Witness*. London: Jessica Kingsley.
Smith, B.H. (1981) Narrative version, narrative theories. In W.J.T. Mitchell (ed.) *On Narrative* (pp. 209–232). Chicago, IL: University of Chicago Press.
Truth and Reconciliation Commission of Canada. (2015) *Calls to Action*. Winnipeg: Truth and Reconciliation Commission.
Weingarten, K. (2003) *Common Shock*. New York: New American Library.

4

THE INTERSECTION OF IMPROV AND MEDIATION

Farshad Farahat, Alexia Georgakopoulos and Charles Goesel

Improvisation, or improv, plays a subtle, yet key role in any thriving mediation practice due to its inherent ability to increase one's propensity to adapt quickly and seamlessly to new information and to assist in breaking old patterns of behaviors and perceptions by improving communication and creative thinking. The ability to engage in and build the capacity for improv is one excellent technique to incorporate into a successful mediation because mediation "benefits from a fresh perspective and a creative mind" (Krivis, 2001, para. 17). In addition, "[m]ediation is indeed an art, not only because style and creativity play such important roles, but also because we as mediators express ourselves through our work" (Kleinberger, 2006, p. 37). Improv plays a significant role in mediation since it provides individuals with a unique platform to express themselves naturally, creatively, and spontaneously. Furthermore, improv enhances discovery and understanding of the self and other, which can lead to a number of positive potential outcomes in mediation.

While most people may not generally associate the infusion of improv, arts, music, theatre, storytelling, poetry, films, and dance as conventional forms of conflict resolution, several chapters featured in this handbook illustrate that they are indeed powerful platforms to promote peace, change, and conflict transformation. As authors of this writing, we provide an example of performance improv in mediation and from the onset of this chapter we call for more individuals who are in the Arts and Performance Arts Fields like artists, musicians, dancers, poets, actors, filmmakers, storytellers and the like to champion conflict transformation and mediation in their work because this work can be sensory stimulating, experientially captivating, unquestionably memorable, powerfully inspiring in nature, but most notably defined as profoundly mediating and mediation where impacts can be far reaching from the stage to the streets. Insofar as participants/audience members are viscerally, mentally, and actively engaged, they can be transformed from observers to change agents who take action for enduring impacts in their communities and world as a result of their participation in these creative and nuanced forms of human expression. A significant aspect of social life draws from the Arts, so there is practical wisdom- along with a growing body of research that substantiates its impact- in being intentional about their prominent placement in the mediation field along with related fields such as peace, justice, human rights, and conflict resolution.

This chapter explores the potential uses of artistic improvisation in mediation by outlining and recommending improv skills, approaches, and techniques applicable to mediation.

Improv, as practiced by stage directors, actors, and musicians, can be translated in principle to enhance mediation sessions by increasing the skills and techniques in a mediator's toolbox. The essence behind improv is in building a shared creative environment that is flexible and changing while discovery and meaning emerge by *being* in the moment. In addition, the opening, body, and closing sections of a mediation session inherently invite performance improvisation concepts, many of which are already well known to conflict resolutionists such as: reflective listening, recognition, empowerment, reframing, transformation, creativity, empathy, flexibility, humor, mutuality, shared interests, new narratives, and cooperative bargaining to name a few. Both mediators and parties to a mediation can benefit from utilizing improv tools and techniques.

Improv defined

Improvisation is the fluidity of performance in life and art that provides an opportunity. It provides mediators and parties with the ability to communicate with openness and authenticity when it is done in a safe and conducive environment. The free flow of ideas in improv allow individuals to freely entertain creative solutions and ideas that are outside the parameters of dominant narratives, rigid structures, and prescriptive scripts, all of which often lead to predetermined expectations or calculated positions. In a theater context, "[i]mprov is a form of live theatre in which the plot, characters and dialogue of a game, scene or story are made up in the moment" (Hideout Theatre, 2016). Improv is a state of constant flux that is characterized by ebb and flow with uncertainty and certainty. It is a dialectical expression of co-constructing meaning by being in the moment and seizing opportunities while responding to unexpected responses. Improv has ancient origins from Greek and Roman cultures where it was used to entertain, yet these performances often involved addressing or tackling conflict. While improv continues to be a significant artistic form in many cultures around the world, improv has also been utilized as an effective conflict resolution approach in contemporary times. For example, the Facilitation Dramatic Problem Solving Model integrates concepts and techniques of performance improv and indigenous conflict management and problem solving (Hawkins & Georgakopoulos, 2010).

Improvisation is defined by two fluid pillars; one, the process of interacting freely with fellow actors within structure; and two, allowing new ideas to flourish. According to Harding (2004), "[t]hrough active listening and reading the cues from the other party … negotiators and comics alike—may be able to explore ideas … Working together they may be able to drive the scene to a more effective result" (p. 210). In a musical context, improvisation is "composing something new which has not been notated, something quite literally 'un-foreseen'" (Harris, n.d., para. 1). It is ultimately the birth of something new by tapping into a storm of creativity and performing a story or meaning on the spot.

From a conflict resolution perspective, we[1] collectively integrate improv with mediation in our work regularly and define improv as the ability to adjust spontaneously to new, shifting, and sometimes conflicting information by being in the moment. Improv requires mediators to listen to parties as they often speak emotionally, yet mediators act as guardians of the process, without controlling the outcome in order to improve parties' understanding of self and other. The outcome of any mediation belongs with parties not mediators; therefore, mediators should invite parties to be a part of the process in order for them to explore possible outcomes. Like the jazz musician or the seasoned actor who use improv, "[m]ediators use information they glean in advance in combination with new information learned 'on the spot' to determine next moves" (Balachandra et al., 2005, p. 426). In all contexts, improv performances take place in the moment and performers must be tuned into those around them in order to craft responses and co-create new emergent meanings, messages, and stories.

Improv enhances the capacity to think and react quickly while fostering a sense of cooperation and collaboration, and opens the door for validating the ideas of the other without the need to abandon one's own ideas (Krivis, 2001). Improv increases the need to connect and truly listen to others while encouraging "openness to creativity and inspiration, willingness to take risks, a lack of judgment, and the capacity to say 'yes' more often than 'no'" (Krivis, 2001, para. 10). Mediation requires one to go beyond simply listening accurately and to listen with empathy (Kleinberger, 2006, p. 37). In fact, improv requires parties to "deal with ... reality ... in real-time rather than continually revisiting scenarios of what they believe could or should be ... Improvising instead of following a script or a plan allows the flexibility to stay nimble, and operate more freely and authentically" (Krivis, 2001, para. 12). Moreover, "[p]eople escalate their conflicts by not being authentic. As they accept themselves more fully they become more accepting of others" (Cloke, 2001, p. 7). Improv aids in building the self-confidence necessary for true self-authenticity and understanding.

Improvising in various film roles enables actors to find instinctual human reactions within the limits of a script and studio benchmarks. In acting as well as in many cultures, storytelling is a tool utilized to pass down life stories from generation to generation, spanning across thousands of years. As each generation hands the oral history through stories down to the next generation, improv often takes place in retelling the story to relate to current times and circumstances. Within the structured walls of folklore, storytellers find spontaneous and captivating human moments to illustrate in improv. Folklore provides the inspiration, but improv tells the new unfolding story. In parallel, improv in mediation can invite the same flurry of human creativity from the opening to the closing of the session as the past, present, and future intersect. It can be used to express disconnection and crisis as well as interdependence and reconciliation between parties. Improv can teach valuable conflict resolution lessons. Performing the issues or problems, parties can face conflict and the past, and this may very well be as important as having parties use improv to perform viable solutions, options, or outcomes for the future. For mediators, improv serves as a tool to harness the strength of being spontaneous and being in the moment with parties rather than being deliberative about next steps. This helps mediators establish trust and rapport with parties as there is a level of exciting vulnerability and openness present in improv.

Improv in mediation

Preparing to improvise

To a certain degree, "mediation is always improv" (Beer et al., 2012, p. 7). Celebrated actors often note that the more you do your homework, the more you are free to be intuitive. This line of thought exemplifies the role of preparation in improv. Any time actors have succeeded in improvising roles, it has been due to countless hours of script and role preparation. Mediators must also thoroughly prepare for every upcoming mediation session (Moore, 2003; Winslade & Monk, 2000). That very preparation allows mediators to have confidence in letting go of the conventional plan and being able to delve into creative and spontaneous improvisation.

Mediators should be prepared to describe the process of improv with clear instructions, objectives, and parameters. They should discuss with parties how improv should be a safe process where parties should communicate their ideas freely. A discussion surrounding how to honor safety throughout the process should be addressed from the onset of mediation improv. In addition, mediators should be prepared to integrate debriefing discussions about improv sessions. These preparations may enhance mediators' abilities because they help mediators become cognizant throughout improv in order to respond and point out shifts, progress, and differences that develop between parties. By being reflective in mediation improv, the mediator may be able to empower the parties to recognize their shared achievements in the session, or mediators may come to recognize their own capabilities to improve understanding and support discovery in the mediation session.

Improv exercise

Improv has proven techniques and exercises that can be utilized by mediators to generate movement in stagnant areas of a session.[2] In fact, being adept at improv can be exceptional for conflict resolution, negotiation, and bargaining. Mediators can utilize vital people skills with help from improv exercises to be proactive in their on-demand interventions to promote momentum in mediation. Improv invites an organic sequence of events that are never imagined or assumed in advance; it is a collaborative process of co-authorship and co-creation that makes it unique. Mediators can focus on improving communication between the parties by incorporating the widely known improv game, "yes, and …" (Leonard & Yorton, 2015). Filmmakers often set up improvisation sessions for their actors to interact loosely within script lines. This tool encourages character actors to acknowledge their counterpart and to validate themselves and their fellow performers within the role, leading to the advancement of creative awareness and shared goals. 'Yes and …' is a back-and-forth improv technique that allows actors to listen to what the first person said and incites the other person to respond to it. The game recognizes counterparts while searching for possibilities in the scene (Parashar & Gupta, 2012). By communicating 'yes and …' with words and nonverbal actions, "parties feel accepted, willing to share more and … [are] more willing to engage in the process of problem solving" (Lee, 2016, para. 13). This approach allows for spontaneous conflict management and bargaining approaches.

"Yes and …" steps

- The mediator can start the exercise by asking the participants to swap seating positions with their counterparts. This allows a physical perspective exchange to take place.
- The mediator can ask one party to voice their position on a soft topic that both groups have roughly agreed upon. The listening party will then be asked to respond by starting with the phrase, "yes and …" Throughout the exercise, parties should be reminded that the idea "is to build upon (and not negate) your partner's ideas" (Lee, 2016, para. 12). In addition, parties should be reminded to refrain from offering approval or criticism of the ideas generated as the point is to stimulate a free flow of ideas.
- This interaction should be repeated for at least five soft questions until there is a common consensus amongst the parties. The goal is to have parties generate ideas, not evaluate ideas.
- Once this trend of interaction is established, the mediator can then apply the formula to the outstanding questions that have created the stalemate or to tackle a new frontier of conflict.

This exercise allows participants to develop skills for acknowledging the other's point of view while highlighting the problem and advancing toward the goal of a resolution. Throughout such improv exercises, mediators can also continually check in with participants and gauge their comfort in the direction of the exercise's questions. The strength of improv occurs when participants are encouraged to make free decisions. By not setting hard ground rules and/or pushing for answers, a mediator can encourage participants to avoid assumptions, while advancing mediation. In addition, "'yes, and' moves things forward, opens up creativity, and creates a collaborative relationship" (Parashar & Gupta, 2012, para. 10). Parties to a mediation often believe that their perception of the conflict is the "right" perception and fear that foregoing their position will lead to the abandonment of their interests. However, if both sides are able to share their stories, they may come to discover and understand the nature of their conflict with a new and enlightening lens. Improv skills greatly increase the likelihood of such occurrences.

It is also important to note the danger of ad-libbing in lieu of improvising in these exercises. If a mediation's finale is preplanned, the session might appear ad-libbed rather than spontaneous, potentially resulting in the participants' disengagement from working toward a shared resolution. In fact, they might simply stop listening altogether. In successful film improv exercises, even when script lines are predetermined, strong directors have not predetermined a character's action and goals. When we, the actors, are left alone to come up with solutions within the boundaries of script lines, innovation, creativity, learning, and spontaneity take hold, allowing improvisation to define and develop the scenes and solutions (Gerardi, 2001). An alternative to this activity is to use the above, but integrate the guiding phrase of "what if ..." as this activity will provide parties with options to test alternatives.

Co-mediators

Improvisation concepts can also guide co-mediators within a mediation session. Trust and mutuality are key components of successful improvisation in film. Whether that trust and mutuality are between directors and producers, or between the actors themselves, they allow the project to move freely (McBroom, n.d.). Trust gives collaborators the tool to follow one another's instincts before passing judgment or projecting solutions. Co-mediators can also utilize the concept of trust in improvisation to allow one another's instincts to operate in a mediation session. When mediators are adept in improv they can trust and follow one another's instincts, mobility, and mutuality—all of which can shape an atmosphere of trust and cooperation for the participants.

Physical attributes

Strong improvisation contains many physical attributes. Throughout each section of a mediation, all participants can exemplify the physical strengths of improvisation. Direct and mutual eye contact is a foundation of improv; it opens the door for shared understandings. In fact, according to actor Barbara Stanwyck (n.d.), "[e]yes are the greatest tool in film." Mediators who continually read from scripts can block eye contact and creative improvisation. Effective vocal projection and clarity are also important in igniting improvised moments within mediation. Fluid posture and movement are the vehicles of that impactful improvisation. Both mediators and participants should mind their body language to better engage in their session. However, it is important to point out that acceptable physical engagement can vary from culture to culture. Therefore, gauging one's atmosphere is most important before delving into productive improvisation.

Mediation introduction

In the opening statement of a mediation session, a mediator establishes credibility with the parties involved (Moore, 2003; Winslade & Monk, 2000; Bush & Folger, 2005). Opening with credentials and necessary background information allows the mediator to gauge the atmosphere and apply improvised personal introductions to calm potential tensions, thereby leaving the parties open to consider new possibilities. Here a key component of improv should be recognized, the gauging of atmosphere. For example, if the room is tense during introductions, contextual humor can loosen the mood. Humor is the essence of improv on stage, and its proper use can smooth over anxiety and tension in a mediation session (Meers, 2009). Conversely, if the room is unfocused and rowdy at the start of a session, a solemn metaphor defining mediation can reinforce the necessary focus of the parties. As with all improv, subtle recognition of the atmosphere is a key in deciphering what could be effective and what could infringe on the productivity of a mediation process. Proper recognition of the atmosphere at the start of a session can set the tone for effectively improvising throughout the mediation.

During the opening statements, a mediator can introduce flexibility by highlighting the session's potential informality, self-determination, and collaboration, all qualities of effective improvisation. Strong and creative producers and directors in the film industry also introduce a role to an actor by injecting self-determination and collaboration. For actors, these introductions allow one to become self-aware within their roles. Self-awareness ignites purpose and ownership. When the participants of a mediation session become self-aware in the mediation, they become vested in the process. Once the mediation parties are vested, the focus can shift to the goals of the mediation session (Moore, 2003; Bush & Folger, 2005). The strongest film performances are not predetermined by producers or directors, but rather they are developed from the ability to guide actors toward owning and harnessing the strength of the role. Likewise, effective mediation can promote its participants to take ownership of their desired goals (Moore, 2003).

Here are five tips for infusing improv into the opening of a mediation:

- Mediators can utilize the improv skill of integrating humor. The appropriate use of humor can calm nerves as well as build and support rapport between the mediator and the parties, and between the parties themselves (Meers, 2009). However, humor should be used carefully, so as not to offend. Humor should be crafted in good taste.
- The improv tool of storytelling can be integrated into introductions by asking each party to introduce themselves by sharing a personal story that expresses something unique about themselves that they would like to share. An improv guiding phrase such as, "tell us a story of who you are" or "what would you like us to know about you" are good ways to begin. Mediators are encouraged to illustrate improv by sharing their story, so parties may understand the process. This process can be done verbally or in a performance based on what is preferred or appropriate for the context.
- Improv can also be used to check in with parties on how much they already know about mediation by asking questions such as, "what does mediation mean to you?" "what do you think mediation is?" or "what is mediation?" These questions give the mediator the ability to gauge what the parties know about mediation while giving parties the ability to share their level of understanding of mediation. The mediator can then improvise on how much s/he needs to share about the process and procedure of mediation.
- Improv can also be used to check in with parties on their expectations by asking parties to share their goals. This can be accomplished by asking questions such as, "why did you come to mediation?" or "what is your hope for mediation?" These questions are

inherently improvisational because they require the mediator to encourage the parties to venture beyond their preplanned positions. In addition, mediators can use the new information provided in a manner that best suits a potential resolution. However, the mediator should stress the necessity of keeping the parties from mentioning specific solutions to the conflict (Moore, 2003).

- Improv can also be used to gain commitment and ownership of the mediation. For example, a mediator may ask parties to share their level of commitment to mediation (Moore, 2003) and why they are committed to utilizing mediation in their dispute by simply asking, "why are you committed to mediation?" or "is it important to be committed to this process?" These responses can then be infused in improv by discussing the possibilities, benefits, or limitations of mediation. This can be very informative for parties.

Body of the mediation

As the body section of the mediation begins, a mediator can invite the parties to verbalize their stories, to express their emotions, frustrations, goals, and fears. Here, the mediator can listen and gather information. Listening is the heart of artistic improvisation. In an 'Inside the Actors Studio' interview, Meryl Streep, the iconic Hollywood actor, says: "Listening is where you live on stage" (Smart, 1998). In film as in mediation, the art of listening closes the door on judgment and assumptions, while opening the door to allow parties to interact uninterrupted. According to Kleinberger (2006), "[i]n mediation, it is not enough to just listen accurately; we endeavor to listen with empathy, to really care" (p. 37). In addition, when parties of a mediation session voice their opinions freely, a mediator allows participants to take the lead (Moore, 2003; Winslade & Monk, 2000; Bush & Folger, 2005). When all parties have a voice that is acknowledged, an atmosphere of neutrality takes hold (Gerardi, 2001). Neutrality is where creativity in mediation can flourish, and more importantly, where self-determination can take root.

When a mediator facilitates the conversation between parties, they can aid in developing the issues at hand through improv activities. These techniques empower the parties to improvise their deliberation, interests, storytelling, bargaining, and decision making voluntarily, rather than simply to restate their positions and desired goals. This tool can encourage mediation participants not only to understand the structure of the session but to acknowledge their own, and more importantly one another's, perspectives (McBroom, n.d.). The participants can now freely play off one another and develop greater awareness of themselves and of the other. This free exploration of one another's perspectives cultivates an atmosphere that can lead to shared resolutions within mediation.

Here are five tips to aid in mediation improv in the body of mediation:

- Improv through storytelling can be used to express the issues surrounding the conflict. For example, a mediator may ask each party to share a story that communicates the issues surrounding the dispute by asking parties, "can you share a story that you perceive will capture the issues surrounding the dispute from the other party's perspective?" This improv practice allows the parties to view the conflict from the other's position. Alternatively, if parties are willing and comfortable, they can perform the improv as performers and perform the story from their perspective or the other party's perspective. This experiential activity allows for recognition.
- Improv can be used to harness common ground. For example, mediators can ask parties to comment or perform: "What does common ground look like to you?" "What does

common ground mean to you?" "What does it look like in action?" "What does it take to establish common ground?" As stated above, these questions and their responses are clearly improvisational by design and require the parties to step out of their own positions.

- Improv can be utilized to provide alternative options through vivid imagery in improv. For example, a mediator may ask parties: "What do you imagine good solutions would look like?" "What would the story look like with solutions in place?" This can be stated verbally or performed in action based on the consent of parties in mediation.
- Improv can be utilized to generate alternative solutions. For example, a mediator may ask parties for good options to resolve the issues by incorporating the priming phrase 'yes and …', rather than 'yes but …'. It is important to have parties alternate as they improv and brainstorm options without evaluating solutions as they provide scenarios to each solution (Moore, 2003).
- Improv can also be used to generate creative solutions in improv skits or performances. For example, a mediator may ask parties to act out solutions or even possible issues or problems to illustrate their points. This allows parties to see the solutions or problems by experiencing them through the performance. This is often done effectively in community mediation or in mediation that involves a number of individuals. However, it can also be used in divorce mediation to illustrate how parents might effectively communicate around their children or how ineffectively their current communication is with children. In corporate mediation, through improv, parties may illustrate what solutions would look like in practice before they are implemented, or through improv, parties can illustrate problems of the status quo to illustrate the severity of the problems. The mediator may ask parties to take a few minutes to envision a scenario and spontaneously act out vivid problems, solutions, or both, to illustrate a problem and a solution to this specific problem. This process is very engaging and involving for parties.

Concluding the mediation

In closing the session, a mediator can review the agreement or conclusions reached by reflecting back the ideas and solutions that were articulated by the parties. This act is in parallel with directors assessing a day's improv work between actors. After an improvised filming session, many directors gather their team of actors and display the results of their work. In these sessions, directors tend to also clarify what parts of the script were addressed or not addressed by the improvisation through a solid debrief.

Mediators can also give an overview and ask parties to reflect on what requires omission, amendment, or acceptance. Mediation is inherently like improv because parties can never completely plan what they will say, do, or agree upon. This gives parties the opportunity to reflect on what they would change as well as giving them the opportunity to focus on the strengths and limitations of the mediation session. However, as in previous steps, coercion cannot be at play when a mediator is reviewing the results of the session. Coercion can stymie future opportunities for improvisation by participants, so it is essential that parties are comfortable with the process. Honest assessment is the key for continued trust in improv and in mediation. Congratulating improvised achievements can also build confidence for participants, encouraging them to engage in future improvisation to finalize outstanding mediation goals. In defining future actions, a mediator can again allow the participants to reflect freely upon their goals, leaving an open door to future improvisation. Improv skills are developmental, so parties may learn to utilize them in the future without the mediator in order to resolve new conflicts.

Here are five tips for improv in the conclusion of a mediation:

- Improv can be utilized in implementing an action plan. Mediators may ask parties or tell parties to perform: "What will an action plan look like in terms of who, what, when, where, why and how?" "What does the solution look like?" "What is required to implement it?" "When will it be implemented and completed?" "Where is the location or address that is tied to the implementation?" "How will the solution be implemented and what aid or resources will be necessary?" Here it might be important for the mediator to improvise by recalling shared agreements and common ground from earlier in the session.
- Improv can be used to ensure understanding of the settlement or outcomes of mediation by checking in with parties to ensure they understand the terms of the agreement and settlement. Mediators may use improv by stating: "Parties please restate what your understanding of the agreement is in your own words or perform this in terms of what the settlement means". This will allow the mediator and the parties to gauge and converge on the accuracy of meanings, while it should invite parties to amend meanings if they are different.
- Improv can be used to discuss consequences. Oftentimes, a solid solution has built-in sanctions in the event that there is a lack of compliance with the settlement terms and conditions. In this event, a mediator may ask parties to use improv to aid in addressing sanctions. For example, a mediator may ask parties to use improv as a guiding question or perform the following: "What should happen if the solution is not implemented or what would the consequences or sanctions look like?", "What if the solution is not implemented?" or "What happens then?" This helps parties build in accountability to their agreed-upon terms.
- Improv can be used to effectively close the mediation session. There is no better way for parties to perceive the mediator in the moment when s/he conveys a solid review of the session based on how it functioned and was completed. For example, the mediator may use improv to help them generate a closing that is authentic, impactful, and meaningful by completing one of these guiding phrases: "This mediation session helped accomplish …" or "this mediation session can be summarized by …" Alternatively, parties can perform a concluding improv to illustrate what the mediation or conclusion symbolized for them.
- Improv can be used to commend parties for their commitment to mediation and ownership of outcomes. For example, a mediator may use these improv guiding phrases: "I commend you for participating in mediation because …", "I thank you for your role in mediation because…" or "I appreciate you for completing mediation because …" These phrases allow the mediator to reveal a spontaneous and authentic statement of gratitude to parties for their involvement in mediation. In addition, the mediator may invite parties to commend each other using the guiding phrases above as well.

Take away

Our hope in writing this chapter is to share how experiences with improvisation in film, art, music, and conflict resolution can be applied to the field of mediation. Farshad Farahat's work in the acting field joined with his conflict resolution work along with Alexia Georgakopoulos and Charles Goesel's roles in incorporating improv into mediation training, coaching, and education have led to the realization of the shared strengths that these disciplines nurture in creative improvisation. Our aspiration is that this chapter will inspire mediators to be more versed and knowledgeable about improv in mediation. It is our hope that mediators will develop and advance the tools of creative improvisation in the ever-evolving discipline of mediation.

A final cut of a successful film can ignite inspiration for all involved, and become a reflection of a script's vision and strength. Likewise, the final product in a mediation session can also be a rousing testament to the creative and unconventional application of improv that benefits mediators and parties by simply harnessing the spontaneity of being in the moment.

Notes

1 The first author is an actor with extensive experience utilizing improv skills and techniques to enhance his roles. The other two authors integrate improv extensively in conflict resolution training and into their teaching philosophies.
2 For a list of improv games that build mediation skills, see appendix 1 of Kleinberger, 2006.

References

Balachandra, L., Barrett, F., Bellman, H., Fisher, C. & Susskind, L. (2005) Improvisation and mediation: Balancing acts. *Negotiation Journal*, 21(4): 425–434.

Beer, J.E., Packard, C.C. & Stief, E. (2012) *Mediator's Handbook*. Gabriola Island, British Columbia: New Society Publishers.

Bush, Baruch R.A. & Folger, J.P. (2005) *The Promise of Mediation*. San Francisco, CA: Jossey-Bass.

Cloke, K. (2001) *Mediating Dangerously: The Frontiers of Conflict Resolution*. San Francisco, CA: Jossey-Bass.

Gerardi, D. (2001) Using improvisation to develop conflict resolution skills. *Mediate.com*. Retrieved from www.mediate.com/articles/geradi1.cfm.

Harding, C. (2004) Improvisation and negotiation: Making it up as you go along. *Negotiation Journal*, 20(2): 205–212.

Harris, W. (n.d.) Improvising as a lost art: The art of realtime composition. Retrieved from community.middlebury.edu/~harris/MusicPapers/MusicAlive.html.

Hawkins, S. & Georgakopoulos, A. (2010) Dramatic problem solving: Transforming community conflict through performance in conflict resolution. *Journal of Alternative Perspectives in the Social Sciences*, 2(1): 112–135.

Hideout Theatre. (2016) What is improv? Retrieved from www.hideouttheatre.com/about/what-is-improv.

Kleinberger, A. (2006) Building skills in mediators: Improvisation as a new technique. Retrieved from crhsgg-studentresources.wikispaces.umb.edu/file/view/Kleinberger_Adam_MP.pdf.

Krivis, J. (2001) Whose trial is it anyway? *First Mediation*. Retrieved from www.firstmediation.com/whose-trial-is-it-anyway/.

Lee, J. (2016) Improv and mediation. *Kluwer Mediation Blog*. Retrieved from kluwermediationblog.com/2016/03/14/improv-and-mediation/.

Leonard, K. & Yorton, T. (2015) *Yes, and: How Improvisation Reverses "No, but" Thinking and Improves Creativity and Collaboration: Lessons from The Second City*. New York: HarperCollins.

McBroom, A. (n.d.) Getting in sync: What improvisational theater has to teach co-mediators. Bellevue Neighborhood Mediation Program. Retrieved from www.ci.bellevue.wa.us/pdf/PCD/Improv_and_Mediation_Skills.pdf.

Meers, W. (2009) The funny thing about mediation: A rationale for the use of humor in mediation. *Cardozo Journal of Conflict Resolution*, 10(2): 657–685. Retrieved from: cardozojcr.com/vol10no2/657-686.pdf.

Moore, C.W. (2003) *The Mediation Process: Practical Strategies for Resolving Conflict* (3rd edn). San Francisco, CA: Jossey-Bass.
Parashar, A. & Gupta, S. (2012) Ding! Mediation improv. Flashpoint Mediation. Retrieved from flashpointmediation.com/ding-mediation-improv/.
Smart, J. (1998) 17 pieces of advice from "Inside the Actors Studio." Inside the Actors Studio. Retrieved from www.backstage.com/news/17-pieces-advice-from-inside-actors-studio/.
Stanwyck, B. (n.d.) AZ quotes. Retrieved from www.azquotes.com/quote/627417.
Tucker, L.M. (2009) Playing by the rules: When mediation is like improv. *Peacewise*. Retrieved from www.peacewisemediation.com/2009/12/playing-by-the-rules-when-mediation-is-like-improv/.
Winslade, J. & Monk, G. (2000) *Narrative Mediation: A New Approach to Conflict Resolution*. San Francisco, CA: Jossey-Bass.

5

VALUE-CENTERED MEDIATION

The centrality and use of meaning and values

Mark Kleiman

Value-centered mediation (VCM) builds upon previous models (problem solving, relationship-driven, facilitative) while integrating scientific frameworks and the Logotherapy of Viktor Frankl (1959). In VCM, the mediator elicits the explicit meaning and value of the conflict for the disputants. This foundation enables the parties to understand what is most important and so they can negotiate in ways that honor each other. The results include a deeper understanding of the conflict, a more nuanced negotiation, and greater wisdom gained from the process.

Prologue

Before I became a mediator, I studied science. I see a direct relationship between conflict resolution and the formation of the physical world. I hope the following informs how we view conflict and provides a rationale for the approach I utilize.

The nature of energy dictates how entities in the universe interact (Greene, 1999). Accepted scientific theory based upon quantum physics holds that every photon of energy has two simultaneous characteristics: that of an individual or point and the other as relational or a wave. After the Big Bang, all matter was formed by collisions, resulting in either their destruction or construction of new and more complex matter (Greene, 1999). The newly formed matter was able to exist when there was stability both internally (individual) and with the environment (relational). Trillions of years of collisions and contacts resulted in the universe we now inhabit. The recent discovery of a new particle, the Higgs Boson (Overbye, 2013), believed to be responsible for giving substance and solidity to the energetically formed entities, presents an additional perspective. The most complex results that have evolved are living things whose lifetime and existence or extinction depends on the same two qualities: healthy stability both as individuals and in relationship to the environment.

I believe that mediation is the healthiest and most balanced way to assist conflicting parties to negotiate conflicts. Mediation serves the individual and their relationships, fostering:

- Individual wisdom through creative problem solving
- Mutual understanding through understanding of and compassion for the other and our environment
- Life lessons and skills for the future

Most important, mediation enables parties to reconcile that which is most meaningful to them as individuals in a collaborative manner, for this is what gives our existence substance. Could this be a manifestation of the Higgs Boson (Overbye, 2013)? Together these are the lessons that are critical to health and survival. Moreover, it is from the value and meaning of conflict for individuals—both within themselves and in relationship to their environment—that value-centered mediation emerges.

Value-centered mediation: defined

Mediation in its basic form is a dispute resolution process in which an impartial third party endeavors to empower the disputants to find a resolution to the dispute. VCM is an integrated mediation model based upon the nature of conflict, the centrality of meaning and values, and how these drive the techniques and objectives of the mediation process. From the early 1900s to William Ury's extensive body of work, interest-based facilitative models have evolved, focusing on rational problem solving (Ury et al., 1989). Implicit in these models has been the value of giving the parties the opportunity to make the best decision to satisfy their needs. This followed a more Newtonian approach to problem solving; the reconciling of two or more forces generated by the value of the interests, rights and power of the respective parties (Ury et al., 1989). In more recent years, models that held the prime values of mediation as understanding and restoration of relationships emerged.

Every model of mediation enunciates values that drive the practice (Bush & Folger, 2005). Transformative mediation uses reflective statements that give recognition to the parties, their presentation and emotions, along with offering opportunities to share what is important to them. These techniques lower the level of conflict to enable the parties to negotiate more effectively. Other techniques such as making suggestions, reframing, or problem solving are considered to be directive, and are therefore rejected (Friedman & Himmelstein, 2009). Understanding in mediation focuses upon the parties presenting their stories and the mediator looping back to create opportunities for new elements to appear. These two models identify relationships as the primary value.

The distinguishing feature of VCM is the degree that conflict, mediation and the needs of the parties are seen through the lens of meaning and values. VCM integrates the best techniques of the problem-solving approach with those emphasizing relationships. VCM is guided by an explicit set of values, which delineate the parameters for acceptable techniques and actions by the mediator. It also focuses on eliciting the meaning and values embedded in the conflict for each party. These are made explicit in order to enable the parties to understand what is most important to the other and thus negotiate in more nuanced ways. This elicitive process deepens the narrative by identifying the motivations and principles that drive the conflict. Therefore, the process often can engender more creative and lasting solutions.

The origins of value-centered mediation

There are three key influences that inform VCM: my early experiences as a lawyer, my introduction to a mentor, and the work of an early 20th-century psychiatrist. In my early experiences as a lawyer, I represented juveniles in the family court as an attorney for the Juvenile Rights Division of the Legal Aid Society. My years there enabled me to appreciate empowering my clients to make decisions on their own behalf. I was respectful, I listened actively to anything they wished to say, I explained the legal circumstances and options they faced, and I gave them a safe, confidential space in which to make their own decisions for their future. Then I fought to have their voices heard. Often I was the first adult to actually listen, to acknowledge and respect these youths. I appreciated the value of both the skills I practiced and the impact they made. Yet, I had not learned about their centrality to mediation until I encountered John Haynes, Ph.D..

John Haynes was the first President of the Academy of Family Mediators and a mentor. It was during the training I undertook with him in 1982 that I understood that a mediator reflected all the qualities that I had valued while practicing law: respect for the parties and their unique circumstances, as well as efforts to empower the clients to make thoughtful decisions about the conflicts they confronted (Haynes et al., 2004). The respectful, self-determinative and future-focused process was a healthy alternative to the polarizing, adversarial and win-lose approach of the courts. John had come to mediation as a Quaker. I was attracted to the fact that his training articulated the value of mediation as a process that represented hope to the parties and gave them the opportunity to act on the "good" in themselves.

VCM is inspired by the work of Dr Viktor Frankl, a psychiatrist who was a contemporary of Freud, Jung, and Rogers (Frankl, 1959). His unique approach to helping people in conflict was based upon the premise that every person's desire is for a life as meaningful as possible and everything we do has some meaning and value to us. Frankl's acclaimed book, *Man's Search for Meaning* (Frankl, 1959), describes an approach very similar to mediation: it is primarily present and future focused; it empowers people to identify and achieve the goals that are meaningful to them. Frankl tested these principles as a prisoner in four different concentration camps during World War II. He found meaning during this time assisting others to identify and act on what was meaningful to them. Even in that most brutal environment, he discovered that those who found some meaning and value in their lives were more likely to survive.

Frankl helps us understand the role that personal values and meaning play in action and choice. In a conflict, each party will be motivated by the depth of the value or meaning he/she attributes to the elements of the conflict (Frankl, 1959). Frankl suggests that we view our lives as the accumulated value derived from:

- Creating a work or doing a deed (what we do or create)
- Experiencing something or encountering someone (experiences and relationships)
- Attitudes toward suffering (which I interpret as the consequences of conflict)

These categories mirror the subject areas contained in any conflict. The objects and actions that make up the conflict are the elements contained in the narratives of the parties. The relationships, and their characteristics and history, are always important to both of the parties and critical to the potential for resolution. The emotional, material or physical consequences of the conflict represent the pain caused, often reflecting values like respect, acceptance, responsibility, loyalty, etc. that have been violated.

The meaning and value to be attained in a conflict include the opportunity to gain wisdom, to better understand the issues, ideas and reasoning of the other, and to transform the emotions resulting from the conflict into feelings of understanding, if not compassion. From this, wiser decisions are made. VCM is a process that facilitates a path to these objectives. The techniques offer opportunities to learn and grow, whether or not resolution occurs. In a successful mediation, the parties are more apt to understand the motivations and perspectives of the other whether they agree with their conclusions or not. The problem-solving process gives both parties the opportunity to make wiser decisions that narrow if not bridge differences. The gift of these experiences continues after the conclusion of the process.

The underlying principles of VCM

If we are to use the model of VCM, we must begin with the values implicit in the model. VCM, like most types of mediation, rests both on principles related to the process—that it is confidential, safe and voluntary—and principles that govern the mediator—that s/he will exhibit humility and impartiality, and promote the clients' self-determination. Of these, the most important quality for the mediator is humility. Humility acknowledges that mediators know very little or even nothing about the parties or their history; therefore, mediators must recognize they do not know what is best for the parties. In fact, only the parties know this. Humility ensures that the mediators will be mindful of remaining as impartial as possible and of acting in ways that allow the parties to perceive that impartial stance. This enables the mediator to more fully promote the empowerment of the parties to make their own decisions on how or even whether they resolve the conflict. In VCM, the mediator avoids techniques that suggest or direct the parties toward any solution.

VCM uses reflective techniques to elicit the narratives, perspectives, and emotions of each party. This promotes the two objectives of the process: fostering understanding and facilitating the knowledge base upon which the parties exercise their wisdom (Hall, 2010). If we think of the required elements of wisdom as knowledge and understanding, analysis and emotions, the mediator must then:

- Elicit the details of the background of the conflict, the facts of the relationships, and the relative importance of aspects of the conflict
- Engage the parties in a process of analysis and problem solving
- Give recognition to the emotions and their meaning

The result will be a wiser decision as well as a wiser person.

The process and techniques of VCM

The structure of the values-centered process would also be familiar to any experienced mediator who uses a facilitative approach. It begins with introductions and information gathering. What differentiates VCM is that in this model, the mediator elicits and fosters a conscious and rigorous exploration of that which has meaning and value to the parties. This creates a more nuanced understanding of each party as well as a vehicle for eliciting the practical elements that underlie those values. This practice, the heart of VCM, distinguishes it from others. Afterwards, reframing issues, problem solving and identifying agreements take place.

The structure of the process, as experienced mediators know, is a mere guide that often loops back on itself as the parties find the need for more relevant information, hear changes in the values and meaning and importance of elements of the conflict, identify more significant issues, and struggle with the process as they strive for solutions.

The primary techniques at each stage of the process and their rationale are listed as follows:

Stage 1: Introduction

A mediator using VCM would frame the process in ways that offer hope and the possibility of a respectful resolution, reinforcing the values of the process and emphasizing that any outcome will be the result of the parties' own creativity. Then the mediator offers the parties the opportunity to ask questions before beginning to elicit the stories. Since the process is voluntary, the parties understand that although there is hope for a resolution, any outcome requires consent by both parties and is not guaranteed to reach a mutually acceptable agreement.

Stage 2: Elicit the narratives

To create ongoing opportunities to gain the knowledge for assessment and eventual decision making, a mediator trained in VCM listens respectfully, reflecting the stories and emotions to acknowledge their importance, and provides opportunities for the parties to better understand each other and expand their perspectives and knowledge.

One exception to this approach is when the value of safety of a party or third party could be at risk. In the case of possible domestic or relationship violence, separate sessions are held so that the mediator has no reasonable suspicion that a threat is present. When the subject is a third party, such as children in a custody matter or disabled elder, it is critical that the mediator be trained to be vigilant to the potential of abuse or neglect. Safety always trumps confidentiality.

In a VCM dealing with conflict around parenting after separation, the process is child-centered. Photos of the children (frequently found now on most people's phones) are placed on the table and the mediator elicits through a series of questions the personalities, characteristics and special qualities of each child. The mediator will have shared some materials prior to the session about the impact of conflict on children depending upon their ages as well as their need for support and stability. This allows the parties to give depth and substance to the picture.

In addition, the mediator asks the parents other questions such as:

- What does the relationship you currently have with each of your children mean to you? What does it mean to be a parent?
- How do you envision your relationships while living in separate households (appreciative inquiry which implicitly elicits values can be used to have them consider better times in the past or an ideal circumstance in the future)?
- What is most important to you going forward to maintain mutual support and stability in all the relationships? What principles should govern the way you deal with each other? The responsibilities?

The mediator writes all the values and principles down on paper or on a computer for the parties to reflect upon, as the details of the parenting plan are discussed. They form a basis for the terms of their future relationship and act as a means of testing present as well as future negotiations.

In these cases, as well as cases involving the elderly or disabled, the perspective of the subject of the mediation must be incorporated into the process as appropriately as possible. In the case of the elderly or disabled, if they are able they should participate appropriately in person, with or without an advocate, or using technology. Children, depending on their maturity, should be told about the process and be able to share information with the mediator. It is up to the mediator to integrate appropriately what is most meaningful and valued by them in the discussions.

Stage 3: Elicit the meaning and value of the objects and actions, the relationships, and the consequences of the conflict

Frequently over time, parties narrow their stories into simpler renditions that blame the other and cast the self as victim. The mediator in VCM elicits information, which provides a deeper understanding of what both parties value, giving them a more nuanced way to evaluate the elements for a potential resolution during the problem-solving stage. A mediator trained in VCM elicits the rationale for the importance of the elements to each party to the conflict.

Utilizing Frankl's framework, the mediator identifies the actions and objects that are at the heart of the dispute and may ask each party to describe the meaning, value, or importance of each to them. The mediator also identifies the relationships and might ask the parties what it means to be a friend, neighbor, relative, parent, employee, boss, landlord, etc. The feelings and perspectives shared may lead to general principles of behavior or responsibilities and help form a framework for an agreement. Finally, the mediator listens for the impact of the conflict on each of the parties. The discomfort, pain, suffering, anger, etc. is a barometer of the importance with which it is associated. Using this approach, VCM offers opportunities to transform the feelings of anger into the desire for a more principled conclusion to the dispute.

Stage 4: Reframe the issues

Reframing is a reflective statement of what the mediator has heard to be the values and goals of the parties. These are an expression of the outcomes each party hopes for. These neutral or positive values and goals depersonalize the problems and use language that is more personally acceptable. A humble mediator offers opportunities for the parties to correct any errors. Using the parenting issue as an example, the values and goals of a party may be convenience, consistency, timeliness, consideration, and/or fairness regarding the drop-off of the child. In VCM, the mediator then can ask the parties to describe what consistency, timeliness, etc. means to them. This can translate the values into anything from specific examples of variables that would be negotiated, principles that should underlie the manner or rationale for the actions of the parties or a recommended solution. Gaining joint definitions creates a framework for the parties to judge any of their suggested solutions and provides a framework for their future relationship.

Stage 5: Foster problem solving

Facilitating problem solving is the promotion of a neutral analytical process in which the parties weigh the variables that make up the conflict. This is a crucial part of the process, enabling both parties to find creative solutions and make decisions with which they feel most comfortable. The mediator, often using flip charts so that parties can examine the information in an objective fashion, captures each of their values and goals, with concomitant meaning, along with any principles they feel should be used to guide the decisions. The mediator asks what variables exist to impact the subject matter or actions associated with the dispute as well as the relationships. In the case of parenting, it could mean time, location, supervision, and manner of transportation. If safety is a concern, it could include trusted adult accompaniment. The parties negotiate the full range of options for each variable or resource and seek to decide which of the choices enables them to achieve their goals. Flexibility, objectivity, and clarity enable creativity, which leads to areas of agreement. The mediator creates opportunities for these, being careful not to be directive. The process fosters wiser decisions.

Stage 6: Design an agreement

The mediator scrupulously allows the parties to negotiate the framework for the agreement. The mediator acts as scribe, making certain that each party understands and agrees with every element. The mediator reflects the areas if the parties are unable to bridge any differences, restating the range of options available for consideration. They always have the court to bridge the final hurdle. Mediation makes this option more acceptable.

Conclusion

The very nature of conflict is a collision of forces that results in new relationships between each entity and its environment. As sentient beings, when we are engaged in a conflict, we have the opportunity to engage in a thoughtful process to gain understanding of our relationships and environment, and use wisdom to create as stable and healthy a result as possible. Mediation offers the skills of an impartial third party to facilitate such a process and to take full advantage of the meaning of conflict. Identifying the meaning and value of the elements of the conflict enables the parties to create an agreement of substance.

Meaning and values are embedded in VCM; they frame the parameters of the process and are elicited from the actions, relationships, and emotions of the parties. They also underlie goals, which lead to a range of options that contain the potential formula for an agreement. This informs a neutral problem-solving approach, which is a thoughtful opportunity to weigh options and design an agreement based upon what is important.

References

Bush, Baruch R.A. & Folger, J.P. (2005) *The Promise of Mediation*. San Francisco, CA: Jossey-Bass.

Frankl, V.E. (1959) *Man's Search for Meaning*. Boston, MA: Beacon Press.

Friedman, G. & Himmelstein, J. (2009) *Challenging Conflict: Mediation through Understanding*. Chicago, IL: ABA Publishing.

Greene, B. (1999) *The Elegant Universe: Superstrings, Hidden Dimensions, and the Quest for the Ultimate Theory*. New York: W.W. Norton & Company, Inc.

Hall, S.S. (2010) *Wisdom: From Philosophy to Neuroscience*. New York: Alfred A. Knopf.

Haynes, J.M., Haynes, G.L. & Fong, L. (2004) *Mediation: Positive Conflict Management*. Albany, NY: State University of New York Press.

Overbye, D. (2013). Chasing the Higgs. *The New York Times*, March 5. Retrieved from mobile.nytimes.com/2013/03/05/science/chasing-the-higgs-boson-how-2-teams-of-rivals-at-CERN-searched-for-physics-most-elusive-particle.html.

Ury, W.L., Brett, J.M. & Goldberg, S.B. (1989) *Getting Disputes Resolved: Designing Systems to Cut the Costs of Conflict*. San Francisco, CA: Jossey-Bass.

6

ELECTRONIC MEDIATION

Daniel Druckman and Sabine T. Koeszegi

In recent years, electronic mediation has proliferated as a dispute resolution method (Turel et al., 2007), predominantly in the context of online dispute resolution (ODR) for settling e-business conflicts (Ebner, 2012; Betancourt & Zlatanska, 2013). ODR tools are designed for resolving disputes-at-a-distance with high-volume caseloads and are discussed by Rainey and Tidwell in this volume. There is also a long tradition in research on electronic negotiation support in which the concepts of e-meditation, electronically supported mediation, or e-negotiation emerged. In this context, e-mediation refers to the use of web-based support systems to facilitate conflict resolution and negotiation processes not only restricted to e-business, but also including such areas as family mediation, labor negotiations, peace negotiations, and environmental conflicts. These support systems are discussed in this chapter.

Advances made in electronic negotiation or mediation suggest that a number of benefits have been realized from these systems for the practice of mediation and related forms of third-party intervention. These benefits include, but are not limited to, speeding online monitoring of developments in negotiation, facilitating the analysis of sources of impasses, making connections between analysis and advice to negotiators, and providing a vehicle for delivering the advice. The variety of web-based support systems is considerable, but only a few of them address the key functions of mediation, which include diagnosis, analysis, and advice.

The aim of this chapter is twofold. One is to connect the various strands of online systems by constructing a framework with examples of application. Another is to focus on web-supported expert systems that serve as mediators who intervene when impasses occur. Two expert mediator systems are highlighted, Negotiator Assistant and its successor Vienna Negotiator Assistant. These systems are discussed in terms of the functions they serve and the research conducted to evaluate their impacts on negotiation processes (flexibility) and outcomes (distributive and integrative). The chapter concludes with a discussion of remaining research challenges and implications for practice.

The many faces of e-mediation

The framework shown in Table 6.1 is organized in terms of phases of conflict resolution and e-mediation systems. The phases are preparation, processes, settlement, and post-settlement.

TABLE 6.1 Types of e-mediation systems by negotiating phase

Phases	*Preparation*	*Processes*	*Settlement*	*Post-Settlement*	*Selected examples*
Aim/target	**Conflict analysis/ modeling**	**Conflict confrontation**	**Conflictresolution**	**Implementation**	
Core activities	Agenda setting, identification of issues and attributes	Exchange of (priority) information	Converging towards agreement	Implementation of agreement and post settlement negotiation	
	Analysis of interests and preferences of parties	Exchange of proposals/offers			
	Planning: BATNA, reservation and aspiration levels	Use of tactics/ persuasion			
	Determination of approach, strategy & tactics				
e-supported mediation e-mediation in its wider sense: human mediators make use of web-based support tools in live mediations to support human agents	Setting the stage, choice of support & communication tools	Process facilitation & shuttle diplomacy	Arbitration	Implementation support	Standard web-based communication platforms that offer chat, video or voice (e.g. Skype etc.)
	Analysis of conflict intensity (questionnaires/ intakes)	Advice			Squaretrade; SmartSettle, Cybersettle, etc. are Online Dispute Resolution services (Ebner, 2012) and offer mediation services to settle e-business conflicts; for further examples see Rainey and Tidwell in this volume
	Diagnosis of conflict situation (ques-tionnaires/intakes)	Reframing			Family Winner, Asset Divider, IMODRE (Bellucci and Zeleznikov, 2005, Abrahams et al. 2012): online family mediation support systems

Phases	*Preparation*	*Processes*	*Settlement*	*Post-Settlement*	*Selected examples*
e-mediation/ e-negotiation e-mediation in its narrower sense: human agents make use of web-based support tools without involving a human mediator	Data Management	Communication support: pragmatic and semantic enrichment, document managment, caucusing & shuttle diplomacy, etc.	Final contract	Suggestion of Pareto-efficient Solutions	Negoisst (Schoop, 2010): Focus on communication support, semantic and pragmatic enrichment of electronic communication as well as decision support
	Preference Elicitation	Decision support: analysis of offers and counteroffers, logrolling and concession advice, optimization models	Analysis of (Pareto-) efficiency of outcome		Inspire (Kersten & Noronha, 1999; Gettinger et al., 2016): Focus on decision support and post settlement Win Win (Qu and Cheung, 2012): Focus on Logrolling and concession advice AC-AT (Vetschera et al., 2014): Focus on concession advice
	Questionnaires	Behavioral support: flexibility & impasse analysis, relationship management and trust, development of shared negotiation cultures	Information presentation (of achieved solution)		Negotiator Assistant, VienNA (Druckman et.al,. 2004; Druckman et.al,. 2014): Expert System, focus on behavioral support and flexibility analysis
	Information presentation (of conflict situation & intensity)	Information presentation (of negotiation process & history)			SIRO-MED (Janssen et al., 2006): graphical land-value maps to show conflict intensity in water management;Talkabout (Sumi and Mizoguchi, 2004): concept tree visualization to support conflict resolution
Automated negotiation artificial agents resolve conflicts of interests	Programming of artificial agents	Exchange of offers and counteroffers	Pareto-efficient solution		Facility Description Language-CR (Lara and Nof, 2002): automated negotiations for conflicting interests in collaborative facility design; ANAC Automated Negotiation Agents Competition (http://ii.tudelft.nl/negotiation/)
Blendede-mediation hybrid forms	Application of e-supported mediation, e-mediation or automated negotiations between human and artificial agents in different phases of conflict resolution process				Discussion Forum (Bollen and Ewuema, 2013): software to exchange asynchronously text-based communication before or during live mediation in divorces

It further distinguishes between the concepts of traditional mediation and the different forms of e-mediation, which include e-supported mediation (mediation is performed by human agents supported by e-mediation tools), e-negotiation/e-mediation systems (support systems take the mediation role between human agents), fully automated systems (artificial agents negotiate with the support of electronic negotiation systems), and blended e-mediation (use of different forms of mediation in the same conflict resolution process or during different phases). The key distinction is between human and non-human support. The table further provides examples of the various support tools or systems.

In e-supported mediation, a human mediator uses web-based support tools to facilitate a synchronous conflict resolution process between two or more parties. These tools are particularly helpful when disputants are in different locations or when tensions between them are high. Asynchronous (parties use the same system at different times), text-based electronic communication may facilitate communication between the disputants by offering the possibility of cooling down by leaving time between communicative acts and revising text messages before they are sent (Pesendorfer & Koeszegi, 2006; Johnson et al., 2009). Furthermore, live mediators can apply web-based communication systems for shuttle diplomacy (messages sent to the other party only through a mediator) or for caucusing (private meetings between the disputants and the mediator before or during the mediation) (Swaab & Brett, 2007; Bollen et al., 2014).

Mediators may also employ electronic communication tools to prepare for live mediation by using online questionnaires (referred to as intakes) to analyze interests of parties, conflict issues and conflict intensity (Bollen & Euwema, 2013). More advanced systems support live mediators or arbitrators with multi-attribute decision support (SmartSettle) or game theoretical applications including concepts of fairness, such as Family Winner, Asset Divider, or IMODRE, to find feasible solutions for live mediation (Bellucci & Zeleznikow, 2005; Abrahams et al., 2012).

Recent studies on electronically supported mediation demonstrate positive effects of web-based support. In the Bollen and Euwema (2013) study, divorce mediators used the system "discussion forum," which allows for the exchange of asynchronous text-based communication where the mediator acts as a go-between or shuttle diplomat for the parties. The study reports not only significantly higher settlement rates in e-supported mediations in comparison to face-to-face mediations, but also very high justice perceptions of the parties.

When conflicting parties decide to use negotiation support systems to facilitate conflict resolution, we refer to e-mediation/negotiation in its narrower sense. Electronic support in mediation consists of communication support, decision support (diagnosis), and behavioral support (diagnosis and intervention) (Vetschera et al., 2013). The early research on electronic negotiation support systems, beginning in the 1980s, focused attention on decision and analytical negotiation support. Regarding analysis, three approaches have been used to increase the understanding and viewpoints of complex negotiation problems: decision analysis (Ulvila, 1990), expert models and rule-based systems (Kersten, 1993), and cognitive mapping (Bonham, 1993). Advice is provided by different solution models that can be applied to negotiation, including optimization models, which search for integrative solutions (Wierzbicki et al., 1993), computer-aided discover and design analyses, which move the process away from create and claim bargaining toward joint problem solving (Samarasan, 1993), and tools that facilitate the development of shared negotiation cultures (Shakun, 1999). These tools demonstrate the usefulness of technical support.

With regard to monitoring, the research on persistent conversation is also relevant (Erickson & Herring, 1999) and consists of technology which manages long-term conversations and contacts by enabling users to track the content and status of conversations, as well as the contact information, skill and proficiency of conversation partners (Whittaker et al., 2002). Related monitoring technology has demonstrated the ability to facilitate collaboration and communication in negotiation settings (Bajwa & Lewis, 2002). Negotiator Assistant (NA) and its successor, Vienna Negotiator Assistant (VienNA), incorporate the third dimension of support: they focus on conflict diagnosis and—as an expert system—offer behavioral advice to disputing parties. The systems are designed to act as a neutral third party, facilitating the core mediation functions without prescribing outcomes.

Mediator functions

Focusing attention on the behavior of mediators, e-mediation systems are designed to move negotiators from generally inflexible postures to a willingness to consider options for agreement. Flexibility varies during the course of negotiation. To capture this variation, an e-mediation system monitors progress by asking where the process is at a particular point in time. The answers reveal how far each negotiator or negotiating team is from agreement on each of the issues being discussed. This is valuable information but does not offer guidance on the steps needed for progress. The guidance comes from an analysis of the sources of the inflexibility that are responsible for the impasse. Those sources can be found in the parties' or delegation's activities, in the issues, in the negotiating process, in the situation, or in a combination of these aspects of negotiation. They point to the areas where mediation assistance is needed.

Advice, which can be considered a function of e-mediation, develops from having performed a diagnosis and analysis. It is tailored to the source of impasse discovered during the analysis phase. For example, if the source is the complexity of issues, negotiators are instructed to exchange information and consider a strategy that fractionates or reduces the size of the issues discussed. If the source is in the negotiating process, where no salient solution has been found, they are encouraged to learn how to use linking or logrolling strategies. If the source is found to be in the situation, where various audiences or stakeholders exert pressures for maximizing returns, the negotiators are encouraged to change the venue from more to less public. The advice is provided through impasse windows that explicitly connect the problem to the advice offered. The progression from diagnosis to analysis to advice is performed electronically, based on self-reported information provided by the negotiators and processed by a set of algorithms that match coded answers to the self-reported questions to categories of sources and types of advice (Druckman et al., 2004). This approach to mediation builds on both developments in electronic communication discussed above and research on flexibility in negotiation (Druckman, 1993).

Effectiveness of e-mediation

Several experiments have been conducted to evaluate the effectiveness of two versions of an e-mediation system. The first set of experiments was conducted with the NA system. It includes the three functions discussed above, diagnosis, analysis, and advice, and is described in Druckman et al. (2002) and in Druckman et al. (2004). The second set was conducted using the VienNA system (Druckman et al., 2014).

The NA system was compared to several other types of intervention including a no mediation condition, a mediator's advice only, and a live mediator implementing the three mediation functions. Three experiments were conducted by Druckman et al. (2004). The first experiment compared access to the NA technology during the between-rounds period with a condition where disputing negotiators were asked to reflect separately between rounds about their progress in a simulated negotiation. The scenario consisted of a negotiation between Anice and Izeria over issues concerned with weapons inspection. It resembled the situation facing diplomats just prior to the 2003 war in Iraq (Druckman et al., 2004).

In that experiment, significantly more agreements were obtained by bargainers with access to the NA system than by those in the reflection condition. The NA negotiators also had more favorable perceptions of the outcome. Interestingly, however, reflection negotiators believed that their activities during the break between rounds were more helpful in planning and evaluating the negotiation as well as in resolving issues than the NA negotiators. The NA negotiators viewed their work with the mediator as not being particularly helpful despite getting more agreements and viewing those outcomes favorably. Thus, while increasing negotiator flexibility, the e-mediator was not regarded as being a positive intervention (Druckman et al, 2004). Further probes of the connection between behavior and perceptions are made in the two experiments to follow.

A second experiment compared NA negotiators with a condition where negotiators received advice during the between-round break period (Druckman et al., 2004). The advice was identical to the advice provided in the impasse window of the e-mediation system. Neither the diagnostic nor analysis functions of mediation were provided. Similar results were obtained: NA negotiators obtained substantially more agreements than negotiators in the advice conditions and believed that differences were reconciled more than negotiators in the advice condition. They did not, however, have more favorable perceptions of other aspects of the negotiation process or outcomes: advice negotiators believed the outcome to be more just and legitimate, viewed the process as fair, and had a higher rate of confidence in their decision making (Druckman et al., 2004). Thus, a similar discrepancy between outcomes and perception occur, although the particular perceptions differ for the two experiments.

The third experiment in this set, conducted by Druckman et al. (2004), compared the e-mediation intervention with a live mediator scripted to carry out the same functions. The NA intervention was divided into two conditions, separate and joint negotiator use of the system between rounds. The e-mediator outperformed the live mediator. Negotiators with access to an e-mediator between rounds obtained a higher percentage of agreements than did those with access to a live mediator. They also stated a higher level of willingness to compromise than their counterparts in the live mediation condition. However, as in the earlier experiments, the NA negotiators perceived the mediator as being less helpful and valuable. In addition, those e-negotiators who worked together between rounds achieved more agreements than those who worked separately. They also attained more integrative agreements than those in the separate condition.

We have learned from these experiments that e-mediation produces benefits to negotiators stuck in an impasse. It produces more agreements than both reflecting and getting advice about resolving the impasses. It performs at least as well, and on some issues better, than a live mediator who implements the same functions. However, these advantages are tempered by the findings on the joint versus separate use of the e-mediation system: the largest differences between electronic and live mediation occurred when negotiators used the system together. They are also tempered by the perceptual data: negotiators at impasse prefer the other interventions designed for these experiments (reflecting, being given advice, and live mediators). Further understanding of this behavioral/perceptual gap awaits more research. First, however, we embarked on research that evaluated the impact of the updated e-mediation system known as VienNA.

VienNA is an advancement of the e-mediation system, Negotiator Assistant. While the functions of analysis, diagnosis, and advice were not altered, VienNA was modified for use in asynchronous and non-face-to-face settings. This involved making changes to the database and information retrieval to give opposing bargainers independent access to the system, thereby allowing partial data to be saved and results to be calculated only after all essential information is available. The advantage of these changes is that bargaining can occur at diverse times and locations.[1]

The VienNA experiment consisted of a two-condition comparison: asynchronous bargaining with or without the e-mediation system. Bargainers were assigned a role of representing one of the two companies (Mihalits or Metallurg) in a bilateral negotiation denoted as the Blue Star joint venture. They negotiated seven issues with opposed positions.

Direct comparisons between the VienNA and control conditions showed strong effects for a variety of process and outcome measures. On process, VienNA bargainers made larger concessions and reciprocated their opponent's concessions more often than the control bargainers. Further, VienNA bargainers discussed the sources of their conflict more often than did control bargainers: they exchanged more relational messages and fewer positional or tactical messages than their control counterparts. These types of messages were correlated with concessions: more relational messages and more concessions. Interestingly, the content of the relational messages was mostly negative. Thus, VienNA bargainers seemed to work through their conflict in conjunction with increased flexibility. Using the e-mediation system in the early stages of bargaining also made a difference: early use led to higher joint gains and less utility distance in the gains achieved.

This pattern of results provides an answer to the Druckman et al. (2014) article: does e-mediation work? The answer is, yes, it does: it produces more flexibility in the process, a willingness to discuss the foundation of the conflict, and leads to satisfaction with their outcomes. However, as found in the earlier study by Druckman et al. (2004), the e-mediation system did not induce satisfaction with the process. A practical challenge is to increase user-friendliness in order to realize the evident benefits of computer-based mediation.

Challenges to e-mediation systems

Research on e-mediation systems without a live mediator faces three challenges to application.

Multi-dimensionality

Conflict resolution processes, like many other forms of communication, can be understood in terms of several dimensions. In particular, one can distinguish a substantive, a communicational, and an affective dimension. Most current negotiation support systems, however, focus on only one or two of these dimensions. For example, systems like Inspire focus on the substantive dimension of the negotiation process, while Negotiator Assistant is oriented to negotiator flexibility and behavior. Negoisst, additionally provides communication support to increase communication quality. There is a need for holistic systems that integrate, the substantive, communicational, and affective dimensions.

Reference models

In order to make inexperienced negotiators aware of potential problems in a negotiation process, a support system would need reference models representing a "normal" or "good" negotiation process in terms of substance, communication, and affective behavior. Existing theories provide such reference models in varying degrees. For substantive outcomes, existing theories already allow for the identification of some desirable properties of negotiation processes. Which patterns in the communication and affective dimensions of negotiation lead to desirable outcomes remains an open question.

Foreshadowing the future

The systems need to alert parties to potential problems as soon as deviations from reference models occur in ongoing negotiations. This monitoring should take place in each of the three dimensions as well as with respect to the coherence of processes along all three dimensions. Current empirical research on face-to-face negotiations indicates that important trends and patterns in negotiation are observed at very early phases (Curhan & Pentland, 2007). So far, existing tools for analyzing electronic negotiation processes focus only on ex-post analysis.

Recommendations for mediators

Three recommendations are suggested for mediators.

Closing the gap with hybrid systems

There is a gap between the analytical support offered by e-mediation systems and their help with facilitating communication. Not surprisingly, calculation is what computers do best. Thus, their primary contribution is to the cognitive challenge of managing problems. These problems are often compounded by relational issues dealt with best by human mediators. Hybrid systems would seem best suited for this dual challenge: improved thinking about the dispute coupled with building trust between the disputants. The combination could also improve the perception of user friendliness for e-mediation systems. For mediators, we recommend introducing e-mediation systems in the context of the total mediation experience.

Timing of interventions

A key challenge for mediators is to manage the timing of electronic and human interventions: where are the opportunities for using the e-mediation tools? As noted above, research shows that early use of the systems leads to better negotiation outcomes. Mediators have control over when to introduce these systems. Less well understood, however, is the relationship between timing and the context of the dispute. We recommend that mediators learn how to adjust the timing to the type of dispute they are dealing with.

Broaden experience with the systems

We have had limited practical experience with e-mediation systems. Questions of timing, user friendliness, and type of systems remain unanswered. Thus, it is important to expand the range of mediation experience with these systems. This entails a willingness by mediators to become computer savvy and to keep up with changes in technologies. A further challenge is to understand the fit between systems and dispute contexts. We recommend that mediation-training programs include modules on the types of electronic systems discussed in this chapter.

Conclusion

In this chapter, we reviewed a variety of e-mediation systems summarized in Table 6.1. The progress made in the development of these systems is apparent. Particularly notable are the improvements made from the NA to VienNA systems. The impacts of these systems on the negotiation process (concessions, reciprocity) and outcomes (compromise, joint outcomes), shown in experiments, are impressive. Clearly, these systems perform the mediator functions—diagnosis, analysis, and advice—well. Yet, as we noted in the previous section, there is a disconnect between effectiveness and proficiency, on the one hand, and user satisfaction on the other. Missing from the systems is a way of dealing with the emotional issues surrounding most disputes. These issues are best handled by live mediators trained to tailor their interventions to situational demands. Thus, hybrid systems would seem suited to accomplish the dual challenges of information processing and trust building. They also have the practical advantage of providing mediators with technical decision aids that complement the human skills of empathy, communication, and interpretation. A question that remains, however, is the timing of these interventions. For researchers, the question of alternative sequencing can be addressed with experiments. For trainers, timing is a question of implementation in the context of a particular dispute. For both, this is the frontier ahead for applications of e-mediation systems.

Note

1 See Druckman et al., 2014 for a description of how this is done.

References

Abrahams, B., Bellucci, E. & Zeleznikow, J. (2012) Incorporating fairness into development of an integrated multi-agent online dispute resolution environment. *Group Decision and Negotiation*, 21(1): 3–28.

Bajwa, D. & Lewis, F. (2002) Current status of information technologies used in support of task-oriented collaboration. In R.H. Sprague (ed.). *Proceedings of the 35th Annual Hawaii International Conference on Systems Science*. Los Alamitos, CA: IEEE.

Bellucci, E. & Zeleznikow, J. (2005) Developing negotiation decision support systems that support mediators: A case study of the family winner system. *Artificial Intelligence and Law*, 13(2): 233–271.

Betancourt, J.C. & Zlatanska, E. (2013) Online dispute resolution (ODR): What is it and is it the way forward? *International Journal of Arbitration, Mediation and Dispute Management*, 79(3): 256–264.

Bollen, K.N.L. & Euwema, M.C. (2013) The role of hierarchy in face-to-face and e-supported mediations: The use of an online intake to balance the influence of hierarchy. *Negotiation and Conflict Management Research*, 6(4): 305–319.

Bollen, K.N.L., Verbeke, A.L. & Euwema, M.C. (2014) Computers work for women: Gender differences in e-supported divorce mediation. *Computers in Human Behavior*, 30: 230–237.

Bonham, G.M. (1993) Cognitive mapping as a technique for supporting international negotiation. *Theory and Decision*, 34(3): 255–273.

Curhan, J.R. & Pentland, A. (2007) Thin slices of negotiation: Predicting outcomes from conversational dynamics within the first 5 minutes. *Journal of Applied Psychology*, 92(3): 802–811.

Druckman, D. (1993) The situational levers of negotiating flexibility. *Journal of Conflict Resolution*, 37(2): 236–276.

Druckman, D., Druckman, J.N. & Arai, T. (2004) e-Mediation: Evaluating the impacts of an electronic mediator on negotiating behavior. *Group Decision and Negotiation*, 13(6): 481–511.

Druckman, D., Mitterhofer, R., Filzmoser, M. & Koeszegi, S.T. (2014) Resolving impasses in e-negotiation: Does e-mediation work? *Group Decision and Negotiation*, 23(2): 193–210.

Druckman, D., Ramberg, B. & Harris, R. (2002) Computer-assisted international negotiation: A tool for research and practice. *Group Decision and Negotiation*, 11(3): 231–256.

Ebner, N. (2012) e-Mediation. In M.S. Abdel Wahab, E. Katsh. & D. Rainey (eds) *Online Dispute Resolution: Theory and Practice: A Treatise on Technology and Dispute Resolution* (pp. 357–387). The Hague: Eleven International Publishing.

Erickson, T. & Herring, S. (eds). (1999) Persistent conversation: An introduction. Special Issue of *The Journal of Computer Mediated Communication*, 4(4).

Gettinger, J., Filzmoser, M. & Koeszegi, S.T. (2016) Do they agree once more? An explorative analysis of the factors that influence agreement in the post-settlement phase. *Journal of Business Economics*, 86(4): 413–440.

Janssen, M.A., Goosen, H. & Omtzigt, N. (2006) A simple mediation and negotiation support tool for water management in the Netherlands. *Landscape and Urban Planning*, 78: 71–87.

Johnson, N.A., Cooper, R.B. & Chin, W.W. (2009) Anger and flaming in computer-mediated negotiations among strangers. *Decision Support Systems*, 46(3): 660–672.

Kersten, G.E. (1993) Negotiation support: Development of representations and reasoning. *Theory and Decision*, 34(3): 293–311.

Kersten, G.E. & Noronha, S.J. (1999) WWW-based negotiation support: Design, implementation, and use. *Decision Support Systems*, 25(2): 135–154.

Lara, M.A. & Nof, S.Y. (2003) Computer-supported conflict resolution for collaborative facility designers. *International Journal of Production Research*, 41(2): 207–233.

Pesendorfer, E.M. & Koeszegi, S.T. (2006) Hot versus cool behavioural styles in electronic negotiations: The impact of communication mode. *Group Decision and Negotiation*, 15(2): 141–155.

Qu, Y. & Cheung, S.O. (2012) Logrolling "win-win" settlement in construction dispute mediation. *Automation in Construction*, 24: 61–71.

Samarasan, D.K. (1993) Analysis, modeling, and the management of international negotiations. *Theory and Decision*, 34(3): 275–291.

Schoop, M. (2010) Support of complex electronic negotiations. In D.M. Kilgour, C. Eden (eds) *Handbook of Group Decision and Negotiation* (pp. 409–424). Dordrecht: Springer.

Shakun, M. (1999) An ESD computer culture for intercultural problem solving and negotiation. *Group Decision and Negotiation*, 8(3): 237–249.

Sumi, K. & Mizoguchi, R. (2004) e-Negotiation via concept tree generation. *Electronic Negotiations*, 13(4): 477–499.

Swaab, R.I. & Brett, J.M. (2007) Caucus with care: The impact of pre-mediation caucuses on conflict resolution. Paper presented at the International Association of Conflict Management, Chicago, IL.

Turel, O., Yuan, Y. & Rose, J. (2007) Antecedents of attitude towards online mediation. *Group Decision and Negotiation*, 16(6): 539–552.

Ulvila, J.W. (1990) Turning points: An analysis. In J.W. McDonald and D.B. Bendahmane (eds) *U.S. Bases Overseas* (pp. 93–105). Boulder, CO: Westview Press.

Vetschera, R., Filzmoser, M. & Mitterhofer, R. (2014) An analytical approach to offer generation in concession-based negotiation processes. *Group Decision and Negotiation*, 23(1): 71–99.

Vetschera, R., Koeszegi, S.T. & Schoop, M. (2013) Electronic negotiation systems. In J.J. Cochran, L.A. Cox, P. Keskinocak, J.P. Kharoufeh & Smith, J.C. (eds) *Wiley Encyclopedia of Operations Research and Management Science, Vol. 8* (pp. 1–8). New York: Wiley.

Whittaker, S., James, Q. & Terveen, L. (2002) Managing long term communication: Conversation and conflict management. In R.H. Sprague (ed.) *Proceedings of the 35th Annual Hawaii Conference on Systems Sciences*. Los Alamitos, CA: IEEE.

Wierzbicki, A.P., Krus, L. & Makowski, M. (1993) The role of multi-objective optimization in negotiation and mediation support. *Theory and Decision*, 34(3): 201–214.

7

MEDIATION AND SPIRITUALITY

Zena D. Zumeta

As a means of connecting or re-connecting isolated and conflicted individuals, mediation is inherently a spiritual activity. Recognizing and fully utilizing mediation's spiritual capabilities can heal mediators as well as parties. This chapter will discuss the spiritual and healing nature of mediation, and explore ways in which mediation can increase healing for parties and the mediator.

Mediation

Mediation is a method of resolving disputes in which a neutral third party assists disputants in listening to one another, discussing potential options for resolution, and negotiating a resolution. In most jurisdictions, the mediator has no authority to resolve the dispute for the parties or to make a recommendation to a court.

Spirituality

Spirituality is the connectedness of all things. It is not religion, although spirituality is a part of most religions. It is also sometimes called an experience of unity, or unity consciousness. Spirituality embraces the connectedness of all things, but also honors and heightens individuality. Spiritually alive individuals honor both their and others' uniqueness and their connectedness to other people and things.

Mediation and spirituality

Connectedness

Mediation mirrors spirituality in many ways. In mediation, we sit in the midst of conflict, perhaps the extreme of disconnectedness. We are asking people to come together to build a resolution, finding a bridge between them; in fact, bridging their disconnectedness. Thus, if conflict is disconnectedness, resolution is connection, or unity. We are helping the parties to find unity consciousness, even if only in one small way. The parties usually come into mediation believing that there is no bridge or common ground. Yet, most of the time, there is.

Even a small amount of unity consciousness is quite often sufficient to move people to bridge their differences enough to reach agreement.

Individuality

Spirituality embraces the connectedness of all things, but it also honors and heightens individuality. We do that in mediation as well. As mediators, we sit at the crossroads of individuality and connectedness. We acknowledge and validate differences, but we also bring people together into agreement. We acknowledge and validate each person's needs and interests, and then use those to bring people together. In acknowledging needs and interests, we encourage empathy between people. We encourage them to acknowledge and validate the needs and interests of the other parties, and then to meet each other's needs and interests.

Conflict as disconnectedness, and resolution as unity

If we think of conflict as the extreme of disconnectedness, we see that parties distrust each other and believe that the other is actively out to hurt them. Parties become very protective of themselves and exaggerate the differences with the other side. They see the differences as a threat to themselves. The primary emotion of conflict is fear. We can also look at complete resolution as unity, the extreme of connectedness. In complete resolution, parties come together as they find mutually acceptable ground to walk upon. In complete resolution, they walk that ground together.

Thus, mediation sits at the crossroads between unity and disconnectedness. We acknowledge and encourage individuality and separate needs and interests, but we also support unity in needs, interests, and, of course, agreements. Mediation focuses on the continuing connectedness of people and their common ground. If fear is the primary emotion of conflict, the primary emotion of mediation is hope.

In divorce mediation, the parties actually are separating. In employment mediation and many business mediations, the parties may have decided to no longer do business together. So helping them keep the connectedness in the midst of parting can be particularly challenging. Yet, that can make parties feel much better about the process. Connection is emotionally and spiritually satisfying.

Divorcing couples and business partners do not want to feel that they wasted the years they spent together. People leaving a job do not want to feel that they were complete failures. So an agreement that can encompass acknowledgement of past caring and connection, and where appropriate, a fashioning of future caring and connectedness can feel emotionally and spiritually satisfying to the parties. Connection is healing. Moreover, in this way, mediation is healing, and inherently spiritual.

The healing nature of mediation

While a mediation can provide healing to the parties, it can also provide healing to the mediator. These are times when there is a deep connection between mediator and clients. There is a quiet trust, a willingness to move beyond settlement, to transformation. Agreements seem stronger and longer lasting. For the mediator, the work is more fulfilling. I see these as spiritual events, spiritual connections.

Not all mediations are spiritual events. The parties may indeed reach agreements, and may even effectively carry out those agreements. However, without the connection and spirituality, the work is emptier and less fulfilling. I feel the disconnection, the separateness of all of us. When I am able to feel that deep connection, I also feel I am helping more, and it is an experience of unity. According to Dass and Gorman (1985), "[w]hen the mind and the heart work in harmony, the barriers between us dissolve" (p. 223). This is what we desire to reach in mindfulness and meditation.

When we say that mediation is healing, it implies an injury that needs to be healed. That injury is the rupture in relationship and connection that people feel in the midst of their conflict. The healing is the reconnection that is made. I often notice that when people can cry together in mediation, healing has occurred. They have reconnected. These are very powerful mediations, and unforgettable in many ways. We surely cannot orchestrate them, but we can encourage them for both ourselves and our clients through the presence of the mediator, naming the connection that remains between the parties, seeing spiritually, quietness practices.

Presence of the mediator

The presence of the mediator is a powerful tool. A mediator may emanate a feeling of calm, peace, acceptance, and non-judgmental attitude. Clients have mentioned to me that they have been able to trust more in my presence, and have been able to say things in a more constructive manner as a result. One believed it was my acceptance that made a difference; another, my deep calm. Some clients are uncomfortable in that atmosphere. For example, one client told me she so resented feeling more forgiving toward her spouse that she was going to quit mediation. Luckily, she did not, and went on to reach resolution. We can be mindful about how our presence affects the parties and the mediation. To make our presence more powerful, we can practice some of the tools of mindfulness—observing, meditating, and sensing. Sensing is that faculty that allows us to pay attention to what is around us without quite knowing how we are aware. It is cultivated and increased through mindfulness and meditation, and serves us well in mediation.

Naming the connection

Sometimes it is helpful to name the original or continuing connection to help people remember, and to value it. In divorce, it is often the children or the family connection. The possibility of a continuing business relationship or friendship might be another connection. Gratitude for mentorship or previous assistance may be named in employment relationships. People forget that there was once a reason they came together, and a gentle reminder can be very powerful.

Seeing spiritually

Seeing beyond the divisions, the conflict, and the emotions can help the mediator and the parties. Quakers talk about finding that which is divine in each person. Even looking for the divine can sweeten our outlook, and then the mediation. Meeting separately with the parties before or during mediation can sometimes allow a spiritual connection to develop or re-develop between the mediator and the parties.

Letting go of outcomes

One of the major tenets of spiritual practice is letting go of outcomes, being in the moment, accepting people and situations for what they are, but working and hoping for the best. This is the same for mediation. For example, if we can let go of outcomes, trust the process, and the parties, and still support and work for agreement, the mediation becomes more stisfying.

Quieting practices

Quieting practices can help keep us open to the spiritual in mediation and include the following:

Meditating prior to the mediation

It can sometimes help to do a short meditation prior to a mediation meeting. A short meditation can relax us and open us up to deeper observation and energy movement in the mediation.

Prayer

Some mediators glance at the St Francis Prayer to quickly shift their attitudes. It starts, "Lord, make me an instrument of your Peace." Other mediators use other prayers.

Nature

Sometimes just looking outside or walking in nature at the sparrows and trees can shift our energy.

Music

Some mediators have healing music that plays in the background or in the waiting room to relax them and the clients.

Objects

Objects such as candles, photographs, or paintings can be used as calming or spiritual reminders for the mediator.

Mindfulness

Practicing mindfulness before and during a mediation can help focus and open the mediator.

Mindfulness can help us as mediators

We take parties as they present themselves. However, if we are able to look at them as a whole we might be able to approach them and their disputes from a different angle. It helps us to get into their heads, or their shoes, by examining aspects of them that they may not have presented initially. This may bring to mind other options for resolution, or other reasons for settlement that can circumvent the obstacles. It is all about observation. Mindfulness allows for a deeper level of observation, which can allow us to make subtle, but very effective adjustments in our interventions in the mediation. The more that we are aware of, the more we can adjust for. The observation can be visual, or it can be energetic.

Working with energy

In addition to observing, mindfulness can help us to work with the energy in the room. An awareness of energy and its movement can make a mediator more alert to subtleties in the atmosphere and use them proactively. I try to be aware of the energy in the mediation room and my office in general. One example of proactive use of energy is the color of the walls in the room, which can calm and warm people. I have received many comments from clients that have noticed my affect and energy to be calming, warm, and supportive.

We can often feel the energy around ourselves, or even see it move, with practice. You may be familiar with the saying "When You're Smiling the Whole World Smiles with You." I like to tell the story of when I was in law school, which is when I started to meditate. My law school had a tunnel between the classroom building and the library, which we all used during the winter months. I used to hate walking in it, because I was facing lines of law students looking angry, depressed, worn, and generally stressed. When I started to meditate, I found myself smiling more often. Then I began to see smiles back at me. This is an example of our energy affecting others around us. It was very dramatic in that tunnel, and I can still see the faces of the students smiling back at me.

We all have energy fields, and it can be helpful in mediation to develop a sense of movement around us even if we are not looking directly at someone. We get a sense that something is going on, and turn to look at them. This enhanced awareness of energy can give us an edge as a mediator.

Mindfulness can bring connection, empathy, compassion, and non-judgment

Sometimes we can feel that we are doing mediation by rote, that we are mediating the same case repeatedly. Connection and empathy can help to overcome the monotony and allow us to be present in the moment with each case and each set of parties. All of these are attributes that help parties to resolve their disputes. This was borne out of research by Margaret Shaw and Steve Goldberg, who asked mediators and the advocates what made the mediators successful. Both the mediators and the advocates named the ability of the mediator to obtain and maintain trust and rapport with the parties as the most important attributes of the mediator in helping with settlement (Goldberg & Shaw, 2007). Connection, empathy, and non-judgment build trust and rapport with parties. Mindfulness seems to build those qualities because a heightened awareness of another person generally builds empathy; and connection, compassion, and non-judgment follow from empathy.

Nurturing the mediator

Mindfulness and quieting the self so we observe better is also a way to energize and renew ourselves. Centering ourselves, exercising, practicing meditation or mindfulness, connecting with friends and loved ones, are all ways to restore ourselves, stay refreshed and open to what is around us. In addition, quieting the mind allows us to listen more, judge less, bring to play all our mental faculties, understand more, and connect better. We become more whole, authentic, and caring. Nurturing ourselves brings out who we really are, and makes our whole self available to ourselves and our clients. This is the hope, goal, and promise of all spiritual practice, including mediation.

References

Dass, R. & Gorman, R. (1985) *How Can I Help: Stories and Reflections of Service*. New York: Knopf.

Goldberg, S.B. & Shaw, M.L. (2007) The secrets of successful (and unsuccessful) mediators continued: Studies two and three. *Negotiation Journal*, 23(4): 393–418.

PART II

Mediating in relational settings

8

TRANSFORMATIVE MEDIATION

Illustrating a relational view of conflict intervention

Joseph P. Folger and Dan Simon

According to transformative theory, human conflict is relational, regardless of the parties' relationship before the conflict or how much interaction they foresee after mediation. This chapter starts by articulating the relational premises that underlie the transformative theory and discusses principles that arise from those premises and that guide the practice of transformative mediation. Finally, we share how those principles played out in two real mediation sessions. This chapter will illuminate the transformative approach to mediation, which is the effort by a third party to support changes in conflict interaction from alienated and destructive to connected and constructive.

Relational premises

Transformative mediation is founded on a relational ideology that shapes both the theory and practice of transformative conflict intervention (Bush & Folger, 1994, 2005). The transformative framework draws heavily from the work of Carol Gilligan and her focus on moral theory and moral development (Gilligan, 1982). Transformative practice is thus based on an ideology that is less individualistic than traditional problem-solving or needs-based views of conflict and conflict intervention. As an alternative to more transactional theories of conflict, the relational view assumes that people are concerned with their self-interests, but they are also simultaneously and pervasively concerned with their connection with others. The human urge to connect is as strong as the human urge to fulfill one's individual needs, but balancing both is often deeply challenging, especially in conflict situations.

Bush and Folger (2005) summarize the core of this relational view of human nature as follows:

> as a matter of basic human consciousness, every person senses that he or she is a separate, autonomous agent, authoring his or her own life, and at the same time senses that he or she is an inherently social being, connected to other people in an essential and not just instrumental fashion. Moreover, in this relational view, awareness of both individual agency and social connection is not just a peripheral characteristic—it is the very essence of human consciousness, the core of our identity as human beings. Each part of this duality—individuality and connectedness—is equally important to our fundamental sense

> of human identity, and we struggle constantly to give each its place and balance … in all of our affairs.
>
> *(Bush & Folger, 2005, p. 60)*

Conflict is difficult because it confronts us with a challenge to our core human nature. We struggle to balance concern for self and connection with others in difficult encounters in family, marriage, workplace, friendship and other conflict settings. This struggle is at the core of who we are as people:

> In effect, the core sense of identity that undergirds the person's life—strong and connected to other—is thrown into question by conflict. This is why the weakness and alienation produced in negative conflict is so repellent to parties in conflict—it violates their very identity, their sense of who they are as human beings. To remain in such a condition is as painful to people as being imprisoned and forced to live in inhuman conditions.
>
> *(Bush & Folger, 2005, p. 61)*

Difficult conflicts tend to destabilize us because both strength of self and connection with other is easily undermined in the face of significant differences. We become relatively weak, uncertain about who we are, how we want to act, what matters to us, and what we want to happen. We also become more self-absorbed, unable, or unwilling to take the perspective of the other and thus become disconnected and alienated from those from whom we differ. When parties in conflict try to interact in these states of weakness and self-absorption, conflict interaction is negative and unproductive, and, at times, violent and destructive. It is not until we are able to shift toward both greater empowerment and recognition (achieving some satisfying balance of strength of self and connection with others) that productive conflict interaction is possible. People who are strong and connected work through difficult conflicts without spiraling into hatred, demonization, or physical and psychological violence. Those who are weak and self-absorbed often suffer the consequences of their destructive efforts and reactive decision making (Folger & Bush, 1996, 2001a; Bush & Folger, 2005; Folger et al., 2010).

An important, but often misunderstood, tenet of the relational view of conflict is that people may decide to end relationships for reasons linked to their self-preservation or needs. For example, they may end relationships to protect their identity, values, beliefs, or psychological well-being. However, even when relationships end, the urge to connect with others is still present and this means that it matters to people how relationships end. Relationships can be terminated in a relational way, rooted in understanding and clarity. The ability to end relationships relationally is at the core of our human capability. It embodies our dual urges for individuality and connection. This aspect of the relational view of conflict clearly distinguishes it from a harmonious view of conflict in which the goal is always to restore relationships, even if it means making oneself subservient to a relationship or community (Folger, 2008).

Principles of relational practice

The principles that shape transformative interventions are directly aligned with the relational premises outlined above (Folger & Bush, 2001b; Bush & Folger, 2005; Beal & Saul, 2001; Della Noce, 2001a, 2004; Charbonneau, 2001; Pope & Bush, 2001). This theory-to-practice connection is important in building the professional identity of transformative mediators and in creating a supportive community of well-grounded practitioners (Pearson d'Estree, 2013). The foundational premises define the mediator's goals and prescribe the mediator's intervention practices—what mediators do *and* do *not* do when they intervene. In the relational framework, the mediator's goal is to support the transformation of the parties' conflict interaction by relying on interventions that foster each party's shifts toward greater empowerment and recognition.

The principles that guide transformative methods are captured by a set of axioms that are included in basic training in transformative mediation. These axioms are not the methods of intervention. They are the guiding principles that mediators rely on as they make decisions about when and how to intervene.[1]

Be comfortable with conflict interaction, including strong emotion and negative patterns of communication among the parties

Parties typically do not need mediators when they are clear and confident about themselves and each other. Consequently, transformative mediators expect that parties' conflict interaction will be negative and, to some extent, unproductive or destructive because people enter mediation without the personal strength and connection they normally have in their day-to-day lives. This requires that mediators are comfortable with parties' difficult conflict interaction and are prepared to work with it, rather than control it or shut it down.

Support parties' choices, including choices about participation in mediation

Supporting parties' empowerment means being willing at all points to accept the decisions parties make about their issues as well as how they want to participate, if at all, in the mediation process. In transformative practice, parties are supported in addressing issues about the way they communicate as well as the more substantive issues that have arisen between them (Pope, 2001).

Be comfortable with a limited understanding of the parties' conflict

Transformative mediators do not diagnose the conflict or determine what "the problem" or "real issue" is for the parties. Instead, the mediator's focus remains on what the parties are saying and how to support clarity, understanding, and deliberation. A commitment to party empowerment means accepting that parties may make choices that are based on information, personal fears, or self-perceptions about their own capability to which the mediator does not have access.

Respect the parties—their behavior, choices, and challenges

Respect for the parties means that mediators are willing to accept (and not evaluate or judge) the way parties express themselves, how they choose to respond to each other, and the choices they make. "The parties['] choices about topic, approach, tone, timing and everything else receive constant support from the transformative mediator" (Simon, 2010, p. 267). One litmus test for a transformative mediator's commitment to party empowerment is whether he or she is willing to accept decisions the parties make, which he or she feels the parties may regret later. This characteristic of transformative practice stands in contrast to prevailing models that rely upon a strong advisory role for the mediator (Baitar et al., 2013).

Be patient with the parties and the process of their interaction

Transformative mediators sustain a belief that no matter how weak and self-absorbed parties may be, they are still capable of making shifts toward greater strength and responsiveness. Being weak and self-absorbed is an unstable and uncomfortable state. This fact supports the work of the mediator and actually sustains the mediator's optimism about the possibility of the parties making constructive shifts. The relational "values encourage mediators to assume that if conflict interaction is supported, parties can find a balance of personal strength and interpersonal connection that may have been lost as they attempted to address a conflict on their own" (Folger & Bush, 2010, p. 456). In some instances, parties may not make significant shifts, but the mediator does not lose the focus on supporting the possibility of such shifts at any point.

Focus on the moment-to-moment events in the parties' interaction

Transformative mediators focus on the parties' interaction as it unfolds, intervening to shine a light on what is being said, fostering parties' clarity about issues, understanding of themselves and each other, and thoughtful deliberation and decision making based on any clarity the parties achieve. Focusing on the unfolding conversation means that the mediator does not analyze the past, diagnose issues, or focus the parties solely on the future. The mediator holds on to the belief that clarity often emerges out of confusion (Folger & Bush, 1996).

Attend to opportunities for empowerment and recognition and choose interventions that support empowerment and recognition shifts

Conflict interaction becomes more constructive and productive for the parties when the mediator supports shifts that create both party empowerment and inter-party recognition. The mediator listens for signs of unclarity, uncertainty, confusion, self-doubt, self-absorption, and misunderstanding and then responds with skills that foster greater clarity about self and other, deeper understanding and supporting more measured deliberation and decision making (Moen et al., 2001; Antes et al., 2001).

Relinquish problem solving and control of the process

Transformative mediators assume that process and content are intertwined during mediation (Folger, 2001). Decisions about process affect the way the content of a conflict unfolds in the parties' interaction. Therefore, parties are encouraged not only to define and address their own issues but also to determine how they want to address their issues. The mediator is constantly attentive to the parties' decisions about how they want to have their conversation and how they want to resolve differences about any process issues that arise, including how they speak to each other, who can be present in the session, whether they talk about past events, etc.

In the next section, we present summaries of two mediation cases. These cases illustrate features of transformative practice that stem from the principles outlined above.[2] Although both of these cases arise from parenting disputes, the principles illustrated apply to disputes in all contexts. Transformative mediation is used in contract disputes, ethno-political conflicts, organizational disputes as well as the full range of court-based conflicts. Each case is summarized from the perspective of the mediator who conducted the intervention.[3] After each case, we provide commentary that points to the links between theory and practice, as illustrated by what occurred in the mediations. These commentaries offer elaborations of one or more of the principles of practice outlined above.

Theory to practice: cases and commentary

1 Carolyn and Victor

Carolyn and Victor lived 30 miles from each other, and they each wanted five-year-old Jakey to attend the school close to them. Carolyn had moved from Golden Prairie (the suburb where she and Victor had lived) to the suburb where her new boyfriend and his child had a home. She and her lawyer felt strongly that at Jakey's age, if he were going to be with one parent more than the other, it should be his mother, and they argued that he should go to school near Carolyn's home. Although Carolyn had created the geographic challenge by moving, she and her lawyer felt that Victor had no business telling Carolyn that she needed to move again. Victor, on the other hand, could not understand how Carolyn's choice to leave him for someone else, and her choice to move away from Golden Prairie (where both sets of grandparents also lived), could possibly mean that Jakey also had to spend school weeks in a strange new suburb far away.

Those are the parts of the conflict I knew about after an hour of conversation. I knew those facts were only a tiny part of the story and that they may have been nearly irrelevant to the question of how I could help Carolyn and Victor with their conflict. I did my best to support their and their lawyers' conversation and I succeeded in staying out of the role of director or decision maker. I had no idea what the best route for them would be or what else they may need to talk about during the session, and I got to see what happened when their lawyers jumped into the conversation and became solution focused in an effort to reach a compromise.

"Have you looked at schools that are halfway between each of you?" asked Victor's lawyer. Victor and Carolyn both rolled their eyes. One of them said, "That's ridiculous. There would be no point to that." The lawyer also asked, "What about just agreeing on a summer schedule now (it was early June) and revisiting the school question in August?" "No, I want this done today—what is the use of putting it off?" Carolyn insisted. The tension rose after both of these suggestions. The lawyers' focus on finding a compromise added to both parents' defensiveness and heightened their anxiety about being pushed to make unwanted or counter-productive choices. Shortly, during a lull in the conversation, I said: "So you've talked about a few different aspects of the situation. Is it OK if I summarize what you've said?"

"As for the school itself, you've both said that either school is fine in terms of quality, but that location is what matters. As for location, Victor, you said you'd like to keep him in Golden Prairie, because that's where all the grandparents are and that's where you went to school. You also said that, since you work near there, you'd be available to Jakey if needed during the school day. Carolyn, you said that since the Apple Park schools are also fine, it makes more sense for Jakey to go there, so he can spend most of the week at your home. Given his age, you said it's especially important that he have a lot of time with you. You also both talked about what to do next about this disagreement. Carolyn, you said that maybe the guardian *ad litem* would make a recommendation. And Joe (Victor's lawyer), you said you don't think that's likely. Instead, you think a custody study will be necessary. Carolyn, you also said that you'd like to be done with these issues today. Another thing you all talked about was the parenting schedule. You all agreed that except for the problem with the school location, a 50/50 schedule would be fine. You also talked about whether there's a fairness issue here. Carolyn you said this isn't about fairness, it's about what's best for Jakey, and Victor you said of course it's about Jakey, but Carolyn caused this problem, so she should be the one who has to do something about it. That seems fair to you." I added a few more details of what I'd heard the parents and the lawyers say. When I finished, all agreed that I'd captured the key points that the parents and lawyers had raised.

My summary gave everyone a chance to think about what they and the others had said, and for them to see how the different perspectives related to each other. I hoped that it also helped them decide whether they had said what they wanted to or whether they had more to say. Everyone appeared to be thinking calmly. I did not know whether this would be a transition point in the conversation, but in hindsight, it appears it was.

Next Carolyn asked a for ten minute break. The lawyers also stood up to take a break. Victor and I remained seated. As Carolyn and the lawyers walked out, I asked, "Is it OK with everybody if I chat with Victor while you're gone?" Carolyn said yes and both lawyers nodded their approval. My request to talk to Victor was not based on any particular instinct I had. I wanted to provide support wherever possible to the parties. I assume it never hurts for me to check in with the parties to allow them to think aloud about the current situation and what they want to do about it.

I told Victor he could use the time to think aloud about how the conversation was going, if he wanted to, and I asked him how he was doing. He said, "Fine. You know we actually got along well before these lawyers got involved. I didn't want to say anything to her during our conversation here, but I've heard from my other kids that Carolyn and her new boyfriend get in fights all the time right in front of the kids. I don't want to bring that up, because it'll really piss her off." (Victor had other children to whom Carolyn had been a stepmother.) Victor shared more of his thoughts with me, some of which I reflected back to him, as he contemplated what he would and would not say when the conversation continued.

When everyone returned, Carolyn made a surprising statement: "OK, here's what I'm thinking. I'm looking for a new job up in Golden Prairie. If that comes through, I'll move back up to Golden Prairie, and Jakey can go to kindergarten there. But I want the visitation schedule to be fully 50/50, and I want it to be understood that Jakey will not see my parents during my time with him." "Fine," Victor replied, "but if the grandparents want to see him during my time, they're going to see him." "Fine," Carolyn stated, "but you know I can't stand my mother, so you had better let her know when Jakey's with me, because she doesn't get to see him then."

The rest of the meeting was anticlimactic. They sorted out the details of how they would schedule their time with Jakey, who would enroll him in school in Golden Prairie, and how Carolyn's move would affect the other kids. At one point, Victor said, "Now what if you don't get the job?" Carolyn said, "I'll move back either way. I'll figure it out." Carolyn had decided that having both parents and all of the grandparents in the same suburb with Jakey was worth any of the other challenges of moving. Finally, the lawyers discussed how they would complete the documentation they felt necessary. I facilitated that discussion as well. As we all stood up to leave, Carolyn and Victor said goodbye to each other comfortably. I shook hands with everyone and the lawyers both shrugged as if to say, "Huh, you never know what's going to happen."

The most striking thing about this session was how unlikely the outcome would have seemed at the start. Until Carolyn made her proposal after the break, there was no indication that she would be open to Jakey going to kindergarten in Golden Prairie, and nothing had been said that indicated Carolyn herself was open to moving back.

If I had relied upon a more settlement-driven approach, I would have intervened in ways that would have made the party-achieved outcome less likely. I might have made suggestions, reminded them how bad parental conflicts are for their son, or reminded them about the costs of litigation. These actions would have raised the tension and defensiveness, as evidenced by the responses to the lawyers' problem-solving efforts. Even if Carolyn had made the same decision about moving back to their original area, a more directive process would have probably made her feel worse about the decision, and would have deprived her of the opportunity to make the choice freely and on her own. The way this conversation played out, Carolyn was able to make a gesture toward Victor that he truly appreciated. She was then able to ask—with strength and clarity—for the other things that were important to her (50/50 time sharing and an understanding about when her mother would have access to Jakey). All of this was done through the natural evolution of their own conversation and decision making, and the opportunities I provided for them to hear and think about what they were saying and how they were responding to each other.

Theory-to-practice commentary

The mediator's account of this session suggests how several of the principles of transformative mediation were demonstrated in this intervention. The mediator remained patient with the parties and their process and, in doing so, relinquished any attempt to push the parties toward problem solving or settlement. The mediator supported the parties as they took the conversation into areas that may or may not have had readily identifiable solutions. There was no attempt to gloss over or understate significant, emotionally laden differences. In fact, the extended summary the mediator offered highlighted these differences without setting an expectation that these issues needed to be solved or settled in any particular way. The mediator did not diagnose or assess the issues; he only highlighted the issues the parties brought up in their conversation and helped the parties see the map of the conflict they were drawing. They were then free to change or alter that map as they wished.

Notice that the mediator treated the lawyers as equal participants in the conversation and did not discourage the lawyers from making whatever contributions they wanted to make at any point in the conversation. This is clearly supportive of the empowerment of all parties at the table. When one lawyer pushed for what the parties thought were premature and unsatisfactory solutions, the parties felt empowered to resist the attempt for closure of their issues. (A transformative mediator would have been equally supportive if the parties wanted to discuss or accept the lawyers' suggestions as well.) The mediator allowed the parties to decide when and whether they wanted to offer any terms of settlement. This demonstrates the mediator's patience with the process—a hallmark of transformative intervention. The parties received no explicit or implicit message that they needed to go anywhere in their discussions or solve any differences they raised. The mediator stayed with where any of the parties—the parents or their lawyers—took the focus at any point in the conversation.

This mediation also illustrates how transformative mediators intentionally accept that they have a limited understanding of the parties' conflict and how this awareness is the foundation for supporting the empowerment of the parties. This was illustrated in the separate meeting with Victor. It was clear that Victor had concerns about his ex-wife that he did not express to her in the joint session. If the mediator had influenced Victor in any way to bring up this or other issues that were related to his views or feelings, it could have alienated and perhaps even frightened him. It is critical that mediators do not assume they know the whole story of the parties' history or the entire set of issues. Transformative mediators try to remain aware of their limited or incomplete knowledge of the conflict because it emphasizes the importance of avoiding suggestions or solutions—or any type of influence—that may be unacceptable or outright dangerous for the parties.

Notice also that the mediator supported Victor's empowerment in the separate session. Victor raised his concern about the fights between Carolyn and her new partner, which he had heard about through his older children. The mediator's role in this separate meeting is only to support the person in getting clearer about whether or not he wants to discuss this issue. This helped Victor to think through his own instincts about raising the issue. This intervention supported his empowerment because it helped Victor decide for sure what he wanted to discuss with Carolyn.

Perhaps most importantly, this custody mediation case illustrates how important it is that any choice a party makes means so much more when it comes from the party themselves. The mediator in this case emphasizes the critical need to support party self-determination in his account of the session. Carolyn's decision to move back to the area where they had previously lived—a clear shift toward recognition of the husband's concerns—was deeply meaningful to Victor only because this decision came from her and her alone—without any prompting or suggesting from the mediator. This allowed the two parties to renegotiate their own relationship as well as to design a settlement regarding the child custody issues. Victor sensed that Carolyn was willing, on her own, to acknowledge him and his concerns, thereby changing how the two parents felt about each other. If the mediator had made the proposal or indicated the need to compromise on this core issue, the mediator sensed that the impact on the relationship would not have been the same. The transformative model, with its emphasis on party empowerment, allowed the mediator to be a helpful part of this difficult conversation for these divorcing parents by supporting the parties in renegotiating their own relationship as well as addressing their substantive issues.

2 Angela and Brett

Angela and Brett had conflict around custody arrangements for two-year-old Charlie. They had not communicated for the six months before the mediation. During that time, Brett saw Charlie only on Saturday afternoons at Brett's mother's house. Brett's mother picked up Charlie every Saturday at Angela's. A court order required Brett to have his mother present when he was with Charlie because of a substance abuse problem. Brett's lawyer told me that Brett hoped to spend more time with Charlie and to remove the requirement that his mother be present.

In my emails with the lawyers, I learned that they felt their presence at the mediation would be helpful to both parties. I also heard from Angela's lawyer that Brett was a real "piece of work" and had serious alcohol problems. I heard from Brett's lawyer that Angela was angry with Brett for leaving her, was exaggerating the alcohol problems, and was being unnecessarily difficult. I told both lawyers that I would be happy to talk to Angela or Brett before our meeting and that it was Brett and Angela's choice whether the lawyers participated in the mediation sessions. I asked the lawyers to forward my introductory email to Brett and Angela.

I met them all at my office. I started by asking whether it would be OK if I said a few words about my role. They all nodded. I said, "I'm here to support you in having whatever conversation you want to have. Although Donna and Ed (the lawyers) arranged this meeting,

I want to make it clear that you are my clients, that I work for you, and that you make all of the decisions about both process and content. You are welcome to contribute to the conversation in any way you want. You all get to decide everything about how we do this. If you want to talk privately with anyone, including me, if you want to take breaks, or if you have any other ideas, by all means, this is your conversation every step of the way. I'll do some things that I hope will enhance the conversation, such as reflecting what one of you has said, or summarizing the different things you've talked about, and if that ever doesn't seem helpful, let me know." I asked if there were any questions or reactions. Everyone nodded and indicated that they were OK. I then said, "So where would you like to start?"

Brett immediately said, "I have a few things I'd like to say." I nodded and looked at the others to indicate that it was OK with me, but that everyone else was welcome to state a different preference if they did not want Brett to start the conversation. Everyone's body language suggested they were OK with Brett speaking, and he began: "I know that I've been very difficult for you to deal with, Angela. I know that I'm an alcoholic and that I've screwed up many times in many ways. I don't blame you for not trusting me at this point. But I want you to know what's been going on for the last six months. Since I got that DUI [driving under the influence], I have been sober. It's one day at a time and I know I don't have any business making any promises, but I'm committed to staying sober today. I've got a great sponsor. I'm going to meetings just about every day, even though I need to get a ride there. And I want to stay sober for Charlie. I know you probably think you've heard this sort of thing from me before. I don't expect you all of a sudden to start trusting me, but I want you to keep your mind open to the possibility that I mean it this time. And I want to know that at some point, if I do not screw up anymore, you will let me spend time with Charlie without all the restrictions." Brett appeared nervous as he spoke. He mostly looked down, as if afraid to see Angela's reaction.

I had no idea how this conversation would start. Transformative practice encourages me to let go of any preference for how the conversation starts or where it goes. My role was to support what the parties were doing and to let them decide what to do going forward. When I observed a pause after Brett spoke, I offered him a reflection of his comments: "So Brett, you're saying you know you've been hard for Angela to deal with ..." and I continued, reflecting the full breadth of what Brett had said, using as many of his exact words as possible. Throughout my reflection, I remained attentive to Brett and alert to any movements or sounds from the others, in case anyone wanted to interrupt me (in which case I would have stopped and moved out of their way). My intention in reflecting what Brett had said was to give everyone present, including Brett, a second opportunity to hear what Brett had said, perhaps to confirm for everyone, including Brett, that he had really said these things, and to highlight the actual details of what he had said.

I then wanted to give everyone the opportunity to make a choice about what to do next. Did Brett want to elaborate? Did Angela want to express doubt or appreciation? Did Angela want to focus on some other aspect of the situation? Did the lawyers want to focus the conversation on the terms of an agreement? I had no idea. My intention at that point was to create the space for all present to make the choices they wanted to make about where to take the conversation.

After my reflection, Angela said, "Well you're right that I've heard most of that before. And more important than you having let me down, you've let Charlie down. And he's at the age now where if I tell him he's going to see you, he'll be hurt if you don't show up. So I'm not ready to trust you on that. I still want your mom to be in charge for now and I don't think more than once a week makes sense either. He's not that comfortable with you."

Brett said, "I can understand that. But how long will it take for you to loosen up on that?" Angela responded, "I don't know." Angela's lawyer, Donna, chimed in at that point saying, "One problem is we haven't seen the results of those UAs." (Urinalysis results showing whether Brett had alcohol in his system.) Brett looked at his lawyer, Ed, who said, "Oh, didn't you get those? I thought we'd sent you those—one from about three months ago, and one from a couple weeks ago?" Donna replied, "No, we haven't seen those results." Brett: "I'll do those whenever you want me to, even though they're a huge hassle." Donna said, "Yeah, I wouldn't be comfortable advising Angela to increase Brett's parenting time, unless we are getting those UAs regularly."

The conversation about UAs continued, with Brett expressing willingness to continue to submit them for a limited period of time, and with him asking for acknowledgement that it was a hassle to do so. Then the lawyers continued to discuss their confusion about whether the UAs had been reported to Ed or not. During a pause, I said, "You've covered a variety of aspects of the situation. Would it be OK if I summarized?" Everyone nodded or said yes.

"So one topic you have been discussing has been the UAs. Brett, you've said you're willing to continue to do those every two weeks after your parenting time, but it's a hassle, and you're only willing to do them for up to a few more months. Ed you've said that you thought you'd sent Donna at least two UA reports—and they were clean. Donna, you said you haven't received those. And Angela, I don't think you said anything about the UAs. Another topic you've discussed is Brett's sobriety and his ability to be reliable for Charlie. Brett, you've said you've been sober for six months, you're going to meetings every day, you've got a great sponsor and you're going to stay sober today, and you want to stay sober for Charlie. Angela, you've said you've heard this before and the important thing to you is that Charlie not be hurt by Brett not showing up. And then you've touched on what you want to do going forward. Angela, you've said you still want Brett's mom involved and that you're not comfortable with Brett seeing Charlie more than once a week at this time. Brett you've said that you'd like to spend more time with Charlie, that you don't think your mother's presence is necessary, and that you at least want to know that at some point, if you don't screw up, that Angela will loosen all the restrictions."

After this summary, Angela made a proposal: "How about this? We keep everything the same for six months. You do the UAs every two weeks. And if those stay clean and there are no other problems, we'll take away the requirement about your mom, and we'll talk about you having more time with Charlie." Brett then replied, "How about three months?" Angela said four, and Brett then agreed. The rest of the conversation involved clarifying the details of the parenting plan and making an appointment for a follow-up mediation session four months later. As everyone walked out, the mood had clearly lightened, and the parties said they were very satisfied with the mediation and its outcome.

Theory to practice commentary

This case illustrates how the mediator's opening comments in a transformative process set the tone of party empowerment of the entire session (Folger & Bush, 1996). The opening creates an expectation for the parties and their lawyers that they will make all of the decisions about both the substance and the process of the mediation. The mediator conveys a strong sense that he will support all of the parties' choices, including their choices about participation in the session. These comments are as important for the lawyers as they are for the parties themselves. The opening allows the lawyers to realize that the mediator is not going to set a direction or an agenda that the lawyers may then have to monitor closely or resist for their clients. It puts them less on guard and in doing so helps the lawyers to support the empowerment of their own clients during the process. They can advise their clients regarding decisions and choices that need to be made but the lawyers have less concern about the mediator taking a directive or evaluative role. This is characteristic of transformative mediation practice when lawyers are present and take part in the conversation with their clients (Miller & Bush, 2010).

This mediator's opening gave a clear invitation to the parties to take the conversation wherever they wanted to, including having an emotional discussion about how they saw each other and the trust between them. This supported Brett's decision at the outset of the session to discuss his substance abuse problem and how it was affecting his shared custody of their son. Brett admitted his personal struggles and was seeking greater trust from Angela. The mediator was supportive of Brett's emotional statement and his desire to discuss how Angela saw him and whether her view would change in the near future. The mediator's openness to emotional expression and the discussion of how the parties view each other counters a known tendency for mediators to selectively facilitate only the discussion of topics that are more tangible and linked to substantive terms of the agreements (Folger & Bernard, 1985; Greatbatch & Dingwall, 1989). In transformative mediation, mediators allow and support parties' expression of emotion because they assume that there are "facts in the feelings" and that the expression of emotion often affords important opportunities to support empowerment and recognition (Folger & Bush, 1996).

The mediator's summary after the conversation between Angela and Brett demonstrates that the mediator is focused on the moment-to-moment events in the parties' interaction. It shows that he stays in the present with the parties and tracks all of the topics and views that are offered by the parties. Summaries cannot be done effectively and comprehensively if the mediator is ahead of the parties, is thinking about possible solutions, or is deciding where the parties should go next in the conversation. Summaries need to include all the topics the parties have discussed as well as the views the parties expressed about those topics. This requires an intensive focus on what the parties have said and accurate recall of their conversation (Bush & Folger, 2010). Executing this skill effectively requires that the mediator be in the moment with the parties.

The mediator had no preference for where the parties went next in their conversation after he completed the extensive summary. This, too, indicates how the mediator stays in the moment with the parties as their conversation develops. There is a sense of openness and receptivity to wherever the parties want to take their conversation at that point. The mediator himself is not sure what direction the conversation will take and he has no preference for its direction. As a result, the summary offered an empowerment opportunity for the parties. The parties had the opportunity to hear and think about what they had just discussed, where they were in addressing their issues, and where they wanted to go next. The parties then initiated and controlled their own negotiation about a plan for the immediate future. The last part of the conversation in the mediation is in some ways a traditional bargaining exchange. Proposals are offered and compromises are reached (about the amount of time Brett still needed to have drug tests), but the parties were not led into this transactional exchange about a temporary agreement and the mediator did not broker or orchestrate the deal making. The parties took the conversation in this direction. In some ways, it was the natural evolution of the party-driven process that was established by the mediator from the very opening of the session.

Conclusion

It should be clear from the cases presented above that although transformative mediation is rooted in a relational orientation to conflict intervention, this does not mean that a transformative mediator attempts to sustain or restore the parties' relationship. Rather, the relational orientation asks the mediator to focus on the quality of the parties' interaction for however long the parties are interacting and are attempting to work though their conflict in the mediation session. This is an important—and often misunderstood—point about the nature of relational practice, which has been described previously as follows:

> the altered interaction which results from transformative shifts during mediation, implies nothing about the choices parties make regarding the nature or status of their relationship moving forward. The relationships the parties develop through shifts in empowerment and recognition can enable them to more deliberately and clearly assess how they want their relationship to be defined. It helps them to decide whether they want to end, change, or continue their relationship as it is. In other words, clear and deliberate choices by the parties—about the current status of their relationship—are made possible by transformative shifts in mediation.
>
> *(Folger, 2008, p. 852)*

Parties make many different decisions about their relationship. They decide to end their relationship, or sustain a minimal connection, or they define their relationship on different terms that they discuss and agree to during the mediation. What needs to be emphasized, however, is that the parties' decisions about the status of their relationship are made based on qualitative changes in the way they interact with each other—changes that the mediator helps to support by focusing on opportunities for greater empowerment and recognition. The interaction among the parties during the mediation evolves from unproductive and, at times, destructive engagement to more productive deliberation, clearer communication, and thoughtful decision making. Whatever decisions parties make about their relationships are made with greater clarity, awareness, and confidence. There is a clear sense that the decisions they make are less reactive and more deliberate and responsive.[4] This is success in the transformative framework, independent of the choices that the parties make about their issues.

The mediator's constant focus on the quality of the parties' interaction means that the mediator takes on a somewhat paradoxical role. The essential role of a transformative mediator is to "proactively follow" the parties as their conversation unfolds. The mediator is constantly active in supporting the parties' voices and facilitating their interaction with each other, but this support is done by following rather than leading the parties (Folger & Bush, 2001b). The mediator allows the parties to draw the map of their conflict and encourages them to see the map they are drawing. The mediator is there to support the parties when they want to edit or modify that map at any point in their discussion. This is highly valuable to the parties because it allows them to understand themselves, each other and the conflict, and it supports them in making choices that are built on that deeper understanding and connection. This somewhat paradoxical role is accomplished by constantly self-monitoring and restraining any tendency to get ahead of the parties or to think that the mediator knows what needs to be discussed or decided.[5]

The self-monitoring process is made easier by the skills that the mediator is asked to master and use during the conflict intervention. Transformative mediators rely on a core set of communication skills that support empowerment and recognition shifts and require a constant focus on where the parties are at any point in the evolving conversation. It is the focused attention on the here and now of the conversation that creates the ability of the mediator to perform the key skills of transformative practice and that sustains the mediator's deep and sustained commitment to party self-determination. In the end, party self-determination is what makes mediation a unique and valuable process for people who are willing to engage those with whom they profoundly disagree.

Notes

1 These principles of practice are included in the Institute for the Study of Conflict Transformation's 2010 manual for the basic training course on transformative mediation. They are presented to participants early in the training and form a foundation for learning all of the transformative skills and interventions.
2 These mediation cases are summarized based on the mediator's involvement in and recollection of the sessions. Quotations provided for the parties or mediator are not taken from verbatim transcripts of the sessions but are recollections/approximations of the language and tone of the communication that transpired during the mediation.
3 The mediation cases were conducted by Dan Simon.
4 It is difficult to convey the full sense of these changes in the parties' interaction during mediation with written case examples. Changes in the quality of communication is actually conveyed best by a video presentation of a transformative mediation where parties' voice and vocal intonations can be heard and their eye gaze, body posture and other nonverbal cues can be observed. We have tried to describe the nature of these changes in the above cases by emphasizing and highlighting some of the key moments and significant shifts that occurred in each case, but it is not possible to describe the full sense of qualitative change that occurred for the parties. (See Folger, 2001b for a discussion of documenting transformative changes in parties' interaction.) Videos of transformative mediations with commentary by the mediators are available through the Institute for the Study of Conflict Transformation at: www.transformativemediation.org..
5 This openness to the parties' control of the direction of their conversation is what necessitates that transformative mediation not be conducted or taught with a phase or stage model of mediation. See Della Noce, 2001b for a discussion of the difference between linear and relational models of mediation process.

References

Antes, J., Folger, J. & Della Noce, D. (2001) Transforming conflicts in the workplace: Documented effects of the USPS REDRESS program. *Hofstra Labor & Employment Law Journal*, 18(2): 429–467.

Baitar, R., Buysse, A., Brondeel, R., De Mol, J. & Rober, P. (2013) Styles and goals: Clarifying the professional identity of divorce mediation. *Conflict Resolution Quarterly*, 31(1): 57–78.

Beal, S. & Saul, J. (2001) Examining assumptions: Training mediators for transformative practice. In J. Folger & R.A.B. Bush (eds) *Designing Mediation* (pp. 9–19). New York: Institute for the Study of Conflict Transformation.

Bush, R.A.B. & Folger, J. (1994) *The Promise of Mediation: Responding to Conflict through Empowerment and Recognition*. San Francisco, CA: Jossey-Bass.

Bush, R.A.B. & Folger, J. (2005) *The Promise of Mediation: The Transformative Approach to Conflict*. San Francisco, CA: Jossey-Bass.

Bush, R.A.B. & Folger, J. (2010) Transformative mediation: Core practices. In J. Folger, R.A.B. Bush & D. Della Noce (eds) *Transformative Mediation: A Sourcebook* (pp. 31–50). Hempstead, NY: Association for Conflict Resolution and the Institute for the Study of Conflict Transformation.

Charbonneau, P. (2001) How practical is theory? In J. Folger & R.A.B. Bush (eds) *Designing Mediation* (pp. 37–49). New York: Institute for the Study of Conflict Transformation.

Coleman, P.T. (2013) Crises and opportunities: Six contemporary challenges for increasing probabilities for sustainable peace. *International Journal of Conflict Engagement and Resolution*, 1(1): 96–113.

Della Noce, D. (2001a) Recognition in theory, practice and training. In J. Folger & R.A.B. Bush (eds) *Designing Mediation* (pp. 96–111). New York: Institute for the Study of Conflict Transformation.

Della Noce, D. (2001b) Mediation as a transformative process: Insights on structure and movement. In J. Folger & R.A.B. Bush (eds) *Designing Mediation* (pp. 71–84). New York: Institute for the Study of Conflict Transformation.

Della Noce, D. (2004) From practice to theory to practice: A brief retrospective on the transformative model of mediation. *Ohio State Journal on Dispute Resolution*, 19(3): 925–935.

Folger, J. (2001a) Who owns what in mediation? In J. Folger & R.A.B. Bush (eds) *Designing Mediation* (pp. 55–60). New York: Institute for the Study of Conflict Transformation.

Folger, J. (2001b) Mediation research: Studying transformative effects. *Hofstra Labor & Employment Law Journal*, 18(2): 385–398.

Folger, J. (2008) Harmony and transformative mediation practice: Sustaining ideological differences in purpose and practice. *North Dakota Law Review*, 84(3): 823–860.

Folger, J. & Bernard, S. (1985) Divorce mediation: When mediators challenge the divorcing parties. *Mediation Quarterly*, 10: 5–23.

Folger, J. & Bush, R.A.B. (1996) Transformative mediation and third party intervention: Ten hallmarks of a transformative approach to practice. *Mediation Quarterly*, 13(4): 263–278.

Folger, J. & Bush, R.A.B. (2001a) *Designing Mediation: Approaches to Training and Practice within a Transformative Framework*. New York: Institute for the Study of Conflict Transformation.

Folger, J. & Bush, R.A.B. (2001b) Developing transformative training: A view from the inside. In J. Folger & R.A.B. Bush (eds) *Designing Mediation* (pp. 169–182). New York: Institute for the Study of Conflict Transformation.

Folger, J. & Bush, R.A.B. (2010) The development of transformative mediation: Past challenges and future prospects. In J. Folger, R.A.B. Bush & D. Della Noce (eds) *Transformative Mediation: A Sourcebook* (pp. 453–474). Hempstead, NY: Association for Conflict Resolution and the Institute for the Study of Conflict Transformation.

Folger, J., Bush, R.A.B. & Della Noce, D. (2010) *Transformative Mediation: A Sourcebook*. Hempstead, NY: Association for Conflict Resolution and the Institute for the Study of Conflict Transformation.

Gilligan, C. (1982) *In a Different Voice: Psychological Theory and Women's Development*. Cambridge, MA: Harvard University Press.

Greatbatch, D. & Dingwall, R. (1989) Selective facilitation: Some preliminary observations on a strategy used by divorce mediators. *Law and Society Review*, 23(4): 613–641.

Halberlin, C. (2001) Transforming workplace culture through mediation: Lessons learned from swimming upstream. *Hofstra Labor & Employment Law Journal*, 18(2): 375–383.

Miller, P. & Bush, R.A.B. (2010) Transformative mediation and lawyers: Insights from practice and theory. In J. Folger, R.A.B. Bush & D. Della Noce (eds) *Transformative Mediation: A Sourcebook* (pp. 207–228). Hempstead, NY: Association for Conflict Resolution and the Institute for the Study of Conflict Transformation.

Moen, J.K., Hudson, D., Antes, J.R., Jorgensen, E.O. & Hendrikson, L.H. (2001) Identifying opportunities for empowerment and recognition. In J. Folger & R.A.B. Bush (eds) *Designing Mediation* (pp. 112–132). New York: Institute for the Study of Conflict Transformation.

Pearson d'Estree, T. (2013) Conflict resolution as a profession and the need for communities of inquiry. *International Journal of Conflict Engagement and Resolution*, 1(1): 83–95.

Picard, C. & Siltanen, J. (2013) Exploring the significance of emotion for mediation practice. *Conflict Resolution Quarterly*, 31(1): 31–55.

Pincock, H. (2013) Does mediation make us better? Exploring the capacity building potential of community mediation. *Conflict Resolution Quarterly*, 31(1): 3–30.

Pope, S. (2001) Beginning the mediation: Party participation promotes empowerment and recognition. In J. Folger & R.A.B. Bush (eds) *Designing Mediation* (pp. 85–95). New York: Institute for the Study of Conflict Transformation.

Pope, S. & Bush, R.A.B. (2001) Understanding conflict and human capacity: The role of premises in mediation training. In J. Folger & R.A.B. Bush (eds) *Designing Mediation* (pp. 61–67). New York: Institute for the Study of Conflict Transformation.

Simon, D. (2010) Transformative mediation for divorce: Rising above the law and the settlement. In J. Folger, R.A.B. Bush & D. Della Noce (eds) *Transformative Mediation: A Sourcebook* (pp. 249–270). Hempstead, NY: Association for Conflict Resolution and the Institute for the Study of Conflict Transformation.

9

NARRATIVE MEDIATION OF FAMILY CONFLICT

John Winslade

If you have ever had the sense of being caught up in a family conflict you did not ask for—it just crept up on you and then seemed to take over—then you will understand why we suggest that family conflict is constructed out of narratives, rather than out of individual motivations. It is always tempting, of course, to blame the other party to the conflict. "She started it!" or, "He is to blame for this mess!" can make family conflict sound like children squabbling. We might laugh at our own silliness in saying such things, were it not for the sense of pain experienced.

This chapter outlines a narrative approach to mediation that builds on this idea. It is an approach that takes the concept of a narrative seriously. Here I will explain: the goals of narrative mediation; the practices of double listening, externalizing and mapping the effects; avenues for generating a counter story of relationship; and finally the return to negotiation on a different foundation. Narrative mediation is an approach to conflict resolution in a range of contexts, although the focus here is on using this approach in the context of family relationships. Key to this approach is the effort to re-author the relationship story first before facilitating the negotiation of resolution in the spirit of this relationship narrative.

What is a narrative?

What do I mean by a narrative? Aristotle taught long ago that a narrative is more than just a story of what happened. It is a story that is organized into a coherent plot, according to a theme, and complete with recognizable characters. He was talking about literary stories but narrative thinking argues that the narrative is a foundational building block for organizing meaning in life more generally.

We do not think in logical propositions all the time, or make decisions on the basis of simple facts, and we are not motivated directly by personal needs and emotions as much as some approaches to mediation might claim. Instead, we mediate all these things through the stories that we tell ourselves, that others tell about us, that we participate in with family members, and the background cultural stories from which we draw templates for decision making. We also work to ensure that the stories we live by are strong enough to live by well. To do so requires the glue that transforms events into an organized narrative.

Family life is no exception. We construct relationships and marriages on the foundation of what we have drawn from happy-ever-after fairy tales, cultural myths and legends, Hollywood romantic comedies, and training in what is right through our schooling, family upbringing, and religion. We recognize the stereotypes of the evil stepmother, the controlling husband, and the cheating sexual partner. We season this mix with a dash of truth from psychological research and a flavor sachet acquired from television talk shows, popular magazines, websites, and social media sound bites. We also know others who have suffered through sibling struggles, relationship misunderstandings, legal battles, gendered violence, and in-law expectations. Michel Foucault (1972) gave us a word for all this: "discourse." His argument was that we live our lives against the background of a "great anonymous murmur of discourse" (Foucault, 1980, p. 27), and draw from it to build up a story of a marriage, a relationship, or a family.

Not all stories, though, are equal. Nor do people in conflict always operate from positions of equality. Some stories are more coherent and some speakers are more articulate than others. In power relations too, differences are not just individual in origin. Michel Foucault (2000) argued that discourses are inseparable in the modern world from the operation of power. Some parties' stories have greater resonance with the dominant narratives in a cultural world. The meanings they embed so deeply in our thinking that we assume they are natural form the basis of much thinking, including the thinking enshrined in law. As power lines up behind cultural assumptions, it affects many things. Foucault's definition of power was, "actions upon others' actions" (Foucault, 1982, p. 220) and there is more that has such influence than direct violent force.

We can represent powerful discursive meanings often in a foundational statement on which other thought is built. Take, for instance, the statement, "a man should be the head of the household." A patriarchal construction still animates many aspects of marriage and family life. This is not to say that is not contestable. Feminist thought has contested it for a long time and has punctured much of its authority. There are now some well-developed counter narratives to those built on such a statement, but it still persists as an organizing idea, despite the resistance to it. Mediators need to be conscious of such discourses and to expect they will show up in many family conflicts. The force exerted by such a statement, just below the surface of a family conflict, and the counter force of female equality are manifest regularly in family mediation.

Such discourse becomes noise in our heads and influences expectations of what others should do and interpretations of where they fail to measure up to norms we just "know" to be right. As a result, we feel justified in feeling hurt, disappointed, angry, vengeful, or outraged when those most intimate to us fail to match up. In this sense, individual persons do not feel pure emotions. How we feel is always shaped by discourse and massaged into narrative patterns, such that how we feel often comes ready-made. It is given by the particular plot in which we partake. It makes little sense, then, to ask persons to own their feelings when the socio-cultural world around them has played such a crucial role in giving them emotional positions from which to respond. It makes equally little sense to blame the other person in a family conflict for not being able to free themselves from such cultural influences.

Goal of narrative mediation

Mediation can be defined as assisting two or more people to negotiate the relational conditions for going forward in a relationship. What narrative mediation aims for is to help people create a small degree of separation from the discourses that have created the conflict and from the narrative performances enacted upon it. Separating momentarily from it allows a small gap within which to consider the possibility of something different. Narrative mediation, therefore, privileges stories, and the meanings within stories, over facts and causes.

Most people who seek help from a mediator find it painful to be caught up in a runaway conflict narrative and are not happy about it. They would prefer things to be in a different place (or, we might say, they would prefer to be living out a different narrative). The goal of narrative mediation is to help people dis-identify with, and separate from, the conflict narrative they experience as problematic, and to step into a different story of relationship, which accords better with what they would prefer.

We refer to this different story as a counter story (Nelson, 2001), because it runs counter to what the problem story has been working to create. It would not be predicted from within the narrow confines of the conflict-saturated story. Rather than escalating conflict, such a narrative might implicate the parties in a story with themes like cooperation, understanding, respect, justice, or whatever else may fit. A counter story should be, as Sara Cobb (2013) argued, a well-formed story. Importantly, however, we do not aim to resolve the conflict story in order to reach greater understanding. Instead, we assume the existence of multiple stories about any relationship. Mediation is about shifting from a story that is not working to another one that might work better.

How does a counter story develop? The key assumption is that there are always pieces of a possible story lying waiting to be noticed. Family relationships are complex enough that we have to select from among available plot elements which to include in the narrative that governs our understanding. There are always bits and pieces that do not make the cut. Something is always left out, usually because it does not fit the story being told. Making a different selection and thus constructing a different narrative is always possible. Identifying the gaps in a story, finding the exceptions that are not consistent with it, listening for expressions of resistance to the logic of the conflict, soliciting the intention to do better, or asking about parties' hopes for something to change—all can open a counter story and give it a chance to flourish.

All this is easier to say than to do, of course. The rest of this chapter will introduce the specific practices of narrative mediation that enable movement toward these goals. On the back of some postmodern and social constructionist assumptions, narrative mediation implements externalizing conversation, double listening, mapping the effects, and counter story construction. These practices will all be described and illustrated.

These narrative shifts set the stage for mutual understanding, which is necessary for satisfying negotiation and lasting settlements. When a counter story has been established, it becomes possible to negotiate an agreement, as happens in other approaches to mediation, but the negotiation of an agreement is built on the counter story and in the spirit it embodies. The development of a counter story of relationship happens first and is followed by the facilitation of negotiation.

Double listening

Mediators are commonly taught to practice active listening—the careful discipline of paraphrasing and reflecting what a person says in order to communicate both acknowledgement and understanding. In an advance on this concept, narrative mediators seek to practice double listening (Monk & Winslade, 2013; Winslade & Monk, 2008; White, 2007). It assumes that what a person says is selective and that there are multiple readings to be made of any conflict story. Therefore, it matters which one(s) we listen to. Even the best active listening selects out some representation of a speaker's experience ahead of other possibilities. If we can listen at the same time for a conflict story and for a counter story, we potentially hear much more than the single story that active listening privileges.

Many family conflicts are constructed on hundreds of moments of interaction fueled by unspoken meanings. When a relationship is going well, the relationship narrative focuses on a desirable account of these interactions. When a relationship turns sour, it is surprisingly easy to drop all recognition of once-desirable experiences, and to select for consciousness only negative events. As a conflict escalates, negative events become the only ones noticed. This is the process of narrative selection at work. There are, however, always events beyond the reach of any selection process. The mediator's work is to listen for these plot elements and to at least acknowledge their existence.

Double listening balances the story of what has gone wrong with the (often implicit) story of hope for something better. For example, even parties' presence in the room speaks to their sense that they would prefer something other than outright war. Rather than focusing only on the story of conflict they are primed to tell, it can be useful to ask about these hopes. *When you came here today, what kind of conversation were you hoping we might have?* Not everyone will respond to this invitation into a counter story but some will. Perhaps someone might say: *I was hoping we might talk things through better than we have been doing. We just seem to be getting nowhere.*

The selection now focuses on whether to pursue the story of what has been "getting nowhere"—the conflict story—or the story of "talking things through" which may open up a counter story. Double listening includes both and contrasts them.

If a person is angry, we can inquire into what the person is not happy about. Anger usually indicates a judgment about a situation in life that someone objects to. The objection and the unhappiness deserve to be acknowledged. Double listening also suggests that if a person is not happy, there must be something different they would prefer. We can also inquire about that. *I hear that you are not happy about the current arrangements for dropping off the children. You sound quite angry about what happened last week. I wonder, though, what you would prefer? What kind of transition might work best for the children and be less of a problem for you?*

Even in the middle of an argument, couples often seek out options for something different. They take steps to prevent a conflict from escalating further—withdrawing from the argument, establishing little truces or breaks of calmness, throwing in humor, implicitly agreeing to skirt around touchy issues, postponing the conflict in order to respond to a child's needs, and so on. Each of these actions potentially opens a counter story, if we hear it and inquire into it. *You seem to both agree it is not worth allowing the argument to escalate further and take over your relationship completely. I wonder what that says about what is more important to you than this argument?*

In a joint mediation, it is possible to listen at the same time for a divorcing couple's arguments over differences as spouses and to their story of themselves as parents who share many values and commitments. Keeping these stories separate and interrupting moments when the spousal conflict contaminates the shared parenting story is often key to family mediation. A mediator can ask: *What is most useful here—to sort out the differences between you as spouses, or to acknowledge you are not planning to continue that relationship and to concentrate more on what will continue—your relationship as parents?*

Often the two stories sit side by side in the same sentence and we can learn to hear this if we listen for the conjunctions that indicate competing stories. The word "but" is especially important and double listening means hearing what is on either side of it. *I understand you were tired and upset at that moment but I still object to the way you spoke to me.* The objection and sense of outrage can easily grab the attention of both the speaker and the mediator to the extent that the other story of "understanding" is lost. Deliberate inquiry into this story can, however, rescue it from potential oblivion. There is no need to integrate these two stories or decide which is truer. They both have truth value within the context of the story they are bound to. They exist simply as pathways leading in divergent directions. We might eventually ask a person to choose between them—express a preference, take a moral stand, or exercise agency.

Double listening also alerts us to exceptions to the conflict-saturated story that exist in moments of cooperation that persist, despite the force of the conflict. They may lie in intentions to create peace (whether or not the actualization of this intention achieved its goal). Sometimes they occur through an effort one party makes to reach out to the other with respect or understanding at a point when the conflict story demands the opposite. Each exception requires curiosity to grow into a counter story of relationship. Each represents a contradiction to the logic of escalation.

Double listening, then, is a general practice that animates more specific mediator responses at any moment in mediation. It allows for the recognition of complexity in people's lives. Being "torn in two directions" need not be heard as a pathological problem, but as a resource. At least there are options! Double listening makes distinctions visible, disentangles knots, and enables choices on the basis of parties' best selves.

Externalizing conversation

Narrative mediation builds on double listening through the practice of externalizing conversation (Monk & Winslade, 2013; White, 2007; White & Epston, 1990; Winslade & Monk, 2000, 2008; Winslade et al., 1998). An externalizing conversation helps parties separate a little from the conflict story through the use of a grammatical shift. The mediator speaks about conflict as a third party and in the third person as if it had a life of its own. "It" (rather than "he" or "she") is no longer closely identified with either of the disputing parties, but is doing things to them. In literary terms, the conflict story is personified. For example, the whole situation in which the conflict has arisen may be externalized as "the dispute," "the argument," or "the rift."

Often a mediator might invite the parties to join in the process of giving the problematic situation a name by asking: *What might we call this whole thing that is coming between you and producing so much distress? What's a name we could agree on to talk about it?* If two parties cannot agree on a name, reverting to "it," or "the conflict," is usually sufficient. On other occasions, the problem does not need to be anointed in such a naming ceremony. The name just pops out of the conversation spontaneously. For example: *So there you have it. It's just a big mess!* An alert mediator might notice this statement and open an externalizing conversation. *It sounds like this big mess is taking over your lives somewhat. Would you say that it has you doing and saying things against your better judgment?*

Troublesome themes in the conflict such as "disrespect," "distrust," or "violation" might be externalized as if they were persons with designs to disrupt the parties' lives. For example: *How is distrust distorting how you respond to each other? How long has the disrespect been living with you? I understand that the violation cast a shadow over your lives. What was it like before the violation did that?*

The key to an externalizing conversation is that the mediator uses the nominalized description of the conflict situation consistently in a series of questions. Doing so once is not enough. The powerful effect of externalizing language relies on repetition. The mediator should attribute the suffering produced by the conflict to the externalized name for the conflict. This attribution interrupts the tendency in conflict for parties to attribute such suffering to each other as blame. *Am I right that the tension has taken you into a place of frustration, so badly that sarcastic exchanges have almost become the norm in a way that they never used to be?* Such externalizing creates a little distance between the problem and the persons. In this space, people can become clearer about what the conflict is doing, or how it diminishes some aspect of living. Guilt and blame are placed on pause and space for a different kind of reflection opens up.

The externalized problem can also be tracked through time. Questions inviting such time travel trace the history of the problem's sway, initiate an audit of its current empire, and stimulate a vision of its (glorious/horrific) future. For example: *How long has it been hanging around? When did it first start? How much time does it occupy in your family right now? If it were to keep on growing its influence, where might your family end up in six months' time? In two years' time? Can you handle that or would you prefer things not to go that far?*

Externalizing language introduces a different way of speaking and therefore opens up the possibility of what Deleuze and Guattari (1977) call "de-territorializing" and "re-territorializing" (p. 196). It disrupts habitual ways of thinking and makes very "striated space" a little bit "smoother" (Deleuze & Guattari, 1987, p. 474). Some people worry that it encourages people to be less responsible. Paradoxically, however, parties are frequently more inclined to take up responsibility. They are released from the expectation that they should assume responsibility for the existence of the problem and are allowed to save some face. From here, they are freer to exercise responsibility for making things better.

Mapping the effects of a conflict

Externalizing leads easily into an exploration of the effects (Monk & Winslade, 2013; White, 2007; Winslade & Monk, 2000, 2008) of the conflict on the parties. The best way to capitalize on the value of externalizing language is to continue a conversation about what the conflict has cost or taken from people, what it has produced in individuals and relationships, domains of living it has contaminated, how far its reach extends, forms of life it has in mind for persons, its somatic manifestations, and the thoughts and feelings it promotes. Such inquiries are what "mapping the effects of the conflict" engages in.

Conflicts can severely narrow people's attention so that their versions of events are compressed (Cobb, 2013). Mapping the effects of a conflict starts to help people notice both the intensity and the extensity (Deleuze & Guattari, 1987) of such effects. Often they are aware of the immediate effects, but can develop greater appreciation for the interlocking web of effects. Noticing the misery these effects have wrought helps people become more motivated for change, even if they are not yet sure what form that change might take.

It is worth taking the time to dwell on mapping the effects of a conflict. Time spent doing so is amply rewarded later. Moreover, the concept of mapping need not always remain metaphorical. An actual diagram can be drawn that records on a whiteboard the network of effects for all to see. The domains that a conflict affects can include: emotions, thoughts, physical experiences, finances, relationships, time spent, work life, values compromised, self-talk, spirituality, career directions, and life goals. Specific questions might include: *How has this problem invited you to respond? Has it affected your personal life? What has the dispute done to your hopes for the future? Has the tension diminished or increased your sense of trust in each other? Has it caused you to lose sleep? Does the whole situation follow you to work and affect you there? Has this argument got you acting out of character?*

Toward the end of mapping the effects of a conflict, the mediator invites parties to weigh up the multiple impacts of all the effects. The parties are asked to sit in judgment of what the problem story has done. Questions like these might be asked: *So what do you think of all these effects that we have been noticing? Is it something you are able to tolerate or have you had enough? If nothing changed, could it get worse? How would you be with that?*

As people make statements about how they do not like what has happened, we can follow up by asking: *Why not?* Whatever a person answers, justifies the need for change. This sequence of questions opens the counter story in earnest. The counter story, however, needs to grow enough substance to stand in for the conflict story. Often people are now ready to focus on the little pieces of experience that can build a counter story.

The counter story

Since no story, even a dominant one, can ever contain all of lived experience, there will always be elements of other possible stories that materialize in conversation. There may be moments of mutual respect, surprising instances of cooperation, agreements on shared goals or aspirations, and even moments of generosity. White and Epston (1990) refer to these moments as unique outcomes. Not all moments of difference can lead to a viable counter story, however. Some are too far back in time to generate much traction, or dead ends that lead nowhere. Others are interesting leads to a totally different narrative, but do not have much connection with the conflict story.

People need time to talk around an issue until a number of disparate events can crystallize into a story of relationship they would prefer to change. People also need to feel acknowledged for the intensity of suffering they have endured at the hands of the conflict before they are ready to move on. If mediation does not provide enough of such acknowledgement, a story of difference will soon drift back into reassertion of the problem.

It is therefore advisable to hold off on the counter story until enough of the conflict story is heard, and its effects examined, and the parties are ready to explore the possibilities for a narrative shift. An alert mediator can still note possible counter plot elements that might be of use later. Double listening has, it is hoped, drawn these moments of contradiction into view. I often draw a line down the center of a page and note, in the parties' own words, what they say about the conflict story and the counter story on either side of the line. Elements of the counter story are often mentioned in momentary asides, subjugated clauses, or throwaway lines that do not fit with the expansion of the conflict. Noting these details makes them available later.

White's (2000) concept of the "absent but implicit" (p. 153) helps notice openings to a counter story. Drawing from Bateson's (1979) notion of double description and Derrida's (1976) deconstruction of presence, White (2000) shows how any statement that negates something implies affirmation of its opposite. People in conflict who speak about disrespect are thus simultaneously speaking about a desire for respect. Emphasis on one thing implies the opposite. A person who complains about distrust implicitly is expressing a preference for trust. A sense of injustice implies a sense of justice. Implied preferences are valuable for a counter story. A mediator can turn over the coin and inquire into what is implied.

The problematic effects of a conflict can thus yield preferences for, say, understanding, and cooperation. Once such preferences are stated, the parties can be asked to locate these themes in events in their relationship. Each such instance is a unique outcome. As they are identified, they can be woven into a counter story. A counter story may feature further thematic elements, such as constructive dialogue, shared values, and instances of agreement. Gradually, these themes and events start to coalesce around a different story of relationship.

Just as there is not one pathway to a counter story, there are also a variety of questions that can be asked to open one up. The aim is always to build a new narrative out of previously neglected story elements, because of the dominance of the conflict story. Here are some examples of different lines of inquiry:

- Exceptions to the conflict story:
  - Are there times when the conflict is less intense?
  - When are you able to cooperate more and what is different about those moments?
  - If I watched a video of those brief periods where resentment has not infected your conversation, what would I see?
- Rejection of the problematic effects of the conflict:
  - Do you mind what the conflict is doing to you both? Why do you find it embarrassing?
- Preference for what does not fit with the conflict:
  - We have talked about the argument and the havoc it is wreaking and you don't want it to keep heading in that direction. So what would you prefer?
- Contradicting the logic of the conflict story:
  - If the tension will not be satisfied until you have worn each other down, what is the opposite of that?
  - If the spousal conflict is contaminating your relationship as parents, how have you found ways to stand up to it? Can you immunize your parenting relationship so that the contamination does not happen so easily?
- Refusing to allow the conflict to escalate:
  - Since last Tuesday, you have both been careful not to re-start the argument. I wonder why that might be important to you?
  - What is the instinct that was restraining you from making a worse mess?
- Resistance to the power of the conflict:
  - Do you ever feel like protesting against the habits of interacting that the dispute keeps talking you into? How would you do that?
- Hidden knowledge of how to handle differences:
  - In the past, how have you sorted out differences and not let them take over?
  - What does your cultural background teach you about handling disputes?
- Intention to act in a more cooperative way:
  - You intended to offer an apology and, if it weren't for the conflict, you might have done so. What might you have said?

Each question represents a line of inquiry with the potential to open a counter story. One question and answer, though, do not make for a coherent narrative. The counter story requires the stitching together of a number of unique outcomes into what Deleuze (1990) calls a series. Once a series of plot events has been accumulated, a mediator can ask about the themes these events might have in common. For example: *On those three occasions, you worked together. What could we call that way of parenting? How is what you would prefer different from what the conflict would want you to do? What is important about your willingness to do things differently?*

The counter story, once established, can be strengthened by some research into its history. For example: *How long has conciliatory thinking been a feature of your relationships?* This type of question strengthens a counter story by lending it a sense of "duration" (Stagoll, 2005, p. 81). Unique outcomes can thus be grown into unique accounts. A series of preferred events can be linked to a person's values and hopes for their lives and relationships. For instance: *What does not allowing the conflict to escalate say about what you value and about the environment you want to create for your children? Is it possible for you to still create this environment, now that you will be living in separate houses? In order to realize this hope, what are some thoughts that will be important to hang onto during the tough times ahead?*

Moreover, in a joint mediation, when one party has suggested a small piece of a counter story, the mediator can build on it by turning to the other party and inviting him or her to make meaning of it. For instance: *What difference does it make to hear what Naomi just said? It's a bit of a relief. I expected her to fight me all the way.* The mediator can then go back to Naomi and ask: *What's it like for you to hear that Charles feels a bit of relief from what you said?* Questions like these can then be asked back and forth between the parties. Each utterance by one party becomes fodder for a response by the other. The significance of a counter story grows moment by moment and a new relational story is generated in front of our eyes. As it grows, it approaches the point where it rivals the conflict narrative.

Once a counter narrative of relationship is established, the mediation can move into the negotiation of agreements to sustain it. Here narrative mediation converges again with a problem-solving or interest-based approach. We might ask: *In the spirit of "mutual respect," what do we still need to sort out and write down as the shared understandings that will keep it alive?* Brainstorming options for resolution can now take place. Each option can be evaluated and negotiated. The difference is that this negotiation is built in the spirit of the counter story. If it is situated, for example, in the spirit of "mutual respect," as already established by the counter story, it is more likely to be fruitful, and to be negotiated more smoothly than if it is attempted in the wake of parties telling the conflict story.

Concluding remarks

If settlements are achieved with only a grudging sense of agreement, there is always a danger that a settlement might quickly unravel as disrespect (or its allies) are reasserted. Narrative mediation seeks to avoid hasty or poorly conceived agreements. The preference is for mediation to focus first on loosening the grip of the conflict story, and then on rescuing parties' best relational intentions. More solid agreements are then possible.

This chapter has outlined some key moves that a narrative approach to mediation might entail. In one brief chapter, I cannot account for all of the details of practice that may be necessary. Other important elements are addressed in greater detail in our books on this approach (Winslade & Monk, 2000, 2008; Monk & Winslade, 2013). To reiterate, however, narrative mediation involves, first of all, becoming proficient in double listening. The development of externalizing conversation helps parties to separate from close identification with a conflict story. Mapping the effects of the externalized conflict on the parties and on their relationship helps grow the motivation for change and establishes the foundation for a counter story. The elaboration of such a counter story can then take place. Finally, the spirit of this counter story can serve as the basis for negotiation.

Narrative mediation has utility in any context where people in relationship are in conflict. My key recommendations, therefore, are that mediators learn to discover for themselves this utility as they: learn to work with narratives; become familiar with how power is always at work in human relationships; practice double listening; develop externalizing conversations; seek out openings to a counter story; and aim to re-author relationships in order to resolve problems rather than resolve problems in order to create relational changes.

References

Bateson, G. (1979) *Mind and Nature: A Necessary Unity*. New York: Dutton.

Burr, V. (2003) *Social Constructionism* (2nd edn). London: Psychology Press.

Cobb, S. (2013) *Speaking of Violence: The Politics and Poetics of Narrative in Conflict Resolution*. New York: Oxford University Press.

Deleuze, G. (1990) *The Logic of Sense*, M. Lester with C. Stivale (trans.). New York: Columbia University Press.

Deleuze, G. & Guattari, F. (1977) *Anti-Oedipus: Capitalism and Schizophrenia*, R. Hurley, M. Seem, H.R. Lane (trans.). London: Penguin.

Deleuze, G. & Guattari, F. (1987) *A Thousand Plateaus: Capitalism and Schizophrenia*, B. Massumi (trans.). Minneapolis, MN: Minnesota University Press.

Derrida, J. (1976) *Of Grammatology*, G.C. Spivak (trans.). Baltimore, MD: Johns Hopkins University Press.

Foucault, M. (1972) *The Order of Things: An Archaeology of the Human Sciences*. New York: Pantheon Books.

Foucault, M. (1980) *Power/Knowledge: Selected Interviews and Other Writings*. New York: Pantheon Books.

Foucault, M. (1982) Afterword: The subject and power. In H. Dreyfus & P. Rabinow (eds) *Michel Foucault: Beyond Structuralism and Hermeneutics* (pp. 199–226). Brighton: Harvester Press.

Foucault, M. (1989) *Foucault Live (Interview, 1966–84)*, Sylvere Lotringer (ed.), J. Johnston (trans.). New York: Semiotext.

Foucault, M. (2000) *Power: Essential Works of Foucault, 1954–1984, Vol. 3*, J. Faubion (ed.), R. Hurley (trans.). New York: New Press.

Monk, G. & Winslade, J. (2013) *When Stories Clash: Addressing Conflict with Narrative Mediation*. Chagrin Falls, OH: Taos Institute.

Nelson, H.L. (2001) *Damaged Identities: Narrative Repair*. Ithaca, NY: Cornell University Press.

Stagoll, C. (2005) Duration (Durée). In A. Parr (ed.) *The Deleuze Dictionary (Revised Edition)*. Edinburgh: Edinburgh University Press.

White, M. (2000) Re-engaging with history: The absent but implicit. In M. White, *Reflections on Narrative Practice: Essays & Interviews*. Adelaide, Australia: Dulwich Centre Publications.

White, M. (2007) *Maps of Narrative Practice*. New York: Norton.

White, M. & Epston, D. (1990) *Narrative Means to Therapeutic Ends*. New York: Norton.

Winslade, J. & Monk, G. (2000). *Narrative Mediation: A New Approach to Conflict Resolution*. San Francisco, CA: Jossey-Bass.

Winslade, J. & Monk, G. (2008) *Practicing Narrative Mediation: Loosening the Grip of Conflict*. San Francisco, CA: Jossey-Bass.

Winslade, J., Monk, G. & Cotter, A. (1998) A narrative approach to the practice of mediation. *Negotiation Journal*, 14(1): 21–42. doi: 10.1111/j.1571–9979.1998.tb00146.x.

10

VICTIM-OFFENDER MEDIATION

A humanistic approach

Mark Umbreit and Toran Hansen

This chapter considers the humanistic approach to victim-offender mediation. This form of mediation comes out of restorative justice scholarship and practice (an alternative to the traditional criminal justice system in responding to incidents of crime), which is briefly discussed here. This context sets the humanistic approach to mediation apart from other forms of mediation that do not focus as much on the harms experienced by conflict parties and may be more settlement-focused (rather than dialogue-driven). This chapter outlines what makes the humanistic approach to mediation so unique, highlighting specific elements of the approach, as well as evidence of its effectiveness. The approach is then illustrated by an example, to give a sense of what humanistic victim-offender mediation looks like in practice.

What is restorative justice?

Restorative justice provides an alternative way of responding to crime, wrongdoing, or rule breaking than is provided by the traditional criminal justice system. In the traditional criminal justice system, a judge or other agent of the court is responsible for determining who broke what specific laws and punishing them accordingly. This is called retributive justice and emphasizes the offender getting their "just deserts" for their criminal behavior (Zehr, 1995). In restorative justice, those most affected by the crime, including crime victims, offenders, and key community members, voluntarily participate directly in the justice process, frequently by having some form of facilitated dialogue with one another. The focus of this dialogue varies, but it centers around meeting the needs of victims and offenders and addressing the root causes of a specific crime. In addition, this dialogue provides a process for offenders to take responsibility for their actions directly to crime victims and to identify the specific obligations created by their crime (the central obligation is for offenders to "make things right" to the greatest extent possible) (Umbreit & Armour, 2011; Zehr, 2002). Offenders then are held accountable to crime victims directly, rather than to the criminal justice system as a whole. In the traditional criminal justice system, the offender breaks the law against the state, rather than against the specific individuals or communities that were harmed (Zehr, 1995).

Restorative justice can therefore be thought of as victim-centered, while the traditional criminal justice system can be thought of as offender-centered (Umbreit & Armour, 2011). Often, in the traditional criminal justice system victims are more peripheral to the process, providing evidence to be used in court or offering a victim-impact statement to be used in the sentencing process. Facilitated restorative justice dialogue offers crime victims an opportunity to speak directly to the offender, asking them important questions about what happened and why, telling the offender about the impact of a crime on their life, and determining with the offender the best (non-harmful and achievable) ways that the offender could make amends for their actions, such as providing restitution in various forms (monetary, working it off, engaging in community service, etc.) (Umbreit & Armour, 2011).

This respectful discussion revolves around the notions of harms and healing, rather than guilt and punishment (Zehr, 2002, 1995). Crime victims share with offenders the harms that they experienced as a result of crimes and the impact of those crimes on them, which reveal critical needs that have emerged as a result, while offenders also reveal their needs (for instance, the need to take accountability and make amends for their actions, needs that led to their criminal behavior, and so on) (Umbreit, 2006; Umbreit & Armour, 2011). Healing occurs when victims and offenders identify the root causes of crimes, share their needs with one another, craft agreements to meet their needs, and carry out their promises to one another after concluding their facilitated dialogue. When this happens, restorative justice "restores" the dignity of crime victims and offenders, fractured interpersonal and community relationships, emotional and material losses, and the capacity of victims and offenders to reconsider the place of a crime in their lives and move forward (Umbreit & Armour, 2011; Zehr, 2002).

The foundations of restorative justice are therefore very different from those of the criminal justice system and its emphasis on retribution and punishment. Zehr (2002) suggests that there are three fundamental pillars of restorative justice that set it apart from the traditional criminal justice system. The first of these pillars is the recognition that a restorative response to harm should focus on the harm done to people and communities, rather than legal infractions against the state. The second pillar involves the understanding that these harms incur obligations, particularly the central obligation for offenders to be accountable to victims for their acts of wrongdoing, understand the impacts of their actions, and take responsibility to "make things right" to any victims, both tangibly and symbolically.

The third pillar indicates that those most directly involved in crime, especially victims and offenders, are offered opportunities to engage in the justice process and participate in direct or indirect dialogue with one another whenever possible. Ultimately, this leads to the following definition of restorative justice, which ensures, "at a minimum that we address victims' harms and needs, hold offenders accountable to put right those harms, and involve victims, offenders, and communities in the process" (Zehr, 2002, p. 25). Zehr (2002) goes further to state that this does not mean that restorative justice and criminal justice processes are diametrically opposed, but rather, they exist on a continuum from more restorative processes to more retributive ones.

What is humanistic victim-offender mediation?

Humanistic victim-offender mediation is a form of restorative justice dialogue used in criminal cases, as well as other forms of rule breaking and wrongdoing. Victim-offender mediation was introduced to the criminal justice system in 1974, in Elmira, Ontario, with the launch of a Victim Offender Reconciliation Program (VORP), when two boys who committed several acts of vandalism were offered the opportunity to meet with the victims of their crimes (Zehr, 1995). The first VORP in the United States was initiated in Elkhart, Indiana in 1978 (Umbreit & Armour, 2011; Zehr, 1995). Its roots, however, go back much further as most societies, at some point in their evolution, developed ways of addressing acts of wrongdoing by those who broke the norms and rules of society using some form of dialogue involving the victim of the infraction, the offender, or both (Umbreit & Armour, 2011; Umbreit et al., 2005).

Since its modern inception in the 1970s, the restorative justice movement has taken the field of criminal justice by storm, with programs in nearly every state and in countries around the world (Umbreit et al., 2005). New Zealand and Northern Ireland have even based their entire juvenile justice systems on a platform of restorative justice. In 2000, the United Nations Congress on Crime Prevention went so far as to draft the *UN Basic Principles on the Use of Restorative Justice Programs in Criminal Matters*, which was later adopted by the United Nations Economic and Social Council (United Nations, 2002). Victim-offender mediation in its current form has been used in all kinds of criminal cases and has had especially large impacts on the practice of such areas as juvenile justice and crimes of severe violence. Although the latter process is modified significantly given the severity of the harms (such as in cases of homicide), requiring mediators to have extensive specialized training (Umbreit & Armour, 2011).

Victim-offender mediation has been found to be a very effective form of mediation, as well as a response to crime and wrongdoing. Typically, about 40–60 percent of crime victims choose to participate in restorative justice programs, although participation rates of up to 90 percent have been reported (Coates et al., 2002). Approximately 80–90 percent of crime victims report being satisfied with victim-offender mediation and nine out of ten state that they would recommend victim-offender mediation to a friend (Umbreit, 1994; Umbreit et al., 2001). Three key reasons why victims report being satisfied with victim-offender mediation are: 1 they felt good about the mediator; 2 they saw the resultant restitution agreement as fair; and 3 they had a strong desire to meet with the offender (Umbreit & Bradshaw, 1999).

Offenders also report feeling satisfied with victim-offender mediation when compared to the traditional justice system (Latimer et al., 2001). Several studies have also found that offender recidivism rates are lower for those who participate in victim-offender mediation (with an effect size between 26–32 percent), and among those who reoffend, they tend to be for less serious charges than offenders who did not participate in victim-offender mediation (Nugent et al., 2003, 2001). Overall, about 90 percent of victim-offender sessions reach a restitution agreement and about 80–90 percent of those agreements are completed (Umbreit et al., 2001). Typically, over 80 percent of participants in victim-offender mediation state that the process and any resultant agreements were fair (Umbreit & Roberts, 1996).

As outlined in Umbreit (2006) and Lewis and Umbreit (2015), there are several hallmarks of a humanistic approach to mediation that set it apart from other mediation models and approaches. First, the process of humanistic mediation is dialogue-driven, rather than settlement-driven, ensuring that having meaningful, frequently emotional, dialogue in the process is considered more critical than actually arriving at a specific agreement or settlement. A second essential feature of the approach is that mediators need to talk with the victim and offender in separate sessions prior to conducting the mediation session. This pre-mediation preparation allows the mediator to explain the mediation process, understand the parties' expectations, hopes, and fears, listen to the parties' narratives, build rapport and trust with them, and ensure that they are willing to participate voluntarily in a mediation session and are ready for it.

Third, within the mediated session itself, the mediator takes a non-directive posture and victims and offenders sit face to face so that the parties speak directly to one another, promoting more meaningful dialogue among them. Fourth, the primary responsibility of the mediator is to ensure the physical and emotional safety of the parties, demonstrating unconditional positive regard for all of them in an impartial manner (caring equally for all the people participating).

Humanistic mediation therefore sets the stage for a safe, if not sacred, space for the parties, which is enhanced when the mediator is centered and recognizes the strengths of all participants. During the mediation, mediators emphasize connection to the parties through "being present," listening deeply, and honoring silences. Quite often, the mediation session will end with an agreement, including some form of restitution; however, this need not be the case for the mediation to be considered successful, as the emphasis is on having high-quality, meaningful dialogue, rather than producing any potential agreement. It is high-quality dialogue that frequently produces transformative effects for parties, including personal and interpersonal development. Mediators are also encouraged to follow up with parties post-mediation to check on their progress.

Humanistic mediation is predicated on several important underlying assumptions and values. An important belief underlying the approach is that we are all interconnected with one another in some way, so treating one another disrespectfully is tantamount to treating ourselves disrespectfully (Umbreit & Armour, 2011). Therefore, all participants (including the victim, the offender, and the mediator) need to endeavor to treat one another with respect and dignity throughout the mediation process. This assumption of interconnectedness also means that every crime, act of wrongdoing, or rule infraction should be viewed as a violation or fracture of relationships (Zehr, 2002, 1995). Humanistic mediation seeks to heal these fractured relationships between crime victims, offenders, and their communities.

Humanistic mediation also presupposes that participants will be honest in conveying their thoughts and emotions. This honest truth telling can have transformative effects, providing a pathway to begin the process of making things right (Umbreit & Armour, 2011). Finally, humanistic mediation is based on the assumptions that we all deserve another chance, every action should be placed within an overarching life context, and that if we give people an opportunity, it is possible that they will learn from their mistakes, develop relationships, and become better people. Every mediation session thus offers such potential for development and transformation.

As indicated by Umbreit (2006) and Lewis and Umbreit (2015), a humanistic mediator should follow some very specific practice guidelines when conducting their work within the mediation session (after essential preparatory work is conducted in separate pre-mediation sessions with victims and offenders). The practice guidelines are as follows:

- The mediator needs to endeavor to connect with the parties as people, remaining centered, mindful, and fully "present" while mediating
- The mediator should elicit the strengths, narratives, and needs of the parties through deep, compassionate listening
- The mediator should care for all parties present, while remaining impartial
- The mediator should respectfully interact with the parties in a non-judgmental manner and honor important silences in conversations
- The mediator should offer the parties (particularly victims) as much choice as possible with respect to the mediation process and the setting
- The mediator must "get out of the way" of the parties, seldom and subtly interjecting in dialogue, helping parties find their own path through their conflict
- The room for the mediation session should be structured in a way to allow the parties to speak directly to one another
- Any agreements should be made by consensus, giving all participants veto power over all elements of any agreements

Hence, two elements of humanistic mediation that help mediators maintain a safe, if not sacred, space are mindfulness and centering. A great deal has been written about mindfulness, making it impossible to explore in depth here, but at its very simplest, it involves staying with the moment-to-moment actions and communication involved in interactions among the parties, putting aside "our stuff" to be available to engage with "their stuff." Each mediator has different ways of centering themselves, some of which may be spiritual in nature; however, one common technique is to use slow, deliberate, and deep belly breathing to relax one's body and calm one's reactions.

One of the primary concerns in victim-offender mediation is to ensure that crime victims do not feel re-victimized by their experience (Umbreit & Armour, 2011). In order to safeguard against this possibility, mediators need to make sure that crime victims participate voluntarily in mediation sessions and that they know they have the ability to end the session at any point if they feel they need to. Mediators should check in with crime victims, perhaps separately in caucus, if they are nonverbally communicating that they may be feeling uncomfortable, unsafe, or even threatened. The session can then be terminated if necessary.

In addition, the preparation phase can reveal the readiness of the crime victim and offender to participate in a mediation session (Umbreit, 2006; Umbreit & Armour, 2011). In particular, the mediator should make sure that the offender is being honest and taking responsibility for their actions and the harm that they have caused any victims; otherwise, the risk of re-victimization will be much higher. A mediator must also be careful not to push victims to forgive offenders in any ways (Umbreit & Armour, 2011). Although this may occur spontaneously as a result of engaging in humanistic victim-offender mediation, any pressure to forgive can be experienced as threatening to crime victims and, for many, their hoped-for outcomes may have little if anything to do with forgiveness (for instance, maybe they would just like to tell the offender the impact the crime had on them or ask them a few questions about it).

Case example: victims meet the burglar and find peace

The Smiths' home had been burgled by a 20-year-old man named Steve while they were gone for the weekend. The neighbors had called them when the police arrived. Mr and Mrs Smith had to travel back to their home in the city from their cabin in the country. They were furious.

Steve, the offender, was arrested. He admitted his guilt, and the judge, before sentencing him, referred him to a restorative justice program called Victim-Offender Mediation. Carol, one of the staff members, initiated the process. She met with the offender first, before even contacting the victims, to check if he had truly owned up to his crime and was willing to enter a mediation process, to talk about what had happened and to develop a plan to repair the harm. He was, although he had many reservations about it. He felt the Smiths were claiming far more damage than he actually did.

Carol called the Smiths, listened to their concerns, and tried to set up a meeting with them. Mr Smith was extremely angry. He would refer to those "stupid punks" that had broken into his home. He talked about how he had been ripped off two times before and it was probably the same idiot who had done it again. His anger prevented him from hearing what Carol was saying about the program. Eventually, he listened and said, "Well, let me give it a little more thought and call me back next week."

Carol called him back the following week and he finally agreed: "Why don't you come out to our home, and we'll be glad to tell you more about how the burglary affected us, and we want to learn more about the program." So Carol, the mediator, went out to their home, did a lot of deep listening, slowly explaining the program in a gentle and down-to-earth way.

Eventually Mr Smith said, "Yeah, I do, I want to tell that punk what it's like to be victimized, what it's like to have all your stuff taken." Sue added, "Well, I know my husband wants to do this, but I don't. So he'll do it by himself."

When Carol got back to the office the next day, she checked in with the director of the program, Eric, and asked for his assistance. The high level of anger by both parties was frightening to her. He agreed to co-facilitate the meeting.

Mr Smith indicated that he preferred having the mediation at a local library conference room in his neighborhood. When Carol and Eric came together at the library with Steve, it was a very tense moment, very awkward. Mrs Smith was with her husband even though she initially said she was not coming. She made it clear that she was concerned her husband would "lose it" and she needed to be there in case he needed to be dragged out of the room.

Despite some hesitancy, the mediators proceeded. There were no handshakes, just brief verbal introductions. They went into the conference room. It was huge, with no tables to sit around so there would be few clear boundaries. All participants therefore sat in an open circle.

When all were seated, Carol began with some brief comments about what they would be doing for the evening, inviting their participation, and thanking them for coming. Eric then added a few comments about the opportunity to take a break at any time and then he opened up the process by turning to Mr Smith and inviting him to speak directly to Steve about how he felt about what happened. He needed little prompting. He was rocking in the chair, arms folded on his chest. Steve was slouched in his chair with his eyeballs glaring at the carpet, looking like he had no interest whatsoever in being there. Mr Smith's energy indicated that he was full of anger.

Within four minutes, the anger got so high, with him calling Steve a punk and other names, that Eric was just about ready to intervene and redirect the conversation, to essentially break the energy of his explosiveness and ask Steve to share his story. However, before Eric did that, Steve actually was getting so agitated by this that he jumped out of his seat and he said, "This is a bunch of crap. I shouldn't have come."

Eric in turn jumped out of his chair, looked at Steve, and said, "Steve, I can understand you wanting to go. Mr Smith is very angry, but I know that he and his wife are here because they want to learn more about what happened. They want to learn more about you and they want to see if some plan to repair the harm can be worked out that seems fair. Can you give it a few more minutes, and then if it's just not working, go ahead and leave?" That appeared to be enough to validate his anger and to encourage him to stick around a little while longer.

This was a powerful lesson in the healing power of releasing toxic emotional energy in conflicts. The outburst of anger by both Steve and Mr Smith was the most pivotal moment in the entire mediation session. It was a transformative event. Before that, their body language was closed. Their voice tone was high and intense. After the verbal explosion of their emotional energy, they both sat up a little more erect and the tone of voices was significantly lower. Mr Smith began asking Steve questions in a very direct way. Steve actually looked openly at him.

Incredible as this might sound, after about 45 minutes there were some moments of silence in the midst of this intense verbal exchange. Mr Smith leaned toward his wife, who was sitting a little behind him and they whispered. Carol and Eric were wondering what in the world was going on but they did not interrupt. They sensed, at an intuitive level, something very powerful was going on.

After they whispered to each other, Mr Smith looked at Steve, bent over closer to him, and in a soft voice tone, said, "Do you know our daughter Sara?" "Yeah," the young man replied. "Was she involved in this? I mean, did she set you guys up to hit our place?" "No, Sara's a good kid. She was not involved at all."

Then Mr Smith leaned back toward his wife and they whispered again. He turned and looked straight at Steve, leaned forward even more closely and in a softer tone said, "Do you ever see Sara? Ever since she ran from that drug treatment program we haven't seen her for the past year." Steve indicated that he saw her every now and then.

Mr Smith, the angry, furious victim looked at Steve, the criminal, the convicted felon and pleaded, "Next time you see Sara, could you tell her that her mom and dad really love her. We miss her. And tell her we'd love her to come home."

Carol and Eric, as mediators, were bearing witness to a powerful shift in energy in the midst of this major conflict. The energy of tension, awkwardness, anger, and hostility, which was so present at the beginning, had now shifted to a very different, gentler form of communication in which the victims were seeking parenting help from the criminal. It was a process of mutual aid. Steve was no longer the convicted felon, the burglar. He was a guy who messed up and was at some level connected with their daughter from whom they were estranged. They needed Steve to help them reconnect with their daughter Sara.

Following discussion of the full impact of the burglary on all involved, the issue of actual losses and the need for restitution were addressed. A restitution agreement was developed by the Smiths and Steve, with clear and specific requirements for Steve to complete.

The meeting was about to wrap up. Carol and Eric could sense the energy of the group was diminishing, and Eric offered the possibility of a follow-up meeting to check out how things were going and to determine if any adjustments might need to be made in the restitution agreement. All agreed that this would be a good idea.

Then Steve looked at Carol and Eric, saying, "I think that would be a good idea. Could we have the meeting at my house?" He then looked at the Smiths and said, "You know, I'm not a burglar. I mean, what I did was wrong, I broke into your house, but I am not some criminal. I'd like you to come to my house sometime and meet my wife and my little baby."

Conclusion

A humanistic approach to conflict resolution, while grounded in thousands of victim offender mediation cases over several decades, is now beginning to be applied in other settings such as marital disputes, family conflicts, neighborhood conflicts, church conflicts, and even in workplaces. Going far beyond simply a settlement-driven process on which most conventional mediation focuses, a humanistic approach draws upon the strength and resilience of the involved parties and is focused on their need to be fully heard, as well as their innate wisdom in constructing some form of repairing the harm that makes sense to them. Research has consistently shown that the involved parties are highly satisfied with a humanistic approach and feel respected and empowered. While it is not settlement-driven, a humanistic approach to victim-offender mediation is remarkably effective at bringing about meaningful "settlements" that have high rates of completion, since all of the parties feel truly heard during preparatory work, the non-directive mediation session, and any follow-up meetings. The unique elements of the humanistic approach also frequently have more transformative effects for the parties that go beyond what traditional settlements offer, as indicated in the example provided above.

References

Coates, R.B., Umbreit, M.S. & Vos, B. (2002) *Systemic Change Toward Restorative Justice: Washington County, Minnesota.* St Paul, MN: Center for Restorative Justice and Peacemaking.

Latimer, J., Dowden, C. & Muise, D. (2001) *The Effectiveness of Restorative Practices: A Meta-analysis.* Ottawa, Canada: Department of Justice, Research and Statistics Division Methodological Series.

Lewis, T. & Umbreit, M. (2015) A humanistic approach to mediation and dialogue: An evolving transformative practice. *Conflict Resolution Quarterly*, 33(1): 3–17.

Nugent, W., Umbreit, M.S., Wiinamaki, L. & Paddock, J. (2001) Participation in victim-offender mediation and severity of subsequent delinquent behavior: Successful replications? *Journal of Research in Social Work Practice*, 11(1): 5–23.

Nugent, W., Williams, R.M. & Umbreit, M.S. (2003) Participation in victim-offender mediation and the prevalence and severity of subsequent delinquent behavior: A meta-analysis. *Utah Law Review*, 2003(1): 137–165.

Umbreit, M.S. (1994) *Victim Meets Offender: The Impact of Restorative Justice and Mediation.* Monsey, NY: Willow Tree Press.

Umbreit, M.S. (2006) *Mediating Interpersonal Conflict.* Eugene, OR: Wipf and Stock Publishers.

Umbreit, M.S. & Armour, M.P. (2011) *Restorative Justice Dialogue: An Essential Guide for Research and Practice.* New York: Springer.

Umbreit, M.S. & Bradshaw, W. (1999) Factors that contribute to victim satisfaction with mediated offender dialogue in Winnipeg: An emerging area of social work practice. *Journal of Law and Social Work*, 9(2), 35–51.

Umbreit, M.S., Coates, R.B. & Vos, B. (2001) *Juvenile Victim Offender Mediation in Six Oregon Counties.* Salem, OR: Oregon Dispute Resolution Commission.

Umbreit, M.S. & Roberts, A.W. (1996) *Mediation of Criminal Conflict in England: An Assessment of Services in Coventry and Leeds.* St Paul, MN: Center for Restorative Justice and Mediation.

Umbreit, M.S., Vos, B., Coates, R.B. & Lightfoot, E. (2005) Restorative justice in the twenty-first century. *Marquette Law Review*, 89(2): 251–304.

United Nations. (2002) *Basic Principles on the Use of Restorative Justice Programs in Criminal Matters.* The United Nations. Retrieved from www.un.org/en/ecosoc/docs/2002/resolution%202002-12.pdf.

Zehr, H. (1995) *Changing Lenses.* Scottsdale, PA: Herald Press.

Zehr, H. (2002) *The Little Book of Restorative Justice.* Intercourse, PA: Good Books.

11

BRAIN SCIENCE BEHIND MEDIATING RELATIONAL CONFLICTS

Thomas DiGrazia

America can be described as a warrior culture. It often feels that America is a war zone of conflict, where deep-seated social, political, and relational issues embroil us in never-ending disagreements, impasse, acrimony, deadlock, and often violence. We cannot seem to get along with our lives on personal, political, or social levels, as we are too eager to watch the next gladiatorial battle, or to embroil ourselves vicariously in a conflict. In this chapter,[1] we will explore one promising tool for mediators and peacemakers dealing with conflict in the divorce field: brain science. The recent scientific findings in the field of brain science can be of inestimable value to mediators and peacemakers in getting to the root of conflict in the marital mediation and dissolution field.

Mediation, which is an assisted form of settlement negotiation, is the fastest growing appropriate dispute resolution process. Mediation involves the participants directly, although lawyers often participate at various stages of the mediation process, particularly in the relational field of divorce. Unless written into a contract, parties to a dispute voluntarily retain the services of a neutral third-party mediator or peacemaker to resolve conflictual issues to their mutual satisfaction.

By definition, mediation is a process of compromise in action. Participants must be ready to forego intractable positions and be willing to be flexible in negotiation. It is best used early on before positions harden in the adversarial process. However, when court ordered, mediation tends to be at a much later stage of the litigation process. The process generally results in significant cost and time savings for participants. Perhaps more importantly, it helps to preserve future personal, familial, and/or business relationships. It allows people to get on with their lives and economic interests without the angst, great expense, and the often all-consuming nature of the adversarial process. For mediators and peacemakers, having more detailed information about the interplay between conflict and brain science is of considerable value in assisting those caught in the morass of a marital dispute in order to avoid the devastating pitfalls of an adversarial divorce.

Conflict and brain science

What is at the root of this warrior culture that so profoundly affects the field of divorce in America? At the root of our warrior culture is conflict. Here we are talking about the conflict that takes place both within and between individuals. Yoga philosophy is most instructive on this subject. It embraces the concept that conflict is based on avidya. Lu DiGrazia, founder of the Yoga School of Kailua and a Yoga teacher with more than 40 years of experience, states that avidya "is simply the lack or absence of awareness, mindfulness; a limited or inhibited awareness in sensitivity; [and] the absence of vision of one's self" (personal communication, October 18, 2014).

Current brain science teaches that conflict, which also according to Krishnamurti (1992a) arises from ignorance of self (p. 54), may be triggered from one or more of any number of real or imagined events. However, the primary source of all conflict is the genetically triggered freeze, flight, or fight response. When unprocessed emotions, such as fear, anxiety or insecurity, all expressions of self-ignorance, hit the pavement of an adversarial divorce system, legal warfare is the most likely result, with emotional and financial exhaustion of the parties its only limit. However, it should be noted that the legal profession's general systemic failure to educate themselves and their clients to cultivate a meditative mind or mindfulness shows some sign of a willingness to change over recent years.

Zen and meditation scholar, Jon Kabit-Zinn (1996), defines a mindfulness approach to life as having two basic parts: the development of an observing attitude toward one's emotions and life experience, and a nonjudgmental receptivity of what is being experienced without feeling a need to do anything about it (pp. 161–170). Adversarial lawyers by disposition, training, and practice as zealous advocates, in general, do not exercise mindfulness as defined above by Kabit-Zinn (1996) in their professional life. Perceiving themselves as warriors, their brain chemical of choice is adrenalin, leading too often to unneeded aggressiveness. This contrasts sharply with the more mindful state of the peacemaker/mediator, whose brain chemical of choice is oxytocin, which allows for a more observant, more receptive, and less judgmental attitude in their interactions towards mediation participants. Oxytocin is also known as the bonding hormone, promoting trust and empathy in relationships—in short, a non-violent approach to conflict resolution (Cloke, 2009, pp. 1–9).

As Lao Tzu (n.d.), a Chinese philosopher, and author of the ancient book of Chinese wisdom, the *Tao Te Ching*, stated, by way of paraphrasing: the greatest revelation is stillness or the meditative mind (p. 1). This stillness begets an environment where peaceful solutions to conflict can occur. Rather than cultivating stillness, the existing adversarial system appeals to the primordial, instinct-driven part of our brain known as the limbic brain. The limbic brain is where issues of daily survival are processed. In the early years of human existence, when we were more likely to be the hunted rather than the hunter, the limbic brain was called upon to make instantaneous lifesaving judgments when confronted with danger. When aggressive animals or humans endangered us, we had to decide whether we would freeze in place, flee, or stand and fight.

Over the eons, however, the human brain has evolved. Our thinking intelligence now dominates in the neocortex or frontal lobe of the brain. This part of the brain uses past knowledge and sensory information to learn how to drive an automobile, use a computer, and learn a new language. It is a much more deliberative and intellectual part of the brain, and capable of abstract thinking.

The raw, often unprocessed emotions generated in a conflicted divorce trigger a direct response from the less highly developed limbic brain. Fears, anxieties, and insecurities abound in highly charged divorces. Separating couples and families are particularly vulnerable to a divorce system based on warfare and violence. The conflict within and between the husbands, wives, and children of divorce is highly susceptible to manipulation by a spiritually bereft legal dissolution process. As Baer (2012) points out, the stress generated by divorce and similar experiences can cause a 20 percent drop in IQ and emotional intelligence (EQ) levels, thus making conflicted disputants more susceptible to often ruinous decision making. He goes on to state bluntly the obvious ethical question for divorce lawyers, who either know or should know that their emotionally distraught clients' effective decision-making abilities are impaired during the divorce process. Baer (2012) posits that family law advocates cannot be sure that the decisions a divorcing client is making are not "significantly impaired" by the emotional trauma of the adversarial marital dissolution process (p. 4).

With the limited capacity of the limbic brain, its instinctive response to conflict is to go into freeze (do nothing), flight (ignore reality, escape) or fight (hire the most aggressive and expensive lawyer you can—even if it means agreeing to place a lien on your home to pay exorbitant legal fees to your chosen warrior) mode. When choosing mediation as the appropriate process to resolve contested divorce issues, participants are able to consider solutions with the more reasoned, and more highly developed frontal lobe of their brains. This type of brain residency allows for a much more nuanced observational, intuitive, and skillful response to the transformative marital dissolution challenge posed for individuals and families. To put it most simply, the difference between a limbic and frontal lobe response is akin to the difference between holding your breath and breathing deeply and fully through the divorce experience.

According to Dr Daniel J. Siegel (2010), a neurological and child psychiatrist, from a physiological perspective when the nervous system is receptive and an individual is centered in the prefrontal lobe, facial muscles and vocal chords relax, and normal blood pressure and heart rate are enjoyed. We are more creative and open to hearing what the other person is stating or proposing. By contrast, when the nervous system is reactive, we are in a limbic or survival mode, physically and emotionally. According to Siegel (2010), in a reactive state we too often twist and bend what we hear to match the things we fear. This causes us to hear, which is a physical act, without listening, which is a neocortical, cognitive event (pp. 214–217). Hearing without listening, by both the divorcing parties and their lawyers, is at the heart of the spiritual morass known as the adversarial divorce process.

One of the principal roles of the peacemaker, who (to use the title of Dr Peter Adler's (2008) book) occupies a place in the eye of the storm, is first to recognize his/her own reaction/receptivity tendencies and then to recognize the reaction/receptivity patterns in the mediation participants' behavior and statements. This recognition can enable the peacemaker/mediator to help move participants from a reactive to a more receptive state.

Well-known peacemaker, Kenneth Cloke (2009) sums up the important interplay between brain science and conflict. He offers that there has been an incredible upsurge in scientific exploration of the inner workings of the human brain. This research upsurge has also provided us with an ability to translate scientific information into practical skills aiding those with whom we work in the divorce and related social fields. He worries that, "[w]ithout an … increase in our ability to use that knowledge openly, ethically, and constructively, and turn it into successful conflict resolution experiences, our species may not be able to collaborate in solving its most urgent problems, or indeed, survive them" (Cloke, 2009, pp. 11–12).

Cloke (2009) goes on to state that all of the increase in violence—in all of its manifested forms of terrorism, environmental destruction, and gridlocked governments—can be traced to the eons-old human brain reflexive response to conflict. Cloke (2009) offers hope that brain science can help us to comprehend the neurological and biological roots of violence, whether in word, deed, or thought. That is, using brain science to help inform our response to legal aggression motivated by fear, insecurity, and anxiety arising from adversarial divorce practice (pp. 1–13).

An additional source of helpful brain and neurological information comes from the experience of Yoga therapists. Many Yoga therapists combine the knowledge, talent and resources of an experienced Yoga teacher and mental health coach in working with patients. Yoga therapists make use of the burgeoning scientific information on the Vagus Nerve (VN) to treat patients with mental health challenges. The experience of Yoga therapists with the VN and its effects on their patients-clients is useful information for the peacemaker to put to use, especially in highly conflicted marital dissolution mediation.

The VN complex is the tenth cranial nerve. It originates in the brainstem and cerebellum and then branches out extensively throughout the torso, making contact with the major organs, the digestive system, and the sex glands. Yoga therapists make use of stimulation of the VN to increase Vagus tone for such symptoms as post-traumatic stress disorder (PTSD) and depression. Low Vagus tone is linked to heart attacks, immune inflammation, loneliness, and negative moods.

The VN is energized mechanically through the application of direct pressure or by stretching the torso. Various Hatha Yoga Asanas can be helpful as a stimulant to the VN, particularly Pranayama exercises such as Ujjayi (slow, rhythmic) breathing, backward bending Asanas (physical postures) like camel pose, wheel, upward and downward bow, and the bridge poses, all of which serve to help stimulate increased Vagus tone. These chest-opening exercises help to lower the heart and metabolic rates and restore a feeling of peace and well-being (Bergland, 2013, pp. 1–11).

Stimulating the VN produces a calmative effect on the parasympathetic nervous system through the production of the neurotransmitter acetylcholine (ACh). Production of ACh has the effect of slowing things down and balancing the "freeze, flight, fright" responses of the sympathetic nervous system. Conscious stimulation of the VN through Hatha Yoga practice, can literally allow access to inner calm on demand!

So, why is the above VN information important for yogis and peacemakers? As Yoga instructors and peacemakers, we often find ourselves in close personal contact with students or disputants who are experiencing feelings of grief or loss. Not only can close proximity to these kinds of feelings manifest in our own bodies, but they are also useful and necessary for us to be familiar with as tools to help our students and mediation participants. The VN stimulating exercises positively affect students' and disputants' symptoms of anger, depression, or anxiety. Among these symptoms may be tightness in the chest, a feeling of heaviness in the heart, or difficulty in breathing. If we only see grief as a purely emotional experience, without realizing the holistic body-mind implications, our abilities to help others or ourselves will be limited and perhaps misdirected.

Physical symptoms such as alterations in breathing, eating, sexual, and sleeping patterns, endocrine and immune function, rapid heart rate, as well as physical pain in the chest area, often accompany the grieving process. It should be noted that grieving can arise from the interruption or ending of a social relationship, including divorce, which ranks number two as a stress-producing experience on the scale of emotional trauma.

Recognition of grief goes far beyond viewing sorrow as the only emotional symptom of grieving. Additional symptoms include anxiety, anger, PTSD, and depression. Yoga therapists recommend that instead of treating grief as something to be gotten over or offering advice to the grieving, our focus needs to be on deep mindful listening. Listening that assures grievers that they are being heard on a compassionate human level, that their feelings of a dissolute sense of self and an involuntary mind-body-heart response to divorcing loss and attachment are normal.

Through compassionate and attentive listening, educative counseling, and Vagus tonal stimulation, we peacemakers can help others and ourselves to cross the body-mind bridge and detach from the causes of grief (Sausys, 2014, pp. 1–11). As peacemakers, when presented with the symptoms of grief in the context of a separation or divorce, we can listen wholeheartedly and reassure mediation participants that they are being heard. We can call a temporary halt to mediation proceedings and direct participants to trained mental health coaches, including Yoga therapists, for counseling and support.

Conclusion

As peacemakers, we can educate our mediation participants in grief self-care, which would include VN and parasympathetic edification, as well as helpful asana and pranayama exercises. We can share information about the fifth Yama, Aparigraha, one of the philosophical precepts found in the Yoga Sutras, for living a balanced and harmonious life. Aparigraha teaches us non-attachment to things, people, and events. It helps us to detach from restrictive memories, toxic relationships, and unhealthy ways of living. Aparigraha teaches us to be content in the present, eternal moment and situation, sometimes called the Eternal Now (Iyengar, 1979, pp. 37–38).

It is important for the reader to take away from the above discussion of brain science, mindfulness, and Yoga in terms of how these tools can be applied to mediators and the mediation process. What can mediators do with the concepts and tools discussed in this chapter?

Recommendations for mediators

- We learned that *hearing without listening* is a concept that mediators must observe within themselves as models of behavior for mediation participants as well as educating those in conflict to overcome if communication between participants is to be useful and conscious. Through modeling for and education of the conflicted, mediators can instruct participants to communicate with each other from the more intelligent prefrontal and receptive part of their brains and not the reactive fight, flight, freeze limbic portion. Such instruction is of inestimable value to mediators in helping to defuse the often highly charged emotions generated in marital dissolution.
- We discussed how utilizing the *yogic* tool of *stimulating the Vagus Nerve* through direct pressure and stretching of the torso (*asana or physical poses and pranayama breathing and energy movement exercises*) could have a calmative effect on the often raw emotions found in family conflict mediation. A mediator can learn for his or her own personal health benefit and teach disputants exercises such as *Ujjayi* and *Nadi Sodhana Pranayama*, breathing and energy exercises that help tone and calm the Vagus Nerve, soothe and cleanse the parasympathetic nervous system, and restore a feeling of peace and well-being to the practitioner. *Ujjayi* and *Nadi Sodhana* can be tools in the mediator's peacemaking toolkit for dealing with the frequent *Cortisol spikes* that arise in highly emotionally charged mediations. These tools help the mediator to lower the emotional charge in the mediation room and raise the emotional intelligence of participants, saving time, energy, money, and angst.
- Another mediator tool of importance is *mindful listening*. People going through the mediation divorce process have a major often-unmet need: to be heard and attentively listened to and acknowledged. A mediation participant's need to be heard is what brings him or her to the mediation process in the first place. By modeling mindful, focused,

and in-the-moment listening, a mediator can help participants to know when they are being reactive vs. receptive in their communication with a co-participant. Cultivating mindful listening in mediation participants is a tool that should not be forgotten by a mediator.

- Mediators may benefit from utilizing the *Meyers-Briggs Type Indicator* (MBTI) in their screening and assessment of mediation participants. The MBTI helps to reveal personality types and behaviors, and how participants' personalities differ from each other. An MBTI summary, which can be provided to mediators by mental health coaches or through the mediator's own testing and assessment of participants, is a tool that can help a mediator quickly to get a handle on the personalities they are dealing with and in framing a more efficient mediation strategy.
- Nonviolent Communication (NVC) seeks to eliminate words and actions in communication that foster guilt, shame, blame, humiliation, force, and threats. In utilizing NVC concepts as a tool, the mediator can help educate participants in private and joint meetings how to communicate more effectively and without the emotional baggage that elicits limbic and non-receptive responses from another disputant.
- A great tool for any mediator dealing with complex family emotions is the use of mental health professionals who can assist participants to be in the mindful present moment by processing their emotions that arise from the dead past of memory or imagined anxiety-fueled future. The use of mental health professionals is a tool that can help relieve the mediator of having to deal with recurrent and unprocessed emotions which can sidetrack the mediation process.

Note

1 This article has been adapted from chapter 4 of the book *Light on Peacemaking: A Guide to Appropriate Dispute Resolution and Mediating Family Conflict*. Business Expert Press, 2015. It is printed herein with the permission of the author and the publisher.

References

Adler, P.S. (2008) Eye of the storm leadership. Resourceful Internet Solutions, Inc. Retrieved from www.eyeofthestormleadership.com.

Baer, M. (2012) Mark Baer's Keynote speech given at the divorce expo in Detroit, Michigan on March 23. Retrieved from www.markbaeresq.com/Pasadena-Family-Law-Blog/2012/March/Mark-Baers-Keynote-Speech-Given-at-The-Divorce-E.aspx.

Bergland, C. (2013) The neurobiology of grace under pressure. *Psychology Today*. Retrieved from www.psychologytoday.com/blog/the-athletes-way/201302/the-neurobiology-grace-under-pressure.

Cloke, K. (2009) Bringing oxytocin into the room: Notes on the physiology of conflict. *Mediate.com*. Retrieved from www.mediate.com/articles/cloke8.cfm.

Iyengar, B.K.S. (1979) *Light on Yoga*. New York: Schocken Books.

Iyengar, B.K.S. (2002) *Light on the Yoga Sutras of Patanjali*. London: Thorsons.

Kabit-Zinn, Jon. (1996) Mindfulness meditation: What it is, what it isn't, and its role in health care medicine. In Y. Haruki, Y. Ishii & M. Susuki (eds) *Comparative and Psychological Study on Meditation* (pp. 161–170). The Hague, Netherlands: Eburon Publishers.

Krishnamurti, J. (1992a) *The Collected Works of J. Krishnamurti, Volume XV, 1964–65*. Dubuque, IA: Kendall/Hunt Publishing Company.

Krishnamurti, J. (1992b) *A Psychological Revolution*. Dubuque, IA: Kendall/Hunt Publishing Company.

Lao Tzu. (n.d.) *Daily Celebrations*. Retrieved from www.dailycelebrations.com/stillness.htm.

Sausys, A.S. (2014) Yoga for grief relief. *Yoga Therapy Today*, Summer, 20–22.

Siegel, D.J. (2010) *Mindsight: The New Science of Personal Transformation*. New York: Random House.

12

MINDFULNESS IN MEDIATION AS A RELATIONAL PRACTICE

Ran Kuttner

This chapter presents the case that what makes a mediation setting relational is the mediator's intention and parties' willingness to perceive the situation through a relational understanding of the Self or of matter, rather than the level to which relationships are involved. Relationality and relationships, for that matter, are very different concepts. What makes a context relational? This chapter suggests that the relationality of a situation is a derivation of and depends on the level of relational awareness that is present in the mediation room. Mindfulness is the manifestation of that relational awareness and mode of interaction. Such understanding of both mindfulness and of relationality, akin to how relationality is understood in various social constructionist writings, sets challenges to the mediator that this chapter will explore.

The relational paradigm

Filtering the world or human interactions through relational lenses requires a transformation of certain foundational assumptions that underlie Western philosophy. It was the Transformative Approach to mediation that first challenged the governing paradigm to understanding the human self and the goals of the mediation process in the name of a relational alternative. Bush and Folger (1994) claimed that transformation is needed from an individualistic view of the self, which is rooted in a vision of the individual as a separate being, autonomous and unconnected, to a relational view of the self, where "[i]ndividuals are seen as both separate and connected, both individuated and similar. They are viewed as being to some degree autonomous, self-aware, and self-interested but also to some degree connected, sensitive, and responsive to others" (Bush & Folger, 1994, p. 242). From the individualistic worldview, they argued, a certain vision—or "story" in their words—of the mediation process is derived, and the transformation involves the cultivation of a relational approach, a different story from what mediation is about, is told: the satisfactions of separately defined individuals' interests and needs should not be the mediator's vision for the process, but rather the transformation of parties' conflict interaction thorough experiencing both their separateness (empowerment of self) and their connectedness (recognition of others).

The narrative approach to mediation, as presented by Sara Cobb (1994) and by John Winslade and Gerald Monk (2000), offers a framework that also challenges foundational assumptions that underlie Western philosophy and challenges both mediators and parties to cultivate a less common view of the Self. Winslade and Monk (2000) also emphasize the fact that the manner in which the self is understood has a foundational effect on how mediators understand the mediation process and on their actions in practice. Following postmodern philosophy, they criticize the idea of the self as possessing a separate, permanent inner core, emphasizing that a shift is required from the parties' firm, fixed, and well-constructed view to a vision of the self as constructed within social and discursive patterns. "Problem-solving and interest-based approaches emphasize the individual as an independent, stable, unitary, self-motivating, and self-regulating identity," they write, while "through the postmodern lens, identity is not fixed, nor is it carried around by the individual largely unchanged from one context to another" (Winslade & Monk, 2000, pp. 44–45).

The questioning of the self as a separate, independent, and fixed entity is one tendency in current alternative dispute resolution (ADR) literature, upon which the transformative and narrative frameworks elaborate. This tendency should be seen in a larger context, as part of a transition in 20th-century thought at large, which involves ontological questioning of Aristotelian metaphysics and Cartesian philosophy regarding the human agent, the subject, or the self. Nietzsche, Heidegger, Wittgenstein, Foucault, and Derrida are prominent thinkers who suggested criticism on common understandings of the self. Phenomenology, Hermeneutics, and Post-Structuralism are central schools in the creation of the intellectual shift, each of them with its unique criticism of the governing Western underpinnings and common concept of "self".[1]

These revolutionary ideas affected all the sciences, and current schools of thought, that stem from more relational understandings of the self are prominent in almost every discipline, from the hard sciences (for example physics, biology) to the soft sciences (among others psychology, communication, political science and international relations). As this volume shows, there is cross-fertilization between the various disciplines and conflict resolution, and relational frameworks of mediation are influenced by the scholarship developed in these disciplines. What is important to note is that regardless of the version of relational worldview that is adopted, relational frameworks of mediation have well-grounded foundations that the mediator should embrace, or rather embody, a way of looking at the world and a way of reeducating oneself with regard to the idea of the self, from which one's mediation practice stems. As presented by the transformative approach and the narrative approach, relational approaches do not advocate for relationships, but for a transformation of worldview, or developing a way of understanding the self as a relational being.

The next section will present the Buddhist worldview, which underlies mindfulness theory and practices, and show how its foundations also challenge us in similar ways, though offering a third, differently nuanced vision of the self, or rather no-self. It is important to note that mindfulness has also caught on rapidly in recent decades, being part of the zeitgeist and complementing well the spirit of the time that seeks an alternative to the ego-centered vision of the separate individual and to the fragmentation and alienation of modern (and post-modern) times.[2] Emphasizing the relational premises, this paper will insist on equating the cultivation of mindfulness to actualization and embodiment of relational awareness in the mediation process, rather than focusing on how mindfulness helps separately situated individuals; it will thus focus on the relational foundations of mindfulness and the added values of mindfulness to the relationally driven mediator.

Mindfulness: a relational framework

As mentioned, mindfulness theory and practices have been integrated in recent decades into almost every discipline. In ADR scholarship, scholars have been adopting mindfulness into the theory and practice since 2002, when Harvard's Program on Negotiation held a symposium on *Mindfulness in the Law and ADR*, followed by a special section under the same title in the same year's issue of the *Harvard Negotiation Law Review*. Since then, vast scholarship has been published (Riskin, 2002, 2004, 2006, 2010; Peppet, 2002, 2004; Freshman et al., 2002; Bowling, 2003; Rock, 2005; Noble, 2005; Freshman, 2006, 2010; Kuttner, 2008, 2010a, 2010b, 2012) and workshops offered to train mediators to cultivate mindfulness for their own benefits and for the mediation setting.

Buddhist philosophy has as its starting point a view that what exists, the nature of matter, is not separately situated, distinct entities or objects, but rather a set of relations that comprise whatever emerges in a specific moment. According to Aristotelian premises, which underlie Western thinking, knowing an object demands knowledge of its "essence," its unalterably fixed and determined inner substance. According to the Buddhist worldview, on the other hand, the challenge is different, even opposite in its basic motivation: knowledge cannot be attained as long as an object's fixed and determined inner substance is sought; while the Western cognition seeks to grasp, delve into the core of something or someone in order to know it/him. The challenge according to the Buddhist philosophy and succeeding psychological perspective is to let go of any grasping or attachment to images of separately grasped entities or selves, outside the relations in which it takes part. A key term in understanding the Buddhist worldview is the term "dependent co-arising" (*pratityasamutpada*): any object—"self" included—is a product of causality, dependently co-arising with other objects that co-arise with it (Izutsu, 1977). According to the principle of dependent co-arising, any given situation is a set of connections and relations in which separate entities arise, entities that through a process of abstraction we grasp as objects, as having characteristics of continuous separate substances. Seeing entities as continuous, separate substances is an abstraction that results from observing a situation from an external perspective and from ignoring the process of dependent co-arising as it occurs in the moment. Illusive images of "Self" and "other" are thus created, abstracted from the immediate context in which they relationally arise. Thus, fragmented images of situations and of society, in which people and entities are designated as situated side by side, are formed, analyzed in separation from the set of relations that co-create the situation that should otherwise be holistically perceived, for example, as comprising the totality of relatings, or relatedness, in it.

The Buddhist practice of cultivating mindfulness is meant gradually to cultivate awareness of one's sensations, feelings, and thoughts as arising in relation to whatever comprises the moment, the felt sense of one's experience. Cultivation of mindfulness is at the same time the letting go of the images of non-relational entities, and the psychological tendency to form and hold to such illusive images of "things," one's and the other's selves included. The human psyche, the Buddhist philosophy tells us, attributes these characteristics because of the human need to arrange the world, enforcing order, and creating an illusory grasping of one's perceived reality (Rahula, 1959; Welwood, 2000). Cultivating mindfulness is the cultivation of the ability to reduce the need for or inclination toward firm, objectified reality, to lessen the tendency to anchor in firm images of oneself, of others, of objects. Cultivating mindfulness is the cultivation of awareness of the interrelated and ever-changing, or impermanent sense of whatever arises in the moment.

Scholarship that is close in spirit to the Buddhist worldview in current Western social thinking can be found among various social-constructionist scholars. Social constructionism emphasizes the socially created nature of social life; that our realities are shaped through our experiences and our interactions with others. Social constructionism questions the taken-for-granted assumption that the individual person, the individual action, or the individual "thought" is the obvious unit of analysis for those wanting to understand the social world, emphasizing instead patterns of interactions and relational processes out of which we construct our individuality. Gergen (2009) argues against the dominant way of thinking in the Western world, which is based on a conception of man as a bounded being. Relationships are no longer perceived as a phenomenon that may occur temporarily when two autonomous individuals converge; rather, relationship precedes the concept of the self, as from it and within it the self emerges:

> all intelligible action is born, sustained, and/or extinguished within the ongoing process of relationship. From this standpoint there is no isolated self or fully private experience. Rather we exist in a world of co-constitution. We are always already emerging from relationship.
>
> *(Gergen, 2009, p. xv)*[3]

It is important to note that dialogue, as understood by prominent thinkers (Buber, 1987 [1923], 2002 [1932]; Bakhtin, 1981 [1930]; Bohm, 2000 [1996]; Taylor, 1991), is a form of engagement in which the primacy of the individual is questioned and in which a relational realization of the self, consistent with that described above, is actualized (Kuttner, 2012). A relational approach that wishes to help embody dynamics that give primacy to the relational space rather than the individual's mind, and to cultivate dialogue, can gain from adopting mindfulness practices, practices directed toward cultivating relational awareness.

Challenges for mediation settings

Entrenchment in the firm sense of our images is, according to Buddhist philosophy, the source of human suffering—also interpersonal suffering in times of conflict with another—and this suffering can be transformed through the cultivation of mindfulness. It is the challenge of the mediator to help parties transform this suffering in practice, in the mediation process, to transform it to an increasing realization of the relationality that underlies their conflict interaction. This is a challenging journey from a well-constructed image of the situation that parties in conflict arrive with to the mediation, and an enormous challenge for the mediator. It is an enormous challenge not only because our social conventions still favor images of individuals, but moreover because in conflict, even more than any other daily state of affairs, people psychologically entrench in a firm perception of their situation, taking sides usually in opposition to others' perspectives and dismissing attempts to let additional, different perspectives, influence them. This is also the essence of positional bargaining: holding firmly to a solidified, well-constructed and unchanging view of the situation that each party pre-determined and fortified well prior to the mediation process.

A mindfulness-based, relational approach to conflict interaction offers a practice that assists parties (who take part and situate themselves, each one in a different part of the situation)—through meditation practices as well as other practices—to become co-partners, to be both mindful of their interdependence in the present moment and reflective of their relatedness, of their co-creation of meaning, whether they like it or not. As the next section shows, such an approach assists parties to partake in a dialogic interaction in which they coordinate meaning, synchronize their actions, and co-construct their understanding of their situation as well as its resolution. This is a gradual process of constructing their common dialogic space, within which their sense of self gets meaning and within which it continues to evolve, rather than on which it is being imposed.

Cultivating mindfulness, as suggested below, can be manifested by helping disputants transform their adversity to a more *collaborative* state of mind and state of affairs. Collaboration, as this chapter claims, does not stand only for the more common understanding within an individualistically oriented framework of collaborative negotiation and mediation, but stands for the potential to cultivate relational awareness and a dialogic mindset and approach.

Within the more common, individualistic tradition, which focuses on the individual as the primary unit for analysis and transformation, the benefits of mindfulness for conflict transformation have been mainly presented in ADR scholarship as baring the potential of aiding the *individual* in various ways: being less distracted and scattered while increasing awareness and attention to present moment occurrences, increased ability to identify one's own habitual behaviors, emotional regulation, developing a non-judgmental stance towards others' perceptions as well as one's own, increasing behavioral, cognitive and emotional awareness of oneself and of others, etc. However, if cultivating mindfulness is understood as the cultivation of relational awareness, it stands also for the development of central interpersonal—or rather dialogical—qualities and skills that the mediator should embody and help disputants gradually embody in the mediational space. In fact, it is important to note that differentiating between individualistically serving and relationally serving qualities of mindfulness is erroneous, as those internally oriented are aimed at developing awareness of the emptiness, illusory sense of a substantial, firm core that projects itself on the situation rather than co-arising within it, and suggest a reconsideration of the internal–external divide altogether.[4]

The individualistically serving qualities thus should also serve the cultivation of relational awareness. However, within an individualistically oriented climate, and in particular in conflict dynamics that reinforce the distinctiveness and party-ness, the more relationally oriented qualities can be easily pushed to the end of the mediator's to-do list in the mediation process. It is thus advised that they are brought back to the forefront. It is advised that the mediator follows the dictum that "dialogue is a conversation with a center, not with sides" (Isaacs, 1999, p. 19), and thus bring more awareness to the joint space, the unit of interaction, the ongoing process of co-arising in the present moment prior to its bifurcation into separately situated parties that are designated, analyzed and addressed in separation of their joint action.

In other words, it is for the mediator to be mindful and help participants gradually cultivate mindfulness, awareness of their relatedness and of moments in which they withdraw from relationality and "take sides," thus developing a different lens for seeing the interpersonal realm and for performing in it. The following is a short list of mindfulness qualities that the mediator who wishes to cultivate a relational awareness and relational mediation space should focus on both developing in oneself and helping parties cultivate during the mediation process.

Presence of mind

A significant feature of the Buddhist practice is the cultivation of the ability to have bare attention to all that occurs and arises in the present moment and be aware of moment-to-moment changes. Such awareness involves an intense focus on occurrences in the present moment, intense and even radical because it manifests a realization of the occurrences as they unfold, dependently co-arise right here, right now. Being in the present moment involves lessening cravings for previously constructed images of the situation or of desired future outcomes to which attachment is developed in the psyche, to which one clings. Being present is at the same time the skill of refraining from withdrawing into the being-entity, the knower, the self behind the occurrences in the present moment, and observing the situation from afar.

Thus understood, letting go of the past does not mean giving up on things and looking ahead to the future instead, but means being non-attached to the past qua past. It means allowing the past to emerge within the situation—right here, right now—by being aware that it, "the past," is also relationally arising in the present.

The mediator's focus is on the dynamics of the moment-to-moment interaction between the parties, and the concern of a mediator, when a party raises issues regarding the past, is to be aware of the context and issues with which it co-arises in the present. The mediator who helps disputants cultivate presence of mind helps them develop openness to new possibilities, trusting the unfolding of the process, aware of the impermanent nature of images clung to, and allowing new situations to co-arise. Such mediators also help parties be aware of moments when their mind is constructing non-contextual images—for example, wandering and not present—and to make a conscious effort in these moments to let go of these constructions and return to the relational dynamics and present-moment unfolding instead. If the focus is on the moment-to-moment interaction, relational awareness is developed, thus assisting the parties to micro-focus on what is happening in a manner exceeding the representation of "one party" and the "other party"; the parties remain focused on the situation as it arises, or "centered"—the center being no longer the center of the self, but of the common space.

Right action

In one of his central teachings, known as the Four Noble Truths, the Buddha teaches the way that one should practice in order to attain the cessation of suffering and dis-ease. The fourth Noble Truth, also known as "the Eightfold Path," is composed of eight different awarenesses that each practitioner should incorporate into his daily life: Right Understanding (*Samma ditthi*), Right Thought (*Samma sankappa*), Right Speech (*Samma vaca*), Right Action (*Samma kammanta*), Right Livelihood (*Samma ajiva*), Right Effort (*Samma vayama*), Right Mindfulness (*Samma sati*), and Right Concentration (*Samma Samadhi*).[5] The word "*right*" (Sanskrit *Sayag*; Pali: *Samma*) repeated in all eight emphases of the eightfold path, which in certain translations is translated into "wholesome," bares a different meaning from the common use of "right." The word "*samma*" has the prefix "sam," which means "to be with," accurately tuned, in a wholesome way. In other words, right action means acting *with* the acted upon with no sense of separate self. Bringing the quality of "right" to every category of daily life calls for moment-to-moment realization of dependent co-arising in every deed (action, speech, etc.), as well as mentally (understanding, thought, etc.). Very much like in the martial arts, practicing right action is the embodiment of an action that is tuned to the other to the point that one does not enforce oneself and act with effort, but rather one's action is a gentle continuation and unfolding of the action of another.

The notion of right action is close in spirit to the social-constructionist idea of coordinated action: whether individuals are together or physically alone, their actions are coordinated. Relationships are processes from which individuals cannot be separated. Thoughts, intentions, experiences, memory, creativity—these are kinds of traits that we usually associate with individual consciousness, but are in fact expressions of our relational existence. As Storch and Shotter (2013) write:

> This approach … leads us into a kind of fluid, process thinking, a shift from thinking of events as occurring between things and beings existing as separate entities prior to their inter-action, to events occurring within a continuously unfolding, holistic but stranded

> flow of events ... Thus rather than inter-actions, we become involved in intra-actions, activities in which we find things happening to us as much as we make things happen in our surroundings.
>
> *(Storch & Shotter, 2013, p. 3)*

Intra-action is a joint action, from within a dialogic situation, and this is something done spontaneously, bodily. Gergen (2009) emphasizes the need to coordinate action and to coordinate rhythm, developing smooth and reiterating patterns of interchange—a dance in which we move harmoniously together. "Without the capacity to coordinate in this way, our actions are rendered unintelligible" (Gergen, 2009, p. 49). It is for the mediator to help parties develop awareness of the relational manner in which each person's moves help constitute those of the other person, how their actions are coordinated and how they make meaning together, or how meaning emerges among them. The mediator's focus is less on personal autonomy and rather on participants' ability to fine tune, to synchronize, and have more constructive inter- and intra-actions.

Right speech

With right understanding in mind, right speech can be understood to mean the realization of speech made from within the common dialogic space. Unlike a picture of a self who brings into the conversation firm positions, insights, notions and pre-suppositions—input from the pre-negotiation preparation or from past memories one clings to or future outcomes one craves for—the quality of *right speech* allows parties to realize the elusive and deluded state of grasping and clinging to independent and firm concepts or notions that encompass separately held, well-constructed meaning. The quality of *right speech* is particularly important, as speech is often used to isolate, discriminate, and form permanent, independent non-contextual meanings. Thus, speech used unwisely contributes to the formation of "party-ness" and to development of the dis-ease of a non-relational mindset. By cultivating mindfulness and right speech, the mediator and participants can let go of the illusive "selfhood" of concepts and understandings, thus being conceptual proliferation of the separately held self and understandings. The fixed objectified self, as well as reality, is manifested in the fixed definition of an utterance.

The notion of right speech is close in spirit to the social-constructionist notion of coordinated meaning, Gergen's (1999) idea that meaning emerges only through and within relatedness, through interacting. Meaning is not the possession of individuals, of separate persons, but rather "an emergent property of coordinated action" (Gergen, 1999, p. 145). The social-constructionist project is to remove meaning from the head of the individual, and locate it within the ways in which people go on together (Gergen, 1999). Social understanding, Gergen (1999) explains, is not a matter of penetrating the privacy of the other's subjectivity, but rather a relational achievement that depends on coordinating action. In dialogue, meaning is perceived to be a joint process and emergent from the interaction; the emphasis on self-expression, valuing the voicing of inner voices that define oneself, is questioned (Gergen et al., 2001) and revisited through right speech. Right speech puts high in the list of emphases the joint process of meaning making rather than the value of self-expression. Awareness of the unfolding coordination of meaning and awareness of dynamics are more of value for learning about oneself than assertion of inner voice. My needs, my interests, my positions, my fears, and my sensations—awareness of the manner in which they relationally co-arise in the present moment—is the focus of the relationally oriented mediator, keeping in mind that "[w]hen any musical phrase is performed, it shapes the next phrase" (Balachandra et al., 2005, p. 428). Within the framework of the Buddhist philosophy and its understanding of mindfulness and right speech, the next phrase is co-arising with that musical phrase and their relationality is what the mediator and parties should be mindful of. The mediator's role is to help parties become partners, to shift from talking and thinking about the world to what Shotter calls withness-thinking, being mindful of the unfolding of meaning and affecting the flow of processes from within our living involvement with them, aware of how abstractions are born out of concrete engagements and only within them make sense (Shotter, 2006). From a relational standpoint, the mediator ought to help parties be mindful of the process of relating itself and of how our sense of who we are and our understanding of conflicting situations co-arise within situations, together with our perceived "other."

Conclusion

A relational approach to mediation should always come back to the foundational premises that underlie its understanding of relationality; a mindful-based relational approach sees the self as co-arising within interactions, unfolding in the here and now and aware of both one's coordinated action in the dialogic space and of withdrawal to preconceived images—pre-scripted, firm understandings of a situation—that the human mind tends to cling to. The challenge of cultivating mindfulness in conflict interaction is the challenge to partake in the continuous relational unfolding of the present moment while letting go of attachment to those securing images. The mediator focuses on helping participants in the mediation process to be mindful of the unfolding present moment, to synchronize and coordinate their actions, and to agree to make meaning together through coordinated, right speech. Mindfulness practices, alongside other practices that scholars have developed, can help cultivate these relational qualities. Cultivation of mindfulness and relational awareness is at the same time cultivation of deep listening, openness to whatever arises with a non-judgmental mind, with no biased perspective—taking or craving for certain, particular outcomes. It assists participants to develop healthy irony toward their standpoints and understandings, to question previously held beliefs, and to evolve curiously and dialogically in and through their present-moment intra-action. A mindfulness-based relational approach puts focus on the quality of interaction among participants; it invites participants to cultivate awareness of the almost automatic process of withdrawing to the separate space where one feels secure and in control, and where a series of monologues takes the place of the dialogue. It invites participants to come back, again and again, to the vulnerable, ever-changing, dialogic space, where from a relational point of view the true relationality is performed.

Notes

1 For an elaborated description of this evolvement in 20th-century thought see Kuttner, 2012, in particular part 1.

2 Moreover, it is important to note that Buddhist philosophy—which is sometimes disregarded when mindfulness practices are implemented (thus not applying the lesson that Bush & Folger and Winslade & Monk also teach us, that a radical change in mindset and in the vision of the self is needed)—is not only part of the zeitgeist but to a large extent a foundational force that boosted the tendency to question the Aristotelian-Cartesian vision of the self in the late 19th century and the early part of the 20th century: Nietzsche's philosophy with its criticism of the self had a tremendous effect on this evolution of Western thought, and he was heavily influenced by Schopenhauer's Eastern-oriented philosophy.

3 For more comparison between social constructionism and Buddhism see Gergen & Hosking, 2006; Hosking, 2012.
4 Emptiness (*sunyata*) is a key term in Buddhist thinking that complements the notion of *dependent co-arising*. Emptiness of self conveys the idea that nothing exists independently, having an internal, substantial and permanent nature of its own; the view of objects with an internal core or inner nature (*svabhava*) is replaced by a view that sees separate entities as products of causality or dependency on other things to which they stand in relation (Garfield, 1994; Hoffman, 1980; Kasulis, 1981).
5 As translated by Rahula, 1959, p. 45.

References

Bakhtin, M. (1981 [1930]). *The Dialogic Imagination*. Austin, TX: University of Texas Press.

Balachandra, L., Barrett, F., Bellman, H., Fisher, C. & Susskind, L. (2005) Improvisation and mediation: Balancing acts. *Negotiation Journal*, 21(4): 425–434.

Bohm, D. (2000 [1996]). *On Dialogue*. London and New York: Routledge.

Bowling, D. (2003) Mindfulness meditation and mediation: When the transcendent meets the familiar. In D. Bowling & D. Hoffman (eds) *Bringing Peace into the Room: How the Personal Qualities of the Mediator Impact the Process of Conflict Resolution* (pp. 13–49). San Francisco, CA: Jossey-Bass.

Buber, M. (1987 [1923]). *I and Thou*. New York: Macmillan.

Buber, M. (2002 [1932]). *Dialogue. In Between Man and Man*. New York: Routledge.

Bush, R.A.B. & Folger, J.P. (1994) *The Promise of Mediation: Responding to Conflict through Empowerment and Recognition*. San Francisco, CA: Jossey-Bass.

Cobb, S. (1994) A narrative perspective on mediation: Toward the materialization of the "storytelling" metaphor. In J.P. Folger & T.S. Jones (eds) *New Directions in Mediation: Communication Research and Perspectives* (pp. 48–63). Thousand Oaks, CA: Sage.

Freshman, C. (2006) Identity, beliefs, emotion, and negotiation success. In M. Moffitt & R. Bordone (eds) *The Handbook of Dispute Resolution* (pp. 99–117). San Francisco, CA: Jossey-Bass and the Program on Negotiation at Harvard Law School.

Freshman, C. (2010) Yes, and: Core concerns, internal mindfulness, and external mindfulness for emotional balance, lie detecting, and successful negotiation. *Nevada Law Journal*, 10(2): 365–392.

Freshman, C., Hayes, A. & Feldman, G. (2002) Adapting mediation to promote negotiation success: A guide to varieties and scientific support. *Harvard Negotiation Law Review*, 7(1): 67–81.

Garfield, J. (1994) The emptiness of emptiness: Why did nagarjuna start with causation? *Philosophy East & West*, 44(2): 219–250.

Gergen, K. (1999) Dialogic potentials. In K. Gergen, *An Invitation to Social Construction* (pp. 142–166). Thousand Oaks, CA: Sage.

Gergen, K.J. (2009) *Relational Being: Beyond Self and Community*. New York: Oxford University Press.

Gergen, K.J. & Hosking, D.M. (2006) If you meet social construction along the road: A dialogue with Buddhism. In M.G.T. Kwee, K.J. Gergen & F. Koshikawa (eds) *Horizons in Buddhist Psychology* (pp. 299–314). Chagrin Falls, OH: Taos Institute Publication.

Gergen, K.J., McNamee, S. & Barrett, F. (2001) Toward a vocabulary of transformative dialogue. *International Journal of Public Administration*, 24(7–8): 697–707.

Hoffman, Y. (1980) *The Idea of Self—East and West*. Calcutta, India: Firma Klm Private Ltd.

Hosking, D.M. (2012) Organising a Buddhist way. In P. Case, H. Hopfl & H. Letice (eds) *Beliefs and Organization* (pp. 66–89). London: Palgrave Macmillan. Retrieved from www.relational-constructionism.org/media/case%20hopfle%20%20letice%20final.pdf.

Isaacs, W. (1999) *Dialogue and the Art of Thinking Together*. New York: Random House.

Izutsu, T. (1977) *Toward a Philosophy of Zen Buddhism*. Tehran, Iran: Imperial Iranian Academy of Philosophy.

Kasulis, T.P. (1981) *Zen Action, Zen Person*. Honolulu, HI: The University Press of Hawaii.

Kuttner, R. (2008) Wisdom cultivated through dialogue. *Negotiation Journal*, 24(1): 101–112.

Kuttner, R. (2010a). What does it mean to do the right thing. *Nevada Law Journal*, 10(2): 407–432.

Kuttner, R. (2010b). From adversity to relationality: A Buddhist-oriented relational view of integrative negotiation and mediation. *Ohio State Journal on Dispute Resolution*, 25(4): 931–974.

Kuttner, R. (2012) Cultivating dialogue: From fragmentation to relationality in conflict interaction. *Negotiation Journal*, 28(3): 315–335.
Noble, B. (2005) Meditation and mediation. *Family Court Review*, 43(2): 295–302.
Peppet, S. (2002) Can saints negotiate? A brief introduction to the problems of perfect ethics in bargaining. *Harvard Negotiation Law Review*, 7(1): 83–96.
Peppet, S. (2004) Mindfulness in the law and alternative dispute resolution. In C. Menkel-Meadow & M. Wheeler (eds) *What's Fair* (pp. 440–453). San Francisco, CA: Jossey-Bass.
Rahula, W. (1959) *What the Buddha Taught*. London: Oneworld.
Riskin, L. (2002) The contemplative lawyer: On the potential contribution of mindfulness meditation to law students, lawyers, and their clients. *Harvard Negotiation Law Review*, 7(1): 1–67.
Riskin, L. (2004) Mindfulness: Foundational training for dispute resolution. *Journal of Legal Education*, 54 (1): 79–90.
Riskin, L. (2006) Knowing yourself: Mindfulness. In A.K. Schneider & C. Honeyman (eds) *The Negotiator's Fieldbook* (pp. 239–250). ABA Section of Dispute Resolution.
Riskin, L. (2010) Further beyond reason: Emotions, the core concerns, and mindfulness in negotiation. *Nevada Law Journal*, 10(2): 289–337.
Rock, E.M. (2005) Mindfulness meditation, the cultivation of awareness, mediator neutrality, and the possibility of justice. *Cardozo Journal of Conflict Resolution*, 6(2): 347–365.
Shotter, J. (2006) Understanding process from within: An argument for "withness"-thinking. *Organization Studies*, 27(4): 585–604.
Storch, J. & Shotter, J. (2013) "Good enough," "imperfect," or situated leadership: Developing and sustaining poised resourcefulness within an organization of practitioner-consultants. *International Journal of Collaborative Practice*, 4(1): 1–19.
Taylor, C. (1991) The dialogic self. In D. Hilly, J. Bohman & R. Shusterman (eds) *The Interpretive Turn: Philosophy, Science, Culture* (pp. 304–314). Ithaca, NY: Cornell University Press.
Welwood, J. (2000) *Toward a Psychology of Awakening: Buddhism, Psychotherapy, and the Path of Personal and Spiritual Transformation*. Boston, MA: Shambahla
Winslade, J. & Monk, G. (2000) *Narrative Mediation: A New Approach to Conflict Resolution*. San Francisco, CA: Jossey-Bass.

13

MEDIATION AND COLLABORATION WITH MULTIPLE DISCIPLINES

The implementation of systemic theory in alternative dispute resolution

Tommie V. Boyd and Randy Heller

> Being a peacemaker is not defined by what role one plays in helping families but by how one provides reconciliation and harmony in interactions with clients, colleagues, opposing parties, children ... judges, court staff, witnesses, experts, and many others.
>
> *(Mosten, 2009, p. 492)*

Casualties of divorce

Statistics in the United States as of 2015 indicate that nearly 40–50 percent of couples will divorce (American Psychological Association, 2016), and that approximately 75 percent of all children born into cohabitating unions will experience the process of the dissolution of their parents' relationship. The termination of such relationships can take a tremendous toll on adults and children alike. These circumstances often increase already existing inter-parental conflict, which directly affects the emotional well-being of each partner and the children (Kazdin, 2000, p. 4128).

Challenges facing families in divorce

When relationships break down, there commonly is an inability between individuals to express emotions, communicate, and solve problems effectively. Couples who experience these challenges during their marriage oftentimes find these tasks are generally more trying during the divorce process and beyond. Divorcing couples must make decisions related to financial matters as well as the sharing, caring for, and co-parenting of their children. Unfortunately, they may not have the skills or emotional readiness to think clearly and make these choices in a thoughtful and amicable way. The emotive responses to separation and divorce can create a less than supportive atmosphere for either spouse and for the children.

Research indicates couples and families going through divorce may experience a wide range of reactions that often last and intensify in the years following the final dissolution of marriage (Lee, 2006). Many of the beliefs that the entire system held to be true about their future as a family are altered in the moment of the final dissolution. Data also suggests that the first year following a divorce may be the most difficult for the family as they move through the transition and reorganization of their family system (Ahrons, 2004, 2007; Kelly, 2007). People going through divorce often endure feelings of anger, guilt, shame, betrayal, loss, isolation, anxiety, sadness, and fear, as well as a multitude of experiences they may not even be aware of. Members of the couple may grieve the loss of a dream, and children typically experience a multitude of emotions as the family they once knew changes its structure and relationships.

Divorce options: litigation vs. ADR

Litigation: the divorce war

When divorcing couples go through litigation, there appears to be an unspoken expectation that the fight in court will avenge all "wrongs" that have been cast upon them, and in doing so, alleviate their negative reactions; unfortunately, it does not. The litigation process, particularly in states where there is no-fault divorce, fails to address the emotional issues stemming from the circumstances that have led up to a divorce. During this process, the financial, emotional, and relational fallout can be so severe that families become casualties of a divorce war, and everyone is shattered at the end of a "lose-lose" process.

Couples who enter the litigation process rely on judicial systems to provide them with guidance while tenuously navigating such issues. Increasingly, judicial systems are turning to "peace-makers" (Mosten, 2009) who engage in a process of alternative dispute resolution (ADR) and utilize interventions to facilitate dialogue between divorcing couples and co-parents to assist them in the process of learning to have different kinds of conversations. In doing so, they are able to lead people to resolve issues in a different way that will directly affect their children and the future of the entire family system. Family mediation can address the needs of families and still offer self-determination and mutually satisfying decisions that may occur outside the court system.

A better way to dissolution: alternative dispute resolution

Mediation

Mediation is a process of ADR, which is on a continuum of options for people desiring to settle disputes outside a litigated court proceeding. In mediation, a specially trained and possibly certified mediator, who is mutually selected by both parties, is a neutral party who will assist the individuals to negotiate their issues toward resolution. Parties can choose to participate in mediation with or without representation by attorneys. A mediator may be a lawyer or non-lawyer, retired judge, or other professional who works together with the participants (and possibly their attorneys) to hear the merits of the issues at hand. Many mediators are private mediators who work outside the courts.

Family mediation

Family mediation is a form of ADR that is geared toward helping couples and their families resolve their marital disputes amicably by taking into consideration the emotional, relational, and financial estate (Emery & Emery, 2008; Mosten, 2009; Tesler, 2008; Ver Steegh, 2008; Webb, 2008). In doing so, members of a couple can discover a better way to converse, minimize conflict, resolve problems, share childrearing responsibilities, and begin to release their destructive emotions and heal.

Family mediators facilitate communication and problem solving by brainstorming and generating options to solve disputes in a non-adversarial process, while taking into consideration each person's needs and interests in a way that will benefit everyone. This type of mediation can be utilized as a beneficial option in diverse relationships with a variety of issues, and can help people from different cultures, and racial and ethnic backgrounds. It can also be a viable option for low- or high-conflict couples. To this end, it is considered common and good practice to remind participants of the following acronym to set the context not only for the agenda, but also for the approach to a successful mediation. When facilitating mediations, it is a good idea to have all parties involved focus on PEACE—Parenting plans, Equitable distribution, Alimony, Child support, and Everything else.

Family mediation from a systemic lens

By definition of their role as neutral facilitators, mediators cannot provide legal advice or therapy. Because of this, the engagement of a family therapist, clinical psychologist, social worker or other mental health professional (MHP) can aid families to help make the outcomes of mediation very successful.

A team approach: mental health professionals and family law

Given our extensive educational background, knowledge and experience in both Mental Health Counseling and Marriage and Family Therapy, we will discuss in detail the various roles of the MHP that can be beneficial to facilitating resolution in conflict and dispute resolution by either working specifically as a mediator, or working in conjunction with a mediator in a multitude of roles to facilitate an amicable resolution.

In many situations, an MHP will take part in what may be called therapeutic mediation, utilizing their clinical skills in conjunction with their education, and training in family systems, child development, and family dynamics to help regulate emotions, facilitate communication, explore options, and focus on issues related to childrearing. An MHP may also collaborate with an attorney and/or a financial professional, to help individuals understand the many underlying causes stifling their ability to come to terms, and guide them to identify what would need to be in place for them to be able to do so. MHPs can also assist divorcing parents to understand the developmental ages and stages that children go through in an effort to support them in the creation of the most viable time-share agreements and parenting plan. Although there may be multiple disciplines working together to assist these families, these processes are client centered and encourage participants to make their own decisions, while promoting negotiation, communication, flexibility, and creativity.

For the purposes of this handbook, this chapter will focus on the ways in which MHPs, working as mediators, in conjunction with mediators, or in various ancillary roles, can assist individuals and couples to move beyond their destructive and oftentimes paralyzing emotions, conflict, and difficulties. This may enable individuals in relationships to discover and tap into their strengths, and settle their disputes in harmonious ways.

Co-parenting: coming together in the midst of differences

In our introduction to this chapter, we pointed out how the dynamics inherent in marital discord that lead to divorce typically render individuals unable to find common ground that would allow them to readily work together and move beyond the obstacles that make termination so arduous. In order to do so, one must have the tenacity to open their minds to another's perspective. Due to the circumstances that preceded the marital injury, negotiation is quite challenging, position based, and adversarial. Effective conciliation is based on an understanding of another's needs and interests combined with a willingness to contribute to that person's expressed desires. This typically does not occur in a failing marriage, and is even less likely to naturally occur during the divorce process when there is anger, distrust, betrayal and hurt involved. In this regard, settling disputes and coming to mutual agreement requires the guidance of people who are specifically trained to understand what is beneath the surface of these feelings and behaviors, as they facilitate an actual appreciation of alternative perspectives. Doing so can facilitate the discovery of solutions that are in the best interest of the entire family and sustainable over time. Ascertaining these solutions might also aid people in finding ways to work together to raise their children to be well functioning adults.

When parents part, they are required by the court to develop a plan for co-parenting, as well as a time-sharing schedule that specifies the required choices and tasks associated with the upbringing of their children. This highly detailed plan outlines everything from how parental responsibility and decision making will be shared, as well as what days and times children will spend with each parent. Additionally the issues that require resolve are related to matters such as health care, school attendance, extracurricular activities, and even religious affiliations. Determinations will also be made regarding the methods and technologies that the parents will use to communicate with their children and each other.

Whose best interest? How is that decided?

Many parents who are not relating well to one another have significant variances in their ideas about what is in the best interest of their children. In these circumstances, a therapist may be called in to assist and help parents make appropriate decisions about raising their children and co-parenting. Additionally, they may be called into conduct therapy with the children and the family prior to mediation, to assist them in communicating their feelings, needs, and desires in a way that they can be heard and understood.

Given that MHPs are well versed in child development, they have the unique ability to provide psychoeducation to parents as well as to assist professionals regarding the needs of children transitioning though divorce. Therapists can meet with parents and their children, either separately or together, to assess their needs and develop action plans to address any challenges that are being experienced. In instances where parents cannot put their resentments aside and act to create a smooth transition for their children, a Guardian ad Litem might be brought onto the case. Guardians ad litem are often MHPs or attorneys who are specially trained to be child advocates. Guardians will consult with MHPs and can attend mediations to provide their input about what is in the best interest of the family, and most importantly the needs of children. A Parent Coordinator (PC), who is also specially trained, is typically a licensed MHP and certified mediator who may also be brought onto a case when parents cannot amicably co-parent. PCs combine all of their knowledge, skills, and abilities to assist parents in the successful implementation and follow-through of their parenting plan. Clinicians working in collaboration with professionals of other disciplines can consult with attorneys, parenting coordinators and guardians ad litem (given the appropriate waivers of confidentiality) regarding information about how they can intervene to help these families to adapt during this potentially tumultuous time. This collaboration can be invaluable as experts from varying disciplines combine their knowledge and skills.

A parent coordinator, who is typically a licensed MHP and certified mediator, may combine all of their knowledge, skills, and abilities to assist parents in the successful follow-through of their plan and co-parenting of their children.

Ages and stages: what divorcing parents need to know

Clearly, MHPs are a necessary resource to educate not only parents, but also all other professionals involved in these children's lives about the anticipatory challenges and changes these children may face regarding their parents' divorce. At various developmental stages there are important things for parents to attend to in order to ensure that children can adapt to the divorce in the best way possible.

Many questions arise about the frequency of contact that children need and the amount of nights away from parents that children can tolerate during the earliest stages of development. According to Strasheim (2002), from birth to 18 months, children are developing their ability to trust. Strasheim's (2002) article outlining the effects of divorce by developmental stages indicates that a significant change in a child's environment, routine, and/or caregiving can disrupt trust because children of this age cannot articulate their distress; therfore they will show signs and symptoms of it. They are sensitive to conflict, sadness, and neglect, and may develop insecurities if their immediate needs are not consistently met (Strasheim, 2002). Consistency and stability are essential at this time.

Children between 18 months and three years are becoming verbal, but are still vulnerable to changes in their environment. Strasheim (2002) goes on to further describe how children at this age are beginning to explore their world, yet still must be confident that they have the security of their caretaker's presence and their environment to return to. They are still predominantly nonverbal, so parents must be attuned to the changes that are taking place (Strasheim, 2002). Since children require more routine and consistency at this time, they may begin to regress from accomplished developmental tasks, act out, and pull away.

From three to five years old, children are becoming more verbal. They also have a form of egocentrism and "magical thinking" that leads them to believe that everything that happens is because of them (Strasheim, 2002). They may begin to fear and articulate that the divorce is their fault and believe that the parent who moves out of the home will be abandoning them and gone forever. These children require continued reassurance. They may feel distressed by the immense changes to their world.

It is suggested in the research that children of this age have frequent daily contact with both parents, and that their adjustment to nights away will really be dependent on how well the mother adjusts (Pruett, 2011). It is also suggested by Pruett (2011) that during separation and divorce, younger children under age four who spend more overnight time with their fathers adjust better and form closer bonds with their fathers.

Between six and nine years old, children are concerned with their whole family being together (Strasheim, 2002). They will miss the other parent and feel responsible for the parent who they view is suffering. They may even believe that they must take sides and display loyalty for one parent. It is essential at this time that they know they can and should love both parents. They may have very strong feelings of sadness, anger, guilt, and/or loneliness. Parents and school personnel may also see these children regressing and acting out. It is important to let children know that although they are missed when they are with the other parent, the at home parent is managing fine.

Between 9–12 years old, children continue to feel torn between their parents. Their anger may be directed at one parent or the other for causing the situation, and they may feel ashamed or embarrassed about the divorce. Parents can help by normalizing these feelings and pointing to others who are managing in similar circumstances.

When children advance into adolescence, they are beginning to develop their own sexual and relational identity. Additionally, they are preparing to leave home and may feel anxiety about that, as well as leaving the parent they are concerned about. They may be insecure about the events of the future and how their parents will handle things, relationally and financially. The may experience resentment that they must "deal with this" at all. These children need to know that there is hope for a positive future for all.

Examples: out beyond right and wrong are the children

Consider a case where a couple has been in such deep conflict in front of their young children throughout the years that as the children develop, they continually believe that they must step in, protect the seemingly "weaker" of the two, align with one and alienate the other parent. In a situation such as this, an MHP may be called in to work with the children and/or the family to enable the children to learn that they have the right to love and be loved by both of their parents. In this safe therapeutic arena, they are given the opportunity to express their feelings, to honor and use their voice, and to be children in the midst of a tumultuous time in their lives. The parents will also be offered psychoeducation to learn how to provide their children with the security that they need at this time, along with the opportunity to love both of their parents.

There are also circumstances where parents decide to sever their relationship subsequent to a baby being born. Often, mothers think they are the only ones who can adequately care for their child at this time. A parenting coordinator might be called into this case to assist the parents in developing and implementing a time-share schedule that allows both parents to adapt to meeting the needs of their baby.

Contemplate a case where one parent leaves the family home in an attempt to protect their children because they believe that the conflict is so severe that it is damaging, and does so without much of an explanation because they do not want to denigrate the other parent. This parent may be viewed by the child as the one who abandons them, does not love them or care about them enough to stay, and ultimately the child aligns with the other parent. In this type of a case, an MHP could be called in to help the parent explain to the children in an age-appropriate and effective way what led them to act in the way that they did, all the while being most concerned about their children's well-being.

We may come across parents who are vying for their children's affection, as well as attempting to gain some sense of power and control and undermine another—one being the *good parent*, and the other the *responsible one*. This may also lead to a child not being certain whose side to be on, and who to love. In many cases, each parent perceives that they are the more reliable, the better, or the more effective parent, and that the children would be best off if they had them most of the time, made the majority of decisions regarding them, and allowed the children merely to visit with the other parent. Additionally, in extreme cases where there may be the suggestion or implication of abuse, neglect, or alienation being encouraged on the part of one parent toward the other, a guardian ad litem could be requested to ensure that circumstances are handled properly and appropriate interventions are taken.

Consider situations where there are new significant others, spouses, and even additional children from outside the initial parent dyad. An MHP could be quite useful assisting in the blending of families, and co-parenting of children and stepchildren. Additionally, these new conditions can create and trigger many emotions that were unanticipated and may stifle effective communication and sound decision making. MHPs can assist in facilitating the regulation of these emotions and the resolution of feelings that arise from these triggers.

MHPs may also be included in mediations to provide directions and make recommendations, so that parents can make the best informed decisions. These professionals, however, cannot function as a mediator at the same time.

A situation might also arise in mediation where one party thinks that the offers for settlement and resolution are equitable and reasonable, while the other party does not agree. After consultation with an MHP, it may become apparent that what is preventing a person from settling on what seems fair, is that person's anger and resentment about the surrounding issues that led to the divorce, and their feelings and beliefs that "nothing about this situation is fair." These intense emotions could thwart an individual's ability to think logically, and come to a consensus. An MHP may be able to help parties understand and manage those emotions so that they can think more logically and come to a degree of acceptance of what is not in their control.

Oftentimes we also may encounter that certain individuals are more ready than others to end their marriage or relationship. In this circumstance, fear of the unknown, or sadness about their reality, renders them unable to let go and move forward. An MHP may be able to help them to become aware of that and ultimately find ways to relate to the circumstances differently.

Also in dependency mediation, the MHP is often sought out when substance abuse may be an issue and parents are losing the children and setting up alternative arrangements for children to live with others while they enter treatment, or if the children need an alternative environment to ensure their safety and security. MHPs may be called in to assist in making decisions that are in the best interest of the child(ren). However, these professionals cannot function as a mediator at the same time.

The presence of an MHP in any or all of these situations may empower and enable people to make decisions and act in a way that is less reflective of their pain and wounds, as well as their beliefs about right and wrong. They may come to develop more hope and believe in the possibilities for their future.

The integration of systems theory as a basis for collaboration and cooperation

Constance Ahrons (1994) drew from the existing research on children in divorce (Hetherington & Kelly, 2002; Wallerstein et al., 2002), and conducted a longitudinal study following families for 20 years after divorce. What remains unchanged in the literature are the notions that families in divorce will experience distress; however, families who work together with each other and professionals to create the most amicable circumstances through this time can and do emerge as resilient (Ahrons, 2004, 2007; Hetherington & Kelly, 2002; Karpf & Schatz, 2005; Schatz, 1999). Ahrons (2004, 2007), coined what is known as the *Good Divorce*. As the need for alternate methods of resolution rises, the literature suggests that more MHPs are becoming equipped to collaborate with professionals and divorcing couples toward successful completion of the process. In this regard, families are the central focus and emerge more successfully (Ahrons & Rodgers, 1987, 1989a, 1989b; Arendell, 1996; Katz, 2007).

Research suggests that when professionals from various disciplines begin to work together in synchronicity, they can share knowledge, skills, attitudes, and behavior that will be useful to each other and divorcing couples (Heller, 2011), which creates a more hopeful future for reorganized families.

Best practices for helping ...

We have some cautions and suggestions that we would like to address for the improvement of the services that MHPs can provide. Oftentimes, MHPs are called in to assist in a case when things have already gone awry; when the mediator cannot handle or manage the depth and number of emotional, financial, and legal issues that arise in very complex matters.

Our recommendations are as follows: screen carefully with much curiosity; learn as much as you can about the clients' histories and issues (mental health and otherwise) before beginning a mediation; bring in professionals at the onset, instead of in a crisis; implement and model the same communication skills with your co-professionals as you are asking of your clients; and know your limitations and remain in your area of expertise. Do not try to be all things to all people; it will not work. Collaboration is not an easy task. Divorce is a legal, financial, and emotional process. Regardless of the discipline-specific skills that each professional brings to any process, it is essential that all of the disciplines work effectively together and integrate their shared knowledge, skills, and attitudes to promote the most positive outcomes (Heller, 2011).

Implications for additional research

In 2013, Baitar, Buysse, Brondeel, De Mol and Rober addressed the lack of literature regarding the mediation process and explored the roles of professionals involved in the mediation and alternative resolution processes. They identified that the success of mediation was a more favorable option to litigation for divorcing couples. There are many resources present today, such as the Association of Family and Conciliation Courts (2016), which is a national organization comprising of mental health, legal, conflict resolution, and financial professionals working in collaboration to assist families going through divorce in more amicable ways.

We are continually reminded that people's experience of divorce is and will continue to be challenging and painful. With the guidance, support, and direction of specially trained mediators working with these families and in effective collaboration with other professionals, families can emerge stable, stronger, and with the necessary tools and abilities to forgive, let go, and rebuild.

References

Ahrons, C.R. (1994) *The Good Divorce.* New York: HarperCollins.

Ahrons, C.R. (2004) *We're Still Family: What Grown Children have to Say about their Parents' Divorce.* New York: HarperCollins.

Ahrons, C.R. (2007) Family ties after divorce: Long-term implications for children. *Family Process*, 46(1): 53–65.

Ahrons, C.R. & Rodgers, R.H. (1987) *Divorced Families: A Multidisciplinary Developmental View.* New York: W.W. Norton & Co.

Ahrons, C.R. & Rodgers, R.H. (1989a). *Divorced Families: A Multidisciplinary Developmental View.* New York: W.W. Norton & Co.

Ahrons, C.R. & Rodgers, R. (1989b). *Divorced Families: Meeting the Challenge of Divorce and Remarriage.* New York: W.W. Norton.

American Psychological Association. (2016) Marriage and divorce. American Psychological Association. Retrieved from www.apa.org/topics/divorce/.

Arendell, T. & College, C. (1996) *Co-parenting: A Review of the Literature.* Philadelphia, PA: The National Center on Fathers and Families.

Association of Family and Conciliation Courts. (2016) Home page. Retrieved from www.afccnet.org.

Baitar, R., Buysse, A., Brondeel, R., De Mol, J. & Rober, P. (2013) Styles and goals: Clarifying the professional identity of divorce mediation. *Conflict Resolution Quarterly*, 31: 57–78. doi:10.1002/crq.21079.

Bateson, G. (1972) *Steps to an Ecology of Mind*. Chicago, IL: University of Chicago.

Emery, R. & Emery, K.C. (2008) Should courts or parents make child-rearing decisions?: Married parents as a paradigm for parents who live apart. *Wake Forest Law Review*, 43(2): 365–389.

Heller, R. (2011) *Exploring Competency and the Role of the Mental Health Professional in Interdisciplinary Collaborative Family Law: What Do "they Do"?* Unpublished doctoral dissertation, Nova Southeastern University, Fort Lauderdale, Florida.

Hetherington, M.E. (2003) Intimate pathways: Changing patterns in close personal relationships across time. *Family Relations*, 52(4): 318–331.

Hetherington, M.E. & Kelly, J. (2002) *For Better or for Worse: Divorce Reconsidered*. New York: Norton.

Karpf, M. & Schatz, I. (2005) The divorce is over—What about the kids? *American Journal of Family Law*, 19(1): 7–12.

Katz, E. (2007) A family therapy perspective on mediation. *Family Process*, 46(1): 93–107.

Kazdin, A.E. (ed.). (2000) *The Encyclopedia of Psychology*. New York: Oxford University Press.

Kelly, J.B. (2007) Children's living arrangements following separation and divorce: Insights from empirical and clinical research. *Family Process*, 46(1): 35–52.

Lee, M. (2006) An ecosystemic look at the rights of children in divorce. In C.A. Everett & R.E. Lee (eds) *When Marriages Fail: Systemic Family Therapy Interventions and Issues* (pp. 37–54). New York: Hawthorne.

Mosten, F.S. (2009) *Collaborative Divorce Handbook: Helping Families without Going to Court*. San Francisco, CA: Jossey-Bass.

Pruett, M.K. (2011) Parenting plans following separation/divorce: Developmental considerations. In R. E. Emery (ed.) *Encyclopedia of Early Childhood Development: Divorce and Separation* (pp. 21–25). Retrieved from www.child-encyclopedia.com/sites/default/files/dossiers-complets/en/divorce-and-separation.pdf.

Schatz, I.M. (1999) *Divorced with Children: Stories of Collaborative Coparenting*. Unpublished doctoral dissertation, Nova Southeastern University, Fort Lauderdale, FL.

Strasheim, C. (2002) How divorce affects children: Developmental stages. *NebFact*, NF548, 1–2. Retrieved from digitalcommons.unl.edu/cgi/viewcontent.cgi?article=1081&context=extensionhist.

Tesler, P. (2008) Collaborative family law: The new lawyer and deep resolution of divorce related conflicts. *Journal of Dispute Resolution*, 2008(1): 83–130.

Tesler, P.H. & Thompson, P. (2006) *Collaborative Divorce: The Revolutionary New Way to Restructure Your Family, Resolve Legal Issues, and Move on with Your Life*. New York: HarperCollins.

Ver Steegh, N. (2008) Family court reform and ADR: Shifting values and expectations transform the divorce process. *Family Law Quarterly*, 42(3): 659–672.

Wallerstein, J.S., Lewis, J.M. & Blakeslee, S. (2002) *The Unexpected Legacy of Divorce: A 25 Year Landmark Study*. New York: Hyperion.

Webb, S. (2008) Collaborative law: A practitioner's perspective on its history and current practice. *American Academy of Matrimonial Law*, 21: 155–169.

Webb, S. & Ousky, R. (2006) *The Collaborative Way to Divorce: The Revolutionary Method that Results in Less Stress, Lower Costs, and Happier Kids—Without Going to Court*. New York: Hudson Street Press.

14

DYNAMIC MEDIATION

Integrating forgiveness

John Zivojinovic

Mediation often seeks to intervene between conflicting parties for the promotion of reconciliation, compromise, or settlement. However, are a person's interpersonal hurt, pain, and brokenness, because of the conflict, ever addressed? In order to frame the question, we need to understand the three predominant mediation models that exist today and their goals.

First, the most common approach is the satisfaction model or problem-solving model of mediation (Moore, 2003). This model, although elaborate and delineated, focuses on getting disputing parties to a place of resolution and settlement. Whether someone is emotionally hurt, relationally broken or experiencing psychological pain is not generally within the purview of this model, although it doesn't prevent their inclusion.

Second, the transformative model of mediation as outlined by Bush and Folger (1994) seeks to empower disputants to make their own decisions and assist them in recognizing the potential for personal growth that can come through conflict. The notion of empowerment is an important aspect of authenticating a person's context for conflict, but it appears the goal of the transformative model is more about improving the interaction at hand rather than addressing the deeper wounds of the disputing parties. The model's principle of recognition could address the emotional component of the conflicting parties. Recognition is "the evocation in individuals of acknowledgment and empathy for the situation and problems of others" (Bush & Folger, 1994, p. 2). To acknowledge and empathize with another are helpful and important, but if relational hurt, brokenness, and pain have not been addressed within, then to acknowledge and empathize are at best short-term solutions.

Finally, the narrative model (Winslade & Monk, 2001) seeks to advocate for change in the narrative of the dispute. Winslade and Monk (2001) see their approach as "outside-in." This means that how conflict is socially understood frames much of the disputing parties' understanding of their own conflicts. Although there is merit to this approach, it seems challenging to think that when one is emotionally hurt, relationally broken, and experiencing psychological pain that social "deconstruction" of the conflict can recognize all the nuances of a person's trauma.

These unique and helpful models of mediation fall short in addressing the deeper dimensions of the individual's emotional hurt, relational brokenness, and psychological pain because they are missing the aspect of intentional forgiveness, which has been researched in a variety of contexts (Altmaier et al., 2011; Exline, 2012; Greenberg et al., 2011; Muhoma, 2012;

Stewart, 2012; Worthington & Langberg, 2012). However, forgiveness studies have not been fully developed and applied to the mediation field. Therefore, this chapter seeks to define and describe forgiveness, demonstrate the benefits of forgiveness and their implications for mediation, and propose ways of weaving forgiveness into mediation practice.

Definitions and descriptions of forgiveness

Defining forgiveness seems to be an elusive task. Often it is better to understand forgiveness by what it is not, than what it actually is (Griswold, 2007). Yet, a variety of different definitions of forgiveness have emerged and assist in giving forgiveness a context with parameters. Enright and Fitzgibbons (2000) explain that forgiveness occurs when rational people determine that despite being treated unfairly, they "willfully abandon resentment and related responses … and endeavor to respond to the wrongdoer based on the moral principle of beneficence, which may include compassion, unconditional worth, generosity, and moral love" (p. 24). The decision to forgive occurs despite the fact that "the wrongdoer, by nature of the hurtful act or acts, has no right" to forgiveness (Enright & Fitzgibbons, 2000, p. 24). Holmgren (2012) states that forgiveness is "understood as a change of heart in which an initial attitude of resentment is overcome and replaced with a positive attitude toward the offender" (p. 32).

For the sake of the discussion at hand, forgiveness will be defined as an emotional and volitional process of choosing to release negative emotions and feelings toward someone who has hurt you in order to embrace and experience a healthy perspective toward the offender. Now that there is context for a definition of forgiveness, it is important to describe the phenomenon of forgiveness. Based on the above definition, the four dimensions that need to be described are emotional and volitional processes, release, embrace/experience, and healthy perspective.

In describing forgiveness, most researchers understand it as a psychological process (Takada & Ohbuchi, 2013; Posthuma, 2012). The process can vary depending on the person, the offense and the circumstances associated with the offense. Worthington (2001) developed the idea that forgiveness must begin with volition or a willingness to forgive. Forgiveness does not just happen. Emotional forgiveness usually takes more time, but cannot happen unless volitional forgiveness is employed. Yet, it is when emotional forgiveness takes place that a person experiences a full sense of forgiveness. Therefore, forgiveness includes both volitional and emotional processes.

The idea of release in describing forgiveness is the idea of *letting go*. Without going into the negative effects of failing to forgive, it should be briefly noted that unforgiveness comes at a high personal, emotional, psychological and relational cost (Harris & Thoresen, 2005; Sapolsky, 2005). Letting go allows the forgiver to process and release the offense. Remember, as noted above, this is a process and depending on the offense it could take a significant amount of time. There is no need to rush forgiving a deep relational hurt. What is important is that a person is processing through forgiveness.

The next key descriptor of forgiveness is to embrace/experience. The core idea of embrace/experience is as you let go or release negative emotions and feelings, you replace those negative feelings with new emotions that are not only cognitively embraced, but experienced. Although Worthington (2006, 2005, 2001, 1998) has developed the notion of replacing negative emotions with positive emotions, there are deep insights to be gleaned from emotion-focused therapy (EFT), especially in the area of exchanging or replacing negative emotions with positive ones. Greenberg (2002) developed outstanding insights in helping clients move from negative emotions to embracing positive emotions by assisting clients in identifying negative emotions and then in assisting them to understand, embrace and experience positive emotions. Embracing positive emotions is a deliberate process in which clients identify other emotions, often very positive emotions that are at work, but have been relegated to the background during the flare-up of negative emotions. Greenberg (2002) highlights eight possible ways to engage positive emotions: "shifting attention, access needs and goals, positive imagery, expressive enactment of the emotion, remembering another emotion, expressing an emotion on the client's behalf and other methods for expressing emotion" (p. 194). If a person is stuck in a pattern of negative emotions over an offense, it may take a significant amount of time to work through exchanging or replacing negative emotions for positive ones. However, positive emotions can be embraced and experienced in people's lives. Cloke (2001) states, "like revenge, forgiveness is possible in every conflict, no matter how painful or serious" (p. 87).

The last descriptor is healthy perspective. As a person is able to work through the process of forgiveness, appropriately letting go of the relational hurt and replacing the negative emotions with positive emotions, one is able to gain a healthy perspective toward the person who harmed them. This healthy perspective is not justifying what happened to you, it is not minimizing what happened to you, nor is it excusing what happened to you, but rather, it is gaining a healthy perspective toward the perpetrator. A healthy perspective connotes freedom from anger, resentment, hatred, and malice toward the person who hurt you (Enright & Fitzgibbons, 2000). An important delineation to remember is that forgiveness and reconciliation are different with different objectives and goals (Worthington, 2001). Just because you have forgiven, does not mean that the relationship has been reconciled, but rather, forgiveness is a bridge toward reconciling, if journeying over the bridge of reconciliation is what a person needs to do.

The benefits of forgiveness and its implications for mediation

The scientific study of forgiveness is a vast field of research (Gonzalez Martin et al., 2011; Olmstead et al., 2009) that gives a real sense of promise and hope. Enright (2001) notes that forgiveness calms angry feelings, changes negative thoughts to more positive thoughts, allows more conscientious actions toward the offender, aids in treating others better, might improve the relationship with the offender, may change the offender's perspective on their offense, and might enhance religious devotion. In addition, Enright (2001) states that forgiveness is the right moral response for one's own good. Moreover, when a deep offense has taken place in a person's life, the implications and ramifications are significant, profound, and pervasive (Takada & Ohbuchi, 2013; Young et al., 2013).

Forgiveness has a significant impact on a person's mental health. Worthington (2006) states, "forgiveness reduces anger, depression, anxiety, and fear" (p. 272). Toussaint and Webb (2005) cite 13 empirical studies that reiterate the positive value of forgiveness on mental health. A summation of the findings can be delineated on the continuum between forgiveness and unforgiveness. Forgiveness as a whole had positive implications for global mental health. Forgiveness contributed positively in addressing depression, anxiety, nicotine use, drug use, vengefulness, phobias, bulimia nervosa, distress, existential well-being, and life satisfaction. Unforgiveness was a contributing factor of depression, anxiety, a lack of life satisfaction and post-traumatic stress disorder (PTSD).

In addition, studies including forgiveness of self, demonstrate positive corollaries between forgiveness and mental health (Webb et al., 2013; Mukashema & Mullet, 2013). Moreover, forgiveness also has positive implications for a person's emotional health. Enright (2012) highlights ten research studies that make the case that forgiveness affects a person's emotional well-being in very positive ways. He concludes that those who forgave improved categorically.

Forgiveness can also positively affect physical health. Witvliet (2005) found that unforgiveness caused eye muscle tension, higher skin conductance levels, and higher blood pressure, whereas forgiveness reduced those same physiological effects. Harris & Thoresen (2005) found that unforgiveness has been framed in the context of a stress reaction. In other words, unforgiveness has the same effects on a person as stress. Therefore, forgiveness is a physiological benefit to those who practice it.

Forgiveness also has a positive impact on relational health. Enright (2001) notes that when a person forgives, they can "experience greater self-acceptance and establish meaningful friendships" (p. 14). He also argues that when a person forgives, anger subsides toward the offender, more positive thoughts emerge toward the offender, actions toward the offender are more positive, and negative interactions with others are lessened. Worthington (2006) deduces several relational benefits of forgiveness: noble intentions, feeling connected to others, humility, less defensiveness, engagement with others, understanding justice in relationships, embracing truth in relationships, trusting others, and responding to stress in relationships. In addition, forgiveness has been documented to enhance relational health in the areas of marriage (Campana et al., 2012; Fatima & Ajmal, 2012), the workplace (Fehr & Gelfand, 2012), close relationships (Gerlach et al., 2012), romantic relationships (Pelucchi et al., 2013), families (Scherer et al., 2012) and groups (López-López, 2013). Therefore, if forgiveness has significant positive ramifications for people and their relationships, should not mediators invite people to think about and experience the power of forgiveness in and through the mediation process?

Recommendations for weaving forgiveness into mediation

Become a more forgiving person

If you take the research seriously about the importance of forgiveness for people, then it would be incumbent to become more forgiving. *The Forgiving Life: A Pathway to Overcoming Resentment and Creating a Legacy of Love* by Robert D. Enright (2012) will walk you through his process of becoming more forgiving. If you struggle with forgiving yourself, Dr Worthington's (2013) book entitled, *Moving Forward: Six Steps to Forgiving Yourself and Breaking Free from the Past* would be a good volume to work through.

Create an environment of forgiveness

Implement some of the characteristics of forgiveness within the very process of mediation. In laying out the ground rules for the mediation, help parties think about how they will talk to one another through the lens of forgiveness. This means not tolerating demeaning words, angry outbursts, or rude remarks. Do not allow the parties to make excuses for previous behavior, but encourage honesty. If emotions arise, handle them appropriately and model a better way. Navigating another person's emotions can be validating to the person expressing emotions.

Coach forgiveness

Many mediators will read this chapter and make the mistake of thinking that forgiveness is a topic for therapists. Forgiveness is a skill that can be taught and learned. Whether in pre-mediation work, during the mediation session(s) or post-mediation work you can coach clients in forgiveness skills. You are not a therapist, so please do not associate coaching with counseling.

Provide resources

In order to safeguard yourself from possibly being seen as someone who might be advocating for forgiveness, which might be misunderstood by one or both parties in mediation as a weakness, provide resources for both parties, such as a list of helping professionals. Let them take the resources home and work through them at their convenience.

Become a networker

Networking with a therapist who utilizes forgiveness therapy in their sessions, can be a transformative move for one or both parties.

Reframe the conflict

You are not trying to minimize or make more of the dispute at hand. Rather, you want to help people see conflict more positively. Conflict is like a dance, and thinking of conflict in this way can create a new metaphor to help disputing parties see each other differently.

Remember your limits

You goal is not to get the parties to forgive one another. However, creating an environment that is forgiving, providing resources about forgiveness, and networking with a therapist can all be professional courtesies in which your practice specializes.

Conclusion

This chapter has sought to present definitions and descriptions of forgiveness, reveal the benefits of forgiveness and its implication for mediation, and give mediators ways to weave forgiveness into their mediation practices. Forgiveness is an agent of transformation, especially of relationships; therefore, it would be expeditious of mediators to consider ways to integrate forgiveness into their everyday mediation practices. Promoting dynamic mediation by integrating forgiveness can have far-reaching implications for conflict resolution in today's world.

References

Altmaier, E.M., Cornick, C., Schultz, J.M. & Tallman, B. (2011) Forgiving significant interpersonal offenses: The role of victim/offender racial similarity. *Psychology*, 2(9): 936–945.

Bush, R.A.B. & Folger, J.P. (1994) *The Promise of Mediation: Responding to Conflict through Empowerment and Recognition*. San Francisco, CA: Jossey-Bass.

Campana, K.L., Gartner, A.L., Hook, J.N., Scherer, M., West, S.L. & Worthington, E.L. (2012) Forgiveness and cohesion in familial perceptions of alcohol misuse. *Journal of Counseling and Development*, 90(2): 160–171.

Cloke, K. (2001) *Mediating Dangerously: The Frontiers of Conflict Resolution*. San Francisco, CA: Jossey-Bass.

Enright, R.D. (2001) *Forgiveness is a Choice: A Step-by-Step Process for Resolving Anger and Restoring Hope*. Washington, DC: American Psychological Association.

Enright, R.D. (2012) *The Forgiving Life: A Pathway to Overcoming Resentment and Creating a Legacy of Love*. Washington, DC: American Psychological Association.

Enright, R.D. & Fitzgibbons, R.P. (2000) *Helping Clients Forgive: An Empirical Guide for Resolving Anger and Restoring Hope*. Washington, DC: American Psychological Association.

Exline, J.J. (2012) Humility and the ability to receive from others. *Journal of Psychology and Christianity*, 31(1): 40–50.

Fatima, M. & Ajmal, M.A. (2012) Happy marriage: A qualitative study. *Pakistan Journal of Social and Clinical Psychology*, 9(2): 37–42.

Fehr, R. & Gelfand, M.J. (2012) The forgiving organization: A multilevel model of forgiveness at work. *Academy of Management Review*, 37(4): 664–688.

Gerlach, T.M., Allemand, M., Agroskin, D. & Denissen, J.J.A. (2012) Justice sensitivity and forgiveness in close interpersonal relationships: The mediating role of mistrustful, legitimizing, and pro-relationship cognitions. *Journal of Personality*, 80(5): 1373–1413.

Gonzalez Martin, M., Rodríguez González, M. & Génova Fuster, G. (2011) Forgiveness in marriage: Healing or chronicity. A dialog between a philosophical and a psychotherapeutic understanding. *Human Studies*, 34(4): 431–449.

Greenberg, L.S. (2002) *Emotion-focused Therapy: Coaching Clients to Work through their Feelings*. Washington, DC: APA.

Greenberg, L., Warwar, S. & Malcolm, W. (2011) Marital and family therapy. *Journal of Psychology and Theology*, 39(2): 164–166.

Griswold, C.L. (2007) *Forgiveness: A Philosophical Exploration*. New York: Cambridge University Press.

Harris, A.H.S. & Thoresen, C.E. (2005) Forgiveness, unforgiveness, health, and disease. In E.L. Worthington (ed.) *Handbook of Forgiveness* (pp. 321–334). New York: Routledge.

Holmgren, M.R. (2012) *Forgiveness and Retribution: Responding to Wrongdoing*. New York: Cambridge University Press.

López-López, W., Pineda Marín, C., Murcia León, M.C., Perilla Garzón, D.C. & Mullet, E. (2013) Forgiving perpetrators of violence: Colombian people's positions. *Social Indicators Research*, 114(2), 287–301.

Moore, C.W. (2003) *The Mediation Process: Practical Strategies for Resolving Conflict*. San Francisco, CA: Jossey-Bass.

Muhoma, C. (2012) Versions of truth and collective memory: The quest for forgiveness and healing in the context of Kenya's postelection violence. *Research in African Literatures*, 43(1): 166–173.

Mukashema, I. & Mullet, E. (2013) Unconditional forgiveness, reconciliation sentiment, and mental health among victims of genocide in Rwanda. *Social Indicators Research*, 113(1): 121–132.

Olmstead, S.B., Blick, R.W. & Mills, L.I. (2009) Helping couples work toward the forgiveness of marital infidelity: Therapists' perspectives. *The American Journal of Family Therapy*, 37(1): 48.

Pelucchi, S., Paleari, F.G., Regalia, C. & Fincham, F.D. (2013) Self-forgiveness in romantic relationships: It matters to both of us. *Journal of Family Psychology*, 27(4): 541.

Posthuma, R.A. (2012) Conflict management and emotions. *International Journal of Conflict Management*, 23(1): 4–5.

Sapolsky, R.M. (2005) The physiology and pathophysiology of unhappiness. In E.L. Worthington (ed.) *Handbook of Forgiveness* (pp. 273–304). New York: Routledge.

Scherer, M., Worthington, Everett L., Jr., Hook, J.N., Campana, K.L., West, S.L. & Gartner, A.L. (2012) Forgiveness and cohesion in familial perceptions of alcohol misuse. *Journal of Counseling and Development*, 90(2): 160–168.

Stewart, D. (2012) Thinking about forgiveness: A philosophical preamble to its cultivation in schooling. *Journal of Thought*, 47(1): 66–95.

Takada, N. & Ohbuchi, K. (2013) True and hollow forgiveness, forgiveness motives, and conflict resolution. *International Journal of Conflict Management*, 24(2): 184–200.

Toussaint, L. & Webb, J.R. (2005) Theoretical and empirical connections between forgiveness, mental health and well-being. In E.L. Worthington (ed.) *Handbook of Forgiveness* (pp. 349–362). New York: Routledge.

Webb, J.R., Hirsch, J.K., Visser, P.L. & Brewer, K.G. (2013) Forgiveness and health: Assessing the mediating effect of health behavior, social support, and interpersonal functioning. *The Journal of Psychology*, 147(5): 391.

Winslade, J. & Monk, G. (2001) *Narrative Mediation: A New Approach to Conflict Resolution*. San Francisco, CA: Jossey-Bass.

Witvliet, C.V.O. (2005) Unforgiveness, forgiveness, and justice: Scientific findings on feelings and physiology. In E.L. Worthington (ed.) *Handbook on Forgiveness* (pp. 305–320). New York: Routledge.

Worthington, E.L. (1998) The pyramid model of forgiveness: Some interdisciplinary speculations about unforgiveness and the promotion of forgiveness. In L. Everett Worthington, Jr. (ed.) *Dimensions of Forgiveness: Psychological Research & Theological Forgiveness* (pp. 107–138). Philadelphia, PA: Templeton Foundation Press.

Worthington, E.L. (2001) *Five Steps to Forgiveness: The Art and Science of Forgiving*. New York: Crown Publishers.

Worthington, E.L. (2005) *The Power of Forgiving*. Philadelphia, PA: Templeton Foundation Press.

Worthington, E.L. (2006) *Forgiveness and Reconciliation: Theory and Application*. New York: Routledge.

Worthington, E.L. (2013) *Moving Forward: Six Steps to Forgiving Yourself and Breaking Free from the Past*. Colorado Springs, CO: WaterBrook Press.

Worthington, E.L. & Langberg, D. (2012) Religious considerations and self-forgiveness in treating complex trauma and moral injury in present and former soldiers. *Journal of Psychology and Theology*, 40(4): 274–288.

Young, R.E., Struthers, C.W., Khoury, C., Muscat, S., Phills, C. & Mongrain, M. (2013) Forgiveness and revenge: The conflicting needs of dependents and self-critics in relationships. *Journal of Social and Clinical Psychology*, 32(10): 1095–1115.

PART III

Mediating in organizational and institutional settings

15

MEDIATION WITHIN AND BETWEEN ORGANIZATIONS

Christopher W. Moore

This chapter[1] addresses the role of mediation in helping people in organizations effectively understand, address, and resolve conflicts. It explores several types of organizational mediators and the diverse approaches and strategies that can be implemented to settle differences. It presumes there is "no one right way" to practice mediation and encourages an integrated approach. The methodology selected should be informed by disputants' expectations, the mediator's relationship with them, an assessment of the assistance parties may need to achieve a successful outcome, knowledge of the issues, and judgment concerning the degree of influence needed or desired by participants to assist them in agreement making. The mediation approaches described specifically focus on the resolution of organizational disputes, but mediators have used these same procedures to settle a range of other conflicts—interpersonal, family, small group, community, inter-ethnic or religious, environmental, business, public policy and international.

In short, mediation is a conflict resolution process in which a third party, not directly involved in a dispute, assists participants to communicate more effectively, improves their working relationships, engages parties in effective problem solving or negotiations to increase common understanding, and/or develops voluntary and mutually satisfactory agreements on issues in question.

Kinds of organizational mediators

Informal mediators are trusted and respected colleagues or friends of disputing parties. These intermediaries resolve the majority of disputes in organizations. Generally, one or more disputants approach an informal mediator, who is not part of the dispute. Occasionally, disputants may request a person in a position of authority for assistance. When serving as an informal mediator, however, the superior acts in his or her personal capacity and not as a representative of the organization or in a formal authoritative position in relation to those involved. Informal mediators may or may not be totally neutral in their relationships with the parties, or totally impartial toward their issues, needs and interests or the outcome of the dispute resolution process. Informal mediators' major means of influence are the relationships and trust they have with all concerned, their capacity to provide a safe forum to discuss problems, and their ability to listen and provide an effective dispute resolution process. They may also, on occasion, offer their perspective on issues in question, or give advice.

In general, informal mediators seek understandings or agreements that are mutually acceptable to all concerned, and do not require parties to take broader organizational policies or procedures into consideration. Informal mediation helped to resolve a dispute between co-workers with different personalities and work styles. The two employees, who had been friends, were in a deadlock over their roles and responsibilities while working on a project together. The parties asked for this type of mediator because they wanted to resolve their dispute privately, and find a way to work together and restore their friendship without involving management or any authoritative decision makers in what they saw as an interpersonal problem.

Peer mediators are organized and mandated by their organization to provide neutral and impartial dispute resolution assistance to co-workers—peers, subordinates or superiors—concerning work-related disputes. Participation is generally voluntary for all concerned, though in some situations the parties' managers may strongly encourage participation. Peer mediation may be conducted by one or more of the disputants' peers, or a combination of their colleagues and members of management. In the latter case, employees and managers usually serve in equal numbers, either as co-mediators or as members of a panel. If managers are involved, they serve in their personal capacities as knowledgeable supervisors in the organization, but do not have any formal decision-making authority over the involved parties or issues in dispute.

Unlike informal mediators, peer mediators are expected to be neutral and impartial. Neutrality pertains to the intermediary's relationship with the disputants. In this regard, peer mediators are not directly involved in the conflict, do not work closely with the parties, or have a reporting relationship with them. Impartiality concerns the mediator's view toward the substance of the dispute, and requires objective treatment of the parties' issues, needs, and interests. Accordingly, peer mediators refrain from taking sides or being an advocate for any party.

In reference to their power and authority, peer mediators cannot make binding decisions for disputants, nor do they have formal authority to pressure them to reach an agreement. Their primary means of influence is their neutrality, impartiality, and capacity to conduct a fair and effective dispute resolution process. Concerning outcomes, peer mediators help parties develop mutually acceptable agreements, which meet their individual and joint interests. When appropriate, they may also encourage parties to consider organizational norms, policies, rules and regulations, and relevant laws when deliberating and crafting solutions to resolve their issues.

Peer mediators helped to resolve a dispute after multiple arguments between co-workers escalated into fistfights over the selection of bundles of clothing to be inspected by quality control inspectors. Each bundle contained different numbers of garments. Payment was based on the number of bundles inspected, which resulted in competition for bundles with the smallest number of garments. After resolving several individual disputes, in which parties agreed not to fight over smaller bundles, the peer mediators identified structural problems in the quality control and payment procedures. They recommended a structural change to management—pay employees according to the number of garments they inspected, rather than the number of bundles they processed—which was accepted. With this change in place, disputes over this issue dropped to zero. Mediation enabled the employer to get beneath the presenting problem and make needed structural changes to work practices that benefited both employees and the organization.

Administrative/managerial mediators are given authority by the leadership of an organization to help members or employees collaboratively address and resolve their differences (Moore,

2014; Kolb & Sheppard, 1985; Morril, 1995). Unlike informal or peer meditators, these intermediaries have administrative or managerial positions and potential or actual decision-making authority over disputants. They also have discretion over whether or not to use this authority, or, based on a variety of factors, to assist disputing parties to reach their own agreements.

Participants in a dispute may be direct reports of the administrative/managerial mediator who assists them, or alternatively be referred to another manager outside their direct chain of command. In both instances, the managerial intermediary retains a degree of influence over involved parties, as their supervisor or by virtue of their position in the organization. Participation in managerial mediation may or may not be voluntary. If a supervisor or manager is one of the parties to a dispute, some organizations require them to participate. Employees, who are subordinates of the involved supervisor or manager, often are not required to participate.

Administrative/managerial mediators are not necessarily impartial. As involved managers, they may have their own interests in the dispute and its outcome, and generally consider the interests, policies, rules, and regulations of the organization in any potential settlement. When administrative/managerial mediators or the organization have specific needs or interests that need to be considered and met in a satisfactory settlement, they may establish parameters for potential understandings or agreements that parties will need to respect in their deliberations and agreement making. Alternatively, when administrative/managerial mediators have no vested interest in the outcome, and the organization's interests, policies, rules and regulations are not at stake, they may allow participants significant leeway to negotiate their own preferred outcomes.

Administrative/managerial mediation was used after an employee threatened to file a charge of discrimination against her supervisor for perceived racism and an unfair performance review. The employee approached her supervisor's manager about the dispute, and he decided to try to mediate to see if the parties could reach common ground, and if possible, address their differences. Rather than make a unilateral decision to settle the issues in question, the manager asked the employee whether, with his help, she would be willing to talk with her supervisor, prior to formally filing a charge of discrimination. She agreed.

The supervisor was initially reluctant to participate in mediation, believing the discrimination charge was spurious and an excuse for poor performance. The senior manager could have ordered the supervisor to participate in mediation; however, after some discussion, he persuaded him that engaging in the process provided an opportunity to address performance concerns, clarify and respond to the discrimination charges, and improve future working relationships. Additionally, the supervisor recognized that a successful outcome might help to avoid an extended, time-consuming, and expensive complaint resolution procedure or lawsuit.

With agreement of both parties, the manager convened and mediated talks that explored the claims raised about the supervisor. After hearing the employee's views concerning his behavior and attitude, the supervisor explained that he had not intended to act in a discriminating manner or dismiss her in any way, and very much regretted if his behavior was seen as such. He said that in the future, he would carefully monitor what he said and how he acted. The employee accepted the supervisor's commitments, and agreed not to follow through with filing a charge of discrimination. The parties also reviewed and clarified the performance review process and criteria, after which the employee acknowledged that she was not performing at the required level. Subsequently, the parties discussed how performance could be improved, set up an improvement plan that included additional training and coaching, and established a time to check in to assess progress.

Independent mediators are intermediaries who are not connected to disputing parties, their work, or social networks, and are impartial concerning issues in dispute. A company, government agency, or non-profit entity experiencing organizational conflict secures this type of mediation assistance from individuals from outside the organization (Moore, 2014; Lederach, 1985). The independence of the mediator is grounded in the objective relationship he or she has with the disputing parties, and his or her stance toward their issues, needs and interests and outcomes of the mediation process. Independent mediators are neutral regarding their relationships with the parties, and generally do not have past, current, or future affiliations with them, which might bias their views. If such relationships exist, the mediator is bound to disclose the nature of the association prior to commencing the mediation. The mediator can only proceed if his or her relationships with the parties are acceptable to all concerned.

Independent mediators have no authority to make substantive decisions for disputing parties. Their role is to help parties make their own decisions. They do, however, have significant influence over the structure of the process used to discuss issues of concern, reach understandings, or develop mutually acceptable agreements.

Independent mediators are also impartial[2] in their views concerning the parties' issues, needs, and interests and take an objective stance toward them. They are also generally impartial and unbiased toward the outcomes of mediation and almost always accept agreements reached by parties without comment, questions, judgments or objections. There are, however, some exceptions when a mediator may raise a concern with parties about a prospective outcome. This may occur when the mediator concludes that the parties are reaching agreement under duress; the parties do not have adequate information to make informed or wise decisions; the parties are not capable of adequately representing themselves or effectively advocating for their interests; the settlement is likely to result in significant psychological or physical harm to one or more participant; the agreement violates a statutory law, rule or regulation, an organizational policy or rule or the rights of potentially affected parties who have not been involved in the mediation process; one or more parties is not negotiating in good faith; or there are questions about whether the agreement is implementable or sustainable. When any of these factors are present, independent mediators may raise their concerns with the parties, individually in private meetings or in joint session, and encourage them to consider and address them as appropriate. In extreme cases, an independent mediator may withdraw his or her services because of a serious concern about some aspect of the mediation process or its outcome.

A team of independent mediators settled a dispute when senior executives and subordinates from different departments were developing a new policy on a controversial and complex issue requiring cooperation between the units, the involvement of joint personnel and financial contributions. Another independent mediator also resolved a dispute after two company CEOs reached an impasse over contested financial agreements where both CEOs believed the other was cheating and had filed lawsuits. In each case, the parties voluntarily decided to engage in mediation and determined that they could best be assisted by an independent mediator from outside their respective organizations. They wanted intermediaries who had no prior relationships with them, and who maintained an objective and impartial view toward issues in question. In the first case, the mediator provided relationship and process assistance to the parties from multiple departments. In the case involving litigation, the mediator provided principally process and substantive assistance (an assessment of the strength of each party's legal case) and a recommendation for a general framework for settlement in which the parties filled in the details.

Four factors that influence the form of mediator assistance

Mediators provide various forms of assistance to disputing parties depending upon a range of factors. Some of them include the: 1) potential or actual causes of the conflict, and the issues, needs and interests that must be addressed for parties to reach mutually satisfactory understandings or agreements; 2) specific targets for intervention and change—individuals, groups, systems or organizations; 3) kinds of help expected or requested by the parties, mediator perceptions of what they may need and types of assistance the intermediary is capable of providing; and 4) the level of influence and direction the mediator believes will be required and what he or she is willing to provide.

Factor one: causes of conflicts

A first step in understanding an organizational conflict is to identify the primary causes of the dispute and other significant factors that may contribute to its development. Information about sources of conflict is usually gathered during meetings between the mediator and individual parties prior to the first joint session and during subsequent joint and private meetings, as required. Figure 15.1 identifies eight potential sources or contributing factors of

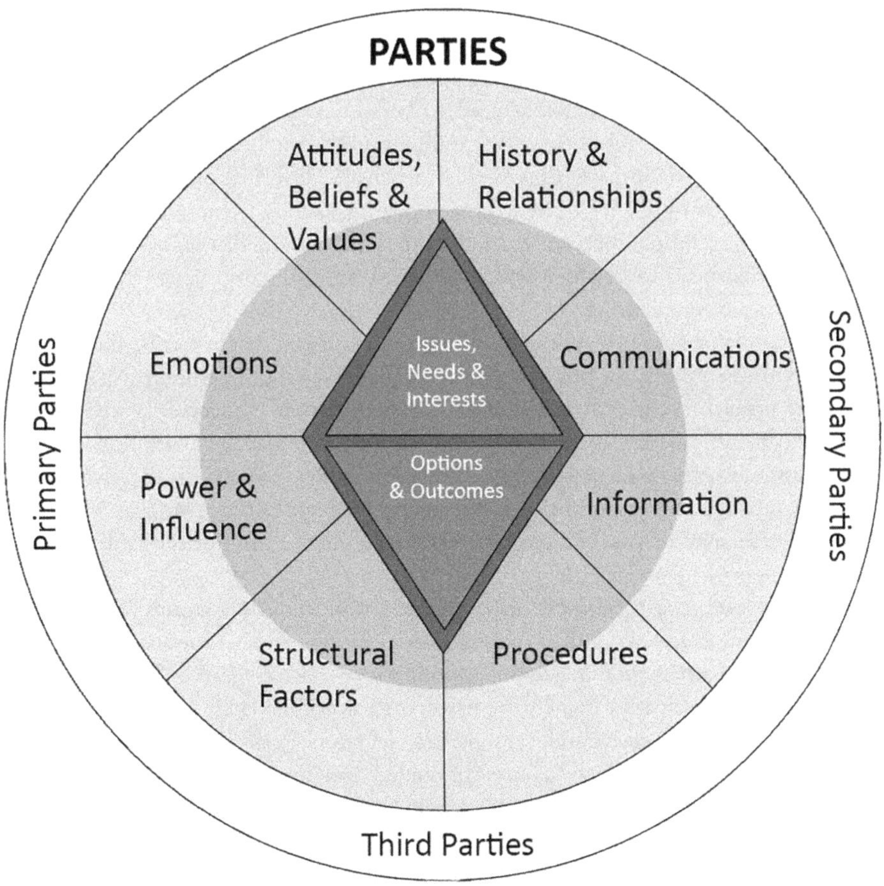

FIGURE 15.1 Circle of conflict: causes of disputes and opportunities for collaboration

conflicts, and areas where parties may potentially find common ground and collaborate (Moore, 2014, p. 110). These include: 1) *parties' histories and relationships*—kinds, duration (immediate, short-term or long-term), interactions and dynamics, and critical events; 2) *parties' attitudes, beliefs and values*—attitudes/preferences or foundational principles concerning what is right/wrong, fair/unfair, just/unjust, seemingly incompatible beliefs or values, or beliefs and values that parties hold in common; 3) *parties' communications*—forms, styles, procedures, frequency, emotions and content; 4) *parties' emotions*—bonds between parties (positive, neutral/ambivalent or negative), strengths (strong, moderate or weak), intensity and means of expression; 5) *information available to the parties*—adequate/inadequate for informed decision making, too little or too much, the wrong kind or misinformation, accuracy, clarity or inaccuracy, broadly understood and accepted or not; 6) *parties' power and influence*—forms, sources and amounts (same or different), willingness to use them, whether or not they have been applied, and risks and opportunities if they are exercised; 7) *procedures utilized to help resolve the parties' dispute*—problematic strategies, tactics or interactions, inappropriate or effective but misused procedures, adversarial or collaborative problem solving or negotiation processes, and unassisted or assisted talks; and 8) *structural factors*—time or timeframes to address the conflict, physical proximity of the parties, different levels of authority or resources, etc.

Closely related to causes of conflicts are the issues parties expect to be addressed through the mediation process. These are in the center of the circle. *Issues* are topics, matters of concern, questions, or problems that people in dispute want to have considered, understood, and, as appropriate, resolved. Issues can be either "presenting problems" or "root problems." Presenting problems are issues for discussion and resolution initially put forth by parties. They may or may not be the real issues that need to be addressed and resolved to ensure a satisfactory settlement. Root problems are the genuine issues at the heart of a dispute, which may take time for parties to disclose, discover, or articulate. Information gathering commonly reveals both kinds of issues. It is often, however, only through extensive discussions, close questioning, and careful conflict analysis that parties and the mediator may fully understand the real topics that need to be discussed, and be able to distinguish between presenting and underlying causes of the conflict.

Either mediators or parties may identify issues for discussion. Issues can be framed in broad or narrow terms, in a partial or one-sided manner incorporating only one party's perspective, or as a joint problem statement that reflects multiple parties' concerns. A key role of the mediator is to help frame the issues in the most constructive way for resolution.

For each issue, parties commonly have a number of needs and interests they want to satisfy, as illustrated in the circle of conflict and the triangle of satisfaction (Moore, 2014, p. 128). Needs or interests may be psychological or relationship, procedural or substantive in nature.

- *Psychological/relationship needs and interests* concern how individuals or groups want to be treated; how they want to feel about themselves and other parties; and how relationships are valued and shaped by participation in a dispute resolution process. Psychological needs and interests commonly include a party's desire to be heard, trusted, acknowledged and respected.
- *Procedural needs and interests* refer to parties' preferences or requirements for the way problem solving or negotiations are conducted and understandings or agreements are reached and implemented. They may include needs for an efficient, fair and timely process; clear understandable steps; opportunities for all parties to present their views; and acceptable procedures to identify or develop mutually acceptable solutions.
- *Substantive needs and interests* are tangible outcomes or benefits a party wants to attain or receive as a result of negotiations or other means of dispute resolution.

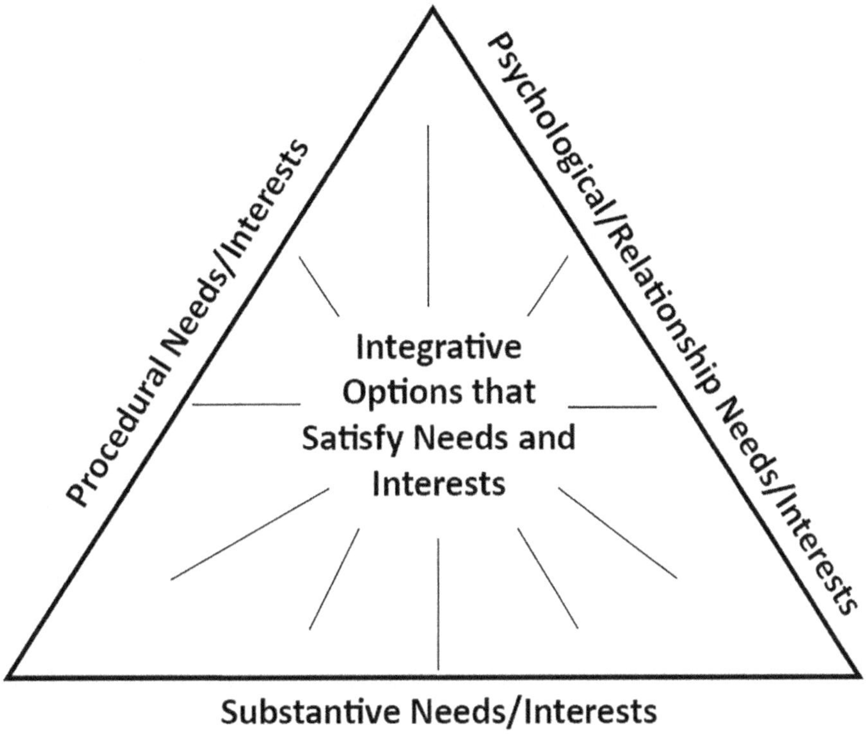

FIGURE 15.2 Triangle of satisfaction

Each case presented at the beginning of this chapter is characterized by one or more sources of conflict, diverse issues, and multiple needs and interests the parties hope to satisfy. The dispute over different work styles centered on a year-long history of seemingly incompatible approaches to work, communication difficulties and frustrations among the co-workers, and their interest in restoring the friendship that existed before the conflict. The discrimination case involved clashes in values concerning what constituted inappropriate attitudes and behaviors, strong emotions, unclear expectations for performance and the performance review process, and a common interest in having fair procedures and outcomes.

Factor two: targets of the mediation intervention

The *target of intervention* refers to the person or group(s) for whom the mediator provides assistance who will need to engage and collaborate to successfully address issues in dispute. The target may be an individual, two or more disputants (peers, superiors and subordinates), a constellation of people within a group (team or subgroup within an organization), or the organization as a whole. As mediators learn more about the perceived and actual causes of a conflict, contributing factors, and the needs and interests of the parties, they are generally able to determine which individuals or groups will need to be the focus of their efforts to promote greater understanding or agreement. They may also identify structural causes of the conflict, which are commonly independent of the parties directly involved, but which may need to be addressed to solve a specific dispute and prevent others from occurring in the future.

The mediators in each case described at the beginning of this chapter had to select specific targets of focus and develop corresponding interventions and strategies for each group or individual. In the discrimination case, the targets were the individuals who were directly involved. The administrative/managerial mediator needed to work with the supervisor in a private meeting to identify whether he did indeed have racist attitudes and behaviors, and if so, what he was willing to do about them. (The mediator may also have informed him that such attitudes and behaviors were unacceptable in the organization, and posed risks for both him and the company.) While the supervisor did not believe that he had alleged attitudes or behaviors, he was willing to listen to the views of the other party, apologize if he had made mistakes, and make an explicit statement that he would not do things in the future that might be perceived as racist. The mediator then had to work with the employee, again in a private meeting, to prepare her to discuss the issues with her supervisor, including her perceptions of discrimination, the performance review process, and criteria used for evaluating employees.

In the case where the organization was mired in the development of a new policy, independent co-mediators identified a range of parties that needed to participate and contribute their views and interests concerning the issues in question. In convening the process, the intermediaries asked the organization to identify participants with the authority to make binding decisions from each of the departments involved, and representative subordinates who would need to be consulted and engaged to ensure successful implementation. Participants included supporters, those neutral to, and opponents of the proposed policy. In the discussions, the mediator focused on supporters and encouraged them to present their views regarding what should be done and the potential benefits to the organization of implementing the proposed policy; opponents to express their doubts and raise questions of concern; and neutrals to assess the various views of other participants. In the course of talks, the mediators identified specific executive and subordinate opinion leaders whose views and interests would need to be considered if agreements were to be reached. At this point, the mediators worked more closely with these individuals, both in private sessions and in whole-group sessions. Several interventions focused on helping the resisters at different levels of the organization to explore and change their views, while other activities encouraged participants to address the concerns and interests of the resistant parties.

Factor three: kinds of assistance provided by mediators

Generally, the focus of a mediator's work is determined by the kind of assistance requested by parties, and the forms of assistance the intermediary is capable of and willing to provide. Intermediaries generally provide three potential kinds of assistance: 1) improving parties' communication and the negotiation/mediation process (procedural assistance); 2) attending to parties' psychological or relationship issues and needs (relationship assistance); or 3) helping parties identify substantive information needed for wise decision making, working with them to generate viable settlement options and assisting them to make proposals that will be accepted and to resolve the dispute (substantive assistance). Each emphasis assumes that a specific type of problem is blocking progress toward achieving greater understanding, settling differences, reaching closure, and ending the conflict. Consequently, the intervention emphasis is tied directly to the issues involved and dynamics presented in each case.

To a significant extent, all mediators focus on improving communication to help people in dispute move toward their goals. However, primary attention to improving the process for effective problem solving and negotiation is required when a non-existent, inappropriate or ineffective problem-solving or negotiation process is prohibiting progress in the mediation session (Moore, 2014; Mayer, 2004; Picard, 2002; Beer & Steif, 1998; Folberg & Taylor, 1984: Stulberg, 1981). This focus assumes that parties need to revise their communication and negotiation procedures to manage and resolve their differences more effectively. Changing the process is expected to improve how parties communicate, understand each other's needs and interests, and conduct effective problem solving. Often, this involves mediators assisting parties to shift from a more positional approach to one focused on identifying parties' needs and interests, and identifying or building potential solutions that satisfactorily address them for all concerned (Moore, 2014; Fisher et al., 2011).

Many informal, peer, administrative/managerial and independent mediators principally provide procedural assistance to help disputing parties reach mutual understandings and agreements.

It should be noted that a major emphasis on improving the problem-solving or negotiation process does not preclude other assistance focused on parties' psychological/relationship issues or needs, or securing or providing needed substantive information to resolve a problem if that is what parties expect or request, and the intermediary is capable and willing to provide it.

Providing relationship assistance by addressing parties' psychological or relationship issues and needs is called for when one or more aspects of a party's psychological makeup and/or the dynamics of multiple disputants' relationships—their perceptions, misperceptions, assumptions, attitudes, emotions, behavior, actions or interactions—are problematic and are key causes or significant contributing factors to a conflict. In such cases the focus of intervention will be on improving disputants' capacities to communicate effectively and engage in meaningful dialogue to increase their insights about themselves, other participants and their relationships, including increasing understanding of their feelings, motivations, expectations, and psychological and relationship needs.

Accordingly, mediators focus on identifying procedures that help participants understand each other; identify, acknowledge, process and creatively respond to feelings; overcome psychological barriers that divide them; and move toward establishing their desired relationships. A relationship-oriented strategy seeks to transform previously conflictual interactions to ones characterized by trust, respect, tolerance, acceptance, and in some circumstances, reconciliation (either acceptance of a current or changed situation, or becoming reunited) and forgiveness.

Therapeutic (Kelly, 1983), *transformative* (Bush & Folger, 1994; Folger et al., 2010; Domenici & Littlejohn, 2001; Burgess, 1997), *narrative* (Monk & Winslade, 2013; Winslade & Monk, 2008; Billikopf-Encina, 2002; Monk et al., 1997; Cobb, 1999, 1994), and *restorative justice* (Umbreit, 2000; Center for Restorative Justice and Peacemaking, 2000) mediation are various approaches for relationship-focused processes. Again, it should be noted that an emphasis on the parties' psychological states or relationships is not always required and does not preclude the mediator from offering other procedural and substantive assistance when desired by the involved parties. Many organizational mediators provide some psychological and relationship assistance to help parties reach mutual understanding and agreement. Such was the case in the dispute involving the co-workers with different work styles. Similarly, the administrative/managerial mediator in the discrimination case also helped the parties to clarify their perceptions and expectations for acceptable attitudes and behaviors and improve their working relationships.

In some disputes, information available to the parties may not be sufficient to allow them to reach satisfactory agreements, and disputants want or need additional data and input from experts to help them make informed and wise decisions. A mediator's focus on substantive information is called for when adequate or acceptable substantive information is a significant barrier to settlement (Freund, 2012; Little, 2007; Freund, 2006; Picker, 2003; Alexander, 2008; Lowry, 2004; Riskin, 1996, 2003, 2009; Bickerman, 1996). Accordingly, mediators may provide various kinds of assistance to help parties assess available information, identify whether more is needed, and develop ways to obtain and evaluate its utility in achieving mutually satisfactory outcomes. Mediators may or may not directly provide information needed or requested by disputants. In some cases, the mediator may elicit what is needed from the parties, or help obtain it from external substantive experts. This approach preserves the mediator's impartiality.

In other circumstances, mediators are selected because of their substantive knowledge and expertise—relationship, psychological, legal, financial, technical, or scientific—and parties expect and want them to provide information that will help them reach understandings or agreements. On occasion, the intermediary may use reality-testing strategies to help parties assess the merits, strengths, or weaknesses of their cases or arguments, or provide these assessments him or herself. In other situations, based on the mediator's knowledge and experience, the intermediary may provide an assessment of potential outcomes if the dispute were to proceed to an administrative dispute resolution process or to court for a judicial decision. Additionally, mediators may be requested to provide standards, criteria, principles or frameworks for possible solutions or agreements; make suggestions for links and trades of items parties value differently; or make general or specific recommendations for how a settlement can be reached. Mediator proposals, if they choose to suggest them, may include agreements in principle, potential positive settlement ranges, options for agreements, specific terms to address individual items, or conceivable components of a package agreement. Again, however, this focus does not preclude the mediator from providing procedural and psychological/relationship assistance where required.

Returning to our earlier vignettes, both the managerial mediator who facilitated the discrimination case, and the independent mediator retained to resolve the lawsuit involving the two executives and their companies, provided substantive input to the parties to help them reach understandings and agreements. In the first case, the mediator provided information to each party in separate meetings. The substantive material included organizational standards and rules governing appropriate interactions between races; what was and was not acceptable in the organization regarding particular attitudes and behaviors; applicable laws, etc. He also provided information on the procedures, standards, and criteria used in performance reviews.

In the second case, the mediator, who was a lawyer, assisted the parties to identify and secure the services of a mutually acceptable independent substantive expert who jointly provided them with information needed to make informed decisions. She also, in private with each party, reviewed their legal cases and commented on what she perceived to be the merits, strengths and weaknesses of each one, and persuaded the parties that they both faced significant risks and costs if they continued to pursue resolution of their dispute in court. After confirmation that the parties wanted to explore possible settlement options, the mediator, at the parties' request, provided several principles and a general framework for settlement that was accepted by both sides. The parties then, with the intermediary's assistance, proceeded to negotiate and fill in the details. These cases illustrate the vital role substantive input, provided by either external experts or an intermediary, can play in overcoming substantive barriers and promoting informed and fair settlements. When appropriate and acceptable to disputing parties, substantive assistance can go hand-in-hand with procedural and relationship assistance as discussed elsewhere in the chapter.

Factor four: approaches to mediator direction

A final variation in mediation procedures is the intermediary's orientation toward how directive or passive he or she is in assisting disputants to better understand each other and reach understandings or agreements. In general, there are two broad mediator orientations: *orchestrators* and *dealmakers* (Kolb, 1983). These orientations occupy the ends of a continuum on which mediators locate themselves, with relatively few intermediaries working at the extremes. Each orientation is based on a number of assumptions about the dispute, the parties, the negotiation process, the appropriate role for an intermediary, and desired or expected outcomes. Orchestrators commonly see conflicts as mutual problems that disputants recognize, and trust that the parties themselves, with some assistance, can resolve the issues in dispute. They maintain that disputants' relationships and views on contested issues and interests, while potentially polarized, are not necessarily irreconcilable. Therefore, orchestrators believe that disputing parties generally require only some relationship or procedural assistance from a mediator, and limited substantive help, to achieve mutually acceptable outcomes.

Regarding information, orchestrators generally consider that data needed to achieve common understandings or agreements is either known by the parties, or can be obtained for them from someone other than the mediator. These intermediaries commonly see their role as catalysts to elicit and clarify information needed for informed decision making, and facilitators of means to secure it from external sources.

Concerning procedures, orchestrators view mediation as an extension of negotiations with procedural and relationship assistance, as necessary, to promote effective joint problem solving. They expect disputants to have major control and final decision-making authority over the dispute resolution process (Stulberg, 1981). Therefore, orchestrators are less active and more elicitive than directive and prescriptive in their interventions. They take their lead from disputants and act accordingly, varying how active or passive they are and how much they elicit suggestions and collaboratively develop the dispute resolution process with parties.

Regarding mediation outcomes, orchestrators presume that with their assistance, parties will achieve integrative solutions that meet their primary procedural, relationship and substantive needs and interests. Orchestrators are likely to intervene and comment on the substantive content of agreements when some of the conditions described in the section above on independent mediators are called into question, such as the good faith or capacities of parties or the durability of the agreement. Informal, peer, and independent mediators with an orchestrator orientation helped in the disputes between the co-workers, conflicts on the shop floor, and the development of the new policy by many departments.

In contrast, dealmakers tend to view the conflicts they mediate as intractable—long-standing, serious, involving contests over values or competition over limited resources and punctuated by a history of failed efforts at resolution (Berkovitch, 2003). Concerning information, mediators with a deal-making orientation perceive that parties commonly negotiate using highly contradictory, inadequate, inaccurate, or unrealistic data. Dealmakers consider disputants to be poor judges of the merits of their views or cases, and unrealistic regarding potential terms for settlements. They believe that parties come to them because they want substantive information or prescriptive advice on the issues that divide them, a perception that is often confirmed by the parties. Indeed, some disputants request the mediator to actively provide knowledgeable appraisals or judgments about the accuracy of data used in deliberations, the merits of their cases, potential risks and outcomes if they cannot reach a negotiated agreement, and suggestions for potential settlement options.

Mediators with a deal-making orientation view parties as having only limited capacity to come together, initiate talks and make sound joint decisions. Therefore, dealmakers, and frequently parties, believe that what is needed to settle a conflict is a strong and active hand both to manage the dispute resolution process and provide substantive input on issues under discussion. Deal-making-oriented negotiations, in the most directive and prescriptive form, involve the intermediary taking a lead role in negotiating with individual disputants in private sessions over the exchange of possible offers. In this process, the mediator helps parties develop, or resort to mediator suggestions, which the intermediary carries back and forth between the parties until an acceptable bargaining range or deal is reached. The intermediary's goal is to narrow the gap between parties' positions to the point where they can agree, or, as a last resort, to suggest a reasonable compromise settlement.

Regarding outcomes, dealmakers generally focus on reaching tangible settlements involving an exchange of what are perceived by parties as scarce resources. Outcomes often take the form of compromises and are distributive in nature, with gains and losses shared in a way that is either acceptable or acceded to by all parties. Improving relationships between the parties is often not seen to be as important as reaching agreements on substantive issues, although it may be a secondary goal or unintended outcome. Mediators displayed a deal-making orientation in the discrimination conflict between the employee and her supervisor, and in the dispute involving litigation between the CEOs. In both cases, the mediators viewed the disputants as entrenched, and concluded that external information and prodding by an intermediary would be needed to help participants reach common understandings and acceptable agreements. In both cases, administrative/managerial and independent mediators were more procedurally and substantively directive than their orchestrator counterparts. In addition to joint sessions, they convened private meetings, a more conducive setting for carrying out deal-making activities, in which they provided relevant party-specific information, conducted reality testing, offered suggestions on potential settlement options and more directly influenced each disputant.

Toward a more integrative view of mediation

Details about mediation and vignettes referenced throughout this chapter illustrate significant variations in the kinds of mediators in organizations, their relationships to parties and issues in dispute, approaches to providing assistance, and the extent of their direction to help parties resolve their differences. While in general most mediators have a preference for a specific kind of mediator role and the kinds of assistance they prefer to provide and utilize general approaches focused on procedural, relationship or substantive assistance, they often borrow from other possible approaches and interventions, adapting and blending them to meet the unique situations of disputants and the context of each dispute. Taking note of these variations, it is safe to conclude that there is not one correct type of mediator, approach, or process for mediation (Riskin, 1996, 2003, 2009; Stempel, 2000, 1997).

Perhaps what most distinguishes an excellent mediator is his or her capacity to be an effective "reflective practitioner" (Schön, 1983). Schön, a philosopher with a specialty in systems and organizational change, first introduced this concept of professional practice and advocated bringing reflection into what professionals do. He posited a process of "knowing in action," in which professionals "think on their feet" and engage in reflection in action to foster personal professional development, improvement and continuous learning. The process involves a practitioner (a mediator in our case) viewing each situation (a dispute or conflict) as new and unique—paying critical attention to its potential causes; those involved and their professed needs, interests and desires for outcomes; and procedures that may potentially be useful to address them. It requires a review of the repertoire of useful theories and practical strategies known to the mediator that might provide guidance for interventions, and then appropriate follow-on activities that cull from the repertoire of the practitioner's own personal and professional experiences—ideas, theories and actions—used to handle similar situations in the past to see what might be applicable and useful in the current situation. Finally, with the above information in mind, the practitioner develops a hypothesis of what might work and tries it out in an experiment—an intervention—while continuously learning as the situation unfolds. The reflection-on-action component of Schön's framework requires building in awareness, observation and a feedback loop so that practitioners can reflect on and assess the impact of their strategies and actions after execution, learn from them and adjust future activities accordingly.

Only by being "reflective practitioners" will mediators be able to work effectively with parties in appropriate roles and designs and that will enable them to implement a customized and effective mediation processes to help disputants successfully address and resolve their differences and move toward more peaceful interpersonal, intergroup, and organizational relationships.

Notes

1 This chapter draws extensively on "The mediation process: Mediator roles, functions, approaches and procedures," in Moore, 2014.

2 It should be noted that many independent mediators do not like the term impartial, as it is seen as showing a lack of concern, or disinterest. Consequently, some prefer the term multipartial, indicating a commitment to help all parties meet their needs and interests.

References

Alexander, N. (2008) The mediation metamodel: Understanding practice. *Mediation Quarterly*, 26(1): 97–123.

Beer, J. & Steif, E. (2001) *The Mediator's Handbook* (4th edn). Philadelphia, PA: New Society Publishers.

Berkovitch, J. (2003) Characteristics of intractable conflicts. *Beyond Intractability*. Retrieved from www.beyondintractability.org/essay/characteristics-ic.

Bickerman, J. (1996) Evaluative mediator responds. *Alternatives to the High Cost of Litigation*, 14(6): 70.

Billikopf-Encina, G. (2002) Narrative mediation: A new approach to conflict resolution. *International Journal of Conflict Management*, 13(1): 100–104.

Burgess, H. (1997) Transformative mediation. Conflict Research Consortium. Retrieved from www.colorado.edu/conflict/transform/tmall.htm.

Bush, R. & Folger, J. (1994) *The Promise of Mediation: Responding to Conflict through Empowerment and Recognition*. San Francisco, CA: Jossey-Bass.

Center for Restorative Justice and Peacemaking. (2000) *Guidelines for Victim-sensitive Mediation: Restorative Justice through Dialogue*. Retrieved from www.ncjrs.gov/ovc_archives/reports/96517-gdlines_victims-sens/ncj176346.pdf.

Cobb, S. (1994) A narrative perspective on mediation. In J.P. Folger & T.S. Jones (eds) *New Directions in Mediation: Communication Research and Perspectives* (pp. 48–63). Thousand Oaks, CA: Sage.

Cobb, S. (1999) Empowerment and mediation: A narrative perspective. *Negotiation Journal*, 9(3): 245–259.

Currie, C. (2004) Mediating off the grid. *Dispute Resolution Journal*, 59(2). Retrieved from www.mediate.com/articles/currieC4.cfm?nl=64.

Domenici, K. & Littlejohn, S. (2001) *Mediation: Empowerment in Conflict Management*. Prospect Heights, IL: Waveland Press.

Fisher, R., Ury, W. & Patton, B. (2011) *Getting to Yes: Negotiating Agreement without Giving in.* New York: Penguin.

Folberg, J. & Taylor, A. (1984) *Mediation: A Comprehensive Guide to Resolving Conflicts without Litigation.* San Francisco, CA: Jossey-Bass.

Folger, J.P., Bush, R.A.B. & Della Noce, D.J. (2010) *Transformative Mediation: A Sourcebook.* New York: Institute for the Study of Conflict Transformation and Association for Conflict Resolution.

Freund, J. (2006) Calling all deal lawyers: Try your hand at resolving disputes. *The Business Lawyer,* 62(1): 37–53.

Freund, J. (2012) *Anatomy of Mediation.* New York: Practicing Law Institute.

Kelly, J. (1983) Mediation and psychotherapy: Distinguishing the differences. *Conflict Resolution Quarterly,* 1: 33–44.

Kolb, D. (1983) *The Mediators.* Cambridge, MA: MIT Press.

Kolb, D. & Sheppard, B. (1985) Do managers mediate, or even arbitrate? *Negotiation Journal,* 1(4): 379–388.

Lederach, J.P. (1985) Mediation in North America: An examination of the profession's cultural assumptions. Paper presented at the National Conference on Peacemaking and Conflict Resolution, Denver.

Little, J. (2007) *Making Money Talk: How to Mediate Insured Claims and Other Monetary Disputes.* Washington, DC: American Bar Association.

Lowry, L.R. (2004) Evaluative mediation. In J. Folberg, A.L. Milne & P. Salem (eds) *Divorce and Family Mediation: Models, Techniques and Applications* (pp. 72–91). New York: Guilford Press.

Mayer, B. (2004) Facilitative mediation. In J. Folberg, A.L. Milne & P. Salem (eds) *Divorce and Family Mediation: Models, Techniques and Applications* (pp. 29–52). New York: Guilford Press.

Monk, G. & Winslade, J. (2013) *When Stories Clash: Addressing Conflict with Narrative Mediation.* Taos, NM: Taos Institute Publications.

Monk, G., Winslade, J., Crocket, K. & Epston, D. (eds). (1997) *Narrative Therapy in Practice: The Archeology of Hope.* San Francisco, CA: Jossey-Bass.

Moore, C. (2014) *The Mediation Process: Practical Strategies for Resolving Conflict.* San Francisco, CA: Jossey-Bass.

Morril, C. (1995) *The Executive Way.* Chicago, IL: University of Chicago Press.

Picard, C. (2002) *Mediating Interpersonal and Small Group Conflict.* Ottawa, Canada: Golden Dog Press.

Picker, B. (2003) *Mediation Practice Guide: A Handbook for Resolving Business Disputes* (2nd edn). Washington, DC: American Bar Association.

Riskin, L. (1996) Understanding mediators' orientations, strategies, and techniques: A Grid for the perplexed. *Harvard Law Review,* 7(8–13): 17–38.

Riskin, L. (2003) Decision-making in mediation: The new old grid and the new grid system. *Notre Dame Law Review,* 79(1): 1–54.

Riskin, L. (2009) Retiring and replacing the grid of mediator orientations. *Alternatives to the High Costs of Litigation,* 21(4): 69–76.

Schön, D. (1983) *The Reflective Practitioner: How Professionals Think in Action.* New York: Basic Books.

Stempel, J. (1997) Beyond formalism and false dichotomies: The need for institutionalizing a flexible concept of the mediator's role. *Florida State Law Review,* 24(949): 972–984.

Stempel, J. (2000) The inevitability of the eclectic: Liberating ADR from ideology. *Journal of Dispute Resolution,* 2000(2): 247–293. Retrieved from scholars.law.unlv.edu/facpub/217.

Stulberg, J. (1981) The theory and practice of mediation: A reply to Professor Susskind. *Vermont Law Review,* 6(1): 85–117.

Umbreit, M.S. (2000) *The Handbook of Victim-offender Mediation.* San Francisco, CA: Jossey-Bass.

Winslade, J. & Monk, G. (2008) *Practicing Narrative Mediation: Loosening the Grip of Conflict.* San Francisco, CA: Jossey-Bass.

16

ORGANIZATIONAL CONFLICT MANAGEMENT SYSTEMS

The emergence of mediators as conflict resolution professionals

Alexia Georgakopoulos, Harold Coleman Jr. and Rebecca Storrow

Conflict is inherent in any system where people are interdependent and rely on others. In organizations, people often spend significant time in their work environments compared to other contexts, and combined with the pressure to perform in a competitive atmosphere conflict may manifest, yet conflict can be constructive, rather than destructive if addressed effectively. Designing a conflict management system (CMS) within an organization may inevitably enhance the overall organizational culture and overall health of an organization, as improved interaction and communication between organizational members tend to yield positive results for everyone involved. Given the paramount importance of preventing, managing, and resolving conflict in organizations, an organizational CMS is not only necessary, but also imperative to the success of contemporary organizations. This is particularly true in today's litigious environment. Mediation serves as one fine example of a conflict management approach whereby mediators emerge as conflict resolution professionals, who enable disputing parties to exercise self-determination, control, and collaboration in their own decision-making processes. Research has shown that mediation is increasingly used as an effective means of dispute resolution in organizations (Cloke & Goldsmith, 2000a; Costantino & Merchant, 1996).

Mediation is generally defined as a non-adversarial and consensual process that includes the assistance of an impartial individual, who serves as a guardian of the process and who assists parties in arriving at mutually beneficial outcomes or decisions. The conceptual definition of mediation certainly is varied across mediation models and it is expected to expand with theory development in mediation as it applies to disparate contexts, people, issues, and conflicts. The notion that mediation has popularly been connected with successful settlement does not capture the depth and breadth of experiences nor outcome possibilities that can emerge from mediation. This resonates with Bush and Folger's (2005) critique of the satisfaction story when the sole outcome of mediation rests predominately on settlement. Indeed, settlement should not be viewed as the sole or perhaps best measure of mediation success; rather, the concept of acceptable outcomes defined by parties may serve as a more enlightening view of mediation success, for it embraces parties' ownership in outcomes. Often mediation results in valuable action plan development or non-materialistic outcomes, so the yardstick of success for mediation is undermined if it rests solely on settlement. In fact, mediation with its application from various models to date has yielded a number of possible positive outcomes (Bush & Folger, 2005; Hansen, 2013; Monk & Winslade, 2013; Moore, 2014; and Cloke, 2001), such as transformation, empowerment, recognition, constructive conflict, improved interactions, restorative relationships, authentic understanding, new narratives, new realities, forgiveness, transcendental experiences, and spiritual growth to name a few possibilities of this effective and largely magical form of conflict management.

The authors of this chapter have years of experience working with multinational organizations of every size in assisting individuals in these contexts with dispute resolution processes and CMS design, so this chapter presents essential recommendations for mediators who want to expand and render their services in this space. In this chapter, we discuss the cost of conflict for organizations, share the benefits of adopting mediation within a CMS, describe how a mediator may assist by serving as a CMS designer, consultant, trainer, or mediator in practice, show how emotional intelligence can be infused into the toolbox of mediators to enhance conflict management approaches, and illustrate how utilizing mediation within an integrative conflict management systems approach that includes progressive and state-of-the-art processes in conflict resolution may be effective.

Costs of conflict for organizations and their members

Organizations often ignore the premise that conflict is significantly controlled, influenced, and impacted by organizations themselves and the attitudes held by organizational leaders about conflict. In educating organizations about the importance of having a CMS in place, it is necessary to build awareness about the costs related to the lack of addressing conflict constructively, so that there may be a movement toward designing an effective and sustainable CMS. Disagreements of values, norms, processes, objectives, and goals are all conflict topics that can arise within an organization. Thus, a CMS would seem to alleviate uncertainty and lead to constructive conflict management, especially when all members are trained in the management system. When conflict prevention and escalation are recognized, organizational members may have less uncertainty and confusion about how to address conflict and this may reduce the potential cost related to conflict. The US Department of Labor's Commission to investigate workplace disputes recommended in-house alternative dispute resolution (ADR) systems (US Department of Labor, 2016). In both the Americans with Disabilities Act of 1990 and the Civil Rights Act of 1991, Congress specifically encouraged alternative methods of resolving discrimination disputes where appropriate and to the extent authorized by the law (US Department of Labor, 2016).

According to a study of managers, nearly half of their time is spent reaching agreements with others when conflicts occur (Watson & Hoffman, 1996). An organization's CMS may be among one of the most significant components in its cost control measures, freeing up time for management and staff to focus on work and operational tasks. There also can be enormous brand costs associated with external conflicts with partners and customers (Nelson et al., 2008). Even more severely, conflict can escalate into hostile workplace environments such as harassment, workplace bullying, workplace violence, or even homicide if organizations lack standards that address conflict preemptively or effectively once it emerges (Georgakopoulos et al., 2011).

In the competitive marketplace, organizations cannot afford to continuously litigate disputes. In a 2012 study by the National Center for State Courts (Washington State Bar Association, 2013), the average attorney costs of a court case were $88,000 for employment cases and $91,000 for contract cases. According to Courtools (2016), the standard percentage of general civil matters disposed or otherwise resolved within 540 days is 98 percent.

However, there is evidence that ADR can reduce time and cost substantially, since according to the American Arbitration Association (AAA, 2016), 56 percent of AAA business arbitration cases in 2015 were resolved through party settlement or voluntary dismissal. Companies that include mediation and arbitration in their contracts may oftentimes resolve matters prior to a court filing (Clausebuilder, 2016).

As globalization and technology increase, contemporary organizations will clearly reap benefits, but challenges and conflicts will also be inevitable, such as the following: 1) communication, including face-to-face and technological interaction, will become more complex; 2) diversity in values and norms will vary across organizational systems in the ever-increasing global marketplace; 3) conflict can cause chaos and crisis when there are no processes in place to address it; and 4) conflict will be costly in an overburdened court system, if appropriate systems are not in place to handle, respond, and resolve conflict early.

Conflict management systems (CMS)

A CMS is a strategic system that involves managing conflict and overall aids in preventing, intervening, and resolving conflict. A CMS can establish a grievance or conflict management process for various types of conflict within the organization between its members, or outside the organization with suppliers, vendors, and/or customers. Preventing future conflict or reducing the escalation of conflict can contribute to the health of relationships associated with the organization. This can reduce corporate costs, improve customer satisfaction, strengthen organizational teams, and support business partners. A CMS includes dispute resolution tools, assessments, interventions, training, and mechanisms to support organizations in effectively addressing conflict from prevention to resolution. The cost of conflict and the multitude of disputes that may arise within organizations should motivate organizational members to consider a solid CMS. A well-established CMS can transform destructive conflict into constructive conflict. What is more, a progressive CMS effectively manages enterprise risk, which is a critical aspect of any organization's strategic management plan.

Benefits of mediation in a CMS

Mediation is one formidable conflict management approach that can save organizations from the aggravation and costs related to conflict. In fact, mediation can be utilized as the primary conflict management approach, given its focus on party self-determination. Mediation combined with other forms of ADR (i.e. negotiation, facilitation, arbitration, ombuds) may be an exceptional match for any organization, yet any form of CMS must be evaluated in relation to the unique organization, people, resources, and needs.

It is essential to recognize that diversity related to any organization presents itself as a strength, yet as a challenge. Negotiating realities in any organization requires that organizational members respond to the demands of diversity, especially in light of the global and multi-faceted organizational environment. Just as individuals are socialized into a complex world of norms and values, organizational culture is an intricately complex woven web of implicit and explicit norms about standard operating procedures about the workplace, conflict, and interactions. Thus, a CMS should have benefits that outweigh costs for its implementation and it should be designed with consideration of the organization's rich diversity. Ultimately, the CMS that is designed for the organization will in turn have a strong bearing on organizational culture and climate.

Just as organizations are diverse, dispute resolution approaches are diverse. Mediation does not have one face; rather, a number of mediation models and theoretical frameworks currently exist with unique variations and objectives (see Table 16.1) and others are expected to emerge in the future.

Therefore, options for mediation abound for organizations. These options are important, given the diverse contexts where mediation may be applied. A CMS may integrate existing models like transformative mediation (Bush & Folger, 2005), narrative mediation (Winslade & Monk, 2000), problem-solving mediation (Moore, 2014), restorative mediation (Umbreit, 2006), or it may integrate a hybrid or mixed approach to mediation like the Generalist approach described by Hansen (2013).

The dispute resolution approach and/or mediation model should be carefully selected with priority placed on people within the organization. According to Costantino and Merchant (1996), there are six principles important to the design phase of a dispute resolution process, as follows: 1) the process should address interests; 2) people should have options that are viable and cost effective; 3) people should have alternative options if earlier methods failed; 4) people should be educated prior to implementation of the method and they should be debriefed after the method; 5) methods implemented should follow rank order from low to high cost; and 6 methods should be bolstered with incentives, reinforcement, and support so they are applied and useful.

Mediation involved with an integrative CMS

When mediation is not sufficient alone, it can be integrated with dispute resolution approaches like negotiation, facilitation, arbitration, or even litigation. Integrative CMS approaches are often nuanced as typically they are designed to meet the unique needs of people and their

TABLE 16.1 Mediation models and theoretical frameworks

	Problem-solving mediation	*Transformative mediation*	*Narrative mediation*
Organization of the mediation	Sequential and linear steps-based model with chronological steps	Fluid and in-flux model, based on movement with parties	Stage-based model with a typical sequence, but ebb and flow permitted between stages
Parties' roles	Parties are viewed as decision makers and problem solvers	Parties largely own both content and process	Parties are co-authors as they co-construct new narratives
Mediators' roles	Mediators are guardians of the process and guide parties through a systematic process	Mediators follow parties in the direction they desire both in terms of content and process	Mediators facilitate parties in constructing new alternative stories
Focus and goal of the model	Focuses on problem solving and beneficial decision making with goals of resolution and settlement	Focus on improved interaction with goals of shifts like empowerment and recognition that support transformation	Focus on deconstructing dominant stories and externalizing the problem to constructing alternative stories of cooperation with goals of changing realities through new narratives
Theoretical focus	Organizational theory and organizational problem solving	Moral theory and development and relational ideology	Social construction theory and postmodern theory

organizations. Essentially, organizational members should take into consideration the preferences of leadership along with employees who are stakeholders in order to build a sustainable CMS. While mediation may be selected as the primary dispute resolution process in a CMS, it alternatively can be offered as one method among disparate conflict resolution methods in the CMS. Given the complexity of conflict, a one-size-fits-all approach to CMS is not recommended as one process may not be sufficient to resolve conflict; therefore, backups are essential (Costantino & Merchant, 1996). Foundational mechanisms for addressing conflict should be dynamic and fluid, so mediation used in conjunction with an integrative CMS may serve as an excellent option in a systemic approach to address conflict holistically.

Typically, it is advisable to use conflict approaches that are informal in initial stages of conflict management and move toward more formal approaches when the conflict is complex or has not been easily resolved by utilizing alternative approaches in the informal stages (Costantino & Merchant, 1996). A continuum that follows initially from informal and largely interest-based approaches toward subsequently formal and rights-based approaches of conflict management can be understood with this sequence: dialogue, negotiation, mediation, facilitation, early neutral evaluation (panel reviews), non-binding arbitration, binding arbitration, and litigation.

Most often, financial costs increase in the continuum with movement toward more formal approaches. This continuum can aid designers and organizational members in their determination of what approaches should be implemented in early or later stages of the CMS. In fact, a CMS can be designed to follow the course of this continuum by which all approaches are applied in sequence until the conflict is resolved, or the CMS may include a few approaches to expedite the process, if time is an important consideration. For example, problem-solving mediation (Moore, 2014) may be selected as a primary method, with binding arbitration as a backup. The authors of this chapter recommend that an integrative CMS should include a primary method with solid backups in order to make the approach concise with clear expectations, so everyone associated with the organization understands the standard operating procedure of the CMS. Pre-screening with intake questionnaires or interviews from the onset should be done with individuals in every conflict scenario to assess if an interest-based approach or a rights-based approach is appropriate.

Mediators emerge as conflict resolution professionals

As Costantino and Merchant (1996) point out, "[c]onflict today is a growth industry" (p. ix). This is a time when conflict conditions are volatile and unprecedented in the history of the human race given the remarkable and unpredictable changes humans face. It seems fitting that mediators should facilitate in the discourse, debates, and action plans that involve mitigating and responding to conflict. We argue that mediators may serve effectively as trainers, designers, consultants, coaches, and/or practitioners if they have solid competencies in mediation and dispute systems design. Many of these tasks are intricately connected, so they require mediators to be dynamic and multifunctional in terms of their work. There are ample opportunities for mediators to assist organizations, so organizations are able to thrive and succeed today and in the future. Mediators, given their skill sets, are well equipped to enter an organization in order to address the following: 1) determine if the types of conflicts typically reported are appropriate and ripe for mediation; 2) educate organizational members on the particular conflict management processes in order to incorporate a good fit with the organization; 3) assist with the implementation of a mediation program within an integrative framework; and 4) provide recommendations and suggestions for how to evaluate the program's effectiveness.

Costantino and Merchant (2002) explain that these activities are encompassed within the four stages of dispute systems design. For example, a mediator who serves as a trainer can educate organizational members to recognize the differences between and among various conflict resolution approaches (i.e. negotiation, facilitation, mediation, arbitration), and distinguish characteristics within each approach such as those inherent to mediation models. They can serve as expert coaches in skill-building stages when individuals are acquiring skills to function as interveners, perhaps as in-house mediators or externally appointed ones. Additionally, mediators may coach individuals on how to navigate within the process of mediation as parties. They can help parties gain an understanding about their roles and skill sets during mediation. In fact, a drawback of any form of ADR is when people are in the dark about an approach and do not understand what it looks like in practice.

In addition, a mediator can serve as a CMS consultant to advise organizational members to design a CMS program with transparency, cooperation, and ownership by individuals who will be directly impacted by it. It will more likely prove to be sustainable and successful in the longevity of the organization when it is co-created and hence co-owned, with the input of stakeholders in the organization. While it may be unconventional for organizational leaders with a top-down or authoritative approach to management to recognize the utility of using an organic cooperative and participatory approach, Cloke and Goldsmith (2000b) have indicated that an inclusive approach that fosters organizational democracy often supersedes people's expectations with positive outcomes. In terms of design stages, a mediator may serve as an excellent designer because they can work with organizational members to design a CMS where mediation may be integrated as the primary or first-step alternative dispute method followed by viable backup options if mediation is not initially successful. Feedback and evaluation should be effectively built into the design of the CMS and new employees should appreciate the origin and customization of this design since it is participatory.

Another vital task required of the designer is to have a CMS that squarely and formally addresses conflict management processes in terms of policy and procedures. These policies and procedures will likely communicate the high value that the organization places on its organizational members and their well-being. For example, if a CMS integrates mediation, the selection of mediators should be approved by appropriate protocol to ensure that mediators can serve as effective and ethical practitioners to mediate disputes. The above examples show that mediators can emerge as conflict management professionals who can be significantly involved with a CMS that ultimately communicates to individuals that addressing conflict as a natural occurrence within an organization serves as an opportunity, rather than as an impediment, to enhance communication, dialogue, and understanding in contemporary organizational landscapes.

Characteristics of a good CMS

Some basic characteristics inherent to an effective CMS include:

- Prevention of conflict by building awareness of how disputes occur in the workplace
- Immediacy in responding to conflict—it should be addressed immediately otherwise if left unresolved, it can escalate and become more costly
- Involvement directly by the individuals involved; conflict is best resolved when addressed

- Sensitivity and respect for the organization's people, history, culture, and accomplishments (Borsa et al., 1999)
- Creation of a "learning organization" (Senge, 1990), building the organization's conflict management competency
- Improvement of morale and results-oriented communication
- Equality in access and ownership of the CMS
- Strategic planning with support of leadership
- Learning and transparency of the CMS
- Feedback and evaluation of the CMS from individuals' perspectives, needs, and challenges

An effective CMS designer: emotional and multiple intelligences

An effective CMS designer should possess many of the tools required of a seasoned mediator or facilitator. Communication, multiple intelligences, flexibility, creativity, and organizational skills are all portable skills that professionals in many ADR fields can apply to CMS consulting and design work.

Perhaps one of the most efficacious areas in which mediators can lend insights and bring value in the training/consulting/coaching mode is emotional intelligence (EI). Also referred to as EQ, EI relates to the self-assessment and management of one's own emotions, as well as to the discernment of those of others as well. Just as IQ is a measure of one's cognitive intelligence, EI is a measure of one's emotional intelligence.

EI is credited for many advancements in business, leadership development, and geopolitical diplomacy, with its focus on people. However, EI benefits are not only for business, but also on a more personal level can result in greater happiness, improved mental and physical health, strengthened social and marital relationships, and decreased stress. Other characteristics of high EI include self-confidence, optimism, persuasiveness, empathy, coping, stress management, self-awareness, self-control, and conflict management.

Although these traits seem desirable for any professional, it would seem that mediators can benefit tremendously by integrating this form of intelligence into their work. In the CMS setting, many companies are downsizing, and with smaller staff come increased stresses. In one recent study, 34 percent of hiring managers said they place greater emphasis on emotional intelligence when hiring and promoting employees (Career Builder, 2011). When asked why emotional intelligence is more important to their selection of staff than high IQ, these hiring managers identified the following attributes as indicative of individuals with high EI: ability to stay calm under pressure, ability to resolve conflict effectively, ability to convey empathy to the plight of team members, ability to lead by example, and ability to effect more thoughtful decisions (Career Builder, 2011).

Ability to improve EI

The good news for professionals is that EI skills can be learned. A major difference between IQ and EI is the fact that IQ is relatively stable over time, whereas EI can improve over time with dedication and guidance. Neuropsychologists posit that the brain has the capacity to develop new neural pathways in response to experience or injury and suggest that with adequate training, people can become more socially adept, altruistic, and compassionate (Cloke, n.d.). This also means that people have the ability to "unlearn" or "learn a better way" to handle their emotions, though one may feel "trapped" in old patterns and habits that are hard to overcome. This news is encouraging for the future of emotional wellness and has spawned a new industry in teaching these skills at all levels of business for executives, managers, and employees. In addition, insightful mediators are particularly well equipped to deliver such trainings in organizational management settings.

Implications for CMS

Mediators, across the board, need to be high-EI individuals. This is because conflict resolution is first, fundamentally, and foremost about people. Mediators may adopt EI principles in their role as CMS designers by first helping organizational leaders to appreciate the importance of this fundamental axiom. In so doing, leaders may be less directed to fault-based forms of dispute resolution and more to forms creating transparency, self-awareness, and communication. Mediators as CMS designers need to help organizational leaders appreciate the fact that the problems employees face belong to the parties (employer and employee alike), and that the best solution, if given the right circumstances, will flow from the parties themselves. Mediators are ideally suited to help others create those best circumstances, conducive to listening and learning, by their EI-based focus on people and constructive interaction.

In the CMS training mode, mediators may train managers and others within the organization in mediation skills and techniques, designed to facilitate the direct negotiation of conflict. In this manner, these individuals might better serve as "conflict coaches" in preparing disputing parties for constructive direct engagement. They can also help disputing parties in becoming more aware of their own emotional triggers and in ways to avoid becoming "emotionally hijacked," which is a frequent cause of workplace conflict. As trainers, mediators may also train internal mediators from select individuals within the organization's workforce, but specifically with those demonstrating a capacity for high EI through their ability to listen, empathize, and communicate productively.

Moreover, mediators in a CMS mode can bring tremendous value to helping parties reframe their negotiating style from one of adversarial posturing to that of cooperative problem solving. Interest-based negotiating produces far more enduring resolutions in the long term, particularly where a relationship is at stake. Interest-based negotiating builds on relationship management principles of EI, such that the parties, with improved understanding born of active listening, are better capable of resolving not only near-term conflicts, but also future ones as well.

The old paradigm that high IQ is enough to succeed in life and in business is dead. IQ is no longer (and may never have been) enough to determine success in today's complex and inter-connected world. While there is no shortage of people with high IQ in professional settings, there is a deficit of people with high EI in these arenas. EI can have dramatic results for every area of life, such as more fulfilling personal relationships, improved business profitability, and increased health and wellness. EI awareness and improvement should be critical tools to be incorporated into a mediator's conflict-coaching toolkit. The good news is that EI can be learned and improved with effort and dedication, and mediators are well positioned to deliver the training required to meet these ends. With increasing focus now placed on cultural competency and diversity in the organizational setting, mediators can bring added value as trainers/consultants/conflict coaches to leverage not only the best in emotional intelligence applications, but also those of multiple intelligences, appreciative inquiry, and related neuropsychological discoveries for sustained organizational success.

Education, tools, and training for conflict management

Training and education are the most frequently used approaches for designing a sustainable CMS. This often requires a "needs-based" approach to the training model, beginning with a training needs assessment (Beebe et al., 2003). Needs assessments can be conducted with surveys, questionnaires, or interviews and a host of other methods. The quality of the CMS depends on a thorough assessment of the following: needs of the organization, the types and patterns of conflict typically found, the resources and barriers to resolution, and the dispute systems design currently in place. There are various models regarding how to conduct needs assessments and a thorough understanding of the appropriate model is helpful to ensure an organization is not investing costly training dollars without a comprehensive strategy (Gupta, 1999).

Second, mediator styles may influence the manner in which the mediator-consultant practices. Mediators with a more collaborative or facilitative style compared to a directive-authoritative style may be more adept at bringing people together, fostering consensus, and promoting ownership. Also, mediators who are intentional about infusing positive consciousness with appreciative inquiry, apply a glass-half-full, rather than glass-half-empty approach and they may effectively prime parties to see mediation as an opportunity that is full of promise and hope. A mediator's style is a state, not a trait, so it is something that can be learned; therefore, it is important for mediators to be intentional about cultivating and crafting their unique styles.

Finally, it is important for mediators to have teaching skills when involved with organizational change. It is wise for mediators to have a solid grasp of adult learning theory (Knowles, 1970) with skill sets to incorporate team-building experiences within their overall instruction. Teaching the skills required for a CMS, mediators should incorporate education about organizational change, as this is an important component when an organization undergoes implementation of a new system. The basic assumption of adult learning theory is that adults engage in learning for personal reasons and that learning adds value to their lives in some ways. Contemporary adult learning in the context of workplace conflict puts the learner center stage and recognizes people as primary agents for change. The adult experience creates the backdrop for learning, and the learning process becomes an organic form of inquiry rather than a set of established truths.

Conclusion

So, what does all this theory and research mean for organizations investing in training and development to address conflict? We know that changes in the modern workplace pose challenges for all workers. The complex and challenging global economy creates the need for continuous learning and updating of competencies and skills that enhance communication and conflict resolution. There is increased need for organizations to establish an environment of continuous collaborative professional growth. The individual's role in his or her own resolution of conflict becomes paramount to leveraging a competitive advantage. Therefore, organizations are wise to expand from traditional approaches of skill-based learning to approaches that include dispute resolution training through technology, communities of learning, and continuous on-the-job learning challenges. Organizations must also create a workplace environment that supports the engagement of ADR on a continuous and long-term basis. Given their unique skill sets, mediators are well equipped to help organizations take this transformative step.

As demonstrated, mediators should be integral to an organization's CMS design. Their focus on people skills and their ability to marry conflict resolution theory with practice, equip them well for the multifaceted roles of conflict assessor, designer, trainer, facilitator, and coach. CMS processes that effectively integrate mediation skills, techniques, and best practices avail much in conflict prevention and resolution. The end results of improved employee morale, strategic risk management, and general organizational well-being should be evident from the consistent application of the CMS design principles outlined above.

References

American Arbitration Association (AAA). (2016) A guide to commercial mediation and arbitration for business people. *ADR.org*. Retrieved from www.adr.org/aaa/ShowPDF?doc=ADRSTAGE2019455.

Beebe, S.A., Mottet, T.P. & Roach, D.R. (2003) *Training & Development: Communicating for Success*. New York: Pearson.

Borsa, L., Cheung, S., Conbere, J., Linden, R. & Wayne, E.K. (1999) Society of professionals in dispute resolution organizational conflict management sector. *Organizational Conflict Management Sector of SPIDR*. Retrieved from adrr.com/adr9/3cq.htm.

Bush, R.A.B. & Folger, J.P. (2005) *The Promise of Mediation: The Transformative Approach to Conflict*. San Francisco, CA: Jossey-Bass Publishers.

Career Builder. (2011) Seventy-one percent of employers say they value emotional intelligence over IQ, according to Career Builder survey. Career Builder. Retrieved from www.careerbuilder.com/share/aboutus/pressreleasesdetail.aspx?id=pr652&sd=8/18/2011&ed=8/18/2099&siteid=cbpr&sc_cmp1=cb_pr652_.

Clausebuilder. (2016) Alternative dispute resolution clausebuilder tool. American Arbitration Association. Retrieved from www.clausebuilder.org/cb/faces/index?_afrLoop=2291125389472410&_afrWindowMode=0&_adf.ctrl-state=bp0q509p_4.

Cloke, K. (2001) *Mediating Dangerously: The Frontiers of Conflict Resolution*. San Francisco, CA: Jossey-Bass.

Cloke, K. (n.d.) Bringing oxytocin into the room: Notes on the neurophysiology of conflict. International Mediation Institute. Retrieved from imimediation.org/oxytocin_ken_cloke.

Cloke, K. & Goldsmith, J. (2000a). *Resolving Conflicts at Work: A Complete Guide for Everyone on the Job*. San Francisco, CA: Jossey-Bass.

Cloke, K. & Goldsmith, J. (2000b). Conflict resolution that reaps great rewards. *Journal for Quality and Participation*, 23(3): 27–30.

Costantino, C. & Merchant, C. (1996) *Designing Conflict Management Systems: A Guide to Creating Productive and Healthy Organizations*. San Francisco, CA: Jossey-Bass.

Costantino, C. & Merchant, C. (2002) *Designing Conflict Management Systems* (2nd edn). San Francisco, CA: Jossey-Bass.

Courtools. (2016) Time to disposition. National Center for State Courts. Retrieved from www.courtools.org/~/media/Microsites/Files/CourTools/courtools_Trial_measure3_Time_To_Disposition_pdf.ashx.

Georgakopoulos, A., Cook, L. & Kent, B. (2011) Workplace bullying: A complex problem in contemporary organizations. *International Journal of Business and Social Sciences*, 2(3): 1–20.

Gupta, K. (1999) *A Practical Guide to Needs Assessment*. San Francisco, CA: Jossey-Bass/Pfeiffer.

Hansen, T. (2013) *The Generalist Approach to Conflict Resolution: A Guidebook*. Lanham, MD: Lexington Books.

Knowles, M. (1970) *The Modern Practice of Adult Education: Andragogy versus Pedagogy*. New York: The Association Press.

Monk, G. & Winslade, J. (2013) *When Stories Clash: Addressing Conflict with Narrative Mediation*. Taos, NM: Taos Institute Publications.

Moore, C.W. (2014). *The Mediation Process: Practical Strategies for Resolving Conflict*. San Francisco, CA: Jossey-Bass.

Nelson, W.A., Weeks, W.B. & Campfield, J.M. (2008) The organizational costs of ethical conflicts. *Journal of Healthcare Management*, 53(1): 41–52.

Senge, P. (1990) *The Fifth Discipline*. London: Century Business.

Umbreit, M.S. (2006) *Mediating Interpersonal Conflict.* Eugene, OR: Wipf and Stock Publishers.
US Department of Labor. (2016) Employment litigation and dispute resolution. Office of the Secretary. Retrieved from www.dol.gov/_sec/media/reports/dunlop/section4.htm.
Washington State Bar Association. (2013) Memorandum. WSBA Office of the General Council. Retrieved from www.wsba.org/~/media/Files/Legal%20Community/Committees_Boards_Panels/ECCL%20Task%20Force/Reports/InterimReport04102013.ashx.
Watson, C. & Hoffman, R. (1996) Managers as negotiators: A test of power versus gender as predictors of feelings, behavior, and outcomes. *Leadership Quarterly*, 7(1): 63–85.
Winslade, J. & Monk, G. (2000) *Narrative Mediation: A New Approach to Conflict Resolution.* San Francisco, CA: Jossey-Bass.

17

EFFECTIVENESS OF MEDIATION IN THE STATE AGENCY GRIEVANCE PROCESS

Jessica Katz Jameson, RaJade M. Berry-James, Dennis M. Daley and Jerrell D. Coggburn

In this chapter, mediation is conceptualized as a form of intervention in which the third party is neutral with respect to the conflict parties and the outcome. As part of an organization's grievance process, mediation offers the grievant and respondent an opportunity to discuss their concerns and interests together and in their own voices, rather than through representatives such as attorneys. The goal is for the parties to construct a mutually satisfactory agreement that prevents further action such as an arbitration hearing or litigation. The organization described in this chapter uses facilitative mediation in which third parties help disputants engage in collaborative problem solving. This is in contrast to evaluative approaches in which mediators might comment on the facts or evidence of the grievant's case and transformative approaches in which mediators focus on the relationship between grievant and respondent. This distinction in mediation style is important because one of the most extensive evaluations of mediation in a government agency is the US Postal Service's REDRESS (Resolve Employee Disputes, Reach Equitable Solutions Swiftly) mediation program, which focuses on different types of disputes (primarily discrimination cases) and uses transformative mediation (see Bingham & Pitts, 2002). The REDRESS studies have demonstrated very high participant satisfaction as well as reduced formal grievance filing, reduced litigation, perceived organizational justice, and overall enhanced organizational climate. We wanted to investigate whether facilitative mediation for a different subset of grievances would show similar results.

The North Carolina Office of State Human Resources (OSHR) implemented a statewide Employee Mediation and Grievance policy to promote an efficient and effective resolution of workplace grievances and provide employees with a less adversarial method for resolving grievances. OSHR invited the authors to perform an independent study to substantiate the benefits of the mediation initiative in North Carolina state government. We compared two state agencies of similar size, the Department of Health and Human Services (DHHS) and the Department of Corrections (DOC).[1] At the time of our study, DHHS utilized the Employee Appeals and Grievance policy, which did not include a mediation option, while the DOC utilized the Employee Mediation and Grievance Process, which included mediation with a co-mediator team in step one. This chapter describes the costs and benefits of adding a mediation option to state agency grievance procedures. We discuss the two agencies we assessed, stakeholders' perceptions of the process where available, and our conclusions. Consistent with other research on mediation, we determined that allowing employees to voice their concerns in a safe environment where they feel acknowledged and treated fairly has long-term benefits for the employee and the organization.

Assessment process

Several sources of data informed our assessment, including meetings with human resource directors at each agency, analyses of mediation surveys completed by grievants and respondents in DOC, as well as reviews of the mediation activity database of the OSHR, Employee Relations Committee reports from DOC, annual human resources reports from DHHS, and Office of Administrative Hearing (OAH) case reports. The OAH acts as an independent quasi-judicial agency to settle state agency cases. It should be noted that dismissals, demotions, and written warnings were the only types of grievances included in the mediation process, and therefore these were the grievances examined across the two agencies in our analyses.

Department of Corrections: Employee Mediation and Grievance Process

At the time of our study, the Department of Corrections included the state prison system and many of the grievants were employed as corrections officers. The context is important, as rules for behavior are especially strict in this environment. Corrections officers must conform to legal requirements and are subjected to oversight from nonprofit and federal agencies. The grievant attends the mediation on his/her own behalf, and is allowed to bring someone with him/her, such as a family member or an attorney. The respondent is not necessarily the grievant's supervisor, but a representative from the agency who has the power and authority to make an agreement. All respondents receive training from OSHR so they are familiar with the process and how to enact their roles (for example, what they are allowed to offer or agree to).

Out of the 403 cases that went through the Employee Mediation and Grievance Process in the assessment period, 59 percent of the cases either did not proceed past intake, were resolved in mediation, or were not carried forward beyond mediation. Only ten cases proceeded to the OAH. The addition of mediation was calculated to save 19 staff hours per case and a minimum of $500 over cases that would have gone directly to the hearing panel if mediation had not been an option.[2] This is a conservative cost savings estimate as it does not include cost savings accrued by preventing cases from going to the OAH (costs of attorneys, time spent in discovery and case preparation, and settlement costs).

Participant evaluation of mediation

It is considered a best practice of organizational dispute system design to perform ongoing evaluation of your grievance process (Lipsky et al., 2003). Following each DOC mediation session, the grievant and respondent are asked to evaluate the mediation process by completing a 14-item survey. These survey questions focus on: 1 *the process* of mediation, such as satisfaction with the facility itself, the timeliness of the process, and whether the process provided an opportunity to discuss the issues; 2 *the relationships* among participants, including the perception of fairness and impartiality on the part of the mediators and the respect or civility accorded to each participant by the others; and 3 *the outcomes*, capturing whether the dispute was resolved and overall satisfaction. We analyzed 867[3] surveys from 429 grievants and 438 respondents using a statistical software package (SPSS). Results are summarized below for each of the three aspects of the mediation covered in the survey.

Research suggests that participants' perceptions of the process are an important component of whether they perceive organizational justice (Shapiro & Brett, 1993; Bingham & Pitts, 2002). The facility where mediation takes place is important, as grievants are especially concerned with confidentiality. If the location allows observers to see who is using it, this may discourage participation due to fear of retribution. In this study, nearly all grievants and respondents were satisfied with the mediation environment and location.

The DOC mediation process requires that mediation be held within 45 days of the filing of the grievance. Nearly all grievants and 100 percent of respondents agreed that their grievance requests were given prompt attention.

Explaining the process of mediation is especially important because it is unfamiliar to most grievants, who are more familiar with arbitration and legal approaches to conflict resolution. One of the biggest advantages of mediation over other third-party processes is that it allows grievants to use their own voices in the process. Nearly all grievants and respondents felt that mediation was explained to their satisfaction and they had sufficient time to tell their stories. There were very high rates of satisfaction in all three areas of the mediation process, although respondents were somewhat more satisfied than grievants.

The socio-emotional aspect of mediation is as important as the content issues discussed. Participants must believe that they will receive a fair and impartial hearing and will be treated with respect. This improves their satisfaction with, and commitment to, the organization. There are also often long-term relationships between grievants and their supervisors (or the respondents) to be considered.

At the heart of mediation is the importance of a fair and impartial hearing with a neutral and objective third-party presence. Since disputants may not trust one another, it is important that they trust the mediator and the process of mediation. Mediators concentrate a great deal of their attention on building and maintaining this trust (Moore, 1986; Slaikeu, 1996).

The DOC mediation process uses two mediators: a senior mediator and an apprentice. In over 90 percent of the cases, grievants and respondents agreed that the mediator and co-mediator were fair and impartial. Around 95 percent of grievants and virtually all respondents agreed they were treated with respect by the mediator and co-mediator. As with previous items, respondents reported a slightly stronger perception of respect than did grievants.

The relationship between the grievant and respondent is also important. A perceived lack of respect from the co-disputant undermines the sincerity and trust that underpins any agreement that might be reached. This survey item showed greater variance in grievant and respondent perceptions. Over 85 percent of grievants agreed they were treated with respect by respondents, while nearly 95 percent of respondents felt they were treated with respect by grievants. This suggests that grievants were somewhat less likely to feel respected by the respondent than vice versa.

Satisfaction with outcomes is measured by examining the extent to which parties believe the final agreement is fair and satisfactory, as well as their overall perception of the mediation session. Approximately 40 percent of grievants indicated satisfaction with the final agreements. Respondents agreed that they were satisfied in around 70 percent of the cases. In 37 percent of mediation cases, both the grievant and respondent agreed that they were satisfied.

The mediation evaluation survey included the option to provide more detailed explanations for participants' assessments of the mediation process. There were more positive than negative comments reported. The most common reasons listed for satisfaction included feeling comfortable due to the non-adversarial environment (for example, "I did not feel like I was on a witness stand"), and the belief that one or both parties left with better understanding (for example, "I learned a valuable lesson from this experience"). Common explanations for dissatisfaction were feeling that the respondent would not listen or negotiate, frustration that the mediator would not impose a solution, and not obtaining the desired outcome (for example, to be reinstated in their old position).

Employee Mediation and Grievance Process summary

While mediation is costly in terms of staff training, hours devoted to the process, and travel, a large percentage of cases did not proceed past step one and very few cases went to the OAH. We know from our examination of the data that the cost of OAH cases (settlements, attorney fees, etc.) is exponentially greater than either mediation or the panel hearing. The fact that an interests-based option, mediation, was available to DOC employees appears to have significant monetary benefits in addition to providing greater flexibility in finding solutions to employee grievances. This finding is especially meaningful given the non-negotiable nature of the types of cases in the DOC: dismissals, demotions, and written warnings. The fact that over a third of cases reached a mutually satisfactory agreement in mediation offers strong support for the value of employment mediation. To examine this claim further, we compared the DOC process to a state agency that did not include the mediation option.

Department of Health and Human Services: Employee Appeals and Grievance policy

The Employee Appeals and Grievance policy process entails three steps. In step one, a grievance form is filed with one's supervisor and human resources. The supervisor has five days to respond. If the grievance is not resolved at this step, the grievant may appeal the grievance to the director at step two. The director reviews the case, speaks with both parties and human resources, and writes a decision. If the grievance is not resolved to the grievant's satisfaction at step two, they may pursue step three, taking their grievance to a hearing officer. This is a formal process that involves general counsel, assignment of a hearing officer, a full discovery process for both sides, settlement conferences among attorneys, and if no settlement is reached, a hearing.

Since the first two steps of this process involve very few people and no additional salaried personnel, the initial costs of this process are lower than the cost of mediation. The hearing process is significantly higher because of the number of people involved, including attorneys. Of the 710 cases we examined, 457 ended after step one, 353 ended after step two, and 169 ended at step three. Forty-two cases went to the OAH.

The data suggest that a large proportion of DHHS cases do not go beyond the initial discussion with one's supervisor, around 50 percent go to the director, and approximately one-third of the grievances we examined went to step three, the hearing officer. It is notable, however, that some types of cases were not eligible for a hearing, and 64 percent of the *eligible* cases did proceed to the more expensive hearing stage. Of the approximately 167 cases that went to step three, 42 were appealed to the OAH and State Personnel Commission, with additional costs for time, travel, attorney fees, and settlements, as described above.

In the absence of evidence from surveys or talking to participants, we do not know how comfortable employees are with the Employee Appeals and Grievance policy process and whether DHHS employees perceive this process as fair. Based on academic studies of employee voice and grievance processes, employees are less likely to pursue a grievance when there is limited separation of management from the third-party process, which often results in fear of retaliation (Blancero & Dyer, 1996; Jameson, 2001, Morrison, 2011). With these two options presented at step one and step two, we conclude that there are likely to be grievances that are not brought to one's supervisor, and it is even less likely that they would go over their supervisor's head and take their grievance to a director. Based on their experience with employees, human resources staff believe hearing officers are perceived as fair and impartial, although it should be noted that very few directors' recommendations were overturned. We also noted a high proportion of recurring cases at DHHS during the three-year period examined (approximately 25 percent). These are defined as new cases that are brought forward from the same grievant.

Employee Appeals and Grievance policy summary

At first glance, the Employee Appeals and Grievance policy process appears to be lower-cost due to lower investment of personnel in steps one and two. However, including mediation at step one may reduce the number of repeat cases, as employees who are more satisfied with the process after their first grievance may be less likely to file additional grievances. Further, the DOC data revealed that only ten of the DOC cases went to the OAH during this time period compared to 42 of the DHHS cases. The higher number of cases that go to the OAH account for exponentially higher costs overall as grievants seek due process from a fair and impartial third party that is not connected to management (Slaikeu & Hasson, 1998). While we do not have data to support the impact of this process on the overall organizational climate, we know from research on alternative dispute resolution that mediation programs encourage employees to seek collaborative, interests-based solutions, while the absence of mediation leads to more adversarial, and ultimately more costly, rights- and power-based orientations to conflict management (Shapiro & Brett, 1993; Ury et al., 1988).

Implications for including mediation in a grievance process

Employee grievances are an inevitable part of the organizational experience. Significant research has concluded that the benefits of including mediation in a grievance process include direct cost savings in employee time, attorney fees, and court costs as well as secondary cost savings in the form of decreased absences and turnover (Burgess & Burgess, 1997; Kasperzak, 1996). The DOC mediation evaluation surveys suggest that participants are extremely satisfied with mediation even when they do not get the outcome they desired. This is especially noteworthy for the context examined here because we only examined dismissals, demotions, and written warnings. Mediation is not likely to result in the grievant's reinstatement, which is their ultimate goal. The fact that there is such high satisfaction in these especially difficult cases, using a facilitative mediation process (as opposed to a transformative mediation approach) is an important contribution to the research on employment mediation.

Notes

1 The Department of Corrections was merged with other agencies to form the Department of Public Safety on January 1, 2012. Because the data reported here are from 2008–10, the DOC is referred to throughout this report.
2 Approximately one-third of the DOC mediations used only a senior mediator, reducing the actual time invested to 15 staff hours or $374.25.
3 Mediation surveys included participants in all mediated cases since the inception of the program for which data were available; this is the only portion of the study that extends beyond the 2008–10 timeframe.

References

Bingham, L.B. & Pitts, D.W. (2002) Highlights of mediation at work: Studies of the national REDRESS® evaluation project. *Negotiation Journal*, 18(2): 135–146. doi: 10.1111/j.1571–9979.2002.tb00256.x.

Blancero, D. & Dyer, L. (1996) Due process for non-union employees: The influence of system characteristics on fairness perceptions. *Human Resource Management Journal*, 35(3): 343–359. doi: 10.1002/(SICI)1099–1050X(199623)35:3<343:AID-HRM4>3.0.CO;2-X.

Burgess, H. & Burgess, G.M. (1997) *Encyclopedia of Conflict Resolution*. Santa Barbara, CA: ABC-CLIO.

Jameson, J.K. (2001) Employee perceptions of the availability and use of interests-based, right-based, and power-based conflict management strategies. *Conflict Resolution Quarterly*, 19(2): 163–196. doi: 10.1002/crq.3890190204.

Kasperzak, R.M. (1996) Using mediation to reduce litigation costs. Dispute Resolution Specialists. Retrieved from www.mediates.com/drsusingmed.html.

Lipsky, D.B., Seeber, R.L. & Fincher, R.D. (2003) *Emerging Systems for Managing Workplace Conflict: Lessons from American Corporations for Managers and Dispute Resolution Professionals*. San Francisco, CA: Jossey-Bass.

Moore, C.W. (1986) *The Mediation Process: Practical Strategies for Resolving Conflict*. San Francisco, CA: Jossey-Bass.

Morrison, E.W. (2011) Employee voice behavior: Integration and directions for future research. *The Academy of Management Annals, 5*(1): 373–412. doi: 10.1080/19416520.2011.574506.

Shapiro, D.L. & Brett, J.M. (1993) Comparing three processes underlying judgments of procedural justice: A field study of mediation and arbitration. *Journal of Personality and Social Psychology*, 65(6): 1167–1177. doi: 10.1037/0022-3514.65.6.1167.

Slaikeu, K.A. (1996) *When Push Comes to Shove: A Practical Guide to Mediating Disputes*. San Francisco, CA: Jossey-Bass.

Slaikeu, K.A. & Hasson, R.H. (1998) *Controlling the Costs of Conflict*. San Francisco, CA: Jossey-Bass.

Ury, W.L., Brett, J.M. & Goldberg, S.B. (1988) *Getting Disputes Resolved: Designing Systems to Cut the Costs of Conflict*. San Francisco, CA: Jossey-Bass.

18

MEDIATION AND DISPUTE RESOLUTION SERVICES IN HIGHER EDUCATION

Neil H. Katz

Colleges and universities in the United States have long recognized the necessity of dispute resolution for the many different stakeholders who come together to live and work in the relatively confined campus community. Traditionally, student, faculty, and staff disputes were handled by offices of student affairs, human resource departments and legal affairs, or other administrative units. On the student side, administrators or student judges presided over disputes among students, infractions over code of conduct, or other policies, and resolved these with either a dismissal of the issues or with imposed sanctions. On the employee side, formal investigation resulted in dismissal of the grievances or punitive actions such as formal reprimands, probation, involuntary leaves of absence, or termination. Occasionally, a decision would prompt costly legal action attempting to overturn a punitive decision. These traditional methods encourage reasonable behavior by rendering a third-party verdict on the violation. However, these systems did not always serve to uncover and help parties grapple with underlying issues, address needs and concerns fuelling the dispute, or assist in the ongoing relationship among the parties. In addition, many of these traditional procedures were costly in terms of time, effort, morale and resources.

Over the past few decades, creative and effective alternative dispute resolution (ADR) services have supplemented these traditional practices at many institutions. These services range from preventative measures such as training and coaching to more formal reactive procedures such as conciliation, facilitation, mediation, and arbitration. These services are more closely aligned with the vision, mission, and values of a modern university emphasizing community, inclusiveness, tolerance, collaboration, emotional intelligence, and life skills, while dealing more effectively with the substantive, procedural, and relational issues at the core of disputes.

This chapter focuses on the use of mediation as one of the most popular alternative dispute resolution processes and illustrates its many uses for student, faculty, and staff disputes within the institutional setting. Some of the data for this chapter were collected by 27 graduate students[1] in a "Peer Mediation and Conflict Resolution in Higher Education" course taught through the Department of Conflict Resolution Studies at Nova Southeastern University. The focus is on college and university centers and programs that provide mediation services primarily to members of the campus community. Data include a summary of over 100 higher education institutions where our, mostly web-based research indicated use of ADR practices.

The institutions in our sample include small private schools, religious academic institutions, prestigious private research universities, and large public universities. The sample programs are diverse in their focus, services offered, client base, funding, housing, and other dimensions. In addition, this chapter makes a case for why mediation and ADR services are congruent with the mission of the modern university and the need to expand their use and effectiveness, particularly in the area of employee disputes. Sections of this article include some major historical milestones of ADR development in higher education, why ADR processes are necessary to mitigate the cost of unproductive conflict, an overview of the variety of ADR options available on campuses today, and the need to expand its use throughout the campus population.

Significant developments in the history of ADR practices in higher education

Conflict is a natural occurrence on college campuses. Over the past 50 years, college administrators have experimented with a variety of procedures and methods to resolve conflict or mitigate its effects. This overview will briefly cover the past 50 years to illustrate some of the most important milestones that propelled the growth and development of mediation services as supplements to the more traditional and punitive ways to handle disputes.

Many of the significant initiatives promoted the use of mediation, a problem-solving process between the primary parties and a third-party neutral who facilitates a collaborative negotiation session that often results in a party-driven agreement while helping bridge relationships going forward. The American Arbitration Association (AAA) established the Center for Mediation in Higher Education in 1979 with the intent of encouraging institutions of higher education to adopt the use of mediation for disputes at all levels—faculty, staff, and administrative. Progress on the student side proceeded quickly. A 1981 study by Folger and Schubert found that more than half of the 741 colleges and universities surveyed had instituted mediation possibilities for student disputes (Warters, 2011, p. 1). The 1980s also included the formation of the National Association for Mediation in Education (NAME) and several publications shone a spotlight on ADR resources available on academic campuses (Warters, 2000, p. 15).

To help propel the growth of the conflict resolution field, the William and Flora Hewlett Foundation provided major funding to universities in the mid-1980s to assist in the development of practice-relevant theory in conflict analysis and resolution (Volpe & Chandler, 1999). This led to 20 prestigious universities, including Harvard, Syracuse, Northwestern, and several of the Big Ten State Universities to develop research, educational courses, and practice activities in conflict resolution, and propelled the use of mediation as a dispute system alternative.

Moving into the 1990s, the scope of mediation and other ADR approaches increased based on the nature of campus conflicts. Practices such as facilitation, conciliation, and negotiation promoted the field with the help of articles in *The Chronicle of Higher Education* such as "Negotiation, not violence, is the rule today when students clash with administrators" (Collison, 1990), which discussed a shift away from using police and force to end student protests. By March 1990, there was ample interest to usher in the first National Conference on Campus Mediation Programs, convened by Professor Neil Katz and Campus Mediation Center Director Bill Warters, at Syracuse University.

Paralleling the rapid rise of campus mediation programs was an even more dramatic acceleration of campus ombudsmen to conduct mediation and other ADR approaches. John

Zinsser (2014) of Columbia University outlined the role of campus ombudsman as being "a great listener, mediator, and conflict coach, a shuttle diplomat, an educator, a quick responder, and an individual with persuasive powers even when s/he has no formal power other than bringing greater clarity to issues and options" (personal communication). The first two campus ombuds programs were introduced in 1966–67 when East Montana State University and Michigan State University began to respond to growing student issues. The idea spread quickly and by 1975, the number of university ombuds had grown to exceed 120 (Warters, 2011). Several ombuds associations now exist to help serve the hundreds of education institutions that have one or more ombuds.

Another important development included initiatives within law schools. By the mid-1990s, more than 30 law schools had entered the area of court-annexed alternative dispute resolution by establishing mediation clinics to treat referral cases from local courts. Nationwide attention was drawn to ADR practices by the Association for Student Judicial Affairs' (ASJA) support of mediation and the National Association of College and University Business Officers (NACUBO) recognized programs that successfully reduced costs and improved the quality of higher education.

In the 21st century, interest and programs in ADR services proliferated. The growth and understanding of ADR benefits was due in part to articles by Sara Lipka (2009) and others in the influential *Chronicle of Higher Education* on trends moving away from legalistic and disciplinary systems. The widespread growth in ADR services at other universities included the University of Georgia system, which trained 3,000 members in conflict resolution skills in its 34 state institutions and 385 designees to handle mediation at institutions other than their own (Fogg, 2008). In 2010, *The Chronicle* published "Workplace mediators seek a role on training faculty bullies" by Peter Schmidt (2010), and reported how the AAA and other conflict management agencies were providing training to help campus members work more effectively with bullying and workplace disputes. In 2013, Morgan State University made a commitment to make conflict resolution training and classroom instruction a mandatory part of students' experiences (Schnoebelen, 2013) in response to mass campus violence. In addition, the Association for Student Conduct Administration (ASCA) "endorsed alternative forms of conflict resolution models as viable conduct administration options … embracing best practices for training conduct professionals" (Schrage & Giacomini, 2009, p. xi).

Costs of conflict

Conflict scholars confirm the commonly negative view of conflict and the human tendency to avoid it whenever possible. Avoidance or mishandling of conflict can have serious economic and psychological costs as well as negative impacts on factors such as recruitment, retention, productivity, and quality. As university administrators, particularly in the private sector, compete for the best students, they are gaining more awareness of the link between student satisfaction and how conflicts with peers, faculty, staff, and administrators are addressed. Recent studies in the area of student disputes confirm that effective conflict resolution services are important in influencing decisions on recruitment and retention (Garrido, 2015). When conflict intervention policies are not effective, there can be a negative impact on student loyalty, alumni relations, and retention.

Beyond student concerns, the costs of unresolved or poorly managed conflict extends to faculty, staff, and administrators. Disputes range from interpersonal differences over schedules and workspace to complex gender, race, or ethnically related controversies (Volpe & Chandler, 1999). Conflicts over issues of grant revenue distribution, civility discord, personality clashes, struggles for power, and frustrations due to limited resources may result in "substantial financial, human, and credibility costs to the organization" (Buss, 2011, p. 54). The effects of employee and student attrition on cost can be broken down into three categories: 1) direct costs, 2) opportunity costs, and 3) indirect costs (Bettes & Sikorski, 2008). Direct costs, for example, can be calculated in the recruitment and retention of employees and students. Even though university enrollment has increased dramatically since the mid-1900s, the ability to keep students in school remains a challenge. Approximately 14 percent of four-year students leave their initial institution after the first year and another 13 percent the following year (Swail, 2004). Nationwide, only about 50 percent of all doctoral students complete degrees, and conflicts with faculty are cited as one of the two most important reasons why they leave before finishing (Warters, 2000, p. 30).

For university employees, "researchers studying exit interview data on voluntary departures state that chronic unresolved conflict is a decisive factor in at least 50 percent of all such departures" (Buss, 2011, p. 56). Voluntary separation costs may include, but are not limited to, unemployment insurance rates, severance pay, exit interviews, outplacement, and fees resulting from possible legal actions (Bettes & Sikorski, 2008). For faculty and staff employees, direct recruitment and placement costs to fill vacant positions range between 100 percent and 150 percent of the predecessor's salary plus benefits (Dana, 2001, p. 22). Several research studies also calculated managers and supervisors spend between 25 percent and 40 percent of their time dealing with conflicts (Dana, 2001, p. 19). This is a considerable use of otherwise productive time for department chairs, deans, and additional supervisors. Furthermore, a study of 808 department chairs at 101 doctoral-granting universities in 1991 found that chairs identified conflict as the major category of stress (Gmelch & Burns, 1993). To ensure recruited employees stay long enough to pay the costs of recruitment, Katz and Flynn (2013) discuss a prevention approach, which includes active dispute resolution practices for maintaining team cohesion because it is directly linked to employee performance and satisfaction.

The cost of conflict also includes opportunity cost. Loss may include limited course offerings due to faculty attrition or decreased quality of teaching and inability to hire the best employees. Furthermore, loss of reputation due to poorly managed conflict can spread quickly through word of mouth and social networks, deterring potential faculty and staff from seeking positions with the institution. Spillover costs include negative effects on student enrollment, limited research and publishing, external grant opportunities, and decreased donations and contributions. Indirect costs can refer to productivity, morale, and negative employee effects. "Productivity suffers when unhealthy conflicts persist" (Buss, 2011, p. 56). Unresolved conflicts have a direct effect on sick days and what is referred to as "presenteeism" the phenomenon of employee(s) giving less than 100 percent attention and effort to task accomplishments until they are able to find another job. Research shows that 60–80 percent of all difficulties in organizations stem from strained relationships between employees, not from deficits in individual employees' skills or motivation (Dana, 2005). The harmful belief that the institution allows self-defeating cycles to exist affects the morale and professional image of the institution.

Variety of ADR services

A review of the services offered by the sample of 100 colleges and universities listed below demonstrated the large variety of ADR services available on campuses across the United States. Services are offered to faculty, staff, and students as well as the community. Some institutions work with governmental agencies. While the ADR services offered fall into the broad categories below, there are differences in the way they are designed and executed.

Mediation services

Mediation services are the most common ADR interventions. Mediation sessions range from student living disputes and relationship issues to mediation for family, court-annexed, community, workplace, and some unique services such as victim-offender mediation, elder, and estate mediation. Noteworthy services include re-entry mediation and social justice mediation. Howard County College offers re-entry mediation in a correctional facility to inmates who are preparing to re-enter the community. Several other types include landlord-tenant disputes, inter-group and intra-group conflicts, matters from judicial proceedings including possible criminal behavior, employment discrimination disputes, and disputes over uncivil behavior, harassment, and bullying.

Restorative justice practices

Restorative justice (RJ) is an innovative mode of conflict resolution that has been gaining popularity at many colleges. At Skidmore College "[a] central practice of RJ is a collaborative decision-making process that includes harmed parties, offenders, and others who are seeking to hold offenders accountable" (Skidmore College, n.d., para. 1). The college offers the service for students and provides training for schools, universities, and the criminal justice system. Illinois State University, another pioneer in restorative justice approaches, offers a variety of RJ services through the Dean of Students Office. RJ provides offenders important life lessons about the impact of their actions on individuals and the community. RJ gives the injured party and/or community a chance to meet the offender face to face and engage in discourse in a safe environment where impact and feelings can be expressed. RJ is an educational process that can be more meaningful and effective than punitive measures.

Community outreach

Several colleges offer services that extend beyond the campus. Southern Methodist University's Resolution Center is geared toward community outreach. Services include mediation, facilitation, arbitration and conflict coaching offered at low cost and are provided by program alumni, faculty, and current students. Syracuse University provides training workshops and other ADR events to non-profit groups in the community in addition to the campus community. The University of North Dakota Conflict Resolution Center serves schools, non-profit organizations, children and youth, families and the elderly. Missouri State University has partnerships with County Mental Health Departments and Green County Juvenile and Youth organizations. They offer free mediation services and training to non-profit organizations and low-cost mediation services to the community. Fresno State University has a unique partnership with the Fresno, California elementary and middle schools in which university student mentors, social workers, counselors and ADR specialists, train and coach over 7,000 teacher and student school mediators.

The Dispute Resolution Center of North Central College in Illinois offers a Campus Outreach Program to assist disputes for local courts, businesses, churches and other organizations. They also have a resource center for conflict resolution information. At Nova Southeastern University, Community Resolution Services (CRS) offers various services through its Voices Family Outreach Program. At Howard Community College, approximately 100 trained volunteers provide mediation and conflict resolution services to the Howard County, Maryland community. Both Kennesaw State University and Salisbury University work locally and globally to research conflict management practices, assess conflict management programs, and provide training in conflict management skills. Virginia Tech also offers workplace mediation services to state government agencies.

Where we are now and where we need to go

The importance of having mediation and other ADR services to supplement traditional procedures is to manage conflicts at their lowest and most effective levels, deal with underlying issues, improve a campus conflict climate, and preserve relationships. Alternative pathways encourage personal empowerment, accountability, and promote creative thinking and skill development. These services help build a safe campus community and model how to resolve conflicts, foster professional relationships and cultivate inclusiveness. Awareness of the benefits and the cost of mismanaged conflicts have led to innovative practices for handling student disputes.

On the employee side, the recognition that dispute interventions are needed for staff, faculty and administrators is growing. One study noted an alarming 250 percent rise in the average legal defense costs for private colleges and universities in just a five-year period (Campus-adr.org, 2011). There are also philosophical and practical grounds for resolving conflicts outside adversarial litigation. A desire to protect the rights of members from unfair institutional policies and practices as well as the benefit of "in-house" settlement procedures makes voluntary agreement more likely and potentially reduces occupational stress (Tallodi, 2015). Many academic offices and support units are enhancing competency in ADR approaches for handling internal disputes. For example, the author of this article recently trained the staff of residential services at Marist College in mediation and conflict management skills, delivered workshops in emotional intelligence, mediation, and conflict management skills for 120 members of the Public Safety force at Syracuse University, and trained over 50 administrative and supervisory staff in workplace mediation at the University of Belize.

Best practice examples

ADR practices offer a "model for promoting individuals' capacities and responsibilities for decisions that affect their lives and others; for building community; for fostering mutual respect and cooperation; for developing fairness rather than power for resolving disputes– values at the core of a University" (Warters, 2000, p. 42). One of the most significant initiatives in recent years is the development of integrated conflict management systems. Examples include Eastern Mennonite University, a small Church-affiliated school in Virginia, and the large state universities of Minnesota, Georgia and Washington. At Eastern Mennonite, the University Accord Office, directed by the university ombudsperson, offers ADR services "to help individuals and groups as they strive to strengthen relationships, and process particular conflicts and concerns" (Reid, personal communication, 2014). Services include RJ dialogue circles where "parties meet in a safe space, tell their stories, identify harms and explore situations to repair harms and rebuild trust" (Reid, personal communication, 2014). Mediation is used to resolve consumer complaints and landlord-tenant issues as well as disputes among faculty and staff. Conflict communication coaching is offered to help participants consider strategies and implications.

The University of Washington has a well-rounded system of ADR integrated in different parts of the university. For example, faculty can access conciliation, coaching, mediation, and referrals through the Ombudsman Office, the University Complaint Investigation and Resolution Office, the Law School Mediation Services, or the secretary of the faculty, depending on the issue. Participants seek ADR services on issues such as unfair tenure/promotion decisions, workplace mistreatment, retaliatory actions, discriminatory practices, and conflict within teams.

At the University of Minnesota, the independent Office of Conflict Resolution (OCR) offers both informal and formal services to all employees, including civil service. Services include private consultation ombuds to conduct data gathering and engage in possible shuttle diplomacy, facilitated difficult conversations with a third-party specialist, and more formal structured mediation. Typical issues for the OCR include conflicts among working groups and academic units, concerns about retaliation and discrimination, disputes over termination, lay-offs, nonrenewal, and disagreements about pay, promotion and performance. In 2013, the OCR celebrated its 20th anniversary and was recognized for interactions with over 3,000 faculty and staff. The OCR received credit for advancing the university's mission by "developing an approach to conflict where disagreements and conflict are seen as natural rather than aberrational and unwelcome irritants … a place where prompt and skilled attention to conflict improves employee's ability to work effectively" (Chalmers, personal communication, 2013). The OCR was also given credit for influencing an 80 percent decline in grievance filings since its establishment.

The University of Georgia system, with a population of over 400,000 students and staff across 34 different institutions, has the most comprehensive integrated conflict resolution system. Until the 1980s, most of the procedures were structured, legalistic, and punitive systems. However, the widely publicized 1983 Jan Kemp affair, that implicated the high-profile football program, the academic remedial program, eventually awarded Kemp $2.5 million for wrongful termination from her job as coordinator of the remedial program served as a major catalyst for change. One of the responses was the appointment of a Blue Ribbon committee to look at the university's dispute resolution system. The committee developed five broad goals (Yarn, 2014, p. 89) for direction: 1 establish a system-wide conflict resolution program that will, 2 decrease the reliance on adversarial processes, and 3 resolve disputes efficiently and fairly at the lowest possible level, and in doing so, 4 foster a healthier community, and 5 lead the nation in ADR for higher education. By 2004, almost all campuses had some form of mediation program or ombuds office. From 1998–2012, over 800 mediations and 4,000 cases were handled (Yarn, 2014, p. 97). Chancellor Stephen Porch noted that the ADR work "saved the system millions of dollars per year in litigation costs" (Yarn, 2014, p. 99).

Furthermore, today some of the most comprehensive dispute settlement systems exist in state and federal government agencies thanks to the Federal Civil Rights Act of 1991, the Americans with Disabilities Act of 1990, and the Administrative Dispute Resolution Act of 1990, which directed federal agencies to expand the use of ombuds and ADR practices to handle disputes. In 1998, President Clinton also issued an executive order requiring all federal agencies "to take steps to promote greater use of mediation, arbitration, early neutral, agency ombuds, facilitation, conciliation, and negotiated rulemaking … and promote interest-based negotiations in their interactions with their unionized employees" (Campus-adr.org, 2011).

In the private sector, a major study by the Institute of Conflict Resolution at Cornell University's School of Labor and Industrial Relations concluded: "research strongly suggests that ADR is firmly institutionalized in a majority of United States corporations, at least for employment and commercial disputes" (Lipsky et al., 2003, p. xvii). Optimistically, the

Cornell authors cited Malcolm Gladwell's "tipping point" phenomenon to characterize the growth and bright future of ADR approaches in the workplace. They predicted, "[g]rowth will get to social and behavioural epidemic proportions where 'everyone will be doing it' and conflict management ... will become as essential to organizational life as other features of human resources" (Lipsky et al., 2003, pp. 139–140).

Unfortunately, the "tipping point" phenomenon in which ADR practices are more the norm than the exception was unfulfilled. Organizations appear to train human resources, equal employment opportunity and legal counsel personnel in a pervading legal frame to address complaints, but they discount the fact that conflict involves differences in perception about behaviors and emotions. Some research suggests that less than 10 percent of complaints meet the test of legal standards, while over 90 percent consist of perceiving actions as offensive and its accompanying emotions (Herrman, 2010). Universities that overlook the essence of disputes are neglecting the research that shows procedural justice, a sense of fairness, a commitment to halting offensive behavior, and psychological satisfaction are just as important for the universities' bottom line as legal protection. Collaborative problem-solving processes are not yet the norm in higher education. The lack of integrated ADR services carries a serious cost in terms of dollars, morale, productivity, retention, a sense of justice and community. Educational leaders are needlessly escalating the cost of poorly managed conflict, and neglecting to promote civil discourse along with creative problem solving for employees and students as the norm rather than the exception. Our institutions that are dedicated to researching, educating and implementing "best practices" for the betterment of individuals and society should be leading, not trailing this trend.

Over time, our research lends evidence that some institutions have evolved from a reactive to a more proactive approach. For ADR practices to grow and become integrated in higher education, critical conceptual shifts must occur in the way conflicts are perceived and resolved. A shift away from rights- or power-based methods to interest- and collaborative-based methods is necessary. The focus is then on preventative training and procedures that address underlying needs and concerns to foster collaborative solutions, rather than focus on protecting the institution from lawsuits and grievance procedures that render dissatisfied parties. As these systems spread and evolve, they will become more integrated into the fabric of the university, address causes instead of symptoms, and treat conflict as normal, functional and expected, rather than aberrational and dysfunctional.

Educational leaders should promote ADR practices as highly congruent with the proclaimed values, mission and vision of higher education. The mission statement for Purdue University's Mediation and Conciliation Center is a model for the skills and concepts that underlie ADR educational practices: "The process of resolving conflict is educational. By establishing a forum where each party is heard, we teach listening. By creating an environment where each party can speak, we teach communication. By mediating disputes, we teach citizenship" (Warters, 2011, para. 2). It is the hope of the author and his student researchers that our documentation of creative ways of handling disputes will increase the likelihood that these services will continue to expand in utilization and effectiveness for all members of the university community.

Note

1 A special heartfelt thanks to the 27 graduate students at Nova Southeastern University who contributed significantly to this chapter through their research and writing, and to Katherine Sosa for her editing and helpful content suggestions.

References

Bettes, K.S. & Sikorski, B. (2008) Financial bottom line: Estimating the cost of faculty/adjunct turnover and attrition for online programs. *Online Journal of Distance Learning Administration*, 9(1). Retrieved from www.westga.edu/~distance/ojdla /spring111/betts111.html.

Buss, H. (2011) Controlling conflict costs: The business case of conflict management. *Journal of the International Ombudsman Association*, 4(1): 54–62.

Campus-adr.org. (2011) Why constructive C.R. matters to staff and administrators. Campus-adr.org. Retrieved from www.campus-adr.org/Staff_Admin_Building/content/rationales_staffadmin/.

Collison, M.N.-K. (1990) Negotiation, not violence, is the rule today when students clash with administrators. *Chronicle of Higher Education*, 36(33), A30–32.

Dana, D. (2001) *Conflict Resolution*. New York: McGraw-Hill.

Dana, D. (2005) *Managing Differences: How to Build Better Relationships at Work and Home* (4th edn). St Petersburg, FL: MTI Publications.

Fogg, P. (2008) Academic bullies. *Chronicle of Higher Education*, 55(3), B10.

Garrido, L. (2015) *The Development of a Theoretically-supported Model of Resolution for Student Complaints in Higher Education*. Doctoral dissertation. Nova Southeastern University.

Gmelch, W. & Burns, J. (1993) The cost of academic leadership: Department chair stress. *Innovative Higher Education*, 17(4): 259–270.

Herrman, M.S. (2010) Understanding and using conflict in the workplace. In S.E. Condrey (ed.) *Handbook of Human Resource Management in Government* (2nd edn) (pp. 326–350). San Francisco, CA: Jossey-Bass.

Katz, N. & Flynn, L. (2013) Understanding conflict management systems and strategies in the workplace: A pilot study. *Conflict Resolution Quarterly*, 4(30), 393–410.

Lipka, S. (2009) With "restorative justice," colleges strive to educate student offenders. *Chronicle of Higher Education*, 55(32), A26.

Lipsky, D.B., Sieber, R.L. & Fincher, R.D. (2003) *Emerging Systems for Managing Workplace Conflict*. San Francisco, CA: Jossey-Bass.

Schmidt, P. (2010) Workplace mediators seek a role in training faculty bullies. *Chronicle of Higher Education*. Retrieved from chronicle.com/article/Workplace-Mediators-Seek-a-/65815/.

Schnoebelen, A. (2013) After shootings, Morgan State U. trains students in conflict resolution. *Chronicle of Higher Education*. Retrieved from chronicle.com/article/After-Shootings-Morgan-State/139051/.

Schrage, J.M. & Giacomini, N.G. (eds). (2009) *Reframing Campus Conflict: Student Conduct Practice through a Social Justice Lens*. Sterling, VA: Stylus Publishing.

Skidmore College. (n.d.) *Project on Restorative Justice*. Retrieved from www.skidmore.edu/campusrj/.

Swail, W.S. (2004) The art of student retention: A handbook for practitioners and administrators. *Educational Policy Institute*. Retrieved from files.eric.ed.gov/fulltext/ED485498.pdf.

Tallodi, T. (2015) Mediation's potential to reduce occupational stress: A new perspective. *Conflict Resolution Quarterly*, 32(4): 361–388.

University of Washington. (2008) A faculty guide to dispute resolution at the University of Washington. Faculty Council on Faculty Affairs in cooperation with the Secretary of the Faculty. Retrieved from www.washington.edu/faculty/files/2014/06/dispute_guide.pdf.

Volpe, M.R. & Chandler, D. (1999) *Resolving Conflicts in Institutions of Higher Education: Challenges for Pracademics*. College of Law CNCR-Hewlett Foundation Seed Grant White Papers (Paper 8). Retrieved from scholarworks.gsu.edu/colpub_seedgrant/8.

Warters, W. (2000) *Mediation in the Campus Community: Designing and Managing Effective Programs*. San Francisco, CA: Jossey-Bass.

Warters, W. (2011) Timeline of major events in higher education dispute resolution. Wayne State University and William Warters. Retrieved from: www.campus-adr.org/CR_Services_Center/content/sample_mission_statements/.

Yarn, D. (2014) Designing a conflict management system for higher education: A case study for design in integrative organizations. *Conflict Resolution Quarterly*, 32(1): 83–105.

Zinsser, J. (2014) Calculating the value return of an organizational ombudsman. Conflict Specialists Show. Retrieved from www.conflictengagementspecialists.com/blog/calculating-the-value-return-of-an-organizational-ombudsman-with-john-zinsser-pacifica-human-communications-llc.

19

MEDIATION AS A TOOL FOR RESOLVING WORKPLACE CONFLICTS

LaVena Wilkin

Mediation is a powerful tool that has numerous benefits for individuals who experience conflicts with one another. First, the process of mediation empowers people to focus on the problem, not the person, to uncover people's underlying motivations, to discuss their differences, and to resolve the issues that are the root of the conflict situation. Second, mediation deals with human interactions by providing a safe process that encourages open, honest, and respectful dialogue. It is often a first step in alternative dispute resolution (ADR) to repairing or improving relationships damaged by conflicts. Perceptions are clarified, and people have an opportunity to open their minds and hearts to see how the world looks through others' different vantage points. Finally, disputants are more likely to feel that the outcomes are fair and justice has been served when their voices are heard. Although mediation provides an opening for people to discuss past damaging behaviors, it often focuses on the future.

Although mediation is often mandated through the courts in cases of litigation, it may be underutilized in cases of workplace conflict. The workplace is a breeding ground for conflict. Consider that organizational culture consists of shared values, beliefs, assumptions, perceptions, and norms. Add to that, the fact that organizations are complex coalitions of individuals, departments, and divisions, and each is competing for scarce resources, such as funding, access to those in power, and time. Stir in a little power imbalance and organizational political posturing. Then, add the fact that today's managers are faced with diversity and cultural issues ranging from race and gender to individual heritage, values, and beliefs, about which we are more vocal. Shake all that together and you have a workplace that is bubbling over with conflicted people and situations, and while you do not have to like your co-workers or invite them home for dinner, you do have to work with them. Organizational mediation can open the lines of communication, begin the problem-solving process, and potentially transform the relationship (Moore, 2003; Bush & Folger, 1994).

Chronic organizational conflicts lead to lower productivity and morale and higher absenteeism and turnover, and these issues are extremely costly to firms. Mediation is a powerful tool for resolving disputes and helping conflicted parties understand other peoples' perspectives. Although the mediation process is best known for its use in intractable, litigated issues, it can also reduce the costs of negative and unproductive conflicts that occur daily in organizations. In addition, the process of mediation is beneficial in resolving equal employment opportunity (EEO) cases, instances of bullying, and contract disagreements. Since mediation gives conflicted parties a voice and provides opportunities to view the world through the other person's lens, it offers benefits for individual employees, as well. Overall, using mediation as a tool for resolving workplace conflicts is a win–win for both the organization and for the employees.

Organizational conflict from a different perspective

Conflict is a naturally occurring part of life, and the world would be a boring and stagnant place without some measure of conflict. It happens, and it happens often because everyone is different. Therefore, even in the best of relationships divergent goals and values result in conflicted situations. Although conflict is a natural, normal occurrence when individuals, groups, or institutions interact, it can become overwhelming. When left unmanaged, conflict is unproductive, costly, and harmful. Costs of unmanaged conflict include wasted time, poor decision making, loss of skilled employees, unnecessary restructuring, lower motivation, and lost work time (Dana, 2001). Many people, when asked to define conflict, assign a negative connotation to the word. In addition, managers who lack conflict management skills may find that when they attempt to intervene, they can make the situation worse.

Conflict, however, can be a positive, healthy, learning, and growing experience. It is a matter of perspective. Although the word often carries a pessimistic implication, conflict can be a positive conduit for organizational changes by improving communication, solving problems, and building trust and cooperation. Using naturally occurring conflict as an opportunity for growth provides a spark that ignites creativity, innovation, and improvements in a dynamic organization (Stitt, 1998). Generally speaking, it is not organizational conflict that is negative. It becomes damaging and unproductive when it causes hurt feelings and fractures relationships, or when productivity drops and the conflicts waste time and zap energy. In part, whether or not damage occurs depends on the strategies used to manage conflict. When conflicts are not managed, or they are mismanaged, the outcomes can be destructive.

Often, when employees feel no one is listening, frustrations can build, and they file a lawsuit believing that is their only recourse. Unfortunately, litigation is generally a lose–lose proposition. The organization may have opportunity costs of time and reputation, even if they "win" the case. Employees generally lose money, time, and peace of mind on the job (or even the job itself). Finding a better way, mediation, may lead to developing an increased appreciation of the employees' and others' needs within the organizations, increasing opportunities to improve the genuineness of the relationships, and discovering constructive ways to engage in inevitable conflicts. Therein lies the promise of mediating organizational conflicts. An added bonus for organizations is that mediation typically costs less than litigation, so it is a win-win for both the individual employees and the organizations. Mediators who are skilled communicators, empathetic listeners, and collaborative problem solvers can help the conflicted employees reach an outcome that is in the best interest of all parties (Williams, 2011).

Mediating intractable workplace conflict situations

Given the previously discussed benefits of mediation, it is easy to see that mediation is an excellent tool for resolving interpersonal conflicts within organizational settings. However, additional side effects of unmanaged conflict include EEO issues, workplace bullying, and contract disagreements. Some would argue that these types of conflicts might not be appropriate for mediation since they involve issues of law or public policy. However, although litigation may give the aggrieved parties financial remuneration, it does not give them a voice. In addition, the cornerstones of transformative mediation, empowerment, and recognition (Bush & Folger, 1994) make it an effective process for dealing with these intractable conflicts. Through listening to understand, instead of listening to respond, it has the potential to empower the conflicted parties to claim control of their situations and their lives and to recognize why the offenders engage in destructive behaviors.

The mediation process

The mediation process and the mediator provide solid arguments for choosing mediation in intractable conflicts. First, the process allows the conflicted parties a forum for dealing with emotions. Emotions can be toxic. If they are held inside, they can destroy the person. However, when people are allowed to express their emotions, they can deal with them and let go of anger and blame. The healing process can begin. Mediation is the avenue for the parties to engage in open, honest, respectful dialogue with one another. When people understand others' motives, it becomes easier to agree on the issues and to move forward.

Second, a third-party neutral assists the parties with communication. Using a third-party neutral, someone who has no vested interest in the outcome, helps build trust in the process and allows people to speak freely and from the heart (Phillips, 2001). During intractable conflicts, parties often become entrenched in their positions or in placing blame and are unable to move past positions to interests. When this happens, the underlying issues are not addressed, and the conflict may continue to raise its ugly head over and over again. By opening the channels of communication and facilitating open, honest, and respectful dialogue, a mediator can help break impasse and encourage employees to generate creative and innovative solutions that address the root of the problem (Moore, 2003).

Finally, mediation is a voluntary and consentual process, and neither party gives up their rights if they cannot agree on a resolution to the conflict. Since what happens in mediation stays in the mediation room, and concessions made during the process are not binding if the parties do not resolve their issues, it makes sense to give mediation an opportunity to work its magic before attempting other rights- or power-based methods of conflict resolution (Moore, 2003).

Rights-, power-, and interest-based resolutions

Although the traditional way to resolve intractable conflicts is grounded in rights- or power-based methods, such as grievances or litigation, the interest-based approach that mediation offers can provide longer-lasting and more satisfying outcomes. Rights- or power-based methods often have negative, dehumanizing, and irrational side effects that leave people angry. Additionally, the conflict may still be unresolved. Furthermore, when the processes for resolving conflicts are structured and narrow such as those based in rights- or power-based processes, they are likened to Max Weber's "iron cage" which traps and surrounds people without providing alternative solutions (Ritzer, 1983).

Moreover, ignoring or dismissing interpersonal or intractable conflicts may be more expeditious, but the resolution is likely to be short-lived. This method generates more harm than benefit to the organization by creating a vicious cycle of disillusionment and frustration that promotes and encourages disputes, competition, sabotage, inefficiency, low morale, and the withholding of information, which are all symptoms of unmanaged conflict gone awry (Costantino & Merchant, 1996).

However, creating an interest-based culture conducive to productively managing conflict will minimize the high costs of turnover, attrition, and negative publicity. Although interest-based systems require a greater investment of time and energy, an individualized process that takes into account the realities and perceptions of the conflicted parties and attempts to see the world through each party's unique lenses will be a more constructive approach to conflict resolution. Ultimately, it costs less and satisfies more (Ury et al., 1988). Therefore, when organizations foster a more humanistic approach to conflict resolution they begin the process of effectively managing conflict. Again, mediation helps organizations promote interest-based resolutions to even the most intractable conflict situations.

Equal employment opportunity (EEO) issues

Cloke and Goldsmith (2000) posit that basic characteristics of mediation, including listening to both parties, validating their pain, acknowledging emotions, and creating a trusting environment can help parties decide to forgive and heal from hurtful behaviors. The mediator can help the disputants recognize and exploit opportunities for moral growth inherently presented by conflict (Bush & Folger, 1994). Empowerment paves the way for recognition, and when the parties understand their own needs better, they often appreciate others' situations. Empowered people understand they are in control of their own destiny; they have options and choices. Likewise, recognition can be given in thoughts, words, or actions. It may take the form of adjusting the lens through which one views the world, openly acknowledging and understanding the other's perspective, or altering one's own conduct. The mediator's role is to help the parties focus on the future by discussing the past and helping them glean a better understanding of the present situation (Bush & Folger, 1994).

One of the most well-known and respected organizations to adopt mediation as a first line of defense in cases of discrimination, harassment, and other EEO claims is the US Postal Service. Their REDRESS (Resolve Employee Disputes, Reach Equitable Solutions Swiftly) model incorporates Bush and Folger's (1994) transformative model of mediation, and since its inception in 1994, 90 percent of the postal workers involved in the process have reported satisfaction with the outcome of the conflict (Bingham, 2004, p. 13). In fact, approximately 95 percent of the employees who filed EEO complaints and then participated in mediation reported they felt respected during the process and believed the mediator was neutral, and reported that the process was equitable (Bingham, 2004, p. 13). Mediation has been such a successful model for resolving EEO claims in the postal service that claims dropped by 30 percent between 1998 and 2004 (Bingham, 2004, p. 13). When asked why they felt respected and believed the process was fair, the complainants noted that open communication and listening resulted in the parties acknowledging one another's perspectives (Bingham, 2004). Even more significant is that complaints involved in these claims and the mediation process often received an apology. This rarely occurs in rights- or power-based processes, such as litigation.

Workplace bullying

Similar to the benefits of mediating organizational EEO claims, instances of workplace bullying are occasionally ripe for mediation. In a study designed to explore how targets of workplace bullies cope with the experience, Wilkin (2010) interviewed ten university faculty members who were bullied by their dean. She found that targets of workplace bullies are better able to cope with the experience if they can release blame and anger, change their reactions to the situation, and develop empathy for the bully. By facilitating constructive dialogue, skilled mediators can help targets express and defuse negative emotions. Storytelling is a foundation of mediation, and when parties listen to one another, they may become more empathetic to how the other person feels. In part, understanding the motivations behind the bullying behavior can address it. A recent study found that some workplace bullies participate in this destructive behavior because they believe the work will not get done if they do not cajole, ridicule, and intimidate others (Castle, 2014). Competition in organizational settings often fuels workplace bullying. Moreover, through listening to understand, instead of listening to respond, mediation has the potential to empower targets to claim control of their situations and their lives and to recognize why the bully perpetuates the destructive behaviors. Mediation provides an opportunity for the bully and the target to address the bullying behavior. When experiences are validated through listening to concerns, individuals are more likely to feel the outcomes are fair and justice has been served (Barry & Shapiro, 2000; De Kremer & Sedikides, 2008).

Mediation is the quintessential arena for helping people uncover commonalities, encouraging open, honest, respectful dialogue, and building trust (Seagriff, 2010). Mediators may empower targets to release negative emotions and help them change their reaction to the mistreatment. Cloke and Goldsmith (2000) state that "[i]n mediation, anger is the map to the source of conflict" (p. 67), and mediation helps people acknowledge, uncover, work through their anger, and decide to forgive. Promoting forgiveness through mediation is underutilized because it is viewed as an irrational, moral issue that does not result in monetary compensation for damages. However, because it deals with the reality of human interaction, it can be the magic bullet that helps amicably resolve disputes involving workplace bullying.

Through constructive dialogue, effective listening, and establishing a safe environment, mediators can help uncover mutual interests that move the bully, target, and leaders away from anger and blame toward psychological closure. Mediators can utilize their communication skills and intuitive abilities to help the parties let go of blame and anger. Additionally, the process helps the parties mend, redefine, or end their relationships, while they maintain their emotional balance, self-esteem, and dignity (Moore, 2003).

Contract disputes

Two industries, construction and entertainment, have used mediation for years to resolve conflicts. The underlying reasons for choosing mediation over litigation in contract disputes were not altruistic, and industry leaders were less concerned about preserving the relationship and more focused on saving money. Mediation is more expedient than litigation. In addition, these contracts may involve several issues, such as salaries, schedules, designs, materials, and copyrights; and mediation provides an opportunity for each of these areas to be discussed and resolved creatively and collaboratively (Newman, 2013). Interestingly, a basic precept of mediation is to focus on the future. Even though the reasons for mediating conflict often center on cost savings, a collateral benefit is that relationships can be preserved.

In the entertainment industry, relationships can be vital to a successful career. An additional benefit of mediating these disputes is that discretion is key and brands can be protected. Court cases are matters of public record, but both what is discussed in the mediation and the outcome of the process are confidential. Public disputes among architects, contractors, subcontractors, and clients can lead to tarnished reputations, and profits may suffer as a result of negative publicity. Moreover, when contract disputes are settled in the courts, a judge or jury decides the outcome. By using mediation to resolve contract disputes, the parties are in control of their own destinies (Blancato & Gibson, 2008).

Conclusion

When conflicts are unmanaged or mismanaged, the chance of entrenchment and resistance increases. While firms that do not productively manage conflict are spending time and resources in litigious warfare, they miss opportunities to adapt to the vibrant, ever-changing competitive environment. Meanwhile, competing counter parts, who have embraced mediation techniques, enjoy profitable results of conflict resolution efforts, the durability of those efforts, and the impact on both internal and external relationships.

Organizational mediation can lead to exciting and inspiring opportunities for change and innovation. In addition, it can be the conduit that not only establishes and strengthens relationships, but also fosters equal opportunity in the workplace and addresses discrimination, harassment, and workplace bullying complaints. Mediation provides an avenue for managed and productive conflict.

References

Barry, B. & Shapiro, D. (2000) When will grievants desire voice? A test of situational, motivational, and attributional explanations. *International Journal of Conflict Management*, 11(2): 106–134.

Bingham, L.B. (2004) Employment dispute resolution: The case for mediation. *Conflict Resolution Quarterly*, 22(1–2): 145–174.

Blancato, W.A. & Gibson, J.A. (2008) Controlling your own destiny: You can with mediation. *Dispute Resolution Journal*, 63(3): 14–21.

Bush, R.A. & Folger, J.P. (1994) *The Promise of Mediation: Responding to Conflict through Empowerment and Recognition*. San Francisco, CA: Jossey-Bass.

Castle, K.M. (2014) *The Workplace Bully: A Grounded Theory Study Exploring Motivational Influences of Bullying at Work*. Retrieved from ProQuest Dissertations and Theses (AAT3636399).

Cloke, K. & Goldsmith, J. (2000) *Resolving Conflicts at Work: A Complete Guide for Everyone on the Job* (1st edn). San Francisco, CA: Jossey-Bass.

Costantino, C.A. & Merchant, C.S. (1996) *Designing Conflict Management Systems*. San Francisco, CA: Jossey-Bass.

Dana, D. (2001) *Conflict Resolution*. New York: McGraw-Hill Publishers.

De Kremer, D. & Sedikides, C. (2008) Reputational implications of procedural fairness for personal and relational self-esteem. *Basic and Applied Social Psychology*, 30(1): 66–75.

Moore, C.W. (2003) *The Mediation Process: Practical Strategies for Resolving Conflict* (3rd edn). San Francisco, CA: Jossey-Bass.

Newman, D.C. (2013) A creative industry needs a creative solution: Why the entertainment industry should adopt mediation as its primary form of dispute resolution. *Dispute Resolution Journal*, 68(3), 71–80.

Phillips, B.A. (2001) *The Mediation Field Guide: Transcending Litigation and Resolving Conflicts in your Business or Organization*. San Francisco, CA: Jossey-Bass.

Ritzer, G. (1983) The McDonaldization of society. *Journal of American Culture*, 6(1): 100–107.

Seagriff, B.L. (2010) Keep your lunch money: Alleviating workplace bullying with mediation. *Ohio State Journal on Dispute Resolution*, 25(2): 575–602.

Stitt, A.J. (1998) *Alternative Dispute Resolution for Organizations*. Toronto: John Wiley & Sons.

Ury, W.L., Brett, J.M. & Goldberg, S.B. (1988) *Getting Disputes Resolved: Designing Systems to Cut Costs*. San Francisco, CA: Jossey-Bass.

Wilkin, L. (2010) *Workplace Bullying in Academe: A Grounded Theory Study Exploring How Faculty Cope with the Experience of Being Bullied*. Retrieved from ProQuest Dissertations & Theses Global (447190).

Williams, F. (2011) The power of social networks: Resolving conflict using informal mediators. *Conflict Resolution and Negotiation Journal*, 20: 35–59.

20

HEALTH CARE MEDIATION

Promoting workplace collaboration and patient safety

Robin Cooper

Given that health care is a matter of life and death, literally, it is self-evident that the health care arena is one of the most stressful workplace environments. Patients and family members are fearful and anxious and often find navigating the health care system confusing and frustrating. Health care providers work long hours under the constant strain of knowing their actions have potentially dramatic consequences. These factors contribute to unique forms of conflict in the health care arena. There are a variety of ways in which mediation can be helpful within the context of the health care system. This chapter focuses on the uses of mediation and mediation skills to address conflict within the health care team or between members of the health care team and patients or their families. For the purposes of this chapter, mediation is defined as a voluntary, confidential process in which an impartial third party assists disputants in discussing their conflict, and in which any settlement is developed and agreed to by the parties.

In the course of treating patients, professionals from a range of different fields—nursing, medicine, physical therapy, to name just a few—must communicate and collaborate, effectively to support positive patient outcomes. Conflict on the health care team not only impacts the workplace experience for these professionals, but can threaten patient safety. When there are negative health outcomes, patients and health care professionals have needs that go beyond financial settlement that can be addressed through mediation. This chapter explores concepts and techniques that promote interprofessional collaboration, as well as conflict resolution between members of the health care team and between health care workers and patients and their families.

Mediation in health care

As compared to many other organizational contexts, the use of alternative dispute resolution (ADR) remains limited in the health care industry, in spite of the fact that organizations such as JAMS, the American Arbitration Association, and the American Health Lawyers Association offer health care-specialized mediators and arbitrators (Thorpe, 2011). Thorpe suggested that this low utilization of ADR may result from health care lawyers having less exposure to mediation and arbitration than lawyers working in other contexts. An alternative explanation is that the limited use of mediation in the field of health care is due to disconnected health care systems and a lack of clarity about the benefits of mediation as well as what type of mediator would be most appropriate (Roscoe, 2010).

One of the questions in any context is whether mediators need to be content experts in addition to process experts. In some contexts, this is more common (for example, trade mediators or foreign policy mediators), whereas in family, community, and workplace disputes, the facilitative style of mediator who is a process expert is generally effective. One of the reasons attributed to the limited use of mediation in health care is the fact that most mediators are not medical experts. "Health care decisionmakers often prefer a mediator with a more comprehensive subject matter expertise than mediation skill" (Roscoe, 2010, para. 5).

There are a range of types of disputes in the health care context that might be considered for possible mediation. Thorpe (2011) outlined six types of disputes in the context of health care:

- Patient safety claims and product liability claims
- Disputes among members of the health care team, whether between members of physician groups or between physicians and other staff
- Various types of fraud
- Transactions involving either mergers and acquisitions or technology transfer and intellectual property
- Payment and reimbursement disputes
- Risk management controversies including insurance issues

To this useful list might be added disputes in which cultural and/or religious factors cause patients and health care providers to disagree about health care decisions. In light of the significant and growing diversity within the United States and across countries in the world, conflict tied to differing cultural views regarding health and medical treatment may well increase. For example, views on immunization or contraception, beliefs about the role of prayer in healing, or cultural dietary restrictions or perceived benefits of certain foods, may impact health behaviors and health care decisions. Mediation can provide a valuable forum, not only to foster greater understanding of varying perspectives on what constitutes "well-being", but also to share information and aid in making decisions on interventions and treatments for patients.

One of the applications of mediation in the health care context is in the aftermath of bad patient outcomes in the form of medical malpractice mediation. This has tended to focus on monetary negotiations rather than addressing the information patients and their families so often desire, such as what happened, how it happened, and how it can be prevented in the future (Liebman, 2011; Roscoe, 2010). Another use of mediation is in the settlement of accusations of health care fraud (Roscoe, 2010; Thorpe, 2011). As in other organizational settings, another application of mediation in the health care context is that of addressing disputes between physicians working in the same practice (Thorpe, 2011).

While the use of mediation may be less common in the health care context than in other organizational settings, Liebman (2011) observed that mediation is starting to become more common in the US health care system to aid communication between health care providers and patients "after an adverse medical event, to ease tensions among members of care-giving teams, to resolve medical malpractice claims, and to help family members and medical professionals make awesome and wrenching decisions at the end of life" (p. 135). At times, there may be different views within families or even within the health care team about whether aggressive end-of-life treatment is "doing everything possible" or prolonging suffering for the patient. Mediation provides a forum to share views, ideas, and information, and work out shared decisions.

Nevertheless, even when mediations take place in the health care context, in many cases physicians do not participate. Reasons for non-participation by physicians in mediation include: busy schedules, wanting to avoid hearing plaintiffs' attacks, the belief that mediation is not a professional custom, or the determination by the physicians' lawyers that their presence was not needed because the physicians could not make decisions about settlement amounts, and the lawyers perceived the mediation as solely about a financial settlement (Liebman, 2011).

In spite of the still-emergent use of mediation in the health care context, Thorpe (2011) highlighted several aspects of mediation that are valuable in this context, including but not limited to: concerns for privacy and confidentiality, reduction of time and costs as compared to judicial proceedings, and management and preservation of relationships. To these general benefits of mediation, Liebman (2011) added a few benefits specific to the health care context: improved patient safety, teamwork, and financial savings for physicians, hospitals, and patients. The benefits of mediation related to teamwork on the health care team, and to interpersonal conflict between members of that team and patients or their families are the focus of this chapter.

Mediation for the health care team

In addition to the demographic changes associated with increasing diversity noted above, the United States, like many countries around the world, is also experiencing demographic changes related to an aging population, especially as the large "baby boom" generation moves into their elder years. A growing older population is associated with higher rates of chronic illnesses such as diabetes and hypertension, which require long-term, interprofessional care from the health care team. In addition, aside from treatment for specific illnesses, elder care requires ongoing, collaborative attention from health care providers. Thus, cooperation among the health care team becomes especially important in responding to this growing segment of the population.

Stemming from the recognition that collaboration among health care professionals is necessary to reduce errors in the health care system, there have been increasing calls over the past several years for training that promotes collaboration on the health care team. Buring et al. (2009) observed that "once health care professionals begin to work together in a collaborative manner, patient care will improve. Interprofessional teams enhance the quality of patient care, lower costs, decrease patients' length of stay, and reduce medical errors" (p. 1). Given the link between effective collaboration on the health care team and the quality of patient care, it is critical to effectively address conflict among health professionals.

One source of conflict among health care professionals is the acceptance of professional stereotypes. "Often health professionals fail to recognize that they carry with them stereotypes or misconceptions of other health professionals that negatively impact opportunities to teach and/or practice collaboration" (D'Amour & Oandasan, 2005, p. 17). These professional stereotypes are associated with what has been called *profession-centrism*, "a constructed and preferred view of the world held by a particular professional group developed and reinforced through training experiences" (Pecukonis et al., 2008, p. 420). Narrative mediation (Winslade & Monk, 2000) can be used to help deconstruct the conflict stories of members of the health care team and support them in recognizing alternate views to understand actions and outcomes.

The mutual listening that occurs in mediation is particularly valuable in helping to develop respect among the members of the health care team. This is critical, given that someone is unlikely to act on information, even if it is accurate, when that information is received from a source that person does not respect. As has been noted, "professional hierarchies created by demographic and professional differences are common but create dysfunctional communication patterns working against effective interprofessional teamwork" (Interprofessional Education Collaborative Expert Panel, 2011, p. 22). The mediation session offers a forum in which all health professionals have equal opportunity to be heard, leveling the communication "playing field" and fostering more effective communication to improve patient safety and health outcomes.

Mediation between health care providers and patients

Bush and Folger (2005) highlight the importance of recognition and empowerment in their transformative model of mediation. The concept of recognition is especially relevant in the context of negative health outcomes. "The need for an apology generally stems from a need to have one's situation and pain acknowledged" (Regis & Poitras, 2010, p. 35). Regis & Poitras (2010) noted that "acknowledging one's unintentional impact on another is just as effective as recognizing one's intentional faults, which suggests that simply recognizing the other's suffering might be enough to bring about some level of reconciliation between parties" (p. 37). Recognizing the potential benefits of this model of mediation within the health care context, Tereanu and Quattrocolo (2011) observed that transformative mediation may be the most appropriate model of mediation for conflicts between patients (or family members) and physicians that are especially emotional.

Aside from offering mediation itself, there have been benefits associated with incorporating mediation skills training. There have been successful programs of training hospital department leaders in "how to employ mediation-type tools to manage the inevitable conflicts that health care delivery produces" (Roscoe, 2010, para. 16). Roscoe (2010) affirmed, "[a]stute health care institutions have learned that when it comes to conflict, prevention and management is easier (and more pleasant) than cure. One day of mediation skills training can improve quality while saving time, money and perhaps even lives" (para. 17).

Physicians are sometimes characterized as difficult and disruptive in the health care setting. Roscoe (2010) suggested this may be "a result of physicians who have not been equipped to deliver services while maintaining effective relationships in an environment of increasing pressures and limited resources" (para. 8). He suggested mediators can both mediate workplace conflicts and also provide some education for physicians about interpersonal communication and behaviors that will reduce conflict and help them meet their goal of providing high-quality care.

"For most users, the quality of their communication and interaction with healthcare professionals is among the main determinants of their perceived quality of medical care" (Tereanu & Quattrocolo, 2011, p. 16). Given the emphasis on communication for patients in determining the quality of their care, health care professionals would benefit from training in the communication skills associated with mediation. Basic interpersonal communication skills such as active listening and reflective listening can go a long way in improving patients' experience and sense of being heard.

Conclusions and recommendations

Although the health care field has not adopted alternative dispute resolution systems as widely as some other professions, there is real potential for mediation to make a significant positive difference in this context. A few suggestions are offered below.

Expanding perceptions of the purposes of mediation

While mediation has largely been perceived as a method to arrive at settlement between disputing parties—and this is certainly a valuable and central purpose of mediation—it would be useful to expand the view of the benefits that may arise from the mediation process. Such benefits include, quality improvement and the identification of actions that may prevent further negative health outcomes. Dauer and Marcus (1997) nearly a decade ago made the case that mediation can play an important role in health care quality improvement. Summarizing their case, they stated, "[i]t can be a safe harbor with therapeutic potential, and can offer its participants the opportunity to address the source as well as the consequence of the immediate problem" (p. 199). Thus, they observed that mediation is a process that can support quality improvement efforts. Given their conclusions, they ask if health care professionals could not "develop a mediation program that had error-risk-reduction as an *explicit* remedial goal" (p. 213).

Along these same lines, Liebman (2011) noted that "hospital administrators reported that they had obtained information from mediation that might lead them to suggest changes in policy" (p. 140). These observations indicate that mediation should be considered not only as a mechanism to arrive at a financial settlement, but as a forum in which critical information is shared that can lead to quality improvement and beneficial policy changes. As Liebman and Hyman (2004) noted, a monetary settlement does not address the desire of the patient or family member to know what happened and what is being done to prevent a recurrence, whereas in mediations in which parties "consider a nonmonetary remedy, such as specific education for staff or a memorial space outside the hospital, both the grieving family and the hospital representatives may feel that the resolution has given meaning to a tragic event" (Liebman & Hyman, 2004, p. 30).

Expanding perceptions of the type of mediator/mediation that is most useful

There are different types of mediators and various typologies to categorize these different mediator styles. For example, Moore (2003) refers to the following types of mediators: social network mediator, benevolent mediator, administrative/managerial mediator, vested interest mediator, and independent mediator. Regis and Poitras (2010, p. 43) contrast two typologies: that of Umbreit (1997), who described two major categories—the traditional, agreement-focused mediator versus the humanistic-transformative mediator who emphasizes the relationship between the parties—and that of Roberge (2007), who identified three types of mediators—"1) Legal expert and risk manager; 2) Expert in problem solving and creating integrative solutions; and 3) Participatory justice facilitator." As perceptions expand to recognize benefits associated with mediation outside those of financial settlement, it would be useful for those in the health care context to consider other types of mediation that could play a constructive role in the workplace, and the various types of mediators associated with those mediation models. A humanistic-transformative mediator, for example, might be most effective if the goal is to facilitate reconciliation within a health care team that has been experiencing conflict in the workplace.

Including physicians in mediations

Regis and Poitras (2010) have advocated for the inclusion of apologies in health care mediation, acknowledging the legal ramifications that must be considered, but also emphasizing the emotional and psychological benefits to both patients and physicians. "In addition to easing the victim's frustration, apologies can also help ease the doctor's sense of guilt and help provide some relief, in the event that the doctor feels guilty as a result of the events" (Regis & Poitras, 2010, p. 36). They clarified that in the context of mediation, the apology may take the form of "regret and sympathy" to avoid legal ramifications of acknowledging wrongdoing (Regis & Poitras, 2010, p. 37). Likewise, Liebman (2011) pointed out that reconciliation between patients and physicians is not possible if the physician is not willing to be present for the mediation. "It also deprives patients of the opportunity to know that the physician involved cares enough about the bad outcome to come and sit with the patient or family in the mediation" (Liebman, 2011, p. 147).

Providing conflict resolution and interpersonal communication skills training

As noted above, aside from mediation itself, the skills associated with mediators would be highly beneficial for those working in health care. Mediators could provide education for physicians about interpersonal communication and behaviors that will reduce conflict (Roscoe, 2010). Liebman and Hyman (2004) recommended "that physicians and other health care professionals develop an awareness of the communication skills most likely to be useful during disclosure conversations" (p. 24). In light of the sensitive nature of disclosing errors and adverse outcomes, they recommended that the hospital staff be provided with a brief introduction to the conflict resolution and communication skills necessary for disclosure conversations, and also to "prepare a core group of skilled and experienced staff members who can help others prepare for disclosure conversations, can participate when appropriate, and can debrief afterward" (p. 25).

As these recommendations reveal, mediation holds significant promise to benefit health care professionals in their working relationships within the health care team, as well as to improve health care quality and relationships between health care providers and patients. Health care affects everyone, is vitally important to everyone at one time or another in their lives, and conflict related to health care decisions has significant financial, emotional, and personal ramifications. As discussed in this chapter, mediation can be beneficial on many levels within the health care arena, and it is hoped that those working in the field of conflict resolution will promote the use of mediation in this unique and important organizational context.

References

Buring, S.M., Bhushan, A., Broeseker, A., Conway, S., Duncan-Hewitt, W., Hansen, L. & Westberg, S. (2009) Interprofessional education: Definitions, student competencies, and guidelines for implementation. *American Journal of Pharmaceutical Education*, 73(4): 1–8.

Bush, R.A.B. & Folger, J.P. (2005) *The Promise of Mediation: The Transformative Approach to Conflict*. San Francisco, CA: Jossey-Bass.

D'Amour, D. & Oandasan, I. (2005) Interprofessionality as the field of interprofessional practice and interprofessional education: An emerging concept. *Journal of Interprofessional Care*, 1: 8–20.

Dauer, E. & Marcus, L. (1997) Adapting mediation to link resolution of medical malpractice disputes with health care quality improvement. *Law and Contemporary Problems*, 60(1): 185–218.

Interprofessional Education Collaborative Expert Panel. (2011) *Core Competencies for Interprofessional Collaborative Practice: Report of an Expert Panel*. Washington, DC: National Academy Press.

Liebman, C. (2011) Medical malpractice mediation: Benefits gained, opportunities lost. *Law and Contemporary Problems*, 74(3): 135–149.

Liebman, C. & Hyman, C. (2004) A mediation skills model to manage disclosure of errors and adverse events to patients. *Health Affairs*, 23(4): 22–32.

Moore, C. W. (2003) *The Mediation Process: Practical Strategies for Resolving Conflict* (3rd edn). San Francisco, CA: Jossey-Bass.

Pecukonis, E., Doyle, O. & Bliss, D.L. (2008) Reducing barriers to interprofessional training: Promoting interprofessional cultural competence. *Journal of Interprofessional Care*, 22(4): 417–428.

Regis, C. & Poitras, J. (2010) Healthcare mediation and the need for apologies. *Health Law Journal*, 18: 31–49.

Roberge, J.F. (2007) La mediation judicaire "innovante" peut-elle ameliorer le systeme judicaire? Synthese et analyse des reponses de la communaute juridique canadienne. *Rencontres juridiques Montpellier-Sherbrooke, Le droit a l'epreuve des changements de paradigms*, 165.

Roscoe, J. (2010) Mediation of health care disputes: An opportunity to heal or a prescription for disaster? Health Care Law. Retrieved from www.jamsadr.com/files/Uploads/Documents/Articles/Roscoe_LI_Healthcare_10-2010.pdf.

Tereanu, C. & Quattrocolo, A. (2011) Transformative mediation in healthcare organizations: A resource. *Management in Health*, 15(1): 16–23.

Thorpe, W. (2011) Effective use of mediation and arbitration in health care disputes. *Bloomberg Law Reports: Health Law*. Retrieved from www.jamsadr.com/files/Uploads/Documents/Articles/Thorpe-Healthcare-Disputes-Bloomberg-2011.pdf.

Umbreit, M.S. (1997) Humanistic mediation: A transformative journey of peacemaking. *Mediation Quarterly*, 14(3): 201–213.

Winslade, J. & Monk, G. (2000) *Narrative Mediation: A New Approach to Conflict Resolution*. San Francisco, CA: Jossey-Bass.

21

INSTITUTIONALIZED MEDIATION AND ACCESS TO JUSTICE IN THE STATE COURT SYSTEM OF THE UNITED STATES

Rebecca Storrow

The State Court System in the United States has come to rely on mediation to achieve the timely resolution of a variety of types of disputes. Mediation allows emotional and complex issues to be resolved outside the courtroom, saving precious judicial resources and allowing for party-driven resolution (Kressel & Pruitt, 1989). Both the court and mediation processes have evolved to achieve a highly functional level of compatibility (Phillips, 2001; Moore, 2003; Fisher, 1991). Sharon Press (1997) defined institutionalization as any entity (governmental or otherwise) that adopts alternative dispute resolution (ADR) procedures as a part of doing business. However, with any system, there is potential to obscure trends that may otherwise have been recognized in a more public process.

History of court mediation in the United States

Since the late 1970s, state courts in the United States have increased the use of mediation in volume and scope of disputes (Scheiwe Kulp, 2013; Hartley, 2002; Folger et al., 2001). Due to increased diversity, complex disputes, and reductions in court funding, courts have relied on mediation and other forms of ADR to manage complex disputes and alleviate caseloads (Winston, 1996; Zylstra, 2001). The National Center for State Courts (2013) reports that civil jury trials represent less than 1 percent of total civil dispositions, creating a large space of opportunity for mediation to intervene in the life of a case.

Pursuant to Title 28 of Judiciary and Judicial Procedures, Statute 652 Jurisdiction requires each district court to provide litigants in all civil cases with at least one ADR process (28 USC § 652). Although state courts have systematically referred domestic issues and small claims to mediation (Zylstra, 2001), the 2008 foreclosure crisis in the United States expanded its use. Nevada, Arizona, Florida, and California led the nation in foreclosure rates, and Florida, for example, implemented a statewide administrative order referring residential foreclosure actions to mediation to reduce the backlog of pending cases (Supreme Court of Florida, 2009). The field added many new mediators to meet new foreclosure mediation caseloads. Simultaneously, the legal profession became more competitive, so attorneys increasingly added mediation to their practices (Zahorsky, 2011). From 2009 to 2013, many regional and statewide foreclosure mediation programs were managed by existing nonprofits that had previously supported the court, large alternative dispute resolution organizations—such as the American Arbitration Association (AAA), and new mediation companies run by mediators or law firms. In support, systems for training mediators, assessments, and technology for case management emerged. The field increased in numbers, organization, and information sharing.

Public satisfaction with mediation in civil matters has also supported its insertion both pre- and post-judgment (Beck & Sales, 2001). Many ADR programs, such as that of the Virginia State Court, report over 90 percent party satisfaction rates (Virginia State Court, 2013). However, in family mediation there are studies that reveal that party satisfaction appears to be significantly related to parents' subsequent perceptions of parenting arrangements and their children's adjustment (Superior Court of the County of Orange, 1991). These post-mediation perceptions are not easily understood in terms of quantitative analysis. Due to mediation's complexity, a more accurate understanding of participant satisfaction might be derived through systematic qualitative research (Storrow & Georgakopoulos, 2012; Finneran, 2006).

Mediation in the courts

Research shows that mediation is particularly amenable to the court system (Center for Analysis of Alternative Dispute Resolution Systems and for Conflict Resolution, 2007; Lawyers Trust Fund of Illinois, 2005). According to Wissler (2004, 2002), most studies report a mediation settlement rate of civil court cases between 47 percent and 78 percent. It has been this author's experience that an additional measure of the default rate on these agreements is needed to provide an accurate assessment of mediation's efficacy. Practitioners have attempted to balance the alternative nature of mediation with the more structured court environment. This has fueled a wider debate among practitioners as to what process defines "true" mediation (Carnevale & Pegnetter, 1985; Kressel, 1979; Kressel & Pruitt, 1985; Touval & Zartman, 1985; Wall, 1981; Wall & Rude, 1985). An example of how court-ordered mediation is framed by the court is in how child-focused approaches are common in court-ordered family mediation, even though child-inclusive family mediation was found to provide significantly more durable agreements (McIntosh et al., 2008).

Legislation, rules, and standards

The Uniform Mediation Act (UMA) was established in 2001 and revised in 2003 by a committee that acted for the National Conference of Commissioners on Uniform State Laws (2003). It defined mediation as a process in which a third-party neutral helps the disputing parties negotiate. The UMA does not cover all types of mediation, but an important aspect is its establishment of the scope of confidentiality, including where it begins and ends in Revised Code (RC) 2710.03 (National Conference of Commissioners on Uniform State Laws, 2003). Further, RC 2710.03 (B) and RC 2711.05 (A) identify which types of mediation communications are privileged. Various forms of this section have been incorporated into mediation rules and statutes throughout the country, supporting a process in which participants feel comfortable communicating and reducing the possibility of privileged information being used in court at a later time.

In 1994, the Model Standards of Conduct for Mediators was developed by the AAA, the American Bar Association's (ABA) Section of Dispute Resolution, and the Association for Conflict Resolution (ACR). Representatives from these organizations revised and approved the standards in 2005. The Model Standards serve as a guide for mediator conduct, inform parties regarding mediation standards, and further promote public confidence, responding to many issues that have been identified surrounding mediation practice.

Ethical standards have also been established in the ACR's Model Standards for Mediator Certification Programs (ACR, 2011), adopted on October 10, 2011. The Model Standards for Mediator Certification Programs guide and increase credibility of mediator certification programs. All of these standards and rules have been informative, and although there is rigorous discourse in professional journals and conferences about mediation having a single entry point or standardization, there is little national, or for that matter international, consensus at this time in regard to a single set of procedures, ethics, and rules.

Certification and qualification

There are two predominant structures for delivering mediation to state courts. One is a process of qualification, in which courts endorse a level of training and expertise. This is sometimes defined by nonprofit mediation programs that receive a substantial portion of their revenue from caseloads referred by the court (Wissler, 2011, 2004; Mosten, 2004; Welsh, 2001). According to a study by Northern Virginia Mediation Service (2013), over half of states have comprehensive statewide standards for mediators who wish to be recognized by the courts and included on court rosters. Another structure is a process of certification in which mediators must be certified through a centralized agency or nonprofit organization, including continuing education, to provide service to courts. Although there are no states that regulate mediation practice, there are several that maintain lists of certified mediators to serve in particular practice areas, such as court-ordered cases.

In October 2011, the Council of the ABA's Alternative Dispute Resolution Section created a Task Force to recommend whether the Section should adopt a policy concerning credentialing of mediators. Their recommendation was to support local initiatives and innovations in the field of credentialing, provided they meet the guidelines set forth in their report (American Bar Association, 2012). Given the lack of consensus regarding the attributes of the mediation process or a process for determining competency, the Section did not support creation of a single nationwide credentialing system. However, some national mediation organizations include, the National Center for State Courts (www.ncsc.org), ACR (www.acrnet.org), the National Association for Community Mediation (www.nafcm.org), and Resolution Systems Institute's Court ADR Resource Center (www.aboutrsi.org), which supports the court ADR programs, and within each state, there may be multiple professional mediator organizations.

Court mediation programs

Court mediation program directors interviewed described a somewhat complex relationship between the "alternative" process of family mediation and the state court legal system (G. Moreno and D. Haataja-Deratany, personal communication, August 15, 2013). Many court mediation programs utilize two types of mediators, court staff mediators, and private contracted mediators who may introduce a more varied approach. Research has indicated that mediators may be influenced to some degree by the court's goals, culture, and interpretation of local rules and statutes (Storrow & Georgakopoulos, 2013; Bush & Folger, 2005; Mosten, 2004; Coleman & Welsh, 2002; Press, 1997; Alfini et al., 1994; Fiss, 1984). Many programs utilize the service of volunteer, pro bono mediators, particularly for small claims caseloads. These mediators provide a valuable public service, but there are perceptions that the use of pro bono mediators may make mediation appear less professional. In addition, since it is predominantly retired individuals who volunteer their time, there may be less diversity in pro bono panels. It is important that there are effective diversity initiatives, that mediators are held to professional standards, and that mediators are provided with appropriate training.

Predominant mediation styles in court programs

The program directors interviewed (G. Moreno and D. Haataja-Deratany, personal communication, August 15, 2013) confirmed the research has shown that most court mediators use a facilitative approach (Moore, 2003). In the facilitative style, the mediator helps the parties create an agenda, look at options, and reach agreement if they so desire. The mediator does not offer opinions or make judgments, managing the process but not the outcome (Zumeta, 2000). Private contracted mediators were viewed by the directors as using a more evaluative style of mediation. The evaluative mediator helps parties reach a resolution using rigorous reality testing, making recommendations, and predicting at times what a judge will decide if the dispute goes to court (Riskin, 1994). These variances in style may be confusing to parties; therefore a neutral provider program adds value by educating parties about the processes of mediation.

Benefits and challenges of court mediation programs

The increase of court mediation programs has catalyzed a symbiosis between court mediation and mediation in the private sector creating benefits and challenges (Shaw et al., 1996). For example, as in many states, Florida clerks of court support pro se parties, those without legal representation, by instituting self-help desks to aid the public with forms and information (Florida Supreme Court Commission on Trial Courts Performance and Accountability, 2011). When parties are better educated, they are better consumers of the process and can participate in more meaningful ways (Moore, 1996). Legal aid is another source of assistance for parties, but this resource has been traditionally underfunded and underutilized (Columbia Law School Human Rights Clinic, 2013). The court's use of mediation has, however, contributed greatly to the professionalization of mediation.

Challenges include a court program focus on maintaining the system of service. George Ritzer (2009) explained that when a culture moves from traditional to rationalized modes of thought and operation, there is a "McDonaldization" or refocusing on efficiency, control, standardization, and rationality. Nancy Welsh (2001) spoke specifically to court-connected mediation's institutionalization, suggesting that there is continued controversy and opposition regarding this symbiotic relationship. Additionally, Thompson (2004) suggests that mediation's positioning in the judicial system may contribute to unfairness and create false expectations in the public. Program directors and mediators interviewed, stated that they feel some judicial pressure for consistency of process and for achieving good and lasting settlement agreements, but do not believe their positions with the court hinge solely upon success rates (G. Moreno and D. Haataja-Deratany, personal communication, August 15, 2013). Other challenges include providing diversity of practitioners and practice styles, access to low-cost, effective legal representation, and maintaining self-determination of parties. Critiques have been leveled against court mediators by private mediators, citing that the rigidity of structure and high volume can create an inferior process (Storrow & Georgakopoulos, 2012; Mosten, 2004). Program directors interviewed stated that volume and the ability to adjourn or schedule longer sessions are areas they are working to enhance (G. Moreno and D. Haataja-Deratany, personal communication, August 15, 2013).

Technology

Technology has had a profound influence on the practice of mediation in the court. There has been an increase in the use of benchmarking of processes, as demonstrated in the National Center of State Courts' Courtools (NCSC, 2013). The implementation of technology programs such as Courtools supports the court's measure of basic performance indicators. Use of these types of technological tools may increase focus on the disposition of cases, again supporting the use of mediation for timely resolution. Technology has also contributed to faster, more efficient practice. Family mediation has shifted to software to calculate child support and alimony. There are online web platforms for the exchange of documents, scheduling the visitation of children, and other detailed parenting plan documents. There is an impetus to leverage technology to get complex matters resolved without multiple post-judgment filings.

Access to justice

There is an important initiative within the courts to promote and preserve access to justice. According to a report by the National Center for State Courts (NCSC, 2013), stakeholders from inside and outside the courts have come together in an effort to remove barriers to civil justice for low-income and disadvantaged litigants. Many low-income and disadvantaged litigants, when selecting mediation, cannot afford attorneys or higher-priced private mediators and opt to use court-staffed mediation programs. There is a burden on mediation program funding to ensure that all parties are receiving fair and just processes. Merely paying the reasonable court mediation program fees can be a barrier for low-income individuals and many programs have waivers or discounted rates subsidized through state funding. Regardless, there is a continued need for pro bono service and increased collaboration and coordination among legal aid providers.[1]

Note

1 I would like to thank Guillermo "Bill" Moreno and Deborah Haataja-Deratany, ADR Court Program Directors for the Fifteenth and Eighteenth Judicial Circuit Courts of Florida, respectively, for their valuable contributions. I would also like to thank Dr Alexia Georgakopoulos as she has been a guide and mentor for so many of us in the field of alternative dispute resolution.

References

Alfini, J., Barkai, J., Bush, R., Hermann, M., Hyman, J., Kovach, K., Bensinger Liebman, C., Press, S. & Riskin, L. (1994) What happens when mediation is institutionalized? *Ohio State Journal on Dispute Resolution*, 9(2): 307–332. Retrieved from ssrn.com/abstract=1435602.

American Arbitration Association, the American Bar Association's Section of Dispute Resolution, & the Association for Conflict Resolution. (2005) Model standards of conduct for mediators. Retrieved from www.adr.org/aaa/ShowPDF?doc=ADRSTG_004416.

American Bar Association. (2012) Alternative dispute resolution section of the American Bar Association task force on mediator credentialing: Final report. *American Bar Association*. Retrieved from www.americanbar.org/content/dam/aba/images/dispute_resolution/CredentialingTaskForce.pdf.

American Bar Association. (2013) Research trends and conclusions: Commercial Mediation 2013. *Who's Who Legal*. Retrieved from whoswholegal.com/news/analysis/article/30713/research-trends-conclusions-commercial-mediation-2013/.

Association for Conflict Resolution. (2011) Model standards for mediator certification programs. *Association for Conflict Resolution*. Retrieved from www.imis100us2.com/acr/ACR/EducationTraining/Model_Sta

ndards/ACR/Education___Training/Model_Standards.aspx?hkey=e53eb47b-1193-4f24-9fd8-8a526 2f9e99e.

Beck, C.J. & Sales, B.D. (2001) *Family Mediation: Facts, Myths, and Future Prospects*. Washington, DC: American Psychological Association.

Bush, R. & Folger, J. (2005) *The Promise of Mediation: The Transformative Approach to Conflict* (2nd edn). San Francisco, CA: Jossey-Bass.

Carnevale, P.J.D. & Pegnetter, R. (1985) The selection of mediation tactics in public sector disputes: A contingency analysis. *Journal of Social Issues*, 41(2): 65–81. doi: 10.1111/j.1540–4560.1985.tb00855.x.

Center for Analysis of Alternative Dispute Resolution Systems and for Conflict Resolution. (2007) *Bibliographic Summary of Cost, Pace, and Satisfaction Studies of Court-related Mediation Programs* (2nd edn). Resolutions Systems Institute. Retrieved from www.aboutrsi.org/pfimages/MedStudyBiblio2ndEd2.pdf.

Coleman, P. & Welsh, N. (2002) Institutionalized conflict resolution: Have we come to expect too little? *Negotiation Journal*, 18(4): 345–350.

Columbia Law School Human Rights Clinic. (2013) Access to justice: Ensuring meaningful access to counsel in civil cases. Retrieved from web.law.columbia.edu/sites/default/files/microsites/human-rights-institute/files/Access%20to%20Justice%20Shadow%20Report%20-%20Final%20(small%20size).pdf.

Finneran, C.M. (2006) Metaphor analysis as a method for holistic PIM research. School of Information Studies: Syracuse University. Retrieved from pimworkshop.org/2009/papers/finneran-pim2009.pdf.

Fisher, R.J. (1991) Family mediation in the United States of America. *Australian Journal of Dispute Resolution*, 2(3): 249–261.

Fiss, O.M. (1984) Against settlement. *The Yale Law Journal*, 93(6): 1073–1090. Retrieved from digitalcommons.law.yale.edu/fss_papers/1215.

Florida Courts. (2015) Instructions for Florida family law rules of procedure form 12.996(a), income deduction order (06/11). Retrieved from flcourts.org/core/fileparse.php/293/urlt/996a.pdf.

Florida Supreme Court Commission on Trial Courts Performance and Accountability. (2011) Recommendations for alternative dispute resolution services in Florida's trial courts. Commission on Trial Court Performance and Accountability. Retrieved from www.flcourts.org/gen_public/court-services/bin/ADR%20Mediation%20Report%2008-2008.pdf.

Folger, J., Della Noce, D. & Antes, J. (2001) *A Benchmarking Study of Family, Civil, and Citizen Dispute Mediation Programs in Florida*. Dayton, OH: Institute for the Study of Conflict Transformation.

Hartley, R.E. (2002) *Alternative Dispute Resolution in Civil Justice System*. El Paso, TX: LFB Scholarly Publishing.

Hedeen, T. (2005) Coercion and self-determination in court-connected mediation: All mediations are voluntary, but some mediations are more voluntary than others. *Justice System Journal*, 26(3): 273–291.

Kressel, K. (1979) *Labor Mediation: An Exploratory Survey*. Albany, NY: Association of Labor Mediation Agencies.

Kressel, K. & Pruitt, D.G. (1985) Themes in the mediation of social conflict. *Journal of Social Issues*, 41(2): 179–198. doi: 10.1111/j.1540-4560.1985.tb00862.x.

Kressel, K. & Pruitt, D.G. (1989) *Mediation Research: The Process and Effectiveness of Third-party Intervention*. San Francisco, CA: Jossey-Bass.

Lawyers Trust Fund of Illinois. (2005) The legal aid safety net: A report on the legal needs of low-income Illinoisans. *Lawyers Trust Fund of Illinois*. Retrieved from www.robparal.com/downloads/legal_needs_study.pdf.

McIntosh, J., Wells, Y., Smyth, B. & Long, C. (2008) Child-focused and child-inclusive divorce family mediation: Comparative outcomes from a prospective study of post-separation adjustment. *Family Court Review*, 46(1): 105–124.

Moore, C. (1996) *The Mediation Process: Practical Strategies for Resolving Conflict* (2nd edn). San Francisco, CA: Jossey-Bass.

Moore, C.W. (2003) *The Mediation Process: Practical Strategies for Resolving Conflict* (3rd edn). San Francisco, CA: Jossey-Bass.

Mosten, F. (2004) Institutionalization of mediation. *Family Court Review*, 42(2): 292–303.

National Center for State Courts (NCSC). (2013) Improving access to justice for self-represented litigants. Center on Court Access to Justice for All. Retrieved from ncsc.contentdm.oclc.org/cdm/ref/collection/accessfair/id/331.

National Conference of Commissioners on Uniform State Laws. (2003) Uniform mediation act. *Uniform Laws*. Retrieved from www.uniformlaws.org/Act.aspx?title=Mediation+Act.

Northern Virginia Mediation Service. (2013) State-by-state guide to court mediator qualification standards. *NVMS*. Retrieved from nvms.us/2015/09/24/nvms-state-by-state-guide-to-court-mediator-qualifications/.

Phillips, B.A. (2001) *The Mediation Field Guide: Transcending Litigation and Resolving Conflicts in your Business or Organization*. San Francisco, CA: Jossey-Bass.

Press, S. (1997) Institutionalization: Savior or saboteur of mediation. *Florida State University Law Review*, 24: 903–917.

Resolution Systems Institute's Court ADR Resource Center. (2013) Retrieved from www.aboutrsi.org.

Riskin, L. (1994) Mediator orientations, strategies, and techniques. *Alternatives to the High Cost of Litigation*, 12: 111–114.

Ritzer, G. (2009) *The McDonaldization of Society*. Los Angeles, CA: Pine Forge Press.

Scheiwe Kulp, H. (2013) Increasing referrals to small claims mediation programs: Models to improve access to justice. *Cardozo Journal of Conflict Resolution*, 14: 361–393. Retrieved from www.aboutrsi.org/pfimages/CAC203.pdf.

Shaw, M., Singer, L. & Povich, L. (1996) National standards for court connected mediations. *Family and Conciliation Courts Review*, 31: 156–225.

Storrow, R. & Georgakopoulos, A. (2012) Mediators and metaphorical coherence: A phenomenological study of Florida family court mediators. *Journal of Conflict Management*, 2(1): 49–68.

Storrow, R. & Georgakopoulos, A. (2013) Mediators and metaphorical coherence: A phenomenological study of family court mediators. *Journal of Conflict Management*, 1(1): 5–24.

Superior Court of the County of Orange. (1991) Client satisfaction survey: A consumer evaluation of mediation and investigative services: Executive summary. Judicial Council of California. Retrieved from www.courts.ca.gov/documents/satsur.pdf.

Supreme Court of Florida. (2009) *No. AOSC09–54. Final Report and Recommendations on Residential Mortgage Foreclosure Cases*. Retrieved from www.floridasupremecourt.org/pub_info/documents/AOSC09-54_Foreclosures.pdf.

Thompson, P. (2004) Enforcing rights generated in court-connected mediation: Tension between the aspirations of a private facilitated process and the reality of public adversarial justice. *Ohio State Journal on Dispute Resolution*, 19(2): 509–572.

Touval, S. & Zartman, I.W. (1985) *International Mediation in Theory and Practice*. Boulder, CO: Westview Press.

Van Epps, D. (2014) Mediators' responses to challenges posed by changes in court administration and practice of law. Live presentation at the Annual 2014 Florida Dispute Resolution Center Conference.

Virginia State Court. (2013) Virginia court-connected ADR. Dispute Resolution Services: Supreme Court of Virginia. Retrieved from: www.courts.state.va.us/courtadmin/aoc/djs/programs/drs/mediation/resources/overview_and_statistics.pdf.

Wall, J.A., Jr. (1981) Mediation: An analysis, review, and proposed research. *Journal of Conflict Resolution*, 25(1): 157–180. doi: 10.1177/002200278102500107.

Wall, J.A., Jr. & Rude, D.E. (1985) Judicial mediation: Techniques, strategies, and situational effects. *Journal of Social Issues*, 41(2): 47–63. doi: 10.1111/j.1540-4560.1985.tb00854.x.

Welsh, N.A. (2001) The Thinning vision of self-determination in court-connected mediation: The inevitable price of institutionalization. *Harvard Negotiation Law Journal*, 6(1): 23–27.

Winston, D. (1996) Participation standards in mandatory mediation statutes: "You can lead a horse to water …" *Ohio State Journal on Dispute Resolution*, 11(1): 187–188.

Wissler, R. (2002) Court-connected mediation in general civil cases: What we know from empirical research. *17 Ohio State Journal on Dispute Resolution*, 641.

Wissler, R. (2004) The effectiveness of court-connected dispute resolution in civil cases. *Conflict Resolution Quarterly*, 22(1–2): 55–58.

Wissler, R. (2011) Court-connected settlement procedures: Mediation and judicial settlement conferences. *Ohio State Journal on Dispute Resolution*, 26(2–3): 271–327.

Yang, H. (1998) The concept of trust and trust building. *A Leadership Journal: Women in Leadership—Sharing the Vision*, 2(2).

Zahorsky, R. (2011) Law job stagnation may have started before the recession—and it may be a sign of lasting change. *ABA Journal Online*, July 1. Retrieved from www.abajournal.com/magazine/article/paradigm_shift/.

Zylstra, A. (2001) The road from voluntary mediation to mandatory good faith requirements: A road best left untraveled. *Journal of the American Academy of Matrimonial Lawyers*, 17: 69–103.

Zumeta, Z. (2000) A facilitative mediator responds. *Journal of Dispute Resolution*, 2000(2): 335–341. Retrieved from scholarship.law.missouri.edu/cgi/viewcontent.cgi?article=1382&context=jdr.

PART IV

Mediating in community settings

22

PROMOTING PEACEFUL COMMUNITIES

The challenges and benefits of community-police mediation

Evan Hoffman

Policing is difficult work and there is always a need to balance public safety with the personal protection and safety of the officer. As such, even the best police officers might from time to time have a public complaint made against them as they go about their daily work. Sometimes these complaints can have a legitimate basis in reality because a violation has occurred; at other times these complaints can simply be the result of a misunderstanding, a misperception, or even a lack of communication. Either way, modern police forces need mechanisms to investigate and resolve these grievances since they are ultimately accountable to the people in the communities whom they serve and protect.

Unfortunately, there is a lack of police grievance statistics in the United States. One report shows that 26,256 complaints were recorded in a single year and only 19 percent of large municipal police departments even had a civilian complaint review board as of 2003, which, of course, makes tracking complaints more difficult (Hickman, 2006). This number in the United States is low, however, when compared to figures from other countries. The Independent Police Complaints Commission (IPCC) noted that 34,863 complaints were recorded in England and Wales during a single year (IPCC, 2015). On the other hand, only 3,114 complaints were filed in one year in Ontario, Canada (Office of the Independent Police Review Director, 2014).

The most common way to resolve these grievances is to have an internal investigations division (sometimes called internal affairs or professional standards) launch a formal inquiry into incidents. These internal investigators often will have already served as a police officer prior to joining internal affairs, so they understand the challenges of policing. When they get a new case, the investigations they launch can be intensive, lengthy, costly, and may ultimately result in officers facing a number of consequences for their actions, ranging from a warning to a suspension to termination.

It can consume a considerable amount of a police department's budget to complete these investigations. In one year alone, at least $346.5 million was spent in the United States on misconduct-related settlements and civil judgments (excluding attorney fees, court costs, and sealed settlements) (Packman, 2010). Chicago alone spent over $84.5 million in just one year on judgments, legal fees, settlements, and other expenses (Shaw, 2014).

Moreover, despite these high costs, the outcomes of these formal investigations show mixed results. For example, almost 11,000 officers in the United States were involved in a formal investigations one year, and of these only 3,238 officers had criminal charges filed against them, and from all of those only about one third of the officers were convicted of the charges or had their charges reduced (Packman, 2010). In another example, 8,542 complaints were recorded over a four-year period in the UK and only 837 were referred to the IPCC. Of these 837 complaints, the IPCC investigated only 21 of them, resulting in 18 officers being prosecuted and 13 officers being found guilty (IPCC, 2013). According to this same source, each year more than 200 police officers retire or resign to avoid being investigated (IPCC, 2013).

An interesting and growing alternative to a formal investigation process is informal, voluntary mediation. Mediation is a structured process whereby a neutral, third-party mediator works with all of the parties to assist them in resolving their conflict. To do this, a mediator may perform many roles such as convening the parties, educating them about the mediation process, facilitating their conversation, removing communication obstacles, and assisting them with drafting any new agreements they may reach.

Mediation, such as this, between members of a community and the police officers who are responsible for maintaining law and order in that community offers a number of benefits for both groups. Because of this, mediation has great potential for strengthening relationships between the police and the public, thus building safer and stronger communities. Yet, for a number of reasons, community-police mediation remains an under-utilized tool for addressing public complaints. These reasons can include a lack of dedicated funding, being unaware of mediation and the benefits it can provide, and not knowing how to establish a mediation program.

In Boston, for example, there have been several false starts to get a new police mediation program up and running, but all this is about to change (Mason & Mashberg, 2015). Apparently, "the Boston Police Department is nearing a deal with its three unions and Harvard Law School to set up a simpler, speedier system for resolving many of the civilian complaints lodged against officers" (Mason & Mashberg, 2015). Under this new program, the most severe cases will still be investigated by internal affairs and the other cases would go into mediation (Mason & Mashberg, 2015).

This chapter will explore how mediation can play a role in addressing public grievances against the police by examining both the benefits and challenges, presenting the basic components of a police mediation program and discussing, more broadly, the need to foster an overall culture of conflict prevention in police departments in order to reduce the number of grievances.[1] First, however, it is necessary to discuss mediation in the context of resolving public complaints against police officers.

What does mediation look like in the context of resolving public complaints against police officers?

There are many styles of mediation that are widely recognized (narrative, facilitative, directive, transformative and so on) and many ways to put these different types of mediation into practice (in small groups, meeting the parties separately in caucus, using co-mediators to guide the process). While the specific needs of each and every police department will vary, broadly speaking, one good approach to mediation in the context of resolving public complaints against police officers is as follows:

Professional, well-seasoned mediators trained in classic interest-based mediation who follow a structured mediation process that is conducted outside the police building (ideally in a safe and private location) should be utilized. Mediation sessions can be approached as short half-day sessions with no outside parties allowed (a complainant's spouse, relative or lawyer, a "witness" or neighbor). That is, in order to create a direct communication line between the parties, just the member of public that filed the complaint and the officer it was filed against should be allowed into the initial mediation session. The nature of the case might mean that bringing other parties into subsequent sessions is desirable and this should be determined on a case-by-case basis.

The overall aim of the mediation session is not to pressure the complainant into withdrawing their complaint. Rather, the session can be seen as an important opportunity for what will most likely be the first face-to-face conversation between the officer and the member of the public since the incident occurred that resulted in a complaint being filed. Each party needs to have the chance to explain, discuss, explore and examine the incident. The mediator can ask the parties to consider how the incident may have been perceived by the other party in the hope of increasing their understanding of why each person acted the way they did. Throughout, the mediator must remain neutral and should not try to explain or justify why certain actions were taken, even if they may agree with or sympathize with one party more than the other.

It is important that the mediator be paid whether a withdrawal of complaint form is filed or not. Otherwise, this pressures the mediator into extending the mediation session until the member of the public does this. The session should only end when there is nothing further to be gained by the parties for staying involved or it has been mutually decided by them that mediation will not succeed and that the case should be referred back to the formal investigation process.

The mediation must remain confidential. That is, there should be no written records of what was said by whom and the mediator should only report back to the police the basic outcome of the session (for example, a second session is needed, the complaint was withdrawn or there is a need to refer the case back to the formal investigation process).

In sum, the main mediator tasks in resolving public complaints against police officers include convening the session, establishing ground rules, facilitating the conversation, encouraging perspective shifts, and reporting on the outcome of the case.

The benefits and challenges of integrating a mediation program into a police department

As noted earlier, mediation can offer a viable alternative to a formal investigation process.[2] In order to do this, a mediation program needs to be established within the police department and be properly resourced. While this offers the department a number of practical benefits there are also challenges involved with doing this, and both of these topics are explored in the next section of this chapter.

There are a number of benefits of mediation that should justify the relatively small expenditure that it takes to get a mediation program up and running within a police department. According to one source (CIIAN, 2012), the benefits of mediation can include the following:

- Participation is voluntary and off the record
- Privacy is maintained
- It creates a neutral and safe space for the problem to be addressed through direct person-to-person communication independent of professional roles
- Mediation does not assign blame or punishment

- Participants have maximum control over any agreement that is reached
- There is great potential to create mutually beneficial, "win-win" agreements
- Trust between the parties can be built or re-established
- Shifts in perspective around the conflict and understanding the impact of one's actions mean that similar conflict is less likely to occur
- A direct communication channel is opened between the parties allowing them to exchange new information or supply missing information to the other party
- Ongoing conflict can be addressed and there is an opportunity for reconciliation to occur

Moreover, there can be significant cost and time savings created by a mediation program, so valuable and limited resources can be reserved for the police and courts. For example, the average time from the point of first contact with CIIAN to the date of the mediation session was 30 days (including weekends and holidays) (CIIAN, 2013) and formal investigation processes can easily be three times as long. One article found that "participants in mediated cases are likely to decrease their use of court and law enforcement after mediation compared to participants in cases not mediated" (Charkoudian, 2010, p. 141). Clearly, there is a growing body of evidence that mediation saves time and resources.

Therefore, while mediation can be a very effective way to handle the right types of grievances and it has the potential to build trust and goodwill between the police and the community members they serve, it is not without some difficulties. That is, only some cases are appropriate for mediation. There needs to be a thorough screening process to ensure that the most serious cases go to formal investigation and that all the other cases flow through to mediation. The question to ask is: can this case be mediated and is it appropriate for mediation? It requires expert knowledge of both mediation and formal police investigations to effectively screen and direct cases to the appropriate channels. Moreover, not every case referred to mediation will proceed past the convening stage. For example, 80 percent of the cases referred to mediation in the Ottawa Police Service Voluntary Alternative Dispute Resolution Program (VADRP) went on to be mediated (CIIAN, 2013). The same report goes on to explain that:

> In one case, the officer withdrew from the VADRP and in the other three it was the complainant that terminated the process. Nevertheless, this is still a very impressive rate and it seems to suggest that once the commitment to use mediation has been made, generally both parties will follow-through on it.
>
> *(CIIAN, 2013, p. 3)*

Additionally, even the best-designed and best-resourced mediation program will be ineffective if no one uses it. There is, therefore, a need to get buy-in from all the parties. In terms of getting buy-in from the officers, it helps to have internal champions for the mediation program. Ideally, this would be the chief of police and other senior ranking officials. However, there may also be a need to work with the police union in order to have the union send supportive messages about mediation to its members. This might entail doing awareness-raising training with the union, circulating question and answer documents about the mediation program, and generally being available to answer any inquiries about the program.

However, getting the program accepted by the police officers is only one side of the equation and there is also a need to work with the public to make them aware of the program. At some point when a member of the public files a complaint, they need to be aware early on in the process that there is a chance their case may be referred to mediation. This means the mediation program has to be integrated into the existing policies and procedures of the police department that is housing it. Indeed, "customizing the program to match the exact needs for the police service and focusing on tying the program into the overall institutional culture is very important" (Hoffman, 2014, p. 17).

The member of public also has to be fully aware that if they choose to go down the mediation route, then their case might be resolved at that level with no further action being taken. That is, some members of the public desire a formal and public investigation process. They may want an officer to get penalized. They may desire their story to be told publically. They may want media attention so that what happened to them will not happen to others. Clearly, mediation is not the right choice in these cases and it illustrates the need only to use mediation under the right circumstances for the right reasons.

Another concern about using mediation relates to power imbalances. Power imbalances can make mediation less effective. If a member of the public feels intimidated or unsafe in the session, then they may not voice their genuine opinions and concerns. It is important that both parties enter the mediation feeling that they are equal. One way to do this is to suggest that officers enter the mediation session in their street clothes and refrain from using technical jargon in order to encourage meaningful dialogue. It is also very important for the mediator to set the right tone for the mediation session at the start by reminding both parties that they have agreed to voluntarily join the session in order to meet each other outside their professional roles.

Another challenge arises if mediation fails. What happens then? If mediation fails then a case can simply flow back into the formal investigation process. In other words, police mediation can be framed as a low-risk, "nothing to lose by trying it out" option.

Components of a basic police mediation program

A basic police mediation program does not need to be complicated. There are four inter-linked components that form a police mediation program:

- An agency to administer and oversee the program
- A program manager
- A mediation roster
- A monitoring and evaluation plan

Perhaps the single most important part of a mediation program relates to the agency that oversees and administers the program. It is important to have a credible, arms-length agency to do this. This provides additional legitimacy to the program and the independence from the police department means that the "highest level of confidentiality can be maintained so that what is said in mediation is strictly off the record and will not be on the officer's file or otherwise available to their superiors" (CIIAN, 2013, p. 1). Moreover, "this helps build trust in the mediation process and it helps generate open, truthful dialogue between the parties" (CIIAN, 2013, p. 1).

Likewise, it is very important to hire a highly experienced and knowledgeable program manager to oversee the work. As mentioned before, the program manager has the difficult job of deciding whether a case is appropriate for mediation or not, choosing the best mediator for the case, and then overseeing the case flow from intake to case closure. The program manager can also be responsible for readying the parties for mediation. This might entail ensuring that both parties sign an "agreement to mediate" document, plus circulating a "tips for mediation" document prior to the first mediation session. The tips for mediation document helps to ensure that the mediation will unfold smoothly because the parties have been prepared to enter the mediation session, whereas the agreement to mediate sets the boundaries on matters of confidentiality and serves as a formal, written commitment that both parties agree to enter the process in good faith.

Another component of a police mediation program is a mediation roster. The agency charged with running the program will need to screen potential mediators and contract with them. Due to the nature of the cases that they will be mediating, they may need to pass security clearances to access case files, and sign non-disclosure agreements. A police mediation roster should comprise professional mediators that have met certain minimum training standards and carry adequate insurance. Utilizing expert mediators who follow the classic interest-based mediation model is critical for success (Hoffman, 2014, p. 17). Moreover, it is best to aim for a diverse mix of mediators from both genders and several different ethnicities.

The fourth and final component of a police mediation program is a monitoring and evaluation component. Ongoing monitoring of the program allows for adjustments to the program to be made when and as needed (Hoffman, 2014, p. 17), whereas evaluation goals need to be set and then customized evaluation surveys developed. Importantly, a police mediation program needs to be clear about what success means. Would a mediation be deemed successful if, and only if, the complainant retracted their complaint or are there other, more robust measures of success that should be measured as well?

In the case of the Ottawa Police Service VADRP a multi-dimensional, short- and long-term definition of success was employed. The evaluation surveys looked at not only whether a complaint withdrawal form was completed,[3] but also whether the parties were happy with the entire mediation process, including things such as:

- Whether the mediator made them feel safe and built trust
- The mediation room set-up and location
- The length of the mediation session

Moreover, in order to capture both short- and longer-term success, two surveys were used. The first was issued electronically exactly 24 hours after the mediation ended (the rationale being that a paper survey issued at the end of the mediation session would not be accurate because people may be rushing to leave the session and not have had adequate time to process how the mediation went). A second, different survey was issued via email six months later to see if the mediation had created a lasting impact.

Building a culture of conflict prevention

As mentioned earlier in this chapter, it should be expected that some types of grievances are inevitable due to the nature of policing work. Nevertheless, there are operational as well as other compelling reasons to build a culture of conflict prevention into police training. We can aim to avoid having grievances arise in the first place if officers become self-aware of their own actions and how they can possibly create or escalate conflicts. That is, officers equipped with some basic knowledge about conflict analysis and resolution are better positioned, not only verbally to de-escalate conflict situations in which they find themselves, but also play an important role in preventing and resolving conflict between members of the public.

All too often police have to respond to repeated calls to the same areas to deal with recurring conflicts and officers equipped with mediation skills can help bring a lasting resolution to these conflicts. This notion is very much in line with the dual roles of police as "enforcers of the law" but also as "keepers of the peace" in the community.

Conclusion

Police mediation holds great promise for efficiently and effectively resolving complaints made against police officers. A basic police mediation program with four inter-linked parts (an agency to administer and oversee the program, a program manager, a mediation roster, plus a monitoring and evaluation plan) can be set up relatively quickly and easily, and does not require a great deal of resources to operate. Once established, a police mediation program can create a number of benefits for both the police service and the members of the community that it serves. However, there are some challenges with setting up and running a police mediation program, but they are not insurmountable. Furthermore, a police mediation program can become a good launching point for creating an overall culture of conflict prevention in a police department by offering officers the chance to complete conflict resolution training. Equipped with such training, officers are well placed to resolve recurring community conflicts.

This chapter provided a basic overview of the type of mediation that can be used to resolve public complaints against the police and how to structure a full program around that. In doing so, it is hoped, this will help inform and inspire greater use of mediation to resolve public complaints against police officers, plus demonstrate that more training in conflict resolution and mediation skills is needed in order to help build more peaceful communities for everyone's benefit.

Notes

1 I am grateful to Yehuda Silverman for the help and support in preparing this chapter and to Detective Ray Aceti (Niagara Regional Police Service) for providing comments on an earlier draft.
2 The discussion that follows is largely based on the author's first-hand experience with setting up and then managing a voluntary ADR program for the Ottawa Police Service in Canada. See www.ciian.org/vadrp1.html. Stemming from this, the author was then invited to develop and deliver innovative and practical conflict resolution training for new recruits joining the force—this being one of very few courses of this type being offered on a regular basis to new police officers in Canada.
3 Some 75 percent of the cases that were mediated by the Ottawa Police Service VADRP were successful in that a complaint withdrawal form was completed after the mediation session (CIIAN, 2013, p. 4).

References

Canadian International Institute of Applied Negotiation (CIIAN). (2012) *Mediation Tips.* Ottawa, Canada: CIIAN.

Canadian International Institute of Applied Negotiation (CIIAN). (2013) *CIIAN Report on the VADRP: Covering the Period July, 2011–December, 2012.* Ottawa, Canada: CIIAN.

Charkoudian, L. (2010) Giving police and courts a break: The effect of community mediation on decreasing the use of police and court resources. *Conflict Resolution Quarterly*, 28(2): 141–155.

Hickman, M.J. (2006) Citizen complaints about police use of force. *Bureau of Justice Statistics Special Report.* Retrieved from www.bjs.gov/content/pub/pdf/ccpuf.pdf.

Hoffman, E. (2014, Winter). Using mediation to resolve public complaints against police officers. *H.Q.—The official publication of the Ontario Association of Chiefs of Police (OACP).* Toronto, Canada: OACP.

Independent Police Complaints Commission (IPCC). (2013) *Eleventh Report of Session 2012–13.* Retrieved from www.publications.parliament.uk/pa/cm201213/cmselect/cmhaff/494/494.pdf.

Independent Police Complaints Commission (IPCC). (2015) *Police Complaints—Statistics for England and Wales 2013/2014*. Retrieved from www.ipcc.gov.uk/sites/default/files/Documents/research_stats/complaints_statistics_2012-13_and_2013-14.PDF.

Mason, E. & Mashberg, T. (2015, May 4). Police, Harvard near deal to mediate civilian complaints. *The Boston Globe*. Retrieved from www.bostonglobe.com/metro/2015/05/03/boston-police-harvard-close-mediation-arrangement/IW77C3mH4zbhjmyFZnLlcL/story.html.

Office of the Independent Police Review Director (OIPRD). (2014) *2013–2014 Annual Report*. Retrieved from www.oiprd.on.ca/EN/PDFs/Annual-Report-2013-2014_E.pdf.

Packman, D. (2010) *2010 Annual Report: The Cato Institute's National Police Misconduct Reporting Project*. Retrieved from www.policemisconduct.net/statistics/2010-annual-report/.

Shaw, A. (2014) City pays heavy price for police brutality. *Chicago Sun-Times*. Retrieved from chicago.suntimes.com/?p=167182.

23

THE PRISON OF PEACE PROJECT

A model for community transformation

Douglas E. Noll

For decades, US mediation and conflict resolution practitioners have struggled with how to embed peacemaking processes within communities. Early efforts at community mediation centers were based on values of empowerment, self-determination, access to justice, and reduction in conflict, especially violent conflict (Hedeen, 2003). As these efforts were often grassroots, funding became and continues to be a major barrier. At best, community mediation is marginalized to traditional court systems and scrapes by on whatever funds can be secured from the courts or philanthropists (Hedeen, 2003). The need for funding has institutionalized community mediation such that the original premise of building peaceful communities through mediation and conciliation has been thwarted. A different model is needed.

This chapter will describe the development of a model of mediation that embeds itself into a community, becomes self-replicating, and ultimately, self-sustaining. The chapter will describe the elements of the model, describe successes and failures to date, and describe how the model is being tested in schools and communities.

The Prison of Peace project: an experiment in radical peacemaking

Prison of Peace[1] (Mayer et al., 2014) is a pro bono project created in 2010 by professional mediators Laurel Kaufer and Douglas E. Noll at the request of inmates at Valley State Prison for Women in Chowchilla, CA. The goals of Prison of Peace (POP) are to help inmates serving life sentences develop skills in emotional intelligence, problem solving, and moral engagement. They are eventually trained as trainers and become the agents of change in inmate populations. By training the general population of inmates within a prison, the Prison of Peace trainers have slowly and powerfully transformed cultures of violence into cultures of peace.

These goals are accomplished through intensive training in verbal communication and listening, convening and conducting peace circles, and convening and conducting mediations to resolve conflicts between inmates. The core training curriculum is a two-part, 12-week program that follows a customized curriculum for mediation training and restorative justice. The training emphasizes interpersonal communications skills especially in high-emotion and high-conflict situations. Participants are required to attend and participate in up to 84 hours of class instruction, practice the techniques and processes outside class, write up their experiences, turn in weekly assignments, conduct five peace circles, and observe two peace circles. If participants continue with the mediation training, they are required to conduct three mediations and observe two mediations and write up their experiences and observations. All new participants now work with an inmate mentor/coach developed from earlier courses.

The inmates in this project have experienced dramatic personal transformations. Prison of Peace has allowed them to discover or rediscover their own humanity, become aware of their own emotions, and begin to understand and reflect back the emotions of others. By learning peacemaking and mediation skills, they are taught how people evade personal accountability and how to morally re-engage those who have become morally disengaged. As a byproduct, they naturally have re-engaged themselves morally. In addition, there has been a qualitative shift in personal interactions in the inmate population. To date, there has been no reported violence involving any inmates certified as peacemakers or mediators. Personal arguments have reportedly reduced in quantity and intensity. Peacemakers and mediators have been able to de-escalate and resolve conflicts among inmates and between inmates and staff. Prison of Peace has been successfully embedded in the two California women's prisons, a men's prison, and the Women's Division of the Los Angeles County Jail system.

The curriculum

Prison of Peace demonstrates: 1 that life and long-term inmates can be trained as powerful peacemakers and mediators; 2 that these inmates can train other inmates in practical peacemaking techniques; and 3 that a culture of violence can be radically shifted by a small group of inmates dedicated to a culture of peace. To achieve these goals, Kaufer and Noll designed and implemented a rigorous mediation-training curriculum. They recognized that there could be no introduction of mediation skills until the inmates were skilled at listening to others and de-escalating strong emotions.

The training begins with an introduction to restorative justice and peace circles. Inmates learn about the six needs of victims and often, for the first time, understand their own responsibility for injuring or killing another. As Anna Humiston stated:

> POP has transformed my thoughts as to how my actions can hurt others. The restorative justice portion of POP has been the most enlightening course I've ever encountered. I now have a much better understanding of those I've hurt with my poor decisions. I've learned to feel empathy and to step into others' shoes to truly understand the effects of my actions.
>
> *(Mayer et al., 2014, p. 207)*

As Ms Humiston's experience indicates, coming to understand the effects of her actions has been powerful and life changing.

The next segment teaches inmates fundamental skills in listening, making agreements, counseling and coaching, and managing strong emotions. The curriculum is based on a collaborative program developed in 2007 between Laurel Kaufer and Ridge Training,[2] known as Essential Problem Solving Skills (EPSS), informed and modified by the work of neuroscientists Matthew Lieberman (2007) and Marco Iacoboni (2008). Based on Lieberman's (2007) fMRI studies showing how the emotional centers of the brain are inhibited by a technique known as affect labeling, Kaufer and Noll enhanced the EPSS curriculum to include skill building that taught inmates to listen to people's emotions, in addition to their words. Iacoboni's (2008) research into mirror neurons led Noll and Kaufer to develop techniques of true empathy using mirror neurons to stimulate positive affect. Thus, the foundation of the Prison of Peace curriculum is formulated on how the human brain processes social and emotional information.

Teaching the inmates how to listen by paying close attention to emotions is very powerful. The skill opened up inmates who were, themselves, emotionally shut down. In addition, deep listening has allowed inmates to create empathic connections with other inmates and with their families. Many inmates were able to truly listen to another human being for the first time in their lives. As inmate Anna Humiston explained: "Prison of Peace has enhanced my life in the most profound way by offering me the gift of communication. In turn, I can give others a most precious gift, just simply listening" (Mayer et al., 2014, p. 207). It was also, for many trainees, profoundly healing to be heard by other inmates at a deep, deep level. The stories and experiences they began to share as they mastered these skills were just as profound.

After four weeks of learning deep interpersonal communication and conflict skills, inmates learn how to convene and conduct peace circles. Peace circles are an ancient community process where listening is paramount, where respect is sacred, and where patience is valued. As the inmates introduce peace circles into a prison population, they report profound changes in relationships. Community is enhanced, understanding is increased and conflict is reduced. Inmates who participate in the circle process, no longer feel alone and isolated. They reconnect with their inner humanity and recognize the humanity of their fellow inmates.

For many inmates, completing the peacemaker training is sufficient. Those students who have demonstrated proficiency in the deep listening, problem solving and peace circle leadership and who wish to be of greater service to others, move on to sophisticated mediation training. The mediation curriculum reinforces the earlier skills and teaches methodologies for the use of those skills in intervention in conflicts that could erupt into violence. Before being allowed to mediate actual conflicts, inmates engage in simulations based upon real prison conflict scenarios. Many inmate mediators report that they have had the opportunity to put their skills to good use. For example, Mike Baldwin, an inmate serving a life sentence at Valley State Prison, reported that "[these] techniques [have] allowed me to go into a room and mediate a conflict between some guys who were on the verge of killing each other. These tools created a process that allowed them to communicate and walk away while saving face" (Mayer et al., 2014, p. 208).

Training trainers

Prison of Peace has been designed from the beginning to be sustainable without outside trainers. What was not known was whether inmates could be trained to be effective trainers. As it turns out, there is almost no statistical margin of difference between the quality of inmate trainers and outside professional trainers. Where there is a slight difference, the inmate trainers outperformed outside professionals in almost every category. This has established that Prison of Peace can be embedded sustainably in a prison without the need of outside supervision.

The training regimen for inmates wishing to become Prison of Peace trainers is rigorous. The inmates must have completed mediation training, demonstrated the ability to teach a group, and model the skills of a peacemaker and mediator in their daily lives. The first step in becoming a trainer is learning how to become a mentor. Mentors are inmates with completed mediation training who sit through the training cycle again with a new group of inmates. They coach inmates through the various phases of the training. After they have successfully mentored one group of inmates, they enter train-the-trainer training.

The curriculum requires each inmate to master the knowledge and skill taught in each segment of Prison of Peace. They must have a firm theoretical foundation, a mastery of the material to be taught, and the ability to present the material in an engaging manner. The trainer manual developed since 2009 by Kaufer and Noll (2016) is over 250 pages long. Each skill is dissected and explained. Teaching scripts are provided as examples of how to present and demonstrate the skills. After the trainers have successfully demonstrated their ability to teach each other all of the segments, they team up, and begin teaching inmates. This training is done under the direct supervision of Kaufer and Noll, who coach and critique each trainer's performance. The trainers must train three complete cohorts of inmates before they are certified as Prison of Peace trainers. The entire process takes 12 months.

The certified trainers are free to conduct Prison of Peace trainings at times of their choosing, subject to prison administration approval. Once trainers have been established in a prison, Kaufer and Noll provide advanced training as requested. In addition, Kaufer and Noll provide the mediation training until trainers have been trained in that process.

Measuring the effects

Following each Prison of Peace training session, the inmates fill out self-reporting surveys to determine programmatic effectiveness. The data show that most participants find Prison of Peace to be effective. Respondents were asked to rank the level of their understanding, before attending the workshop, in five skill areas on a scale from 1 through 4, with 1 indicating a level of low or no understanding and 4 indicating a level of high or thorough understanding. Of those responding, 60.08 percent indicated a moderately low to low level of understanding of communication skills in general, and 39.92 percent indicated a moderately high to high level of understanding of those skills (Mayer et al., 2014).

With regard to the specific communication skills (i.e. active listening, results-based listening, agreement and managing strong emotions) 70.54 percent of respondents indicated a moderately low to low level of understanding, with 35.46 percent at the lowest level, as opposed to 29.46 percent who felt that before this workshop they had a moderately high to high level of understanding, with only 11.73 percent indicating a high level. In contrast to their reports of skill level prior to attending the workshop, 90.34 percent of respondents report their understanding as moderately high to high in all categories, upon completion of the workshop, with only 9.66 percent still reporting a moderately low level of understanding, with less than 1 percent at low understanding (Mayer et al., 2014).

Again on this same scale, respondents were asked to rate the usefulness of the EPSS workshop training for them overall. Some 96.86 percent of respondents rated it moderately high to high, with 75.29 percent giving it a rating of 4 or high. Some 99.2 percent of respondents also reported that the workshop introduced them to new skills for use in solving problems or conflicts in their lives and/or communities. The majority of respondents reported improved communication skills and ability to manage strong emotions. Most inmates also reported positive changes in the prison environment (Mayer et al., 2014).

Development of a model

The Prison of Peace project has demonstrated one way to embed peacemaking and mediation practices into a community. The elements of the model are: 1) a dedicated and highly competent cadre of outside professional trainers committed to the long-term success of the community; 2) continuous recruitment of community members called to become peacemakers and willing to undergo rigorous training over 18–24 months; 3) a personal commitment from each community trainer to conduct two complete training cycles per year for five years; 4) space, time, and resources to do the training; 5) a curriculum designed from the beginning to be replicable and scalable; 6 adherence to high standards of performance through various types of assessments, evaluations, and feedback loops; and 6) a defined community within which to embed the project.

The model developed in Prison of Peace has been adapted for use in transforming a school district from a zero-tolerance discipline philosophy to a restorative practices philosophy (Noll, 2014). The outside trainers teach teachers and administrators, who themselves will become trainers of other teachers and administrators. The curriculum is rigorous and demanding. The process moves slowly to build confidence, competence, and awareness. The goal is to eliminate the need for outside professional help within two years so that restorative practices become self-sustaining within the school district.

At this writing, the adaptation to the school district is entering its second academic year. The early indications show similar indications of success. Teachers and administrators desire more training; a cadre of potential future trainers is emerging; and school sites where the process had begun are showing early signs of cultural transformation. Other adaptations of the model are in process design. They include projects in deeply entrenched poverty- and crime-ridden neighborhoods and adaptive leadership development to create a cadre of leaders capable of managing the polarization of ideologies that thwart community growth and transformation.

Conclusion

Prison of Peace has proven successful at several levels. Inmate mediators and peacemakers provide role models for the general population, demonstrating that there are choices beyond violence for resolving conflict. They provide informal conflict resolution services as deep empathic listeners, circle keepers, and mediators. Prison of Peace peacemakers and mediators have stopped prison riots, mediated incipient violence, worked with mentally ill inmates, dealt with gang problems, and have been general problem solvers within their prison community. They inspire other inmates to seek peace and to behave responsibly.

As peacemakers and mediators, inmates serving life sentences live a life of service. For many of these inmates, Prison of Peace has become a life vocation. Through the work, Prison of Peace inmates have experienced profound personal transformations. The project has demonstrated its efficacy in reducing prison violence and transforming lives. Most importantly, Prison of Peace shows that even the most violent human beings can redeem themselves into powerful peacemakers.

The development model is being adapted to systems and cultures outside prisons. It appears that a long-term, focused effort at building a cadre of dedicated trainers and mentors can change a community culture to the values of peace, problem solving, and constructive dispute resolution. Instead of relying on institutionalized mediation centers, the model trains community members to be peacemakers, mediators, mentors, and trainers so that they have the skills and confidence to work within their neighborhoods and school sites.

Notes

1 For more information see prisonofpeace.org.
2 Ridge Training provides courses in performance management, interpersonal communication, coaching, and team development, among others. More information is available at www.ridge.com.

References

Hedeen, T. (2003) Institutionalizing community mediation: Can dispute resolution "of, by, and for the people" long endure? *Penn State Law Review*, 108(1): 265–276.

Iacoboni, M. (2008) *Mirroring People: The Science of Empathy and How We Connect with Others*. New York: Picador.

Kaufer, L. & Noll, D.E. (2016) *Prison of Peace Mediator Training Manual*. Copyright manuscript.

Lieberman, M. (2007) Putting feelings into words: Affect labeling disrupts amygdala activity in response to affective stimuli. *Psychological Science*, 18(5): 421–427.

Mayer, J., Kaufer, L. & Noll, D. (2014) Prisoner facilitated mediation: Bringing peace to prisons and communities. *Cardozo Journal of Conflict Resolution*, 16: 187–219.

Noll, D. (2014) Safe schools project. *DougNoll.com*. Retrieved from www.dougnoll.com/safe-schools-project/.

24

SUSTAINING PEER MEDIATION

Assessing challenges and opportunities for peace educators

Cheryl Lynn Duckworth

For the past several decades, youth advocates, scholars of peace education, teachers, administrators and some parents have worked to build the rationale, database, infrastructure and curriculum necessary to generate a movement for peace education, and in particular the teaching of interpersonal conflict resolution and peer mediation skills. This chapter will explore the challenges and opportunities shaping the reality of peer mediation programs today, as they continue to form the bulk, at least in the USA, of what we consider to be "doing" peace education. I will focus in particular on the apparent difficulty of sustaining peer mediation and other peace education programs, as research suggests that this remains a significant challenge for practitioners.

Many researchers, myself included, view sustainability as our most important challenge for the peer mediation and peace education movement (Bickmore, 2001, 2002; Duckworth et al., 2012; Johnson & Johnson, 1996; Sellman, 2002; Ford, 2002). Sustainability challenges seem to have emerged from a number of common sources, based on case studies reviewed (Johnson & Johnson, 1996; Casella, 2000; Ford, 2002; Johnson et al., 1996; Duckworth et al., 2012; Sellman, 2002; Sandy, 2001; Bickmore, 2001, 2002). I will explore resources and relevance, two key challenges to program sustainability. Finally, I will recommend deepening community partnerships, as well as direct legislative and policy advocacy where needed, as paths forward towards mainstreaming and sustaining peer mediation and other kinds of peace education programs. This chapter defines mediation as an organic, interpersonal process, involving an often professional third party, whereby individuals or groups in conflict, dialogue about the sources of the conflict and creatively develop solutions. Peace education, related but distinct, is education both about and for peace; it facilitates student understanding of the causes of especially violent conflict and war, and engages them in actions to reduce those causes (Duckworth, 2015b, pp. 351–367).

In assessing the difficulty of sustaining peer mediation programs, we must ask what the current context is in shaping the content, focus, and structure of contemporary programs. How often, indeed, are such programs offered and where? What can we say about how successfully we, as peace educators and peer mediators, have actually addressed the critiques that have been made over the past several decades? Most importantly, what seems to be preventing sustainability, where peer mediation programs are not sustained? This chapter will explore the context and source of these two continuing challenges, and suggest possible ways forward.

Such considerations are important when considering community mediation for several reasons. One, peer mediation and peace education programs are distinct, but of course related. The values, knowledge, and skills they impart lay the groundwork for the advancement of community mediation in the future, continuing the consolidation and expansion of our field, and building the capacity of a community as a whole to address conflicts. Second, youth leadership for peace is essential in both domestic US and international contexts. Young people are consistently either overlooked, or framed as the problem rather than a possible solution, to a given community's conflicts. Yet, perhaps most importantly, peer mediation and peace education programs can and should partner with one another, potentially addressing one of the most serious barriers to such programs at the K-12 (kindergarten to 12th grade) educational level, which remains sustainable funding. Addressing these barriers is key as they are deeply entrenched, especially the funding barrier, and so likely to remain a difficulty for the foreseeable future without sustained effort on the part of the peace education community.

Sustaining relevance

Where programs are not reflective of or developed in genuine and equitable partnership with the local community, or implemented with care and expertise, the relevance of the program may be questioned, causing it to be shut down. Relevance may also be questioned when programs are too narrowly conceived, capable of only addressing small interpersonal conflicts. Like other peace educators, and mediators, I have been critical of a narrow view of peace education, arguing that a critical theory-based approach best enables mediation and other peacebuilding skills to be capable of fostering social justice. Critical peace educators (Bajaj, 2008; Duckworth, 2011), mediators (Cobb, 2013, Winslade & Monk, 2008) and conflict resolution scholars generally (Hansen, 2013), have held social justice as essential for creating and sustaining positive peace. While negative peace refers to a lack of violence, positive peace suggests the presence of relationships that are consensual, equitable, and respectful, in the broader context of people being able to meet their basic human needs. Critical theorists, including critical mediators and peace educators, have been skeptical of some peer mediation programs on these grounds, arguing that we cannot assume they will have a social justice orientation or that they will be capable of interrupting the kinds of inequalities of power and resources that often drive conflict, including many of the interpersonal conflicts students and teachers face in the classroom.

For example, much of what we commonly call bullying today is directed at LGBT or minority students, such as those thought to be Muslim, as my recent research on the teaching of the terrorist attacks of September 11, 2001 revealed (Duckworth, 2014). In my own region of south Florida, conflicts often manifest between US-born and immigrant students. Such examples cannot be understood as mere miscommunications or excessive tension or anger as they clearly reflect larger social, even political, conflicts. In view of this, I believe peer mediation is best implemented as one part of a larger peace education program. Interestingly, similar critiques have sometimes been made of peace education itself, noting that it can narrow its focus too often to intercultural appreciation or dialogues without interrogating history and power (Bajaj, 2008). Peace educators and mediators alike have thus worked to develop models, theories, and a curriculum that would address previous blind spots.

Without the ability to sustain a peer mediation program in a particular school, much precious time and financial resources are wasted, something schools can ill afford in an age of budget cuts and unfunded mandates. This is the reason, I stress community partnerships so often as a means of sustaining peer mediation and peace education programs (Duckworth, 2015a). Depending on the commitment and motives of the partner, such partnerships are likely to prove key to a particular peer mediation (PM) or conflict resolution education (CRE) program's success. Community partners can provide resources, of course, but also visibility, areas of expertise that might not exist within the school system, moral support (not to be underestimated) and increased credibility beyond the school walls. Yet the community partners, in current economic reality, often struggle for funding themselves, even large, public universities, and whether this will change remains uncertain.

One source of a perceived lack of relevance is a lack of "buy in" from school administrators or teachers, who among other issues are concerned about relinquishing real power to students (Bickmore, 2001; Casella, 2000). Training for teachers and administrators has commonly been employed as a means of generating support and confidence in PM programs. Yet, one cannot simply carve out an afternoon for an in-service and build the necessary trust and relationships needed for the kind of commitment that will sustain a program. Especially for schools and communities that experience high levels of conflict, regular opportunities to teach, learn, and reflect on the school culture as a whole, and the peer mediation program in particular, will surely increase commitment and faith that the time and resources invested are worthwhile.

This remaining question in some minds is one reason why so much of the literature on peer mediation in schools has tried to point to evidence that such programs reduce violence, boost attendance, reduce disciplinary referrals, and even improve academic work (Johnson & Johnson, 1996; Johnson et al., 1996; Lantieri & Patti, 1996). Oddly, as Kathy Bickmore (2001) notes, peer mediation programs, and peace education in general, are still viewed as "feel-good" and worthwhile in some respects, but not directly related to academic achievement. Advocates must directly address this if we are to expand and sustain peer mediation programs nationally.

Scholars and practitioners alike must also continue to build the body of work that offers evidence demonstrating PM programs can improve a school climate, reduce violence, effectively teach mediation and conflict resolution skills, and yes, boost grades and test scores. As Ian Harris (2003) argues, the literature on peace education and peer mediation that explicitly addresses evaluation remains surprisingly thin, given how long now peer mediation and peace education programs have existed. Harris (2003) specifies some of the difficulties of evaluating these sorts of programs, given how complex the causes of conflict and violence are. Rather than overpromise, he recommends advocates of such programs focus on the impact PM programs and other sorts of peace education can have on the students involved (Harris, 2003).

We must also address shortcomings in our program evaluations (Cantrell et al., 2007). For example, an inordinate number of studies that argue they prove the successes of PM programs seem drawn from a few programs—the Winning Against Violent Environments (WAVE) program in Cleveland or the Resolving Conflict Creatively Program (RCCP), for example. The authors do seem to make their case for the success of these programs, but other programs need to be evaluated similarly. Useful case studies along these lines include Ford (2002) and Casella (2000). Too often, evaluations can read as an advertisement for the program, especially when written by creators or directors of the curriculum. Far fewer are willing to be appropriately critical as needed (Mark, 2013). In my reading of the literature, few studies asked if PM programs were having an impact at all on the larger community, though some research suggests that this can be the case (Duckworth, 2006).

Quality of implementation is also essential for program sustainability. Daunic et al. (2000) suggest, for example, that too many PM programs suffer from a lack of consistency over time.

University or other partners come to the end of their grant cycle or move on to another project. Bickmore (2001) observes that peer mediation is excellent for the peer mediator, in that they learn new skills, gain a stronger college application, and build confidence. Yet, she notes that too often peer mediators were typically the students with the highest social and economic status. Where this is the case, interest in the program, and therefore sustainability, will almost certainly wane. Sustainable programs need diverse groups of students and adults with a variety of backgrounds and outlooks on what conflict itself is, what might be driving a particular conflict, and how best to resolve it.

Bickmore (2001) makes another observation useful to my discussion of sustainability. The more trust adults were able to place in the young people to actually do the mediating, the more likely the program was to be successful. Just as we are in an age of budget austerity, especially at the state and local levels relevant to most education funding, we are in an age of securitization of nearly every sector of society (Duckworth, 2014). In such an environment, it may prove difficult for teachers and administrators to trust students, especially lower-income or otherwise marginalized students, enough to allow them to truly problem solve with other students. Yet, this is necessary for the success and impact of PM programs. Designers and implementers of such programs, then would be well advised to incorporate school-wide community and trust-building activities into their PM program design.

A related issue remains the limited ability of peer mediation programs to fundamentally address social justice. Especially when not connected to the local community, PM programs risk missing issues of power and access to needed resources for meeting one's basic human needs. This is not inevitable, and certainly, models of peer mediation exist that are intended to be aware of student realities outside the classroom. I argue that PM programs will prove the most successful, and therefore sustainable, when integrated with restorative justice practices, nonviolence workshops, service learning and activism outside the classroom and other means of building an overall school culture, and indeed community culture, of peace. In this manner, peer mediation programs would be viewed as one aspect of what we must undertake to build more peaceful communities. Peer mediation programs are more likely to be successful in the context of a school that, for example, practices cooperative learning (Johnson & Johnson, 1996). Too often, this methodology is viewed as an end point of a program to improve school culture, not a beginning.

What students are learning about conflict, and its resolution, has also been an area of contention and concern among PM scholars and practitioners. Will students emerge believing conflict is "bad"? Johnson and Johnson (1996) emphasize the importance of teaching the positive and productive potential of conflict when it leads to an integrative solution. Casella (2000), however, cautions again about individualizing and decontextualizing conflict. Do peer mediation programs risk inadvertently teaching that interpersonal conflict is removed from larger policy, economic and cultural contexts, and dynamics? What does it mean for long-term processes of advancing social change, he wonders, when students learn from PM programs that "conflict is a result of inappropriate behavior, for which various forms of behavior modification techniques were recommended?" (Casella, 2000, pp. 332–333). I share this concern and wonder where in a PM program or other curriculum students will be taught about systemic change or larger processes, dynamics and institutions related to oppression and social justice.

As an example, in a limited but real way, a peace education program I evaluated in 2012 (Duckworth et al., 2012) moved toward this broader systemic impact in that students were invited to write and produce an anti-violence musical about causes and prevention of bullying. This opened the door to students creatively and critically analyzing school and community dynamics, such as adults not providing a safe environment, the role of the media, racism, and homophobia. Students even had the opportunity to be critical of adult responses to school violence and bullying, which they often viewed as absent or even actively harmful (in the sense of setting a poor example). Relatedly, some research has attempted to understand the broader context of school-based conflicts by examining bystanders (Pöyhönen et al., 2010). This is important given that we, at least in the USA, remain in a predominantly victim-blaming culture, constituting a conceptual and cultural barrier to peer mediation and peace education programs. Again, we see that PM programs are likely to be most effective when implemented with other curriculum or activities that incorporate learning about broader social causes of conflict and violence.

Indeed, serious criticisms regarding impact and content must still be addressed if we are to see the continued expansion and sustainability of peer mediation programs nationally. Casella (2000) makes this point effectively, writing: "When peer mediation programs lose sight of the realities of life in poor cities, it joins together with other policies and programs that view youth misbehavior as essentially personal or individual matters—a problem having to do with their own cognitive and sometimes neurological deficits" (p. 332), rather than social inequalities or manifest structural violence. This is the fundamental, urgent critique of peer mediation.

Reflective of Western cultural biases toward individualism, PM programs are sometimes unable to address or even see larger groups or community dynamics. This is especially a concern with a student who may be trying to mediate a peer conflict, which is driven by sexism, racism or other kinds of structural or cultural violence. Bickmore (2001), Beckerman and Zembylas (2012), and Davies (2004) make a similar point. Psychologizing the conflict, rather than being cognizant of its systemic roots, perpetuates the structural violence that is likely a driver of the conflict to begin with. The student is viewed as the problem, not a source of a possible solution, perhaps the reason why so many programs are likely to select peer mediators from the upper classes of the school who have received good grades and not had disciplinary referrals (and so teachers and administrators can conceive of releasing them from class). Unaddressed are important questions of authority, obedience and what constitutes so-called good behavior. Who defines this and why? Is obedience always the best choice for a student? How can we educate thoughtful, critical citizens who are able to function in a free society if our schools do not allow for meaningful participation by students in decision making? Case studies and evaluations of peer mediation programs suggest similarly (Ford, 2002; Casella, 2000). Critical pedagogues have been asking such questions, of course, since Apple and King (1977) and Dewey (2008) during the 20th century. Given that such habits as victim-blaming, individualism and psychologizing the conflict, while overlooking systemic root causes, remain ingrained in the policies and culture of many US school systems, this critique is likely to remain relevant for some time to come. The current reality in schools systems today is quite mixed, given that disciplinary and curriculum decisions remain made at the school system or even building level.

If peace educators and peer mediation practitioners can innovate viable answers to such questions (as they have been doing in some small but tangible ways), we will go a long way toward improving the sustainability of peer mediation. Such innovations would also enable peer mediation programs to not just teach students nonviolent conflict resolution skills (a worthwhile enough use of resources), but to impact the broader school and its community over time. Bickmore (2002) calls for such awareness on the part of PM program implementers, lamenting the lost potential of programs limited only to within a school or, even more narrowly, to a small group of students who receive the training. Such wider impact cannot be taken for granted or assumed as automatic. Community partnerships will be essential. Ford (2002) describes such involvement of community partnerships sustaining a CRE program. Not only school leaders but also local leaders, to include local media—business and civil society leaders—in general must begin to see the possible contributions young people can make to community conflict resolution and development. I refer to this way of thinking about peer mediation and peace education as forming "multi-track schools" to emphasize the need for conceptualizing schools as centers of community life (Duckworth, 2015a).

Sustaining resources in a neoliberal era: a question of political will

Like the rest of the public sector, public K-12 schools today operate in a neoliberal context of budget austerity. Schools in particular are under threat of closure via the diversion of public money to charter schools, or if they are deemed to be failing by officials who may or may not have any background in education (Ravitch, 2013). To my mind, this is the most compelling contextual factor, which can explain the lack of sustainability of peer mediation programs. Such austerity has impacted teaching and learning broadly (Duckworth, 2014), and any program perceived as extraneous to the basics, and thus not relatable to standardized tests. Professional mediators and peace education scholars, not necessarily a part of the K-12 system on a daily basis, may well underestimate the extent to which state objectives have crowded out all else. Teachers can be fired for student lack of achievement on such tests. States can seize control of schools deemed to be failing (Ravitch, 2013). Teachers express concern about straying at all from activities and objectives not related to the prescribed curriculum (Duckworth, 2014). As an example, consider that commonly, state standardized testing can take a full month or more to complete. Students are often required to complete them on computers, and when only about 20 or so computers are available at a time in the school's technology lab, with several hundred children to test, classrooms are interfered with for prolonged periods of time. In this kind of context, dedicating the particular staff and resources essential to the long-term sustainability of peer mediation programs is often simply not a priority. Cultures of fear rarely allow for innovation or learning. Our work as peace educators and peer mediation practitioners is as much policy-based and legislative as it is curricular in this sense, and given the politicization of public schools over the past several decades, this reality may not change in the foreseeable future.

Another problem, perhaps related, remains a lack of resources in the form of time and specified staff to design and implement the programs (Bickmore, 2001, 2002; Daunic et al., 2000) not just within the school but at the community partner level as well. As one scholar and implementer of peer mediation recently noted in an observation worth quoting at length:

> We lost touch with the middle schools we worked with simply because we moved on to other funded projects and had our plates full with implementing other programs. We offered our help for anyone interested in continuing the CR/PM program, but we had used a train-the-trainer model, so there were trained personnel at the schools (and they had the materials), and we didn't get any requests for consultations.
>
> *(A. Daunic, personal communication, May 2014)*

Sustainability after researchers pull out is a central issue, and many programs are hard to continue without external resources. In her words:

> We tried to design something that would be feasible to implement with typical school resources, but there are always costs involved in reproducing materials, training new implementers, time, etc. With the push for academics that has increased since our CR project, I'm afraid many social-emotional learning related programs have taken a back seat.
>
> *(A. Daunic, personal communication, May 2014)*

Another researcher and program implementer in Maryland had a similar experience. She writes:

> We worked on this project for a few years but were not able to sustain funding to keep it going and [it] ended in 2010. We initially had some funding through the law school here. We also had staff changes, which made it difficult.
>
> *(C. Weiss, personal communication, June 2014)*

Clearly, there remain resource difficulties at the community partner level; often these partners are universities or local non-profits whose involvement is dependent on a temporary grant or non-profits with similar funding structure. Yet, very little of the literature on peer mediation (or similar terms such as peace education or citizenship education) seems to examine, for example, grant structure or formats, or peer mediation/peace education programs in the context not just of school climate or improving education, but in the larger public policy context of community development. Much of the literature that discusses sustaining or implementing PM or peace education programs examines this issue with the school itself as the unit of analysis, with less examination of the dynamics or structures at universities or community organizations that might be constituting barriers for schools. Teachers and administrators have long cited the need for tangible support from communities, manifested in financial resources but also in investment of time and building relationships, and this chapter highlights that ongoing need.

Concluding observations

Based on the research and observations above, then, I would put forward the following recommendations for public officials, funders and educators alike. First, funders must grapple with the sustainability question and acknowledge that the typical grant window of 12–18 months is not likely to be sufficient for a peace education program that will last. Building trust and relationships with school staff will take time. Second, as some program designers and educators are already doing, care must be taken to ensure that programming is accessible to all students, not merely those who are the best academic performers. Third, program designers must ensure that peer mediation is seen as only one part of a larger effort to build a school culture of peace. The curriculum must go beyond interpersonal dynamics to address root causes of structural violence and social justice. Relatedly, local public officials, media and business leaders must commit to genuine partnership and engagement with schools, resisting a culture of fear and standardization, and working to address community conflicts, which may be impacting the school climate. Resources are always a question of public priorities, and thus always a *political* question. The lack of sustainability of peer mediation, and related peace education programs more broadly, reflects a public policy decision that such citizenship education and conflict resolution education is not urgent, at least not when compared to other priorities.

Arguably, these two challenges to program sustainability have a common source. As readers know, we continue, especially at the state and local levels in the USA, to be in an age of budget austerity. Privatization by another name through such policies as parent triggers, centralizing curriculum, and tying standardized tests to teacher retention, have contributed to a climate of fear and tension in many schools. Risk taking, so essential to integrative solutions and innovation, seems impossible for most teachers and administrators in such an environment. Peer mediation and even more so peace education, while well enough known in educational and conflict resolution circles, remain off the center of the public radar screen. Reflective of the culture in the USA at large, we continue to address school safety and violence prevention from a limited, narrow negative peace approach, though recent experimentation with restorative justice in schools suggests this may be beginning to change. Negative peace, of course, defines peace as a lack of violence. The goal is security. Positive peace, more deeply rooted, defines peace not as a mere lack of violence but as the sustainable presence of relationships that are equitable and based on trust and respect. The more entrenched the current, wrongheaded culture of centering the life of a school and a student around testing becomes, the less likely administrators are to take the risk of incorporating peer mediation and peace education into the school's life and culture as needed for genuine impact. As I have written elsewhere (Duckworth, 2014), ultimately a deep cultural shift is necessary with respect to how we view the purpose of education. No dialectic is perfect, but public policy approaches to education can roughly be understood as reflecting one of two views: education's purpose is to produce critical, ethical, and well-rounded citizens, or education is to produce workers for the economy. Both have merit, of course, and both are needed. Yet the climate of polarization brings the two into conflict and increasingly, since the 1980s and 1990s when peer mediation and peace education programs were being developed at a rapid pace, they are in danger of being viewed as a distraction from what schools really ought to be about.

As an example, Bickmore (2001) cites one harried administrator as saying, "[w]e don't have time for conflict!" (p. 148). Yet, the greater risk is to continue with a failing status quo, in which too many students, especially in our most troubled districts, are dropping out, arrested, or even killed related to community and school-based conflicts. These are not conflicts that form in school and emanate outwards into the community; rather the reverse. This suggests that we may be approaching the question wrongheadedly when we ask merely how to make schools safer or how to improve school climate. Those are important questions, but should not be allowed to obscure asking how we can make *communities* safer and improve *community climate*. This cannot help but positively impact schools and families. By addressing the challenges described above, in particular the questions of resources and relevance, and by rethinking schools as centers of community life, urgently needed peer mediation programs in schools can become more effective and sustainable.

References

Apple, M. & King, N. (1977) What do schools teach? *Curriculum Inquiry*, 6(4): 341–358.

Bajaj, M. (ed.). (2008) *Encyclopedia of Peace Education*. Charlotte, NC: Information Age Publishers.

Beckerman, Z. & Zembylas, M. (2012) *Teaching Contested Narratives: Identity, Memory and Reconciliation in Peace Education and Beyond*. Cambridge: Cambridge University Press.

Bickmore, K. (2001) Student conflict resolution, power "sharing" in schools, and citizenship education. *Curriculum Inquiry*, 31(2): 137–162.

Bickmore, K. (2002) Good training is not enough: Research on peer mediation program implementation. *Social Alternatives*, 21(1): 33–38.

Cantrell, R., Parks-Savage, A. & Rehfuss, M. (2007) Reducing levels of elementary school violence with peer mediation. *Professional School Counseling*, 10(5): 475–481.

Casella, R. (2000) The benefits of peer mediation in the context of urban conflict and program status. *Urban Education*, 35(3): 324–355.

Cobb, S. (2013) *Speaking of Violence: The Politics and Poetics of Narrative in Conflict Resolution*. Oxford: Oxford University Press.

Daunic, A.P., Smith, S.W., Robinson, T.R., Miller, M.D. & Landry, K.L. (2000) Implementing schoolwide conflict resolution and peer mediation programs: Experiences in three middle schools. *Intervention in School & Clinic*, 36(2): 94–100.

Davies, L. (2004) *Education and Conflict*. London: Routledge.

Dewey, J. (2008) *Democracy and Education*. Radford, VA: Wilder Publications.

Duckworth, C. (2006) Teaching peace: A dialogue on Maria Montessori. *Journal of Peace Education*, 3(1): 39–53.

Duckworth, C. (2011) Restorative classrooms: Critical peace education in a juvenile detention home. *Peace and Conflict Studies Journal*, 18(2). Retrieved from nsuworks.nova.edu/pcs/vol18/iss2/3.

Duckworth, C. (2014) *Teaching Terror: 9/11 and Collective Memory in America's Classrooms*. New York: Routledge.

Duckworth, C. (2015a). History's hardest questions in the classroom: History, memory and peace education. *Peace and Change*, 40(1): 167–193.

Duckworth, C. (2015b). International and peace education in the twenty-first century: Acknowledging differences, optimizing collaboration. In M. Hayden, J. Levy & J. Thompson (eds) *The SAGE Handbook of Research in International Education* (pp. 351–367). London: SAGE.

Duckworth, C., Allen, B. & Triguba Williams, T. (2012) What do students learn when we teach peace? *Journal of Peace Education*, 9(1): 81–99.

Ford, E. (2002) Oregon's SCRIP model: Building school conflict resolution capacity through community partnerships. *Conflict Resolution Quarterly*, 19(4): 465–477.

Hansen, T. (2013) *The Generalist Approach to Conflict Resolution*. Lanham, MD: Lexington Books.

Harris, I. (2003) Peace education evaluation. Retrieved from files.eric.ed.gov/fulltext/ED480127.pdf.

Johnson, D.W. & Johnson, R.T. (1996) Teaching all students how to manage conflicts constructively: The peacemakers program. *The Journal of Negro Education*, 63(3): 322–335.

Johnson, D.W., Johnson, R., Mitchell, J., Cotton, B., Harris, D. & Louison, S. (1996) Effectiveness of conflict managers in an inner city elementary school. *Journal of Educational Research*, 89(5): 280–285.

Lantieri, L. & Patti, J. (1996) *Waging Peace in Our Schools*. Boston, MA: Beacon Press.

Mark, B. (2013) Khalil, Khalil, Khalil! In C. McGlynn, M. Zembylas & Z. Beckerman (eds) *Integrated Education in Conflicted Societies* (pp. 171–184). New York: Palgrave.

Pöyhönen, V., Juvonen, J. & Salmivalli, C. (2010) What does it take to stand up for the victim of bullying? *Merrill-Palmer Quarterly*, 56(2): 143–163.

Ravitch, D. (2013) *Reign of Error: The Hoax of the Privatization Movement and the Danger to America's Public Schools*. New York: Alfred A. Knopf.

Sandy, V.S. (2001) Conflict resolution education in the schools: "Getting there." *Conflict Resolution Quarterly*, 19(2): 237–250.

Sellman, E. (2002) Peer mediation, school culture and sustainability. *Pastoral Care in Education*, 20(2): 7–11.

Winslade, J. & Monk, G.D. (2008) *Practicing Narrative Mediation: Loosening the Grip of Conflict*. San Francisco, CA: Jossey-Bass.

25

ENCOURAGING EFFECTIVENESS THROUGH COMMUNICATION COMPETENCE IN COMMUNITY MEDIATION

Brian L. Heisterkamp

Disputants arrive at community mediation centers for a variety of reasons including the fact that they previously were unable to resolve disputes with other parties. The mediators encountered by disputants employ a variety of approaches to assist the parties in effectively negotiating and reaching an agreement. While agreement is not always possible, many mediators approach the process with the view that their intervention affords disputants an opportunity both to express their position and to find common ground with the opposing party. The communication approaches associated with effective mediation are the focus of this chapter.

This chapter begins by defining community mediation and explaining the various areas of community mediation practice. Then, the classification of mediation approaches into different styles is discussed. While research on mediator style has waned over the past few years, the categorization of mediator style remains important because parties often select mediators based on style, and programs often highlight their use of a particular style (Kressel & Wall, 2012). Next, the chapter turns to a discussion of specific interventions mediators use with the aim of transforming the conflict situation. Facets of the mediation context—including gender, culture, and conflict type—are discussed in relation to their importance for effective mediation. Finally, pre-mediation concerns and mediation session activities such as intake inquiries, room set-up, and agenda setting are addressed.

Community mediation

The philosophies of empowerment and self-determination distinguish community mediation (Faulkes & Claremont, 1997). Community mediation centers seek to empower citizens "to learn and use conflict resolution and problem-solving skills, rather than relying on third parties, such as courts [and] police officers" (Zondervan, 2000, p. 111). Community mediation centers are resources for citizens to take back control of their lives from courts or other government institutions that are often viewed as inefficient, oppressive, and unfair (Hedeen, 2004). The goals of community mediation centers range from "clearing crowded court dockets, to increasing the parties' ability to communicate with each other, to saving parties' time and/or money" (Zondervan, 2000, p. 113).

Community mediation centers can be categorized as either government sponsored or community based (Hedeen, 2004). Government-sponsored programs include those housed within the courts that handle small-claims cases or serve as an initial attempt to resolve disputes before entering the traditional adjudicative system. Police departments utilize mediation through mediation awareness and mediation skills training for officers (Volpe & Phillips, 2003), which can significantly decrease police calls to conflict situations (Charkoudian, 2005). In the school setting, peer mediation programs provide students with the opportunity to learn conflict resolution skills and may reduce students' need to access traditional disciplinary procedures for relatively minor conflicts (McWilliam, 2010).

Community-based programs include neighborhood mediation projects that seek to resolve disputes between neighbors which may involve noise complaints, parking disagreements, or property upkeep differences. Programs such as CeaseFire in Chicago and Baltimore seek to reduce neighborhood violence (Whitehill et al., 2014). Dialogue-based approaches to restorative justice, such as victim offender mediation, bring together victims and offenders with the aim of holding offenders accountable, repairing harm done, and developing understanding and respect (Coates et al., 2006).

In most of these settings, community mediation centers utilize volunteers from various backgrounds who often begin practicing after a relatively brief period of training (Hedeen, 2004). As discussed above, community mediation occurs in various contexts ranging from courthouses to schools to neighborhoods, and involves disputes that could range from barking dog disputes between neighbors to playground fights between students. At first glance, mediators seemingly need a great deal of content-level expertise. However, mediators are primarily process professionals—experts in understanding and applying a process (Faulkes & Claremont, 1997). Content-level expertise lies with the disputants, while mediators bring conflict management and negotiation skills to the table.

Mediator style

Mediator style, which refers to a cohesive set of strategies that characterize the manner in which a mediator conducts a case (Kressel, 2006), offers a means for researchers to categorize the communicative approach used by mediators. The evaluative-facilitative typology developed and later refined by Riskin (1996, 2003) is perhaps the most well-known categorization of styles. Kolb (1983) identified these styles as orchestrators, similar to the facilitative style, and dealmakers, similar to the evaluative style. Evaluative mediators help parties realistically assess their negotiating positions, while facilitative mediators help parties identify and express their interests (Kressel, 2007). The facilitator, formulator, and manipulator represent another typology of mediator styles (Touval & Zartman, 1985). The transformative style of mediation has received a considerable amount of attention because of the view that "parties' participation in mediation can help them develop increased capacity for self-determination and responsiveness to others" (Folger & Bush, 1996, p. 277). Most community mediation centers lean toward the facilitative approach (Hedeen, 2004).

Evaluative mediators may believe disputants want or need their direction (Charkoudian et al., 2009), which often results in mediators providing a reality check on disputant negotiation positions (Kressel, 2007). The role of the mediator is seen as providing a balanced and realistic assessment of disputant positions (Kressel, 2006). The manipulative mediator is similar to the evaluative mediator in that this approach to mediation involves the use of influence to shift the bargaining process (Beardsley et al., 2006). Della Noce (2009) delineates competencies for evaluative mediators including "structure persuasive arguments to yield concessions" and "undermine each party's confidence in the merits of his or her own case" (p. 208). In disputant ratings, this style was not associated with perceptions of fairness of the mediator or the mediation process (Alberts et al., 2005).

Facilitative mediators view their expertise as lying within the mediation process (Mayer, 2004), and they direct their efforts toward helping parties identify their interests and needs in an effort to identify areas of agreement and possible compromise (Kressel, 2007). Rather than attempting to persuade parties to accept an agreement, facilitative mediators guide disputants through a communication process in which they are able to voice their thoughts and feelings (Mayer, 2004). There are similarities between the facilitative and formulative mediator because the mediator does not pressure the parties to endorse a particular outcome (Wilkenfeld et al., 2003). The focus community mediation centers place upon the facilitative style leads to training that emphasizes "interpersonal skills, rapport building, empathy, and reframing" (Zondervan, 2000, p. 114). This approach was associated with disputant perceptions of fairness and satisfaction (Alberts et al., 2005).

Mediator interventions

Much of the skill associated with competent mediation emerges from choices related to mediator interventions. Mediators must engage themselves in such a way that the parties perceive progress and settlement as contingent on the mediator's presence (Kolb, 1985). Mediators must be capable of determining when a party's behavior could be an impediment to forward movement (Donohue et al., 1985). While disputants may attempt to affect a mediator's behavior, successful community mediators gain control of the interaction by drawing from their repertoire of strategies and tactics. A recent review of the literature identified approximately 100 mediator techniques that have been categorized into approximately two dozen strategies including bottom-up, differentiated, evaluative insight, problem solving, power broker, and neutral (Wall & Dunne, 2012). Categories are often associated with a particular style of mediation. Posthuma, Dworkin and Swift (2002) identified the specific categories of pressure, negotiation process, friendliness, avoiding negative emotions, and discussing alternatives; while Mayer (2004) more generally identified tactics including asking questions, validating parties' points of view, and assisting parties in finding options for resolution.

Regardless of the manner in which tactics are categorized, a key to successful community mediation includes the perceptive use of those tactics. Strategies can range from communication facilitation to procedural to directives, and can vary from low to high involvement intensity (Bercovitch & Houston, 2000). Mediators who encounter one disputant attacking another may need to interrupt the attack, enforce ground rules, and reframe or terminate the discussion (Donohue et al., 1985). Paraphrasing, attention to emotion, and encouraging problem solving may help produce turning points in the mediation that lead to greater understanding and resolution (Jameson et al., 2014). Mediators who offer solutions and encourage the discussion of those solutions give disputants the space to consider options in a more favorable environment (Jones, 1988). Empathetic listening leads to rapport building between parties in order to establish trust, which is key to successful mediation (Goldberg, 2005). Given the vast array of strategies and tactics available to mediators, one must be responsive to the current situation in order to increase the effectiveness of the negotiation situation.

Recognizing the integrative or distributive structures embedded within the disputants' stories is one avenue for recognizing appropriate mediator intervention. Disputants introduce these different conflict structures, which can be transformed or reinforced by mediators through their intervention tactics (Sinclair & Stuart, 2007). Distributive or differentiation structures refer to patterns of interaction with sharp distinctions between positions (Putnam, 2010) and often involve attempts to distribute resources by focusing on single issues (Olekalns, 2003). While distributive structures are fundamental to working through conflict (Putnam, 2010), disputant use of integrative conflict structures is more likely to result in constructive conflict resolution and agreement generation (Sinclair & Stuart, 2007). These integrative structures build on joint gains, include behaviors that work toward problem solving, and discover mutual benefits (Olekalns, 2003). Mediators who recognize the more constructive integrative conflict structures used by disputants are encouraged to extensively summarize or reframe those structures while very briefly summarizing distributive structures with the aim of encouraging disputants to devote more time to integrative structures (Sinclair & Stuart, 2007).

Regardless of style or tactic, community mediators should remember that they do not control disputants' behavior. Mediation is an interactive process involving mutual influence (Wall & Dunne, 2012). Conceptualizing mediation as a storytelling process embraces the view of interaction and mutual influence and situates the mediator within the role of moving the disputants from story to settlement (Stewart & Maxwell, 2010). Therefore, effective mediators are able to combine and use a balance of strategies in order to assist the parties in reaching an agreement (Beardsley et al., 2006).

Context sensitivity

A variety of context-related issues may influence both the mediators' and the parties' behavior. These factors could include the intensity of the conflict, the nature of the issues, the identity of the mediator, the relationship between the parties, and the mediation environment (Bercovitch & Houston, 2000). Conflict type, culture, country, and mediation institution are other contexts or environments mediators face (Wall & Dunne, 2012). When confronted with intense antagonism between the parties, mediators may use active strategies such as suggesting concessions the parties can make or changing expectations in order to prevent conflict escalation (Bercovitch & Wells, 1993). Mediators working with parties who have unrealistic expectations, may attempt to change these expectations through an evaluative approach in which they explain the unrealistic nature of a party's position (Carnevale & Pegnetter, 1985). Attention to these environmental factors can exert significant influence on mediator strategy selection with the aim of tailoring style and strategy to the individual characteristics of the dispute at hand.

While the issue of mediator gender impact on the process has been limited and inconclusive (Stuhlmacher & Morrissett, 2008), some researchers found that mediator gender is not a relevant discriminator in terms of participant perception of the process (Alberts et al., 2005). Still, some research suggests that male mediators are perceived more positively than their female counterparts (Stuhlmacher & Morrissett, 2008). Female mediators may be perceived as less controlling, despite their equivalent use of a controlling, interventionist style of mediation that is similar to their male counterparts (Burrell et al., 1988). Maxwell (1992) suggests that a feminine style of mediation involving a more integrative bargaining style may be better suited to the emotional factors some disputants bring to a conflict. The different sensibilities and perceptions a mediator's gender brings to the mediation suggest the continued need to examine communication behavior from this perspective.

Cultural differences and stereotypes complicate effective community mediation because disputants may not share the same expectations, norms, or communication styles (Salmon et al., 2013). Not all intercultural disputes are alike, and mediators are advised to match tactics to disputant characteristics (Salmon et al., 2013). Factors to consider in intercultural disputes include openness to mediation, willingness to concede, trust, and cultural intelligence, which is an individual's ability to function in culturally diverse situations (Salmon et al., 2013). Given that cultural intelligences predict intercultural negotiation effectiveness, programs should train mediators on the facets of cultural intelligence or select mediators based on cultural intelligence (Imai & Gelfand, 2010).

Pre-mediation concerns

Aside from communication-specific issues related to mediator style and intervention tactics, effective community mediation also involves a number of pre-mediation concerns including making intake inquiries, timing the sessions, and arranging the environment. The mediator's ability to make pre-mediation inquiries with the parties depends upon how the case is brought to mediation. Among other reasons, cases reach community mediation centers by party submission, court order, prior contract, or legal requirement (Frenkel & Stark, 2012). For example, court staff typically schedule cases heard in small-claims court. Thus, mediators arrive for the scheduled mediation and are able briefly to review the claims brought by each party shortly before the mediation session begins. In other cases, mediators may have more advance opportunity to make inquiries with the parties. Such inquiries could include gathering data from the parties about the history of the dispute and assembling information regarding the positions and interests of the parties (Frenkel & Stark, 2012). At this point mediators can also determine if there are any ethical concerns related to serving as the case mediator, including having a prior relationship with one of the parties or an inability to be neutral (Spencer & Brogan, 2006).

The timing of the mediation session can also be determined if the mediator has advance contact with the parties. Some conflict may be too recent and involve heightened emotions that inhibit effective mediation. For example, if the dispute involves a very recent car accident some parties may be too upset to negotiate effectively. The passage of time may aid the parties in terms of their readiness for mediation because of the opportunity to consider their own interests while remaining at an impasse with the other disputant. The need for a quick decision in a dispute is another factor to consider. Again, in the case of the car accident, one party may need immediate compensation for his/her automobile because of transportation needs. Therefore, the mediator must consider a number of factors including scheduling, party readiness, and the need for a quick resolution when determining appropriate timing for the mediation sessions.

The environment for the mediation session can also be determined in advance. The selection of a neutral and convenient location is important. Neutral locations avoid problems associated with one party having an advantage over the other (McCorkle & Reese, 2014). The location should be convenient in terms of transportation for each party (free parking or access to public transportation). Another environmental concern includes the set-up of the mediation room itself. The most important consideration is that the mediator should have each party within his/her gaze, which can be accomplished with a round or rectangular table or no table at all. Chairs should be equal in size to avoid situations in which one party has a larger or more comfortable chair (McCorkle & Reese, 2014). Ideally, there should be additional space for caucusing with individual parties if necessary (Frenkel & Stark, 2012). Parties should have access to restrooms and water. Access to computers, telephones, and copy machines may also be important if parties need to gather or share information with others (Moore, 2014). The increasing popularity of online mediation necessitates the consideration of other concerns related to the accessibility of appropriate technology (Goodman, 2003).

Mediation session activities

As the mediation session begins, other topics community mediators must consider include making an opening statement, establishing ground rules, and setting the agenda. The opening statement is particularly important when parties have no prior mediation experience and when the mediator did not have the opportunity to meet with the parties before the mediation session. Elements to include in the opening statement are introductions, discussion of the role of all in attendance, determination of authority to settle the dispute, and a discussion of the sequence of events (Spencer & Brogan, 2006). Mediators may also want to explain their roles and highlight the benefits of mediation (Frenkel & Stark, 2012). The sequence of events to mention during the opening statement often includes ground rules, party opening statements, caucusing, possible solutions, and resolution.

Discussing ground rules helps establish the tone of the mediation session. Ground rules may describe the neutrality of the mediator and the confidentiality of the process. Noting the neutrality of the mediator aids parties in understanding the role of the mediator in facilitating the process. Mediators may also mention the need to focus on the future rather than the past so that parties avoid rehashing past events. Establishing ground rules related to avoiding hostile or demeaning talk helps preempt this type of negative interaction and is a useful tool for stopping such talk should it begin (Frenkel & Stark, 2012).

After the parties make their opening statements and the issues have been clarified, the agenda can be set. The agenda includes those issues that require negotiation (Menkel-Meadow et al., 2014) and have been recognized by the disputants or the mediator (Spencer & Brogan, 2006). These issues can be written on a flipchart or whiteboard by the mediator to show that all parties have been heard and to ensure that no issues are missed (Spencer & Brogan, 2006). Neutral language should be used to avoid showing favoritism to one party or the other. For example, "breach of contract" could be reframed to "obligations under the agreement" to avoid assigning blame or limiting discussion (Spencer & Brogan, 2006). Issues should also be framed concretely (Frenkel & Stark, 2012). For example, the parties needing to address "how they communicate" might be reframed as "giving and receiving performance feedback."

A final issue related to the agenda concerns the sequencing of items. Several different approaches are suggested including ranking by importance, discussing the easiest issues first, or developing a simple agenda (Moore, 2014). Ranking involves first determining which issues are most important and then developing agreement on those issues. This approach hinges on the parties agreeing on which issues are most salient. Similarly, the "easiest first" approach centers on parties agreeing upon which issues are "easy" with the hope that agreement on those issues will develop momentum toward agreement on other, more difficult issues. The simple agenda involves discussing the negotiation issues in the order they were raised by the parties.

Conclusion

This chapter has illustrated that through extensive study, researchers linked mediator communication to various effectiveness measures including participant satisfaction, perceptions of fairness, and settlement rates. Styles of mediation, ranging from facilitative to formulative to manipulative, enable researchers to relate certain strategies and tactics to mediation approaches and to mediation outcomes. Mediator use of particular tactics enables mediators to intervene in conflict with the goal of transforming parties from differentiating conflict structures to integrative conflict structures, which are more likely to lead to agreements. Researchers should continue to focus upon issues that mediators and program designers can adjust including intervention strategies, agenda setting, and pre-mediation inquiries.

With the aim of providing practical advice, researchers should continue to focus on identifying strategies and tactics that lead to positive assessment and that can be integrated into mediation training (Lande, 2004). While searching for these factors, researchers should not lose sight of the fact that mediation is a process and an interaction, not a "black box" from which these variables can be retrieved (Sinclair & Stuart, 2007). There is no "magic bullet" tactic that will lead parties to an agreement—rather skilled mediators know they must build trust with the parties and facilitate the process by responding to the changing needs and dynamics of the mediation context (Jameson et al., 2014). This suggests that discourse analysis may be especially useful in mediation research because it allows for interpretation of strategies employed in mediation's changing interactional context (Glenn & Susskind, 2010).

Community mediation centers are an integral part of the communities they serve, and they are resources for conflict management, training, and education. The communities in which mediation centers are situated are stakeholders in the outcome of these disputes because the centers play a role in maintaining a peaceful, harmonious community (Faulkes & Claremont, 1997). The volunteer community mediators who serve these organizations are educators and facilitators of social change in places ranging from schools to courthouses. The possible spillover effect of their work provides hope that the constructive, nonviolent behavior of some will lead to the same behavior in others (Hedeen, 2004).

References

Alberts, J.K., Heisterkamp, B.L. & McPhee, R.M. (2005) Disputant perceptions of and satisfaction with a community mediation program. *International Journal of Conflict Management*, 16(3): 218–244.

Beardsley, K.C., Quinn, D.M., Biswas, B. & Wilkenfeld, J. (2006) Mediation style and crisis outcomes. *Journal of Conflict Resolution*, 50(1): 58–86. doi: 10.1177/0022002705282862.

Bercovitch, J. & Houston, A. (2000) Why do they do it like this?: An analysis of the factors influencing mediation behavior in international conflicts. *Journal of Conflict Resolution*, 44(2): 170–202. doi: 10.1177/0022002700044002002.

Bercovitch, J. & Wells, R. (1993) Evaluating mediation strategies: A theoretical and empirical analysis. *Peace & Change*, 18(1): 3–25. doi: 10.1111/j.1468–0130.1993.tb00591.x.

Burrell, N.A., Donohue, W.A. & Allen, M. (1988) Gender-based perceptual biases in mediation. *Communication Research*, 15(4): 447–469.

Carnevale, P.J.D. & Pegnetter, R. (1985) The selection of mediation tactics in public sector disputes: A contingency analysis. *Journal of Social Issues*, 41(2): 65–81.

Charkoudian, L. (2005) A quantitative analysis of the effectiveness of community mediation in decreasing repeat police calls for service. *Conflict Resolution Quarterly*, 23(1): 87–98.

Charkoudian, L., Ritis, C.D., Buck, R. & Wilson, C.L. (2009) Mediation by any other name would smell as sweet—or would it? The struggle to define mediation and its various approaches. *Conflict Resolution Quarterly*, 26(3): 293–316.

Coates, R.B., Umbreit, M.S. & Vos, B. (2006) Responding to hate crimes through restorative justice dialogue. *Contemporary Justice Review*, 9(1): 7–21. doi: 10.1080/10282580600564784.

Della Noce, D.J. (2009) Evaluative mediation: In search of practice competencies. *Conflict Resolution Quarterly*, 27(2): 193–214.

Donohue, W.A., Allen, M. & Burrell, N. (1985) Communication strategies in mediation. *Mediation Quarterly*, 10: 75–89.

Faulkes, W. & Claremont, R. (1997) Community mediation: Myth and reality. *Australian Dispute Resolution Journal*, 8(3): 177–181.

Folger, J.P. & Bush, R.A.B. (1996) Transformative mediation and third-party intervention: Ten hallmarks of a transformative approach to practice. *Mediation Quarterly*, 13: 263–278.
Frenkel, D.N. & Stark, J.H. (2012) *The Practice of Mediation* (2nd edn). New York: Wolters Kluwer Law & Business.
Glenn, P. & Susskind, L. (2010) How talk works: Studying negotiation interaction. *Negotiation Journal*, 26(2): 117–123.
Goldberg, S.B. (2005) The secrets of successful mediators. *Negotiation Journal*, 21(3): 365–376. doi: 10.1111/j.1571-9979.2005.00069.x.
Goodman, J. (2003) The pros and cons of online dispute resolution: An assessment of cyber-mediation websites. *Duke Law & Technology Review*, 2(1): 1–16.
Hedeen, T. (2004) The evolution and evaluation of community mediation: Limited research suggests unlimited progress. *Conflict Resolution Quarterly*, 22(1–2): 101–133. doi: 10.1002/crq.94.
Imai, L. & Gelfand, M.J. (2010) The culturally intelligent negotiator: The impact of cultural intelligence (CQ) on negotiation sequences and outcomes. *Organizational Behavior and Human Decision Processes*, 112(2): 83–98. doi: 10.1016/j.obhdp.2010.02.001.
Jameson, J.K., Sohan, D. & Hodge, J. (2014) Turning points and conflict transformation in mediation. *Negotiation Journal*, 30(2): 209–229. doi: 10.1111/nejo.12056.
Jones, T.S. (1988) Phase structures in agreement and no-agreement mediation. *Communication Research*, 15: 470–495.
Kolb, D.M. (1983) *The Mediators*. Cambridge, MA: MIT Press.
Kolb, D.M. (1985) To be a mediator: Expressive tactics in mediation. *Journal of Social Issues*, 41(2): 11–26.
Kressel, K. (2006) Mediation revisited. In M. Deutsch, P.T. Coleman & E.C. Marcus (eds) *The Handbook of Conflict Resolution: Theory and Practice* (2nd edn) (pp. 726–756). San Francisco, CA: Jossey-Bass.
Kressel, K. (2007) The strategic style in mediation. *Conflict Resolution Quarterly*, 24(3): 251–283. doi: 10.1002/crq.
Kressel, K. & Wall, J. (2012) Introduction to the special issue on mediator style. *Negotiation and Conflict Management Research*, 5(4): 334–339. doi: 10.1111/j.1750–4716.2012.00110.x.
Lande, J. (2004) Commentary: Focusing on program design issues in future research on court-connected mediation. *Conflict Resolution Quarterly*, 22(1–2): 89–100.
Maxwell, D. (1992) Gender differences in mediation style and their impact on mediator effectiveness. *Mediation Quarterly*, 9(4): 353–364.
Mayer, B. (2004) Facilitative mediation. In J. Folberg, A.L. Milne & P. Salem (eds) *Divorce and Family Mediation: Models, Techniques, and Applications* (pp. 29–52). New York: Guilford Press.
McCorkle, S. & Reese, M.J. (2014) *Mediation Theory and Practice*. Los Angeles, CA: SAGE Publications.
McWilliam, N. (2010) A school peer mediation program as a context for exploring therapeutic jurisprudence (TJ): Can a peer mediation program inform the law? *International Journal of Law and Psychiatry*, 33(5–6): 293–305. doi: 10.1016/j.ijlp.2010.09.002.
Menkel-Meadow, C.J., Love, L.P. & Schneider, A.K. (2014) *Mediation: Practice, Policy, and Ethics* (2nd edn). New York: Wolters Kluwer Law & Business.
Moore, C.W. (2014) *The Mediation Process: Practical Strategies for Resolving Conflict* (4th edn). San Francisco, CA: Jossey-Bass.
Olekalns, M. (2003) Phases, transitions and interruptions: Modeling processes in multi-party negotiations. *International Journal of Conflict Management, 14*(3/4): 191–211. doi: 10.1108/eb022898.
Posthuma, R.A., Dworkin, J.B. & Swift, M.S. (2002) Mediator tactics and sources of conflict: Facilitating and inhibiting effects. *Industrial Relations*, 41(1): 94–109. doi: 10.1111/1468–232X.00237.
Putnam, L.L. (2010) Communication as changing the negotiation game. *Journal of Applied Communication Research*, 38(4): 325–335. doi: 10.1080/00909882.2010.513999.
Riskin, L.L. (1996) Understanding mediators' orientations, strategies, and techniques: A grid for the perplexed. *Harvard Negotiation Law Review*, 1(7): 7–51.
Riskin, L.L. (2003) Decisionmaking in mediation: The new old grid and the new new grid system. *Notre Dame Law Review*, 79(1): 1–53.
Salmon, E.D., Gelfand, M.J., Çelik, A.B., Kraus, S., Wilkenfeld, J. & Inman, M. (2013) Cultural contingencies of mediation: Effectiveness of mediator styles in intercultural disputes. *Journal of Organizational Behavior*, 34(6): 887–909. doi: 10.1002/job.

Sinclair, L.E. & Stuart, W.D. (2007) Reciprocal-influence mediation model: A guide for practice and research. *Conflict Resolution Quarterly*, 25(2): 185–220. doi: 10.1002/crq.

Spencer, D. & Brogan, M. (2006) *Mediation Law and Practice*. New York: Cambridge University Press.

Stewart, K.A. & Maxwell, M.M. (2010) *Storied Conflict Talk: Narrative Construction in Mediation*. Amsterdam: John Benjamins Pub. Co.

Stuhlmacher, A.F. & Morrissett, M.G. (2008) Men and women as mediators: Disputant perceptions. *Management*, 19(3): 249–261.

Touval, S. & Zartman, I.W. (1985) *International Mediation in Theory and Practice*. Boulder, CO: Westview Press.

Volpe, M.R. & Phillips, N. (2003) Police use of mediation. *Conflict Resolution Quarterly*, 21(2): 263–267. doi: 10.1002/crq.61.

Wall, J.A. & Dunne, T.C. (2012) Mediation research: A current review. *Negotiation Journal*, 28(2): 217–244. doi: 10.1111/j.1571-9979.2012.00336.x.

Whitehill, J.M., Webster, D.W., Frattaroli, S. & Parker, E.M. (2014) Interrupting violence: How the CeaseFire program prevents imminent gun violence through conflict mediation. *Journal of Urban Health*, 91(1): 84–95. doi: 10.1007/s11524-11013-9796-9799.

Wilkenfeld, J., Young, K., Asal, V. & Quinn, D. (2003) Mediating international crises: Cross-national and experimental perspectives. *The Journal of Conflict Resolution*, 47(3): 279–301. doi: 10.1177/0022002703252365.

Zondervan, D.B. (2000) Community mediation in the USA: Current developments. In M. Liebmann (ed.) *Mediation in Context* (pp. 111–125). London: Jessica Kingsley Publishers.

26

THE SPACE OF CONFLICT

Aesthetic lessons for mediators

Dorit Cypis

This chapter frames lessons on recognizing the knots of chronic conflict through considering the spatial nuances of human identity and social relations. As an artist and mediator, I use the double lens of aesthetics and mediation to explore identity as psychic spaces within bodies and politicized spaces surrounding bodies that mirror, inform, and extend each other. If we miss this reflexive relationship between internal and external spaces, we miss a large part of the story of human identity differences and what fuels conflict between and within people. My artist practice has always explored identity and social relations through aesthetic genres of performance, photography, and social sculpture. I became a mediator to extend out from the studio to the street, to explore conflict embedded in identity and social relations.

Early in my mediation career, I came across a critical question posed by Bernard Mayer (2004) in *Beyond Neutrality*: how can conflict resolution processes root out systemic social causes of conflict and not cover them over with neutrality and resolution? As an artist, I understand that identity is contextual and rooted in the individual and the collective culture. As identity and conflict are inseparable, I now understand that to resolve conflict on the individual level does not necessarily address the social level where many conflicts are rooted. Mayer's (2004) suggestion opened mediation to a finer volume control of engaging rather than resolving conflict. My practice of mediation is as a conflict specialist with a toolbox of skills and approaches, highly inquiring and thoughtfully responsive to each conflict situation uniquely.

The lessons of this chapter are aesthetic as they question the form and meaning of space, calling on perceptual and sensorial strategies to reveal nuanced threads often not seen. Artists disturb the peace of our quotidian lives to unmask hidden threads of form and meaning. As a mediator I employ aesthetics to mediate conflict dangerously, to unmask hidden threads of conflict with "a deep and dangerous level of honesty and empathy" (Cloke, 2001, p. 5). Celebrated mediator, Kenneth Cloke (2001) encourages mediators to open Pandora's Box, to listen more deeply and explore conflict even when it seems out of control. The following aesthetic lessons on the experience of space are meant to build the mediator's capacity to more fully recognize and embrace sensorial and perceptual strategies as core to mediating conflict toward deeper engagement and, it is hoped, individual and social transformation. You never know who your next teacher is.

Prelude: recognize the attributes of physical space

In our information age of online communication, we have become more unaware of the attributes of physical space and how these affect our face-to-face relations. As a mediator, how often do you walk into a space and immediately sit down without first moving through the space to experience its attributes? When you look across a space, do your eyes scan the surfaces, missing detail? Do you notice how the furniture is arranged, the spaces between objects, the way light falls over various areas, the colors, the textures, the height of the ceiling, the ways sound is filtered, whether there are windows that can be opened, or window shades that can be drawn closed?

Next time you enter a space check out these variables and explore them as if this was a playground. Ask yourself if the spatial variables connote inclusion, trust, and expansion or exclusion, fear, and contraction. Honestly, how do you feel in the space? Empathize with the conflicted parties who will fill this space to sense how they might feel. Is the space conducive to setting a tone of equity between parties? Consider that intentionally shifting spatial variables would dramatically alter the physical space and increase or diminish trust between people, encourage or discourage sight lines for people's eyes to connect, soften or enhance power dynamics between them, and add calm or anxiety to any conflict engagement.

We so readily accept the conditions of our environment, even as they often distance us from each other. Recognize how easy it can be to animate a space for more dynamic engagement. Take the time to look more deeply at the ways that space can be made dynamic and flexible for all parties, no matter their status or culture. An animated spatial environment reframes experience from contraction, mistrust, hesitation, to expansion, trust, and attention, allowing for more open dialogue. Arrive early to your next mediation site to explore the spatial nuance of the environment that will frame the mediation.

Lesson one: practice dynamic listening

As mediators, we are highly prone to our own unrecognized bias riding the coat tails of our internalized memories of past experience. We are vulnerable to being triggered by parties involved in the conflict we are mediating. Listen to how you listen. Ask yourself if you are hearing the present or your own past circumstances blocking you as mediator from engaging the conflict more honestly and more empathically.

Gaston Bachelard, philosopher of phenomenology, wrote on the human capacity to hear dynamically from within, to be more available to deeply sense the subtle qualities of the present, in objects, space, and in people, stating that "[t]he subconscious is ceaselessly murmuring, and it is by listening to these murmurs that one hears its truth" (Bachelard, 1971, p. 59). Memory is in the present—it is our past perceived in the present. How do our filters of the past held within spaces of our bodies affect our perceptions of present circumstances? What inner murmurs may be filtering and biasing how you are hearing yourself and others? How do you sense murmurs internalized within and between people in conflict?

- Contracted. Dense. Tense. Tight.
- Claustrophobic. Dark. Shallow. Full.
- Opaque. Anxious. Refracted. Breathless. Blind.

Dynamic Listening is a tool I created to expand on Active Listening, which is to listen at once to the one speaking, to the spatial environment, and to yourself as listener. To hear the murmurs of your own subconscious, whether whispering in your head or tingling somewhere in your body, is to more fully recognize yourself. These murmurs are current memories of past experiences that clamor for attention, offering you recognition of what may be blocking you from more deeply hearing the one speaking, or from recognizing how the nuances of the space around you may be filtering what you are experiencing, perhaps even sustaining inequitable power relations between the parties. Listen. According to Cloke (2001), "[p]eople escalate their conflicts by not being authentic. As they accept themselves more fully they become more accepting of others" (p. 7).

My path to learning how to listen dynamically included many years of working with dancers. Simone Forti was the first to teach me the capacity of the human body to listen dynamically. In the late 1960s, Forti spent many hours at zoos watching animal movement to better understand how primal body movement responds to the Earth's gravity. Forti recognized an animal's capacity to tune in to their bodily experience, detecting the nuance of sensation that informs their place in the immediate spatial environment, to trust, fight, or flight. While animals are keenly sensorially aware of their relationship to space, humans must be reminded to tune in and listen. Forti created a dance form to listen subtly to the resonance of her body's sensorial experience of physical space. Forti (1974) describes the experience: "As I sat in the chair … I felt my body occupying the same space, as had the body of the original player. I could feel and even smell the player" (p. 12). She inspired me to develop strategies to teach mediators to listen to their bodily responses to spaces they inhabit—to attune to present experience and recognize how space may confuse our perception of present and past.

The following scenario reflects on how listening dynamically to one's experience of space can expand dialogue between parties in chronic conflict. A few months after the 2009 Israel–Gaza war, I arranged travel to Israel for myself and two other members of Mediators Beyond Borders,[1] to visit Neve Shalom Wahat al Salam (NSWAS),[2] an Israeli village of Jewish and Palestinian residents dedicated to peace, coexistence, and reconciliation. Abdesalam Najar, a Palestinian founding member of NSWAS, had initiated a series of cross-cultural mediation training sessions for Jewish and Palestinian Israeli educators, community leaders, and community mediators. The week we were there was their third and final session. The three of us came to listen and share tools. Feeling sensitive to the palpable post-war tensions between the bi-cultural participants, I presented a dynamic listening exercise of spatial movement and attention.

I intentionally chose a large room, empty except for a few chairs, to provide a safe and open space for everyone to have the same opportunity to explore. Over the next hour, I guided the participants to walk through the room at their natural gait in silence and gradually, while focusing on their breath, to slow the pace of their walk and pay more subtle attention both to the physicality of the outer architectural space and to the spatial experience within their moving body. After time enough for each person to acclimate to this dynamic attention, I asked them to individually gravitate to an area of the room that was most compelling, either because of feeling pulled toward or feeling pushed away from this space. In conclusion, each person was asked to share an experience triggered by the spatial qualities and the location they chose to be in.

What was revealed brought us to an intimacy of mutual recognition that we would not have arrived at if we had started directly with facilitated dialogue. While most of the Jewish participants gravitated to open spaces that were light filled, most Palestinian participants tended to spatially hover closer to walls, away from windows and direct light. The ensuing dialogue amongst us resonated with feelings of who felt safe where, of spaces of trust, mistrust, pride, fear, and fearlessness. We existed in the same physical space but for the participants, vulnerable and less vulnerable, their psychophysical experience of this space mirrored their respective experience of the political conflict in which their daily lives were embedded. Their psychic internal spaces mirrored the external political circumstances surrounding them. Sharing these experiences did not resolve the political power imbalance between Israeli Jew and Palestinian, but did allow for deeper mutual recognition and empathy.

John Paul Lederach (2005) reminds us that listening takes more than technique alone, but must also employ the subtlety of aesthetics, "akin to the haiku moment … attending to what things mean … achieved through aesthetics and ways of knowing … a capacity and pathway that rely on intuition more than cognition … moments of the aesthetic imagination" (p. 69). When involved in mediating difficult conflict conversation, ground the group's sensation and memory in an awareness of the present spatial environment. Give people time to explore and experience themselves in silence so they can hear their interior bodily voices and memories. Once trust is gained, the conflict conversation can be engaged expansively rather than be resisted.

Lesson two: design the space for everyone's trust

Spatial variables within a meeting space can mitigate, frame, and sustain an existing conflict especially when the conflict is chronically embedded in the community and the community lacks trust. I was witness to a public dialogue in South Central Los Angeles, which can instruct mediators in why it is so important to recognize the power relations between parties in conflict and to intentionally design the physical dynamics of a meeting space to gain everyone's trust.

The City of Los Angeles Human Relations Commission invited the Neighborhood Council Commissioners elected to serve South Central LA, to hear community members express what they considered to be excessive police force that had resulted in the multiple deaths of their black youth[3] and to make recommendations on the future of policing in their community. Most people were seated in 25 linear rows, while some stood against the outer walls holding cardboard cutouts of coffins with drawings and names of local youth killed by police bullets. The community members faced four neighborhood commissioners who sat at the front of the hall behind a long table raised on a platform. Noticeably, a 15-foot cavernous space separated the community and the commissioners—an abyss of dead space. A podium with a microphone was placed in front of the seated community.

This spatial format is called proscenium design, where two groups face one another framed by a separation that can easily become adversarial. In this case, one group was also seated higher than the other, adding another spatial attribute of power differentiation. The result was two groups facing each other across a spatial gulf in a binary configuration evoking power and separation. How would this spatial design support reciprocal dialogue and listening?

Community members came up to the podium to address the commissioners, expressing grief, anger, and frustration. To them nothing had shifted procedurally to change their experience of oppression, victimhood, and perceptions of the police department as racist. As this spatial format did not inspire a mutual trust necessary for dialogue, community members and commissioners could not listen or respond thoughtfully to each other, nor could they hear their inner murmuring to recognize thresholds between their past memories of oppression and the present. Harvard School of Negotiation Professor and author William Ury (1991) coined three ways that people often react when trust is absent: avoidance, accommodation, or attack.

FIGURE 26.1 Francis Alys, *L'imprevoyance de la Nostalgie*, 1999

The ensuing event seemed like scripted theater. A community member took the microphone off the podium, stepped into the spatial divide, and asked why the community was positioned to be so isolated from the commissioners. Other members then occupied the spatial gap activating it as a space of conflict. The commissioners immediately left to avoid their fear of further confrontation. The possibility for dialogue turned to mayhem. The spatial divide symbolized yet another oppression and impossibility. Although this was a clear public representation of systemic racial oppression as a root to this conflict, the public officials could not see it and could not be adaptive and responsive. The intended dialogue did not take place.

The lesson to mediators: spend time to recognize your parties' cultural histories and perceptions of power. Know what the conflict issues are before mediation. Carefully assess the physical attributes of the space you are using for dialogue or mediation. Recognize that physical space will trigger psychic space. Allow space to engage with the conflict, not stifle it with neutrality and resolution before it can be expressed and honest dialogue can happen. Allow for dynamic shifts. What if the public officials who had organized the meeting had been adaptive and responsive, recognizing that elements in the space mirrored the community's experience of separation and isolation? What do you imagine they could have done spatially to encourage options to suggest possibilities for engagement and inclusiveness?

Lesson three: witness the experience of others

James Baldwin (2014) spoke eloquently of the experience of being made "other." How a dominant (white) culture blind to its racism is blind to the experience of a (black) minority group, unable to look directly into their eyes to recognize them. This double blindness mirrors itself, maintaining the status quo, theirs as well as yours. Baldwin (2014) states: "In order to learn your name, you are going to have to learn mine" (p. 22).

America knows this symptom well, and we can transpose it onto any other chronic cultural conflict. In the Middle East, there seems to be no end to the high cost on human life waged by political conflict between Israeli Jews and Palestinians. We are used to seeing media images of this human cost, but what can we viscerally understand by looking at pictures when we are entirely distanced from the physical context of their space and time?

Traveling through Israel in 2015, I was moved to contact Machsom,[4] an activist peace group of women initiated in 2000, courageously and humbly working as witnesses to the daily crossings of Palestinian laborers who live on the other side of the Israeli border wall, bringing attention to the human costs of political and spatial restriction. As witnesses, Machsom women dare to cross the spatial divides imposed by politics and culture, to stand close and become intimate with others behind the wall. Their roles are of a conflict specialists, shifting between advocates, witnesses and conflict engagers, present to hear, see, feel, acknowledge, apologize, facilitate, and channel communication. They are an answer to Bernard Mayer's (2004) question.

On two consecutive mornings, I accompanied Machsom members to witness crossings at three border checkpoints, including two checkpoints along the West Bank where Palestinian farmland is divided by the Israeli boundary wall. Day workers, farmers, and teachers cross daily into Israel from their homes in occupied territory, waiting two hours in line from 5.00 a.m. to "enter" Israel, and waiting two hours crossing to return home nine hours later. Witnessing this event was humbling, deeply disturbing, and stupefying. Feeling my internal conflict at being witness to their humiliation was palpable and visceral, mirroring the spatial conflict of their physical reality. In wanting to turn away, I was reminded that refusing to look and see their anguish framed in physical space, was to negate the conflict, negate them and negate myself. This became a huge challenge for me, and ultimately a huge lesson that I now carry proudly.

The words of James Baldwin (2014) echo my sentiments: "If you can examine and face your life, you can discover the terms with which you are connected to other lives, and they can discover too, the terms with which they are connected to other people" (p. 31). Recognizing my conflicted psychic space focused me to more honestly reach into the unspoken spatial divide between us. One by one, I wished each person crossing a good morning and shared eye contact. Most people passed by me, looking back into my eyes reflecting a vulnerable acknowledgement of our mutually awkward positions, yet with an appreciation for sharing a human glance across intractable conflict. If only for a moment, we engaged the conflict with an intimacy that overshadowed the divided space between us—between Israel and Palestine.

On day two, I accompanied Nura Resh, a founding member of Machsom, to one of the larger border checkpoints at Irtach, where 6,000 Palestinian laborers take two to three hours to cross into Israel each morning, and back home at the end of each workday. We arrived early to witness a throng of men and women in a deafening silence clicking through a quarter mile of turnstiles. Nura later wrote in her journal: "The unrelenting line of laborers moves incrementally through the clicking, squeaking turnstiles." Zachariah, a laborer, gives Dorit a rosebud, "on behalf of all the laborers. Dorit is stunned. Through her eyes I see freshly the terrible injustice" (personal communication).

Indeed, I was stunned and took photographs constantly hoping to learn something more through the collapsed space between my camera lens and the eyes of men and women who would look back at me. A shallow, full, listless, anxious space with no breath is the space of systemic institutionalized conflict. Once more, I recognized that here only the intimacy of eyes meeting empathically could contradict the spatial impossibility for connection. According to Butler (2004), "[t]o ask for recognition, or to offer it, is precisely not to ask for recognition for what one already is. It is to solicit a becoming, to instigate a transformation, to petition the future always in relation to the Other" (p. 44). In my moral imagination, this is a conflict specialist's aesthetic form for engaging conflict.

Recommendations

1 Recognize the attributes of physical space

Use elements of the space to animate the environment, to challenge expectations and habits—consider lights, chair/table positions, windows, curtains, and objects. Keep your eyes and ears open. Be inventive. Engage the environment so all participants feel safe, yet fluid.

2 Practice dynamic listening

Grow your capacity to recognize what is present and what is past experience. Pay attention to your parties' gestures, movement, tone, gaze, and body positions to recognize how they may be holding conflict internally. Allow them space and silence to recognize their experience and their difference. Notice how parties in conflict inhabit space, feeling safe or unsafe.

3 Design the space for everyone's trust

Recognize how external social space can reflect internal psychic space to connote power, cultural difference, isolation, and separation. Ask how people feel. Notice if the physical space replicates and mirrors aspects of the conflict between the parties. Be open to engaging a party's triggered memory of conflict. Be adaptable to shift spatial attributes to suggest options and possibilities.

4 Witness the experience of others

Acknowledge your own experience of chronic social conflict. Be open to an intimate moment of eye contact. Allow for space, time, and silence for tiny intimate gestures to occur—the movement of an arm, a breath, a smile, a direct empathic gaze, a moment of shared silence—these are core attributes of deep connection even in intractable conflict.

Conclusion: lessons learned/knots untied

Conflict takes place in the many spaces we inhabit—interior and exterior. We may be unaware of narratives of conflict that seem distant from our daily lives, but are reflected within our psyches and in the environments we inhabit daily. Conflict that lives between us also lives within us. Reflecting critically on the spaces where conflict takes place reveals something about us—how the memories we carry silently drive reactive habits, and how spatial contexts we inhabit mirror our relationship to feeling safe or unsafe. We inhabit multiple spaces simultaneously: our thoughts, our memories, our somatic body, and the environmental, architectural, social, and political spaces that we move through daily. Spatial awareness can stimulate us to recognize how we may be contributing to and responding to conflict, and allow us insight to shift from habitual reaction to thoughtful recognition of ourselves and of others, the backbone to engaging and transforming conflict into generative relations.

Notes

1 For more information on this project see: mediatorsbeyondborders.org/what-we-do/projects/past-projects/.
2 Neve Shalom/Wahat al Salam and Wahat al Salam/Neve Shalom, Arabic and Hebrew for Oasis of Peace—an intentional community jointly established by Jewish and Palestinian Arab citizens of Israel in 1976. For more information see: www.wasns.org.
3 Ellison, Treva & Lenz, Colby (2016). Mapping police violence in Los Angeles. *The Scholar and Feminist Online*, 13(2), Spring. sfonline.barnard.edu/navigating-neoliberalism-in-the-academy-nonprofits-and-beyond/treva-ellison-colby-lenz-mapping-police-violence-in-los-angeles/.
4 Machsom Watch, a volunteer organization of Israeli women observing and reporting on the Occupation of Palestinians living in the West Bank, daily monitoring West Bank checkpoints, separation fences, agricultural gates, since 2001. For more information see: www.machsomwatch.org/en.

References

Alys, F. (2007) *Politics of Rehearsal*. Hammer Museum. Regents of the University of Los Angeles.

Bachelard, G. (1971 [1960]). *The Politics of Reverie: Childhood, Language, and the Cosmos*, D. Russell (trans.). Boston, MA: Beacon Press.

Baldwin, J. (2014) *James Baldwin: The Last Interview and Other Conversations*. New York: Melville House Publishing.

Butler, J. (2004) *Precarious Life: The Powers of Mourning and Violence*. London: Verso.

Cloke, K. (2001) *Mediating Dangerously: The Frontiers of Conflict Resolution*. San Francisco, CA: Jossey-Bass.

Forti, S. (1974) *Handbook in Motion*. Nova Scotia: The Press of the Nova Scotia College of Art and Design.

Lederach, J.P. (2005). *The Moral Imagination: The Art and Soul of Building Peace*. Oxford: Oxford University Press.

Mayer, B. (2004) *Beyond Neutrality: Confronting the Crisis in Conflict Resolution*. San Francisco, CA: Jossey-Bass.

Ury, W. (1991) *Getting Past No: Negotiating in Difficult Situations*. New York: Bantam Books.

27

FROM PEERS TO COMMUNITY

Transferring peer mediation skills from school to community

Vitus Ozoke

Today's youth are in many major ways different from their counterparts two decades ago. In this age of the internet and its allied digital and media technologies, today's 12-year-olds are exposed to more information than a 30-year-old was two decades ago. This exposure has huge implications for child and youth development. With this exposure comes the acquisition of social and other life skills on an accelerated scale unimaginable just a couple of decades ago. One remarkable area of this accelerated development for 21st-century youth is in problem solving and conflict resolution. Through peer mediation programs in schools, today's youth have demonstrated remarkable skills and abilities in mature and constructive handling of conflict. A recent pre-test/post-test experimental research study by Kasik and Kumcagiz (2014) analyzed the effect of peer mediation and conflict resolution training received by 20 seventh graders in primary schools on their self-esteem and conflict resolution skills. Using the "Self-Esteem Scale" (Ziller et al., 1969) to measure self-esteem and the "Scale for Conflict Resolution Behavior" to define students' conflict behavior, the study found that a peer mediation and conflict resolution skills training program produced a significant effect on students' levels of self-esteem and conflict resolution skills.

Like traditional mediation, which involves adult mediators, peer mediation is a communicative process in which schoolchildren, with the assistance of a neutral third party, work collaboratively to resolve issues. Peer mediation is designed to help schools become healthier and safer learning environments. This objective is achieved through the empowerment of children and young people to manage conflict and, in the process, transform relationships. Every well-designed and -implemented peer mediation program inculcates in student peer mediators the skills and strategies for handling conflict, including effective communication and decision making, critical perspective taking, and greater self-esteem. Yet, with all these skills, young people have not been welcomed and utilized as resources for conflict resolution beyond school settings. Even as members of their communities, young people with proven mediation skills have not been incorporated as valuable resources in community mediation and other community conflict resolution settings.

This chapter makes the case for the inclusion and utilization of young people, who have been trained as student peer mediators, in the mediation of community conflicts. This position is predicated primarily on two factors: 1) peer mediation training equips young people with useful, usable, and transferable conflict resolution skills; and 2) today's youth are more mature and more knowledgeable in life's common routines than their counterparts in past time. They are, therefore, much more able, more equipped, and more comfortable and confident to handle more complex tasks than society has been willing to trust them with. A major ambition of this chapter is to propose this idea as a new model of mediation, one that draws from social psychology and allied theories. In advancing this proposal, the chapter rests on the fundamental premise that mediation skills, including those acquired in peer mediation settings, are transferable.

The chapter provides a general overview of peer mediation, including its evolution, its underlying philosophy, and its mechanics. It presents a six-step model of peer mediation as an illustration of the similarity between the principles and processes of peer mediation and those of conventional mediation. Using the Peacemakers Program (Johnson & Johnson, 1996) as evidence, the chapter makes a closing argument for the transferability of peer mediation skills to community settings. The chapter concludes with an evaluative success story. The goal of the evaluative component is to highlight not just the successes of the initiative in promoting healthier and safer learning environments in schools, but also the transferable valuable skills and resources with which it equips young people going into their communities.

The concept and the emergence of peer mediation in schools

Neither the notion nor the theories of conflict resolution programs in schools are new. As early as the 1970s and the early 1980s, schools across America had been developing ways and means to "improve the school climate by building conflict resolution skills among members of the school community" (Hakim, 1992, p. 15; Tolson et al., 1992). The 1980s and 1990s had seen a dramatic upsurge in school violence across the United States. However, it was not just the United States; the pervasiveness of school violence is one that has been amply documented on a global scale. From the United States (Roberts et al., 2012), Africa (Liang et al., 2007), Asia (Chen & Astor, 2012), the Middle East (Khoury-Kassabri et al., 2009), to Europe (Smith, 2002), it is the same sad story. At the root of most school violence is the unprovoked repeated harassment of one or more students by another or a group of others—verbally, physically, and, in our postmodern world, virtually through cyber bullying (Berkowitz, 2014; Smith & Brain, 2000; Furlong et al., 1995).

For American children particularly, modernity has brought with it a wave of never-before-seen violence (Children's Defense Fund, 1991; DeVoe et al., 2003). The menace of gun violence has become a major threat to the safety and well-being of both children and school personnel in American urban school districts. As noted by Loupe and Shepard (1993), one out of every three school children in metro Atlanta admitted to knowing someone who brought a gun to school. As American schools reflectea microcosm of the general mood of home and community violence, teachers and administrators are challenged to come up with measures to curb growing school violence and make school environments safe (Johnson & Johnson, 1996). Different schools and school personnel respond in different ways. Some adopt different regimes of punishment, including suspension and expulsion from school, random weapons sweeps and locker searches, and metal detectors (Harrington-Lueker, 1992). Others take a more fundamental and transformative approach, teaching their students the lessons and benefits of alternative dispute resolution. The virtue of nonviolence provided a ready theme for this latter group (Harris, 1996). It was in the rank of this latter group that peer mediation, as an alternative conflict handling approach, evolved (Bell et al., 2000; Powell et al., 1996). As noted by Deutsch (1991), teachers and school administrators across the United States are adopting the insights of peace education under various names, including peer mediation, multicultural awareness, and violence prevention. Peer mediation initiatives are being developed and implemented in school districts across America as a response to the rising wave of violence in schools and society generally (Close & Lechman, 1997) and this is also the case around the world.

Purpose of conflict resolution programs in schools

Johnson and Johnson (2004) have identified two principal purposes for conflict resolution programs in schools. The first purpose is to ensure that schools are safe places where students are not just able to learn, but are also able to interact with one another in constructive ways. The second purpose is to "socialize children, adolescents, and young adults into the competencies and attitudes they will need to resolve conflicts constructively for the rest of their lives ..." (p. 68). The importance of constructive handling of conflict, especially among children and young people cannot be overstated. Available evidence suggests that in the absence of conflict resolution training, children and young adults approach conflict in rather destructive and unproductive ways (Johnson & Johnson, 2004).

Conflict resolution training invites children and young adults to engage in integrative negotiations of conflict and teaches them skills useful in mediating their schoolmates' conflicts. It also empowers them to engage in effective decision making and resolve their own conflicts without needing adult intervention—a valuable life skill (Close & Lechman, 1997; Guanci, 2002). This is a view equally held by Maxwell (1989) who noted that the mediation process for children and young people is self-empowering, enabling them to "make decisions about issues and conflicts that affect their own lives" (p. 150).

In their analysis of the Winning Against Violent Environments (WAVE) program—the first school-based peer mediation program in the entire state of Ohio—Close and Lechman (1997) concluded that students who take part in the program are capable of resolving conflicts without adult help. They learn how to state positively and confidently what they need in order to resolve the problem. They also learn very useful skills in decision making, effective communication, and negotiation which they find very valuable later in life (see also Cueto et al., 1993; Schomberg, 1992; Jacobson & Lombard, 1992; Guanci, 2002). Experienced WAVE mediators are not just peer mediators in their high schools; they are also "trainers of other students and adults" (Close & Lechman, 1997, p. 12).

Therefore, it is not just that peer mediators learn how to manage conflict constructively and maintain peaceful and safe learning environments; they are also able to transfer and apply their learned skills to conflict situations beyond the classroom and school contexts and into family and community settings (Johnson & Johnson, 2004). One of Johnson and Johnson's (2004) findings of a meta-analysis of 16 research studies, carried out between 1988 and 2000, on the success of the Teaching Students to be Peacemakers (TSP) program in eight different schools in the United States and Canada, was that students did in fact use the procedures taught in the program in family settings. A specific inquiry in those analyses was whether students who participated in the TSP program transferred the negotiation and mediation procedures to situations beyond the school and classroom. In reporting their findings on that specific line of inquiry, Johnson and Johnson (2004) stated: "Our studies demonstrated that students did, in fact, use the negotiation and mediation procedures in the hallways, lunchroom, and playground. In addition, students used the procedures in family settings" (p. 75).

Six-step model of peer mediation

There may be minor stylistic variations in process elements from program to program; however, the following six-step model of peer mediation has become established (Stevahn, 2004).

Step one: consenting to peer mediation

As a general rule, mediation is a voluntary process. The consent of parties must not only be voluntary; it must be informed. Parties to peer mediation must understand what the process is about and give their informed consent. Any person who has either a direct personal stake in the problem or a formal interest in a resolved outcome can request mediation. It could be a student, a teacher, the principal, the school counselor, or any other. A Peer Mediation Request Form can be used to secure consent to mediate. The form contains the date, names of students involved in the conflict, their grade levels and their teachers, where the conflict occurred (classroom, hallway, cafeteria, or outside the school), a brief description of the conflict, the requester, and the requester's signature. Part of this step is party introductions and the establishment of ground rules. The ground rules usually include a promise to tell the truth, not to interrupt, not to call names, to work on the problem with an open mind, and to "stay cool" until the problem is resolved.

Step two: information gathering

Even though the requesting party has offered a brief description of what happened in the request form, in this second step, the requesting party is asked to explain fully what happened. The other party or parties are also given the opportunity to present their version of what happened. It is during this time that the mediator reminds parties of the ground rules established in step one—no interruptions, no name-calling. After all parties have offered their explanations of what happened, the mediator asks each person whether s/he has anything to add.

Step three: exploring common interests

Mediation is an integrative and collaborative process. Parties in peer mediation are urged to explore areas where their interests cohere. The mediator guides the parties away from positions and toward interests. It is at the level of interests that common ground is found. When interests have been explored, the mediator and the parties determine what interests are common to the parties and summarize them.

Step four: generating options

Based on shared interests identified in step three, parties, with the assistance of the peer mediator, generate possible options for resolution of the problem. This involves brainstorming solutions, during which parties are encouraged to feel free to make as many suggestions for resolving the problem as they like without the fear of their suggestions being simultaneously judged and evaluated.

Step five: evaluating the options

From a possible longlist of options generated in step four, the mediator and the parties now evaluate the options, noting one or two options that have the best prospect of resolving the problem in a way that meets the best mutual interest and satisfaction of the parties.

Step six: crafting an agreement

Based on what parties agree to in step five as the option that best satisfies their common interests, the mediator writes up an agreement, reads it to the parties, and if they are satisfied with it, they sign it and shake hands.

The six-step model of peer mediation is adapted from the problem-solving, integrative negotiation approach of Johnson and Johnson's (1995) TSP work. Apart from reflecting a common methodological process in the more conventional mediation, the Peacemakers program also offers strong support to the case for transferring peer mediation skills to communities.

Transferring peer mediation skills to community settings—the Peacemakers program

Using the Peacemakers program as a case study, Johnson and Johnson (1996) examined the transferability of the procedures and skills learned in peer mediation to non-classroom and outside school settings. They used three types of measures to determine the extent of what they termed "school-to-home transfer for students receiving Peacemakers training" (p. 331). First, they assessed students' spontaneous use of the learned negotiation and mediation skills and procedures in non-classroom, outside school settings. Second, they analyzed students' written reports of conflicts in which they were involved in outside school settings. Third, they conducted a methodical observation of students in outside school settings.

They found that students effectively transferred the integrative negotiation and mediation skills and procedures, learned at schools implementing the Peacemakers program, to non-classroom and non-school situations (Johnson & Johnson, 1996, p. 331). They also indicated that students reported using the procedures and skills in the home. They corroborated the students' reports with those of parents who reported that their children who were trained in the Peacemakers procedures were "better able to mediate conflicts constructively at home and in other contexts away from school" (Johnson & Johnson, 1996, p. 331). They included anecdotal accounts of some of the parents whose children were trained in the Peacemakers program. One such parent reported that a daughter in the third grade effectively used the Peacemakers procedure to mediate a disagreement between her daughter's older sister and the older sister's boyfriend while all three of them were at a movie. Another parent reported that a fourth grade child interrupted and mediated a heated argument between both parents. The child was able to "take her parents through all the steps of constructive resolution" (Johnson & Johnson, 1996, p. 333). Even the teachers acknowledged the transferability of mediation skills from school settings to family and community settings. According to the authors, one teacher commented:

> The negotiation and mediation skills we are teaching our students will have a definite positive impact on the way our students interact with each other … these skills go beyond the scope of the classroom, and contribute to the betterment of our community, and our world.
>
> *(Johnson & Johnson, 1996, p. 333)*

Evaluation of peer mediation

Evaluation results of peer mediation programs across the United States have revealed the benefits of the initiative (Lam, 1989; Johnson & Johnson, 1992). The results have shown positive effects not only for individual participants, but also for schools and communities (Burrell & Vogl, 1990; Crary, 1992; Harrington & Schine, 1989; Kock, 1988; Metis Associates, Inc., 1990; Stuart, 1991; Bell et al., 2000; Hanson, 1994; Johnson & Johnson, 2001; Johnson et al., 1995; Powell et al., 1996; Graham & Pulvino, 2000; Johnson et al., 1994). From teachers, there has been a remarkable positive shift in their students' attitudes and behaviors (Metis Associates, Inc., 1990). Teachers have also reported a dramatic drop in the number of conflicts they have to deal with (Johnson et al., 1992). These positive changes in school settings, observes Crary (1992), have taken place even in schools where there are significant culturally diverse student bodies.

With these testimonies, it is little wonder, therefore, that peer mediation programs have witnessed a dramatic explosion in American schools and across the world. When the National Association for Mediation in Education (NAME) was formed in 1984, there were already in existence about 50 mediation programs in school districts across the United States. In 1995, NAME reported over 5,000 such programs across the country (Girard, 1995; Miller, 1994). Hakim (1992) announced that California's attorney general in 1994 extolled peer mediation as "one of the most effective means to deter violence in public schools" (p. 8).

The beauty of peer mediation in schools is that it not only enables students to resolve immediate conflicts, but it also equips them with problem-solving skills that are transferable to, and replicable in, future disputes. As noted by Gentry and Benenson (1992), as children learned and took part in the process of peer mediation, there was a significant decline in the rate of sibling conflict, resulting in a reduction in parents' intervention in sibling disputes. This also led to an increase in children's self-esteem and self-confidence (Malia et al., 1995).

Conclusion

This chapter began with the recognition of a major generational shift in children's and young people's cognitive development. It observed that in this age of the internet, social media, and various other forms of digital exposure, today's children and young people are much more informed than their counterparts in past times. They have heightened awareness of the relational and interactional processes, including conflicts, which go on as life's daily routine. The chapter discussed that with peer mediation training, these children and young people learn very useful skills in conflict handling. They learn skills that are not peer-specific, but are applicable and transferable to non-school and non-peer settings such as the family and the community.

Yet, through a misplaced sense of adultism, society misses out on a huge opportunity to tap into the skills that well-trained peer mediators could bring into traditional, non-peer conflict settings, such as the community. The chapter identified the gap in the logic that recognizes the positive results of peer mediation programs in training young people to become competent conflict mediators, yet refuses to offer them needed empowerment and opportunity to take their skills home to their communities.

The chapter reviewed the concept and the emergence of peer mediation as a response to the violent, unsafe, and unhealthy school environment across the world, and particularly in America in the second half of the 20th century. It discussed the purpose of peer mediation and conflict resolution programs in schools, highlighting their success in teaching young people transferable skills in constructive handling of conflict. The six-step model of peer mediation not only mirrors the process of conventional mediation, but also reflects the six-step approach used in the Peacemakers program. One of the findings by Johnson and Johnson (1996), using the Peacemakers program as a case study, is that peer mediation skills are transferable to settings outside the school, including the community. Communities will be better served if and when the energy, skills, and experiences of peer mediators are granted access into community dispute resolution processes.

References

Bell, S.K., Coleman, J.K., Anderson, A., Whelan, J.P. & Wilder, C. (2000) The effectiveness of peer mediation in a low-SES rural elementary school. *Psychology in the Schools*, 37(6): 505–516.

Berkowitz, R. (2014) Student and teacher responses to violence in school: The divergent views of bullies, victims, and bully-victims. *School Psychology International*, 35(5): 485–503.

Burrell, N.A. & Vogl, S.M. (1990) Turf-side conflict mediation for students. *Mediation Quarterly*, 7(3): 237–250.

Chen, J.K. & Astor, R.A. (2012) School variables as mediators of the effect of personal and family factors on school violence in Taiwanese junior high schools. *Youth and Society*, 44(2): 175–200.

Children's Defense Fund. (1991) *The State of America's Children*. Washington, DC: Children's Defense Fund.

Close, C.L. & Lechman, K. (1997) Fostering youth leadership: Students train students and adults in conflict resolution. *Theory into Practice*, 36(1): 11–16.

Crary, D.R. (1992) Community benefits from mediation: A test of the "peace virus" hypothesis. *Mediation Quarterly*, 9(3): 241–252.

Cueto, S., Bosworth, K. & Sailes, J. (1993) *Promoting Peace: Integrating Curricular to Deal with Violence*. Paper presented at the annual meeting of the American Educational Research Association, Atlanta, GA.

Deutsch, M. (1991) Educating beyond hate. *Peace, Environment and Education*, 2(4): 3–19.

DeVoe, J.F., Peter, K., Kaufman, P., Ruddy, S.A., Miller, A.K., Planty, M., Snyder, T.D. & Rand, M.R. (2003) *Indicators of School Crime and Safety: 2003*. Washington, DC: US Department of Education Justice.

Furlong, M.J., Chung, A., Bates, M. & Morrison, R.L. (1995) Profiles of non-victims and multiple-victims of school violence. *Education and Treatment of Children*, 18(3): 282–298.

Gentry, D.B. & Benenson, W.A. (1992) School age peer mediators transfer knowledge to home setting. *Mediation Quarterly*, 10(1): 101–109.

Girard, K.L. (1995) Preparing teachers for conflict resolution in the schools. *Eric Digest: ED387456*. Retrieved from eric.ed.gov/?id=ED387456.

Graham, B.C. & Pulvino, C. (2000) Multicultural conflict resolution: Development, implementation, and assessment of a program for third graders. *Professional School Counseling*, 3(3): 172–181.

Guanci, J.A. (2002) Peer mediation: A winning solution to conflict resolution. *Educational Digest*, 67(6): 26–33.

Hakim, L. (1992) *Conflict Resolution in Schools*. San Rafael, CA: Human Rights Resource Center.

Hanson, M.K. (1994) A conflict resolution/student mediation program: Effects on student attitudes and behaviors. *ERS Spectrum*, 12(4): 9–14.

Harrington, D. & Schine, J. (1989) *Connections: Service Learning in the Middle Grades*. New York: Center for Advanced Study in Education/CASE, the Graduate School and University Center of the City University of New York.

Harrington-Lueker, D. (1992) Blown away by school violence. *Education Digest*, 58(11): 50–54.

Harris, I.M. (1996) Peace education in an urban school district in the United States. *Peabody Journal of Education*, 73(3): 63–83

Jacobson, M. & Lombard, R. (1992) Effective school climate: Roles for peers, practitioners, and principals. *Rural Research Report*, 3(4): 1–6.

Johnson, D.W. & Johnson, R.T. (1992) Positive independence: Key to effective cooperation. In R. Hertz-Lazarowitz & N. Miller (eds) *Interaction in Cooperative Groups: The Theoretical Anatomy of Group Learning* (pp. 174–199). New York: Cambridge University Press.

Johnson, D.W. & Johnson, R.T. (1995) *Teaching Students to be Peacemakers*. Edina, MN: Interaction Book Company.

Johnson, D.W. & Johnson, R.T. (1996) Teaching all students how to manage conflicts constructively: The Peacemakers program. *Journal of Negro Education*, 65(3): 322–335.

Johnson, D.W. & Johnson, R.T. (2001) Peer mediation in an inner-city elementary school. *Urban Education*, 36(2): 165–178.

Johnson, D.W. & Johnson, R.T. (2004) Implementing the "Teaching Students to be Peacemakers program." *Theory into Practice*, 43(1): 68–79.

Johnson, D.W., Johnson, R.T. & Dudley, B. (1992) Effects of peer mediation training on elementary school students. *Mediation Quarterly*, 10(1): 89–97.

Johnson, D.W., Johnson, R.T., Dudley, B. & Acikgoz, K. (1994) Effects of conflict resolution training on elementary school students. *Journal of Social Psychology*, 134(6): 803–817.

Johnson, D.W., Johnson, R.T., Dudley, B. & Magnuson, D. (1995) Training elementary school students to manage conflict. *Journal of Social Psychology*, 135(6): 673–686.

Kasik, N.C. & Kumcagiz, H. (2014) The effects of the conflict resolution and peer mediation training program on self-esteem and conflict resolution skills. *International Journal of Academic Research*, 9(1): 179–186.

Khoury-Kassabri, M., Astor, R.A. & Bebnbenishty, R. (2009) Middle Eastern adolescents' perpetration of school violence against peers and teachers. A crosscultural and ecological analysis. *Journal of Interpersonal Violence*, 24(1): 159–182.

Kock, M.S. (1988) Resolving disputes: Students can do it better. *NASSP Bulletin*, 75(504): 16–18.

Lam, J.A. (1989) *The Impact of Conflict Resolution Programs on Schools: A Review and Synthesis of the Evidence*. Amherst, MA: National Association for Mediation in Education.

Liang, H., Flisher, A.J. & Lombard, C.J. (2007) Bullying, violence, and risk behavior in South African school students. *Child Abuse and Neglect*, 31(2), 161.

Loupe, D. & Shepard, B. (1993). A common sight for students: Guns at school. *Atlanta Constitution*, April 13, A1.

Malia, J.A., Cunningham, J.L., MacMillan, E. & Wynn, E. (1995) Expanding the policy infrastructure for resolving family-related disputes: Mediation as a technology. *Family Relations*, 44(1): 19–27.

Maxwell, J. (1989) Mediation in the schools: Self-regulation, self-esteem and self-discipline. *Mediation Quarterly*, 7(2): 149–155.

Metis Associates, Inc. (1990) *The Resolving Conflict Creatively Program: 1988–1989—Summary of Significant Findings*. National Criminal Justice Reference service (NCJ Number: NCJ 160433).

Miller, E. (1994) Promising practices: Peer mediation catches on, but some adults don't. *Harvard Education Newsletter*, 3(3), 8 NCJ 160483.

Powell, K.E., Muir-McClain, L. & Halasyamani, L. (1996) A review of selected school-based conflict resolution and peer mediation projects. *Peer Facilitator Quarterly*, 13(3): 31–38.

Roberts, S., Zhang, J., Truman, J. & Snyder, T.D. (2012) *Indicators of School Crime and Safety: 2011*. Washington, DC: National Center for Education Statistics, US Department of Education, and Bureau of Justice Statistics, Office of Justice Programs, US Department of Justice.

Schomberg, R. (1992) *A Developmental Approach to Conflict Resolution*. Paper based on presentation at the annual conference of the National Association for the Education of Young Children, Anaheim, CA.

Smith, P.K. (2002) *Violence in Schools: The Response in Europe*. London: Routledge.

Smith, P.K. & Brain, P. (2000) Bullying in schools: Lessons from two decades of research. *Aggressive Behavior*, 26: 1–9.

Stevahn, L. (2004) Integrating conflict resolution training into the curriculum. *Theory into Practice*, 43(1): 50–58.

Stuart, L.A. (1991) *Conflict Resolution Using Mediation Skills in Elementary Schools*. Charlottesville: The University of Virginia, Curry School of Education. (ERIC Document Reproduction Service No. ED 333 258).

Tolson, A.R., McDonald, S.E. & Moriarty, A.R. (1992) Peer mediation among high school students: A test of effectiveness. *Social Work in Education*, 14(2): 86–93.

Ziller, R.C., Hagey, J., Smith, M.C. & Long, B.H. (1969) Self-esteem: A self-social construct. *Journal of Consulting and Clinical Psychology*, 33(1): 84–95.

PART V

Mediating within environmental settings

28

CONFLICT, CLIMATE CHANGE, AND ENVIRONMENTAL CATASTROPHE

How mediators can help save the planet

Kenneth Cloke

The oil spill by BP in the Gulf of Mexico several years ago highlights an escalating set of difficulties in our responses to environmental catastrophes, with echoes that resonate and reverberate with experiences responding to Hurricane Katrina in New Orleans, earthquakes in Haiti and Peru, firestorms in Russia, flooding in Pakistan, tsunamis in Indonesia and Japan, and others. As population, technology, and globalization continue to expand, so undoubtedly will environmental deterioration, including global warming, allowing us reasonably to anticipate, and perhaps predict, the following outcomes:[1]

- Environmental disasters will become more widespread, severe, impactful, costly and common
- Conflicts will be triggered by these events, and escalate as more individuals, groups, nations and ecosystems are impacted
- These conflicts will accumulate around the failures in local, national, and global emergency response systems
- The ability to resolve these conflicts quickly and effectively will have a direct impact on the degree of damage they create
- Mediation, collaborative negotiation, and allied conflict resolution methodologies will be used to address and resolve climate change and environmental disaster disputes

The logical chain

As human populations have grown more numerous and technologically advanced, we have naturally had a greater ecological impact on the planet. Simply by not paying attention to these impacts for centuries and seeking to maximize our separate competitive short-term advantage as nations, corporations, and separated communities, we have wasted exhaustible resources, despoiled and desecrated our environment, and created the preconditions for mass extinctions and global catastrophe. Consequently, it is no longer possible to pursue non-sustainable approaches to survival, particularly those that aggravate these problems. Instead, these problems demand not only the collective attention of everyone, but respectful, collaborative, democratic ways of communicating; complex, creative, paradoxical ways of solving problems; and interest-based methods for negotiating, discussing, and resolving conflicts over how to address them. Without these shifts, it is likely that many people around the planet will not survive.

A number of far-reaching environmental changes have been taking place on a global scale for some time, and increasing in their pace, momentum, and potential to inflict disastrous consequences on human societies internationally. Perhaps the most important of these changes is that the *rate* of change is itself changing, in an exponential direction. Changes in the natural world can, of course, take place incrementally and piece by piece, or exponentially, with increasing rapidity. Exponential changes look something like Figure 28.1.

Many of the most serious problems we face today reveal rates of change that can arguably be plotted along this curve. These include, but are by no means limited to, the following:

- Size and density of human population
- CO_2 and methane emissions that increase global warming
- Species extinctions
- Loss of tropical rainforest and woodland
- Desertification, erosion, and loss of arable land
- Decreasing genetic diversity in agricultural commodities
- Loss of biodiversity
- Loss of fish stocks
- Resistance to antibiotics
- Pollution, loss of biodegradability, and use of toxic chemicals
- Increasing severity of natural catastrophes and weather conditions
- Vulnerability to pandemics
- Rising cost of medical care
- Loss of potable water
- Disruption of weather patterns
- Migration as a result of these environmental changes
- The global effect of local, relatively minor environmental decisions

In addition to these, we are facing worldwide problems in other areas that can easily trigger severe environmental consequences, escalate conflicts, and make it more difficult for us to solve these problems, including:

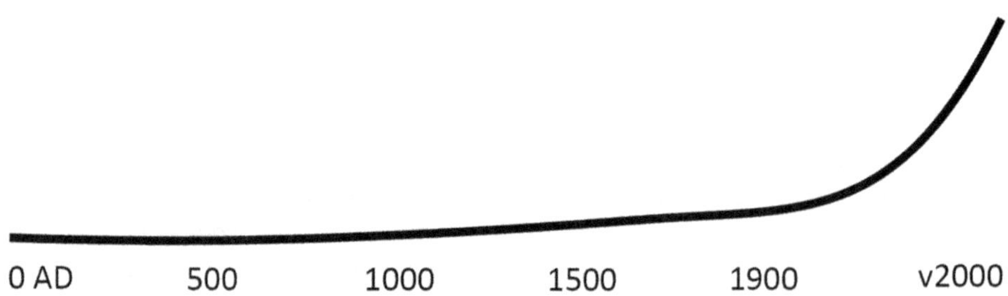

FIGURE 28.1 Exponential changes

- The increasing destructive power and availability of military technology
- Willingness to use war and resort to violence
- Nuclear proliferation
- Intentional targeting of civilians in warfare
- Terrorism and unending cycles of revenge and retaliation
- Acceptability of the use of torture and cruelty in response
- Global financial crises
- Unregulated economic transactions
- Financial cutbacks in government services, especially in education, corporate regulation, and science and violence
- Increasing poverty, social inequality, and economic inequity
- Destabilization due to political autocracy and dictatorship
- Hostility to immigrants, refugees, minorities, and outsiders
- Rise in prejudice and intolerance
- Genocidal policies and ethnic cleansing
- Growth of the drug trade, sexual trafficking, and organized crime

Jared Diamond (2004) argues from a somewhat different premise that we are presently facing 12 sources of ecological and social collapse, each of which is growing steadily and has to be solved correctly in order to avoid catastrophic consequences:

- Deforestation and habitat destruction
- Water management problems
- Soil problems (erosion, salinization, and soil fertility losses)
- Effects of introduced species on native species
- Overhunting
- Overfishing
- Human population growth
- Increased per capita impact of people
- Human-caused climate change
- Energy shortages
- Buildup of toxic chemicals in the environment
- Full human utilization of the Earth's photosynthetic capacity

In Diamond's (2004) well-researched account, it was rare for earlier societies to face more than one of these crises at a time, or for them to spread beyond local environmental limits, yet all seem to be occurring today. Moreover, globalization has introduced a synergistic element into the feedback loop, allowing each of these crises to deepen and aggravate the others, speeding the rate of collapse and spreading it around the world. Diamond (2004) provides a framework for assessing the likelihood of environmental collapse, which includes a quantitative and qualitative assessment of the following criteria:

- Environmental damage
- Climate change
- Hostile neighbors
- Friendly trade partners
- Society's responses to its environmental problems (including whether elites believe they can escape the problem)

Diamond (2004) does not explicitly cite funding for education, science and technology, or support for the use of a rich array of conflict resolution methods, yet the willingness to use mediation, collaborative negotiation, public dialogue, group facilitation, conflict resolution systems design, and similar conflict resolution techniques needs to be included in any realistic assessment of the likelihood of eventual ecological collapse. This is extremely important for our purposes, since it places conflict resolution skills at the center of international efforts to prevent and respond to environmental disasters.

A number of scientific experts in different fields were asked in 2010 by *Scientific American* to estimate the limits on growth, citing preindustrial levels, current levels, and their best estimate of the boundary beyond which more serious consequences might occur (Foley, 2010). Their results are in Table 28.1.

In most of these cases, there is a growing scientific consensus that we are well beyond the boundary conditions that permit environmental sustainability. A wide range of scientific reports from around the world confirm the existence of these problems, the urgent need for solutions, and the devastating consequences of failing to address them. In addition, a number of these problems are synergistically related to others, so that deterioration in one will likely cause increased deterioration in others. Narrowing our focus to the issue of climate change, even conservative scientific studies document the following significant shifts in recent years, with each appearing to increase irregularly on an annual basis, but significantly over decades. To demonstrate that global warming is happening, the following statistics for the 20th century were presented in scientific papers circulated at the United Nations (UN) Copenhagen

TABLE 28.1 Estimated limits of growth

	Preindustrial	*Current*	*Boundary*
Climate change	CO_2 = 280 parts per million (ppm)	387	350
Ocean acidification	Aragonite saturation = 3.44 Omega units	2.90	2.75
Stratospheric ozone depletion	Value = 290 Dobson units	283	276
Nitrogen removal	Value = 0 tons/year nitrogen removal from atmosphere	133	39
Phosphorous cycle	Value = 1 ton/year into oceans	10	12
Freshwater use	Value = 415 cubic kilometers/year	2,600	4,000
Land use	Value = negligible conversion to cropland	11.7%	15%
Biodiversity loss	Value = 0.1 to 1.0 species per year	100	10
Aerosol loading	Value = negligible particulate concentrations in atmosphere	undetermined	undetermined
Chemical pollution	Value = negligible amount emitted to or concentrated in the environment	undetermined	undetermined

Source: Foley, 2010.

Climate Change Conference in 2009, which I attended with a team from Mediators Beyond Borders:

- Global average surface temperature increased by 0.6 °C over the 20th century
- There has been a 10 percent reduction in snow cover ice since the late 1960s
- The 1990s was the warmest decade and 1998 the warmest year in the last 1,000 years in the Northern Hemisphere, exceeded only by the decade that followed it
- There has been a 2–4 percent increase in the frequency of heavy precipitation events in the Northern Hemisphere mid and high latitudes over the latter half of the 20th century
- Over the last 50 years, night-time minimum temperatures have increased by about 0.2 °C per decade
- There has been a reduction of about two weeks in the annual duration of lake and river ice over the 20th century
- Northern Hemisphere spring and summer sea-ice extent has decreased by 10–15 percent since the 1950s
- There has been a 40 percent decline in late summer Arctic sea-ice thickness in recent decades
- Global average sea level has increased by 10–20 cm during the 20th century
- There has been a widespread retreat of mountain glaciers during the 20th century
- There has been a 0.5–1 percent per decade increase in Northern Hemisphere mid-latitude precipitation during the 20th century

More recent studies (UN Framework Convention on Climate Change—UNFCCC) have developed forecasts for the future impact of climate change that conservatively, to my mind, include the following projections:

- Global average surface temperature is expected to increase by from 1.4 °C to 5.8 °C by 2100, a rate of warming that is unprecedented in the last 10,000 years
- Global average precipitation will increase over the 21st century, with more intense precipitation events and irregular precipitation in areas that have become accustomed to stable rainfall
- Land areas will warm more than the global average
- Snow cover and sea ice are projected to decrease dramatically
- There will be a loss of agricultural stability as crops require temperate weather
- Global mean sea level is projected to increase by 9–88 cm or more by 2100, and in some reports, by as much as 2–5 meters
- Glaciers and icecaps are projected to continue their widespread retreat

The list of evidence continues, yet somehow exceeds our ability to grasp it. One reason may be that we are surrounded with so many other, more immediate and palpable catastrophes. Another may be that the news media make so much of catastrophe in order to attract customers to secure the advertising that pays their way, and do not want to cover anything that might be bad for business or advertising revenues. A third reason may be that while many of these changes are taking place rapidly, and in some cases exponentially, several interdependent yet equally critical changes are taking place only gradually, allowing us to feel that something is in fact being done about them. Moreover, responding to global environmental disasters and climate change will inevitably have to include finding solutions for a much broader range of social, economic, and political problems, such as:

- Implementation of solutions to poverty and hunger
- Reduced vulnerability of civilian populations to terrorism
- Reductions in bigotry and prejudice
- Fewer assertions of territoriality
- Decreased willingness to use warfare, torture, and threats of force
- Increased effectiveness of national and international regulatory institutions
- Responses to amplified vulnerability to infectious diseases
- Less openness of political institutions, including in the USA, to corporate influence, bribery, and control
- Greater acceptance, expanded training, and widespread institutionalization of conflict resolution
- Regulation of currency speculators, hedge funds, and multinational corporations
- Improved methods of international cooperation
- Increasing life expectancy and reducing child mortality
- Reducing the rising cost of medical care
- Elimination of illiteracy
- Improvements in the treatment of women and children
- More rapid government responses to ecological problems
- Far greater awareness of the extent, seriousness and exponential increase in many environmental and climate change indicators

The last item deserves a more detailed explanation. One of the main difficulties in responding to exponential changes is that our awareness and understanding are not equipped to recognize it, and inevitably lag behind even the hardest scientific evidence. As Albert Einstein (1945) ominously wrote following the explosion of atomic bombs over Hiroshima and Nagasaki, "[e]verything has changed, except our way of thinking." Yet the way we think is perhaps the largest part of the problem, reminding us that, as Einstein also famously observed, "[t]he significant problems we face cannot be solved at the same level of thinking we were at when we created them" (Calaprice, 2005).

There is a wonderful story told by science writer K.C. Cole (1997) that illustrates the difference between exponential and incremental change, and highlights our difficulty in assessing its importance. Assume for a moment that two bacteria are living inside a bottle, and that they reproduce and double in number once each minute, allowing us to predict that at the end of one hour they will completely fill the bottle. How much advance warning will they have that they are about to do so? The answer is nearly none, since at 58 minutes, before the hour, with only two minutes remaining, the bottle is only a quarter full. At 59 minutes, with one minute remaining, the bottle is still only half full. In another minute, the bottle will be filled, and in another, the bacteria will fill an entire second bottle. It is unfortunate, yet entirely possible, that we are now just a cycle or two from irreversible environmental collapse.

Global interdependency

We know from the scientific study of chaos and complexity that the flapping of a butterfly's wings in the Amazonian rainforest can trigger a tornado in Texas. Is it not equally possible for the killing of an unarmed civilian by a US soldier in Baghdad to spark a hurricane of political anger that results in the death of equally unarmed civilians in an unrelated city elsewhere on the planet? Or for a small mistake in the hierarchical transmission of safety information at BP to devastate an entire ecosystem?

The scientific definition of chaos is "sensitive dependence on initial conditions" (Gleick, 1987). As any system approaches criticality and begins to undergo a phase transition, its previously stable systemic makeup becomes increasingly unstable and dependent on minor fluctuations in its environment. This scientific metaphor suggests that instability in the social, economic, political, and environmental conditions in one region can dramatically impact people in other regions. The science of ecology reveals that the loss of even a single important species can rapidly turn catastrophic for others, triggering a cascade of consequences vastly greater than anything we might have imagined beforehand. The same can be said of seemingly isolated events, such as those that followed the elimination of apartheid in South Africa, the collapse of Enron, or the assassination of Archduke Ferdinand prior to World War I.

If we consider, for example, avian influenza, or bird flu, it is clear that extreme poverty and a consequent reliance on domestic poultry for survival anywhere in the world will create favorable conditions for the H5N1 or similar virus to mutate into a form transmissible by air between human beings. The ease of international travel, panic, and a desire to escape infection could then spread the virus rapidly to other countries, creating global pandemic. Similarly, without a coordinated international response, scientists are nearly unanimous that significant temperature increases will occur before the end of the current century, leading to rising sea levels that will inundate many of the world's urban centers, triggering mass migrations, heightened competition for scarce resources, militaristic responses, and political polarizations that will make environmental problems more difficult to solve. As we become more interdependent, a disaster in one part of the planet can easily turn into a catastrophe elsewhere, making it clear that global problems require global solutions. As climate is naturally chaotic and unpredictable, even small, seemingly insignificant changes can produce vastly larger ones later.

The problem with existing solutions

To solve any of the problems I have cited, and others we will inevitably confront as we develop and expand, we need better ways of communicating with each other, expanded skills in open and honest dialogue, and better techniques for solving problems, negotiating collaboratively, and resolving disputes without warfare, coercion, and other adversarial methods. This may sound simplistic, even idealistic. Clearly, our history of working together to solve pressing social, economic, political, and ecological problems offers few reasons for unabashed confidence. Instead, it reveals an astonishing record of avoidable disasters, pointless miseries, and needless deaths. For centuries, we have gotten away with murder, and no longer have resources to waste. Indeed, none of the following well-established, centuries-old problem-solving mechanisms by themselves can succeed in solving these problems:

- Military force
- Power-based diplomatic negotiations
- Negotiated treaties and international agreements
- Legal interventions, litigation, and the rule of law
- Administrative rules and regulations or policies and procedures
- The United Nations, as presently constituted
- Capitalism and market principles
- National political leaders and institutions

So what is left? The answer is, *we* are, we as citizens and we as mediators. Mediation can make a difference. As our problems have multiplied, so has our social and technological ability to solve them. We have vastly increased our scientific and technological capabilities in recent years, and have also enormously improved our understanding and skills in effective communication, group facilitation, creative problem solving, public dialogue, conflict coaching, collaborative negotiation, prejudice reduction and bias awareness, mediation, conflict resolution system design, and similar methods. These are precisely the skills we need in order to "save the planet."

If we consider the BP gulf oil spill as an example, there were numerous well-recognized long-term problems that led to that environmental disaster, or contributed to making it worse. In my mind, these include:

- Dependence on fossil fuels
- Powerful oil and gas companies with assets and sales larger than the gross domestic products of all but a handful of nations
- Inadequate market mechanisms to dampen the lust for quick profits, creating an incentive to cut corners on costs, including safety
- Regulatory agencies that are led, managed and lobbied by people who pay greater attention to corporate influence than public safety and environmental sustainability
- Disputes over how to manage the off-shore platform that were resolved hierarchically, bureaucratically, and autocratically, leaving those with direct experience of the problem without the power or authority to solve it
- Concentration of the problem-solving authority in the hands of those who were more concerned with company profits than with safety or environmental damage

In the BP spill, as in the *Exxon Valdez* spill before it, there was a concerted effort in political circles and the media to find someone to blame for what happened. Yet a secondary effect of blaming individuals is that the systems that permitted, caused, or encouraged the mistake are ignored and let off the hook, increasing the likelihood of fresh occurrences in the future. Without mediation and a systemic approach to future disasters, relief will be less effective, and delayed for years, if not decades. In responding to BP and similar disasters, and in efforts to negotiate climate change issues at Copenhagen and similar international problem-solving endeavors, political leaders, envoys, and delegates continue to rely on classic international diplomatic processes, which are, for the most part, adversarial, reactive distributive and power based, and tend to have the following characteristics:

- Complex rules, protocols, policies, and procedures that make the process arduous, bureaucratic and confusing, and discourage conversation, participation and informal problem solving
- Large, formal, highly structured meetings with processes that are influenced by political agendas, that attempt to consider multiple wide-ranging proposals to modify the language of proposed legal agreements
- Limited opportunities for small, informal, unstructured conversations with open agendas, collaborative dialogues, and creative processes designed to satisfy common interests
- Public declarations, official statements and pronouncements in which positions are elaborated without engaging in genuine exchanges, admitting mistakes, or stopping to discuss important questions, critiques and alternative approaches

- Disagreements over diverse approaches and proposals that escalate into hardened positions and avoidable conflicts that result in impasse because there are no conflict resolution processes or professionals available who are empowered to assist in clarifying communication, brainstorming options, facilitating dialogues, and mediating solutions
- Traditional behind-the-scenes "hardball" negotiations, with arm-twisting, hidden agendas and adversarial, competitive bargaining tactics in which the largest, most powerful and wealthiest parties "win," while others "lose" and leave feeling excluded, disempowered and disrespected

There are much better ways of reaching agreements, using mediation, facilitation, collaborative negotiation, and informal problem solving. It would be possible, for example, for the UN, without significant financial investments, to measurably improve the quality of its meetings and negotiations at important climate change events in at least the following 20 ways, by:

- Conducting an in-depth, broadly inclusive, collaborative evaluation of the process used in Copenhagen and other climate change meetings to identify what worked and what could be improved
- Developing a comprehensive set of process recommendations for future talks and securing agreement to implement them prior to the session, and brief delegates on them before they arrive
- Consulting widely with diverse public and private sector organizations and individuals who have experience designing dispute resolution systems and can provide ways of improving the entire negotiation process
- Reaching agreement on a variety of next steps that can be taken when consensus is not reached, including dialogue, informal problem solving, collaborative negotiation and mediation
- Asking each delegation to future talks to include among their members one or more trained mediators, collaborative negotiators, ombudsmen, or small-group facilitators who can assist in bridging differences as they occur
- Appointing fast-forming, diverse problem-solving teams with experts representing all nations, regions, groups, types of alternatives and ranges of opinion, with professional facilitators and recorders to aid them in their work
- Facilitating meetings of climate change experts and scientists to develop consensus-based recommendations, including them on problem-solving teams, and convening meetings of diverse specialists to advise delegates on specific topics
- Conducting frequent open dialogue sessions on critical topics without attempting to reach agreement and providing multiple opportunities for free-ranging small-group discussions, and open recommendations for ways of reaching consensus
- Offering free training sessions throughout the process for individual delegations and teams in collaborative negotiation, group facilitation, and conflict resolution
- Continuing to search for preventative measures that can be adopted by all parties and UN organizations, that will help reduce the severity of future problems
- Appointing facilitators, ombudsmen, and mediators in advance for every meeting and asking them to recommend ways of improving the meeting
- Allowing facilitators to stop the process if it is not working, discuss it openly, invite suggestions, and propose ways of improving it

- Assigning UN mediators or ombudsmen to every delegation, and to each small-group and problem-solving meeting
- Periodically conducting process checks to make sure everything is on track and making improvements as needed
- Focusing not only on reaching a single comprehensive agreement, but also on smaller, specialized, limited, tentative, provisional, national, regional and bloc agreements as well, then work to accumulate and amalgamate them into a single draft
- Considering the entire multi-year agreement drafting process as a conflict system and using conflict resolution systems design principles to develop better ways of responding to obstacles, impasses and conflicts as they occur
- Drastically simplifying and reducing the rigidity and formality of protocols, rules and official processes, especially as they effect the negotiation and agreement-writing process
- Shortening large meetings and breaking participants up into small, diverse, informal teams to brainstorm alternatives, agree on common goals or shared values, and reach consensus recommendations on specific problems, led by facilitators and mediators
- Sending experienced negotiators, facilitators, ombudsmen, and mediators to meet with the parties in advance of conferences and negotiating sessions to help set targets and timetables and encourage compromises that could lead to better and quicker agreements
- Creating international negotiation and conflict resolution protocols, model mediation language, and annexes to existing agreements that encourage a broad range of collaborative interest-based dispute resolution processes, including mediation, ombudsmen, facilitated dialogue, and similar methods

In these ways, it is possible for professional mediators, collaborative negotiators, ombudsmen, group facilitators, and conflict resolution systems designers to contribute to making climate change and other UN meetings more effective and collaborative. Mediation and conflict resolution can also be used to resolve conflicts that arise after agreements have been reached, and a culture of conflict resolution can be systematically reinforced throughout the community of nation-states.

A great deal is riding on the success of these negotiations, and the world's most experienced conflict resolution professionals, if asked, would be honored and pleased to work together to create a more thoughtful and acceptable set of recommendations for action. Thus, there is little to lose and much to gain from asking for their help, analyzing new approaches, and beginning to experiment with them. This does not mean it will be easy to move away from existing processes or alter methods that are familiar and understood, even when they prove in practice to be ineffective, inefficient, and time consuming. Mediators and conflict resolvers with the right approach have experience convincing conflicting parties to try new ways of achieving their goals and designing more successful agreements.

What needs to be done

Our ability to act in harmony with ecological limits is also reduced by our dependence for social status on luxuries and material possessions, our unrelenting economic expansion and competitive pursuit of profits, and our division into hostile, undemocratic nation-states, adversarial political parties and factions, and intolerant religious orthodoxies. Each of these sources of chronic conflict reduces our ability to think and act globally.

A revealing report by an official British commission on global warming chaired by Sir Nicholas Stern (2006) reported that climate change "is the greatest and widest-ranging market failure ever seen" (p. 1). Former head of the US Fish and Wildlife Service, Mollie Beattie (n.d.), wrote: "In the long term, the economy and the environment are the same thing. If it's unenvironmental, it is uneconomical. That is the rule of nature." Still, the USA, China, and other governments continue to act in isolation, using aggressive and hostile bargaining techniques, competitive market principles, power diplomacy, and threats of economic sanction or military force to achieve their goals, all of which increase resistance and reduce the likelihood of solving environmental problems.

If we are to solve environmental problems internationally and sustainably over a period of decades, if not centuries, it is becoming increasingly clear that we will not be able to do so without helping people in less developed countries improve the quality of their lives, or by enforcing the changes we want by military force or coercive adversarial negotiations. Instead, we will require honest communication, egalitarian financing, genuine collaboration, democratic decision making, and a massive infusion of interest-based processes, conflict resolution initiatives, and interest-based interventions on all levels.

As a result, we will not be able to require problem-solving methods that allow the wealthiest countries to predetermine outcomes and processes in advance, or that pursue selfish economic policies, or that stack the deck in favor of wealthy nations that are already technologically advanced. If we do, others will dig in, drag their feet, and change efforts will falter. Instead, we require a collaborative attitude that encourages participatory problem solving, greater use of consensus, and a shift from relying on power or rights to trying to satisfy everyone's interests.

Over the last several decades, we have developed a powerful, complex set of methods and techniques that enhance collaboration and conflict resolution. These have proven highly successful, even with committed adversaries. While our skills have improved substantially, we have yet to fully acknowledge the need to adapt them to reducing environmental conflicts, or assuaging the chronic social, economic, and political hostilities that fuel them; or the need to implement them globally in a large-scale, organized, and coherent way.

At the moment, we are not even close to being able to respond sensibly or successfully to global disasters, let alone accept responsibility for solving the far more arduous problem of becoming ecologically sustainable and halting global warming in the long run. What is worse, the skills we need to leverage these changes are widely regarded as optional, too expensive, "touchy-feely," and threatening to the social, economic, and political status quo. How, then, do we overcome these obstacles?

Saving all sentient beings

There is an ancient Buddhist command that directs each of us to personally save all sentient or conscious beings. I have always thought this meant that no matter how difficult or seemingly impossible the task, it is important to extend compassion to others, focus on what blocks our growth and commitment, be mindful of our impact on others, and dismantle the pessimistic attitude that assumes it cannot be done.

Changing times, however, require fresh interpretations, and I now believe this command needs to be taken quite literally. I believe it is uniquely the task of this generation to harness the power of conflict resolution and associated techniques and contribute to actually saving as many sentient beings as possible, principally by bringing conflict resolution to bear on environmental problems, building preventative global systems, and working to transform and transcend conflicts at their internal and external sources.

There is a famous story about two people walking along a beach that is strewn with thousands of dying starfish washed up from a storm. As one of them begins tossing the starfish back into the ocean, the other remarks: "What difference can that make?" The first person answers, "it made a difference to that one." They both begin throwing them back (Eiseley, 1969). More deeply, the Dalai Lama wrote: "'We' and 'they' no longer exist. This planet is just us. The destruction of one area is the destruction of yourself. That is the new reality" (Ritter, 2005).

Just as our personal development reaches a limit in our capacity for affection and compassion, which is revealed in our external relationships with those who differ from us, our ability to make heartfelt connections with others rests on our internal capacity for affection and compassion. We cannot save ourselves without saving the world, or the world without saving ourselves. In this way, the original paradoxical meaning of the command endures. In order to save others and ourselves, we need to become more aware of the environment and our impact on it. This leads to the profound realization that we and our environment are one. We will only finally succeed in dismantling selfishness, apathy, prejudice, greed, and brutality by becoming aware of their sources internally within ourselves, and by redesigning the social, economic, and political systems that sustain them, transforming, and transcending them in each of their locations.

As science and technology revolutionize our understanding of natural phenomena, they exponentially expand our capacity to manipulate and change the world. However, our compassion, open-heartedness, and wisdom have not grown at the same pace. In the past, when science has outstripped wisdom, we have discovered that a lot of knowledge and very little heart can be an extremely dangerous thing.

The way forward

So how do we help save the planet? I believe we start by educating ourselves regarding global problems and accepting responsibility for improving them, including ourselves. Next, we realize that neither we nor any group or nation can succeed in isolation, and that the depth, seriousness, and reach of our problems require international collaboration. Finally, we recognize that our capacity for collaboration will remain limited in the absence of:

- Profound appreciation of value and importance of diversity as a basis for unity
- Strategic insight into the chronic sources of social, economic, and political conflict
- Willingness to apply advanced communication, negotiation, and conflict resolution skills to the ways we interact socially, economically, and politically
- Concerted efforts to develop more skillful approaches to resolving conflicts before they result in intolerable, irreversible damage
- Readiness to redesign our social, economic, and political institutions and practices from a conflict resolution perspective

It is possible that we will not succeed, but are these not worthwhile goals in any event? Might they not lead to significant improvements in the quality of our communication and relationships, regardless of their eventual outcome? Do not our very lives, and those of our environmentally inseparable cousins among other species increasingly depend on our doing so? As the brilliant anthropologist Margaret Mead (n.d.) presciently wrote, "[w]e are continually faced with great opportunities which are brilliantly disguised as unsolvable problems."

The problems we now face offer immense opportunities for improving our condition and rethinking our social, economic, political, and ecological relationships. Doing so will develop our capacity to prevent, resolve, transform, and transcend conflicts at their chronic sources, and allow us to see that the solutions to our problems are already imaginable and being lived every day. Mostly what is lacking is our realization that we can indeed make a difference. The world is waiting.

Note

1 Excerpted from Cloke, K. (2013). *The Dance of Opposites: Explorations in Mediation, Dialogue, and Conflict Resolution Systems Design*. Goodmedia.

References

Beattie, M. (n.d.) Environmental education quotes. *Western Kentucky University*. Retrieved from www.wku.edu/cees/ee_quotes.php.

Calaprice, A. (2005) *The New Quotable Einstein*. Princeton, NJ: Princeton University Press.

Cole, K.C. (1997) *The Universe and the Teacup: The Mathematics of Truth and Beauty*. Orlando, FL: Harcourt Brace & Company.

Diamond, J. (2004) *Collapse: How Societies Choose to Fail or Succeed*. London: Penguin Group.

Einstein, A. (1945) Goodreads. Retrieved from www.goodreads.com/quotes/17014-the-release-of-atomic-power-has-changed-everything-except-our.

Eiseley, L. (1969) The star thrower from the unexpected universe. *Papu*. Retrieved from www.eiseley.org/Star_Thrower_Cook.pdf.

Foley, J. (2010) Boundaries for a healthy planet. *Scientific American*, 302(4): 54–57.

Gleick, J. (1987) *Chaos: Making a New Science*. New York: Penguin Books.

Mead, M. (n.d.) Goodreads. Retrieved from www.goodreads.com/author/quotes/61107.Margaret_Mead.

Ritter, K. (2005) Rutgers hears Dalai Lama push for peace. *Philly.com*. Retrieved from articles.philly.com/2005-09-26/news/25428561_1_tibetan-people-14th-dalai-lama-tenzin-gyatso.

Stern, N. (2006) Stern review: Economics of climate change. Retrieved from www.wwf.se/source.php/1169157/Stern%20Report_Exec%20Summary.pdf.

UNFCCC. (n.d.) *United Nations Framework Convention on Climate Change*. Retrieved from climate-l.iisd.org/events/unfccc-cop-21/.

29

MEDIATORS AS ADVOCATES IN CLIMATE NEGOTIATIONS

The power of neutrality

Thomas Fiutak

Too often, those within the mediation world become focused only on the interaction of the parties rather than understanding the importance of the cultural process that brought the parties and mediator together. This phenomenon acts as a barrier when attempting to create the incentives that reinforce the parties to convene and actually address common concerns. No other topic than the reality of climate change now and in the foreseeable future poses the need for us to reconsider how the concept of mediation and the role of the mediator can have a profound effect on how effective and successful all nations of the world will be in addressing a common interest of survival.

Toward this end, this chapter addresses three themes where mediators can play critical leadership roles relative to climate change: advocacy in the public policy sector; informed intervention; and complex community processes. Based on my five years of experience as an observer of the United Nations Framework Convention on Climate Change (UNFCCC)[1] for Mediators Beyond Borders,[2] we need to refine the strategies for advocating for the understanding and inclusion of mediation practices within complex climate change policy formation. Mediators must become familiar with both the contesting practices and theories that intersect the climate question and to recognize at what junctures the particular skills of the mediator can best be put to use. Of particular interest is how to lead from a base of neutrality. Finally, we need to redefine the mediation process to include an understanding of arena building (Fiutak, 2009), where invitation and convening of large group interactions of multiple stakeholders fosters real-time collision of interests inherent to climate change debates.

As my purpose is to broaden the concept of mediation and its advocacy within this increasingly complex world, it is important to understand how I wish the reader to interpret my definition of mediation, actually as meta-mediation, which is the mediating of the process by which we can mediate. Within this context of the global negotiations regarding climate change, mediation should be understood as an intentional intervention by a neutral party for the purpose of resolving disputes among or between individuals, groups, organizations and systems, which is inclusive of the culturally appropriate processes by which the stakeholders who are necessary and sufficient to resolve the disputes are identified, invited, and convened prior to the facilitation by the neutral.

Advocacy in the public policy sector

At its inception in 2009, Mediators Beyond Borders, International (MBBI) had recognized the critical nature of the negotiation process inherent in the UNFCCC relative to the climate policy development, and their application. Beginning with the Conference of the Parties in Copenhagen (COP15) in that year, a delegation from MBBI had been granted observer status, which allowed a limited number of members access to the UNFCCC negotiation process as regulated by the UNFCCC Secretariat. This meant that along with the other organizations with observer status, we could interact with the country delegates and their staff; attend plenaries and those working groups that were open to observers; present side events that highlighted specific interests or informed analysis regarding climate issues specific to the observer organizations utilizing space and resources provided by the Secretariat; and attend both formal and informal briefings from UNFCCC leadership regarding the status and direction of the negotiation process.

Within this context, MBBI framed three initial goals for their involvement. First, to develop an understanding of the complexities of the UNFCCC negotiation process; second, to advocate on behalf of all mediators throughout the world for application of mediation principles, including the use of mediators where appropriate to culture and available expertise, in the creation and application of climate-related policies; third, to advance the inclusion of language, where appropriate, that includes mediation and other neutrally supported processes.

Informed intervention

While the common denominator of mediation is the focus on process that is inclusive to the stakeholders involved, those mediators intending to be involved in climate issues are burdened with the need to go deep into the complexities of climate policy process to begin to understand the many and constantly changing parties and their evolving relationships (Glavovic et al., 1997). Just for starters, there are over 220 acronyms in the UNFCCC vocabulary list.[3] It truly was walking into a parallel culture with its own vocabulary and rituals. We knew it would take years to be accepted into the culture, and we were correct.

Of particular concern was that while the majority of MBBI members attending the UNFCCC were American, we were aware of the caveats that come with the perception of a Western bias to the concept of mediation (Meierding, 2010). When interacting with literally every country in the world, one's own cultural biases needed to be constantly updated as they were tested daily. It became essential for our teams to have MBBI members from multiple countries and cultures in order to reflect the intent that our efforts were well informed culturally as well as in process and content.

Complex community processes

The scope of the undertaking was all the more difficult for the lack of experiential models normally faced by those who practice mediation. With 194 countries each with varying numbers of delegates, who often change from meeting to meeting, we needed to find an efficient methodology to deal with the changing calculus of the members. While we had made personal contact with members of approximately 160 of the member countries, discovering the shifting coalitions of like-minded countries was a more effective arena of communication. Conversations were more likely to be in short interactions over the course of days rather than *ad seriatim*. This demanded that there was a premium on the internal communication within the MBBI team in order to keep all informed of the multiple, disjointed interactions with a wide variety of country delegates. Small groups of interested delegates were organized. Follow-ups from minor to major delegates within a country delegation needed to be pursued.

The discipline of neutrality

The MBBI Climate Team had made a decision early on that was essential to the success we had in gaining entry into the UNFCCC culture. To be perceived as neutrals we needed to be neutral (Damary, 2014). This meant that our purpose was to advance the understanding and application of mediation as a method to bring about more durable agreements—for all parties whatever their political or policy slant. Of the nearly 1,500 nongovernmental organizations (NGOs) registered with the UNFCCC, MBBI was the only NGO without a substantive or policy agenda. This meant that MBBI would reject any request to enter into a conflict within the parties or between them. If we had, the chances were great that MBBI would be associated with the outcome or with the parties to the dispute, both of which would compromise the perception of the balanced, impartial neutral. This was important to reinforce our privileged role of representing the field of mediation in all its manifestations in cultures throughout the world.

Our outcomes

Since Copenhagen in 2009, to 2015 and COP21 in Paris, MBBI has been present in 20 UNFCCC sessions including Barcelona, Doha, Panama, Lima, Bangkok, Warsaw, Bonn, Durban, Paris, and Cancun (UNFCCC, 2014). After COP15 in Copenhagen, all or part of each of these sessions were attended by a member of the MBBI Climate Leadership team along with other members. For the 20 sessions since Copenhagen, approximately a dozen MBBI members have attended multiple meetings totaling 52 nominations to attend. Our purpose was to build an authentic arena[4] in which the understanding of the use of mediation could be presented, discussed, and demonstrated. Almost all delegates we met had a fundamental understanding of the facilitation of a mediated dispute. What was being sought was how to identify, invite, and convene those stakeholders most effected by the mediated outcomes.

Outcomes of MBBI climate change team

As noted by Bercovitch (2007), there are both subjective and objective criteria to measure the outcomes of a mediated event, and in the case of international arenas, an even more complex assessment by virtue of intermingled cultures and multiple stakeholders. However, there are clearly several positive outcomes for which we have a high degree of confidence. The consideration of the use and application of mediation within the larger issue of climate change has been discussed and acknowledged by delegates from over 150 member nations. In so doing, there has been a discovery of linkages among like-minded delegates, which increases the probability that neutral intervention can take place. These connections are enhanced by the recognition that MBBI has been acknowledged within the UNFCCC and the Secretariat as a legitimate voice for the process of mediation and facilitated negotiation. As evidence of this legitimacy, MBBI has crafted language that has been accepted (posted) by the Secretariat for inclusion in UNFCCC policy if sponsored by a national delegation. MBBI is one of a handful of NGOs to succeed in this complex process. The net result has been that MBBI has received requests from several national delegations to sponsor and support this mediation-related language when the specific crafting of language is appropriate within the agreement process.

As noted, there is substantial evidence that our efforts have supported the creation of a better environment for future conflict management within the UNFCCC. Subjectively, MBBI is approached as an example that strives for fairness and neutrality, a welcome alternative to the competitive actions of contesting nations.

Suggested development and cautions for mediators involved in climate issues

As mediators we need to not only practice the skills we have learned and earned, but vigorously push ourselves outside the boxes where we feel most comfortable. Learning takes place on the margins of doubt and exploration. Environmental mediation brings with it demands on our skills and knowledge that must be balanced by our keen recognition of our limitations. Competency is the key. We must put in the effort to build our knowledge base regarding primarily the policy complexities of climate and yet have enough familiarity with the associated science to comprehend how the policies and practices interrelate.

Recognize that the skills of invitation and convening authentic arenas for negotiation are essential steps before leading to the mediation of a dispute. Groups, organizations, and systems have specific cultural rituals that provide the rubric for how stakeholders are invited (and authentically not invited). Finding culturally knowledgeable confederates is essential to moving through these complex systems. You do not need to be an expert in all cultures. You just need to know how to locate your reliable guides. This becomes most important in approaching environmental issues because our undiscovered naiveté has the real potential for undue risk and long-term harm.

Seek out experience in medium-sized and large group mediation practices. It may seem like a leap of faith but once confident in your fundamentals of mediation, taking these core principles and applying them to larger groups can bring systemic changes that are worth the effort and sense of risk. In the culture of the UNFCCC, it starts with acquiring a working knowledge of the UNFCCC's vocabulary and acronyms. The commitment deepens with your understanding of the role organizational as well as national and ethnic cultures play in dealing with disputes. For this there is little one can do other than seek out neutral interactions with multicultural stakeholders and find your cultural guides. Lastly, begin thinking of mediation in terms of the comprehensive steps of invitation, then convening and facilitating. Our worth as mediators is as great if not more significant as advocates for the arenas where stakeholders feel secure; where their self-esteem is enhanced and their respect in their community is honored. Finally, learn to work as a team of mediators with emphasis on internal team communication.

Mediators have a tendency to see themselves as primarily individual actors where at best we co-mediate in a dispute. Team interactions, which advocate for the culture of mediation take patience and acceptance of the far horizon. For many, this rigor takes them out of their comfort zone because forces us to reflect on our own perception of mediation in contrast with the multiple adaptions that mediation has undergone throughout the world. Environmental mediation is not a good fit for every mediator. Yet if you understand the power of advocacy of mediation as a path to shifting away from unquestioned competition, you will leave a legacy for generations.

Notes

1 For more information, see: www.wmo.int/pages/themes/climate/international_unfccc.php.
2 For more information, see: www.mediatorsbeyondborders.org.
3 See: unfccc.int/resource/cd_roms/na1/ghg_inventories/english/8_glossary/Glossary.htm.
4 "An authentic arena for negotiation is a physical and psychological space, embedded in a culture that defines the process by which disputes are resolved and frames the definitions of durable outcomes" (Fiutak, 2009, p. 53).

References

Bercovitch, J. (2007) Mediating in international conflicts: Theory, practice and development. In W. Zartman (ed.) *Peacemaking in International Conflict, Methods and Techniques* (pp. 163–194). Washington, DC: United State Department of Peace.

Damary, M. (2014) On being neutral: Reflections on neutrality in humanitarian action. *Professionals in Humanitarian Action, Assistance, and Protection.* Retrieved from phap.org/system/files/article_pdf/Damary-OnNeutrality.pdf.

Fiutak, T. (2009) *Le médiateur dans l'aréné: Réflexions sur l'art de la médiation.* Toulouse: Ères.

Glavovic, B., Dukes, E. & Lynette, J. (1997) Training and educating environmental mediators: Lessons from experience in the United States. *Conflict Resolution Quarterly*, 14(4): 269–292. doi: 10.1002/crq.3900140403.

Meierding, N. (2010) Mediators: Staying culturally relevant in a multi-cultural world. *Mediate.com.* Retrieved from www.mediate.com/articles/meierdingN1.cfm.

UNFCCC. (2014) UNFCCC—20 years of effort and achievement: Key milestones in the evolution of international climate policy. UNFCCC. Retrieved from: www.unfccc.int.timeline.

30

THE ROLE OF MEDIATION IN LARGE-SCALE COLLABORATIVE INITIATIVES ON FOREST RESOURCE MANAGEMENT

Marcelle E. DuPraw

The world of environmental and public policy mediation encompasses conflicts over many issues, from air quality to land use. Such conflicts may be place-based or policy oriented. The place-based conflicts unfold from the project level to the international level. This chapter focuses on the role of mediators in place-based controversies over forest resource management, and specifically, those that play out at the landscape scale. The chapter begins by explaining the context for this particular type of conflict, reviews traditional definitions of mediation and facilitation, and discusses how these practices manifest in this niche. The author makes the case for an emergent hybrid of mediation and facilitation in this arena, and identifies implications for mediators and facilitators.

Context

The national forests of the United States are "living, contentious public lands" (DuPraw, 2014). National forest management conflicts brought the US Forest Service to its knees in the latter part of the 20th century, as environmental interest groups filed appeal after appeal of forest management plans. Conflicts arose over differing preferences for how particular forest resources should be managed – e.g., which portion of a given forest should be open to logging versus protected as wilderness; which methods of logging are acceptable; and how to make good management decisions when faced with high levels of scientific uncertainty. Conflict is inevitable, given the mission of the Forest Service: "to sustain the health, diversity, and productivity of the nation's forests and grasslands to meet the needs of present and future generations" (US Forest Service, 2014). The agency must balance its management efforts to ensure that timber, rangelands, water, recreational assets, and wildlife are available in perpetuity. National forest management conflicts are never going to disappear, but can be minimized and managed constructively.

The desperate need to reduce catastrophic wildfires underscores the valuable contribution that mediators and facilitators can make in this arena. The Forest Service established the Collaborative Forest Landscape Restoration (CFLR) Program for three purposes: 1) "to encourage the collaborative, science-based ecosystem restoration of priority forest landscapes"; 2) to reduce wildfire risk; and 3) to create jobs (US Forest Service, 2012). At the five-year anniversary of the CFLR Program, the Forest Service reported remarkable accomplishments from the 23 landscape-scale collaborative initiatives it had funded around the USA, including over 1.45 million acres treated to reduce wildfire risk (US Department of Agriculture, 2015).[1] Based on the author's study of collaborative capacity building in this program, she suggests that landscape-scale collaboration is a phenomenon that requires impartial "third parties" to provide an integrated blend of mediation and facilitation (DuPraw, 2014).[2]

Landscape-scale collaboration, mediation, and facilitation defined—initially

Landscape-scale collaboration

The CFLR Program defines "landscape-scale" as a geographic area of 50,000 acres or more. In collaboration at this scale, diverse stakeholders work together to identify and achieve common forest landscape management goals. This does not usually happen by itself or without conflict. Virtually all CFLR projects have impartial third parties who have helped to organize stakeholders' collaborative processes and coordinate their efforts on an ongoing basis. Are these third parties facilitators, mediators, or a hybrid of the two? This chapter argues a hybrid.

Environmental and public policy mediation and facilitation

Fisher and Tees (2005) provide an excellent discussion of the similarities and differences between mediation and facilitation, as they have been understood in the public policy arena over the last three decades (pp. 126–127). They describe facilitation as "a process where a person who is acceptable to all the members of the group, substantively neutral, and has no decision-making authority, intervenes to help the group improve the way it identifies and solves problems and makes decisions" (p. 126). They draw upon an early definition of mediation, but the expanded version of the definition of mediation is provided by Moore (2014) as: "Mediation is a conflict resolution process in which a mutually acceptable third party, who has no authority to make binding decisions for disputants, intervenes in a conflict or dispute to assist involved parties to improve their relationships, enhance communications, and use effective problem-solving and negotiation procedures to reach voluntary and mutually acceptable understanding or agreements on contested issues" (Moore, 2014, p. 8).

Using the above definitions, Fisher and Tees (2005) note that mediation and facilitation are similar in that both are interventions by an impartial third party. Mediators and facilitators seek both to enhance participants' analytical approach to their shared problems and to help participants use constructive behaviors to arrive at mutually acceptable decisions. However, Fisher and Tees note, mediation assumes that the participants are engaged in conflict, which they have not been able to solve and have thus requested the mediator's assistance (Fisher & Tees, 2005, p. 127). In contrast, the authors assert, when facilitation is used, there may or may not be conflict present, but the conflict is not the driver for seeking the help of an impartial third party; facilitation, they say, focuses on improved decision making and problem solving. While these definitions have been widely accepted for years,[3] this chapter questions whether mediation and facilitation actually are distinct forms of practice in the context of landscape-scale collaboration.

Linkages between landscape-scale collaboration, conflict, and conflict resolution

DuPraw (2014) found that conflict is the very context for landscape-scale collaboration, and inseparable from it. Respondents said: "There's gonna be conflict" ... "It totally came out of conflict" … "Differing missions means we may not ever agree" … "Conflict is the name of the game" … "Conflict is the underlying narrative" … "Conflict is a complicated, essential part of the collaborative process" … "Conflict is the background for everything" … "Conflict created 'em!" (speaking of the collaborative processes in which this person has been involved) … "Conflict is the background and history of the collaborative processes I've been involved in—it's fundamental" … "Conflict is inevitable when you have a really diverse group of people" … "It's about conflict!" … "There's a history of conflict on this landscape" … "The collaborative process is a perfect prism of all the conflicts in the area that have developed over the last 400 years."

Conflict is more prevalent at the landscape scale than other scales due to the high degree of scientific uncertainty, coupled with the potential magnitude of the impacts of making a mistake when working at the landscape scale. By definition, landscape-scale collaboration encompasses very large sweeps of land with so many data gaps that decision making will play out over years; thus, these conflicts tend to be macro-scale, diffuse, chronic conflicts (e.g. whether to manage national forests for maximum economic vs. ecological benefits) rather than acute, discrete, focused conflicts. Conflict is often a catalyst for collaborative processes. Stakeholders see collaborative forums as venues in which to negotiate mutually acceptable solutions to forest resource conflicts. Moreover, the painful memory of conflict keeps participants at the table.

DuPraw (2014) identified four types of conflict resolution strategies seen in the collaborative forest landscape restoration initiatives she studied—macro-level, second track diplomacy, dispute resolution system design, and strategies applied in the context of a particular, place-based controversy. In the latter, an impartial third party uses an integrated blend of mediation and facilitation to help participants in a particular landscape-scale collaborative initiative pursue their common goals and resolve conflicts as they come up. The third party helps stakeholders draw upon: a) their knowledge of the natural resources that are at the center of the controversy; b) their understanding of the legal and policy context of the issues under contention; c) their dedication to the goals of the problem-solving effort; and d) any political support that the stakeholders may be able to enlist in service of the joint problem-solving process. Mediation takes place informally, within the context of facilitated consensus building and without naming it as such; it has become integrated with facilitation in this particular practice area.

Conflict resolution: a necessary competency for landscape-scale collaboration

DuPraw (2014) found that landscape-scale collaboration requires collaborative capacity at four levels—the individual collaborator, the constituent group, the collaborative stakeholder group as a whole, and the sponsoring organization where there is one (e.g. the Forest Service). She also found that skilled process management (a term that encompasses both mediation and facilitation) is one of nine competencies required for effective landscape-scale collaboration (DuPraw, 2014). She suggests that process management skills are most salient at the level of the individual collaborator (who may suggest a particular strategy and participate in enacting it) and at the level of the stakeholder group as a whole (who must put in place conflict resolution procedures). However, constituency groups also have to understand the range of conflict resolution strategies available to them so they can choose whether to participate in them and support their representatives in doing so effectively. Sponsoring agencies also need to understand the range of available conflict resolution strategies to ensure that their budgeting, contracting, personnel management and other systems enable the use of these strategies.

Recognizing a valid hybrid of facilitation and mediation

Virtually every respondent in DuPraw's study of collaborative capacity building in the CFLR contact indicated that facilitation is central to productive landscape-scale collaboration (DuPraw, 2014). Virtually no one mentioned mediation. However, in examining respondents' expectations of facilitators, the composite picture painted is an amalgamation of facilitators and mediators. Respondents offered insights on desired abilities, attitudes, and behaviors in facilitators, recommending someone with "enough credibility with the group that people would do things for them" (DuPraw, 2014). They suggested the facilitator's style be not too prescriptive, not conflict averse, and not too light-handed. One person described the desired function as "leaderful facilitation" (DuPraw, 2014). She suggested that stakeholders in this arena have come to value facilitators who go beyond giving everyone an opportunity to speak, and ensuring that all the agenda topics get airtime, to bringing a certain amount of subject-matter expertise to bear in shaping the discourse.

One of the skills that respondents associated with effective facilitators of landscape-scale collaboration was managing conflict, such as by helping collaborators align around shared priorities and by directing conflict away from individuals and toward issues and interests. Respondents look to their third-party helpers to make good judgment calls on: 1 when to stick to the agenda and when to release it to focus on something pressing that has come up, such as a conflict; and 2 when participants need the flexibility to finish a conversation. They appreciate it when the third party encourages the group to provide process suggestions, welcomes group feedback, discourages over-reliance on the third party, and nurtures group members' own sense of agency. They look to the third party to keep discussions on track and sustain group momentum, to reframe issues, and to help disputants move through their positions and fears to focus on underlying interests. Respondents find it helpful when the third party draws participants out so that all contribute to the group discussion and discuss the core issues. They value third parties who notice if a participant is not maintaining an effective linkage with his or her constituency, and coaches the representative on strengthening this relationship. They appreciate third parties who recognize problematic attitudes or behaviors on the part of a representative and, if necessary, persuade the parent organization to coach the representative on more effective behavior at the negotiating table.

Recall that Fisher and Tees (2005) assert that the main difference between public policy mediation and facilitation is that *mediation assumes that the participants are engaged in conflict, which they have not been able to solve and have thus requested the mediator's assistance* (p. 127). After reading the description of facilitation in the context of CFLR initiatives, try replacing the word mediation in the above italicized phrase with the word facilitation and see if it makes sense. When stakeholders use the term *facilitator* in the CFLR context, they do assume that the participants are engaged in conflict, which they have not been able to solve, and have thus requested the *facilitator's* help.

Recall also that Fisher and Tees (2005) explained that, in contrast to mediation, there may or may not be conflict present when facilitation is used, but the conflict is not the driver for seeking the help of an impartial third party. Rather, facilitation focuses on improved decision making and problem solving. In CFLR initiatives, this statement often holds true. As described above, this is because while conflict is ubiquitous in landscape-scale collaboration, it tends to be taken for granted, almost like background noise. It also sometimes flares up, takes more visible forms, and requires varying levels of conflict resolution intervention by the facilitator.

What stakeholders in CFLR processes refer to as facilitation meets the conventional definitions of both facilitation and mediation. Why might stakeholders prefer the term facilitator?

Conventional wisdom might suggest it is because no one likes to admit they have a conflict they cannot solve without outside help. However, in this context, stakeholders do not seem to have any problem asking for facilitation help. More likely, this preference ties to a distinction in the traditional use of the terms facilitation and mediation that did not surface in the Fisher and Tees (2005) discussion.

The distinction is that facilitation has historically been a proactive intervention, while mediation has historically been a reactive intervention. Landscape-scale collaboration tends to be an extremely proactive phenomenon; it often takes a tremendous amount of foresight and planning to launch and sustain such an effort. There is nothing reactive about it. Thus, if a stakeholder associates mediation with reactive interventions, s/he might not think that it is a mediator whose help is needed to manage such a process. It would be a facilitator who would come to mind—but a facilitator who can mediate when necessary, and then slide easily back into a collaboration coordinator mode.

The solution to this interesting situation is not to correct the terminology used by stakeholders, but rather to acknowledge, accept, and learn from this evolution in the world of conflict resolution. Two practical implications of this situation are that: 1) mediators who wish to be of service in this arena may find such opportunities framed as requests for facilitation assistance; and 2) mediators and facilitators working in this arena need to have a toolkit that includes both mediation and facilitation skills.

Conclusion

Landscape-scale collaboration offers a "sweet spot" for addressing forest resource management challenges, minimizing unnecessary conflict, channeling unavoidable conflict toward positive outcomes, and reducing risks of catastrophic wildfire. The remarkable results achieved through the CFLR Program reflect participants' dedication to the forests that are special to them, the growing awareness of how much more can be achieved when we work together, and the simple logic of working at the scale on which the ecosystem that collaborators are trying to restore actually functions. The assistance of experienced, highly skilled facilitators has been a key ingredient in the CFLR Program's winning recipe. In this chapter, the author has made the case that the facilitation involved has actually evolved into an integrated blend of mediation and facilitation, that this has served stakeholders well, and that in this arena, it makes little sense to adhere to the traditional distinction between facilitation and mediation.

Notes

1 Other accomplishments reported by the CFLR Program at its five-year anniversary included: 1) timber sales on over 84,570 acres for the purpose of improving forest health; 2) over 1.33 million acres of improved wildlife habitat; 3) weeds and invasive plant species removed on 73,600 acres; 4) over 1,256 million board feet of timber sales generated through restoration activities; 5) $661 million in local labor income generated; 6) an average of 4,360 jobs per year; and 7) over $76.1 million in partner match funds (US Department of Agriculture, 2015).

2 "Third party" refers to a person who helps others solve a problem in which the helper has no stake. It implies a mediator or facilitator. It should be considered a term of art in the public policy arena because, while it implies there are only two disputants, there are typically many more than two disputants involved in public policy controversies.

3 One aspect of these definitions that has generated debate is the question of whether anyone can be truly neutral (see, for example, Mayer, 2004).

References

Charmaz, K. (2011) *Constructing Grounded Theory: A Practical Guide through Qualitative Analysis.* Washington, DC: Sage Publications.

DuPraw, M.E. (2014) *Illuminating Capacity-building Strategies for Landscape-scale Collaborative Forest Management through Constructivist Grounded Theory* (Doctoral dissertation). Retrieved from ProQuest Dissertations and Theses (3666697).

Fisher, F. & Tees, D. (2005) *Key Competencies for Improving Local Governance—Local Elected Leadership Series Volume 3—Concepts and Strategies: For Each of the Roles and Competencies.* UN Habitat. 92-1-131728-2.

Mayer, B. (2004) *Beyond Neutrality: Confronting the Crisis in Conflict Resolution.* San Francisco, CA: Jossey-Bass.

Megason, P. (2015, May 1). State's wildfire season now runs year-round. *Sacramento Bee*, A17.

Moore, C. (2014) *The Mediation Process: Practical Strategies for Resolving Conflict.* San Francisco, CA: Jossey-Bass.

Omnibus Public Land Management Act of 2009. (2009) *Pub. L. No. 111–111. Title IV (Forest Landscape Restoration).* Codified at 16 USC. Chapter 92.

US Department of Agriculture. (2015) *Collaborative Forest Landscape Restoration Program 5-Year Report.* FS-1047. March.

US Forest Service. (2012) *People Restoring America's Forests: 2012 Report on the Collaborative Forest Landscape Restoration Program.* Retrieved from www.fs.fed.us/restoration/documents/cflrp/CoalitionReports/CFLRP2012AnnualReport20130108.pdf.

US Forest Service. (2014) *About the Agency.* Retrieved from www.fs.fed.us/about-agency.

US Government Accountability Office. (1999) *Western National Forests: A Cohesive Strategy is Needed to Address Catastrophic Wildfire Threats.* (GAO Publication No. GAO/RCED-99–65). Retrieved from www.gao.gov/products/GAO/RCED-99-65.

31

MEDIATION AT THE NEXUS OF CLIMATE CHANGE AND CONFLICT

Oliver Leighton Barrett

Climate change is in essence about water: too little where there once was plenty; too much where there once was too little. This chapter explores how acute water scarcities across the world are increasing the likelihood of violent conflict in general, and how international mediators in particular can facilitate the peaceful resolution of emerging water wars. It is important that both fledgling and seasoned mediators alike begin to familiarize themselves with the linkages between climate change and conflict (specifically, climate change as a catalyst for conflict) since this nexus will require the kind of services that only skilled conflict resolution practitioners can deliver.

This chapter endeavors first to describe how climate change will accelerate instability across already vulnerable countries and regions, and second, how international mediators can facilitate the de-escalation of tensions and the achievement of equitable and enduring agreements.

Context

In his 2015 State of the Union address, President Obama stressed the need for the United States, and the world, to respond to climate change through an unprecedented global campaign to mitigate and adapt to impacts of the phenomena that some have characterized as a "slow-moving emergency." In the speech, the president referenced that 2014 was the planet's warmest year on record and warned that "if we do not act forcefully, we'll continue to see rising oceans, longer, hotter heat waves, dangerous droughts and floods, and massive disruptions that can trigger greater migration, conflict, and hunger around the globe" (Obama, 2015). Intelligence assessments such as the *2012 Intelligence Community Assessment on Global Water Security* support President Obama's call for action by warning that "climate change will cause water shortages in many areas of the world" (Defense Intelligence Agency, 2012, p. 1).

Further, a series of regional research and conference reports conducted by the National Intelligence Council (NIC, 2009) titled the *Impact of Climate Change to 2030* amplifies the aforementioned assessment, projecting severe impacts, particularly on freshwater scarcity across the globe, especially across North Africa. In addition, Mr Salman M.A. Salman, lead counsel and water law advisor at the World Bank in a 2006 article titled "International water disputes: A new breed of claims, claimants, and settlement institutions," explained that global water security challenges are a result of "the steady increase in population, urbanization, environmental degradation, and industrialization" (p. 1). Salman (2006) continues to explain that water shortage challenges are giving rise to growing international disputes "involving not only states, but also legal entities, corporations, and individuals against other states. The claims now go beyond the traditional water quantity issues, and involve water quality, border lines across boundary rivers, and water rights issues" (p. 1).

Environmental variability poses a near-term risk to the security of states and communities of all sizes because shifting climatic patterns not only create new problems, but also exacerbate vexing underdevelopment problems as well. Populations across failing and fragile states especially will be hardest hit, but there will also be increased risk for the West as globally minded violent religio-political movements, as well as illicit organizations, find more under-governed or totally ungoverned spaces from which to plan, recruit and launch operations. Larger swaths of permissive surrounding areas across the Middle East and North Africa (henceforth referred to as "MENA") will be fertile ground for on-the-march terrorist groups like the Islamic State in Syria (henceforth referred to as "ISIS"), Boko Haram, and al-Shabaab. Further, political and security breakdowns across the Levant (Syria, Lebanon, Israel, Jordan and the occupied Palestinian territory) and Iraq, especially, will exacerbate a worsening security condition and might lead to a further diffusing of the terrorist threat for regional nations most specifically, but also for Western nations. It is within this context—at the nexus of climate change, political volatility, underdevelopment, and resource scarcity—that third-party interventions can help disputing parties and conflicting countries/regions reach peaceful resolutions.

The opportunity

A special issue of the *Journal of Peace Research* found significant linkages between climate change and intra-state conflicts in East Africa and Central Asia, and explained that water conflicts are becoming more numerous, and in some instances, deepening due to climate change effects—principally drought (Gleditsch, 2012). Though it is unreasonable to expect that international mediators can facilitate the resolution of all intrastate and transnational conflict (especially those that have already turned violent), mediators can have incredibly consequential impacts of a range of scenarios including those exacerbated by climate change effects. This is especially true of environmentally related mediation interventions.

Environmental mediation can be defined as the application of processes aimed at helping parties to resolve water, land use, and agricultural disputes in ways acceptable to all key stakeholders. Environmental mediation at the climate-water-conflict nexus aims to foster and advance dialogue, understanding and a give and take that results in equitable water-sharing agreements that factor into the resolution calculus not only current scarcities, but also likely future ones as well. Such efforts lead to comprehensive and enforceable agreements that mitigate violent conflict over water scarcity and can even become the basis for cooperation on other issues. Third-party conflict resolution practitioners can play a transformative role in helping factions that are near or in conflict to formulate agreements oriented on the axis of resource sharing before natural and man-made trends converge to reach crisis tipping points. Credible and seasoned mediators can be invited into pre-conflict scenarios to intervene and to help disputants to frame positions and interests with the aim of jointly formulating prospective solutions out of crisis.

Case study

Disputes resulting from the competing demands between diverse sets of water stakeholders at all strata of society and government (municipal, state, regional and international) are only broadening and becoming more complex, not only across traditionally water-stressed regions such as the MENA, but also across other parts of Africa and Southeast Asia. As water flows and volumes lessen due to changes in precipitation patterns (and dramatic increases in usage), popular unrest can ensue, and in some cases turn violent as people resort to arms to assert their rights. However, with skilled mediation and the commitment of the parties to a resolution process, crisis can be averted, as was the case across the extremely environmentally vulnerable Nile Basin 20 years ago.

The Nile Basin has historically faced water-related pressures compounded by high demographic growth rates (in seven of the 11 riparian countries, population will double in the coming 20–25 years) and by the demands of faster economic growth (Nile Basin Initiative, 2016). Climate change impacts in particular are expected to compound water scarcity across these Nile riparian communities, exacerbating food, water and energy insecurities. Mediators played pivotal roles in resolving water conflicts in the Nile Basin at least as early as 50 years ago. For example, an agreement resolving transnational water rights, and Egypt's construction of the High Dam (which would have significantly affected water availability of other states), was memorialized in an agreement entitled *Agreement for the Full Utilization of the Nile Waters* in 1959. However, seven other riparian states of the Nile at the time of execution of this agreement were left out of the process, resulting in a demand for a more comprehensive and inclusive follow-on agreement that would address the legitimate water needs of all the affected 238 million water consumers. This outcry led to a subsequent road-to-settlement process that ended in the Nile Basin Initiative (NBI) mediated by the World Bank and the United Nations in 1999. The mediated NBI process succeeded in bringing together for the first time riparian states at the national ministerial level which worked together to develop a water-sharing framework that is still in effect today. The NBI is a model of intergovernmental partnership—a platform—that enables joint planning and management of water resources and which has helped to foster peace and security across one of the world's most expansive basins.

A growth industry

Mediators Beyond Borders (MBB, 2008) is one American organization working at the nexus of climate-related conflicts and mediation. The organization cites a few notable water stress-related disputes including cross-border conflicts resolved by skilled third-party interventions in recent years. Representative examples include:

- Acta de Brasilia Negotiations between Peru and Ecuador
- Agacher Strip Mediation between Burkina Faso and Mali
- The Middle East Climate Change Assessment
- Lake Michigan—USA Mediation
- Coeur d'Alene Lake Management Plan Mediation

In the above instances, mediators, facilitators and even researchers helped disputing parties (and other stakeholders) to explore prospective solutions to resolve water disputes—long-standing or nascent. These cases are evidence of the fact that conflict resolution practitioners can successfully intervene at all points along the conflict continuum through varied intervention tools and approaches (MBB, 2008). The performance record of third-party mediators as agents of conflict resolution is well established; however, the value of researchers (even student researchers) as interventionists is very much under-appreciated. This should change.

The Middle East Climate Change Assessment (Roth et al., 2009) is an example of how even a neutral analysis can raise awareness of nascent resource conflicts and compel stakeholders to take near-term mitigating actions to avert crisis. In 2009, the International Institute for Sustainable Development (IISD), an independent Canadian environment and development research institute, conducted a neutral analysis of the security threat that climate change poses to the Levant populations. The Levant has experienced more than 60 years of conflict and is of acute political and security interest to the US government due principally to strategic alliances in the region, on-the-march terrorism, and traditional energy security concerns. To accomplish this assessment, the group conducted online research, in-person consultations and extensive interviews (in Amman, Beirut, Damascus, Jerusalem, Ramallah and Tel Aviv) to learn about the positions, interests and equities of all Levant stakeholders. From these investigative activities, the team formulated suggested strategies for mitigating emerging conflicts to include a recommendation for the establishment of a Regional Center for Adaptation to Climate Change that would develop and disseminate innovative ways to deal with drought and maximize water and energy efficiency (Roth et al., 2009).

Conclusion

The referenced reports and case studies shared in this chapter point to the growing concern about the security consequences of climate change as a stressor on states and populations. The decline in precipitation (or change in precipitation patterns)—arguably the most consequential effect of climate change—will impact MENA states most due to political fragility, simmering unrest and their inability to absorb environmental shocks. However, such shocks will not be confined to MENA states. They will likely also occur in Central Asia, Southern Europe, Southern Africa, Latin America, and the Caribbean, and even in the relatively more resilient United States (especially the southwest region because of the rise in red water levels). Populations will have to do their best to mitigate what can be mitigated but also to adapt to outcomes that are already locked in if they are to maintain state stability, livelihoods, and quality of life. In almost all of these contexts, water supply (and rights to these supplies) will become intensifying pain points, and if claims are not adjudicated or otherwise resolved through legitimate and credible conflict resolution processes, parties may resort to violence to assert their claims. Given the intensifying impacts of climate change, it is a worthwhile endeavor for conflict resolution practitioners to consider pursuing environmental mediation as a specialty practice. However, those who choose this specialty pathway must establish the kind of foundational knowledge base that is not imparted through traditional academic and mediator credentialing processes. It will especially require a multidisciplinary approach with a focus on the interplay between climate change, environmental degradation, urbanization, and geo-political imperatives. However, with this foundational knowledge, a skilled mediator can aptly facilitate mitigating processes that help the representatives of climate-vulnerable populations to step away from the brink of conflict. Fostering understanding and enabling joint decision making in an increasingly resource-scarce world will require the kind of maturity, judgment and skills that committed and thoughtful conflict resolution practitioners can bring to bear.

References

Defense Intelligence Agency (2012) *Global Water Security*. Washington, DC: Office of the Director of National Intelligence. Retrieved from www.dni.gov/files/documents/Special%20Report_ICA%20Global%20Water%20Security.pdf.

Gleditsch, N.P. (2012) Whither the weather? Climate change and conflict. *Journal of Peace Research*, 49(1): 3–9.

Mediators Beyond Borders (MBB). (2008) Case studies demonstrating the use of mediation, consensus building and collaborative problem solving in resolving environmental and climate-related conflicts. Retrieved from www.riverstoneresolutions.com/files/MBB%20COP15%20Case%20Summaries.pdf.

National Intelligence Council (NIC) (2009) *Executive Summary: In North Africa: The Impact of Climate Change to 2030*. Washington, DC: National Intelligence Council.

Nile Basin Initiative. (2016) *Understanding the Nile Basin*. Retrieved from nilebasin.org/index.php/about-us/the-river-nile.

Obama, B.H. (2015) *Remarks by the President in State of the Union Address: January 20, 2015*. The White House: Office of the Press Secretary. Retrieved from www.whitehouse.gov/the-press-office/2015/01/20/remarks-president-state-union-address-january-20-2015.

Roth, A., Pelaez, J., Valbh, A. & Group, S. (2009) Case studies demonstrating the use of mediation, consensus building and collaborative problem solving in resolving environmental and climate-related conflicts. *Middle East Assessment* (Rep. No. S/2009/189).

Salman, M.A.S. (2006) International water disputes: A new breed of claims, claimants, and settlement institutions. *Water International*, 31(1): 2–11. Retrieved from www.internationalwaterlaw.org/bibliography/articles/Salman/InternationalWaterDisputes.pdf.

32

THE PUBLIC SECTOR AS MEDIATOR

The role of public institutions in environmental collaboration and conflict resolution

William Hall and Michael Kern

Environmental collaboration and conflict resolution (ECCR) can be defined as an umbrella term for a diverse set of practices—mediation, facilitation, community-based collaboration, consensus building—involving a neutral third party to develop and implement environmental policy (Dukes, 2004; Office of Management and Budget & Council on Environmental Quality, 2012). Since the mid-1980s, federal and state agencies and public universities across the USA have established public sector ECCR institutions to serve as centers of expertise and service (Hall, 2013, 2014), which reflects a similar trend in the broader conflict resolution field. Kriesberg (2007) characterizes that trend as a period of differentiation and institutionalization, in which the practice of conflict resolution became specialized for use in particular substantive areas. During this time, the US Congress passed laws to promote the increased use of dispute resolution in government activities, agencies have established dedicated ECCR programs, and ECCR centers have been founded at public universities.

The institutionalization of ECCR practice in the public sector has occurred without much explicit attention to what makes such institutions effective interveners in contentious environmental and natural resource issues. We aim to address this gap in scholarship and contribute to an important conversation about how public sector institutions provide effective ECCR services, offering examples for others who are practicing, or seek to do so, within this institutional setting. First, we offer some background on our own organizations—the Conflict Prevention and Resolution Center (CPRC) at the US Environmental Protection Agency (EPA) and the William D. Ruckelshaus Center (Ruckelshaus Center, or the Center) at Washington State University (WSU) and the University of Washington (UW). We then draw on our organizations' experiences to explore attributes that contribute to public sector ECCR institutional effectiveness and the types of functions they may serve in preventing and resolving environmental conflicts. We conclude by highlighting some of the unique roles public sector ECCR institutions can play as environmental mediators.

Public sector ECCR institutions in the United States

ECCR institutions in the public sector take many forms in the USA. Some are separate government organizations, such as the US Institute for Environmental Conflict Resolution in Tucson, Arizona. Others are housed within government agencies that have a broader mandate, such as the Office of Collaborative Action and Dispute Resolution at the US Department of the Interior. Publicly funded universities have established organizations dedicated to promoting ECCR practice and scholarship, such as the University of Virginia's Institute for Environmental Negotiation. Some institutions originally located in state government (such as Florida State University's FCRC Consensus Center) have migrated to public universities, often as a result of shifting state budget priorities. We provide background on the purpose, history, and structure of our respective organizations, as different examples of such institutions. We then discuss how each has become an effective ECCR intervener, and functions each serves to that end.

The CPRC was founded in 1999 to consolidate all of the EPA's national ECCR practice in a single organization, following more than a decade of entrepreneurial efforts by individuals working in multiple parts of the agency to promote ECCR, particularly in regulation development and enforcement activities. Although the CPRC is located within the EPA's Office of General Counsel, its organizational charter specifies that it is programmatically independent and directly responsible to the agency's administrator. Its director and seven staff members provide a range of services to all EPA environmental programs, including process advice/design, convening, mediation/facilitation, training, and evaluation.

The CPRC handles approximately 80 ECCR cases per year, many of which feature drinking water or surface water quality, or hazardous waste cleanup issues. Approximately one quarter are focused on challenges to agency decisions, such as final regulations or permits, or on enforcement of environmental laws. Both of these are situations where the parties are usually engaged in resolving a dispute, often in the context of administrative or federal court litigation. One example of such cases is the Barrick Cortez gold mine administrative enforcement ECCR case (United States Environmental Protection Agency, 2013). By contrast, the majority of the CPRC's ECCR processes contribute to decisions that have not yet been made (such as development of regulations or standards) or assist with ongoing decision-making processes (for example at hazardous waste sites, where cleanup activities may take place over many years). In some cases, an external mediator is engaged to manage a single public meeting; in others, a mediator may work with a group of stakeholders for years. One example of pre-decisional ECCR processes is the Oregon Fish Consumption Rate and Water Quality Standards Rule facilitated dialogue (United States Environmental Protection Agency, 2012).

The William D. Ruckelshaus Center was established in 2004 and renamed in 2006 after William D. Ruckelshaus (the first and fifth EPA administrator), who is the Center's founder and Advisory Board chair. The Center's mission is to act as a neutral resource for collaborative problem solving in the State of Washington and the Pacific Northwest. The Center is a joint effort of Washington's two research universities, hosted at UW by the Daniel J. Evans School of Public Policy and Governance, and at WSU by WSU Extension, which also provides its administration. Its director and core staff are guided by an advisory board of prominent local, state, and regional leaders representing a broad range of constituencies and geographic locations. The Center is dedicated to assisting public, private, tribal, non-profit, and other community leaders in their efforts to build consensus and resolve conflicts around difficult public policy issues. The Center also brings real-world policy issues into the academic setting.

The Center's program areas/services include pre-assessment, situation assessment, facilitation/mediation/dispute resolution, applied research and fact finding, neutral forums and policy discussions, and collaborative capacity building and training. The Center has helped the State of Washington and others in the Pacific Northwest resolve challenges and conflicts on large and small issues involving disaster response, health care, economic development, good governance, and other topics, but the majority of its work has been on environmental conflict and natural resource management (Kern, 2013). Examples of prominent Ruckelshaus Center ECCR projects include the Voluntary Stewardship Program (William D. Ruckelshaus Center, 2010), Chehalis Basin Strategy (William D. Ruckelshaus Center, 2014), and Columbia River Salmon and Steelhead Assessment (Oregon Consensus & William D. Ruckelshaus Center, 2013).

Attributes and functions of public sector environmental mediation institutions

Practitioners working to create effective public sector ECCR institutions should attend to several important institutional considerations, including: 1) establishing appropriate party-mediator relationships; 2) ensuring mediator competence; and 3) providing an adequate resource base for efficient access to ECCR services. These characteristics enable important ECCR program functions, including early awareness of opportunities for intervention, brokering of mediation services, convening, capacity building, providing or identifying sources for funding, and routinized systems for accessing ECCR practitioners. These considerations are described below.

Party-mediator relationships

First and foremost, ECCR institutions and practitioners must be acceptable as interveners to the parties they serve. Parties' acceptance of a mediator determines whether an individual has a sufficient platform for successful intervention in a given situation. If any party does not accept the mediator, that party is unlikely to feel the process is fair and impartial. Mediators gain the trust and credibility of parties by having an appropriate relationship with them, and by having sufficient competence in both conflict prevention and resolution processes and the substantive aspects of the issues at stake.

Moore (2014) highlights three bases for an appropriate mediator relationship with parties—social network, authority, and independence. The first is grounded in the parties' and intervener's involvement in the same social network and reflects an emphasis on maintaining long-term positive relationships among group members. This relationship may support a public sector institution's early awareness of ECCR opportunities and help its staff influence decision makers to consider ECCR. The second mediator-party relationship derives from the mediator's authority over one or more parties, usually because of status or position, administrative responsibility, or vested interests. This type of relationship is typically how one thinks about US government agencies relative to potential ECCR parties. Moore's (2014) third category of mediator is independent from and has no authority over the parties, and is invited to assist them primarily to foster effective decision making.

Having multiple real or perceived types of relationships with the parties may enhance ECCR institutional effectiveness, a notion consistent with suggestions that practitioners embrace more complex mediator-party relationships than those of strict neutrality (Mayer, 2004). We examine the types of relationships that the EPA's CPRC and the Ruckelshaus Center have with the parties they serve as examples to practitioners of how ECCR institutions have addressed the mediator-party relationship.

For the CPRC, the primary relationship with parties is a significant degree of programmatic independence from the agency's other functions, buttressed by the voluntary nature of the services the CPRC offers to parties and confidentiality protections that exist for appropriate cases, pursuant to the agency's policy on alternative dispute resolution (United States Environmental Protection Agency, 2000). That independence is further bolstered by the CPRC's access to external independent practitioners through its Conflict Prevention and Resolution Services Contract. In addition, because the CPRC is situated within a larger agency, its staff members are part of the social network of the organization and build long-term relationships with their EPA clients. This affords the CPRC staff with opportunities to both learn about potential situations in which ECCR may be useful and educate and influence EPA colleagues in the direction of appropriate dispute prevention and resolution, similar to what Lederach (1991) describes as "insider-partial" mediation. While the CPRC has no responsibility for making decisions regarding the matters in which it intervenes, its position within the EPA may also enable its staff to persuade some otherwise reluctant nongovernmental parties to participate in ECCR.

Whether the Ruckelshaus Center is an acceptable convener is one of the primary criteria the Center uses to determine if a potential project is a good fit for the organization. An important aspect is the parties' determination that the Center is independent from and has no authority over them. The Center's university setting is often conducive to being perceived in this way, though it can limit the Center to working with faculty, staff, students, and practitioners who are not perceived as having taken strong positions on the issues at hand. The Center's core and project faculty, staff, and practitioners often maintain robust connections in the public policy social networks that Moore (2014) describes, providing more opportunities for early awareness and influence on decision makers contemplating ECCR than are likely available to most private and nongovernmental sector practitioners. These connections are greatly expanded by the extensive networks of the Center's advisory board, comprising prominent current and former public, private, and nongovernmental sector leaders. While the Center has no authority over those whose projects it facilitates, its strong reputation and record of success (more than 25 projects successfully completed over the last five years, resulting in several pieces of high-profile, broadly supported legislation, and almost $100 million in total investment from the State Legislature) allow it to work effectively with governors, legislators, tribal chairs, agency heads, and other leaders to establish the legitimacy of collaborative processes.

A notable distinction between the CPRC and the Ruckelshaus Center in mediator-party relationships concerns where they are housed. The CPRC's association with the EPA's overall clout in environmental matters affords the opportunity to persuasively interact with EPA regulators serving as parties in ECCR matters and may convey a sense of importance to non-EPA parties as well. However, this quasi-authority mediator relationship may also narrow the CPRC's perceived independence in a few cases; the Center, by contrast, may have somewhat greater independence in its public university setting.

Mediator competence

Competence is another important component of intervener acceptability. While the elements of mediator competence are certainly a function of the specific situation and the expressed preferences of the parties involved, a general assessment of mediator competence necessarily includes relevant conflict prevention and resolution skills (Herrman et al., 2001; Wehr, 1979). Mediators in the ECCR domain also require a degree of expertise in the substance of the particular environmental and natural resource issues that may be a stake in a particular situation (Society of Professionals in Dispute Resolution, 1992) and understanding of the relevant organizational cultures. The way in which the CPRC and the Ruckelshaus Center have established and maintained mediator competence may be instructive to current and prospective public sector mediators.

The EPA recruits all staff members into the CPRC based in part on conflict resolution skills and experience, gained through previous work for other public and private sector conflict resolution organizations, or through graduate studies in conflict resolution theory and practice. Once on the job, staff members hone their skills through targeted training and practice. Equally important is the staff's understanding of the EPA's environmental programs, the substance of which frames collaboration opportunities and disputes where the CPRC may become involved. Some staff members came to CPRC having worked in one or more of the EPA's environmental programs. All staff members gain environmental knowledge through training courses, temporary assignments to environmental programs, or by working on cases. This knowledge uniquely positions the in-house staff to provide advice to internal and external clients, convene parties in preparation for mediation, and occasionally serve as mediators in appropriate cases.

The Ruckelshaus Center ensures that every project team it assembles contains the elements of mediator competence described above. The Center's five-member core faculty has over 90 years of collective experience in public policy conflict resolution and collaborative policy-making, and advanced degrees in relevant fields, such as public policy, marine affairs, law, and land use planning. They have practiced in academic, private, non-profit, and governmental settings, which helps them understand differing organizational cultures. University requirements for faculty promotion encourage them to contribute to the field through research and scholarship, further developing their expertise and areas of competence. The Center's in-house expertise is augmented by an extensive pool of faculty, staff, students, and practitioners at the state's two premier research universities.

Because of its emphasis on "on the ground" and "in the community" application of academic expertise, WSU Extension is a good place to identify faculty with facilitation skills and interests, though the Center has worked with talented university-based mediators drawn from public policy, business, law, marine affairs, and many other disciplines. In some situations, private sector practitioners are also involved. The Center's Collaborative Capacity Building and Training program helps develop conflict resolution expertise among extension faculty and others. The Center's graduate student internship program seeks to create collaborative competence among the next generation of policy leaders. University faculty and students are often seen as a source of impartial applied technical, scientific, and social data that help establish a common and trusted information base (Kern, 2012; Policy Consensus Initiative, 2005).

Practitioners need to keep in mind that the mediator-party relationship and degree of competence are two sides of the same coin for public sector ECCR institutions—neither alone is sufficient. Having an appropriate connection to parties is essential for having access to intervene in complex or controversial environmental issues. Having the right set of process skills and substantive background promotes a staff member's credibility and enables them to be successful practitioners once they become involved.

Resources for ECCR and party access to services

Effective public sector ECCR institutions possess or have the capacity to locate sufficient resources to provide ECCR services. They also must develop and implement systems to provide easy and rapid access to these services. Practitioners working in public sector settings may find the CPRC and Ruckelshaus Center's approaches to these challenges informative.

The small CPRC staff is funded as part of the EPA's Congressionally appropriated budget and thus effectively offers its services at no additional cost to internal and external parties. The CPRC also has some limited contract funding to support ECCR cases and to enhance agency staff members' capacity to engage effectively in ECCR. Offering funds for cases is often a critical incentive for initiating ECCR. CPRC staff can also work with various parts of the EPA to find funding for ECCR services when the immediate participants may not have it. For example, CPRC can inquire within EPA headquarters to see if resources are available to fund ECCR use in one of the agency's ten regional offices.

Having funding is, however, only part of the equation. The nature of environmental controversies is such that ECCR services are often needed quickly for an effective intervention. The CPRC has addressed this challenge through a mission contract for ECCR services, which is available to all parts of the agency on a fee-for-service basis and eliminates the inefficiencies of developing a separate contract for each ECCR case. The EPA typically spends more than $5 million each year through the Conflict Prevention and Resolution Services Contract. One of the contract's most distinctive aspects is that basic practitioner qualifications and a roster of service providers are established at the contract level, rather than being determined on a case-by-case basis. This allows rapid access to a wide range of providers, sometimes putting a facilitator on the job in less than a week.

The Ruckelshaus Center's funding is a mix of public and private sources, including modest core funding from the universities; fee-for-service contracts to involve university faculty, staff, students, and practitioners in projects; and private philanthropy through the Ruckelshaus Center Foundation. The latter is a particularly unique way to support ECCR through the Center's institutional base within a public university. Through giving from advisory board members, grants from private and public charitable foundations and institutions, and large and small gifts from private donors, the Center has established a multi-million-dollar Endowment for Excellence. The Endowment is intended to preserve in perpetuity the Center's ability to remain flexible and independent; get involved in the pre-assessment and design phases of a project, or stay involved when contract funds are expended, but an agreement is not quite complete; contribute supplemental resources when the project scope exceeds the client's available funding; and take on tasks for the benefit of the ECCR field, such as scholarship and evaluation.

Parties access the Center's services by contacting its director or other members of the core faculty and staff for initial consultation, discussion and conceptualization. That may lead to a pre-assessment (to apply the Center's project criteria), then to designing, scoping, budgeting, and contracting the project. An important part of the latter phase is identifying and securing the services of university faculty, staff, students, and practitioners to serve on the project team. At any of these steps, the Center or the involved parties may determine that a non-university-based provider is more appropriate, at which point the Center will refer them to private sector practitioners. The Center only gets involved if there is something unique about university involvement that makes a successful outcome more likely.

As this review of resources for and access to mediation services underscores, mediators in the public sector setting need to carefully construct and implement strategies to ensure adequate funding for the conflict prevention and resolution practice they support. Both the CPRC and the Ruckelshaus Center have modest funding for basic functions, but rely largely on a fee-for-service model to support specific projects or cases. The fee-for-service model has the advantage of promoting clients' shared responsibility for the success of an ECCR process, but it can lead to situations in which the substantial benefits of ECCR may be out of reach for parties struggling with a controversial, yet resolvable matter. As public sector ECCR institutions, the CPRC and the Center are able to meet this challenge by seeking out funding in various ways that parties considering ECCR may not be able to do on their own. For the CPRC, this can mean reaching out to other parts of the EPA and other federal agencies to identify sponsors. For the Center, it can involve engaging private donors who see the value to society in making effective use of ECCR.

Conclusion

Public sector ECCR institutions are not the appropriate interveners for all collaboration and dispute resolution opportunities. Many times parties will appropriately gravitate toward private sector environmental mediators instead, for example, when no public entities are involved, when complete independence is perceived as necessary, or when a government agency or academic ECCR institution would not add anything valuable to the process. Organizations like the CPRC and the Center are often uniquely situated, however, to further the practice of ECCR.

One reason is that public sector institutions can have a diversity of mediator-party relationships, including those derived from key social networks and established connections to entities with relevant legal authority, to a greater degree than private sector mediators, whom parties may sometimes keep at arm's length, viewing them more as consultants than colleagues. Public sector ECCR institutional relationships provide increased awareness of potential intervention opportunities and influence to promote capacity building and initiation of ECCR cases. While the specific foundations for productive mediator-party relationships do vary on a case-by-case basis, the comparison between the CPRC and the Center on the intervener-party relationship dimension reinforces the value of maintaining a range of public sector institutions with a diversity of relationships to parties, which maximizes the possibility of having an organization with an appropriate platform to intervene in a given situation.

Public sector institutions also contribute greatly to ECCR practice by brokering case funding and services. There are no obvious market incentives to establish these coordination functions in the private sector, especially since so many environmental issues that may be the subject of collaboration or conflict resolution involve government agencies. What has emerged is a model in which modest amounts of base funding for public sector ECCR institutions allow their staffs to seek out and match funding and practitioners from a variety of sources to cases that would benefit from environmental mediation. These characteristics of public sector ECCR organizations do not place them in opposition to private sector mediators. The two loci of ECCR practice are complementary, with public sector ECCR practitioners often providing the opportunity and means for private sector practitioners to intervene efficiently in important environmental and natural resource decisions and controversies. This fruitful public-private ECCR partnership, established over several decades, is likely to flourish into the future.

References

Dukes, E.F. (2004) What we understand about environmental conflict resolution: An analysis based on empirical research. *Conflict Resolution Quarterly*, 22(1–2): 191–220.

Hall, W.E. (2013) Environmental collaboration and conflict resolution in the USA: Reflecting on the first 40 years … and opportunities for research. *Signal*, 28(3): 6–8.

Hall, W.E. (2014) *Turning Points in Environmental Negotiation: Exploring Conflict Resolution Dynamics in Domestic and International Cases*. Dordrecht, the Netherlands: Republic of Letters.

Herrman, M.S., Jerry Gale, N.H. & Foster, M. (2001) In practice: Defining mediator knowledge and skills. *Negotiation Journal*, 17(2): 139–153.

Kern, M.A. (2012) Why collaborate? Why involve universities? *Evans School Review*, 2(1): 1–4.

Kern, M.A. (2013) Fostering collaborative solutions to environmental conflicts on the ground: The William D. Ruckelshaus Center. *Signal*, 28(3): 9–10.

Kriesberg, L. (2007) The conflict resolution field: Origins, growth, and differentiation. In I.W. Zartman (ed.) *Peacemaking in International Conflict: Methods and Techniques* (revised edn) (pp. 25–60). Washington, DC: United States Institute of Peace.

Lederach, J.P. (1991) Of nets, nails, and problems: The folk language of conflict resolution in a Central American setting. In K. Avruch, P.W. Black & J.A. Scimecca (eds) *Conflict Resolution: Cross Cultural Perspectives* (pp. 165–186). New York: Greenwood Press.

Mayer, B.S. (2004) *Beyond Neutrality: Confronting the Crisis in Conflict Resolution* (1st edn). San Francisco, CA: Jossey-Bass.

Moore, C.W. (2014) *The Mediation Process: Practical Strategies for Resolving Conflict* (4th edn). San Francisco, CA: Jossey-Bass & Pfeiffer Imprints, Wiley.

Office of Management and Budget & Council on Environmental Quality. (2012) *Memorandum on Environmental Collaboration and Conflict Resolution*. Washington, DC: Office of Management and Budget, and Council on Environmental Quality.

Oregon Consensus & William D. Ruckelshaus Center. (2013) *Columbia River Basin Salmon and Steelhead Long-term Recovery Situation Assessment*. Portland, OR and Pullman and Seattle, WA: Oregon Consensus and William D. Ruckelshaus Center.

Policy Consensus Initiative. (2005) *Finding Better Ways to Solve Public Problems: The Emerging Role of Universities as Neutral Forums for Collaborative Policymaking*. Portland, OR: Policy Consensus Initiative.

Society of Professionals in Dispute Resolution. (1992) *Competencies for Mediators of Complex, Public Disputes: An Overview Developed by the Environmental/Public Disputes Sector*. Washington, DC: Information Services Federal Judicial Center.

United States Environmental Protection Agency. (2000) *Policy on Alternative Dispute Resolution*. Washington, DC: United States Environmental Protection Agency.

United States Environmental Protection Agency. (2012) *FY 2011 Template ECR Policy Report to OMB-CEQ*. Washington, DC: United States Environmental Protection Agency.

United States Environmental Protection Agency. (2013) *FY 2012 Template ECR Policy Report to OMB-CEQ*. Washington, DC: United States Environmental Protection Agency.

Wehr, P. (1979) *Conflict Regulation*. Boulder, CO: Westview Press.

William D. Ruckelshaus Center. (2010) *A Framework for Stewardship: Final Report on the Work of the Agriculture and Critical Areas Committee*. Pullman and Seattle, WA: Washington State University and University of Washington.

William D. Ruckelshaus Center. (2014) *Chehalis Basin Strategy: Governor's Chehalis Basin Work Group 2014 Recommendation Report*. Pullman and Seattle, WA: Washington State University and University of Washington.

PART VI

Mediating in international and intercultural settings

33

THINKING LOCALLY, ACTING GLOBALLY

Mediating beyond borders and integrated global capacity building

Kenneth Cloke

While listening to news about the latest international disasters from wars to terrorist attacks, I sometimes fantasize about what would happen if, instead of dropping bombs on civilian populations, mediators by the tens of thousands were parachuted into war zones to initiate conversations across battle lines; if, instead of shooting bullets, we organized public dialogues and shot questions at each other; if, instead of mourning the loss of children's lives by visiting equal or greater losses on "enemy" children, we turned every lost life into the name of a school, hospital, library, road or playground dedicated to those who died because we lacked the skills and capacity to communicate and solve common problems.

This raises the question: what would we actually *do* after parachuting in and hitting the ground? We can begin to see that it is possible for each of us to have an impact, even on embittered, intransigent, warlike opponents. We can do so, for example, by building their capacity to communicate, and even celebrate their differences; by strengthening their skills in designing and facilitating dialogues, negotiating collaboratively and resolving their disputes; by mediating beyond and across the borders that divide them; by thinking locally and acting globally; and by acting in ways that reduce their willingness to murder and terrorize each other.

What can be done?

It is clear that conflict resolution as a profession has developed the knowledge, skills and experience needed to begin thinking and planning how we might contribute, even in small ways, to building the capacity of people around the world to resolve chronic conflicts.

In the process, we have learned that deeply entrenched social, economic and political conflicts can be prevented, resolved, transformed and transcended; that doing so means working collaboratively to design culturally respectful conflict resolution approaches and integrating them with prejudice reduction, group facilitation, public dialogue, collaborative negotiation, victim-offender mediation, community building, collaborative law and similar interest-based methodologies. Doing so also means forming international conflict resolution teams that can train indigenous "conflict revolutionists," build integrated conflict resolution capacity both locally and globally, enlist international support and train trainers who can provide commitment, depth, insight and continuity to these strategies.

While many mediators have largely done so as individuals, we have now reached levels of skill and experience that allow us collectively to make a difference. Parachuting mediators into war zones may not be realistic, but convening groups of dedicated dispute resolution professionals to work a few weeks a year over several years with people in highly conflicted areas is quite feasible. All that is lacking is our resolve, in-depth understanding of the dimensions, potential pitfalls and complexity of the problem, and a practical, strategic and integrated way to begin.

The most effective international projects, in my experience, are those that extend over decades with people returning year after year to follow up, learn what worked and what did not, and provide fresh information, more advanced techniques and nuanced advice as circumstances evolve and needs change. Clearly, it takes considerable effort and lasting commitment to design and implement such projects. Yet, as conflict itself has no borders, neither does resolution—nor, for that matter, do empathy, compassion and the willingness to commit to making a difference. We can only choose whether we will be distant, helpless victims of what we mistakenly regard as other people's tragedies or active participants in resolving disputes in our own human family, regardless of where, how or among whom they are occurring.

Conflict as a border or boundary condition

All conflicts take place *between* people—that is, at the borders or boundaries that separate them as individuals, cultures, organizations and nations. Every conflict can therefore be regarded as creating or reinforcing a border or boundary that divides people, drawing a line of demarcation that separates them into opposing sides, isolating and alienating them from one another. Boundaries are then indirect efforts to reduce conflicts through separation, based on a fear of outsiders who are thought likely to use power-based methods in pursuing their self-interests, or of insiders who create internal conflicts and are seen as diminishing the ability to compete effectively with outsiders.

Yet every boundary is also a place of interface and connection, a potentially unifying field, a space where two sides are able to come together. As a result, we can regard conflict resolution as a consensual crossing of the borders and boundaries that separate us. Non-consensual border crossings are experienced as boundary violations and are often vigorously resisted. Consensual border crossings are precursors to collaboration, problem solving, forgiveness and reconciliation.

Conflict, in this sense, is a chasm cutting us off from commonality, a fault line isolating us from our own estranged family, a schism within wholeness. As a result, conflicts can be prevented, resolved, transformed and transcended by identifying the boundaries that separate us and consensually crossing them. There are two principal reasons for doing so: first, to create positive, enjoyable learning relationships; and second, to solve common problems more effectively and sustainably. While the first is optional, the second is becoming mandatory. The problems we are increasingly required to confront have no borders, threaten our survival and cannot be solved except collaboratively.

What would it take to successfully cross these borders and mediate social, economic and political conflicts globally? If time, money, laws, bureaucracy, expertise and willingness to participate were not obstacles, what methods and programs could we employ to reduce unnecessary bloodshed and return to peace and unity after violence subsides? What might the United Nations, national governments and nongovernmental organizations (NGOs) do to discourage evil, war, injustice and terrorism before they begin, and encourage a global transition of organizations and institutions to interest-based conflict resolution processes?

Social, economic and political conflicts are simultaneously public and private, intellectual and emotional, procedural and structural, preventive and reactive, relational and systemic. Because these disputes are highly complex and multilayered, successful dispute resolution efforts need to focus on supporting diverse local initiatives, coordinating efforts internationally and developing unique, culturally supported, integrated combinations of techniques and approaches.

Over several decades, conflict resolvers have invented, discovered and developed a wide range of techniques for successfully communicating across far smaller, less defended, yet remarkably similar interpersonal borders and cultural divides, and resolving disputes in families and communities without warfare or coercion. It is precisely these skills we now need to solve global problems.

Why we need integrated global capacity building

We now face a steadily increasing number of difficult problems and complex conflicts, each of which requires us to move beyond personal, organizational, national and cultural borders in order to solve them. The most important of these, in my view, include:

- Global warming
- Exhaustion of the oceans
- Species extinction
- Decreasing bio-diversity
- Air and water pollution
- Deforestation and loss of arable land
- Resort to warfare
- Nuclear proliferation
- Drug-resistant diseases
- Global pandemics
- Overuse of fertilizers
- Religious intolerance
- Terrorism
- Torture
- Prejudice and intolerance
- Genocide and ethnic cleansing
- Sexual trafficking and abuse
- Vaccinations for diseases
- Population increase
- CO_2 and methane emissions
- Destructive technologies
- Cyclical economic crises
- Unregulated currency trading
- Organized crime and narcotics smuggling

Here is a list of the most powerful problem-solving mechanisms and institutions we have developed over the course of centuries that will not be able to solve these complex conflicts sustainably:

- Military force
- Treaties and international agreements

- Legal interventions and rule of law
- Traditional rules and regulations, policies and procedures
- Diplomacy
- Nation-states
- Capitalism and market principles
- The United Nations, as presently constituted

What is left? The answer is international, collaborative, democratic, interest-based, integrated capacity building, using methods that range from open dialogue, communication and informal problem solving to consensus building, collaborative negotiation and mediation. Here is a 15-step chain of common sense reasoning that supports this conclusion:

- The problems we now increasingly face can no longer be solved locally, nationally or sustainably by a consortium of the largest nation-states
- Conflicts and diverse opinions are widespread over whether these problems exist, who is responsible, and how to solve them
- There are no international organizations presently capable of solving them
- None of these problems can be completely solved using military force or litigation, violence or coercion, hierarchy or bureaucracy, power or rights
- Conflicting political beliefs, perspectives, processes and relationships are blocking agreements, timely solutions, and working preventatively
- International power- and rights-based dispute resolution mechanisms are incapable of sustainably resolving disputes, and hinder collaborative, democratic solutions
- If we do not solve them fully and in time, devastating consequences may occur that will seriously impact hundreds of millions, even billions of people
- It is likely that as greenhouse gases accumulate, the climate will change and thousands of species will become extinct, causing the Earth to become uninhabitable
- Each of these problems is likely to increase as population expands, economies grow and we become more interconnected and interdependent
- The only way we can solve these problems and increase our chances of survival is by building global capacity to communicate across differences, collaboratively negotiate solutions and implement them internationally
- To improve our capacity for voluntary collaboration in solving these problems, we need to reduce the systemic sources of chronic conflict and resistance to change
- It will therefore become necessary to reduce social inequality, economic inequity and political autocracy, as these hinder international cooperation and slow problem solving
- It will also be necessary to reduce social prejudice and discrimination, economic greed and unregulated market practices, political nationalism and bureaucracy
- To achieve any of these goals, we need to vastly increase our skills and capacity in cross-cultural communication, prejudice reduction and bias awareness, creative problem solving, group facilitation, public dialogue, collaborative negotiation, mediation, conflict resolution systems design and similar interest-based methodologies
- In short, we require a *conflict revolution* if we are to substitute integrated, global, interest-based processes and relationships for the predominantly power- and rights-based practices we use today

Six integrated intervention strategies

There are dozens of ways of assisting people to recover from conflict and learn practical methods for preventing, resolving, transforming, and transcending them. To recover from severe social, economic, and political disruptions, a broad range of integrated skills and capacities in multiple areas needs to be developed. We can identify six intervention strategies that will be useful and important in building local capacity:

- Combine responses to grief, loss and trauma with conflict resolution
- Build skills in responding to stereotyping, prejudice and discrimination
- Adopt an elicitive approach to working in and between cultures
- Integrate skills in dialogue, mediation and all interest-based processes
- Encourage empathy and forgiveness, truth and reconciliation
- Design preventative systems and institutionalize conflict resolution

Combine responses to grief, loss and trauma with conflict resolution

The first strategy is to actively integrate trauma recovery and emotional intelligence with conflict resolution skills, for example, by encouraging the open expression of grief and processing the rage triggered by the conflict, while at the same time creating a context, process and setting that are constructive and oriented to prevention, conflict resolution, emotional completion and reconciliation, such as that used by the South African Truth and Reconciliation Commission.

Grief, denial and rage are natural emotions in processing trauma and loss. Conflict creates trauma, and trauma feeds conflict. Healing comes when people face their losses, express their grief, tell stories about what happened, describe their feelings, listen empathetically to each other's experiences, open their hearts to forgiveness and reconciliation, and collaboratively seek ways of preventing future hostilities.

Every culture has its own rituals for handling painful emotions and these rituals should be respected and included in the conflict resolution process. Yet there are times, places and individuals for whom these rituals will be inapplicable or ineffective, and all rituals can be improved and supplemented by creative insights drawn from the experiences of parties in conflict resolution. A capacity-building response to loss can then be seen as taking place in the following steps:

- Design a process and an environment within which it is possible to safely encourage and support expressions of grief and anger
- Critically examine prejudicial views about "the enemy" and collaboratively explore alternatives such as forgiveness, reconciliation and using heartfelt communication
- Develop skills in turning grief and anger into problem solving, negotiation, dialogue and mediation
- Build a sense of diverse, democratic, inclusive community

By way of illustration, hostile racial, religious and ethnic groups can be asked to meet in mixed or self-same teams to discuss and answer the following questions:

- What is one thing you lost as a result of this conflict, or one thing that happened that you are still grieving over?

- What is one thing someone said or did to you or others that you find difficult to forgive, and never, ever want to experience again?
- What is one thing someone said or did that supported you or others when this happened, or which gave you strength and courage or helped you recover?
- What is one thing the people who are here could do right now to help make sure that what happened to you will never happen again?
- What is one thing you are willing to do to help make sure that occurs?
- What is one wish you have for your future relationship with each other, or the relationship between your children and grandchildren?
- What is one thing you would be willing to do starting right now to help those children have the relationship you want them to have?

Build skills in responding to stereotyping, prejudice, and discrimination

A second strategy is to systematically dismantle stereotypes, prejudices, biases, and discriminatory attitudes toward the "enemy." Conflicts grow out of biases and prejudices regarding culture, ethnicity, gender, religion, politics, nationality, language skills, disabilities, sexual orientation, and countless other differences that can be surfaced and often successfully overcome. Creative interventions, techniques, and exercises can assist people in becoming more aware of their biases and realizing that differences can be a source of strength and celebration. Storytelling to elicit empathy and person-to-person understanding and encourage group presentations and recommendations to promote learning from each other is powerful.

Specific conflicts can then be analyzed through simulations and alternative solutions generated through joint analysis of group experiences. The following exercises[1] have proven useful, even in large community groups, in reducing prejudices, biases and cross-cultural conflicts:

- *Introductions*: Ask people to turn to the person next to them and introduce themselves by describing their personal history and cultural background
- *Reclaiming pride*: Ask participants to state their names, the groups or cultures with which they identity, and why they are proud of belonging to them
- *What's in a name?*: In mixed dyads, ask people to describe the origin and meaning of their names and how they came by them
- *Storytelling*: Each person finds someone from a different group or culture and tells a story about what it felt like to grow up as a member of that group or culture
- *Assessing group identity*: Participants discuss what they get by identifying with a group and what they give in return
- *Personalizing discrimination*: In mixed dyads or small groups, participants describe a time when they felt disrespected or discriminated against and compare their experiences
- *Reframing stereotypes*: In mixed or self-same dyads, people describe the stereotypes and prejudices others have about their group while their partners write down key descriptive words and phrases, which they later compare and reframe as positives
- *Observing discrimination*: In mixed dyads, participants describe a time when they witnessed discrimination against someone else. What did they do? How successful was it? What might they have done instead? What kept them from doing more? How could they overcome these obstacles?
- *Owning prejudice*: Participants in teams write down all the prejudicial statements they can think of, analyze them, identify their common elements and read these elements out to the group to brainstorm effective responses

- *Overcoming prejudice*: In dyads, participants describe a personal prejudice or stereotype they had or have, what they did or are doing to overcome it, then ask for and receive coaching, preferably from someone in that group, on what else they might do
- *Which minority are you?*: Participants list all the ways they are a minority, report on the total number of ways and discuss them
- *Explaining prejudice*: Participants in self-same groups identify the prejudices and stereotypes other groups have of them, and explain the truth about their culture and answer questions others have about their group but were afraid to ask
- *A celebration of differences*: Participants stand and are applauded for their differences, in age, family backgrounds, skills, languages, cultures and personal life experiences

Adopt an elicitive approach to working in and between cultures

It is therefore critical in working across and beyond borders that we learn ways of communicating, working collaboratively, solving problems and resolving conflicts in and between cultures that are not our own. Among the most effective approaches in developing conflict resolution capacity and working with diverse cultures is the *elicitive*, collaborative, democratic methodology developed by Mennonite mediator John Paul Lederach (1995). This method focuses on supplementing rather than replacing indigenous problem-solving and conflict resolution strategies, while simultaneously learning from other cultures and developing improvements in everyone's methods and practices. Here are some techniques in bridging cross-cultural enmity in mediations and facilitations:

- Take time to warmly welcome, meet and get to know each person and both sides. Serve food or drink and break bread together. Ask each group to create a culturally appropriate heartfelt context and opening for the conversation they *most* want to have with each other
- Ask them to clarify who they think you are, how they define your role and what they expect of you and the mediation process
- Ask each side to identify the ground rules that will make them feel respected, communicate most effectively and be better able to resolve their disputes
- Elicit a description of conflicts from each side. What are the words for different kinds of conflict in their culture? Which are most serious and which are least? What is commonly done in response to each? Compare similarities and differences between cultures, then do the same for conflict styles and resolution techniques
- Ask people to rank their perceived options from war to surrender and explore the reasons they might choose one over another
- Ask people to state, pantomime, role-play, draw or script how conflicts are resolved in their culture. To whom do they go for assistance? What roles do third parties traditionally play? Which techniques do they use, when and why? How do they mediate, forgive and reconcile? Where do they get stuck and why?
- Invite volunteers from opposing cultures to jointly design a culturally inclusive, enriched, multilayered, comprehensive conflict resolution system to help avoid future disputes
- Ask each side to meet separately and list the words that describe the communication, negotiation or conflict style of the opposing culture and next to it, the words that describe their own. Exchange these lists and ask each side to respond. Do the same with conflicting ideas, feelings such as anger, attitudes toward change or values
- Establish common points of reference by asking someone from each culture to indicate their values or goals for their relationship with the other, or aspirations for the resolution process

- Ask questions like: "What does that mean to you?" "What does the word 'fairness' indicate or imply to you?" "Can you give an example?"
- Acknowledge and model respect for differences, and ask questions if you are not sure what words or behaviors mean
- Ask each person to say one thing they are proud of with regard to their culture, ethnicity or group, and why
- If appropriate, ask if there is anything they dislike about the aforementioned and why
- Ask groups in conflict to say what they most appreciate about the other and why
- Ask them to bring cultural items, such as poems, music or artifacts, and share stories that would help an outsider understand and appreciate their culture
- Ask each side to identify a common stereotype regarding their culture, what it feels like and why. Then ask them to describe what their culture is actually like, why the stereotype is inaccurate and what they would most like others to know about them, then invite the other side to ask the questions they always wanted to ask
- Ask what rituals are used in each culture to end conflicts or reach forgiveness, such as shaking hands, then design combined, integrated or simultaneous rituals for release, completion, closure or reconciliation

In many countries or cultures that lack significant long-term experiences with social, economic and political democracy, there are ancient indigenous tribal and societal conflict resolution traditions that emphasize collaborative, democratic and interest-based interactions. In some cases, these were gradually subordinated to conformist, competitive, autocratic, caste- and class-bound power-based processes that relied on directives and hierarchical authority from above. While both of these approaches have been useful in ending conflicts, prevention, resolution, transformation and transcendence occur more frequently when ancient interest-based resolution processes are revived and reintegrated using collaborative, democratic, and elicitive techniques.

Integrate skills in dialogue, mediation and all interest-based processes

A fourth intervention strategy is to develop integrated skills within local neighborhoods and communities in implementing these processes, including multiple, diverse interest-based methods such as group facilitation, public dialogue, strategic planning, collaborative negotiation, and peer mediation. Teams of volunteers then coach and conduct skill-building workshops for conflict resolvers, mixed groups of neighbors, community activists, therapists, clergy, managers, union leaders, judges, attorneys, government officials, and leaders in civil society. For example, in Los Angeles following the civil unrest in response to the beating of Rodney King, I helped train Federal Emergency Management Agency (FEMA) workers to facilitate dialogues between hostile racial and ethnic groups who went door to door to de-escalate potentially explosive conflicts. Here are some of the exercises I used:

- *Communication and miscommunication*: Self-same groups identify the communications, behaviors and signals they or others do not understand about their culture, present them in a skit, suggest ways to clear up misunderstandings and answer questions from others
- *Mock cultural conflict*: Participants demonstrate a typical cross-cultural conflict in a fishbowl while observers describe their reactions and volunteers offer suggestions on how to mediate or resolve it

- *Offensive remarks*: A volunteer starts to make an offensive comment or joke, then stops mid-sentence and observers offer coaching on effective ways to respond
- *Observing cultural bias*: As homework, participants collect examples of biases and prejudices from the media, family members and peers, and share and analyze them
- *Social change*: Cross-cultural teams discuss what they could do to change prejudicial attitudes and behaviors at work and among family, friends and peers, brainstorm suggestions and agree to implement them
- *Institutional change*: Participants discuss what their organizations and institutions could do to counteract prejudice, and what they might do together to support community dialogue and encourage people to change
- *Breaking bread*: Ask participants to invite someone from other groups or cultures in their community to their home for a potluck dinner and exchange music, poetry, artifacts and stories from their cultures. Then ask their guests to do the same next month and pass it on
- *What I will do*: Each person indicates one thing they learned and are willing to do differently in the future to reduce cross-cultural conflict

Encourage empathy and forgiveness, truth and reconciliation

A fifth strategy is to encourage empathy and forgiveness along with truth and reconciliation by inviting former adversaries to engage in profound, spiritually informed, open-hearted communications and direct, heart-to-heart dialogue. I discuss these techniques in *Mediating Dangerously* (Cloke, 2001) and *The Crossroads of Conflict* (Cloke, 2006), and have found it useful to ask adversaries to:

- Recall what they experienced and how it felt, then imagine and describe what the other person may have experienced and felt
- Tell their opponent directly what they most want or need to hear in order for the conflict to be over for them
- Acknowledge the positive intentions or character of the other person or group
- Apologize for what they did or did not do in the conflict that was counterproductive
- List all the reasons for not forgiving them, and the costs for holding onto those reasons
- Clarify through stories the cost of the conflict and why it is difficult for them to forgive
- Say what they most want to say to each other, straight from the heart, as though this were the last conversation they were ever going to have with each other
- Articulate what they each believe are the most important lessons they learned from their conflict and what they are willing to do differently
- Design a ritual of release, completion or closure that expresses their desire for forgiveness and reconciliation, and agree to execute it

Design preventative systems and institutionalize conflict resolution

A sixth strategy consists of designing preventative systems and institutionalizing conflict resolution skills so that future chronic disputes can be avoided and resolved without violence or coercion. This strategy consists of using conflict resolution systems design principles to identify what the organization, institution, or system contributed to the conflict, then working together to change it. For example, I have created mixed "conflict audit teams" to identify the systemic sources of conflict in workplaces, organizations and institutions by asking the following questions, revised from *Resolving Conflicts at Work* (Goldsmith & Cloke, 2000):[2]

- How much time, money, and effort have been spent on unresolved conflicts?
- How much time are people spending in preventing, managing, and resolving conflicts? At what cost?
- What has been lost due to conflict-related illnesses, injuries, and turnovers?
- How much time has been spent on rumors, gossip, lost productivity and reduced creativity and collaboration due to conflict?
- What impact has conflict had on morale and motivation?
- How many conflicts have recurred because they were never fully resolved?
- What personal, familial, social, and organizational opportunities have been lost?
- Where might the people, the organizations, communities, families and others be by now if it had not been for these conflicts?
- What are the unspoken expectations and values in the organization, family, community, or culture regarding conflict?
- What are the main messages sent by the organization, family, community, or culture regarding conflict?
- Are negative conflict behaviors being rewarded? If so, how?
- How do leaders typically respond to conflicts? How might they respond better?
- Have people been trained in conflict resolution techniques? If not, why not?
- What do different people do when they experience conflicts? Where do they go for help?
- Is there an established conflict resolution procedure? Who is allowed to use it? How often is it used? Do people know about it? How successful is it?
- How satisfied are people with existing conflict resolution processes?
- How skilled are they in using these processes?
- What skills do people need to resolve their conflicts more successfully?
- What hinders prevention, resolution, transformation, and transcendence of conflicts?
- How can people be motivated to resolve their disputes more quickly and completely?
- What systemic changes might prevent, reduce, or help resolve future conflicts?

A 12-step program for integrated capacity building

Taken together, these strategies and techniques suggest a simple, generic 12-step plan that could be used to increase the capacity of families, communities, groups, organizations, and cultures to help prevent, resolve, transform and transcend their conflicts.

- Identify potential partners and allies and convene a cross-cultural team of experienced trainers to conduct action research, facilitate group discussion and deepen understanding of what might be useful in resolving disputes
- Interview leaders of opposing groups, cultures and factions, listen empathetically to their issues and clarify cultural mores, values, interests, goals and concerns regarding conflict
- Meet again with leaders of hostile groups, cultures or factions to secure agreement on a common process and plan, build trust and encourage ongoing support
- Elicit from each group, culture or faction the methods currently being used to resolve disputes and identify ways of validating, supplementing and expanding these core strategies while introducing new ones to adapt and determine which are most successful

- Select or elect a team of volunteers from each group to be trained as co-mediators, facilitators and trainers
- Form cross-cultural teams of volunteer co-mediators and facilitators to work with families, communities, schools, workplaces, government offices and other sites
- Train volunteer co-mediators and facilitators in techniques for processing grief and loss, reducing prejudice, facilitating public dialogues, organizing truth and reconciliation commissions, mediating community disputes and similar methods
- Train more advanced teams to facilitate public dialogues, arbitrate disputes, encourage forgiveness and reconciliation, and conduct conflict audits
- Form cross-cultural teams to train trainers in these techniques throughout civil society and support them in training others
- Conduct periodic feedback, evaluation, audit and course correction to improve the capacity of volunteers and collaboratively identify where future support may be required
- Develop case studies revealing successes and failures and build ongoing popular, financial and institutional support for continuing resolution programs
- Design conflict resolution systems for civil society, economic organizations, political parties and government agencies that provide increased opportunities for early intervention, open dialogue, problem solving, collaborative negotiation and mediation

Implementing these global steps and modifying them to fit local conditions will allow us to substantially reduce the destructiveness of conflict and create a platform on which deeper social and political changes might take place. As global problems extend their reach and increase in importance and severity, it is essential that we discover better, more complex and integrated ways of responding to contentious social, economic, and political issues; that we come together across and beyond borders to improve our ability to listen, ask questions, discuss and understand them, and begin to act together in solving them.

It is therefore essential that we continue building bridges that connect us with those who are seeking to resolve conflicts in other countries and cultures, and not allow ourselves to become silent or passive as difficult, dangerous and polarizing events drag us into their downward logic. However, the efforts that will make the greatest difference are those that are as protracted, global, complex, networked and systemic as the conflicts they seek to address. More profoundly and importantly, by responding to global conflicts in these preventative, heartfelt and systemic ways, we will help prepare the groundwork for what I believe is the next great leap in human history—the leap beyond chronic social, economic and political conflicts and invented, anachronistic borders—into genuine international collaboration, participatory democracy and conflict prevention.[3]

Notes

1 Some of these are drawn from work by the National Coalition Building Institute.
2 Conflict audit teams in communities, organizations and countries can adapt these questions to their own conditions and cultures, and join with dispute resolvers and leaders in families, communities, organizations and institutions to design programs that provide a broad, scalable array of resolution alternatives aimed at preventing social, economic and political conflict.
3 This chapter is revised and adapted from a chapter in Cloke, 2015.

References

Cloke, K. (2001) *Mediating Dangerously: The Frontiers of Conflict Resolution*. San Francisco, CA: Jossey-Bass.

Cloke, K. (2006) *The Crossroads of Conflict: A Journey into the Heart of Dispute Resolution*. Santa Ana, CA: Janis Publications.

Cloke, K. (2015). *Conflict Revolution: Designing Preventative Systems for Chronic Social, Economic, and Political Conflicts*. Dallas, TX: Goodmedia Press.

Goldsmith, J. & Cloke, K. (2000) *Resolving Conflicts at Work*. San Francisco, CA: Jossey-Bass.

Lederach, J.P. (1995) *Preparing for Peace: Conflict Transformation across Cultures*. Syracuse, NY: Syracuse University Press.

34

INTERNATIONAL MULTIPARTY MEDIATION

Siniša Vuković

This chapter will reflect on the unique nature of international multiparty mediation by highlighting a number of essential aspects: who gets involved as a mediator and why, the benefits and liabilities of a process conducted by multiple third parties, and the challenges of achieving cooperative and coordinated efforts by those third parties. The chapter will conclude by recommending a set of skills and competencies that would help professional mediators to conduct multiparty mediation efforts in an efficient and timely manner.

Following the eruption of violence in Syria, a United Nations (UN)-backed Action Group held a closed meeting in Geneva, where the participants discussed and subsequently reached an agreement that outlined the necessary steps for a peaceful political transition in a country that was rapidly being ravaged by an escalating conflict. The list of participants was quite impressive, chaired by UN-Arab League Joint Envoy for Syria Kofi Annan, the meeting was attended by the foreign ministers of China, France, Russia, the United Kingdom, the United States, Turkey, Iraq (chair of the Summit of the League of Arab States), Kuwait (chair of the Council of Foreign Ministers of the League of Arab States), Qatar (chair of the Arab Follow-up Committee on Syria of the League of Arab States) and the European Union high representative for foreign and security policy (Action Group for Syria, 2012). Although it might seem peculiar that this meeting was not attended by a single representative of the conflicting parties in Syria, in contemporary international conflict management, this has become common practice.

In an international system devoid of central authority, international conflicts regularly draw the attention and consequent involvement of actors with interests as heterogeneous and competing as the ones that characterize relations between the conflicting parties themselves. As mediation represents the most cost-effective form of conflict management, the increase in mediation efforts on the part of various international actors seems to be less a matter of choice and more a fact of life (Crocker et al., 1999). The case of Syria is just one of many examples of how crowded and diversified the field of international mediation has become. In fact, following the meeting in Geneva, the newly appointed UN envoy for Syria, Lakhdar Brahimi, started working on an international peace conference for Syria. Confronted with the unyielding and deeply entrenched positions of the conflicting parties, which were also gradually becoming more fragmented, Brahimi sought support from a number of external actors with the capacity to bring the parties to the negotiating table. Eventually, more than

30 states and intergovernmental organizations sent their representatives to the peace conference held in Geneva and Montreux, Switzerland (Brahimi Press Conference, 2013).

International conflicts frequently generate a partial or complete breakdown of communication between the parties, whose relations are tainted by high levels of mutual distrust and suspicion. As the parties become either unable or unwilling to find a solution on their own, the management of the dispute is often delegated to an external actor that assumes the role of mediator. Mediation represents a form of negotiation that is assisted by an external actor in a voluntary and ad hoc manner and is inherently non-coercive and based on legally non-binding measures. The mediator's tasks range from facilitating communication between the parties, to assisting them in formulating viable solutions and transforming their conflictual relationship. In the most resistant cases, mediators may also use material and non-material side payments to incentivize the parties to accept a negotiated solution that may have been outside their initial calculations. They do this by increasing the costs of continued conflict and increasing the utility of cooperation (Bercovitch et al., 1991).

Today, mediation is increasingly conducted by a wide range of international actors that are willing and able to manage international conflicts. These activities, in which more than one international actor mediates a conflict, are generally referred to as *multiparty mediation*, and include sequential, simultaneous and composite involvement of more than one external actor or group in mediating a dispute. The involvement of traditional mediators that represent interested states is now complemented by that of representatives of international and regional organizations, nongovernmental agencies, and prominent individuals. Each one of these actors brings a unique blend of capabilities and interests to the peacemaking process. Depending on their relative will and skill, different mediators may enter the dispute at various stages of the conflict and assume different tasks throughout the process that could be instrumental in terms of the overall outcome.

The crowded stage of international mediation

Mediators never engage in the peacemaking process without an aim. They may gain entry upon invitation by the conflicting parties or by offering their mediation services to these parties. Moreover, they may also start the process based on previously made arrangements that specify mediation as an appropriate method of conflict management. Publically and officially, this involvement is often justified on humanitarian grounds. In cases where an escalating conflict could generate a large-scale violation of human rights, such as genocide or forced dislocation of people, mediators might face mounting public pressure that induces them to draw on a sense of moral imperative to intervene. However, humanitarian concerns should not be confused with pure and unconditional altruism. While for many actors, humanitarian issues are at the core of their involvement, the fact that they still incur certain costs by allocating both material and non-material resources to managing the dispute indicates that they may expect something in return as well (Zartman & Touval, 1996). In fact, even when mediators lack strong strategic interests in a specific conflict, they may benefit from improved reputation and an increased role in international affairs. Therefore, mediation should be understood as a very practical foreign policy tool, used to advance one's particular interests through non-coercive means. As experience has shown, there have been many instances that have required and would have benefited from a mediated peacemaking process, but which were not able to attract the involvement of an external actor as mediator (Young, 1972). Evidently, as mediators' activities are driven by cost-benefit considerations, the very fact that they get involved at all is an indication that they have something at stake.

States

Over the past 60 years, more than 38 percent of all mediation activities have been conducted by states (Greig & Diehl, 2012, p. 63). The bulk of these activities (more than 50 percent) has been carried out by the five permanent members of the UN Security Council—the United Kingdom, France, Russia, China and the United States—commonly regarded as global superpowers (Touval, 1992). The drivers of their activities can best be described as a blend of offensive and defensive motives. Russian mediation efforts in countries that were once in the Soviet sphere (now commonly regarded as the Russian "near abroad," including Georgia, Moldova, Tajikistan, Ukraine, Armenia and Azerbaijan); American mediation of the conflicts in the Balkans and the Middle East; Chinese peacemaking in Cambodia and in the context of the Six Party Talks on North Korea; or French and British peace initiatives in their former colonies—all may serve as useful illustrations of the various motives that trigger state involvement in mediation. These interests range from reasserting a state's zone of influence (and, by the same token, limiting that of their rivals), preventing or containing detrimental spillover effects of escalating conflicts or establishing a more assertive role in future regional and global politics. While superpowers may have been the most active mediators, small and medium-sized states, such as Norway, Finland, Switzerland, Qatar, and Algeria, have also used mediation to strengthen their reputation, credibility, and relevance at the international level, or to prevent regional instability from damaging their interests.

International and regional organizations

Escalating conflicts around the globe that are not prioritized by state actors are often delegated to intergovernmental organizations that have a very unique role at the international level. For many international and regional organizations, one of their most fundamental *raisons d'être* is the promotion of peace and security. As such, they are often engaged in mediation processes in order to contain escalating conflicts, reduce human suffering, promote principles and norms of international law, and foster long-term constructive engagement between the disputing parties (Bercovitch, 1996). While they generally lack the resources and operational capabilities at the disposal of their member states, international and regional organizations rely in large part on the legitimacy they derive from their status as actors capable of pooling diverging interests and distilling a common one; their credibility as international actors, their internal cohesiveness and/or experience from previous mediation efforts (Fretter, 2002, p. 98).

The United Nations has been the most active mediator of all international organizations. Although its overall involvement has been declining steadily from nearly 50 percent of all mediation activities in the 1940s and 1950s, to around 35 percent in the 1990s, evidence of the UN's continued relevance in mediation can be found in the fact that is has been tasked with managing the most resistant cases at the global level (Greig & Diehl, 2012, p. 68). With its reputation of being a bastion of international morality, the UN has the ability to offer a multilateral setting in which international actors can address the most salient international conflicts, while at the same time serving as a legitimizing agency for unilateral conflict management efforts conducted by various state and non-state actors (Rubin, 1992; Fretter, 2002, p. 100). However, due to a variety of contextual (the UN is frequently tasked with managing the most intractable conflicts), systemic (principles of state sovereignty and non-interference) and operational (decision-making processes) constraints, the UN has faced mounting criticism of its inability to handle escalating conflicts properly (Touval, 1994). Not surprisingly, it has increasingly delegated or shared responsibility for mediation with various regional organizations, like the European Union, the Organization for Security and Co-operation in Europe (OSCE), the African Union (AU), the Organization of American States (OAS), the Arab League (AL) and many others. The comparative advantage of these organizations in the realm of peacemaking relates to the perception that regional organizations more closely reflect the socio-political, economic, and cultural character of the conflicting parties. Parties to a conflict may find the regional expertise and cultural sensitivity of regional organizations as essential features that make them uniquely qualified for the job.

Nongovernmental organizations and eminent individuals

The least conspicuous international actors (at least when it comes to their interests) able to act as mediators are nongovernmental organizations (NGOs). A distinctive feature that qualifies these actors as mediators is their perceived lack of particular interests that parties may perceive to be intimidating, intrusive, and imposing. Their activities may range from the distribution of humanitarian assistance, to monitoring the degree to which the principles of human rights have been upheld and the effectiveness of measures promoting socio-economic development (Dunn & Kriesberg, 2002). At the same time, thanks to their continuous presence in conflict-affected areas, various development, humanitarian, and/or religious NGOs may develop a strong local expertise and establish important connections with relevant local players. As a result, they may be well placed to adequately and rapidly recognize the underlying issues that drive the conflict and to identify actors that should be engaged in the peacemaking process. In light of their relatively innocuous interests, they may be able to gain entry in the very early stages of conflict, at which point the conflicting parties may still be reluctant to internationalize their dispute, as this may put more pressure on the parties and reduce their flexibility and capacity to compromise.

Similarly, many illustrious individuals have acted as international mediators, either through their NGOs (Martti Ahtisaari's mediation efforts in Aceh conducted through his Crisis Management Initiative—CMI), or by their own initiative (Jimmy Carter's 1994 mediation of nuclear issues in North Korea). What sets these individuals apart as mediators is their unique mediation expertise and experience as diplomats. As they are not mandated by a state or international organization, these individuals might use their existing network of contacts and established international reputation to de-escalate conflicts.

Benefits and liabilities of multiparty mediation

Since it is nearly impossible to find a single international actor that is either capable of or willing to invest the necessary material and non-material resources required to manage a conflict (which increasingly include elevated levels of commitment), multiparty mediation has become a very useful method of addressing contemporary conflict. Since each mediator may bring a distinct set of capabilities to the process that can be used to incentivize the parties to achieve a negotiated solution, a multiparty endeavor allows the mediators to pool their resources and develop a unique set of incentives that would be unavailable to a single actor (Crocker et al., 2001). At the same time, while working in concert, the mediators may also share the costs of peacemaking activities—be they material (such as logistics) or non-material (such as reputational political costs)—and divide the labor and responsibilities across the coalition (Beber, 2010). Furthermore, the coalitions can include external actors that are sensitive to the interests of all conflicting sides. When mediators manage to achieve internal balance of their (competing) interests, this in turn increases their legitimacy in the eyes of the conflicting parties and allows mediators to exercise their influence with less objection. Also, as mediation represents a calculated choice, deeply embedded in a network of preferences pursued by actors at the international level, mediators may use this collective engagement to improve damaged relations and restructure regional and global affairs.

However, none of these advantages can be exploited if the mediators are unable or unwilling to develop a shared understanding of the conflict and lack the capacity to promote a common solution. In the event that mediators fail to act based on a common script, mixed signals may be sent to the conflicting parties, exacerbating the existing complexities of the conflict (Crocker et al., 2001). Such mixed messages may reduce clarity around the leverage and strategies the mediators aim to apply and, as a consequence, confuse the parties regarding the direction in which the mediators intend to take the overall peacemaking process. The fact that diverse mediators express their intention to join the mediating coalition does not guarantee that they will commit to the peacemaking process. While mediators may be attracted by the prospects of a collaborative endeavor that has the potential to generate an "easy win," as soon as the conflict proves to be more resistant to mediation initiatives, mediators may reduce their commitment and begin free-riding in the process. As different mediators shift responsibility to other coalition members, avoid the application of their resources, and push the parties toward an agreement, the overall process may be seriously jeopardized.

The more the parties believe that mediators are working at cross-purposes, the more they might be inclined to exploit these divides to conduct negotiations for nefarious purposes that have little to do with reaching a mutually acceptable solution (Richmond, 1998). For instance, the parties may use these circumstances to stall and buy time to rearm and regroup. Faced with competing mediators, parties may also engage in forum shopping for a mediator that offers a solution more in line with their specific interests.

Evidently, effective multiparty mediation efforts are contingent upon the mediators' ability to reach the required convergence of interests and their ability to coordinate their activities. Although there is clear evidence that increasing the number of available and willing mediators may improve the effectiveness of the overall process (Frazier & Dixon, 2006), the increase in numbers could also have adverse effects on establishing and maintaining congruence among them. The diverse nature of various mediators is not only reflected in the set of resources and leverage they bring with them, but is also evident in the variety of interests and views they have regarding the conflict itself. Therefore, an increase in the number of mediators will inevitably increase the likelihood that the mediating coalition is characterized by competing or incompatible interests within the mediating coalition, which only adds to the complexity of the overall peacemaking process. Larger coalitions yield higher organizational costs, as they require more sophisticated regulation mechanisms to promote cooperative efforts. Looking at the nexus between pooling of leverage and mounting organizational costs, smaller coalitions seem to outperform larger ones (Böhmelt, 2011). An enlargement of the mediating coalition certainly offers opportunities that can significantly increase the effectiveness of mediated peace processes, but this is only true as long as the coalition does not become overcrowded and difficult to organize and synchronize.

Fostering cooperation and coordination

Cooperation

In order to generate expected benefits and minimize potential liabilities, collective efforts must foster adequate cooperation among the mediators and subsequent coordination of their activities in the mediation process (Vuković, 2012). Cooperation can be understood as "a situation where parties agree to work together to produce new gains for each of the participants that would be unavailable to them by unilateral action, at some cost" (Zartman & Touval, 2010, p. 1). It represents a process in which actors (even those with competing interests) decide to pool their resources and capabilities in order to achieve joint gains. This decision is not driven by impulse or coincidence. It is a calculated choice, made by actors interested in overcoming their differences as a means of creating new opportunities. Cooperation generates organizational costs, especially in ad hoc formats, as parties need to develop and maintain predictable and mutually acceptable regulatory mechanisms that promote cooperative activities. Cooperation costs also include the trade-offs that participating actors willingly accept as part of the reciprocal exchange that takes place in cooperative endeavors (Hopmann, 2010). Therefore, by agreeing to cooperate, participants automatically accept that they will have to settle for less than what they initially aimed for.

In multiparty mediation, cooperation takes place on three distinct yet highly interrelated levels: between conflicting parties, between conflicting parties and mediators, and between mediators themselves. Consequently, success in a complex peacemaking process is directly dependent upon the maintenance of cooperation on all three levels simultaneously. As experience has shown, it is not rare for initially cooperative mediators to begin opting for defection strategies, ranging from procrastination to complete abandonment of the peacemaking process. However, in multiparty mediation, defection also includes instances at which mediators refuse to work together, start developing irreconcilable diagnoses of the conflict, promote competing and mutually exclusive solutions, or demonstrate unwillingness to apply all of their resources to move the conflicting parties toward a negotiated solution. The evident lack of cooperation between mediators is a practical manifestation of an escalating conflict between them.

If not managed properly, the conflict between mediators may exacerbate the actual conflict that is being mediated. Interests and resources that mediators bring with them to the peacemaking process translate into their specific biases (Carnevale & Arad, 1996). On the one hand, their interests are projected into specific formulas for the final outcome. As such, mediation is often influenced by mediators' "bias of outcome." Effective mediators should never ascribe international legitimacy to and endorse a solution that violates their interests (Vuković, 2015). On the other, the decision to manage a conflict is often influenced by pre-existing relations between external actors and particular parties in conflict. Contemporary conflicts are increasingly internationalized in the sense that one or more external actor offers material and non-material support to one or more conflicting sides (Themnér & Wallensteen, 2014). While conflicting actors are inclined to accept multiparty mediation activities because they expect that their external partners in the mediating coalition will help them reach the best mediated solution possible, the rest of the mediating coalition is also aware that this "bias of actor" may be used to leverage a particular conflicting party toward an agreement that might not be accepted otherwise (Zartman & Touval, 1996). However, a non-cooperative attitude on the part of a mediator with close ties to one of the conflicting parties may send a signal that defection is an acceptable course of action and thus decrease the potential of finding a compromise-based solution to the conflict.

Just as the decision to cooperate is based on a cost-benefit analysis, so is the decision to eschew cooperation. However, in large part, non-cooperation reflects external actors' short-term calculations. In fact, while this decision may prove its utility in the short term, it will most likely yield fewer benefits than cooperation in the long term (Vuković, 2015). By remaining outside the mediating coalition, an external actor will be deprived of the possibility of controlling and influencing the overall peacemaking process toward an outcome that is in line with its interests and needs. Furthermore, the outcome mediated without its cooperation has the potential to be less attractive and beneficial to their partners in conflict. This, in turn, might damage that external actor's international reputation and credibility, and ability to exert control over future conflict management activities.

Since mediation is a foreign policy tool and no foreign policy decision is made in a vacuum, significant developments at the system level, caused by pivotal socio-political, economic, or natural events, may induce external actors to reconsider their defection strategies and engage in cooperative activities. For instance, if external actors engaged as mediators in a particular conflict are confronted with a new parallel conflict that is rapidly escalating; this may induce them to reconsider their priorities (Kriesberg, 1991). Similarly, catastrophic events caused by nature or human behavior can elicit a shakeup of the established strategies of all actors involved in the peacemaking process. The decision to alter foreign policy preferences might come from the incumbent regime or from a completely new political elite because the confrontational strategies pursued (by incumbent elites) proved to be inefficient and harmful. In all of these instances, finding a solution through cooperative mediation efforts might prevent external actors from depleting their resources and overstretching their capabilities.

In addition to these exogenous geo-political shifts, external actors may also reframe their priorities in response to changes in conflict dynamics. This is especially true if the confrontational strategies of their partners in the conflict are no longer yielding expected results and, instead, are becoming harmful and unbearable. Mediators may be the first ones to perceive or produce a deadlock and can project this on their partners and other parties involved in the conflict with the aim of creating a mutually hurting stalemate (Stedman, 1991). Finally, external actors can foster a sense of cooperation not only after a geo-political shift or change in conflict dynamics, but also in response to a realization that non-cooperative behavior may damage reputations and relationships with other international actors in the end. Therefore, they may engage in a negotiating process to produce necessary trade-offs with other members of the mediating coalition, clarify the formula for the lasting solution and improve the overall structural relations with their rivals (Zartman, 2010).

Coordination

Once the mediators manage to achieve sufficient convergence of interests and engage cooperatively, they still need to coordinate all of their activities. Coordination represents a subset dynamic of the wider cooperation process and refers to the logistical aspects of dividing tasks effectively and clarifying who needs to do what, when and how (Strimling, 2006). Coordination is achieved through information sharing, collaborative analysis and strategizing, resource sharing, building, and maintaining formal partnerships and other means of synchronizing and/or integrating activities (Nan & Strimling, 2006). All of these activities help mediators prevent any possibility of working at cross-purposes and thereby jeopardize the achievement of shared goals.

Clarity regarding roles within the coalition, especially when it comes to leadership, diminishes the potential of an uncoordinated process. However, at the international level, where actors are reluctant to lose their autonomy in terms of decision making, the choice of assigning (or assuming) the leading role appears to be quite context dependent and is often done in an ad hoc manner. The appointment of a leading actor is best understood as a combination of opportunity, conflicting parties' demands, capabilities and resources of interested mediators to sustain that role and their credibility vis-à-vis other members of the international community (Whitefield, 2010). As experience has shown, leadership roles may be taken by powerful states due to their ability to muster the most resources and assume an assertive role throughout the process. However, powerful states often bring with them very strong preferences and biases, which, in turn, may affect the internal balance of the mediating coalition. By leaning toward one of the parties and/or a particular outcome that favors one of the parties, the multiparty efforts may not be accepted by all conflicting parties (Jones, 2002). For this reason, a large proportion of multiparty mediation efforts are conducted under the formal leadership of an international or regional organization. Distinguished by their legitimate power, these actors are able to project an image of balance and global convergence of interests (Touval, 1994).

Conclusion and policy recommendations

International mediation is increasingly conducted by more than one interested external actor. While these actors may encompass a wide variety of international players—ranging from states of different sizes and capabilities, to a variety of non-state actors such as international and regional organizations, NGOs, and eminent individuals—the effectiveness of mediated efforts depends on their ability to reach convergence of interests over a solution they aim to pursue. Once they decide to work from a common script, mediators may agree on an adequate coordination mechanism, which would assemble their specific resources and leverages in order to produce attractive incentives for parties to move toward a mutually acceptable agreement. In practice, such coordination mechanisms are often designed in an ad hoc manner. As such, multiparty mediation may be conducted through a group endeavor—with the most notable format being the Contact Group—or through a process that has a clear leader, whose efforts are supported and complemented by various relevant external actors.

Regardless of the format, the benefits of multiparty mediation may turn into liabilities if the external actors are unable to work from a common script. Thus, before entering the peacemaking process, it is recommended that potential mediators discuss and come up with a common understanding of the conflict and the range of potential solutions that they are willing to explore and potentially suggest to the conflicting parties through a multiparty mediation process. Mediators' unwillingness or inability to develop a shared idea of the conflict has the potential to bolster already intransigent positions of the conflicting sides and significantly reduce the likelihood of reaching a negotiated solution. Therefore, success in mediation is dependent on the ability to promote complementary efforts not just between conflicting parties, but between participating external actors as well.

References

Action Group for Syria. (2012, June 30). *Final Communiqué*. United Nations. Retrieved from www.un.org/News/dh/infocus/Syria/FinalCommuniqueActionGroupforSyria.

Beber, B. (2010) *The (Non-)efficacy of Multi-party Mediation in Wars Since 1990*. New York: New York University. Retrieved from www.operationspaix.net/DATA/DOCUMENT/4628~v~The__Non-_Efficacy_of_Multi-Party_Mediation_in_Wars_Since_1990.pdf.

Bercovitch, J. (1996) The United Nations and the mediation of international disputes. In R. Thakur (ed.) *The United Nations at Fifty: Retrospect and Prospect* (pp. 73–87). Dunedin: Otago University Press.

Bercovitch, J., Anagnoson, J.T. & Wille, D.L. (1991) Some conceptual issues and empirical trends in the study of successful mediation in international relations. *Journal of Peace Research*, 28(1): 7–17.

Böhmelt, T. (2011) Disaggregating mediations: The impact of multiparty mediation. *British Journal of Political Science*, 41(4): 859–881.

Brahimi Press Conference. (2013). *Transcript of Press Conference by Joint Special Representative for Syria (JSRS) Lakhdar Brahimi*. United Nations, December 20. Retrieved from www.un.org/sg/offthecuff/index.asp?nid=3212.

Carnevale, P.J. & Arad, S. (1996) Bias and impartiality in international mediation. In J. Bercovitch (ed.) *Resolving International Conflicts: The Theory and Practice of Mediation* (pp. 39–53). Boulder, CO: Lynne Rienner.

Crocker, C.A., Hampson, F.O. & Aall, P.R. (1999) *Herding Cats: Multiparty Mediation in a Complex World*. Washington, DC: United States Institute of Peace Press.

Crocker, C.A., Hampson, F.O. & Aall, P. (2001) A crowded stage: Liabilities and benefits of multiparty mediation. *International Studies Perspectives*, 2(1): 51–67.

Dunn, L. & Kriesberg, L. (2002) Mediating intermediaries: Expanding roles of transnational organizations. In J. Bercovitch (ed.) *Studies in International Mediation* (pp. 194–212). London: Palgrave Macmillan.

Frazier, D.V. & Dixon, W.J. (2006) Third-party intermediaries and negotiated settlements, 1946–2000. *International Interactions*, 32(4): 385–408.

Fretter, J. (2002) International organizations and conflict management: The United Nations and the mediation of international conflicts. In J. Bercovitch (ed.) *Studies in International Mediation* (pp. 98–126). London: Palgrave Macmillan.

Greig, J.M. & Diehl, P.F. (2012) *International Mediation*. Cambridge: Polity.

Hopmann, P.T. (2010) Synthesizing rationalist and constructivist perspectives on negotiated cooperation. In I.W. Zartman & S. Touval (eds) *International Cooperation: The Extents and Limits of Multilateralism* (pp. 95–110). Cambridge: Cambridge University Press.

Jones, B.D. (2002) Challenges of strategic coordination. In S.J. Stedman, D. Rothchild & E.M. Cousens (eds) *Ending Civil Wars: The Implementation of Peace Agreements* (pp. 89–116). Boulder, CO: Lynne Rienner.

Kriesberg, L. (1991) Formal and quasi-mediators in international disputes: An exploratory analysis. *Journal of Peace Research*, 28(1): 19–27.

Nan, S.A. & Strimling, A. (2006) Coordination in conflict prevention, conflict resolution and peacebuilding. *International Negotiation*, 11(1): 1–6.

Richmond, O. (1998) Devious objectives and the disputants' view of international mediation: A theoretical framework. *Journal of Peace Research*, 35(6): 707–722.

Rubin, J.Z. (1992) Conclusion: International mediation in context. In J. Bercovitch & J.Z. Rubin (eds) *Mediation in International Relations: Multiple Approaches to Conflict Management* (pp. 249–272). New York: St Martin's Press.

Stedman, S.J. (1991) *Peacemaking in Civil War: International Mediation in Zimbabwe, 1974–1980*. Boulder, CO: Lynne Rienner.

Strimling, A. (2006) Stepping out of the tracks: Cooperation between official diplomats and private facilitators. *International Negotiation*, 11(1): 91–127.

Themnér, L. & Wallensteen, P. (2014) Armed conflicts, 1946–2013. *Journal of Peace Research*, 51(4): 541–554.

Touval, S. (1992) The superpowers as mediators. In J. Bercovitch & J.Z. Rubin (eds) *Mediation in International Relations: Multiple Approaches to Conflict Management* (pp. 232–248), New York: St Martin's Press.

Touval, S. (1994) Why the U.N. fails: It cannot mediate. *Foreign Affairs*, 73(5): 44–57.

Touval, S. & Zartman, I.W. (2001) International mediation in the post-cold war era. In C.A. Crocker, F.O. Hampson & P. Aall (eds) *Turbulent Peace: The Challenges of Managing International Conflict* (pp. 427–443). Washington, DC: United States Institute of Peace Press.

Vuković, S. (2012) Coping with complexity: Analyzing cooperation and coordination in multiparty mediation processes. *International Negotiation*, 17(2): 265–293.

Vuković, S. (2015) *International Multiparty Mediation and Conflict Management: Challenges of Cooperation and Coordination*. London: Routledge.

Whitefield, T. (2010) *External Actors in Mediation: Dilemmas and Options for Mediators*. Geneva: Centre for Humanitarian Dialogue.

Young, O.R. (1972) Intermediaries: Additional thoughts on third parties. *Journal of Conflict Resolution*, 16(1): 51–65.

Zartman, I.W. (2010) Cooperation and conflict management. In I.W. Zartman & S. Touval (eds) *International Cooperation: The Extents and Limits of Multilateralism* (pp. 213–237). Cambridge: Cambridge University Press.

Zartman, I.W. & Touval, S. (1996) International mediation in the post-cold war era. In C.A. Crocker, F.O. Hampson & P. Aall (eds) *Managing Global Chaos: Sources of and Responses to International Conflict* (pp. 445–461). Washington, DC: United States Institute of Peace Press.

Zartman, I.W. & Touval, S. (2010) *International Cooperation: The Extents and Limits of Multilateralism*. New York: Cambridge University Press.

35

EXPLORING INTERNATIONAL MEDIATION

Past, present and beyond

Lynn Cole

In the last decade, the use of mediation worldwide has exploded. Mediation's meteoric growth mirrors the rapid expansion of international business as large and small companies in a myriad of countries are shifting to a global vision. e-Commerce enmeshes the globe like a giant intricate silk web. Far fewer commercial transactions are tied to national boundaries in contemporary times. Mediation based on traditions arising centuries ago in the tribes of the Arabian deserts and African savannahs—and fostered today by governments and business—has developed into the emergent dispute resolution tool in the world.[1]

Today, international business transactions cover longer periods; create multifaceted financial, legal, and technical relationships; and involve many participants from diverse nations, including multinational corporations, international organizations, global financial institutions, sovereign governments, and state enterprises (Salacuse, 2002). In fact, "[p]arties from countries throughout the world are negotiating and carrying out these complex transactions in an environment of diverse cultures, political instability, conflicting ideologies, differing bureaucratic and organizational traditions, inconsistent laws, and constantly changing monetary and economic variables" (Salacuse, 2002, para. 2).

As globally linked commerce increases, so too does the likelihood of disputes. Fostered by these increased organizational and transactional complexities, international commercial disputes are increasing. Mediation has increased exponentially to meet international business and commercial dispute resolution needs.

Cultural impacts of mediation

Cross-cultural impacts

Due to the cross-polarization of disputes, the impact of culture in mediation cannot be overstated. However, despite its imperative in international mediation, this chapter does not explore cultural differences and how they impact mediation to any degree of depth. Nonetheless, as a general matter, it is vital that international mediation practitioners, before engaging in cross-cultural mediations, understand the cultural environment and ethnic differences, preferences, and social codes of each mediation participant.[2]

Cultural aspects are expressed in society's values, norms, and ways of thinking, feeling, and behaving, all of which are expressions transmitted in mediation. These cultural aspects contextually are expressed in the differences of national, regional, ethnic, religious, linguistic, gender, generational, social class, organizational, department, and corporate levels. Therefore, it is reasonable to expect individuals from different cultures to attach different meanings to a personal interaction and to react differently to signals from others. Before mediating, always meaningfully explore those differences; rather than seeing them as a threat because culturally determined differences can be viewed as a cross-cultural win-win strategy.[3]

Neither can the impact of traditional mediation be underestimated. The practice of mediation in various locations around the globe is not only influenced by current culture, but also by the historical and traditional use of mediation in that particular culture. Mediation is not a new process, although its application by court systems is relatively contemporary, as are "professional" mediators. Present-day practice of professional mediation is a mere nanosecond in the history of mediation. Ancient people practiced mediation for centuries using the core principles of empowering the parties to make their own decisions in private sessions, and employing a respected communal neutral. In fact, "[m]ediation is, historically and certainly, more ancient than the Anglo-Saxon adversarial system of law" (Cole, 2009).

A society integrating modern mediation into its social laws and social and economic fabric best designs its model by assimilating its traditions of conflict resolution and mediation. Incorporating its traditions is particularly appropriate in the design of programs for developing the rule of law, such as court-based mediation. Although the American concept of court-based mediation is successful and aspects of it have been incorporated in a number of non-Western mediation systems, it is not necessarily and routinely followed as a model; rather, most countries developing mediation blend traditional mediation techniques with modern-day concepts.

For centuries, communities across India used an information dispute resolution akin to mediation: village elders (often high-ranking family members) called the disputing parties together to resolve community and family disputes. This tradition of *Panchayat* continues today in many Indian communities (Xavier, 2006). Likewise, Bedouin tribal elders in the Arabian deserts practiced a similar traditional style of mediation centuries ago. The ancient tribal tradition of *wassata* involved a tribal elder bringing the parties together in a private setting to resolve disputes between warring tribes and families.[4] In kinship with this practice, tribal chieftains practiced Ubuntu, originating in the South African savannas. This belief system advocates the connection of all humanity. Because it was used for centuries as a successful philosophic basis to resolve tribal disputes, the South African government embedded this concept in many of its mediation statutory provisions (Joubert, 2012).

Rather than being village- and tribal leadership-based, China's ancient practice of conciliation and mediation emanated from a philosophic base found in the Confucian belief system. As such, the emphasis in this form of mediation is to preserve the values of compromise, self-criticism, and natural social harmony. Recorded history shows us that as early as 1146 BC the Chinese practiced this form of mediation (Mealey-Lohmann, 2010). Based upon its unique history, China's mediation represents the emergence of a unique culture of mediation's close cousin, conciliation.

Mediation is the preferred resolution process

From these ancient traditions of mediation, modern mediation is proliferating around the world. Advocates of mediation have long claimed that mediation is the most cost-effective and time-efficient alternative dispute resolution (ADR) process to resolve international disputes (Barkett et al., 2010). Although there is a paucity of data, corporate surveys evidence mediation as the fastest growing ADR method of choice in the business community; across diverse jurisdictions, overwhelmingly, mediation is preferred over other ADR practices (Smith, 2007).

We know there are several reasons for this preference. A primary one is that participants take resolution of the case into their own hands and away from third-party strangers to the disputing party, such as judges and arbitrators. Mediating parties are specifically encouraged and empowered to do so by a neutral third party. Courts must follow the strict confines of evidentiary and procedural rules and, while arbitrators have greater latitude, they still are constrained to procedural and evidentiary parameters. In mediation, the parties have the opportunity to create a resolution tailored to the inimitable circumstances of their dispute, oftentimes assisted by neutral mediators who are industry experts. Some courts have discretion to shape equitable remedies. Nevertheless, in mediation, the parties not only can be equally creative, but can also address and resolve potential future contentious issues. The outcomes traditional in court-related litigation and arbitration—the quintessential "winner and loser"—can be much more expansive in mediation.

It is well known that the use of mediation reduces costs (De Palo et al., 2011) and curtails the delay endemic in litigation and arbitration. Add to these factors, routine reports by authorities from around the globe, that mediation settlements have a higher rate of compliance than decisions made by outside parties. Many ascribe this attribute to the fact that the parties in this voluntary process ultimately control the outcome of the agreement. The parties "own" their decision because they are empowered by a trained neutral to create a resolution designed to be fair and capable of performance.

Mediation is a process unlike any other, because of its consistent imperative on confidentiality. This fact alone makes mediation appealing in commercial disputes. In the mediation laws being promulgated in various countries around the world, most if not all of them have provisions requiring confidentiality. Especially in developing countries attempting to incentivize trade and tourism, they have promulgated civil mediation laws prominently including a provision of confidentiality. In some countries, mediation laws make violation of mediation confidentiality an illegal act (Cole, n.d.).

In some types of commercial situations, confidentiality can be and often is critical to the successful resolution of a dispute. For example, the protection of trade secrets involves matters relating to formula, process, device, or other business information that must be kept confidential in order to maintain a competitive advantage. In cases involving patents, proprietary information and other sensitive commercial information, mediation's confidentiality is a significant enticement to use the mediation process. In the growing area of technology and intellectual property disputes, especially where the technology at issue in the dispute is not patented, the mediation process allows outside expertise to be brought into the intellectual property dispute resolution. By discussing all aspects of issues and interests in order to protect their trade secrets and proprietary information, mediation's confidentially provides a real opportunity to reach a business-oriented solution.

Mediation success rates

As a practical matter, if mediation is heralded as such a productive tool, is there any proof that mediation is actually working? Efforts are being made to capture mediation success rates around the world. Surveys in the more sophisticated mediation markets such as the UK and the USA demonstrate overwhelming success. The data indicate that the settlement rate for mediation approaches 80 percent (Posin, 2004). Moreover, "[m]ediation success rates for business disputes … cases that result in settlement during or shortly after the mediation … generally are in the 80%-90% range" (Kaskell, 2002, p. 61). The International Chamber of Commerce (ICC) has collected more recent data from mediations of disputed amounts ranging from below US$20,000 to over $500 million, involving parties from over 70 nationalities, and for the period December 31, 2012 to January 1, 2014. These data confirm that in less than four months after the file was transferred to a mediator, over 80 percent of the cases were settled after a first meeting with the mediator (ICC, n.d.). Mediation is no longer the alternative in dispute resolution—it is the choice.

The drivers of modern mediation

New enforcement of the mediation settlement agreement

As a dispute resolution tool, most agree that mediation is well established in the "legal ethos and procedural rules of most common law jurisdictions, such as the United Kingdom, the United States, Canada and Australia" (Pribetic, 2008, p. 37). In civil law countries, where the principal source of law is the code, the practice of mediation generally relies upon passage of a mediation law, rule, or regulation. However, failure to enact a specific mediation law, rule, or regulation necessarily has not curtailed the practice of mediation; arbitration laws or various procedural rules requiring settlement efforts for cases within various countries allow settlement of mediation without a specific mediation law. Even in those countries without a promulgated mediation law, many civil law countries are catching on fast to mediation.

There are occasions when, after the mediation is concluded, circumstances may cause a party to breach or attempt to breach the mediation agreement. Fortunately, given the increasing numbers worldwide of successful mediations, litigation of the mediation agreement appears to be the rarity rather than the norm. Although there is a paucity of statistics to support this position, anecdotal evidence is coming in from international sources (Coben & Thompson, 2006). Nonetheless, many mediation scholars argue that the use of mediation in court systems has been revolutionary (Singer & Lewis, 2008).

Despite commercial mediation's obvious benefits, businesses may be wary of the unpredictable enforcement mechanisms based upon varied national policies. Fortunately, there appear to be a number of multi-jurisdictional enforcement mechanisms, which generally include enforcement as an arbitral award and enforcement as a judgment within the disputants' jurisdiction; these procedures give hope to the concept of enforcing a mediation settlement without additional litigation.[5] There are several avenues to validate a mediation settlement agreement based upon the entry of an arbitration award.

According to Miccioli (n.d.), "[c]ountries may agree bilaterally to enforce arbitral awards, sometimes through a treaty of friendship, commerce, and navigation or through a bilateral investment treaty (BIT), of which there are now an estimated 2000" (p. 6). Alternatively, a multilateral agreement may be implemented. The United Nations Commission on International Trade Law (UNCITRAL) Model Law on International Commercial Conciliation (MLICC), Article 14, provides that a settlement agreement reached in mediation is enforceable; however, it fails to provide a mechanism for such enforcement, instead leaving enforcement to the enacting states (United Nations, 1994).[6]

The UNCITRAL Model Law on International Commercial Arbitration, adopted in 1985, provides that if the parties reach agreement and the agreement is not the result of the arbitrator's action, the arbitral tribunal shall "terminate the proceedings and, if requested by the parties and not objected to by the arbitral tribunal, record the settlement in the form of an Arbitral Award on agreed terms" (Article 30). This law has impacted the national arbitration legislation of more than 50 countries. As of the writing of this chapter, there is an UNCITRAL Working Group II, which is working on a proposal to put mediation settlements on the same footing as arbitral awards (McIlwrath, 2014). The author strongly supports this mechanism to bring a universal consistency and balance to mediation settlement agreements.

International organizations supporting commercial mediation

Several private international organizations focus on providing not only arbitration, but also mediation. Three of the largest and most well-known international and for-profit organizations offering arbitration and mediation from the United States include: the International Center for Dispute Resolution (ICDR) of the American Arbitration Association; the International Institute of Conflict Prevention and Resolution (CPR); and JAMS, Inc. There also are a number of other organizations that offer institutionalized arbitration and mediation, such as the London Court of Arbitration, the Stockholm Chamber of Commerce, and the World Intellectual Property Organization (WIPO). These organizations develop lists of selected and trained neutrals (mediators and arbitrators) to work in international mediation and arbitration. Each has its own suggested methods of enforcement.

The International Centre for Settlement of Investment Disputes (ICSID) of the World Bank is another reputable organization supporting mediation enforcement. By its rules, an award of an ICSID tribunal "is binding on all of the parties to the proceedings" and may be "enforced by the Courts of any ICSID Member State" (ICSID, 2016).[7] Instituted under the Convention on the Settlement of Investment Disputes between States and Nationals of Other States, the ICSID is an autonomous group of over 140 member states. An older and powerful global organization, the Paris-based ICC, adopted ADR rules granting status and effect of mediation awards as a final award. Its revised mediation rules, promulgated in January 2014, are patterned after the US practice of mediation and signal the ICC's recognition that mediation is co-equal to arbitration.

The European Union

European Directive, Mediation in Civil and Commercial Matters, passed in 2008, made uniform certain attributes of enforcement of mediation in civil and commercial settlements throughout the European Union (EU).[8] The objective of mediation is for commercial parties to settle their disputes amicably without reference to a tribunal, and the Directive makes clear that mediation "should not be regarded as a poorer alternative to judicial proceedings" (Friel & Toms, 2011).

That more and more countries are promulgating their internal mediation laws exponentially increases the potential to file judicially for a mediation award or mediation judgment. If a lawsuit has been filed before the mediation has commenced, it is possible in many jurisdictions to have the court enter the settlement agreement as a consent decree and incorporate it into the dismissal order. Even where a lawsuit is not filed, in those countries with mediation laws, enforcement can be by submission to a public notary or by using a court in a summary proceeding.

Mediation's meteoric drivers

Multiple drivers are working to sustain mediation's meteoric rise. One such driver is an abiding philosophy that mediation is essential to a strong business climate and a rule of law's robust judiciary. A second paramount driver is a bevy of international funding organizations subsidizing mediation development. Each works to establish mediation law programs internal to various countries, especially in developing rule of law countries.

The business driver

Coincidental with its philosophy that mediation is essential to a robust business climate is the widely accepted philosophy—and proof—that mediation within judicial programs is viewed as essential to improving an investment climate and private sector development. Larger multinational "blue-chip" companies have been using mediation for several years. Small and medium-sized business enterprises and entrepreneurship also are quickly discovering that in order to flourish within a country, there needs to be an environment conducive to mediation, often through the courts, where the rule of law is practiced through a fair and transparent judiciary. If the current judicial process in the region is time consuming, expensive, or corrupt, it often leads to less desirable outcomes—or no outcomes at all. Mediation offers an important route to mitigating these issues by offering an alternative to the court process. In most of the emerging rule of law countries, including many of the more sophisticated countries of Europe, the judiciary and the courts are not as flexible as they need to be to address the increasingly complex economic and communication demands that globalization has created.

International businesses now have clients all around the world and need a method of dispute resolution, which is faster and less expensive than traditional judicial adjudication. Countries addressing court-based mediation programs understand that mediation simultaneously and significantly advances growth potential for increased international trade and commerce. Mediation promotes increased access to justice.[9] It is also well documented that it strengthens the judiciary by increasing the ability of court systems to deliver services in a more transparent, independent and accountable ways. Lastly, mediation advances judicial reform as a corollary to best practices of case management, increased transparency, and better-qualified staff. These types of judicial reforms using mediation are rapidly growing worldwide.

The governmental driver

Governmentally, the most widely recognized driver of mediation is the United Nations. In June 2011, the UN Security Council in a unanimously passed resolution (65th Session), proclaimed the first primary and paramount resolution on supporting global peace through the use of mediation. As the first such globally accepted mediation resolution of its kind, it also set out principles on how to carry out mediation activities in order to prevent armed conflicts in a world where conflict becomes a part of daily life in many regions.[10] The resolution not only supports mediation in member states, but also: promotes regional civil organizations, especially those benefiting women; requires annual compilations of guidelines; and requires the secretary-general to report annually on peace mediation to the General Assembly. This resolution was adopted unanimously. Mediators from around the world celebrate this unique resolution for its peacebuilding capacity.[11] It is this author's opinion that this powerful UN resolution brings increasing respect and interest worldwide to the use of mediation, not only in disputes between and among countries, but also to the political and economic stability necessary for the burgeoning growth of international commercial mediation.

Perhaps the most heavily funded global providers of rule of law programs, including developing court-related mediation, is the United States Agency for International Development (USAID). USAID's publicly stated foreign-policy mission is to "further America's interests while improving lives in the developing world" (USAID, 2016). USAID works in over 100 developing countries in partnership with private voluntary organizations, indigenous groups, universities, American businesses, international organizations, other governments, trade and professional associations, faith-based organizations, and other US government agencies. It contracts with or grants money to over 3,500 companies and over 300 US-based private voluntary organizations. USAID has become one of the leading governmental funders of justice sector reform programs, including mediation.[12]

The EU Commission, another organizational, international funder of mediation programs, awards grants to nongovernmental organizations (NGOs) in order to implement projects or activities in relation to EU policies. It supports the implementation of its 2008 Directive where at least one of the parties is domiciled or habitually resides in one of its member states.[13]

The International Finance Corporation (2015) of the World Bank Group is the largest global development institution focused on the private sector in developing countries. As the private-sector arm of the World Bank Group, its mission is to provide financing to help businesses employ more people and supply essential services, mobilize capital from others, and deliver advisory services, all to promote sustainable development. Its 178 member countries provide its share capital and collectively determine its policies.

Conclusion

Mediation's traditional and ancient practices still are expressed in today's mediation essential processes. Several of the member countries that voted for the UN resolution on mediation practiced ancient societal traditions of mediation. The UN has joined farsighted corporations, large and small, in proclaiming mediation as the solution for disputes in our shrinking globe. Economic communities increasingly view mediation as a universal supra-judicial option for dispute resolution. For many developing and economically transitioning countries suffering from poor contract enforcement and corrupt and inefficient justice systems, mediation is viewed as a necessity to attract foreign investors and business. Mediation—and its communal use as a civilizing tool—empowers individuals in all walks of society to resolve their own disputes; this in turn strengthens developing nations' judiciaries and business environments. Nations and individuals are empowered to make choices in their disputes: avoid them or suffer the economic consequences. When mediation filters down from the courts, through business, governmental institutions, and into general communities and societies, mediation is a proven transformational tool for good governance, economic growth, and ultimately, peace.

Notes

1 Excerpted from Cole, L. (2012). What's driving the global growth of mediation in business and commerce? *International Law Quarterly*, Spring, 55–58. Retrieved from www.scribd.com/doc/99466273/International-Law-Quarterly-2012-Spring-Issue.

2 For a discussion by the authors who have developed a working list of recommendations in cross-cultural mediations, see Lücke & Rigaut, 2002.
3 There are currently several books, articles and scholarly papers focusing exclusively on cross-cultural aspects. International counsel, prior to experiencing a cross-cultural mediation, will find it helpful to review any one of many books and articles focusing extensively and insightfully on cultural differences in international mediation. Recently, a new online virtual academy has opened which seeks to empower mediators and others working in conflict resolution by training them in core intercultural competencies. Explore BRDGES Academy at www.BRDGESAcademy.com.
4 This practice is captured today in Jordan's 2005 mediation law which permits use of "Special Mediators," such as statesmen or high-ranking judges held in high esteem.
5 Contractual remedies are available as a mechanism for enforcing a mediation settlement agreement, but litigating a contract again in another posture is oxymoronic to the concept and purpose of mediation.
6 This Model Law recognized that "many practitioners put forth the view that the attractiveness of conciliation would be increased if a settlement reached during a conciliation would enjoy a regime of expedited enforcement or would for the purposes of enforcement be treated as or similarly to an arbitral award."
7 For more information, see Parra, 2007.
8 The Directive ensures that "it is possible for the parties, or one of them with the explicit consent of the others, to request that the content of the written agreement be made enforceable … by a court of other competent authority in a judgment or decision or in an authentic instrument in accordance with the law of the member state where the request is made …"
9 In particular, ADR processes are of significant importance to justice systems when effective establishment of alternative means of dispute resolution can significantly reduce the number of *minor* disputes before the civil courts, helping to improve the availability of judges for cases that must be tried.
10 By the terms of the resolution "Strengthening the Role of Mediation in Peaceful Settlement of Disputes, Conflict Prevention and Resolution," the Assembly invited its member states to optimize the use of mediation and other tools outlined in Chapter VI of the United Nations Charter for the peaceful settlement of disputes, as well as conflict prevention and resolution. It also encourages member states, where appropriate, to develop national mediation capacities in order to ensure coherence and responsiveness, and in that context, to promote women's equal, full and effective participation. The resolution was adopted without objection.
11 There are several NGOs internationally that work with mediation as a peacebuilding tool, including Mediators Beyond Borders, International. MBB has as its mission: "Building sustainable conflict resolution capacity for a more peace 'able' world." See, www.MediatorsBeyondBorders.org.
12 The author has worked as a Mediator Specialist designing court-related mediation systems for USAID in Bulgaria, Jordan and Kosovo.
13 In 2014, it completed its funding of a countrywide mediation system in Kosovo. As another example of mediation funding, in December 2008, the EU granted €1 million to the Philippines, a grant that included a component on mediation.

References

Barkett, J., Martin, T., Burt, D.H., Cheng, T., Baum, S., Wolrich, P.M., Ulicny, S. & Martinez, L. (2010) International mediation. In A.W. Rovine (ed.) *Contemporary Issues in International Arbitration and Mediation: The Fordham Papers*. Retrieved from www.brill.com/contemporary-issues-international-arbitration-and-mediation-fordham-papers-2010.

Coben, J.R. & Thompson, P.N. (2006) Disputing irony: A systemic look at litigation and mediation. *Harvard Negotiation Law Review*, 11(43): 43–146.

Cole, L. (2009) Court-based mediation: Expanding access to justice in developing societies. *Paralegal Resource*. Retrieved from www.theparalegalresource.com/articles/view.php?article_id=3529.

Cole, L. (n.d.) Jordan leads the way in mediation in the Arab Middle East. *National Academy of Distinguished Neutrals*. Retrieved from www.nadn.org/articles/ColeLynn-JordonLeadsTheWay.pdf.

De Palo, G., Feasley, A. & Orecchini, F. (2011) Quantifying the cost of not using mediation: A data analysis. European Parliament. Retrieved from www.europarl.europa.eu/document/activities/cont/201105/20110518ATT19592/20110518ATT19592EN.pdf.

Friel, S. & Toms, C. (2011) The European Mediation Directive: Legal and political support for alternative dispute resolution in Europe. *Bloomberg Law Reports—Alternative Dispute Resolution*, 2(1). Retrieved from www.brownrudnick.com/uploads/117/doc/Brown_Rudnick_Litigation_European_Mediation_Directive_Friel_Toms_1-20110.pdf.

ICSID. (2016) *Recognition and Enforcement: ICSID Convention Arbitration*. World Bank Group. Retrieved from icsid.worldbank.org/apps/ICSIDWEB/process/Pages/Recognition-and-Enforcement-Convention-Arbitration.aspx.

International Chamber of Commerce (ICC). (n.d.) Mediation and ADR statistics. Retrieved from www.iccwbo.org/Products-and-Services/Arbitration-and-ADR/Mediation/Introduction/Mediation-and-ADR-statistics/.

International Finance Corporation. (2015) About IFC: Overview. Retrieved from www.ifc.org/wps/wcm/connect/corp_ext_content/ifc_external_corporate_site/about+ifc_new.

Joubert, J. (2012) Embedding mediation in South African justice. *Mediate.com*. Retrieved from www.mediate.com/articles/Joubertj1.cfm.

Kaskell, P.H. (2002) Is your infringement dispute suitable for mediation? *Fordham Journal of Corporate and Financial Law*, 20(3): 45–61.

Lücke, K. & Rigaut, A. (2002) Cultural issues in international mediation. Retrieved from aloys.rigaut.free.fr/pdf/Cultural_issues_mediation.pdf.

McIlwrath, M. (2014) UNCITRAL to consider proposal for convention on enforcement of mediated settlements. *Kluwer Arbitration Blog*. Retrieved from kluwerarbitrationblog.com/2014/07/07/uncitral-to-consider-proposal-for-convention-on-enforcement-of-mediated-settlements/.

Mealey-Lohmann, L. (2010) Using mediation to resolve disputes: Differences between China and the United States. *China Insight*. Retrieved from www.chinainsight.info/culture/chinese-3/526-using-mediation-to-resolve-disputes–differences-between-china-and-the-united-states-.html.

Miccioli, G. (n.d.) International commercial arbitration. American Society of International Law. Retrieved from www.asil.org/sites/default/files/ERG_ARB.pdf.

Parra, A.R. (2007) Enforcement of ICSID Arbitral Awards, 24th Joint Colloquium on International Arbitration, Paris, November 2007. Retrieved from www.arbitration-icca.org/media/0/12144885278400/enforcement_of_icsid_awards.pdf.

Posin, D.Q. (2004) Mediating business disputes. *Fordham Journal of Corporate and Financial Law*, 9(2): 449–474. Retrieved from: ir.lawnet.fordham.edu/jcfl/vol9/iss2/4/.

Pribetic, A.I. (2008) A strategic functionalist approach to international commercial mediation. *Journal of Alternative Dispute Resolution*, 7(2): 37–58.

Salacuse, J.W. (2002) Mediation in international business. International Mediation Institute. Retrieved from imimediation.org/jeswald-salacuse-article?

Singer, L.R. & Lewis, M.K. (2008) Looking forward in mediation: Today's successes and tomorrow's challenges. *Dispute Resolution Magazine*, 14(3–4): 15–18. Retrieved from www.americanbar.org/content/dam/aba/publishing/dispute_resolution_magazine/dispute_magazine_DR_Sp_Sum_2008_Final_LOWRESOLUTION.authcheckdam.pdf.

Smith, H. (2007) The inside track: How blue chips are using ADR. Retrieved from www.herbertsmithfreehills.com/-/media/HS/Insights/Guides/PDFs/Alternative%20dispute%20resolution%20-%20the%20inside%20track/1%206398ADRreportD4.pdf.

United Nations. (1994) *UNCITRAL Model Law on International Commercial Conciliation*. Retrieved from www.uncitral.org/pdf/english/texts/arbitration/ml-arb/06-54671_Ebook.pdf.

United Nations General Assembly Sixty-fifth Session. (2011) Agenda item 33 10–52952, Resolution adopted by the General Assembly [65/283], strengthening the role of mediation in the peaceful settlement of disputes, conflict prevention and resolution. *United Nations*. Retrieved from www.un.org/depts/dhl/resguide/r65.shtml.

USAID. (2016) Who we are. USAID. Retrieved from www.usaid.gov/who-we-are.

Xavier, A. (2006) Mediation: Its origin and growth in India. *Hamline Journal of Public Law and Policy*, 27. Retrieved from www.arbitrationindia.com/pdf/mediation_india.pdf.

36

CULTURE, RELIGION AND POLITICS IN INTERNATIONAL MEDIATION

Mohammed Abu-Nimer and Timothy Seidel

In 2012, while conducting an evaluation on intercultural dialogue in Egypt, Mohammed encountered a foreign consultant. The consultant had arrived a few months earlier to Cairo to complete an assessment and design an intervention to mediate between two different nongovernmental organizations (NGOs) in Egypt that received funding from the same donor. In the course of the conversation, when sharing the details of the assignment, the consultant repeatedly indicated that they were facing challenges in gaining access and the trust of the parties. Although the consultant recognized the context of post-revolution Egypt, they were not able to account for the sub-cultural differences when dealing with these organizations. They neglected to recognize the distinctiveness of Egyptian in comparison to Syrian and Jordanian contexts, and when challenged with such questions, the immediate reaction was: "but you are all Arabs." This particular statement delegitimized the consultant's credibility among both organizations in Egypt.[1]

As this story illustrates, attending to the role of culture and religion in mediation can be complicated but essential when working in international, intercultural, and multicultural settings. It is a matter of crossing boundaries—whether in terms of individual, communal, or national identities—both for parties to a conflict as well as for the mediator. However, this notion of crossing boundaries in ways impacted by culture and religion has not always received proper attention in the field of conflict resolution, and when it has, it is not always in a way that attends to the role of the mediator in the process.

Indeed, in the fields of international relations and to some extent in conflict resolution, culture and religion have often been seen as irrelevant, or worse an obstruction, to an effective resolution of conflict.[2] This approach is not unrelated to the perspective that a society's development into a modern state requires relegating culture and religion to the periphery where politics does not *really* happen, which begs the question: what roles do culture and religion play in conflict resolution?

In this chapter, we will look at the role of culture and religion in mediation and conflict resolution practices and will argue that an approach that relegates culture and religion to the periphery can be ineffective and even inadequate. More specifically, it will explore the role of culture, religion, and identity and their impacts on mediation contexts and processes with particular attention to the often Eurocentric character of mediation models, especially in international contexts, that ignore the power dynamics introduced by third parties intervening in conflict situations. In this regard, we are examining mediation as a form of *intervention* in conflict contexts, an inherently political act. We will argue that attention to culture and religion is critical to *politicizing* mediation processes and interventions. As we will discuss below, by politicizing we mean attending to the power dynamics of conflict contexts by both interrogating the claims to neutrality of third parties and underscoring the importance of relationships and relational approaches to mediation.

Culture, religion, and conflict resolution

Although we are exploring ways in which cultural and religious identities have been neglected in mediation and conflict resolution, it is clear that a comprehensive discussion of the two concepts is outside the scope of the chapter. There is a great deal of research and discussion on the definition, nature, and relationships between these two terms (for example, by some estimations there are at least 160 definitions of culture in anthropology; see Avruch, 1998). This chapter deals with religion and culture as two examples of marginalized factors in the process of conflict resolution. Our objective is to focus on the common neglect that these two aspects of identity have faced in the conceptualization and practice of conflict resolution frameworks and models of intervention.[3]

The discussion on the role of culture, as well as religion, in conflict resolution is quite diverse. For example, some approaches such as a Basic Human Needs approach do not view culture as relevant to a conflict resolution process that is concerned with universal, generic human needs (Burton, 1987; Zartman, 1993). A second perspective recognizes the relevance of culture but only as one variable among many in a still fairly instrumentalist approach to conflict resolution (Bercovitch, 1996; Cohen, 1997). A third view sees cultural variation as fundamentally significant to the narration and analysis of conflict and its subsequent resolution (Augsburger, 1992; Lederach, 1995; Abu-Nimer, 1996a; Avruch, 1998). Among these three views of culture, conflict, and conflict resolution, one can identify a sort of descending order of resonance with positivist perspectives on behavior that totalize the categories of conflict and conflict resolution. For example, it is within the theoretical tradition of the Basic Human Needs approach that one finds greatest resonance with a universal explanation of behavior and its relevance to conflict resolution, in which the assumption is that all humans have the same basic needs and that they differ only in the way they seek ways to satisfy such needs. This resonance decreases with the second approach and arguably disappears in the third, with its emphasis on particularity and local knowledge.

The role of religion has also received some attention in the field of conflict resolution (Johnston & Sampson, 1994; Abu-Nimer, 1996b; Appleby, 2000; Gopin, 2000; Abu-Nimer, 2003). Often this has included explorations of the role of religion and religious symbols in the analysis of conflict—how conflict is expressed in religious terms—and the role of religion in the resolution of conflict—attending to religion and religious identity amongst conflicting parties as well as with the identity of the mediator and appealing to religion for transformative moments in conflict.[4]

Johnston and Sampson (1994) argue that religion should be taken seriously because, among other reasons, it functions as a "complicating factor" in many post-Cold War conflicts and can create opportunities for "spiritually motivated peacemakers" (p. 332). Sampson (1997) explores the roles of religiously or spiritually motivated peacemakers such as advocate, intermediary, observer, and educator (p. 276). She points out that there are aspects of peacebuilding and conflict resolution that are best understood in religious terms, not least because of their emergence from religious, not secular, contexts. In this literature, the "ambivalence of the sacred" (Appleby, 2000) presents the potential for religion to work as both a resource for violent conflict and war, and for promoting peace and the nonviolent resolution of conflict. This has underscored for some not the tensions between religions but the tensions that exist within religious traditions, with the possibilities of constructive and destructive effects. However, as the discussion below will illustrate, these descriptions of culture and religion leave intact problematic categories that when interrogated have the potential to open up productive lines of inquiry and practice.

Abu-Nimer (2003) argues that like other religions, in the case of Islam, religious discourse (based on scripture and tradition) can be the base for developing effective frameworks of peacebuilding and nonviolent resistance. Without such anchoring of the framework in these local religious and traditional discourses, the peacebuilding intervention programs to rebuild fragile states will continue to be perceived as foreign knowledge and expertise.

Culture, religion, and the state: the secular bias in IR (and CR)

While some attention has been given to the roles of culture and religion in conflict resolution (CR), it has been an understudied point in the broader field of international relations (IR) and conflict resolution. One explanation for this can be found in Talal Asad's discussion on religion, the secular, and secularism. Asad argues that the liberal nation-state is required to define the genuinely "religious" in order to lay claim to the secular (Asad, 2003, p. 17). Similarly, Cavanaugh (2009) argues that the religious-secular distinction does not identify facts about the world, but rather "authorizes certain arrangements of power in the modern West." The "myth of religious violence," argues Cavanaugh, replicates "a story of salvation from mortal peril by the creation of the secular nation-state," identifying "Others and enemies, both internal and external, who threaten the social order and who provide the requisite villains against which the nation-state is said to protect us." The result is that "it legitimizes the direction of the citizen's ultimate loyalty to the nation-state and secures the nation-state's monopoly on legitimate violence" (p. 226).

The decision to engage religious and cultural identity in the intervention process is certainly an important step. However, the style and intention behind such engagements matter. For example, one might argue that self-described "secular" peacebuilding and conflict resolution organizations are compelled to define themselves in opposition to religious groups and religious parties. They must define the "religious" in order to carry out their work as "secular" organizations. It is precisely their "secular" status that compels them to delineate and circumscribe the "religious." This engagement is a tenuous process that leads to homogenized and static definitions of people and groups, as well as limiting organizations' ability to provide advocacy and policy guidance to parties in a conflict. However, most importantly, it grants secular institutions the power to name and (de)legitimize religious organizations. For example, when politicians mediating a conflict in Afghanistan confine their contacts and framework to an exclusive secular diplomatic set of interaction, the process and results of this mediation will remain within the small group of Afghan political elite whose values and belief system correspond with the Western, secular approach. This will inevitably lead to the majority of the remaining leaders as well as the larger community feeling alienated from the discourse and framework of negotiation as it has been introduced.

Instrumentalizing religion can have negative effects. To return to the example in Afghanistan, a mediation process that does consider a role for religion, but maintains this hard and fast religious/secular distinction, may include simply injecting a few prayers in the initial or final ceremonies, or by getting the blessing of tribal leaders when the agreement is signed.

Instead of bolstering the mediation process, the incorporation of such instrumentalized religious symbols may actually add to the delegitimization of the agreement itself and those religious leaders who blessed it because it treated religion as an add-on to a fundamentally secular process. Such an approach was reflected in many cases of US government policy when engaging the indigenous councils of Afghan tribes. While it was completely ignored in the early stages of the war, military commanders and politicians gradually realized they needed tribal leaders and their cultural structures to certify and legitimize any new policy or reality on the ground. Thus, politicians began utilizing the Loya Jerga cultural structures in their attempts to market new policies.[5]

This reflects what Mavelli (2012) calls a "secular bias" in our international engagement. A "postsecular" alternative, he argues, has the potential to open up new possibilities because it reimagines our understanding of the boundary between the secular and the religious as the product of multiple regimes of power and knowledge, rather than a natural divide; and our understanding of the international, in a perspective, which acknowledges the European genealogy of secularity (p. 1078).

This again has to do with the role of categories like "religion" in these processes. Chakrabarty (2000) writes, "it is impossible to think of anywhere in the world without invoking certain categories and concepts, the genealogies of which go deep into the intellectual and even theological traditions of Europe" (p. 4). Chakrabarty (2000) is not only referring to the ways that histories of non-Western nations are written as variations on or derivatives of a master narrative called "the history of Europe" (see Chatterjee, 2010), but he is also speaking to what is seen as the proper role of religion. That is, while religion, properly disciplined, may occasionally be a means to a more just society, it can never be an end in itself. Religion is only instrumental to a goal that is privileged over and above it: the well-being of the nation-state.

If the above critique of existing categories and concepts of religion and religious identity in peacebuilding, mediation, and international relations are accepted, then the processes of peacebuilding and conflict resolution intervention will look differently. When accepting religious and cultural identities as central, and not peripheral or marginal, to conflict resolution, mediation and public diplomacy models will be constructed and practiced more from within and less from above and outside the parties involved in any conflict.

Why and how culture and religion matter: power and politics

It matters *how* we consider culture and religion. In our discussions and conceptions of mediation, how do binaries such as religion/secular present themselves? How do they contribute to our ability to imagine and (de)legitimize new possibilities? For example, the tendency to cast the religious (as irrational) against the secular (as rational—where the "political" really operates in history) can be observed in the public diplomacy and peace work of many European government organizations and agencies. Empowering secular civil society in Middle Eastern and Muslim societies is the intended impact in their interventions. Supporting local or regional religious associations and organizations is rarely considered.[6]

This is a critical reason why Jabri (2006) takes the field of conflict resolution to task, namely for what she feels is its tendency to depoliticize conflict. She holds that the standard elements of conflict resolution are subject to controversy and hence "steeped in political contestation" (p. 69). Therefore, she makes the case for bringing politics (and ethics[7]) back into our thinking about conflict resolution and change.

Thus, when US diplomats intervened in the political dynamics of the Arab Spring, or when international NGOs implemented a conflict resolution project in such a context, they ran into direct contradictions with local cultural and religious agencies. Recognizing these local, contextual realities ought to determine the nature of their interventions.

One of the ways this happens, Jabri observes, is when the complexity of conflict in international or intercultural contexts is reduced to the interpersonal. Focusing on the dynamics of the interpersonal has its attractions and even benefits (e.g. in terms of focusing on more manageable conflict elements), but it has the effect of dehistoricizing and "dislocating" conflict from a specific time and place. This denial of particularity is no neutral act as it serves to enable (even naturalize) some institutions and institutional practices—such as the state and the international political economy—while constraining others. This has profound implications, notes Jabri, "for the choices available to parties involved in conflict just as they do in determining not just the capacities of potential third parties but the discourses they draw upon in conceptualizing a conflict" (p. 71).

To summarize, while one of the most overused concepts (and most difficult to define[8]), the appeal to "culture" is a helpful corrective to the appeals to "nature" and corresponding tendencies to reify or "naturalize" behaviors. This reification not only delimits the range of possibilities in responding to conflict, but also serves as a pretext for outside (i.e. Western) interventions into conflict situations with liberal modern intentions that resemble historical trends of *mission civilisatrice* or a governmentalizing attempt at controlling populations—both having a depoliticizing effect (also see Jabri, 2010).

We argue that attention to culture and religion, not only opens up productive lines of inquiry, but can also serve to destabilize dominant modes of mediation practice by challenging the mediator to address and interrogate the ways in which culture, religion, and identity are reified in mediation processes, and how these categories produce limitations for the mediator. For example, when identifying the issues and sorting their priorities and importance to the parties as a first step in a problem-solving model, cultural and religious values and beliefs determine the process. The religious values shape the views of the individual or leaders and thus determine to a large extent the response and actions, or at least the discourse. Protecting the *karamah* (dignity) of the individual affiliated group is often a crucial factor in gaining access and legitimacy for the mediators in an Arab traditional cultural setting. A mediator has to take such factors into consideration in the opening to, during, and at the end of the process of intervention.

This relates to a consideration of culture and the state. Attention to culture and religion destabilizes the state-centric approach to conflict resolution in general and international mediation in particular, raising the specter of intercultural (and intracultural) mediation. However, this also raises several possibilities, particularly as it relates to power in conflict. Appeals to culture have the potential to both ignore and obfuscate or uncover and challenge power in conflict, identifying and locating power as it is expressed other than by the state.[9]

Culture, religion, and politics in international peacebuilding

The importance of including and incorporating cultural and religious identity in international mediation and peacebuilding can be seen in the work of many faith-based organizations. In her discussion on the similarities and differences between faith-based and secular humanitarian organizations, Elizabeth Ferris (2005) notes how faith-based humanitarian organizations have a constituency that is broader than humanitarian concerns, and that faith-based organizations tend to embrace a justice agenda that does not make the principle of neutrality their priority. This means that the sharp distinction traditionally seen in the roles played by human rights NGOs and humanitarian NGOs does not hold up well for faith-based organizations, which usually engage in both human rights and humanitarian work. Ferris (2005) points out the difference between human rights or advocacy and humanitarian assistance departments in "many Northern faith-based organizations ... However, local organizations rarely draw such clear lines and see advocacy and assistance as part of a holistic response. Faith-based organizations, with their commitment to justice, tend to further blur the distinctions" (p. 321).

With these observations, Ferris (2005) seems to begin to identify some of the categorical instabilities marking modernist discourse which, if followed through, would lead to a deeper interrogation of the secular-religious distinction. For example, Ferris points out that governments have long used humanitarian assistance as an instrument of foreign policy, but that the war on terrorism has intensified this trend. For example, in Afghanistan and Iraq, concerns that their work could be perceived "as supporting US political objectives ... led many US NGOs to decline US financial support for their programmes there" (Ferris, 2005, p. 323). In addition, "[t]he role of military forces in providing humanitarian assistance in those two countries has also increased pressure on NGOs to think more carefully on what humanitarian action means in such situations" (p. 323).

Ferris (2005) also points out the challenges and possibilities found in relations between Christian and Islamic NGOs. She underscores a point made by Serge Duss of World Vision, who observed that, in some non-Christian countries, a Christian identity enhanced their ability to work with local communities and national governments. "Unlike Western society," Duss observed, "which separates the spiritual from the physical, Islamic societies in particular integrate the spiritual into every aspect of their lives," pointing to a common conviction for Christians and Muslims that sees "a witness of faith through charity that is a way of life and expression of obedience to God" (Ferris, 2005, p. 324). This theme is echoed by Abdel-Rahman Ghandour, who reports that Islamic NGOs "do not understand (or do not accept) that a humanitarian gesture, whatever its origin, could be made outside the scope of religious values, considering that religion is the guarantor of morals, charity, good behaviour and virtue" (Ferris, 2005, p. 324). In addition, Ferris (2005) posits, "Islamists cannot conceive of self-respecting Western humanitarian NGOs as anything other than religiously inspired" (p. 324).

In a similar manner, Chantal Logan (2007), who worked for several years with the Mennonite Central Committee (MCC) in Somalia, observed that some international NGOs, which saw themselves as "neutral" because of their secular identity, had difficulty understanding how a religious organization such as MCC could be regarded as a valuable and trusted partner by Somalis. She observed: "They had difficulty seeing that it was because we were religious people that the Somalis appreciated working with us" (Logan, 2007, p. 62). They envied MCC relationships, but could not understand how they were forged. She goes on to describe that while teaching in Djibouti, another Islamic country, she found that Muslims appreciated knowing her faith commitment. "Muslim colleagues, students, and neighbors thus looked to me as somebody with whom they had something in common. Like them, I believed in God, and we could connect because we shared a religious world view" (Logan, 2007, p. 62). She goes on to explain that "[l]ike other Mennonite workers in Somalia, I found out working with Somali partners that overt use of religious language was an advantage in building trust and relationships" (p. 62).

The acknowledgment piece was crucial for Logan. She noted that "the one thing worse than an infidel for a Muslim is a hypocrite. Those who disguise their Christian identity (either at the personal or agency levels) are much more despised that those who acknowledge it openly" (Logan, 2007, p. 62). This speaks again to the importance of transparency and honesty, critical especially in those contexts where we engage in relationships with those who have too-often experienced inequity and imbalances of power vis-à-vis the West and where suspicions may run high. In addition, such an example reflects the need to design the peacebuilding intervention from within the cultural and religious context as opposed to using a generic formula of intervention that supposedly cuts across cultural and religious contexts.

With these examples, we are calling the secular-religious distinction itself into question in an attempt to illustrate the overlapping and shifting relationships that constitute religious identity and peacebuilding work around the word today. Unsettling this distinction allows us to explore the ways that "Muslim," "Christian," "religious" and "secular" categories are products of contingent and fluid relationships, rather than static identities.

Conclusion: principles and lessons learned

There are several implications to be drawn from this discussion. An obvious one is the critical importance of recognizing and acknowledging cultural and religious differences among conflicting parties. Such differences should be assessed as to their potential impact on the communication process generally or how it invokes the framing of needs, values, and identities in a given conflict setting. This requires a mediation process and design to be more complex and less simply facilitative in nature or free of religious discourse.

As we discussed above, this approach also aids in identifying and interrogating the state-centric biases that persist in international conflict resolution. The persistence of a realpolitik that maintains a state-to-state focus falls short because of its neglect of issues regarding culture and religion. International power politics have an effect on the local and regional cultural identities and their manifestation in shaping the conflict dynamics (escalation and de-escalation), evaluation of peacebuilding and mediation outcomes, and design and credibility of peace intervention models.

However, this recognition must also extend to those differences between the parties and the mediator. In other words, the role and impact of the mediator must be accounted for (not only using generic secular measures, but implications on the religious discourse, too can be part of the formula to evaluate the mediation or peacebuilding intervention). As we have demonstrated above, the cultural, religious, and political location or identity of the mediator him- or herself matters. This speaks to a sort of reflexivity and humility a mediator needs to recognize their (in)ability to fully understand and comprehend the cultural and religious codes and discourses, acknowledge biases, and monitor their effects. The mediator as reflective practitioner attends to these insider/outsider dynamics. In addition, while we do not explore this at length here, the role of gender and the gender identity of the mediator is another important consideration.

Finally, there have been significant changes implemented in the last decade in which international organizations such as the United Nations, World Bank, UK Department for International Development, German Technical Cooperation Agency (GTZ), and other major governmental donor organizations have begun to engage faith-based organizations and religious institutions. Even some US government agencies began exploring different methods for introducing basic packages of information on how to engage faith-based organizations in USAID and State Department programs. Thus, new introductory manuals or guides for government officers who work overseas on how to work with faith-based organizations became available.

The lesson to be learned here is not simply one of mediator capacity and competency, but mediator impact. We understand this also as an issue of politics and power. What we might call a politicizing of conflict resolution through giving attention to culture and religion is in many ways about the ethics of international mediation. Traditional dispute resolution has not always addressed these issues, but the entry of the mediator or mediation team not only can significantly affect the power relations in the dynamics of the mediation but, indeed, becomes a part of the conflict itself. Again, it is a question of the role and the social location of the mediator that can either normalize certain social realities or problematize them by identifying their political and structural elements. No matter how thoughtful the design, how rigorous the approach, power sits and is at work in mediation, making self-awareness and reflexivity on the part of the mediator critical. Beth Roy (2008) describes the power of the mediator as "a fluid and complex matter. Who the mediator is, of what cultural heritage, matters of gender and race and age, language spoken, transparency, and so much more—all affect the flow of power in the course of the work" (p. 181).[10] In this context, religious leadership and institutions have isolated themselves and been marginalized by existing international systems and agencies from contributing to the resolution of their own societies' problems. Thus, further inclusion and reflections are urgently needed to systematize the crucial role that such agents of change can offer.

Notes

1 Based on an encounter with an evaluation team in Cairo, Egypt, June 25, 2012.
2 For example, in both of our experiences we have observed the neglect or even marginalization of religion in international peacebuilding and conflict resolution. This observation was also confirmed in interviews with other scholar practitioners.
3 In addition to a survey of the literature, primary research, and personal experiences and reflections, we conducted interviews with two scholar practitioners as we developed this chapter. The time of interviews was 2014 and the selection criteria included those working with interreligious and intercultural identity conflict.
4 The increased attention to the role of religion in international relations is also reflected in the creation of a number of international organizations such as KAICIID (King Abdullah International Center for Intercultural and Interreligious Dialogue), which focuses on closing the gap between religious leaders and institutions and policy makers (www.kaiciid.org).
5 For example, the crucial decision of the presence of US military forces in Afghanistan was debated in this tribal cultural structure; see Associated Press, 2013.
6 See European Union grants and awards given to Middle Eastern or Muslim organizations between 2010–15.
7 For a critical examination of ethics in mediation and conflict resolution see Laue & Cormick (1978). Whereas they talk about ethics primarily in terms of attention to power and empowerment in conflict resolution processes, Jabri articulates the ethical more in these terms of bringing politics (back) into conflict resolution—a framing that also seeks to acknowledge power not only in the material aspects of a conflict but in the relational and discursive production of a conflict.
8 Avruch (1998) offers a helpful discussion on culture in conflict resolution that resists a "reified or stable or homogenous view of culture," but rather understands that culture "is to some extent always situational, flexible, and responsive to the exigencies of the worlds that individuals confront" (p. 20). The same destabilizations could be presented in a definition of religion as well.
9 As Abu-Nimer (2001) has pointed out, peace interventions in conflict areas such as Northern Ireland, former Yugoslavia, the Middle East, and elsewhere reveal the critical role of culture and religion in individual and collective identity in a way that shapes and informs both the values and norms of participants to a conflict as well as the resources available in peacebuilding processes.
10 Nader (1991) talked about this in terms of the effect of "harmony models" in conflict resolution that can be used ideologically as a powerful form of direct and indirect control. "Harmony" can be used to suppress peoples by socializing them toward conformity and against the contentious. This "movement to control the disenfranchised, and the loss of concern with rights created a model of law that was intolerant of conflict, its causes, and its expression" (p. 52).

References

Abu-Nimer, M. (1996a). Conflict resolution approaches: Western and Middle Eastern lessons and possibilities. *American Journal of Economics and Sociology*, 55(1): 35–52.

Abu-Nimer, M. (1996b). Conflict resolution in an Islamic context: Some conceptual questions. *Peace and Change*, 21(1): 22–40.

Abu-Nimer, M. (2001) Conflict resolution, culture, and religion: Toward a training model of interreligious peacebuilding. *Journal of Peace Research*, 38(6): 685–704.

Abu-Nimer, M. (2003) *Nonviolence and Peace Building in Islam: Theory and Practice*. Gainesville, Fl.: University Press of Florida.

Appleby, R.S. (2000) *The Ambivalence of the Sacred: Religion, Violence, and Reconciliation*. New York: Rowman & Littlefield.

Asad, T. (2003) *Formations of the Secular: Christianity, Islam, Modernity*. Stanford: Stanford University.

Associated Press. (2013, October 19). Afghanistan Loya Jirga will determine whether U.S. troops remain after 2014. *The Guardian*. Retrieved from www.theguardian.com/world/2013/oct/19/afghanistan-loya-jirga-us-troops-2014.

Augsburger, D.W. (1992) *Conflict Mediation across Cultures: Pathways and Patterns*. Louisville, KY: Westminster/John Knox.

Avruch, K. (1998) *Culture and Conflict Resolution*. Washington, DC: United States Institute of Peace.

Bercovitch, J. (ed.). (1996) *Resolving International Conflicts: The Theory and Practice of Mediation*. Boulder, CO: Lynne Rienner.

Burton, J.W. (1987) *Resolving Deep Rooted Conflict: A Handbook*. Lanham, MD: University Press of America.

Cavanaugh, W.T. (2009) *The Myth of Religious Violence: Secular Ideology and the Roots of Modern Conflict*. Oxford: Oxford University.

Chakrabarty, D. (2000) *Provincializing Europe: Postcolonial Thought and Historical Difference*. Princeton, NJ: Princeton University.

Chatterjee, P. (2010) Whose imagined community? In *Empire and Nation: Selected Essays* (pp. 23–36). New York: Columbia University.

Cohen, R. (1997) *Negotiating across Cultures: International Communication in an Interdependent World*. Washington, DC: United States Institute of Peace.

Ferris, E. (2005) Faith-based and secular humanitarian organizations. *International Review of the Red Cross*, 87(858): 311–325.

Gopin, M. (2000) *Between Eden and Armageddon: The Future of World Religions, Violence and Peacemaking*. Oxford: Oxford University.

Jabri, V. (2006) Revisiting change and conflict: On underlying assumptions and the de-politicisation of conflict resolution. In D. Bloomfield, M. Fischer & B. Schmelzle (eds) *Berghof Handbook Dialogue Series No. 5: Social Change and Conflict Transformation* (pp. 69–76). Berlin: Berghof Research Center for Constructive Conflict Management.

Jabri, V. (2010) War, government, politics: A critical response to the hegemony of the liberal peace. In O.P. Richmond (ed.) *Palgrave Advances in Peacebuilding: Critical Developments and Approaches* (pp. 41–57). New York: Palgrave Macmillan.

Johnston, D. & Sampson, C. (eds). (1994) *Religion: The Missing Dimension of Statecraft*. Oxford: Oxford University.

Laue, J. & Cormick, G. (1978) The ethics of intervention in community disputes. In G. Bermant, H. Kelman & D. Warwick (eds) *The Ethics of Social Intervention* (pp. 205–232). Washington, DC: Halstead.

Lederach, J.P. (1995) *Preparing for Peace: Conflict Transformation across Cultures*. Syracuse, NY: Syracuse University.

Logan, C. (2007) Reflections on Mennonite interfaith work in Somalia. In P. Dula & A. Epp Weaver (eds) *Borders and Bridges: Mennonite Witness in a Religiously Diverse World* (pp. 57–65). Telford, PA: Cascadia.

Marshall, K. (2005) Faith and development: Rethinking development debates. World Bank. Retrieved from go.worldbank.org/XRHTISAQB0.

Mavelli, L. (2012) Postsecular resistance, the body, and the 2011 Egyptian revolution. *Review of International Studies*, 38(5): 1057–1078.

Nader, L. (1991) Harmony models and the construction of law. In K. Avruch, P. Black & J. Scimecca (eds) *Conflict Resolution: Cross-cultural Perspectives* (pp. 41–59). New York: Greenwood.

Roy, B. (2008) Power, culture, conflict. In M.A. Trujillo, S.Y. Bowland, L.J. Myers, P.M. Richards & B. Roy (eds) *Re-centering Culture and Knowledge in Conflict Resolution Practice* (pp. 179–194). Syracuse, NY: Syracuse University.

Sampson, C. (1997) Religion and peacebuilding. In I.W. Zartman & J.L. Rasmussen (eds) *Peacemaking in International Conflict: Methods and Techniques* (pp. 273–316). Washington, DC: United States Institute of Peace.

Zartman, I.W. (1993) A skeptic's view. In G. Faure & J. Rubin (eds) *Culture and Negotiation: The Resolution of Water Disputes*. London: Sage.

37

INTERNATIONAL MEDIATION

Some observations and reflections

Sean Byrne

> The challenge confronting all of us is to recognize the diversity, strengths, and limitations of mediation, and then use its most effective range of tools where appropriate. Given the amount of destruction resulting from today's conflicts and tomorrow's potential crises, this is one challenge we cannot afford to ignore.
>
> *(Bercovitch, 2009b, p. 349)*

Article 33(1) of the United Nations Charter provides for states to resolve their differences by availing themselves of a mediation process to resolve complex and intractable disputes that have political, psychocultural and/or economic dynamics (Bercovitch, 1993). Conflicts are complex and the mediation Track 1 diplomacy procedural and directive process can assist in managing relationships where there is a zero-sum stalemate especially as leaders protect their state's sovereignty (Bercovitch & Houston, 1996). The third-party intermediary needs to be aware of the historical context of the relationship, the issues involved in the dispute, and be acceptable to the disputing parties due to his or her legitimacy as head of state, and the prestige and the attributes s/he brings to the table (Bercovitch & Houston, 1996).

Mediators have their own interests and wish to increase their security and influence with the disputing parties (Zartman & Touval, 2007, p. 438). Third-party mediators typically are small and large states, individual practitioners, official and unofficial, intergovernmental organizations (IGOs), nongovernmental organizations (NGOs), transnational and regional organizations that are impartial or biased and are invited or indeed noninvited to mediate a dispute by conflicting parties (Bercovitch, 1993; Zartman & Touval, 2007). "Biased mediators" often succeed because they change their behavior to "equalize the outcome" and have carrots and sticks—i.e. power, resources and knowledge to bring to the table (Carnavale & Arad, 1996, p. 42). "Insider-partials" who hold a relationship with one or more of the disputing parties, comprehend the underlying dynamics of the conflict, are acceptable to both parties, and can use their influence and resources to be successful in mediating successful outcomes in the same way that "outsider-impartials" are able to (Carnavale & Arad, 1996, p. 42). The mediator seeks to improve the communication between the parties, formulate the problem, provide creative and innovative solutions, and manipulate the parties into reaching an agreement (Zartman & Touval, 2007, p. 446). "Mutually hurting stalemates" and "crises bounded by a deadline" can motivate the parties to accept mediation and assist the mediator in pushing the parties forward toward negotiating an agreement (Zartman & Touval, 2007, p. 445). The use of "soft realism" or soft power through the mediation process is effective to manage conflict when there is a "hurting stalemate" (Hampson, 2007, p. 391). The parties will accept the mediator who brings analytical, process, and content strategies to the process because mediation is "low risk" and they can blame the mediator for any failure of the process, as mediation is an "expression of the parties' commitment" to negotiate especially when their citizens are suffering from war-weariness (Bercovitch, 1993, p. 7).

The mediation process has been derived over the centuries as a tool to manage interpersonal and organizational disputes at the local and national levels and as a diplomatic tool to manage interstate conflicts (Bercovitch, 2009a). The process has ranged from directive, problem-solving, and transformational to more contemporary hybrid forms. I draw on the extensive literature on international mediation to highlight a number of contemporary models to manage elite interstate and intergroup conflicts to determine what some of the important lessons are that can be taken away regarding the centrality of international mediation as a critical conflict management tool in cross-cultural settings.

This chapter begins by outlining Kleiboer's (1998) conceptual four-model framework of mediation. A number of contemporary mediation models are then highlighted to illustrate the diversity of mediation approaches to manage interstate and intergroup conflicts in the peace and conflict studies (PACS) field. The chapter then provides some discussion of the lessons learned from mediation intervention in international disputes. The question that propels this chapter is as follows: What is international mediation, and how useful is it in resolving interstate or intrastate conflicts? This chapter also offers some critical ideas with regards to some of the lessons learned about the role and importance of international mediation.

International mediation differs from interpersonal or transformational mediation as it involves external (or sometimes internal) third-party intermediaries who are individuals, states or organizations with power, resources and often strategic interests that use directive or problem-solving nonviolent mediation processes to manage elite conflict within a complex and reflexive political milieu.

Marieke Kleiboer's conceptual mediation model

Conflict resolution strategies are contingent on the nature of the conflict's "escalation or de-escalation," the many parties and tangible and intangible issues involved, and the relationship and characteristics of the parties (Kriesberg, 2001, p. 416). Mediation is often voluntary and nonbinding. Providing a framework to understand the nature and motivation behind the use of effective mediation in international disputes provides a useful conceptual lens to understand the long-term consequences of mediation.

Marieke Kleiboer (1998) outlines four conceptual frames or models to understand the roles and impact of international mediation. "The power brokerage" model connects to the idea that states are rational unitary actors operating in an anarchic global milieu in which the balance of power prevents war (Kleiboer, 1998, p. 42). Mediation assists states in enhancing their relationships with other states, settling disputes, as well as pursuing their national interests. "Power makes mediation successful" (Kleiboer, 1998, p. 45). States use mediation to secure the national interest and to provide stability in the global system. Disputing parties agree to mediation to save face, seek favorable settlements, and to improve relations. "By studying the structure of the international system (the whole), the rational behavior of states (the parts) can be understood" (Kleiboer, 1998, p. 46).

"The problem-solving" model allows state leaders to improve pipelines of communications with each other, to analyze conflict, to change perceptions of the other, and to manage conflict. "Foreign policymaking is a process of double-edged diplomacy" (Kleiboer, 1998, p. 51) because international policymaking is affected by what happens domestically and vice versa so it is important to understand the "psychological, organizational and political reasons" behind why elites make decisions (Kleiboer, 1998, p. 50), so that the decision-making process is looked at from the "inside-out" (Kleiboer, 1998, p. 57). Conflict can spiral into ultimate chaos so the mediator desires to change elite decision-makers' perceptions, worldviews, and enemy images (Kleiboer, 1998, p. 56). The mediator needs to explore each dispute individually to grasp fully the underlying dynamics if the conflict is to be successfully managed and contained (Kleiboer, 1998, p. 57).

"The domination" model allows core states to resolve both manifest and latent conflicts in peripheral states and in internal peripheries in core states through mediation that does not alter dependent core-periphery relationships or advocate for a New International Economic Order (NIEO) (Kleiboer, 1998, p. 64). Many peripheral states are enslaved by the "political, ideological and social consequences of economic forces" (Kleiboer, 1998, p. 59). Mediation is used to settle manifest conflicts in peripheral states while ignoring the deeper structural roots of global inequalities between core and peripheral states, and within core states.

"The humanist restructuring relationships" model ensures that a mediator facilitates a process that empowers states and ethnic groups to pursue their basic human needs by analyzing the deep underlying roots of their conflicts in a fair process that focuses on long-term change (Kleiboer, 1998). If a group's basic human needs are ignored and constructive consensual change does not occur then the resulting violent conflict may shape intergroup or interstate relations. Informal rather than power broker mediators can level the playing field, creating a process that is empowering, fair and respectful for all of the parties so that they can influence procedures and decisions together (Kleiboer, 1998, p. 78).

Some mediation models

In this section, I outline some of the mediation models that are used in interstate and intrastate mediation processes to manage and transform conflict.

Quasi and primary mediators

"Quasi mediators" have personal and group stakes in the end result of a conflict resolution process and work to de-escalate conflict (Kriesberg, 1991, p. 31). Quasi mediators often work at multiple levels of a Track 2 grassroots process to till the soil and connect to other conflict transformation approaches (Kriesberg & Dayton, 2011). "Higher primary mediators" have their own strategic interests and bring resources, capabilities, and political leverage to the table to nudge the parties toward resolution (Princen, 1991, p. 7). "A principal or primary mediator has benefits to deny; it can threaten harm. It can rearrange payoffs to create an acceptable zone of agreement. But it can neither play the role of full-fledged protagonist nor of a neutral facilitator" (Princen, 1991, p. 26).

Transformative mediation

"Transformative mediation" empowers conflicting parties to understand each other's perspectives to identify issues and decide together settlements that work (Busch & Folger, 1994,

p. 3). The process empowers people to grow morally by recognizing the other party; to produce more compassionate people and fulfill their basic human needs rather than solely finding the optimum solutions to problems (Busch & Folger, 1994, p. 29). The problem with the problem-solving mediation approach that is concerned with winning and losing means that a new vision of conflict and a radically different approach to mediation is necessary (Busch & Folger, 1994, pp. 75, 111). Transformative mediation is distinct from, yet continuing a direction started by the problem-solving mediation approach (Busch & Folger, 1994, p. 88). Transformative mediation assists parties in expressing consideration for each other, focusing on the here and now, making informed choices about their situation, finding transformative possibilities in each participant's story, and exploring intangible issues such as enemy images, trust building, and fears (Busch & Folger, 1994, pp. 135–138). Transformative mediation reflects a much-needed paradigm shift in terms of our understanding of conflict, human nature, and the civic culture (Busch & Folger, 1994, p. 255).

External ethno-guarantor mediators

"External ethno-guarantors" (EEGs) are regional mediators who have historical, cultural, identity, and political ties with internal co-nationals embroiled in protracted ethnopolitical conflicts, and who can ameliorate or exacerbate the conflict between rival ethnic groups destabilizing the situation as they become embroiled in a dependent relationship with their internal ethnic allies (Byrne, 2006). For example, Greece and Turkey, Britain and Ireland, respectively, were the EEGs involved in preventing the conflict from being resolved in Cyprus, and in working together to manage the conflict and impose solutions in Northern Ireland. The USA as primary mediator (and the European Union in Northern Ireland) in both cases used influence, power and resources to get the EEGs to cooperate, and to deter them from intervening in support of their ethnic allies that would lead to an escalation of conflict between the EEGs (Byrne, 2006).

Elicitive and prescriptive approaches to mediation

Lederach (1995) critiques the prescriptive conflict resolution approaches that are developed and disseminated in other cultural contexts and instead proposes an "elicitive" approach where local cultural resources are used in conflict transformation (p. 7). Practitioners need to develop appropriate training and processes through expression, perception, and interpretation that empower local people so that they can create appropriate models to address their conflicts (Lederach, 1995, p. 39). The prescriptive approach uses external experts where the trainer's knowledge is valued more than the local people's knowledge, and that expert designs and controls the training (Lederach, 1995, p. 48). The elicitive training approach is an "opportunity aimed primarily at discovery, creation, and solidification of models that emerge from the resources present in a particular setting and respond to needs in that context" (Lederach, 1995, p. 55). The trainer facilitates an open process where the local participants are the primary resources and are empowered to develop the conflict resolution process to transform their conflict. Storytelling and proverbs can assist local people to understand and to work through conflict and its transformation (Lederach, 1995; Senehi, 2000, 2002, 2009a, 2009b). Lederach (1995) uses the storyboarding process that is built on facets, functions, forms, and formulas that combine prescriptive and elicitive conflict resolution approaches (p. 93). Elicitive role-play is also an important tool of discovery and creativity in conflict analysis, and in empowering local people to build appropriate mediation models (Lederach,

1995, p. 102). The elicitive approach is critical in multicultural settings so that the trainer facilitates a process whereby local people are empowered to analyze the conflict in its cultural setting, and to be aware of self in context (Lederach, 1995, p. 112).

Humanistic and directive problem-solving interpersonal mediation

Mark Umbreit (1995) defines mediation as "an informal, but structured process in which one or more impartial third parties assist disputants in talking about the conflict and in negotiating a resolution to it that addresses the needs and interests of the parties. Mediators do not impose a settlement and participation in the process is usually voluntary" (p. 24). A humanistic non-directive mediation model can address emotional issues and move conflict from a destructive to a constructive mode of interaction (Umbreit, 1995, p. 6). In contrast, directive problem-solving mediation has the mediator take a direct role in defining the issues, setting the agenda, looking for interests behind positions, and developing and accessing options for settlement in a bargaining process that ends in the parties signing a final agreement (Moore, 1996). The process is settlement driven rather than centered on transforming relationships between the conflicting parties.

Some lessons learned

There are a few lessons to be learned from this chapter. Here I explore eight of them.

- Higher or primary mediators have their own strategic interests in intervening in interstate and intrastate conflict that influence the mediation process, and the mediator's role (Bercovitch, 1993; Princen, 1991). Biased mediators use power, influence, and resources to nudge and cajole disputing parties into accepting an outcome that ends violence (Carnavale & Arad, 1996).
- Only hawks or extremist political actors can transcend seismic political fault lines and sell a mediated outcome to their intransigent constituents who trust these fiery individuals to make an intractable conflict tractable (Byrne, 2002). For example, Gerry Adams and Martin McGuinness had the trust and confidence of the Catholic Nationalist Republican community and David Trimble and the Reverend Dr Ian Paisley had the support of the Protestant Unionist Loyalist community to be able to sell the 1998 Belfast or Good Friday Agreement settlement to their respective constituents in Northern Ireland. In South Africa, Nelson Mandela and F.W. de Klerk co-created the CODESA (Convention for a Democratic South Africa) process and were able to keep their respective constituents in line. Similarly, Yitzhak Rabin and Yasser Arafat were able to enforce the 1993 Declaration of Principles for peace between the Arabs and Israelis among their respective constituents although it cost Prime Minister Rabin his life.
- There is a plethora of different types of mediators at all levels who are invited or non-invited to mediate conflicts such as large and small states, IGOs and NGOs, powerful actors such as Henry Kissinger and Hillary Rodham Clinton, as well as third-party intermediaries with no power, resources or prestige such as Adam Curle, Loraleigh Keashly, Celia Cook Huffman, and John Paul Lederach—all of whom can make a difference in waging conflict constructively (Bercovitch, 1993; Zartman & Touval, 2007).
- External conflict resolution and peace-building processes in intragroup conflicts are often "supply-led" rather than "demand-led" as the needs of the external actors are deemed more important than the parties as peace is "done unto them" and not "by them" (Mac

Ginty, 2006, p. 164). The elements of an "ideologically neutral" democratic peace that include the business negotiation model, elections and democracy, a free market economy, civil society and good governance, hierarchically defined groups, liberal optimism, and a one-size-fits-all peacebuilding template are flawed and unstable, culminating in a negative frozen peace (lack of social justice) (Mac Ginty, 2006, pp. 174–176). "Securing peace is a long-term and expensive endeavor, likely to outlast program and project cycles of a few years" (Mac Ginty, 2006, p. 165). Many ethnic conflicts fail to transition out of a "depressed economies" after a peace accord has been delivered, and may never "fully recover" (Mac Ginty, 2006, p. 133), operating within "an unforgiving global economy" (Mac Ginty, 2006, p. 134). A real pragmatic peace must come from local actors working in concert with external actors to build trust and security to address the macro-structural dynamics of conflict and spoiler violence if a real peace is to be achieved and sustained (Mac Ginty, 2006, p. 172). "Hybrid models" combining "everyday peacemakers" with external actors, and Western and indigenous methods of mediation and peacemaking have a better chance of crafting a sustainable rather than a frozen peace (Mac Ginty, 2011).

- In peacebuilding processes, there are top-down and bottom-up peacemaking efforts with middle-tier elites acting as the mediator conduit between both levels (Lederach, 1997). The information and knowledge derived from professional middle-tier participation in dialogue groups and problem-solving workshops informs both the elite decision-making policy process as well as furnishing important information to the grassroots (Lederach, 1997; Olson Lounsbery & Pearson, 2008).
- Indigenous processes of mediation have been an integral part of traditional communities' restorative processes of peacemaking for thousands of years (Rice, 2011). Clearly, it is imperative that traditional mediation approaches that have evolved from their own cultural contexts are front and center in peacemaking and peacebuilding processes.
- The time is optimum for mediation efforts to commence when a zero-sum stalemate arises in interstate or intrastate conflicts, when the protagonists' realization that they cannot defeat the other is combined with the war-weariness that exists in the grassroots (Bercovitch & Houston, 1996; Hampson, 2007; Zartman & Touval, 2007). The opportunity is there to deconstruct and reframe the "chauvinistic nationalism" that has fueled the violence and instead replace it with a focus on social justice (positive peace), civic culture, and democratic values (Anastasiou, 2009, p. 41).
- It is important to bear in mind that mediation efforts form an integral part of a much-needed multilevel, multi-modal and multi-track coordinated and complementary integrated and holistic peacebuilding system that includes all actors and activities in the cross-level processes, which interacts simultaneously and sequentially to address tangible and intangible issues (Byrne & Keashly, 2000, p. 97; Diamond & McDonald, 1996, p. 6).

Conclusion

This chapter reviewed the international mediation process and briefly outlined a number of mediation models. The chapter also highlighted Kleiboer's (1998) conceptual approach to frame international mediation. Finally, the chapter explored some of the lessons learned in exploring the role of international mediation in addressing interstate and intrastate conflicts. This analysis indicates that despite the different approaches, there are similar perspectives, such as de-escalating conflict, preventing or ending violence, improving communication, and deep analysis of the underlying issues in conflict, changing perceptions of the enemy other, developing a shared understanding of the problem as well as reaching some kind of agreement on what to do.

PACS intervention processes directly engage with direct, cultural and structural violence (Galtung, 1996). Conflict resolution processes and techniques that include mediation are often perceived as building negative peace (the absence of war) rather than building positive peace (social justice) (Barash & Webel, 2002). Sometimes mediation is important in stopping wars and preventing the further loss of life and bloodshed as conflict is contained and managed. However, other peacebuilding and peacemaking processes become equally important in transforming relations and structures to build an equitable and just peace.

International mediation is a critical intervention tool for the management of interstate and intergroup elite-driven conflict as it improves the communication flow by focusing on the critical issues that escalate the intensity of conflict. The procedural, process, and practice skills of international mediators combined with the timing of the intervention often function to alleviate and de-escalate conflict. The new hybrid forms of international mediation and the range of actors involved ensure that in the years to come international mediation will remain an important conflict management tool for the international community in mediating interstate and intergroup conflicts.

References

Anastasiou, H. (2009) Encountering nationalism: The contribution of peace studies and conflict resolution. In D. Sandole, S. Byrne, I. Staroste-Sandole & J. Senehi (eds) *Handbook of Conflict Analysis and Resolution* (pp. 30–42). London: Routledge.

Barash, D. & Webel, C. (2002) *Peace and Conflict Studies*. Thousand Oaks, CA: Sage.

Bercovitch, J. (1993) The structure and diversity of mediation in international relations. In J. Bercovitch & J. Rubin (eds) *Mediation in International Relations: Multiple Approaches to Conflict Management* (pp. 1–29). Basingstoke: Palgrave Macmillan.

Bercovitch, J. (2009a). Mediation and conflict resolution. In J. Bercovitch, V. Kremenyuk & W. Zartman (eds) *The Sage Handbook of Conflict Resolution* (pp. 340–357). Los Angeles, CA: Sage.

Bercovitch, J. (2009b). Mediation and international conflict resolution: Analyzing structure and behavior. In D. Sandole, S. Byrne, I. Staroste-Sandole & J. Senehi (eds) *Handbook of Conflict Analysis and Resolution* (pp. 337–349). London: Routledge.

Bercovitch, J. & Houston, A. (1996) The study of international mediation: Theoretical issues and empirical evidence. In J. Bercovitch (ed.) *Resolving International Conflicts: The Theory and Practice of Mediation* (pp. 11–38). Boulder, CO: Lynne Rienner.

Busch, R.B. & Folger, J. (1994) *The Promise of Mediation: Responding to Conflict through Empowerment and Recognition*. San Francisco, CA: Jossey-Bass.

Byrne, S. (2002) Toward tractability in South Africa and Northern Ireland. *Irish Studies in International Affairs*, 13(1): 135–150.

Byrne, S. (2006) Mired in intractability: The role of external ethno guarantors and primary mediators in Cyprus and Northern Ireland. *Conflict Resolution Quarterly*, 24(2): 149–172.

Byrne, S. & Keashly, L. (2000) Working with ethnopolitical conflict: A multi-modal approach to conflict intervention. *International Peacekeeping*, 7(1): 97–120.

Carnavale, P. & Arad, S. (1996) Bias and impartiality in international mediation. In J. Bercovitch (ed.) *Resolving International Conflicts: The Theory and Practice of Mediation* (pp. 39–54). Boulder, CO: Lynne Rienner.

Diamond, L. & McDonald, J. (1996) *Multi-track Diplomacy: A Systems Approach to Peace*. West Hartford, CT: Kumarian.

Galtung, J. (1996) *Peace by Peaceful Means: Peace and Conflict, Development and Civilization*. Thousand Oaks, CA: Sage.

Hampson, F.O. (2007) Parent, midwife or accidental executioner? The role of third parties in ending violent conflict. In C. Crocker, F.O. Hampson & P. Aall (eds) *Leashing the Dogs of War: Conflict Management in a Divided World* (pp. 387–406). Washington, DC: United States Institute of Peace Press.

Kleiboer, M. (1998) *The Multiple Realities of International Mediation*. Boulder, CO: Lynne Rienner.

Kriesberg, L. (1991) Formal and quasi mediators in international disputes. *Journal of Peace Research*, 28(4): 29–42.

Kriesberg, L. (2001) The growth of the conflict resolution field. In C. Crocker, F.O. Hampson & P. Aall (eds) *Turbulent Peace: The Challenges of Managing International Conflict* (pp. 407–426). Washington, DC: United States Institute of Peace Press.

Kriesberg, L. & Dayton, B. (eds). (2011) *Constructive Conflicts: From Escalation to Resolution*. Lanham, MD: Rowman and Littlefield.

Lederach, J.P. (1995) *Preparing for Peace: Conflict Transformation across Societies*. Syracuse, NY: Syracuse University Press.

Lederach, J.P. (1997) *Building Peace: Sustainable Reconciliation in Divided Societies*. Washington, DC: United States Institute of Peace Press.

Mac Ginty, R. (2006) *No War, No Peace: The Rejuvenation of Stalled Peace Processes and Peace Accords*. Basingstoke: Palgrave Macmillan.

Mac Ginty, R. (2011) *International Peacebuilding and Local Resistance: Hybrid Forms of Peace*. Basingstoke: Palgrave Macmillan.

Moore, C. (1996) *The Mediation Process: Practical Strategies for Resolving Conflict*. San Francisco, CA: Jossey-Bass.

Olson Lounsbery, M. & Pearson, F. (2008) *Civil Wars: Internal Struggles, Global Consequences*. Toronto: University of Toronto Press.

Princen, T. (1991) *Intermediaries in International Conflicts*. Princeton, NJ: Princeton University Press.

Rice, B. (2011) Relationships with human and non-human species and how they apply toward peacebuilding and leadership in indigenous societies. In T. Maytok, J. Senehi & S. Byrne (eds) *Critical Issues in Peace and Conflict Studies: Theory, Practice, and Pedagogy* (pp. 199–277). Lanham, MD: Lexington.

Senehi, J. (2000) Constructive storytelling in inter-communal conflicts: Building community, building peace. In S. Byrne, C. Irvin, P. Dixon, B. Polkinghorn & J. Senehi (eds) *Reconcilable Differences: Turning Points in Ethnopolitical Conflict* (pp. 96–114). West Hartford, CT: Kumarian.

Senehi, J. (2002) Constructive storytelling: A peace process. *Peace and Conflict Studies*, 9(2): 41–63.

Senehi, J. (2009a) Storytelling to transform conflicts constructively. In D. Sandole, S. Byrne, I. Sandole-Staroste & J. Senehi (eds) *Handbook of Conflict Analysis and Resolution* (pp. 199–212). London: Routledge.

Senehi, J. (2009b) The role of constructive, transcultural storytelling in ethnopolitical conflict transformation in Northern Ireland. In G. Irani, V. Volkan & J. Carter (eds) *Regional and Ethnic Conflicts: Perspectives from the Front Lines* (pp. 227–237). New York: Prentice Hall.

Umbreit, M. (1995) *Mediating Interpersonal Conflicts: A Pathway to Peace*. West Concord, MN: CPI Publishing.

Zartman, W. & Touval, S. (2007) International mediation. In C. Crocker, F.O. Hampson & P. Aall (eds) *Leashing the Dogs of War: Conflict Management in a Divided World* (pp. 437–454). Washington, DC: United States Institute of Peace Press.

38

SUCCESS AND FAILURE OF INTERNATIONAL MEDIATION

Examining causes and conditions that impede or assist process success

Brian Polkinghorn, Anthony Yost and Matt Swiderski

International mediation can mean many things to many people. The definition we are adopting here is the deliberate *use of a third party, be it a group, an entity or actors who intervene* (in a sometimes neutral, sometimes unbiased and sometimes non-partisan manner) *in a dispute or conflict arising among two or more state actors with the intent of helping them resolve a problem.* However, many others provide their own definition (e.g. Mitchell & Webb, 1988; Burton, 1972) which signals that there are more definitions beyond how we define it here. Similarly, mediation itself conjures up many connotations, as in Latin it means to cut in half, in Chinese it indicates the act where someone comes between two others to help them solve their problem, and in Arabic it might entail a sense of manipulation. For others it is simply a process that is used to help solve problems (Wall & Lynne, 1993).

Many studies have been conducted over the last decade using a variety of databases to examine the results occurring in international mediation efforts. For example, Bercovitch and Gartner (2006) conducted a thorough examination and analysis and came to the conclusion that mediation had occurred in 70 percent of all international conflicts since 1945. Indeed, when mediation is used, the probability of a peace agreement appears six times more likely when third-party intermediaries are present. Yet success is more than reaching an agreement. One measure we found to be missing is an examination of "mini wins" or partial agreements that arise partially due to conditions on the ground that demand an incremental focus, rather than a one-time opportunity to strike a grand deal. After reviewing the literature on international mediation outcomes, we argue that the definition of success (and failure) needs to be broadened past the typical outcome of the process to include contextual and relational changes.

This begs the question of whether or not international mediation is so unique that it needs its own framework, models and theories. Vuković (2014) makes a strong argument that international mediation should be considered a special arena or a distinct form of conflict intervention/management. While there are similarities to be found among mediation practices in other venues, the degree of uncertainty, lack of predictability of the parties, complexity of the case, contextual complications and the propensity of a less clear structure within which to operate, arguably make international mediation a unique arena of application deserving of its own focus of study, research and theoretical development. We concur with Vuković's (2014) arguments.

Factors impacting success and failure

Several authors have examined what mediation success looks like from a variety of perspectives (Kleiboer, 1996; Wallensteen & Svensson, 2014); others have sought to distinguish the dynamics of international mediation efforts and their subsequent consequences and provide insight on the most important factors affecting mediation (Wickboldt et al., 1999). Some have focused on particular characteristics of international disputes and how they affect the performance and effectiveness of mediation (Bercovitch & Langley, 1993). Still others have examined the effectiveness of mediation styles on outcome variables (Beardsley et al., 2006). Beardsley et al. (2006) conclude that "facilitative mediation is best able to resolve commitment problems and secure a reduction in post crisis tensions … more intrusive or coercive forms of third-party intervention are apparently not necessary to manage or resolve conflicts" (p. 83). Beardsley's (2013) examination of mediator leverage provides a sense of caution that a one-size-fits-all approach to intervention and process choices will not work and, given this, mediators must be careful in terms of what style they choose to adopt.

Getting parties to the table is an understated task. Sometimes it takes incredible effort on the part of many outside actors, be they governments, international organizations, or individuals. Techniques range from creating incentives with reciprocation via confidence-building measures to outright threats of other parties in the international community joining in on another side. How parties get to the table is, therefore, not as clear-cut as one might conjure up with the standard conflict analysis and intake process. Given the impediments that arise in getting parties together, it might be prudent to consider it a mini-win if they come to the table. We will now explore several factors that impact parties getting to the table and the outcome of the process.

Zartman (1991) provides several interesting landmark determinants regarding the success of international mediation and what persuades parties to trust mediation. These concepts include mutually hurting stalemate (MHS) and ripe moments for conflict resolution. Zartman (1991) advances the idea that "conflict, and its resolution, is not just a matter of contending wills but of the costs and advantages inherent in the context at any given time" (p. 12). The cost-benefit analysis of disputing parties plays into the concept of ripe moments for conflict resolution. "The basic component of a ripe moment is a deadlock that keeps both parties from achieving their goals" (Zartman, 1991, p. 16), which can be viewed as an MHS. Zartman (1991) defines this as a "stalemate that hurts both parties enough to make them feel uncomfortable and unable to break out by an escalation with acceptable costs" (p. 16).

Timing is everything; attempts to intervene too early—that is, before issues are clear and the commitment of resources is fully established—can lead to a premature failure. On the other hand, intervening too late—that is, after parties are psychologically and materially overcommitted—can diminish the impact of future means for outside parties to intervene. The impact of MHS on timing occurs when the parties feel as though they are trapped in a costly conflict from which they cannot escape through victory (Zartman, 2000). Mack and Snyder (1957) also examine conditions when parties will begin to pursue types of de-escalatory options. In short, it often comes down to a calculation of the exposure to future risk added to the overall costs of continuing the conflict, versus cutting losses now and ending the conflict episode. Seeking a way out is more likely to occur when conflict intensity is high, opponents possess similar strength, and the crisis has gone on for a fairly long period of time (Beardsley, 2008). Then again, mediating a peace agreement under these types of conditions can produce strong short-term impacts but can, if left to linger, also act to inhibit long-term peace. If agreements are not fulfilled or mediation creates long-term artificial incentives that allow the agreement to linger, then some might argue that timing of intervention certainly impacts the efficacy of reaching an agreement (Beardsley, 2008).

Two other interesting studies shed more light on Zartman's (2000) ripeness theory. In the case of Cambodia, Amer (2007) sees the value of ripeness theory although its primary area of impact and applicability is limited to the stakeholders' ability to assess their circumstances. Zahar (2010) likewise examines the spoiler in international intervention and thinks this role impacts the conditions leading to the "ripeness" for mediation to occur. In this case, it is the context, and not so much the actors, that it is most important to watch for signs of ripeness.

Types of interveners

For our purposes here, the focus is just on mediation efforts. It is probably best to think of these ideas on several continua. The first deals with types of mediators considered, and we find inspiration in the work of Spitka (2015). On one end of the continuum are mediators who are there purely to support process functions. Their focus is on providing a time and space within which to hold a structured problem-solving process. Then, on the other end of the continuum are mediators who not only manage the process but, because of their knowledge and expertise of the case, also take part in shaping issues and otherwise engaging in substantive matters. These mediators may not focus as much on the process as on the substance and outcome. They are there to get an agreement and they bring influence to the table. Mediators who bring (dis)incentives or otherwise impact how the disputants interact are, in essence, working to drive the process toward a preferred set of options.

What we know is that a process-oriented intervener may have more difficulty getting the parties to come to the table and to reach an agreement, but if the intervener do succeed then they are more likely to remain involved and help to work out the implementation and enforcement issues. On the other hand, we know that the more influential or powerful mediator who brings resources and other incentives is often better at getting an agreement, but not as good with the follow-up post-mediation implementation and enforcement issues. Heavy-handed third-party involvement that relies on threats or promises may not be the right tool for the job and should be considered with great caution (see Beardsley, 2013).

So how do we moderate between the process-oriented "hands-off" mediator and a substance-oriented "hands-on" mediator? It all depends on the other aforementioned factors, as well as the parties' confidence in the mediator. For instance, high confidence in the mediator's ability to achieve preferred outcomes increases the probability of acceptance or request to mediate (Maundi et al., 2006). Also of note are those mediators who have previously helped parties reach an agreement, having a 19 percent greater probability of acceptance by the parties (Greig & Regan, 2008).

Types of intervention

Intervention can come in the form of a single mediator such as President Jimmy Carter at Camp David, through a team such as the one led by Senator George Mitchell for the All-Party Peace Talks in Northern Ireland (Curran & Sebenius, 2003), or the team led by Richard Holbrooke in Bosnia, where, Curran, Sebenius and Watkins (2004) go to lengths to point out that, it is imperative to be cautious in developing any firm conclusions leading to generalizations as to what can lead to a successful international mediation. Even so, Frazier and Dixon (2006) assert that multilateral actors such as these can lead to a greater chance of reaching a negotiated settlement, as multilateral actors are often perceived as more legitimate than individual state actors or ad hoc coalitions. Part of that perception may arise from a sense of enhanced independence, a greater sense of neutrality and the ability to be more effective with resources.

Multi-track diplomacy as a systems approach

Joe Montville is credited with the development of the concept of Track II diplomacy which generally refers to non-state or nongovernmental actors who use informal contacts to work toward peace (Davidson & Montville, 1981; Montville, 1991). Diamond and McDonald (1996) expanded the two-track system to nine, in an effort to more fully explore the range of actors throughout society, down to the grassroots, who are working toward similar goals. This expanded multi-track model is couched in a systems approach to peacebuilding and conflict resolution. Research points toward the finding that higher track involvement along with higher enforcement capabilities and resources used as leverage (Low, 1985; Touval & Zartman, 1985; Bercovitch & Houston, 1996), combined with lower track grassroots involvement increases effectiveness due to pooled resources, decreased uncertainty, and more local support for such efforts (Bohmelt, 2010; Regan & Aydin, 2006; Frazier & Dixon, 2006; Diamond & McDonald, 1996). Comparatively, Frazier and Dixon (2006) indicate that Track I used along with international governmental organizations can more likely lead to success. It may also be the trend to move away from the single actor to multi-party and multi-track approaches (Greig & Diehl, 2012).

Impact of substantive bias and mediator stance

Another factor that may impact mediation success involves bias in the form of substantive expertise. At first glance, one might expect an unbiased approach by the mediator to be more desirable by the disputants, although biased mediators are on average more successful than unbiased ones in helping parties reach agreement (Savun, 2008; Favretto, 2009). We might cautiously consider linking this finding to the power-based mediator to see if this increases the chances of reaching an agreement.

Impact of process approach bias and mediator stance

Mediator approaches to managing the process have already been discussed. What we are doing here is taking two types, power mediators, and pure or facilitative mediators, (Svensson, 2007; Spitka, 2015) and comparing their ability to reach an agreement. As noted, power mediators are more successful at reaching settlements and pure (or facilitative) mediators are better at reaching issue resolution. Pure mediators are also more effective in reaching territorial and political power-sharing arrangements (Svensson, 2007), while power mediators might be more effective in minimizing potential cost and increasing potential benefits. One thing power mediators possess is the ability to induce and issue rewards and threats which research indicates is positively associated with success in mediation (Sisk, 2009; Susskind & Babbitt, 1992). Other research shows that the power mediator is more effective in getting parties to sign a peace agreement (Bercovitch & Gartner, 2006). Svensson (2007) used the Uppsala Conflict Data Program (UCDP) to determine who amongst trust (minds) or power (muscles) mediators is more likely to bring about conflict resolution. Svensson (2007) found that all types of mediators—pure mediators, power mediators and a combination of both—have a positive effect on the likelihood of peace agreements. The findings also revealed that mediators usually do not make things worse and, more often positively, increase the prospect for agreements.

There appears to be an argument for power mediation on the front end and facilitative on the back end of peace processes. The basic idea is that a combination of types of mediation may be more effective in reaching a peace agreement with more durable institutional arrangements within agreements (Svensson, 2007; Beardsley et al., 2006; Carment et al., 2009). Research on the impact of substantive expertise of the mediator along with a higher degree of process control and persuasion might lead to an agreement.

Types of agreements

International mediation operates across a wide array of circumstances and contexts where a variety of agreements are possible. Reaching no agreement may not spell failure, but rather be an indication that the timing was incorrect, that a party is acting in bad faith, or that there is some other issue that must be attended to in order to get the parties to the table when conditions are more suitable. Likewise, partial agreements or mini-wins may be the best that can be achieved at any given moment. A partial agreement might buy time by getting some issues settled while regrouping to figure out how to address the remaining items. The reality is that in order for agreements to work, they have to reflect the ability of the parties to individually carry out what they have committed to doing. In some instances, parties have agreed to certain conditions that they do not have the capacity to fulfill or do not have the backing of their constituents.

Sometimes agreements are meant to be temporary, with a more comprehensive version being developed in the future. This incremental approach is more likely to occur in instances of protracted conflict where the conditions described by Mack and Snyder (1957) are present with no clear path to victory for any of the combatants and mounting costs of engagement piling up.

Why are some agreements essentially self-sustaining and others doomed to fail? There are many factors that come into play and they would fill an entire book. We will generally examine just a few. Sometimes "external guarantors" take part in an international mediation agreement as agents who are there to support whatever terms the parties decide, although the guarantor often comes with conditions that also need to be met. Having an outside benefactor who is there to support the implementation and enforcement of the agreement, as well as provide further potential resources, can be highly beneficial, as long as their demands/agenda can be integrated in such a way as not to tip the balance so that one party feels ganged-up on.

So what helps move the process along toward an agreement? One suggestion is to generate a high degree of specificity on tangible issues. Getting a clear understanding on who, when and how parties will fulfill their obligations, helps implementation. Creating built-in guarantees that certain actions will be carried out also increases confidence in the process and each other. Another is the inclusion of power-sharing arrangements. Caution is needed here because there are agreements that possess these characteristics but still fail to work, as was the case in the Indo-Sri Lankan agreement. This case also has the distinction between short-term success—signing an agreement—and long-term success which includes realistic implementation and sustainable goals (Bercovitch & Simpson, 2010). Hartzell and Hoddie (2003) also indicate that a higher number of power-sharing provisions in an agreement and the presence of a third-party guarantor decrease the likelihood of a return to violence and reduce the risk of settlement failure.

Conclusion

In conclusion, the findings from research studies reviewed here provide useful insights, some of which contradict each other, but in all still provide more clarity than confusion. Success and failure do not need to be predicated solely on problem-solving process outcomes, but can also be considered in regard to increased dialogue, improved relations and the reduction of dehumanization. Mediators would be well advised to keep in mind the non-contractual and less obvious benefits of their intervention when considering how to frame success and failure. Similarly, moving from a rigid stance to a more fast and flexible posture when dealing with changing needs and demands of the parties may improve results. In the end, labels aside, if we truly expect something new, then we must be prepared to consider doing things in new and unique ways.

References

Amer, R. (2007) The resolution of the Cambodian conflict: Assessing the explanatory value of Zartman's ripeness theory. *Journal of Peace Research*, 44(6): 729–742.

Beardsley, K. (2008) Agreement without peace? International mediation and time inconsistency problems. *American Journal of Political Science*, 52(4): 723–740.

Beardsley, K. (2013) Using the right tool for the job: Mediator leverage and conflict resolution. *Penn State Journal of Law & International Affairs*, 2(1): 57–65.

Beardsley, K.C., Quinn, D.M., Biswas, B. & Wilkenfeld, J. (2006) Mediation style and crisis outcomes. *The Journal of Conflict Resolution*, 50(1): 58–86.

Bercovitch, J. & Gartner, S.S. (2006) Is there method in the madness of mediation? Some lessons for mediators from quantitative studies of mediation. *International Interactions*, 32(4): 329–354.

Bercovitch, J. & Houston, A. (1996) The study of international mediation: Theoretical issues and empirical evidence. In J. Bercovitch (ed.) *Resolving International Conflict: The Theory and Practice of Mediation* (pp. 11–38). London: Lynne Rienner.

Bercovitch, J. & Langley, J. (1993) The nature of the dispute and the effectiveness of international mediation. *The Journal of Conflict Resolution*, 37(4): 670–691.

Bercovitch, J. & Simpson, L. (2010) International mediation and the question of failed peace agreements—improving conflict management and implementation. *Peace and Change*, 35(1): 68–103.

Bohmelt, T. (2010) Why many cooks if they can spoil the broth? The determinants of multiparty mediation. *Journal of Peace Research*, 49(5): 701–715.

Burton, J.W. (1972) Resolution of conflict. *International Studies Quarterly*, 16: 5–29.

Carment, D., Samy, Y. & El Achkar, S. (2009) Protracted conflict and crisis mediation: A contingency approach. In J. Bercovitch & S. Gartner (eds) *International Conflict Mediation: New Approaches and Findings* (pp. 216–239). New York: Routledge.

Curran, D. & Sebenius, J.K. (2003) The mediator as coalition builder: George Mitchell in Northern Ireland. *International Negotiation*, 8(1): 111–147.

Curran, D., Sebenius, J.K. & Watkins, M. (2004) Two paths to peace: Contrasting George Mitchell in Northern Ireland with Richard Holbrooke in Bosnia-Herzegovina. *Negotiation Journal*, 20(4): 513–537.

Davidson, W. & Montville, J.M. (1981) Foreign policy according to Freud. *Foreign Policy*, 45: 145–157.

Diamond, L. & Ambassador McDonald, J. (1996) *Multi-track Diplomacy: A Systems Approach to Peace* (3rd edn). West Hartford, CT: Kumarian Press.

Favretto, K. (2009) Should peacemakers take sides? Major power mediation, coercion, and bias. *The American Political Science Review*, 103(2): 248–263.

Frazier, D.V. & Dixon, W.J. (2006) Third-party intermediaries and negotiated settlements, 1946–2000. *International Interactions*, 32(4): 385–408.

Greig, J.M. & Diehl, P.F. (2012) *International Mediation: War and Conflict in the Modern World*. Malden, MA: Polity Press.

Greig, J.M. & Regan, P.M. (2008) When do they say yes? An analysis of the willingness to offer and accept mediation in civil wars. *International Studies Quarterly*, 52(4): 759–781.

Hartzell, C. & Hoddie, M. (2003) Institutionalizing peace: Power sharing and post-civil war conflict management. *American Journal of Political Science*, 47(2): 318–332.

Kleiboer, M. (1996) Understanding success and failure of international mediation. *The Journal of Conflict Resolution*, 40(2): 360–389.

Low, S. (1985) The Zimbabwe settlement: 1976–1979. In W. Zartman & S. Touval (eds) *International Mediation Theory and Practice* (pp. 91–105). Boulder, CO: Westview Press.

Mack, R. & Snyder, R.C. (1957) The analysis of social conflict: Toward an overview and synthesis. *The Journal of Conflict Resolution*, 1(2): 212–248.

Maundi, M., Zartman, W., Khadiagala, G. & Nuamah, K. (2006) *Getting in: Mediators' Entry into the Settlement of African Conflicts*. Washington: United States Institute of Peace Press.

Mitchell, C. & Webb, K. (1988) Mediation in international relations. In C. Mitchell & K. Webb (eds) *New Approaches to International Mediation* (pp. 1–15). Santa Barbara, CA: Greenwood Publishing.

Montville, J. (1991a). Track two diplomacy: The arrow and the olive branch. *The Psychodynamics of International Relations*, 2: 160–175.

Montville, J. (1991b). Track two diplomacy: The arrow and the olive branch: A case for track two diplomacy. In V.D. Volkan, J.V. Montville & D.A. Julius (eds) *The Psychodynamics of International Relations: Vol. 2. Unofficial Diplomacy at Work* (pp. 161–175). Lanham, MD: Lexington Books.

Regan, P.M. & Aydin, A. (2006) Diplomacy and other forms of intervention in civil wars. *Journal of Conflict Resolution*, 50(5): 736–756.

Savun, B. (2008) Information, bias, and mediation success. *International Studies Quarterly*, 52(1): 25–47.

Sisk, T. (2009) *International Mediation in Civil Wars: Bargaining with Bullets*. New York: Routledge.

Spitka, T. (2015) *International Intervention, Identity and Conflict Transformation: Bridges and Walls between Groups*. New York: Routledge.

Susskind, L. & Babbitt, E. (1992) Overcoming the obstacles to effective mediation of international disputes. In J. Bercovitch & J. Rubin (eds) *Mediation in International Relations: Multiple Approaches to Conflict Management* (pp. 30–51). New York: St Martin's Press.

Svensson, I. (2007) Mediation with muscles or minds? Exploring power mediators and pure mediators in civil wars. *International Negotiation*, 12(2): 229–248.

Touval, S. & Zartman, W. (1985) *International Mediation in Theory and Practice*. Boulder, CO: Westview Press.

Vuković, S. (2014) International mediation as a distinct form of conflict management. *International Journal of Conflict Management*, 25(1): 61–80.

Wall, J.A. Jr. & Lynne, A. (1993) Mediation: A current review. *The Journal of Conflict Resolution*, 37(1): 160–194.

Wallensteen, P. & Svensson, I. (2014) Talking peace: International mediation in armed conflicts. *Journal of Peace Research*, 51(2): 315–327.

Wickboldt, A., Bercovitch, J. & Piramuthu, S. (1999) Dynamics of international mediation: Analysis using machine learning methods. *Conflict Management and Peace Science*, 17(1): 49–68.

Zahar, M.J. (2010) SRSG mediation in civil wars: Revisiting the "spoiler" debate. *Global Governance: A Review of Multilateralism and International Organizations*, 16(2): 265–280.

Zartman, W.I. (1991) Conflict and resolution: Contest, cost, and change. *Annals of the American Academy of Political and Social Science*, 518: 11–22.

Zartman, W.I. (2000) Ripeness: The hurting stalemate and beyond. In P. Stern & D. Druckman (eds) *International Conflict Resolution after the Cold War* (pp. 225–250). Washington, DC: National Academy Press.

39

MEDIATION AND THE CHALLENGE OF FOSTERING RECONCILIATION IN ETHNO-POLITICAL DISPUTES

The case of Guyana

Perry Mars, Frederic Pearson and Marie Olson Lounsbery

This study is dedicated to the memory of Dr. Perry Mars.[1]

Ethno-political disputes that tend to be intractable and prone to violence, as in the Guyana case, demand serious and sustained efforts towards reconciliation and stabilization. International mediation is considered here as a most effective approach to addressing this problem, particularly in light of the repeated failure of domestic interparty efforts toward this end over the years. Mediation is the facilitation by independent third parties of constructive dialogue and negotiation toward an agreed settlement. Guyana is selected as an extremely informative case of efforts along these lines in a situation of persistent political and social conflict mainly along an ethno/racial divide.

The major challenges to fostering resolution in Guyana reside in the typical intransigence of ruling parties that resist attempts to share or mutually accommodate political power, the lack of cultural and political infrastructure conducive to mediation and negotiations over power or governance issues, and the limited time horizon mediators give themselves in attempts to deal with protracted and sensitive political and/or ideological issues in such troubled democracies. Given evidence of severe splits in divided societies such as Iraq, Syria, Afghanistan, the Democratic Republic of the Congo, Bosnia, Lebanon, and other struggling polities, Guyana's experience affords important caveats about approaching civil unrest and instability through mediation.

The focus is on the role of international mediation efforts in the post-Cold War era, regarding both electoral monitoring and further attempts at political reconciliation and peacebuilding between two major ethno-political contenders. These interventions will be assessed in relation to the best practices in international mediation and facilitated negotiations across the globe, particularly in developing countries. Mediated conflict resolution is important for a country such as Guyana, which over the years has persistently witnessed serious ravages to its democratic political life, stemming from both foreign Cold War interventions and the political dominance of a particular ethnic group over the others. A peaceful outcome away from the often-deadly conflict process has relevance for the prospects of "good governance" that is usually said to be associated with democratic inclusiveness and equitable distribution of resources.

Mediation standards and strategies

Mediation in the international context can range from the offer of diplomatic "good offices," to the dispatch of notable envoys acting as dialogue intermediaries. Factors that must be considered in mediation of civil disputes include the questions of timing, the identity, and status of the mediator, and the level of approach to involving intrinsic participants to assist in the process (Zartman, 2014). Mediation effectiveness can also depend on the level of approach used, for example, involving grassroots participants, or elite-level bargaining. Of course, all these levels and distinctions must be considered in predicting and accounting for mediation outcomes (Pearson, 2001). Much of mediators' effectiveness can depend on both the political and social culture being faced. Indeed, the full history of the conflict needs to be mapped out and addressed by any third party hoping to progress toward settlement (Wehr, 1998).

Integral to the conflict mapping process are mediators' feel and skill in identifying the propitious time for initiating or renewing talks, or maximizing settlement potential. This involves reading parties' readiness to seek cessation of hostilities, or addressing issues of power balancing, resource distribution, and probable "spoilers" who might shoot down (literally) any agreement. Zartman (2014) has suggested that a "mutually hurting stalemate" may be a precondition for productive talks. Mediation also may be complicated when, as in Guyana and in the majority of intrastate conflicts currently, one of the disputing parties holds the reins of government while the other is a non-state actor (or, as in Syria, actors) representing aggrieved minority or majority factions; at the extreme, of course, such situations have resulted in outright civil wars. Indeed, Walter (1999) has also noted the importance of mediation in cases of rebellion in her finding that "governments and rebels are 39% more likely to bargain successfully with the help of a mediator than on their own" (Kydd, 2003, p. 607). The issues discussed, however, tend to remain tangential to the issues of grievance without significant outside pressure or presence (Olson Lounsbery & Cook, 2014).

Wehr and Lederach (1991, pp. 90–98) and others (Watkins & Winters, 1997, p. 123) have summarized some of the expected best practice in ethno-cultural mediation and have identified three basic elements: 1 deliberate citizen and volunteer presence (taking into account the often unrecognized importance of the grassroots); 2 mixed teams of outside-neutral and inside-partial mediators in order to maximize the advantages of each; and 3 a resident and persistent conflict-transformation or peacebuilding group working on deep-seated issues. Key reference points in the processes include solving problems involving mutual recognition and legitimacy, logistics, and "transparency"—for example, verification that the terms are being met. Since power asymmetries and issues of discrimination (Olson Lounsbery & Pearson, 2009) also frequently characterize civil disputes and rebellions, provisions constructively addressing such asymmetries must be built into terms of settlement.

Another set of best practices has been formulated by Kumar and De la Haye (2011) involving efforts to bridge the gap between international norms and practices and local conflict management mechanisms, a form of hybrid mediation for conflict transformation in some 30 countries, including Guyana where they assisted in fostering a Social Cohesion Program that included national dialogue and a network of local community mediators to ease tension. However, they have also identified troublesome confounding effects, such as the penetration of violence beyond the elite level and primary antagonists down into the society itself, often driven to criminal behavior by fear and desperation bred of poverty and insecurity. Kumar and De la Haye (2011) refer to the establishment of an infrastructure of peace, which combines external mediation and assistance with the necessary extension of negotiations to internal actors themselves at various societal levels.

Background to Guyana's ethno-political conflicts

Guyana gained its independence from British colonial rule in 1966. Ethnic diversity of the Guyana population was occasioned by a colonial history of forced or enslaved labor importation from Europe, Africa, China, and India, not to mention the earlier enslavement of the native Amerindian population also. The European colonial approach to maintaining control of the diverse population was through a policy of divide and rule that pitted one of the major ethnic or racial groups against the other. In the Guyana case, this was East Indian versus African descendant segments of the population. The current ethnic distribution of the population as outlined in government of Guyana 2002 statistics is as follows: East Indians (43.45 percent), Afro-Guyanese (30.20 percent), mixed (16.73 percent), native Amerindians (9.16 percent), Chinese (0.19 percent), Portuguese (0.20 percent), whites (0.06 percent), and others (0.01 percent) (Guyana Statistical Bureau, 2002).

Following an intensive spate of violent ethno-political conflicts in the 1960s, the major ethnic groups became polarized along partisan political lines, with mostly East Indians supporting the People's Progressive Party (PPP) originally led by anti-colonial activist Cheddi Jagan, while most Afro-Guyanese gravitated towards the People's National Congress (PNC) originally led by the relatively moderate Forbes Burnham. The "mixed" segment of the population was divided about equally between PPP and PNC, while the Amerindians, Chinese, Portuguese and whites tended towards smaller third parties such as the then United Force (UF).

The 1964 elections saw the defeat of the PPP government and succession to power of a coalition government comprising the moderate Afro-dominated PNC, and the small pro-British ethnically mixed UF. This coalition government took Guyana into political independence in 1966. The PNC very soon ditched its UF coalition partner and proceeded to rule unilaterally following rigged elections between 1968 and 1985. Under PNC rule, resistance by the then opposition parties, mainly the PPP and a new party called the Working People's Alliance (WPA), was met with a variety of state repressive measures including the violent disruption of opposition meetings and political campaigns (Mars, 1998).

When free and fair democratic elections returned to Guyana in 1992, it became clear that ethnic voting had not disappeared from the scene. The 1992 elections were not only ethnically divisive, but also resulted in some political violence, and a change of regime from PNC to PPP. Despite many prior efforts to mediate or resolve the inter-party conflicts, this change of government made little or no difference to the frequency or intensity levels of political-ethnic conflict that soon morphed into criminal violence in the country.

Guyana's historical attempts at mediation and resolution

Responding to the pre-independence violence of the 1960s, Cheddi Jagan, the then leader of the ruling PPP, approached both regional and international actors to help mediate the conflicts—in particular the then President Kwame Nkrumah of a newly independent Ghana, and the then Prime Minister Eric Williams of neighboring Trinidad and Tobago (Jagan, 1972). Both of these individuals had advantages of international prestige and relevant cultural identity as "Third World" and regional notables. However, the opposition party leaders at the time, Forbes Burnham of the PNC and Peter D'Auguar of UF, rejected this offer with a view to distancing themselves from the Marxist Jagan and the PPP.

After independence in 1966, Burnhamist approaches included instituting ruling party "paramountcy" or dominance over the government and people, augmenting the militarization of the state and society, and unilaterally imposing a new constitution in 1980, which among other things instituted Burnham as president for life (James, 2006). In opposition, Jagan and the PPP responded with a mix of civil protest (strikes, parliamentary boycott) and reconciliatory approaches including calls for a national front government (NFG) to be shared between the PNC and PPP, and eventually the offer of what the PPP termed "critical support" to the PNC government. Burnham eventually decided to accommodate Jagan's request for peace and collaboration following pressures from Cuba to foster working-class unity in the pursuit of socialist objectives (Majeed, 2005). However, Burnham died in 1985 before these reconciliation initiatives could materialize, and was succeeded by President Desmond Hoyte.

Ultimately, in the late 1980s, Jagan in conjunction with other opposition and third-party forces, particularly the WPA, again appealed for international mediation of the now hurting (though not clearly mutually hurting) stalemate in the country. This time the opposition parties were focused on the speedy resolution of the rigged electoral process, ending the continuing ethnic divisiveness and polarization, and initiating constitutional change. Among the international observation groups approached were the Commonwealth Secretariat, The Caribbean Community (Caricom), and The Carter Center.

Carter Center electoral and reconciliation efforts

The Carter Center's intervention involved electoral monitoring, identity/diversity considerations and some deeper-seated interests as well. Former President Jimmy Carter's approach to mediating the 1992 elections was quite adequately summarized in a report by two of The Carter Center's main officials familiar with the region, David Caroll and Robert Pastor (1993). Violence of a limited scale did occur on the very day of the 1992 elections when angry crowds in PNC strongholds claiming disenfranchisement stormed the Elections Commission headquarters in the capital and two other urban areas. However, most probably due to Carter's influence, the violence was quickly contained (Caroll & Pastor, 1993). The report further detailed the following lessons learned: 1) that international observers need to help all sides to focus on the most important issues that divide them and assist in finding solutions; 2) that observers need to withdraw from the process if it ever becomes seriously flawed; and 3) that observers should be involved in encouraging public confidence and participation in the national healing process.

Carter's successes in monitoring the 1992 electoral front included fair counting at the polls, peaceful transition of power, and mitigation of sporadic violence. Thus, the new ruling party, now renamed the PPP/C (because of its inclusion of what it called a "civic" component), again invited Carter in 1993 to mediate the broader Guyana conflict situation in the areas of sustainable economic development, electoral reform, and ethnic reconciliation. Carter returned to Guyana in 2001 to monitor what turned out to be peaceful and above-board elections held that year (The Carter Center, 2001). Carter remained engaged with the parties up to 2006, when he again monitored elections held under the new Jagdeo PPP/C regime. Meanwhile, in 2004, Carter proposed a list of measures focused on issues such as electoral reforms and good governance.

The most prominent of these 2004 recommendations were the restructuring of the Elections Commission, implementation of a National Development Strategy (NDS), constitutional reform, instituting a Commission of Inquiry into death squad activities and connections, change of parliamentary representation from proportional representation (PR) to constituency-based parliamentarians to cut across entrenched ethnic voting patterns, serious governmental efforts to deal with corruption and drug trafficking, and inclusiveness of opposition parties in dialogue, parliament, and the government-controlled media (Carter, 2004). However, most of Carter's recommendations were either slighted or rejected by the then President Jagdeo (Carter, 2004). Carter was also critical of the constitutionally spawned Ethnic Relations Commission (ERC) in Guyana as being of "high ambition but limited experience" (Carter, 2004, p. 2). Yet, Carter encouraged the civil society leaders to form some kind of public forum with which The Carter Center "could relate," since, as Carter asserted, it was necessary to bypass the "stalemated political party structure" (Carter, 2004, p. 2) which he regarded as an obstacle to peaceful resolution of the Guyana conflict situation.

It has been well noted in other conflict-ridden zones, as in West Africa and even Northern Ireland, that political and factional leaders gain material and status rewards and interests in keeping conflicts going (O'Brien, 1986). Indeed, Carter's request that Guyana's civil society be politically independent led to expressions of what Carter recalled as "fear of losing government contracts, licenses, etc" (Carter, 2004, p. 2). Carter himself left the Guyana scene in 2004 in frustration, to say the least, as he concluded: "Of all countries I have visited in the world, Guyana has the most unrealized potential" (Carter, 2004, p. 3).

Comparisons with Commonwealth, Caricom, and UNDP approaches

Following massive electoral violence that accompanied the 1997 elections, Caricom, on the invitation of both the new PPP President Janet Jagan and the PNC opposition leader Desmond Hoyte, became involved in a relatively substantial intervention for conflict resolution, this time in the brokering of peace between the two parties. A peace settlement came in 1998 in two parts: first, in the form of what came to be known as the Herdmanston Accords, and the second, as the St Lucia Statement.

The Herdmanston Accords of 1998, mediated by the heads of government of the various Caribbean countries comprising Caricom, encouraged the parties to work by themselves on a solution through continuous dialogue, and to establish a constitutional commission to institute policies and programs to ease or resolve traditional racial tensions. The St Lucia Statement admonished the two leaders to observe the first accords (Herdmanston), particularly referencing the recommendations for constitutional change. Like The Carter Center, Caricom emphasized the importance of consulting civil society as an important lever in the resolution of conflicts and disputes in Guyana (Caribbean Community Mission, 1998, p. 2). However, as Clifford E. Griffin (2007) contends, Caricom had been "largely unsuccessful in bringing about long term solutions" to such conflicts principally because of what he regarded as "Caricom's political culture" of lack of expertise, as well as organizational and operational capacity for conflict mediation (p. 309).

The Commonwealth Secretariat also mediated the Guyana elections and conflict situation between 1992 and 2006. The Commonwealth's special envoy, the late Sir Paul Reeves, a former archbishop and governor of New Zealand from 1985–90, was in Guyana between 2002 and 2006 to help rekindle the failing inter-party dialogue (Commonwealth Network, 2014). His approach focused on the use and upgrade of parliament as the best site for inter-party dialogue (*Guyana Chronicle*, 2003). Reeves also relied on civil society initiatives, particularly facilitating local mediation efforts. In the end, Reeves asserted, "parliament began to work noticeably better" (Commonwealth Network, 2014, p. 2). However, the question of meaningful dialogue getting at underlying interests between the two main parties remained in abeyance by the time Sir Paul left Guyana in 2006.

The United Nations Development Programme (UNDP) initiative in instituting what it called the Social Cohesion Program (SCP) was perhaps the most far-reaching of these additional mediation and facilitation efforts in Guyana (UNDP Guyana, 2007). The SCP facilitated a series of community dialogues among the various civil society stakeholders, inclusive of the major ethnic and competing groups, across the country. Further, this approach to multi-ethnic communal dialogue influenced similar efforts by the government-appointed Ethnic Relations Commission (ERC). This SCP program, however, despite the overwhelming financial resources and expertise expended on it, also failed to get the two major parties on a course to improving their mutual stances on dialogue and political reconciliation. The main, potentially lasting, contribution of the UNDP is its likely inspiration of the new governmental Ministry of Social Cohesion, made possible by a change of government in 2015. However, only time will tell if this ministry will be more fruitful than the UNDP itself in realizing ethno-political reconciliation and inclusive governance in Guyana.

Assessing mediation successes and failures in the Guyana case

The frustrations awaiting international mediators in the Guyana context were overwhelming. The first obstacle was the unfathomable depths in which the political leaders entrapped themselves in negative ethnic tit-for-tat politics, complete with resource incentives to persist in the quest for unrivaled political power. President Carter, for example, could not get President Jagdeo to budge on accommodating the more important demands of the opposition, although the governing party had the greater responsibility for ensuring success of peace initiatives. At the same time, mediation efforts seldom went below the level of the traditional civil society groups to engage grassroots citizens and neighborhoods directly, something attempted elsewhere on a small scale in places such as Israel–Palestine (Handelman, 2011). Also evidently lacking was significant external economic and political pressure or incentives from major powers such as the US government, of the type seen, for example, in Northern Ireland (Anglo-Irish accords and European Union (EU) incentives).

Second, the Guyana civil society upon which mediators pinned considerable hopes to facilitate and force reconciliation was largely misunderstood. Far from being a cohesive and independent force to institute reconciliation pressures, civil society in Guyana represented a much too weak entity and link, being itself highly fragmented and polarized along partisan and sectarian lines. The voices of trade unions and the Guyana diaspora, for example, were largely ignored. Within Guyana's civil society, therefore, divisive forces constantly subdued the forces for peace and reconciliation. The peace initiatives tended to suffer from inadequate knowledge of the history of the Guyana conflicts and recognition of relevant contending interests among the participating groups, particularly the poorer classes, radicalized workers' representatives, and other elements of the non-traditional civil society.

Third, the opposing ethnic-based political parties failed to accept their own share of responsibilities for inciting or exacerbating the conflict situation. The two main parties accused the other of the same misdeeds while denying their own culpability. For this reason, there was no consensus on what constitutes the end game, which is political reconciliation and inclusiveness in governance. With no workable agreement on what an inclusive democracy would look like and what institutions would support or undermine it, reconciliation remains remote. Available proposals by both contending parties on the issue of democratic or "good" governance, for example, tended to be either unrealistic or ill conceived (PNCR, 2003; People's Progressive Party, 2003), and thus betrayed a lack of readiness by the parties for the negotiation and bargaining process.

The big question for mediators then is how to call into question the arguments associated with each governing party's assumption that it is possible to attain inclusive and democratic governance without the assistance of the other. So far, mediations seemed to have been taken up with the worthy goal of ending violence, rancor, electoral fraud and disputes as a mark of accomplishment, although the absence of violence or shouting is not necessarily the beginning of peace, let alone good governance and inclusive democracy that might lead to long-term cooperation and political reconciliation.

Conclusion

In transitional societies like Guyana, post-colonial conflicts tend to be rather persistent in nature. Struggles to form governing institutions tend to be a function of a violent and divisive colonial past and persistent discriminatory policies aimed at opposition groups. As elites maneuver to maintain or to gain advantage, they tend to rally support by employing instrumentalist tactics. In the process, parties based in colonial identities (and the probable resulting animosities) become calcified. Actors/elites who come into power in such a way are likely to resist efforts to significantly alter a system from which they benefit. Mediation in such contexts, while it may secure short-term gains such as peaceful elections or frameworks of reform, will often fail, as the actors involved, especially without sustained foreign or grassroots pressure, may be unwilling to make a good-faith effort at achieving a lasting peace.

Despite numerous efforts by outside actors to influence and transform political relationships and institutions in Guyana, deeply divisive conflict, distrust and resentment persisted. As presented here, while the political dispute had repercussions for all of Guyana's society, the conflict itself appeared to be elite-driven. Outside actors attempting to bring about resolution have largely done so with less than forthcoming elites, without involving the "streets," and without much settlement pressure from outside actors.

A massive economic assistance program conditional upon parties resolving their differences might also have constituted the type of inducement to peace that evidently played a role, for example, in the Northern Irish accords in relation to the EU (White, 2013). Such incentives are important for the building of institutions and momentum for the infrastructures of peace. In terms of Lederach's summary of success criteria, there is need in Guyana and similarly divided societies for a more concerted citizen and volunteer presence or representation in the various mediative efforts and a more conspicuous and lasting resident conflict transformation cadre to persist in exploring the deeper issues separating the parties and involving their constituents (Wehr & Lederach, 1991).

How to navigate these challenges will ultimately depend upon: 1) the extent and timing of international pressures that are applied to reluctant or intransigent parties; 2) whether mediators' engagement with the parties is transient or sustained; 3) the willingness to involve and prioritize community and grassroots participation within the overall civil society mobilization process; and 4) the interest and capability of international actors in the education and training of local mediation teams for protracted, regionally inclusive, engagement with difficult, intransigent, ethnic-based parties and groups, in fragile developing democracies such as Guyana, or for that matter Iraq. Significant and sustained outside pressure, beyond offers to mediate, may be necessary to bring parties to the table in good faith. It would seem that while the mediation efforts in Guyana were genuine, and while some procedural successes were scored, what they lacked was muscle. Concerted external pressures generally make it more difficult for the status quo to continue whereby the contending parties in civil disputes benefit from ethnic divisiveness and conflict.

Note

1 This study is dedicated to the memory of our colleague Dr. Perry Mars, who was tragically killed during a robbery in Guyana in 2016. In addition to being an outstanding scholar, teacher and researcher on the challenges of international peacemaking and inter-ethnic understanding, he was fully devoted to the welfare and development of his homeland. Few people understood the history and needs of the region so well, which compounds this terrible loss.

References

Caribbean Community Mission. (1998) *Guyana, Herdmanston Accord.* Retrieved from www.gecom.org.gy/pdf_laws/Herdmanston%20Accord.pdf.

Caribbean Community Secretariat. (1998) *Guyana: The St Lucia Statement.* Retrieved from archive.caricom.org/jsp/communications/meetings_statements/st_lucia_statement.jsp.

Caroll, D. & Pastor, R. (1993) Moderating ethnic tensions by electoral mediation. The Carter Center. Retrieved from www.cartercenter.org/documents/1205.pdf.

The Carter Center. (2001, March 21). Postelection statement on Guyana election. The Carter Center. Retrieved from www.cartercenter.org/news/documents/doc644.html.

The Carter Center. (2016) Waging peace: Guyana. The Carter Center. Retrieved from www.cartercenter.org/countries/guyana-peace.html.

Carter, J. (2004) President Jimmy Carter visits Guyana, August 11–13. The Carter Center. Retrieved from www.cartercenter.org/news/documents/doc1802.html.

Commonwealth Network. (2014) Good offices for peace. *Commonwealth Network.* Retrieved from www.commonwealthofnations.org/commonwealthinaction/good-offices-for-peace/.

Griffin, C.E. (2007) Caricom: Confronting the challenges of mediation and conflict resolution. *Commonwealth and Comparative Politics*, 45(3): 303–322.

Guyana Chronicle. (2003) Sir Paul Reeves: Guyana needs to draw on selfless spirit in service. September 29. *Guyana Chronicle.*

Guyana Statistical Bureau. (2002) 2002 population & housing census—Guyana national report: Chapter 2—population composition. Retrieved from www.statisticsguyana.gov.gy/census.html.

Handelman, S. (2011) *Conflict and Peacemaking in Israel-Palestine: Theory and Application.* Oxford: Taylor & Francis.

Jagan, C. (1972) *The West on Trial: My Fight for Guyana's Freedom.* Berlin: Seven Seas Publication.

James, R. (2006) *The Constitution of Guyana: A Study of its Dysfunctional Application.* University of Guyana, Institute of Development Studies.

Kumar, C. & De la Haye, J. (2011) Hybrid peacemaking: Building national "infrastructures for peace." *Global Governance: A Review of Multilateralism and International Organizations*, 18(1): 13–20.

Kydd, A. (2003) Which side are you on? Bias, credibility, and mediation. *American Journal of Political Science*, 47(4): 597–611.

Majeed, H. (2005) *Forbes Burnham: National Reconciliation and National Unity, 1984–1985.* New York: Global Communications Publishing.

Mars, P. (1998) *Ideology and Change: The Transformation of the Caribbean Left.* Detroit: Wayne State University Press.

O'Brien, C.C. (1986, June 1). Thinking about terrorism: Two stereotypes dominate discussions of terrorism. They cloud thought and inhibit effective action. *The Atlantic.* Retrieved from www.theatlantic.com/magazine/archive/1986/06/thinking-about-terrorism/305045/.

Olson Lounsbery, M. & Cook, A. (2014) Negotiating your way out of rivalry: Unassisted conflict resolution efforts in Southeast Asia. *International Negotiation Journal*, 20(2): 242–268.

Olson Lounsbery, M. & Pearson, F.S. (2009) *Civil Wars: Internal Struggles, Global Consequences.* Toronto: University of Toronto Press.

Pearson, F.S. (2001) Dimensions of conflict resolution in ethnopolitical disputes. *Journal of Peace Research*, 38(3): 275–287.

People's Progressive Party. (2003) Towards greater inclusiveness in governance in Guyana: Building trust to achieve genuine political co-operation. Presented by the PPP Government, State House, February 8.

PNCR. (2003, July 5). Shared governance in time for 2006. *Guyana Caribbean Politics*. Retrieved from guyanacaribbeanpolitics.com/?p=1117.

United Nations Development Programme (UNDP) Guyana. (2007) Can fostering a culture of dialogue change the course of a nation? An evaluation of the social cohesion program, key findings and summary recommendations. UNDP-Guyana. Retrieved from erc.undp.org/evaluation/documents/download/1521.

Walter, B. (1999) Designing transitions from civil war. *International Security*, 24(1): 127–155.

Watkins, M. & Winters, K. (1997) Intervenors with interests and power. *Negotiation Journal*, 13(2): 119–142.

Wehr, P. (1998) Conflict mapping. In *International Online Training Program on Intractable Conflict, Conflict Research Consortium*. Boulder, CO: University of Colorado. Retrieved from www.colorado.edu/conflict/peace/treatment/cmap.htm.

Wehr, P. & Lederach, J.P. (1991) Mediating conflict in Central America. *Journal of Peace Research*, 28(1): 85–98.

White, T. (ed.). (2013) *Lessons from the Northern Ireland Peace Process*. Madison: University of Wisconsin Press.

Zartman, I.W. (2014) Ripeness: The hurting stalemate and beyond. In P.C. Stern & D. Druckman (eds) *International Conflict Resolution after the Cold War*. Washington, DC: The National Academies Press.

40

MEDIATING IN THE SHADOW OF CONFLICT

United States Special Operations Forces in unconventional warfare

Christian Ramthun, Raffi Mnatzakanian and Patrick James Christian

> Natura abhorret vacuum (*nature abhors a vacuum*).
>
> *(Aristotle)*

Within the US Department of Defense, elite teams of Navy SEALs, Green Berets, Civil Affairs, and Psychological Operators are employed against violent extremist organizations seeking to fill ungoverned spaces of failed or failing political states. Once there, they operate against extremist organizations that have taken advantage of weak or non-existent governance to install radical versions of human organization. This struggle between elite special operations teams and violent extremist organizations usually occurs in the vacuum of hope and social authority, far from easy interference by collective international security. In this vacuum, rule of law is replaced by rule of force that trades minimum psychological and social survival for maximum authoritarian control.

US Special Operations field teams deploy into these vacuums of law and social order to help indigenous communities successfully negotiate their internal acceptance or rejection of extremist ideology and authoritarian domination. They are third-party neutrals who practice a proven form of mediation in places of extreme communal violence in failed and failing states around the world. The men and women of these Special Operations Forces, collectively referred to as "SOF," are organized for unconventional warfare. These unconventional operators use mediation as both action and process to reduce or even (ideally) resolve violent conflict between family, village, and tribe inside ongoing intra-state conflicts. Their use of mediation as action and process plays a central role in their ability to understand and engage the ongoing violence.

In the extreme context of working to counter the spread of terrorist insurgent organizations in ungoverned spaces outside the control of state governments, mediation is complicated. SOF teams are the central weapons of advanced skill-craft used to combat the roots of terrorism, insurgency, and the nihilist ideology of chaotic and disintegrating social structures. While they may be armed with the best equipment available, their most powerful tools involve non-kinetic human interaction. Their missions focus on the interaction between human beings rather than physical terrain.

Once deployed, SOF teams are not limited by diplomatic protocols to speak exclusively at the governmental level. Instead, SOF personnel work in the spaces that exist below the governmental level, from the individual citizen to the nation and all areas between. They practice field conflict mediation through a cultural lens using a historical narrative model to reduce or resolve intractable communal violence. The Special Operations soldier learns through training and experience to commit to empathy with community members who are at once victims and perpetrators. These specialized warriors find that while the existence of the collective narrative may be non-negotiable, the micro-stories that bring the narrative into conflict can be mediated.

The shift in violent conflict resolution

The battlefields of intra-state conflicts are quite different from those of interstate warfare of generations past. In the latter, the focus was on the battle formations of the enemy other. Damaged, violated civilian populations existed, but the need for participating armed forces to survive the terror of high-intensity warfare tends to marginalize their ability and/or willingness to internalize the plight of unarmed civilians, especially those populations of the enemy. Civilian casualties do often occur in interstate warfare as collateral damage, but what is different in intra-state conflict is the "intentionality" of the casualties and focus on the people rather than the combatants as the true target to destroy—in some cases, the care to which one side or the other took to ensure that maximum suffering occurred amongst their enemy other. What combatants of intra-state war are protecting is not merely life itself, but the survival of the psychosocial self-love across boundaries of death and metaphysical salvation.

This is why armed forces' practice of interstate warfare fails to resolve intra-state conflict; the participants to ethnic and cultural conflict often cannot negotiate that which they are not able to surrender: identification of self as it is known through historical narrative and existential memorialization to future generations. The intra-state conflict participants fight each other as politicized proxies against the physical fear of psychic annihilation. Such conflicts can never be negotiated because one cannot negotiate away identity and memory. However, the underlying stories in violent contest can be rewritten through mediation of the conflict narratives.

The context and applicability of mediation in SOF field operations

> Mediators operate in the shadow of the law, SOF mediates in the shadow of conflict.[1]

SOF Mediation is the concept of exposing core grievances between parties entrenched in violent conflict through engagement and dialogue that fosters opportunities capable of unraveling seemingly intractable conflict stories from non-negotiable historical narratives. Modern SOF conduct military operations that carry a significant amount of political, military, and informational gravitas at the strategic level of national defense based on their unique capabilities and the sensitivity of their missions. SOF missions specifically address security issues around the globe such as terrorism, insurgency, transnational crime, and communal violence by competing militias or violent extremist organizations in fragile and failing states. During intra-state conflict, these security issues often are a result of tribal, ethnic, or political tensions. In an effort to treat the underlying causes of violent conflict rather than just the symptoms, SOF planners and operators construct broad mission parameters that employ a mix of lethal skills traditionally seen in modern warfare and non-lethal solutions we refer to as "soft power." These are used to influence populations, as well as train and orient key actors and their communal organizations who are most directly engaged within the conflict. Distinctively, SOF employs mediation and negotiation as significant non-lethal skills that complement traditional lethal means of achieving national security objectives.

During intra-state conflict, clearly and accurately defining the problem is tantamount to success. In any situation, often the view from the balcony greatly differs from the view on stage, and this is especially true when analyzing conflicts at the national level down to the tribal level. For example, in Iraq today some may easily write off problems between Iraqis as simply a deviation between Sunni and Shia. However, when you peel back the layers, a more complex picture becomes evident, unique to each family, tribe, or locality. Pursuant to mission success, SOF directly attempts to create dialogue with various parties to the conflict in an effort to foster stability and reconciliation. Creating this dialogue is, unfortunately, often easier said than done because SOF are often active only in areas that present significant security risks or where extreme violence is employed by parties in conflict. This environment sharply contrasts with normative ideas of mediation and negotiation in secure conference rooms furnished with rich mahogany round tables and plush leather chairs.

During the course of SOF Mediation, the indigenous inhabitants that we in SOF engage with are often initially reticent to openly communicate with us because of a misperception that as foreigners, we just will not understand them. However, we have found that people will often erupt with strong emotions based on seemingly simple questions. During mediations in developed societies with strong rule of law systems of justice, emotions run high, but seldom lead to deaths. We go to places where emotions run high, but failing to negotiate or reach agreement often leads to a gunfight, someone's car being blown up or years of bloody insurgency. Our ranks epitomize a distinctive dynamic by simultaneously seeking to resolve the conflict on a personal level, but also being prepared to utilize lethal force in order to walk away safely if negotiations collapse.

During any attempt to understand intra-state conflict's true origins on a personal level, whether it be ethnic, religious, or political tensions, people may associate the interloper as either part of their problem or part of their solution. As people convey their story, a potent mix of hope, loss, longing, rage, and even despair are expressed in an effort to push us away or pull us deeper into their reality. We frequently operate in very small teams, maintain a non-aggressive disposition, and dress in local garb in order to be more approachable and build better rapport. During conversations either on the street or in people's dwellings, the mood can get tense, becoming clearer that our behavior is tantamount to success or failure. Strong emotions tied to death of family members, loss of livelihood, and disenfranchisement are not simply subjects that can be casually listened to, but core aspects of a person's identity with which they want us to empathize.

All the while, militias, insurgents, and terrorists who employ violence as a means of expressing their grievances are watching and judging how to react to our discreet or overt presence. During intra-state conflict, not every person directly employs violence as a means of addressing the problem. The baker on the corner who sells bread may feel that his greatest contribution to the fight is with moral and economic support, while another family feels it is their duty to enlist their children as fighters for their cause. Violent extremists who share certain ideological goals that demand brutality and carnage, like the core cadre of Islamic State in Iraq and Syria (ISIS), will attempt to snuff out all dialogue that is in contradiction to their narrative. The very identity of extremist ideology is at risk if we can create opportunities and possibilities for alternative ways of resolving conflicts. These alternatives can degrade, mitigate, and possibly eliminate key nodes of support that devout extremists rely on to thrive.

In order to address this, SOF mediation facilitates dialogue, builds rapport, provides access to individuals and groups who are part of the larger conflict. Essentially, mediation at the micro-level of the conflict between individuals or families will help to minimize grievances that act as the metaphorical fuel to the fire. Specifically, SOF employs mediation heavily during two of its many mission sets: counter-insurgency operations (COIN) and civil-military engagement (CME). These mission sets incorporate mediation as a form of non-lethal effects toward supporting operational success.

SOF conduct COIN at the micro-level, tailored to specific villages or towns that pose strategic or operational importance. Village Stability Operations were heavily used in Afghanistan to enable local security and re-establish local governance mechanisms that represent the populations, such as *shuras* and *jirgas* (decision-making councils), and which promote critical local development to improve the quality of life within village communities. In theory and practice, SOF efforts at the village level expand to connect village clusters upward to local district centers, while national-level governance efforts connect downward to provincial centers and then to district-level centers (Connett & Cassidy, 2011). SOF are the primary candidates to conduct these missions due to their unique capabilities and ability to place themselves in areas otherwise denied to traditional mediators or peacekeepers.

CME programs, at best, provide the US government with a means of maintaining its influence with key actors in particular countries by building partner capacity to handle internal issues. CME programs, at worst, maintain open lines of communication, build rapport with key actors, and foster greater situational awareness (Mnatzakanian, 2015). Mitigating the historical conflict narrative requires time and tact; particularly, though, the use of violence to justify that narrative can be mitigated through continuous dialogue, material aid, and training capabilities that alleviate immediate grievances (lack of essential services, education, medical treatment, etc.). Creating dialogue not only between representatives of the US government and the parties, but also between the parties themselves, will help foster pathways out of the conflict. CME programs offer one of the best opportunities to utilize mediation as a means to gain influence and build situational awareness by seeking to gain a fuller appreciation for the nature of the conflict.

Field mediation in communal violence in intra-state conflict

The ability to mediate complex social conflict is a necessary skill for field teams that operate within the intimate spaces of violent, communal conflict. Daily life for the teams and tribes they engage are often in the most austere conditions of societies that live on the edge of survival—both physically and psychologically. It is in this intimacy of shared space that the basis for effective intervention in violent psychosocial conflict through daily phenomenological inquiry into the lived experiences of the conflict community they are engaging. SOF teams establish a sociocultural competency of the conflict communities' historical narrative in order to mediate the elements of the conflict story that is calling its members into positions of violent response. From within their intimate position of shared space, SOF field teams build trust with leaders of village and tribe, helping them to rewrite their conflict story while preserving their larger historical narrative.

Sociocultural competence of the historical narrative and its conflict stories

Sociological and cultural competence of the historical narrative and its inner conflict stories is the enabling basis of mediation for SOF field teams. This is because at the village and tribal levels of social organization, the larger communal historical narrative harbors a sub-story of unmediated conflict that has turned destructive. This sub-story in dispute creates competing interpretations of the larger narrative that can appear to undermine the psychological identity coherence and dependent social reality of the conflict parties.

Elements of the individual sub-stories that are locked in violent contest include issues such as Sunni and Shia versions of Muslim doctrine, patriarchal and tribal social organization, sharia and secular legal systems, male and female social roles or rights, ethnic and cultural hegemony, or social dominance. Communities with devolving or unsustainable narratives are nearly always involved in violent conflict. The devolving narrative creates fears of psychic annihilation from loss of identity definition (Christian, 2013). Simultaneously, the unsustainable narrative threatens the collective memorialization of past and present across future generations that is critical to the psychological and emotional health of the community (Attias-Donfur & Wolff, 2003).

The community's historical narrative consists of an inherited structure of historical events; collections of emotion-laden meanings that are attributed to those events; and culturally specific ways that events and meaning are celebrated, mourned, and memorialized (Stein, 1994). Sociocultural competence involves three interactive components: the sociological structure of community, the psychological organization of individual and group psychology, and the typical patterns of emotional conjugation that emanate from psychosocial behavior of families and clans.

The sociological structure can be found in the geologic, geographic, and climatologic analysis of habitat combined with sociopolitical and economic position of the conflicted communities. To the foundation of sociological organization, SOF operators overlay an even deeper analysis of the psychological organization of the communities, one that determines the communities' positional basis on the sociocentric–egocentric scale of group identity and accompanying locus of member control, external in the former and internal for the latter (Lindholm, 2008). Finally, the sociological structure and psychological organization yield an understanding of how interior constructive and destructive emotions are conjugated from social actions and phenomenological meaning given to events and objectified ideas like ideology.

The power of the narrative and persistence of the conflict story

The psychological coherence and esteem that a persistent conflict story provides its community members is usually the same thing that is killing them and denigrating their ability to adapt rapid, external change. The use of mediation to engage the communal historical narrative and expose the conflict story to the outside reality of ongoing suffering and loss "is not about relieving suffering, it's about repairing one's relationship to reality" (Scheff & Retzinger, 1991, p. 100).

The power of the historical narrative lies in the existential memorialization of the thousands of individual personhood identities of the community—past and present. Its effects can be seen and felt during narrative oral storytelling of the collective glories and traumas of generations past. As the narrated stories deepen, village members—men, women, and children—gather to hear these familiar recitations. They are literally "called into emotional positions" of listening, vicariously participating in the recital of their shared history of origination.

This "call to position" has a powerful psychological and emotional pull on the community's members. What begins with a stranger's simple inquiry into their past becomes a shared re-cohering of social binds that renew collective belonging and group self-esteem. Normal human anxiety over subconscious mortality awareness is relieved by the public remembering of loved ancestors long dead; anxiety relieved by the renewed faith that each in their turn will be equally remembered and cared for.

The persistency of the conflict story is deepened when it establishes prototypical identification with ancient types (archetypes) of heroism ideals commensurate with past communal mythology. The conflict story may also have already resulted in deaths of members past, resulting in the conflict story being the vehicle for member sacrifice-made (sacred) to save the community. These "member sacrifice-made" actions become chosen glories and traumas that brush particles of heroism upon all of the community members bringing coherence and esteem to levels sufficient enough to sustain nearly intractable violence (Volkan, 2005).

Mediating the conflict story within

Mediating the conflict story contained within the community's historical narrative follows a logical process of narrative mediation that includes conflict story identification, externalization, deconstruction, reimagining and metaphorically rewriting within the oral stories of the owning community (Winslade & Monk, 2000). The single goal of this narrative mediation of the conflict story is to help it conform to reality as a precondition of halting the violence and preserving the historical narrative (White, 2008).

Externalizing the conflict story

Mediating reality in the midst of violent, communal, even at times genocidal conflict is not for the faint of heart. The injury and death of beloved family members in this type of conflict creates levels of emotion that steal away the power of reason even as they strip away the humanity of its victims. Returning reason to those we mediate with is only possible through an exercise of what is called externalization, which involves helping victims externalize the painful (and powerful) emotions of shame, grief, and rage away from themselves and onto the inanimate conflict story. In the psychopathology of victimization, guilt and shame are often directed inward for perceived failure to protect vulnerable loved ones. Shame then interferes with normal mourning process and psychological acceptance of losses creating totalizing extremes of violence-laden emotion. Relieving the most acute symptoms of violent emotions through externalizing dialogue by the mediators is the first step in the mediation process. During one of my team's mediation efforts in the Darfur conflict, more than once we found ourselves working to help nearly suicidal victims externalize overwhelming grief and shame in a race to prevent an onset of uncontrollable rage.

Deconstructing the conflict story

The second step in narrative mediation re-examines past assumptions about blame, guilt, motives, and intention, against the value potentials of revenge and retribution. Deconstruction of the conflict story from its safe harbor in the historical narrative is only possible after some level of externalization of the story (Winslade & Monk, 2000), a precursor event that reduces the "fever" of painful violent emotion. In the externalization process, the victims being mediated desire to find relief from their agony of guilt and shame, but they are not sure they deserve it. Alternatively, they feel as though they cannot silence the calls of their dead or dying loved ones to reassume the destructive positions of revenge. In the deconstruction process, the victims being mediated are presented with cold realities that include their responsibilities to those still living and to the future memorialization of those now deceased. The responsibility to ensure continuity of the family, village, and tribe in order to be able to memorialize the dead and the past is often a powerful and sobering reality that is rarely denied if the conflict story has been successfully externalized (Christian, 2014).

Reimagining and rewriting the conflict story

The SOF mediator's successful efforts at externalizing the conflict story lead him/her to guide the conflict party through deconstructing that story and separating its elements out from the non-negotiable historical narrative. As the conflict story is separated out from the sacred narrative, so too are the emotional "calls to position" of violent conflict such as revenge and retribution. With the negotiable conflict story safely separated out from the non-negotiable historical narrative, the mediator uses dialogue, suggestions, questions and, at times, outright argument to push the conflict parties to explore and evaluate alternative meanings and ending to this conflict story that is killing their children and their capacity to memorialize love and existential history. Each of these three steps (externalize, deconstruct and reimagine-rewrite) are enormously complex and although the process is based on the science of psychology and emotion, the application can be as much art as science. While field mediation has no guarantee of success, as a tool of soft power conflict resolution, its use allows SOF teams to penetrate into the interior spaces of violent communal conflicts and work to resolve, or at least mitigate the worst of the violence. As we have seen in Rwanda, the Balkans, and now Syria and Libya, violent communal conflict left unchecked does not remain within political boundaries.

Restoring trust amidst betrayal

If warfare is an extension of social-political dialogue between states, then violent communal conflict is an emotional eruption of betrayal that involves the breakage of a common social reality. Repairing that reality requires the mediator to intellectually and emotionally comprehend the participants' opposing versions of the conflict. Most conflicts align with "the structure of the original passion play, recounting the death and resurrection of Jesus. There is a wrongful act alleged, a suffering endured and the dénouement in justice being served—either by righteous revenge or an act of God" (Benjamin, 2002).

This conflict structure plays out endlessly in communal conflicts throughout the deployment sites of SOF operators. In Colombia, SOF mediated between the villagers' ideological alliance with the FARC (Revolutionary Armed Forces of Colombia) and the government's efforts to cohere rural society into national allegiance. The structure of their conflict story was strewn with issues of murdered families, unresolved survivor grief, and vengeance gained through their support to the rebels (Christian, 2007). In Sudan, we mediated between Muslim Arabs and Muslim Africans in a bitter war over identity, where the denial of ethnic origination and counter-accusations of slavery sparked a conflagration of communal betrayal leading to near-genocidal cross-vengeance (Christian, 2013). Most recently, in the central Sahel, we mediated between Africans and Tuaregs, where both sides battled over the meaning of racial color and existential identities that were expressed in ways that precluded the coexistence of an enemy other (Christian, 2015).

In each case, the goal was the externalization of the conflict story as a precondition for deconstruction, and deconstruction as a precondition for reimagining and rewriting or re-authoring the conflict story in a way that resolved or avoided their continuing participation in the ongoing violence. SOF teams conducting mediation in conflict communities are successful only because they operate one village at a time, "one tribe at a time" (Gant, 2009).

Future applications in SOF mediation

Mediators employ various styles of mediation (caucus or non-caucus models) that are tailored to their client's cultural backgrounds, legal systems, and overall interests in mediation. We shape our mediations at the micro-level with tribes or groups that are tailor-made models with cultural norms at the forefront and bearing in mind the law may be irrelevant simply because violence is the primary coercive force away from the table. The future relevance of SOF Mediation rests upon a standardized model, institutional training development, and collaborations of mediating intra-state conflicts with professional mediators.

SOF Mediation standardized

At this time, SOF does not possess a model of mediation that is employed consistently in the field, but rather ad hoc methods based on natural ability are created to help address situations as they develop. This presents challenges not only to mediators, but also to military commanders and planners at higher levels who may not understand SOF's concept of mediation and the desired effects at the micro- and macro-levels of the conflict. A standardized model would provide a baseline for SOF in the field to utilize and tailor to the situation instead of having to fabricate one on the spot. A standardized model of mediation for SOF would also provide a means for military commanders to understand how the process works and what kinds of risk, support requirements, and time may be required when conducting SOF mediation.

Training SOF mediators

Currently, US Special Operations Command (USSOCOM) requires SOF units to undergo negotiations and mediation training prior to any CME missions (USSOCOM, 2015). Within USSOCOM's units, there are some established training standards for negotiations during various SOF qualifications courses, but they often fail to distinguish between negotiation and mediation training. During routine SOF exercises, there is emphasis on developing intra-state war-centric scenarios using professional role-players. These scenarios are developed to provide soldiers with a chance to hone their skills, but without formal mediation methods or standards, it is difficult to evaluate. More importantly, soldiers miss the opportunity to improve or validate in a field environment on various mediation techniques, nuances, or styles employed by professional mediators.

Outside the schoolhouse, operational SOF units possess their own means of training, but typically not in mediation. This often leads to contracting training through agencies that specialize in mediation or attending seminars through academia (Mnatzakanian, 2015). It is through these agencies that SOF has the most to benefit by building mediation programs within their own formations, building their network of professionals who deal with conflict, and ultimately developing reach-back to possibly assist SOF mediators in the field in mitigating violent conflicts.

Building the SOF Mediation network

Law schools maintain some of the best schools for mediation around the world. As the law has evolved over the years, many courts have imposed mediation as a means of mitigating potentially colossal transactional costs (legal fees, duration, etc.) of legal battles and avoiding the risk of coercive judgment imposed in court. SOF can benefit from learning how experts with years of research and practice in conflict resolution or related fields apply their models to real conflicts. Simultaneously, SOF provide mediators with the reality that conflict in the world is not always settled through a legal framework, but through the way of the gun.

Expanding the network includes exchanges of guest lectures, joint seminars by USSOCOM and academic institutions, and real-time consultation during SOF mediations. SOF provide opportunities to apply mediation models to conflict areas where SOF are deployed, and academia provides SOF with a network of experts who have years of theory, practice, and research experience. Professional mediators and SOF mediators both seek to mitigate and resolve conflict (violent or nonviolent), and thus their shared interests dictate the need for a professional network and enterprise.

Conclusion: understanding the difference between negotiated war and mediated conflict wars among nations

We can think of interstate war as "*negotiation*" between two sides, involving dialogue and violence that creates suffering as sacrifice for national objectives of the governing majority or elite. Interstate warfare armies practice negotiation on battlefields where controlling physical terrain and the forced surrender by military and political leadership is the only objective. Each side's military force is, in effect, negotiating with the other side using applications of calculated violence on each other's territory and defensive structures. What is central to remember is that interstate war is organized violence by interested parties in dispute that is intentionally conducted for real or perceived objectives thought to be important enough for the accompanying suffering as sacrifice.

Wars among communities

From the perspective of developed nations that are used to dealing with interstate conflict, intra-state conflict requires an intervention into the affairs of others whose inability to resolve their violence threatens regional or even global stability. Several important differences characterize intra-state violence from interstate war, most notably underlying drivers of the conflict and inhibitors of resolution:

- While the political state in which the conflict is occurring may or may not be party to the conflict, the state is unable to resolve the conflict and halt the violence at the expense of its deteriorating legitimacy. This is why states with seemingly intractable conflicts are described as failed or failing states.
- Whereas interstate conflicts are usually fought over terrain or access to shared common pool resources, in intra-state conflicts the underlying causes often do not involve recognizable utilitarian objectives.
- Intra-state conflicts often have inhibitors to resolution that would-be interventionists are unable to easily perceive, such as traumatizing social conditions, disintegrating social structures, and devolving psychological organization of large-group identity.

From negotiated warfare to mediated intervention: the changing face of intra-state conflict resolution

The focus of nation-state war has always been about national self-preservation from immediate threat of physical attack against its national boundaries. Violent conflicts in distant lands have only in the past half-century or so become strategically important issues for developed and developing nation-states. Some of the reasons for this include:

- The growth of ethnic minorities living in diaspora and the rise of multi-ethnic societies whose psychological identities extend back to homeland countries
- The growth of audio and visual communication capacity to the lowest levels of social organization
- The growth of trade, travel, and transportation systems that span continents and the oceans in between

Faced with disintegration of national identity due to these global changes, nation-states recognize the need for mediation. Special Operations Forces, who are trained to mediate, mitigate, and resolve conflict, have begun intervening to protect nations from the fallout of intra-state conflict. Only through active mediation at the forefront of conflict can hope to be restored. SOF personnel equipped with their unique skill to mediate in a physically demanding and hostile environment where both person and mind are tested to the extreme will remain at the forefront of interventionist deployments to intra-state conflicts.

Note

1 This quote was inspired by Professor Robert N. Mnookin while attending his seminar at Harvard's Mediating Disputes Seminar in June 2015. It serves to demonstrate that the law holds primacy in resolving mediations or bargains. Conversely, in intra-state armed conflict, coercion and violence hold primacy and the law is nearly irrelevant.

References

Attias-Donfur, C. & Wolff, F.C. (2003) *Generational Memory and Family Relationships*. Paris: CNAV.

Benjamin, R. (2002) Mediation as theater and negotiation as performance art. Mediate.com. Retrieved from www.mediate.com/articles/benjamin5.cfm.

Christian, P.J. (2007) Guerrillas in the midst: U.S. planning, advisory and training team helps Colombian army build skills. *Special Warfare*, 20(3): 16–22.

Christian, P.J. (2013) Darfur—ground zero for Africa's crises of identity: A psychohistoriography of tribes in conflict. *African Security*, 6(1): 1–38. Retrieved from dx.doi.org/10.1080/19392206.2013.759457.

Christian, P.J. (2014) A reformulated model of narrative mediation of emerging culture conflict. *International Journal of Conflict Engagement and Resolution*, 2(2): 76–94.

Christian, P.J. (2015) Between warrior and helplessness in the valley of Azawaɣ—The struggle of the Kel Tamashek in the war of the Sahel. ProQuest Dissertation Press. doi: 10.13140/RG.2.1.4879.4320.

Connett, T. & Cassidy, B. (2011) Village stability operations: More than village defense. *Special Warfare Magazine*. Retrieved from www.soc.mil/SWCS/SWmag/archive/SW2403/SW2403VillageStabilityOperations_MoreThanVillageDefense.html.

Department of Defense. (2007) *Irregular Warfare Joint Operational Concept*. Washington, DC: US Department of Defense.

Department of Defense. (2015) *Department of Defense Dictionary of Military and Associated Terms*. Washington, DC: US Department of Defense.

Gant, J. (2009) One tribe at a time. *StevenPressField.com*. Retrieved from www.stevenpressfield.com/wp-content/uploads/2009/10/one_tribe_at_a_time_ed2.pdf.

Lindholm, C. (2008) *Culture and Identity: The History, Theory, and Practice of Psychological Anthropology*. Oxford: Oneworld.

Mnatzakanian, R. (2015, September 7). SOF mediators: The application of understanding based mediation as a non-lethal effect. *Small Wars Journal*, 3.

Scheff, T.J. & Retzinger, S.M. (1991) *Emotions & Violence: Shame and Rage in Destructive Conflicts*. Lexington, MA: D.C. Heath & Company.

Stein, H.F. (1994) *The Dream of Culture*. New York: Psych Press.

USSOCOM. (2015) *USSOCOM Directive for Civil Military Engagement 525–38*. Macdil AFB: US Special Operations Command.

Volkan, V.D. (2005, December). Large group identity and chosen trauma. *Psychoanalysis Downunder*, 6: 1–32.

White, M. (2008) Narrative therapy. Retrieved from www.massey.ac.nz/~alock/virtual/white.htm.

Winslade, J. & Monk, G. (2000) *Narrative Mediation: A New Approach to Conflict Resolution*. San Francisco, CA: Jossey-Bass.

41

RELIGION AND MEDIATION

Strange bedfellows or natural allies?

S. Ayse Kadayifci-Orellana

Although the involvement of faith-based actors in conflict resolution processes such as mediation is not a new phenomenon, the constructive role religion can play in peacebuilding did not receive sufficient attention until recently. This chapter attempts to fill this gap by exploring this role and by analyzing how faith-based actors can contribute to effective mediation. Linking it to mediator identity, this chapter argues that the religious identity of the mediator can play an important and complementary role in resolving disputes in ethno-religious conflicts. The chapter first discusses advantages of faith-based mediators, such as legitimacy, motivation, leverage, and resources, and explores some of the potential impacts of faith-based actors during mediation including trust building, facilitating communication, enhancing shared identities, and altering perceptions, attitudes, and behaviors.

Mediation and peacebuilding

As a dynamic and complex process, mediation in this chapter is broadly defined as a conflict resolution tool where a third party assists involved parties with ending violence and finding a peaceful solution to conflict. It is a process that is "related to but distinct from the parties' own efforts ..." (Bercovitch, 1992, p. 8). In mediation, parties seek the assistance, or accept an offer of help from a third party to change, affect, and influence their perceptions or behavior without resorting to physical force or invoking authority of the law (Bercovitch, 1998, p. 8). It is a non-binding, non-coercive, and voluntary process, where parties in the dispute retain control of the outcome of their conflict and mediators do not have an authoritative decision-making power, but they do try to influence the behaviors, attitudes of the parties, and the outcome of the conflict. The overall aim of mediation is to reduce violence, change the hostile attitudes and behaviors of the parties and to help reach lasting peace. From this perspective, mediation is not only a conflict settlement mechanism, but also a peacebuilding strategy that mediators can employ at all stages of conflict (Bercovitch & Kadayifci-Orellana, 2002, p. 21).

All conflicts respond differently to different conflict resolution mechanisms, and developing a strategy that will successfully resolve the conflict requires a good understanding of the particular circumstances and the context of the conflict. Mediation is clearly affected by the context and characteristics of each conflict situation. The specific contextual factors, beliefs, attitudes, behaviors, and symbols of the disputants affect the mode of behavior adopted by a mediator and the parties, and to a large extent, impact the success or failure of mediation.

Mediating ethno-religious conflicts

In many current-day conflicts, such as those in Iraq, Nigeria, Sri Lanka, Somalia, and Afghanistan, among others, political and religious leaders have used religion to justify violence, intolerance, oppression, and hatred. Referred to as *ethno-religious identity conflicts*, these conflicts involve parties that are defined along religious lines, societies in which religion is an integral aspect of social and cultural life, and religious institutions represent a significant portion of the community. Religion, in this sense, is a key element underpinning these conflicts.

Traditional conflict resolution tools developed as responses to interstate conflicts in the post-World War II/Cold War era, fall short of addressing and resolving ethno-religious identity conflicts. For that reason, scholars and practitioners are developing new approaches and tools to address these complex and intractable conflicts. Engaging different segments of the society, these approaches are holistic and multi-dimensional, and acknowledge the potential of religious traditions as sources of peace and the contributions religious actors can make. They also recognize that although many conflicts and acts of violence are instigated because of religious differences, religion offers unexpected avenues toward peacemaking, as virtually all religious traditions incorporate values and principles that promote peace and justice (Rasul, 2009).

Identity conflicts

While religion itself is rarely the cause of conflicts, it plays an important role in delineating the identities of the parties. Identity is related to the way in which one fits into social groups and society overall. A wider social recognition of identity—for example, the way people and/or groups see, understand and define themselves—and effective participation in social, economic and political processes are recognized as basic needs of all humanity (Kelman, 1998; Burton, 1990).

Identities are formed as a result of the complex, multi-dimensional and dynamic workings of symbolic orders, experiences, social norms, pre-existing discursive and institutional continuities, and others' perceptions of one's own identity. Different aspects of identity (for example, ethnicity, gender, race, nationality, religion, etc.) become salient under different circumstances, and across time are influenced by interpersonal and intergroup dynamics (Block & Siegel, 2011, pp. 417–418). During conflicts, shared identity aspects are often undermined and identity cleavages are emphasized, rendering conflicts even more intractable. Identities incorporate psychological, physical, and social dimensions, and are intrinsic elements of the "self." Perceived threats to identity or denial of its legitimacy often lead to a sense of victimization and frustration. Actors who share salient identity aspects share, to a certain extent, norms, customs, and perceptions of the world, which can facilitate communication and assist the resolution of conflicts (Block & Siegel, 2011, p. 418). Carefully chosen third parties may be able to foment shifts in the salience of shared identity at times, even without diminishing the salient identity cleavages developed during the course of the conflict (Block & Siegel, 2011, p. 418).

Religio-cultural traditions play a vital role in identity construction, as they form an aspect of social identity and bring with them particular practices and modes of understanding that at the same time confer identity and suggest frames of identification of distinct groups in society (Jabri, 2007, p. 141). Amina Rasul (2009) recognizes that "[r]eligion is a strong basis for identity, particularly when religious difference coincides with other demarcation lines such as political, ethnic, economic or geographic," and adds, "[r]eligious identities are more or less inclusive or exclusive in relation to outsiders" (Rasul, 2009, p. 3).

Religion answers some of the most profound questions regarding right and wrong, life and death, good and evil, among others (Kadayifci-Orellana, 2009). It serves to delineate sharp distinctions between parties during identity conflicts and inform the believers where they belong. "An identity with a religious source may, therefore, be exceptionally robust: religion tells you where you belong and where to proceed" (Harpviken & Roislien, 2008, p. 354). This unique power to mobilize populations toward spiritual and political religious traditions has often been instrumental in defining group identity and legitimizing violence. A mediator who understands the centrality of religious identity, religious traditions, and the ways in which they inform conflict can help parties resolve their conflicts more effectively.

Centrality of mediator identity for effective mediation

The identity of the mediator influences the success of the process because mediation as an interactive process occurs around the influence and impact mediators wield. The identity of the mediator affects the mediator's influence, legitimacy, resources, and strategies as each mediator has different strengths and shortcomings in different contexts. For instance, the identity of the mediator was important during the mediation between Iraq and Iran, which led to the Algiers Accord of 1975. As Lieb (1985) notes, Iran and Iraq agreed on mediation by Algerians, specifically by Boumedienne, a Muslim leader and a member of the community: that is, a member of the "same Muslim family" (p. 82).

Faith-based actors as mediators

The religious identity of the mediator can play an important and complementary role in resolving disputes in ethno-religious conflicts. Faith-based mediation where the third party is a faith-based actor, including organizations, institutions, and individuals who are motivated and inspired by their religious and spiritual traditions, principles, and values to undertake peace work (Bercovitch & Kadayifci-Orellana, 2009, p. 185) can have an impact on advocating peace, building trust among disputants, fostering a shared identity, assisting communication, facilitating changing behaviors, attitudes and perceptions, providing relief, and helping heal traumas (Bercovitch & Kadayifci-Orellana, 2009). Faith-based actors may include those who may explicitly identify themselves as religious, or others who may take their religious identity as a given and may not emphasize it explicitly, or official religious leaders whose religious leadership role is seen as the basis of intervention, or secular leaders inspired by faith traditions to intervene in conflicts, while employing religious principles, values, and texts to resolve conflicts.

In faith-based mediation, the religious/spiritual identity of the mediator, institutions, and creed play an important role in the acceptability of the mediator and effectiveness of the process. Some of the characteristics that distinguish faith-based mediators from secular ones may include: 1) intervention of faith-based actors such as religious leaders or institutions; 2) explicit emphasis on spirituality and/or religious identity; 3) use of religious texts; 4) use of religious values and vocabulary; and 5) utilization of religious or spiritual rituals during the process (Bercovitch & Kadayifci-Orellana, 2009, p. 185).

The involvement of faith-based actors in conflict resolution processes, such as mediation, is not a new phenomenon. Throughout centuries, Muslims have used mediation (*wasatah*) to resolve their disputes based on the model of the Prophet Mohammed, who mediated various conflicts among Muslims and between Muslims and non-Muslims alike. Mediation is also deeply rooted in Jewish tradition under laws of compromise and justice known as *p'shara.* Aaron, brother of Moses, is recognized as the first mediator. Nonviolent activists such as Martin Luther King Jr., Thích Nhất Hạnh, and Mahatma Gandhi, among many others, were also inspired by their faith traditions. In 1947, the Friends Service Committee (Quakers) was awarded the Nobel Prize for Peace for its efforts in reconciliation among peoples.

One of the most well known and frequently cited cases is the successful mediation the Rome-based Community of Sant'Egidio in Mozambique. Mediation efforts of the Sant'Egidio Community were successful in assisting parties to end the civil war in 1992 (Smock, 2006). Pope John Paul II also successfully mediated the Beagle Channel conflict between Chile and Argentina in the 1980s. The Pope's identity as the religious leader of the Catholic community was an important consideration for his intervention to be accepted by both Argentina and Chile, whose populations are largely Catholic.

Mediator legitimacy

In order for mediation efforts to be successful, parties in a conflict must be willing, committed, and motivated to accept and engage in mediation (Bercovitch & Kadayifci-Orellana, 2002, p. 27). Mediation legitimacy refers to the credibility and acceptability of the mediators by the disputants to become involved in their conflict and help them find a peaceful solution. Provided that meditation is a voluntary and non-binding process, trustworthiness, acceptability and credibility are critical components of mediation efforts.

The acceptability of the mediator largely depends on the identity of the mediator. Faith-based actors are often considered insider mediators with the moral and spiritual legitimacy to influence their communities. It is important to note that faith-based actors cannot be effective in every conflict or in every community. Religious leaders and faith-based organizations may have a unique opportunity and an advantage in conflicts in which religion plays a key role in the social, political, and cultural life of the parties, and religious leaders are highly respected and recognized as legitimate and moral guides.

In the Philippines, for example, the involvement of the Ulema in the peace process was welcomed among the Muslim population since they were very influential and trusted by their communities. Amina Rasul (2009) points to a survey conducted in 2006, in which over 80 percent of the Muslim respondents indicated that they had "much trust in their religious leaders," 89 percent trusted the imam and 85 percent trusted the *ulama*, compared to the 79 percent trusting the elected *barangay* (village) captain and 69 percent trusting the traditional leaders (Rasul, 2009, p. 5).

Again, Sant'Egidio's religious identity gave them legitimacy and credibility to mediate between the Islamic Salvation Front (FIS) and the National Liberation Front (FNL). Although both parties were Muslim and the Sant'Egidio Community was not, their religious identity in connection with their peace work was accepted by the parties. Their religious identity was also closely linked to their perception as a moral religious body with integrity, long-term commitment and an open-ended attitude to the conflict (Appleby, 1996, p. 835).

Mediator motivation

Motivation of a mediator is critical as it determines not only if the mediator will intervene, but also whether or not the mediator's efforts will contribute to building trust and credibility among the parties, and whether they will be perceived as even-handed and fair. If parties believe that the mediator is sincerely interested in reducing the violence and resolving the conflict, they are more likely to trust the mediator. Therefore, mediator motivation is closely tied to the legitimacy of mediators and the mediation process.

Many scholars commonly accept that mediators have an interest in the outcome of the mediation process. For instance, Carnevale and Arad (1996) argue that influence in mediation stems from either the mediator's interests and bias or impartiality (p. 40). Stulberg (1987) states that, in addition to being impartial, mediators must be neutral outsiders who have no personal preference that the dispute be resolved in one way or another, and objective in the sense that they can transcend the rhetoric and the emotion of the parties (p. 37). In this model, legitimacy and credibility stem from the mediator's "neutral-impartial-objective" approach.

Wehr and Lederach (1996) challenge this impartial-neutral mediator model and argue that in various contexts, such as Latin America and the Middle East, acceptability of the mediators is rooted in the connectedness and positive trusted relationships with the parties. In this "insider-partial" model, trust comes partially from the fact that the mediators do not leave post-negotiation, and are considered insiders to the conflict. This model also assumes accumulated and sometimes intimate knowledge shared by the parties and the mediators, which is the source of trust between them (p. 58).

Bercovitch and Kadayifci-Orellana (2009) conclude that acceptability, legitimacy and credibility of mediators depend on the parties and issues involved (p. 186). For example, in Sierra Leone or Nicaragua, mediation by an insider who knows the parties as well as the context, with a vested interest in conflict resolution, receives more credibility and legitimacy (Francis, 1998, p. 47). In both insider-partial and outsider-neutral models, motivation of the parties is key to the legitimacy of the parties. If parties believe that the mediator has a sincere interest in reducing violence and resolving the conflict, it is more likely that they will accept and trust the mediator.

The identity of the mediators, especially insider-partial mediators, is closely related to common bonds, shared history, and common experiences. Faith-based mediators are highly respected and their opinions are valued. In Nigeria, the Quakers were able to earn the trust of the parties due to their religious identity and spiritual motivation. As Cynthia Sampson (1994) notes, "the Quakers were the sole third party that won the complete trust of both parties to the conflict, and they sustained that trust for the duration of the war" (p. 111). Their religious identity was instrumental in promoting peace together with their unofficial status and denominational disinterest. Their convictions led them to endure hardships, tensions, and face dangers of traveling into conflict zones without having any guaranteed protection (Sampson, 1994, p. 107). Their willingness to take such risks without having any other motive, save that of God, earned the respect of both parties. Representatives of the parties' answers to the question, "what motivated the Quakers?," which ranged from "God" and "belief in God and humanity," to "an absolute dedication to humanity," clearly exemplify this (Sampson, 1994, p. 110). This conviction also allowed them to be perceived as fair and even-handed.

Mediator leverage and resources

Mediator leverage, or power, is an important element of influence during the mediation process. Leverage is related to the potential influence mediators have based on their tangible and intangible resources, to alter disputants' incentives so that they may reach an agreement.

Bercovitch and Houston (1996) insert that to exercise any degree of influence, mediators need "leverage" or resources to search for information to move parties away from rigid positions, and to facilitate the resolution of the conflict (p. 26). In fact, Bercovitch and Schneider (2000) note that mediators are asked to mediate because they supposedly have the ability to promote an agreement by using their leverage, power potential, and influence, not because of attributes such as neutrality. In the case of faith-based actors, leverage has different components that may include the following:

- *Rank*: One of the important sources of mediator leverage is often considered to be their rank and status. Each mediator has varying types of power and each brings different resources and capabilities according to their experience and rank. Bercovitch and Houston (1993) find that there is a positive association between high rank and successful outcomes of mediation. Faith-based actors such as religious leaders are often viewed as high-ranking individuals with sources of legitimacy based on custom and religious tradition (Kadayifci-Orellana, 2007).
- *Spirituality and morality*: Faith-based actors also have a unique spiritual and moral leverage that is unavailable to secular mediators, based on their moral and spiritual authority. These spiritual resources such as values, principles, norms, and rituals rooted in religious traditions can encourage parties to embrace a new reality, change their behavior, and form new relationships. The use of spiritual and religious resources during mediation aims to connect the participants to the benevolence, mercy, and forgiveness of the Divine. It also aims to generate a sense of connectedness of God's creatures to foster a sense of unity among the participants. A spiritual dimension can also create a sense of engagement and commitment to the process (Abu-Nimer, 2001, p. 686).
- *Financial and human resources*: Mediation is often a long and costly process and requires human and financial resources. Various faith-based actors like Quakers, the Sant'Egidio Community, the Vatican, and Islamic Relief Services have a broad base of committed individuals and well-established regional and global networks to which they can turn for institutional and financial resources. Religious leaders and organizations have access to community members through mosques, churches, temples, community centers, and educational institutions such as Bible or Quranic schools. The same base also endows them with financial resources through charities and donations, which are critical for the continuation of the mediation process, especially in the post-agreement phase. Through their sermons, lectures and educational programs, they can reach out to a large number of people in their societies. As middle-range leaders, they are often in a unique place to reach out to both grassroots and high-level leaderships.
- *Time as resource*: For mediation to be effective, mediators need to have a long-term engagement in the communities and continue to offer assistance on a sustained basis with local structures and actors in the post-agreement phase to ensure its implementation. However, mediation is considered an expensive, time-consuming yet a short-term, ad hoc event that ends with the signing of an agreement. After the mediation, parties are often left on their own to implement the agreements without a mechanism to monitor, enforce, or facilitate this difficult process.

Faith-based actors often have a long history of service in community affairs, which indicates their commitment to the communities and adds to their credibility. Because they have the necessary financial and human resources, they can invest in long-term involvement in the communities. Many religious groups, especially the local ones, also stay involved in the post-agreement phase and help parties heal, build social institutions, and seek justice. Therefore, they are often in a better position to offer long-term continuous support before, during, and after the conflict. For instance, the negotiators in the Sant'Egidio Community emphasized the importance of time as a resource. Emberti Gialloretti noted that because mediators were free to take the time needed and to patiently work throughout the process, they were able to build trust with the parties (Hegertun, 2010, p. 55). According to Mario Rafaelli, too, this ability to take time was one of the most important contributions of Sant'Egidio Community (Hegertun, 2010, p. 54).

Potential impacts of faith-based mediators

Empirical findings and an analysis of case studies indicate that faith-based actors can have a number of impacts on peacebuilding and mediation (Abu-Nimer & Kadayifci-Orellana, 2005) which include building trust, facilitating communication, enhancing shared identities, and altering perceptions, attitudes, and behaviors.

Build trust

One of the main impacts of faith-based actors is to help parties build trust during the mediation process. In deep-rooted identity conflicts in particular, conflicting parties are "not simply disputing over material interests but are suffering from deeply damaged social relationships" and a strong sense of mistrust (Notter, 1995, p. 8). This deep sense of mistrust hinders communication, collaboration, and cooperation between parties. Trust building during mediation "facilitates creative or integrative bargaining and cooperative solutions to the many conflicts that arise between interdependent and interactive parties" (Lindskold, 1978, p. 777). Parties who trust each other are more likely to enter into negotiations with good faith and to implement agreements.

Faith-based actors can move parties toward an agreement by building trust between disputants by engaging the moral and spiritual resources that emphasize shared identities and experiences, common moral and spiritual values. By encouraging parties to see commonalities between their values and by invoking trust in a higher power they can open a window to the deeper and spiritual realities of the disputants. For example, in Nicaragua, mediators were able to overcome mistrust by employing religious and spiritual values and symbolism, including prayers and other rituals, which opened a window to a transcendent dimension at both the personal level (prayer, forgiveness, and reconciliation) and in political terms (peace, and political and social accords), and helped build trust between the parties. This allowed the representatives of both parties to speak with each other, and to see beyond their individual preoccupations to goals shared by the other (Nichols, 1994, p. 84).

Facilitate communication

Similar to other mediators, faith-based actors can also facilitate communication between parties during the mediation process. At times of conflicts, deep levels of mistrust, negative stereotypes, and perceptions of the "other" can undermine communication by fostering suspicion and fears. Misinformation or lack of understanding makes communication particularly challenging. Therefore, some of the most important roles of the mediator are to facilitate communication, clarify and remove misunderstandings and misinterpretations, and provide practical know-how when it is necessary (Bercovitch & Kadayifci-Orellana, 2009, p. 189).

Often perceived as trusted, credible and legitimate, faith-based actors can employ spiritual and religious values and varieties of communicative, procedural and directive strategies to help parties overcome mistrust and suspicion, and to reach an agreement. Through religious rituals such as prayers, they can ease the tensions and break the ice. For instance, during the conflict in Nigeria, Quakers played a critical role by opening the lines of communication and were specifically asked to carry messages between the leaders of the two parties (Sampson, 1994, p. 95). They were also actively involved in removing obstacles in negotiations, such as suspicions, misperceptions, and fear, through listening emphatically to the fears and concerns of the parties.

Enhance shared identities

Faith-based mediators can also help parties enhance shared identities during the mediation process. During identity conflicts, shared identity aspects are often undermined and identity cleavages are overemphasized due to mistrust and perceived threats. Block and Siegel (2011) observe that third parties who deliberately and repeatedly display the shared identity aspect of the disputants can alter the negotiation context toward that of commonality between the parties more effectively than a generic third-party mediator (p. 439). This can be helpful especially in conflicts where parties share the same faith, as it was with the case of Argentina and Chile—both Catholic countries—during the Beagle Channel conflict. The papal mission was able to emphasize the common values, principles and shared history of the parties by highlighting religious commonality and asking them to submit to the will of God.

In conflicts where parties do not share the same faith, it may not be possible to emphasize same-faith identity. As Starkey et al. (2005) observe, "when racial, ethnic, and religious differences are involved, contrasting appearances, roles, and rituals often block the abilities of negotiators and the broader societies they represent to find what they share—some common values in addition to their competing ones" (p. 75). However, faith-based actors may be still able to help parties identify common values and principles and emphasize shared humanity during the mediation process. For instance, Imam Asafa and Pastor Wuye of the Interfaith Mediation Center in Kaduna, Nigeria, have been able to identify shared values and principles such as forgiveness, peace, respect, compassion, and kindness in their respective traditions and emphasize the shared history of the parties (Little, 2007, p. 12).

Change attitudes, perceptions, and behaviors

Deep injuries and suffering experienced by the parties reinforce the negative stereotypes of the "other" and fuel resentment, anger, and dehumanization. In ethno-religious conflicts, these attitudes and behaviors are supported by religious myths and stories, and create modes of inclusion and exclusion as was the case during the conflict in the former Yugoslavia, where religious institutions and images were used to dehumanize the "other" and foment violence. Abu-Nimer and Kadayifci-Orellana (2005) note that religious leaders have been effective in altering behavior, attitudes, negative stereotypes, and mind frames, and in rehumanizing the "other." Local imams, sheikhs, priests, monks and rabbis often know the history and traditions of their communities, so as insider-partial mediators, they have a good sense of their physical and emotional needs. By invoking religious myths, sagas, and stories that support peace, reconciliation, and compassion toward each other, and emphasizing common identities and values, they can inspire a change in the behavior toward the "other" (see Abu-Nimer & Kadayifci-Orellana, 2005).

Conclusion

Ethno-religious identity conflicts continue to challenge mediators, as religious bigotry and hostility make them particularly intractable. In these conflicts, religious actors politicize religion, draw sharp borders between identity groups, and incite violence and conflict. However, as this chapter argued, faith-based actors, such as imams, priests and rabbis, or representatives of religious organizations, such as Quakers, inter-religious councils and the Vatican, can play important roles in conflict resolution and peacemaking. Their respectable positions in the communities and their moral and spiritual authority give religious actors legitimacy and credibility that is not available to secular organizations. Many faith-based actors often know the parties, the history of the conflict and have a good understanding of the needs and interests of their communities. Their long-term commitment to the communities they work in and their ability to devote the necessary time help them to build rapport and trust with the parties and to help heal and rebuild broken relationships. Perceived as fair and even-handed, mediators who know the tradition and can interpret the sacred texts in a new perspective to highlight values such as justice, mercy, acceptance of accountability, compassion, and forgiveness, among others, can set a moral example as peacemakers and can help find a lasting solution to the conflict and help rebuild relationships. These advantages increase the impact of faith-based actors in a variety of areas such as facilitation and communication, emphasizing shared identities, trust building, and make them effective mediators in ethno-religious conflicts.

References

Abu-Nimer, M. (2001) Conflict resolution, culture, and religion: Toward a training model of interreligious peacebuilding. *Journal of Peace Research*, 38(6): 685–704.

Abu-Nimer, M. & Kadayifci-Orellana, S.A. (2005) *Muslim Peacebuilding Actors in Africa and the Balkans*. Washington, DC: Salam Institute for Peace and Justice.

Appleby, R.S. (1996) Religion as an agent of conflict transformation and peacebuilding. In C.A. Crocker, F.O. Hampson & P. Aall (eds) *The Challenges of Managing International Conflict* (pp. 821–840). Washington, DC: United States Institute of Peace Press.

Bercovitch, J. (1992) The structure and diversity of mediation in international relations. In J. Bercovitch & J.Z. Rubin (eds) *Mediation in International Relations* (pp. 1–29). New York: St Martin's Press.

Bercovitch, J. & Houston, A. (1993) Influence of mediator characteristics and behavior on the success of mediation in international relations. *International Journal of Conflict Management*, 4(4): 297–321.

Bercovitch, J. & Houston, A. (1996) The study of international mediation: Theoretical issues and empirical evidence. In J. Bercovitch (ed.) *Resolving International Conflict: The Theory and Practice of Mediation* (pp. 11–35). Boulder, CO: Lynne Rienner.

Bercovitch, J. & Kadayifci-Orellana, S.A. (2002) Exploring the relevance and contribution of mediation to peace building. *Peace and Conflict Studies*, 9(2): 21–40.

Bercovitch, J. & Kadayifci-Orellana, S.A. (2009) Religion and mediation. *Journal of International Negotiation*, 14(1): 175–204

Bercovitch, J. & Schneider, G. (2000) Who mediates? The political economy of international conflict management. *Journal of Peace Research*, 37(2): 145–165.

Block, R. & Siegel, D. (2011) Identity, bargaining, and third party mediation. *International Theory*, 3(3): 416–449.

Burton, J. (1990) *Conflict: Resolution and Provention*. New York: St Martin's Press.

Carnevale, P.J. & Arad, S. (1996) Bias and impartiality in international mediation. In J. Bercovitch (ed.) *Resolving International Conflicts: The Theory and Practice of Mediation* (pp. 39–53). Boulder, CO: Lynne Rienner.

Francis, D. (1998) *Mediating Deadly Conflict*. Cambridge, MA: World Peace Foundation.

Harpviken, K.B. & Roislien, H.E. (2008) Faithful brokers? Potentials and pitfalls of religion in peacemaking. *Conflict Resolution Quarterly*, 25(3): 351–373.

Hegertun, N. (2010) *Faith-based Mediation? Sant'Egidio's Peace Efforts in Mozambique and Algeria* (Master Thesis). Universitet I Oslo.

Jabri, V. (2007) *War and Transformation of Global Politics*. London: Palgrave Macmillan.

Johnston, D. & Sampson, C. (1995) *Religion, the Missing Dimension of Statecraft*. New York: Oxford University Press.

Kadayifci-Orellana, S.A. (2007) *Standing on an Isthmus: Islamic Approaches to War and Peace in Palestine*. Lanham, MD: Lexington.

Kadayifci-Orellana, S.A. (2009) Ethno-religious conflicts: Exploring the role of religion in conflict resolution. In J. Bercovitch, V. Kremenyuk & I.W. Zartman (eds) *The SAGE Handbook of Conflict Resolution* (pp. 264–280). London: SAGE.

Kelman, H.C. (1998) The place of ethnic identity in the development of personal identity: A challenge for the Jewish family. In P.Y. Medding (ed.) *Coping with Life and Death: Jewish Families in the Twentieth Century* (pp. 3–26). Oxford: Oxford University Press.

Lieb, D. (1985) Iran and Iraq at Algiers, 1975. In S. Touval & W. Zartman (eds) *International Mediation in Theory and Practice* (pp. 67–90). Boulder, CO: Westview Press.

Lindskold, S. (1978) Trust development, the GRIT proposal, and the effects of conciliatory acts on conflict and cooperation. *Psychological Bulletin*, 85(4): 772–793.

Little, D. (2007) *Peacemakers in Action: Profiles of Religion in Conflict Resolution—Tanenbaum Center for Interreligious Understanding*. Cambridge: Cambridge University Press.

Nichols, B. (1994) Religious conciliation between Sandinistas and the East Coast Indians of Nicaragua. In D. Johnston & C. Sampson (eds) *Religion, the Missing Dimension of Statecraft* (pp. 64–87). New York: Oxford University Press.

Notter, J. (1995) *Trust and Conflict Transformation*. Occasional paper No. 5. Washington, DC: The Institute for Multi-Track Diplomacy.

Rasul, A. (2009) The role of religion in peace making. Presented at the CSID 10th Annual Conference. Retrieved from www.csidonline.org/documents/pdf/Amina_Rasul_Role_Religion_CSID_Paper.pdf.

Sampson, C. (1994) To make real the bond between us all: Quaker conciliation during the Nigerian civil war. In D. Johnston & C. Sampson (eds) *Religion, the Missing Dimension of Statecraft* (pp. 88–118). New York: Oxford University Press.

Smock, D.R. (2006) *Religious Contributions to Peacemaking: When Religions Bring Peace, Not War*. Washington, DC: United States Institute of Peace.

Starkey, B., Boyer, M.A. & Wilkenfeld, J. (2005) *Negotiating a Complex World: An Introduction to International Negotiation*. Lanham, MD: Rowman & Littlefield Publishers.

Stulberg, J.B. (1987) *Taking Charge/Managing Conflict*. Lexington, MA: Lexington Books.

USIP (2001) Faith-based NGOs and international peacebuilding. Special Report, 76. Washington, DC: United States Institute of Peace.

Wehr, P. & Lederach, J.P. (1996) Mediating conflict in Central America. In J. Bercovitch (ed.) *Resolving International Conflict: The Theory and Practice of Mediation* (pp. 55–74). Boulder, CO: Lynne Rienner Publishers.

42

MEDIATING PEACEBUILDING IN PROTRACTED CONFLICTS

An interactive design framework

Benjamin J. Broome

International conflicts can sometimes be exceptionally complex, resisting even the most determined attempts at resolution. Variously labeled as deep-rooted conflicts (Burton, 1987), protracted social conflicts (Azar, 1990), and intractable conflicts (Kriesberg, 1998), they are frequently characterized by ethnic victimization, unaddressed historical grievances and traumas, economic asymmetries, unequal distribution of resources, and structural inequalities (Coleman, 2003). With such a diverse and complex set of forces revolving around ever-changing dynamics, protracted conflicts can result in severely fragmented and highly polarized societies. Building bridges across such deep divides requires concerted and systematic peacebuilding efforts, usually with assistance from third-party mediators. Mediation in the context of protracted conflict is typically multilateral, with multiple parties representing themselves, organizations, or diverse constituencies.[1]

The demands of protracted conflicts present special challenges for mediation involving multiple parties, including traumas of past events (Montville, 1993), a near total loss of trust (Agger, 2001), a flourishing of enemy images (Mack, 1990), negation of identity (Kelman, 1987), a legacy of polarization (Oberschall, 2001), painful memories of personal and collective losses (Volkan, 1990), and ethnocentric nationalism (Anastasiou, 2008). Such circumstances often prevent parties from reaching agreements, or else parties are forced into making unsatisfactory compromises that often lead to an eventual breakdown of agreements that were reached. With contact usually limited or non-existent between the conflicting parties, all sides are often caught in a web of destructive communication habits, and interpersonal and group dynamics become exponentially more complex (Cormick, 1989). Adding to the complexity, each situation has its own distinctive set of underlying forces, as well as many unknown variables. Attempts to intervene in such conflicts usually follow an uncertain and unpredictable track, meaning the challenges can be overwhelming for even the most seasoned mediator.

In their classic book *The Promise of Mediation*, Bush and Folger (1994) differentiate between three dominant frameworks of practice in the field of mediation: problem-solving, harmony, and transformative. They suggest that the problem-solving framework is grounded in individualistic ideology, the harmony framework is rooted in organic ideology, and the transformative framework is based in relational ideology. The problem-solving approach is directive and outcome-oriented, emphasizing the generation of mutually acceptable settlements. The harmony approach is aimed primarily at relationship restoration, with an emphasis on conflict-constraining or -preventing strategies. The transformative approach emphasizes empowerment and recognition as primary goals, promoting understanding, and respect of each party's needs, interests, and perspectives, while helping to build greater listening and communication skills. Although Folger (2008) believes that it is important to make clear distinctions among these frameworks, taken together they reflect the primary goals of mediation in protracted conflicts that involve multiple parties.

In my own research and practice over the past 25 years, I have worked within an "interactive design" framework that is characterized by elements from all three approaches proposed by Bush and Folger (1994), although it does not fit clearly within any single framework. The roots of interactive design lie in systems thinking, and it was originally developed to help resolve complex issues (Warfield, 1994). The primary goals of this process are to engage a group of stakeholders often representing multiple constituencies holding a variety of perspectives in: 1) constructing together a framework for interpreting the situation they are facing; 2) jointly envisioning a future in which they can work together collaboratively; and 3) building an integrated set of actions for realizing their collective vision. Important secondary goals are to instill new communication patterns and build stronger relationships among the participants. Although these secondary goals are not usually a direct focus of the interactive design sessions, the methodologies are designed to promote these relational outcomes.

Thus, the interactive design approach shares goals with each of the three frameworks proposed by Bush and Folger (1994), including the outcome goal of the problem-solving framework, the empowerment goal of the transformative framework, and the co-existence goal of the harmony framework. In protracted conflicts, an interactive design framework can help individuals and groups progress through the maze of content and relational difficulties with which they are confronted. It does this by helping participants explore critical issues in depth and develop a vision and strategies for working together collaboratively. Over the past two decades, I have had opportunities to apply this interactive design approach in mediating peacebuilding in the eastern Mediterranean, primarily on the divided island of Cyprus (see Broome, 2005, 2006, 2009). Although a mutually acceptable settlement has not yet been reached at the political level, the individuals and teams involved in these peacebuilding sessions have taken significant steps to bridge the differences that divide the two primary communities, involving thousands of people in locally-driven peacebuilding activities and preparing the ground for successful implementation of an eventual peace agreement.

In this chapter I will describe the interactive design process in more detail, providing an overview of the framework, a summary of the practice of interactive design, and an outline of the major responsibilities, competencies, and skills of the mediator within this approach. Afterwards, I will discuss some of the challenges and limitations of using the interactive design framework in protracted conflicts.

An interactive design framework for mediation with multiple parties

Overview of interactive design

The interactive design framework is based on John Warfield's (1994) science of generic design. With initial applications primarily in organizational contexts, the process was originally called Interactive Management (IM).[2] The theoretical constructs that inform IM, which was developed over the course of more than three decades of practice, draw from both behavioral and cognitive sciences, with a strong basis in general systems thinking. IM gives emphasis to balancing behavioral and technical demands of group work while honoring fundamental design laws concerning variety, parsimony, and saliency.

IM was developed as a generic process, applicable to a wide range of settings, and was specifically developed to respond to the demands of complexity. Complex issues are generally characterized by the following: 1) a variety of perspectives involving different segments of society; 2) conflict about both basic issues and associated values; 3) rigidity and inflexibility of thought by both leadership and group/organizational/societal members; 4) high degrees of uncertainty and instability within the overall system in which the issues are embedded; 5) the inability of any single person or entity to comprehend the entire set of issues and understand what is required in order to address them; and 6) incomplete, contradictory, and changing requirements for resolving the situation. For such complex issues, it is often the case that attempts to solve the problem are frustrated by the changing nature of the problem itself. A protracted conflict possesses all or most of these characteristics of complexity.

Complex problems are inherently multidimensional, and a wide variety of perspectives are necessary in such situations to guard against under-conceptualization. Multiparty mediation in complex problem situations requires methodologies that can fully utilize multiple voices in helping the group identify the relevant dimensions of the problem situation. Unless the dimensionality of the solution-space matches the dimensionality of the problem-situation, agreements are likely to fail. In addition, participant contributions should be rooted in their own concrete experience, with discussion grounded in participants' lived experiences. Understanding and treating participants as experts not only enhances the possibility of uncovering the relevant dimensions of the problem, but can also lead to empowering everyone's voice and validating differing perspectives that exist among the parties to the conflict.

Interactive design in practice

In a typical interactive design session, a group of stakeholders representing multiple parties are brought together to engage in structured dialogue on a set of issues they have identified through prior discussions with the mediator. Participants are given full responsibility for contributing ideas and the mediator takes responsibility for choosing and implementing selected methodologies for generating, clarifying, structuring, interpreting, and amending ideas. In a series of facilitated sessions, sometimes taking place over several months, participants are engaged in: 1) developing an in-depth understanding of the situation they face; 2) establishing a collective basis for thinking about their future; and 3) producing a framework for collaborative action. In the process of moving through these phases, participants usually develop a greater sense of teamwork and gain new communication and information-processing skills.

A carefully selected set of idea generation and structuring methodologies are used in interactive design sessions. Methodologies are matched to the phase of group interaction and the requirements of the situation. In the process of moving through these phases, group members engage in structured dialogue guided by the implementation of specific methodologies, including the *nominal group technique* (Delbeq et al., 1975) or NGT, *ideawriting* (Warfield, 1994), *interpretive structural modeling* (Warfield, 1994) or ISM, and *field representation/profile methodologies* (Warfield & Cardenas, 1994). NGT and ideawriting are employed for the purpose of generating ideas, which are then structured using ISM and field methodologies.[3]

Creative idea generation, flexibility of organization, and involvement of a wide range of relevant stakeholders are particularly important in multiparty mediation in protracted conflict situations. Participants need methodologies that help break destructive thinking patterns, open new avenues for thinking about the future, and involve a broad cross-section of society.

While there are no guarantees of success, a properly designed and implemented set of interactive design sessions can support multiparty mediation in a number of ways. First, the idea-generation methodologies allow the emergence of a dynamic set of ideas that adjust and grow as new learning takes place and as circumstances change. This flexibility is key to keeping the discussion open to new perspectives and opinions, without which participants in protracted conflicts can remain stuck in perceptions rooted in the past. Second, the structuring methodologies help participants to view their situation as a systemic whole. When parties with diverse viewpoints are engaged in structured dialogue that allows them to see the larger picture, it is easier for them to understand how the conflict developed, what issues are driving it, and how they might be able to make a difference in resolving it. Third, the overall set of interactive design methodologies support full participation in the planning process. The structured turn taking used in the idea generation methodologies and the systematic steps of the structuring methodologies allow regular opportunities for everyone to contribute and prevents any single individual or party from dominating the discussion. A set of inclusive methodologies can bring everyone actively into the process, helping to ensure that all perspectives are considered, while promoting creativity. If a plan of action or set of recommendations can be accomplished with full participation, there is a greater chance that progress can be made in implementation of the results.

The interactive design mediator: responsibilities, competencies and skills

Promoting collective learning and meaningful outcomes in a multiparty setting is challenging work that requires a sophisticated understanding of participatory planning, productive and efficient group dialogue, and problem solving. In general, the mediator role in the interactive design approach falls within what Moore (2014) calls the process-focused school of mediation, which he calls "facilitative mediation." In this school, mediators primarily provide assistance with procedures, methods, techniques, and other aspects of the process, rather than offering advice about content issues. In interactive design work, the facilitative mediator takes on five important responsibilities.

Developing a collaborative working relationship with participants

Before an interactive design session can take place, the mediator must work with liaisons from all constituencies in order to design the group sessions. It is critical to gain a clear picture of the context in which the design sessions are embedded. This could entail several discussions with representatives from the parties in order to understand the problematic situation, decide on the goals of the session, and identify the participants who will take part in the dialogue. Often the mediator will need to serve in the role of an educator in explaining what can/will be done in an interactive design session and how much time will be required.

Planning interactive design sessions

After the mediator has a clear sense of the purposes and goals for the mediation sessions, the next task is designing a detailed plan for session activities and preparing the necessary materials for use in the sessions. A critical component of this planning process is selecting the methodologies and the sequence of activities that will be carried out during the process. Most interactive design sessions involve both idea generation and structuring, and often there are multiple instances of each, depending on the goals of the sessions. For idea generation, decisions have to be made about wording of guiding questions, and for the structuring process, choices have to be made about the type of relationship to be used in exploring the connections between ideas. Importantly, the methodologies and the wording should be tested with liaisons and/or representatives of the parties to make sure they are appropriate.

Managing logistics

Although logistics are often considered as a mundane concern, it is very important for the mediator to give attention to tasks such as making arrangements for the meeting room, gathering the materials that will be used in the session (such as marker pens, paper, etc.), and making sure that the necessary food and drink have been arranged to sustain participants during the long and demanding set of mediation sessions. While many of these tasks can be delegated to support staff, it is advisable for the mediator to keep a close eye on logistics, since they are not only necessary in order for the session to flow smoothly, but also because participants can become distracted by small disruptions that could be easily prevented by proper attention to details.

Facilitating the interactive design sessions

A central role of the facilitative mediator is to create and sustain an inclusive and participatory climate during the dialogue sessions. It is not easy in any group, no matter the composition, to manage group dynamics effectively. Constant interruptions, domination by a few vocal members, constant shifts in focus, and other problems plague attempts of most groups to work together successfully. One of the vital roles of the facilitative mediator is to prevent the sessions from becoming platforms for individual presentations, or a forum for debate or political posturing. Although groups are usually composed of individuals with various levels of status and prestige, the mediator promotes respect for everyone's contributions and guides the discussion to help participants understand diverse points of view. It is critical to encourage a variety of perspectives while disallowing premature evaluation. Participants must be persuaded to adopt a posture of individual and collective willingness to listen to and learn from each other. While it is not expected that everyone will agree with every aspect of the final products, the goal is to bring participants to a place where they are committed to and willing to support the outcomes.

Guiding parties to their desired outcomes

Interactive design sessions usually result in both improved relations among the participants and a set of products that can be implemented after the interactive sessions. By engaging in dialogue through a carefully structured process, participants can develop new communication patterns that carry over outside the sessions, and a higher level of trust may develop among the participants. The primary focus of the interactive design sessions, however, is usually on the task outcome; the objective is to help the participants gain a clearer understanding of the situation they are facing and to design an appropriate response to it. Depending on its purpose and goals, the interactive design sessions could lead to a number of different products, such as a collective vision statement, priority structure of needs and interests, a set of proposals to pitch to political leaders, or a detailed plan of action to address the situation. An important function of the facilitative mediator is to keep the group on track toward their desired outcomes by implementing the planned methodologies, while making necessary adjustments in response to the continually evolving dynamics and changing needs of the parties. This may involve interventions such as reminding the participants about the context of their work, summarizing and synthesizing progress at various points along the way, displaying interim results, recognizing when the discussion veers off on a tangent and redirecting the participants to their task, varying the pace of the work to keep everyone engaged, and bringing attention to the objectives and goals of the session. Finally, in addition to facilitating the interactive design sessions, the mediator is usually involved in the follow-up discussion to help the parties interpret and implement the outcomes. Especially when the mediator has worked extensively with other conflicts, he/she can serve as a valuable resource and offer sage advice in regard to carrying through with the agreed-upon plans.

Challenges and limitations

Although the interactive design framework was developed for complex problem situations and has been used successfully for over 30 years, there are many challenges and limitations that must be considered when applying it to protracted conflict situations. One of the first questions to ask is if the stage of a conflict is appropriate for such an intervention. When armed conflict is still taking place, or when tensions are extremely high, peacekeeping may be more important than peacebuilding. Separating the parties, rather than bringing them together, may be the most appropriate action. It is true that even in the midst of violence, there are almost always individuals on both sides who are ready to meet and discuss ways to stop the violence, and this could open opportunities for applications of interactive design mediation. Nevertheless, the process is more likely to be effective after hostilities have ceased and individuals on each side recognize the need for peacebuilding and commit themselves to the long and difficult process required for the interactive design process.

A second challenge is to identify who should be part of the dialogue. Multiple perspectives are necessary, so an attempt should be made to include participants with a wide range of views. However, those with extreme positions can severely hamper the group's work, often deliberately. Sometimes, it is best to bring a group together slowly, starting out with individuals who are committed to peacebuilding, and then later make an attempt to include in the group individuals with views that might be more difficult to integrate. In addition, it can be helpful to have people in the group who are close to the political leaders, since one goal of many peacebuilding groups is to filter their ideas up to decision makers. However, having them in the group can significantly inhibit the free flow of ideas, and because of their position, those who are closer to top officials can feel constrained in their own contributions. Additional considerations in identifying participants include ensuring an appropriate range of ages and professions, as well as an appropriate male-female balance (when societal norms allow mixed groups).

Third, a serious commitment is required on the part of both participants and mediator. An interactive design is time consuming and time intensive. Moreover, it cannot be forced upon unwilling subjects. In order to make progress, there must exist (or must be cultivated) a committed core of individuals who see the value of the activity and are willing to devote significant amounts of personal time to take part. In addition, internal clashes or sporadic breakouts of violence can bring peacebuilding to a halt, as can high-tension events that occur outside the conflict areas. If this happens, the sessions may not continue without a strong commitment on the part of participants. Sometimes there are attempts by officials, or others who feel threatened by the dialogue sessions, to make the work difficult or to discourage individuals from participating. Maintaining the participants' focus, or even keeping them together, can be a major challenge in peacebuilding.

Commitment and dedication are required not only of the participants, but also of the third-party mediator. Few third-party mediators are in a position where they can devote the time, energy, and other resources necessary for success. Without a long-term commitment on the part of those involved, including those funding the work, it may be better to refrain from initiating a participatory planning and design project in a protracted conflict than to start something that might create false expectations or endanger the limited supply of goodwill that exists in such situations. Fortunately, when the multiparty mediation can continue for an extended period, their commitment can serve a reinforcing purpose, driving future interaction in a productive direction. A positive dynamic may develop, with forces pushing toward continued interaction, which can, it is hoped, resist the inevitable attempts to stop it.

A fourth challenge concerns the cultural appropriateness of applying US- or Western-based approaches to mediation (Avruch, 2012; Lebaron, 2003). Cultural groups are grounded in shared values, worldviews, identities, communication styles, and a host of other variables that bind them together. Communication patterns and styles do not always fit with Western-style dialogue, and decision-making processes do not necessarily follow Western logic. Most societies have native mediation procedures, and bringing in a Western model could easily conflict with local ways of resolving disputes. Methodologies and approaches brought in from the outside may be unworkable or even harmful. The mediator has to be cognizant of possible incompatibilities and adjust accordingly. At the same time, it should be noted that one of the advantages of third-party intervention in protracted conflicts is the ability to introduce new methods which help break destructive cultural patterns that may be keeping parties from moving forward. There is sometimes a fine line between cultural imperialism and the introduction of new methodologies, and it is not always easy for the mediator to make decisions about how best to adapt a particular mediation technique or process to the local cultural environment.

Even when the imported approach is compatible with or is adapted appropriately to local cultural processes, mediators coming from a Western orientation have to continually monitor their own behavior and their interpretations. The facilitative mediator will constantly face questions of when and how to intervene on the micro-level. Does an intense and pointed exchange indicate anger, or is it just a sign that everyone is engaged? If most people arrive half an hour past the stated start time, does this mean that their commitment level is low, or is it simply a more relaxed approach to time? Are long periods of silence a time for the facilitator to interject a probing question, or is it culturally appropriate simply to allow this time for reflection and absorption of difficult topics? These and many other questions confront the facilitative mediator when working in an unfamiliar cultural setting, and establishing an appropriate level of competence requires acute awareness, ability to recover from mistakes, rapid learning, plenty of experience, and a trusted group of local advisors.

Finally, it is important to keep in mind that multiparty peacebuilding activities are only one small part of a much larger picture. Structured dialogue is not likely by itself to lead to a successful resolution to a protracted conflict, for several reasons. First, even though, it is hoped, the ideas and goodwill generated through such activities will "filter up" to official decision makers, there is never a guarantee that this will happen in a way that significantly influences negotiations or strategizing at the top level. Second, even when peacebuilding activities expand to include larger numbers and a broad cross-section of society, there is always the danger that it will not spread among enough of the population to make a real difference in changing societal perceptions. Third, even the best ideas of groups involved in design activities can be either ignored or severely criticized by both officials and the media, making implementation extremely difficult or impossible. Fourth, when funding and third-party assistance are from external sources, there is always suspicion from the larger society about their possible motives or their agenda. Even when the planning and design work is successful, others may not view it as legitimate or accept the results.[4]

Conclusion

The interactive design approach described in this essay offers the possibility of building alliances and developing the collaboration that can become the backbone of multiparty peacebuilding efforts in protracted conflicts. Although there is no assurance of success, by engaging multiple parties in structured dialogue using a set of carefully selected and specially developed methodologies, the interactive design framework promotes holistic understanding of the complexity that is inherent in protracted conflicts. Participants can explore a wide range of options for promoting peace and construct an integrated plan for achieving their goals. As parties work progressively through the phases of an interactive design process, they often build new communication skills and cultivate new relationships that can withstand the inevitable breakdowns brought on by internal and external events. In this way, an interactive design framework provides a possible means to achieve the three primary goals of mediation involving multiple parties in protracted conflicts: a mutually agreed outcome, empowerment of group members, and movement toward harmony and co-existence.

Notes

1 Moore (2014) defines this as multiparty mediation, where "multiparty" refers to several parties involved in the conflict. Others define multiparty mediation as intervention by more than one third party (Crocker et al., 1999; Vuković, 2015). In this essay, I am using Moore's definition of multiparty mediation, although I recognize that in the international mediation literature, Crocker's definition is widely adopted.
2 Alexander Christakis, who played a primary role in developing the practice of Interactive Management, and has been a leading practitioner for over 35 years, calls IM a "Structured Design Process" (Christakis & Bausch, 2006). My colleagues in Ireland refer to IM as "Collective Intelligence" (Hogan et al., 2015).
3 Space limitations do not permit detailed description and presentation of examples of these methodologies, but applications can be found in Broome (2006) and in Warfield and Cardenas (1994).
4 There are many additional challenges, cautions, and limitations that space constraints prevent bringing into this discussion, including factors discussed by Mohammed Abu-Nimer and Timothy Seidel (in this volume), in particular the power dynamics associated with third parties who mediate in international conflict situations.

References

Agger, I. (2001) Psychosocial assistance during ethnopolitical warfare in the former Yugoslavia. In D. Chirot & M.E.P. Seligman (eds) *Ethnopolitical Warfare: Causes, Consequences, and Possible Solutions* (pp. 305–318). Washington, DC: American Psychological Association.

Anastasiou, H. (2008) *The Broken Olive Branch: Nationalism, Ethnic Conflict and the Quest for Peace in Cyprus (Vol. I: The Impasse of Ethnonationalism)*. Syracuse, NY: Syracuse University Press.

Avruch, K. (2012) *Context and Pretext in Conflict Resolution: Culture, Identity, Power, and Practice*. Herdon, VA: Paradigm Publishers.

Azar, E.E. (1990) *The Management of Protracted Social Conflict: Theory and Cases*. Aldershot: Dartmouth.

Broome, B.J. (2005) *Building Bridges Across the Green Line: A Guide to Intercultural Communication in Cyprus*. Nicosia: United Nations Development Programme.

Broome, B.J. (2006) Applications of interactive design methodologies in protracted conflict situations. In L.R. Frey (ed.) *Facilitating Group Communication in Context: Innovations and Applications with Natural Groups* (pp. 125–154). Cresskill, NJ: Hampton Press.

Broome, B.J. (2009) Building relational empathy through an interactive design process. In D.J.D. Sandole, S. Byrne, I. Staroste-Sandole & J. Senihi (eds) *Handbook of Conflict Analysis and Resolution* (pp. 184–200). New York: Routledge.

Burton, J.W. (1987) *Resolving Deep-rooted Conflict: A Handbook.* Lanham, MD: University Press of America.

Bush, R.A.B. & Folger, J.P. (1994) *The Promise of Mediation: Responding to Conflict through Empowerment and Recognition.* San Francisco, CA: Jossey-Bass.

Christakis, A.N. & Bausch, K.C. (2006) *Co-laboratories of Democracy: How People Harness their Collective Wisdom to Create the Future.* Boston, MA: Information Age Publishing.

Coleman, P.T. (2003) Characteristics of protracted, intractable conflict: Toward the development of a metaframework. *Peace and Conflict: Journal of Peace Psychology*, 9(1): 1–37.

Cormick, G. (1989) Strategic issues in structuring multi-party public policy negotiations. *Negotiation Journal*, 5(2): 125–132.

Crocker, C.A., Hampson, F.O. & Aall, P. (eds). (1999) *Herding Cats: Multiparty Mediation in a Complex World.* Washington, DC: United States Institute of Peace Press.

Delbeq, A.L., Van De Ven, A.H. & Gustafson, D.H. (1975) *Group Techniques for Program Planning: A Guide to Nominal Group and Delphi Processes.* Glenview, IL: Scott, Foresman.

Folger, J.P. (2008) Harmony and transformative mediation practice: Sustaining ideological differences in purpose and practice. *North Dakota Law Review*, 84(3): 823–860.

Hogan, M.J., Johnston, H., Broome, B.J., McMoreland, C., Walsh, J., Smale, B., … Groarke, A.M. (2015) Consulting with citizens in the design of wellbeing measures and policies: Lessons from a systems science application. *Social Indicators Research*, 123(3): 857–877.

Kelman, H.C. (1987) The political psychology of the Israeli-Palestinian conflict: How can we overcome the barriers to a negotiated solution? *Political Psychology*, 8(3): 347–363.

Kriesberg, L. (1998) Intractable conflict. In E. Weiner (ed.) *The Handbook of Interethnic Coexistence* (pp. 332–342). New York: Continuum.

Lebaron, M.D. (2003) *Bridging Cultural Conflicts: New Approaches for a Changing World.* San Francisco, CA: Jossey-Bass.

Mack, J. (1990) The enemy system. In V.D. Volkan, J.V. Montville & D.A. Julius (eds) *The Psychodynamics of International Relationships Vol. I: Concepts and Theories* (pp. 83–95). Lexington, MA: Lexington Books.

Montville, J.V. (1993) The healing function in political conflict resolution. In D.J.D. Sandole & H. van der Merwe (eds) *Conflict Resolution Theory and Practice. Integration and Application* (pp. 112–127). Manchester: Manchester University Press.

Moore, C.W. (2014) *The Mediation Process: Practical Strategies for Resolving Conflict.* San Francisco, CA: Jossey-Bass.

Oberschall, A. (2001) From ethnic cooperation to violence and war in Yugoslavia. In D. Chirot & M.E.P. Seligman (eds) *Ethnopolitical Warfare: Causes, Consequences, and Possible Solutions* (pp. 119–150). Washington, DC: American Psychological Association.

Volkan, V.D. (1990) An overview of psychological concepts pertinent to interethnic and/or international relationships. In V.D. Volkan, J.V. Montville & D.A. Julius (eds) *The Psychodynamics of International Relationships. Volume One. Concepts and Theories* (pp. 31–46). Lexington: Lexington Books.

Vuković, S. (2015) *International Multiparty Mediation and Conflict Management: Challenges of Cooperation and Coordination.* New York: Routledge.

Warfield, J.N. (1994) *A Science of Generic Design: Managing Complexity through Systems Design* (2nd edn). Salinas, CA: Intersystems.

Warfield, J.N. & Cardenas, A.R. (1994) *A Handbook of Interactive Management* (2nd edn). Ames: Iowa State University Press.

CONCLUSION

The future of mediation in a changing world

George A. Lopez

The chapters and parts of this handbook reveal the remarkable diversity of mediation thinking and practices in various aspects of our social and public life. They also highlight, whether in the changing context of families, complex organizations, local communities, or the global human community, the mediation dilemmas that have been confronted successfully, and will continue to challenge mediators in the future. That the parts of this handbook reflect and are organized by the context in which mediation unfolds—as well as address the competencies, skills, and techniques employed by mediators—demonstrates the new era of mediation we have been experiencing over the last two decades. In this new era, and as appropriately portrayed throughout this volume, mediators not only assist parties to problem solve jointly in handling discord, but they also empower them with the skills to meet new challenges in their shared future. From working with families, communities, or large-scale conflicting actors, the skills and techniques detailed throughout this volume indicate where and why there is (and must continue to be) a strong linkage between theory, research, and practice in contemporary mediation.

These developments underscore the evolving definition of mediation in conflict situations to which I would subscribe. Beginning with the insights developed by Folger and Bush (1996) and as resounds in these chapters, both practitioners and scholars now consider mediation to have moved far beyond the notion of an impartial (in the most stale and placid sense) facilitator to a transformative and engaged practitioner who is proactive for the parties in a dispute in major ways. First, is the mediator's recognition of and interaction with each party regarding his/her claims and worldviews as a means of increasing a party's capacity to see "the other" and to consider those perspectives and claims in a more empathetic light. Second, through this process and the use of a range of techniques, the mediator enhances each party's capacity for greater self-determination. This, in turn, enhances the responsiveness of each party to one another and the changing aspects of their situation. Thus, mediation has become much more of a transformational dynamic that opens new possibilities for more productive relationships among parties going forward, and creates and legitimizes new spaces for a range of emotions, expressive tools, and actions, which were heretofore serendipitous at best.

Building from this definitional perspective and the range of themes explored in the parts of this book, this concluding chapter explores the future of mediation through some particular lenses. I begin with a brief sketch of the recent history of mediation that brought our theory and practice to the critical space that this handbook aptly illustrates and our current state-of-the-art occupies. Second, this chapter highlights and amplifies crosscutting themes that emerge in the handbook because these provide the foundation stones of our mediation thinking and techniques as we move into the future. In the final section of the chapter, I will discuss some themes regarding the substantial potential that this future provides, whether we be seasoned researchers or practitioners in the field, or the varied citizens, groups and leaders engaged in mediation from the many contexts addressed in this volume.

A glimpse of the past to understand the present and the future

In the early 1980s, I was asked by colleagues in the American Library Association who knew of my teaching and training to write a review essay for their magazine, *CHOICE*, about the new approaches that were coalescing in the conflict resolution literature. I welcomed the task, not the least of the reasons being that I had recently completed my own training in mediation. Thus, I had command of more professional techniques and case examples to provide in illustrating what the academic research meant in practice. I now realize, of course, that in writing the essay (Lopez, 1984), I very much lacked at the time the critical self-reflection emphasized by Alexia Georgakopoulos in her Introduction to this handbook.

Thus, I failed to recognize the gap between a number of the academic writings and the techniques in which experienced negotiators and mediators had trained me! My "practice self" was content to have a well-laden toolbox of newly honed techniques that were the standard fare of the mediators of the time. I accepted without question that the more distanced role of the scholarly analyst was to look over the shoulder of the mediator and document what worked and why. I had not yet recognized that one of my responsibilities as a scholar-practitioner of mediation was to close the gap between theory and practice. I did not follow the rubric set out so well by Anthony Bing (1989), who posited that our task was to think our way into new forms of action and act our way into new forms of thinking.

The chapters and parts of this handbook testify that this dynamic reinforcement is now standard in our field, but to arrive at this interconnection between theory and action, between the findings of academic research and the growth of an array of skills and techniques honed in mediator practice, the field traversed a number of developments that merit our attention.

The first rationale for this brief historical survey is to underscore how and where the clear and direct linkages to "the present" of this handbook are somewhat foreshadowed by the developments and growth of the field prior to 2000. The second reason to discuss the developments of the past is to remind ourselves that mediation activity has never been far from—and in many cases has been intimately connected to—struggles for justice, whether it be gender, race and power dynamics within families, communities, or the workplace. In addition, it has been dealing with unprecedented environmental developments, as well as the challenges facing disputants in a shrinking world where the local and the global meet. In short, the history of mediation informs our present and future in many ways that merit our examination.

The breakthrough period for closing the gaps between theory and practice in the field of conflict resolution generally, and mediation in particular, occurred in the early 1980s. A number of trends in thinking and research developed to move beyond simply recording best practices, to applied research that developed new models and methods of practice. At the same time, mediation practice itself moved into new areas of work that changed how academics would engage in research on social conflict and its resolution. Although not explicitly dealing with mediation, Roger Fisher and William Ury's bestseller, *Getting to Yes* (1981; see Fisher et al., 2011), created a significant citizen consciousness that there was a much better way to resolve disputes then the strong-armed adversarial manner that typified domestic and internal disputes and the realpolitik that guided world leaders. Its focus on interest-based approaches to resolution provided mediators with a more creative lens by which to move intractable conflicts among hostile parties to a potential new basis of dialogue and problem solution.

As far-reaching as the success of the Harvard Negotiation Project work was, it was only one part of the boom decade of the 1980s for mediation and conflict resolution. Within the US culture, two trends were in their takeoff stage in the early part of the decade. The first was the acknowledgment within the American legal community that the backlog of court cases for low-level disputes and crimes combined with new thinking about local community conciliation and problem solving to create court-appointed mediation and the emergence of victim-offender resolution processes. This extended as well to alternatives to divorce court and legal alternatives for dealing with non-violent youth offenders. Most notably, this endorsement of the alternative dispute resolution movement within its own profession by the American Bar Association (ABA) increasingly legitimized the teaching of that approach—and related areas such as community mediation—within US law schools (Cole et al., 2011; Goldberg et al., 2012). Today, the ABA (2016) section of Dispute Resolution, created in 1993, has over 18,000 members.

Second, in the wake of violence that erupted in US cities, but also in light of the victories in the Civil Rights Movements of the 1960s and early 1970s, many who had been veterans of those movements, as well as professionals who had worked for the US Department of Justice Community Relations Service, recognized the moment of new civic engagement where the prevention of violence in essentially justice and social group-based disputes had to be addressed in a focused manner using all new tools available. Thus, local community organizers and agencies, backed by the legal community, began creating local mediation centers for resolving interracial and community disputes. These, in turn, led to the resurgence—in a very short period of time—of the Society for Professionals in Dispute Resolution (SPIDR, originally founded in 1972), and the creation of the Academy of Family Mediators (1982). Further, the Ford Foundation established the National Institute for Dispute Resolution (1983) to advance alternative dispute resolution (ADR) practices nationally. In many ways, Part III's focus on organizational contexts of mediation and Part IV on community disputes, reflects the maturation of these developments of three decades ago.

A final set of critical developments occurred when the US Congress created the United States Institute of Peace (USIP) in 1984 to advance the use of knowledge and techniques of mediation and peacemaking internationally. From 1983–91, the Hewlett Foundation supported the development of professional graduate- and master's-level programs aimed at bridging the gap between theory and practice in conflict resolution and mediation (Lewis, 1993). The creation of USIP and the funding and convening by Hewlett of the growing number of graduate programs, provided a significant boost to the field in many reinforcing ways. In particular, Hewlett's focus on state-of-the-art graduate training in skills development for mediators and negotiators as standing alongside the ever-growing theories and concepts of conflict resolution created a new post-civil rights generation of mediators ready to tackle the widening contexts in which they were needed, as very much reflected in the parts of this volume. For its part, USIP undertook further development of mediation in internationally focused graduate programs, funded research studies on emerging post-Cold War intractable conflicts, and developed a USIP Press to publish—via a wide variety of formats—practical case studies as well as theoretical advances in the field.

The decade of the 1980s also witnessed the full emergence of environmental conflict management and thus environmental mediation as a booming area of work. Many factors, of course, led to this. The creation and operation of the Environmental Protection Agency (EPA) in the USA in 1970 dramatically changed the prospects that community groups and US labor and identity groups could gain redress from polluters, corporations violating the EPA rules, or poor practices of state government management in the environmental area. At the same time litigation was not always the answer to resolving what was becoming known as "the socio-scientific dispute" (Wessel, 1982). This gave rise to the need for expert mediators in environmental issues who were also trained in the expanding world of mediation techniques. Thus, as we fast-forward 30 years to the chapters in Part V, it is not surprising that one of the most substantial issues among our future challenges, climate change, is becoming the subject of both research and practice in the environmental mediation realm.

In the 1990s, many of the mediation associations, individual practitioners, and experts in the USA found themselves going fully global. The post-Cold War world created a period of perilous transition, particularly among Eastern European states, that led mediators in the USA and Western Europe to respond to both the social and environmental crises faced by a variety of the emerging democratic states. Because much of the Eastern European peaceful revolution (the Yugoslav wars being the exception) had been made possible by the development for over a decade of effective civil society organizations, the structural foundations were strong for dispute resolution becoming a central part of the emerging new social and political order. Thus, experts in constitution making, labor relations, and community and environmental mediation were in high demand in these national cultures where new political systems were anxious to learn from Western mediation successes, but were also committed to retaining their own control and autonomy in solving their own problems.

This was also the case with some of the most serious justice struggles of the 1990s that were able to arrive at a political space for resolution. Most notably the wars in Central America, especially in El Salvador, benefited greatly from the ideas and work of both the Harvard Conflict Management Group and United Nations (UN) officials skilled in such mediation. In the case of South Africa, a number of the professionals associated with SPIDR who had been deeply involved in US civil rights struggles were helpful across a number of South African communities. At the highest level of the final negotiation, so too were groups of US church mediators and the Conflict Management Group.

The post-1990s, moving to the present, was a diverse period in which two larger trends emerged. First, as well illustrated in this handbook, there was a broadening across a number of different lateral contexts of the work of mediation in domestic spheres of many countries. Thus family, community, church, school, larger community entities and national governments themselves manifested divisive and sometimes violent internal conflicts. Second, at the more regional and global level, the UN, transnational nongovernmental organizations (NGOs) and new groupings emerged to immerse themselves in deeply volatile and ongoing wars with new forms of mediation and beyond. The UN proclaimed a new era of peacebuilding and structural changes that increased its role in peacekeeping and mediation (Bellamy and Williams, 2010). Indicative of the new UN focus in this period, was the deployment of special mediator-style advisors and special representatives of the UN secretary-general (SRSG) to particular conflict zones. So too was the centrality of more institutionalized mediation within the UN structure by 2006 with the creation of the Mediation Support Unit of the UN.[1] Illustrative of new changes and adaptations in the NGO sphere was the

2004 merger of Roger Fisher's Conflict Management Group with the well-known and effective humanitarian agency Mercy Corps. We see the fruition of these developments in Part VI of the volume, complete with a necessary and added focus on the contemporary dimensions of culture and religion.

Crosscutting themes of this volume

Against this rich historical background, the parts of this handbook reflect the new developments in thinking and practice that have occurred in the last decade and a half. Thus, they build from the effective emergence of mediation within the USA and parallel developments globally. In this section, I want to accent the critical themes reflected in the book that push what researchers and practitioners will encounter and explore in the future.

Theme one: at the end of the day all mediation is local

One of the distinctive strengths of the volume is that it presents strong interlocked parts by examining family mediation, community mediation, and organizational contexts in which mediation unfolds. If these were the only contributions of the handbook, these alone would be a huge benefit to our field, but in this volume, these dimensions have been placed alongside the other major themes explored that rightly demonstrate the significant breadth that the field has developed in a short time.

Particularly striking about the expanding dimensions of family mediation in Part III are the importance of a variety of understandings and skills the mediator must now possess about identity, emotion, power positions, and values. I will address the emergence of these in detail in the next sub-section of this chapter. However, I raise them here because their prominence in the development of family mediation illustrates how the latter cannot be considered distinct from the larger context of extended identity groups, neighborhood, and community dislocations that happen interactively with a family's local context. This, then, as Part II details, warrants the increased emphasis on moving from working out specific dimensions of divorce disputes to applying methods that aim at authentic forgiveness or restorative justice, and entail transformative mediation, narrative mediation, and other collaborative approaches. This directly relates to the transformative approach that has also been so critical in social disputes that tackle reconciliation in communities. In this wider view, new techniques are expanded and intensified.

The concern with community conflict and the focus of community policing discussed in Part IV of this handbook could not be more relevant for the US domestic context. The explosion of violence in the decade after 2010 of long-simmering fissures in local communities beset by an increasing distance between neighborhoods afflicted with criminal violence and the rising violence directed at devoted and professional law enforcement officers—and police violence, has created a national crisis. The events in Ferguson, Missouri, and Baltimore, Maryland, to name only two high-profile situations, the emergence of national movements like Black Lives Matter, highlight the contemporary challenge that will dominate the near- and longer-term future of community conflict and policing in the USA.

If—as I would argue is a "must"—US communities are to be able to engage in preventive violence and to close the gap among groups sharply divided by the racial, class, and justice challenges that they face, then dispute resolution and mediation must become the new citizen education of our time. In addition, imperative for the future is the need for anyone engaged in family mediation—most especially clergy leaders—to be well trained in the skillsets that they need. We may need more fully credentialed independent persons and agencies in the mediation field, some of which is discussed as characteristic of our new age in Part I of the volume.

Theme two: mediation in schools pays off and must be accelerated in the future

As chapters in this handbook argue, we will always need the most dedicated and highly trained professional mediators, but in communities, organizational settings and even in families, we also need more individuals with a "mediation mindset." As with other perspectives and skills that are integrated into an individual's personality and social being, engaging with and training in mediation must begin early in one's socialization as several chapters in Part IV discuss. The growth of anti-bullying campaigns in schools adds to the multi-decade recognition that students, teachers, and school boards must be prepared to deal with the realities of conflict and violence as part of their educational responsibility. Several chapters address these issues directly, illustrating and arguing for comprehensive programs in training younger students to work out their disputes among themselves through peer mediation.

In this, we must recognize the new challenges to university-based teacher education—and to statewide teacher improvement and mid-career training—programs that must produce the next generation of teachers competent in and committed to such mediation roles. What the future calls for, I believe, are more innovative programs for students aiming for careers in local school systems that provide graduate-level training in the theory and practice of conflict resolution, in learning the extensive peace education literature for youth and the techniques of tolerance and mediation that flow from there and can be incorporated into everyday classroom situations.[2]

As a scholar-practitioner who has spent 95 percent of his time within universities, I found Part III discussions of the emergence of disputes and ways to mediate them within higher education settings particularly relevant. If recent developments in US academic institutions are at all instructive, US campuses will increasingly be playing out the wider societal and local conflicts noted above regarding race, class, gender, cultural communication, and policing. The myriad high-profile disputes that have engulfed large flagship universities and smaller, church-affiliated colleges alike begs the question of whether these educational entities are capable of forging the equivalent internal changes for their situations that have been occurring at the K-12 (kindergarten to 12th grade) range regarding mediation for tolerance, non-violence, and justice.

Theme three: culture, values, emotions, and deep-rooted sentiments are central in mediation

It would be unfair to suggest that one of the outcomes of the Harvard approach to mediation and the successes of interracial and environmental mediation of earlier times skewed our understanding regarding what must transpire in effective community conflict mediation. However, much of the literature that analyzed those outcomes and prescribed the manner in which mediators might apply tools to disputes was more distanced, analytical, rote, and over-determined gender-wise, than it was focused on the emotive. In hindsight, it quite possibly was less suited to and accurate regarding certain dimensions of the intensity of both domestic and international disputes.

All the parts of this handbook, wherein the chapters present both the theory and practical success of how mediators elicit from participating parties the full contours of the value dimensions, emotions, and cultural divides that dominate their dispute, are indispensible. No doubt effective mediators have recognized for a long time that many disputes are neither interest based, nor lend themselves to a kind of Solomon solution of splitting the differences. This handbook rightfully recognizes that more typical of our era must be the deep engagement by mediators in helping parties sort out "claims," because they are most dear to them—are simply not up for negotiation or compromise. Thus, it is not surprising to read in various chapters a recognition that whether it be family, or other community conflicts, one role of the mediator is to help protect the values and culture of the participants while moving them to more transformative understanding of what they can do with the disputes they face.

The mediation and wider peacebuilding fields owe an intellectual debt to John Paul Lederach (2003) whose *Little Book of Conflict Transformation* specified quite clearly that the reason the traditional international negotiation-mediation model was failing in justice-based conflicts was because it reinforced the skewed power relationships between the parties that sparked the conflict in the first place. Moreover, the work of mediators traditionally of addressing one by one the potential resolution of multi-issue conflicts privileged compromise among unequal parties without helping them to build a new and future relationship in which multi-issue complexity could be better mediated. Conflict transformation embraces—rather than holds distant or constant—the relational dynamic among the parties and requires the key elements of culture, values, emotions, and deep-seated sentiments.

Theme four: mediation must embrace greater human expression and the arts in its training and practice

As editor Alexia Georgakopoulos notes in her Introduction, "Revealing the world of mediation is also about a story," and by extension it holds that if our preceding theme three is going to be embedded successfully in mediations and have any meaning, this can only occur if those who have been both participants and victims of violence have a way to tell their stories, expressed wherever and however they seek. Various chapters in this handbook underscore what practitioners have long understood and used in this area. Former US Ambassador Cynthia E. Cohen stated it clearly regarding even the most painful and divisive violent conflicts: "arts can be crafted to engage people compellingly, but non-coercively, in the issues that confront their communities … this power can be felt in the transformation of energy in a theater or in changes in relationships evoked by a poetry workshop" (Cohen, 2015).

Until recently, scholarship about the arts and mediation/peacebuilding has lagged terribly behind the effective use of it as a technique by practitioners. The latter group has known for a good while that cultural expression via the arts can provide an avenue for dialogue and relationship building that is based more on reciprocity and connectivity than the kind of power or domination manifest in violent conflict. As conflicts have increased in their complexity, such as when conflicting parties do not share a spoken language, or when cultural, religious, or linguistic issues fuel violence, then dance, music and related forms of artistic performance can be critical in communicating core values of peace and participation. Finally, the horrific violence witnessed in various nations over the past two decades has created new levels of community dislocation, significant numbers of people, especially children, having experienced traumatic events that defy full description. These experiences, memories, and traumas sometimes can be processed and partially relieved through various art forms, such as instrumental music and expressive movement.

As Shank and Schirch (2008) argue, scholar-practitioners must engage in a better assessment of the very real conceptual framework guiding the use of arts in mediation, reconciliation, and conflict transformation. Whether it is drawings by children, the emergence of street theater, the healing provided by narrative circles, or other forms of expression that will bring people together, a growing subfield of the arts and peacebuilding relevant to the future of mediation now exists and must be mobilized.

Theme five: the future of mediation—like many patterns of modern life—will be increasingly tied to new communication technologies

In Parts I, III and VI of the handbook, we read of current and prospective use of new creative communication technologies for online dispute resolution, e-mediation, and interactive management. In light of how such technologies are changing most other areas of our private and social lives, these developments should not be a surprise, but that does not make them any less significant. These new technological realities help advance at least two cornerstones of effective mediation: parties work best together when there is full disclosure and equal access to all information, and when the mediator strives for consistent contact with each of the parties to forge ongoing relationships with them and their constituents to build support for a mediated agreement.

In this important dimension of information access then come new advantages in working with violence reduction and mediating disputes beyond US boundaries as well. Much of US society benefits from everything from strong internet access in virtually all parts of the country and the predominance of handheld devices as modes of access; however, this is much less true in cross-cultural and international disputes. To change this disadvantage, NGOs such as Search for Common Ground have made it their continued priority to build cell phone distribution and internet access into their programming for empowering communities to better report outbreaks of violence to gathering together groups for immediate responses to the breakdown of peace accords.

Similarly, the USIP created the PeaceTech Lab (2012) as a way of integrating new technologies into their work with overseas partners engaged in mediation and conciliation. The rapid nature of change in this area, as well as the willingness of many private sponsors to be part of these expanding possibilities, led the PeaceTech Lab to be spun off as an independent entity in 2015. Two of the most significant mediation techniques they have developed is the ability to engage communities in Burma to use handheld device apps as networks that immediately test and verify claims of violent action, and to identify and counter hate speech that is often generated by popular media.

Looking to the future of mediation in a changing world

In surveying the broad reach of the parts of this handbook, I want to close with further examination of some significant areas and themes of mediation going forward that illustrate the relevance, importance, and diverse contributions that effective mediation will have on our political and social order. The first lies in the future of mediation in climate change. The chapters in Part V of the handbook do an excellent job of detailing recent successes in practice and new approaches to how US communities have been able to resolve certain disputes that clearly are related to climate changes in their region. As climate change specialists are increasingly concerned with the gap between the rapid pace of that change and its lack of recognition by politicians and others who are failing to take appropriate action to deal with this reality, these cases of adaptive and successful mediated progress are important guideposts to the future.

Recent scholarship regarding the anticipated impact of climate change on myriad global trends and problems portrays the larger societal dislocations that lie ahead. Whether it involves the prevention of predicted "water wars" (Klare, 2012; Welzer, 2013) or the dislocations that lead climate to generate refugees who spark tensions that end with violence, mediators are faced with a set of new complex dilemmas. How can we bring to bear on the potential for violent disputes generated by climate change the knowledge and practice that we have regarding incompatible values, emotion-laden conflicts, and dealing with competing truth claims? How do we become more transformative of the entire climate change enterprise by recognizing a shared fate where time is running out and where it is less a concern about partial solutions?

Because all areas of our globe are affected by these environmental conflicts, the small victories shared in Part V of this volume are noteworthy and deserve full scrutiny. Cases like these presage the wider "process" disagreements among those who still reject climate change as a threat, those who believe that whatever is changing can be managed incrementally over time, and those who believe that the disaster has already begun and we need fundamental change of historic portions. These divergent views will likely require a mediation approach beyond what we have seen in any of our past successful practice, and for which we will need any number of relevant, useful theories.

A second future trend to consider is the imperative of analyzing successes and failures of conflict resolution including mediation in international contexts, which is exceptionally featured by the authors in Part VI of this handbook. I leave the reader with two additional contemporary cases to illustrate the importance of analyzing, at opposite poles of the continuum, successful versus failed mediation. In the former is Colombia, which appears on the verge of finalizing a mediated settlement of a 50+-year civil war that has been beset by human rights atrocities, international criminal drug rings, and past failed processes. In addition to the courage and political will of the contending parties of the Colombian government and its FARC (Revolutionary Armed Forces of Colombia) adversary, some other elements have produced a peace that was quite elusive in earlier attempts. Clearly, this outcome results from a range of ongoing, local peace processes with which were blended international mediation assistance to lead to an unprecedented set of ceasefire and peace agreements. This case like other successful cases should be used as significant learning opportunities to investigate how and why processes worked, the contribution of insider and external mediating agents, and the lessons they hold for ongoing civil wars should be a major focus of practice and scholarship for our immediate future.

The Colombian peace accord stands in stark contrast to the failure of international mediation to end the carnage and full national destruction that has unfolded in the past half decade in Syria. It would require its own substantial volume to address the failures of the international community to assist in developing a mediated solution (if one were possible) in Syria, and obviously, neither the best of mediation practitioners, nor scholars, are the primary culprits in the failure to end the war, as local parties and the Assad government waged an atrocity-filled war. However, as brutal hot wars like Syria that involve multiple internal and external forces, and the intractable sporadic violent conflicts that in Congo and Palestine continue to defy mediated settlements, we are faced with recognizing there is a lot of work to be done to close the gap between current war realities and ineffective mediation approaches. Svensson and Wallensteen (2010) stated how we might close part of this gap in the opening of their important book, *The Go-between*. "The gap between theory and practice has to be narrowed. Mediation theory needs more input on how mediators actually mediate, and policymakers would benefit from analytical tools in deciding on optimal mediation strategies" (Svensson & Wallensteen, 2010, p. xi). The authors in Part VI in this handbook problematize this gap while they discuss a number of recommendations for international mediators that aid in their development. This would appear a high-priority agenda item that urgently needs our immediate and continued attention.

As I close, I note my admiration for the manner in which the contributing authors of this handbook and its editor, Alexia Georgakopoulos, have so well accomplished its aims, while not shying away from the challenges we face in the changing world of mediation that spans the local to the global. The parts of this handbook provide a significant service in locating the strides made in the field, the linkage between thought and action, and the emerging requirements for effective mediation faced by scholars and practitioners in the future. The world desperately needs this kind of expertise and the commitment it requires, and this is the future that this volume competently and convincingly launches.

Notes

1 For more information see peacemaker.un.org/mediation-support.
2 One example can be found at www.utoledo.edu/education/depts/efl/cnde.html.

References

American Bar Association (ABA). (2016) American Bar Association Section of Dispute Resolution: About us. Retrieved from www.americanbar.org/groups/dispute_resolution/about_us.html.

Bellamy, A. & Williams, P.D. (2010) *Understanding Peacekeeping* (2nd edn). Cambridge: Polity Press.

Bing, A. (1989) Peace studies as experiential education. *The Annals of the American Academy of Political and Social Science*, 504(1): 48–60.

Cohen, C.E. (2015) Arts and building peace: Affirming the basics and envisioning the future. United States Institute for Peace. Retrieved from www.usip.org/insights-newsletter/arts-and-building-peace-affirming-the-basics-and-envisioning-the-future.

Cole, S.R., McEwen, C.A., Rogers, N.H., Coben, J.R. & Thompson, P.N. (2011) *Mediation: Law, Policy, and Practice* (3rd edn). Eagan, MN: West Publishing Co.

Fisher, R., Ury, W. & Patton, B. (2011 [1981]). *Getting to Yes: Negotiating Agreement without Giving In*. New York: Penguin.

Folger, J.P. & Bush, R.A.B. (1996) Transformative mediation and third party intervention: Ten hallmarks of a transformative approach to practice. *Mediation Quarterly*, 13(4): 263–278.

Goldberg, S.B., Sander, F.E.A., Rogers, N.H. & Cole, S.R. (2012) *Dispute Resolution: Negotiation, Mediation, Arbitration, and Other Processes* (6th edn). Frederick, MD: Wolters Kluwer Publishing Co.

Klare, M. (2012) *The Race for What's Left: The Global Scramble for the World's Last Resources*. New York: Picador.

Lederach, J.P. (2003) *The Little Book of Conflict Transformation*. Intercourse, PA: Good Books.

Lewis, S.W. (1993) Peacemaking and conflict resolution: A decade of development. *The Institute for Conflict Analysis and Resolution*. Retrieved from scar.gmu.edu/op_6_lewis.pdf.

Lopez, G.A. (1984) Bringing people together: The literature on dispute settlement and conflict resolution. *Choice*, 22(3): 383–392.

Lopez, G.A. (1989) Trends in college curricula and programs. *The Annals of the American Academy of Political and Social Science*, 504(1): 61–71.

PeaceTech Lab. (2012) Retrieved from www.peacetechlab.org.

Shank, M. & Schirch, L. (2008) Strategic arts-based peacebuilding. *Peace & Change*, 33(2): 217–242.

Svensson, I. & Wallensteen, P. (2010) *The Go-between. Jan Eliasson and the Styles of Mediation*. Washington, DC: United States Institute of Peace Press.

Welzer, H. (2013) *Climate Wars: What People Will Be Killed for in the 21st Century*. Cambridge: Polity Press.

Wessel, M.R. (1982) A rule of reason approach to socio-scientific dispute resolution. *Jurimetrics*, 22(4): 445–450.

INDEX

eBooks

from Taylor & Francis

Helping you to choose the right eBooks for your Library

Taylor & Francis eBooks

Add to your library's digital collection today with Taylor & Francis eBooks. We have over 50,000 eBooks in the Humanities, Social Sciences, Behavioural Sciences, Built Environment and Law, from leading imprints, including Routledge, Focal Press and Psychology Press.

ORDER YOUR FREE INSTITUTIONAL TRIAL TODAY

Free Trials Available

We offer free trials to qualifying academic, corporate and government customers.

Choose from a range of subject packages or create your own!

Benefits for you

- Free MARC records
- COUNTER-compliant usage statistics
- Flexible purchase and pricing options
- 70% approx of our eBooks are now DRM-free.

Benefits for your user

- Off-site, anytime access via Athens or referring URL
- Print or copy pages or chapters
- Full content search
- Bookmark, highlight and annotate text
- Access to thousands of pages of quality research at the click of a button.

eCollections

Choose from 20 different subject eCollections, including:

- Asian Studies
- Economics
- Health Studies
- Law
- Middle East Studies

eFocus

We have 16 cutting-edge interdisciplinary collections, including:

- Development Studies
- The Environment
- Islam
- Korea
- Urban Studies

For more information, pricing enquiries or to order a free trial, please contact your local sales team:

UK/Rest of World: **online.sales@tandf.co.uk**
USA/Canada/Latin America: **e-reference@taylorandfrancis.com**
East/Southeast Asia: **martin.jack@tandf.com.sg**
India: **journalsales@tandfindia.com**

www.tandfebooks.com

For Product Safety Concerns and Information please contact our EU representative GPSR@taylorandfrancis.com
Taylor & Francis Verlag GmbH, Kaufingerstraße 24, 80331 München, Germany

www.ingramcontent.com/pod-product-compliance
Lightning Source LLC
LaVergne TN
LVHW080804011026
849160LV00015B/1528

* 9 7 8 1 1 3 8 1 2 4 2 1 9 *